C. W. LEADBEATER

THE FIRST COLLECTION

A Yesterday's World Publishing

Published by A Yesterday's World Publishing
Copyright © 2025 A Yesterday's World Publishing
First impression 2025
ISBN - 978-1-916923-99-7

CONTENTS

AN OUTLINE OF THEOSOPHY

		PAGE
CHAPTER I.	INTRODUCTORY.	01
	What it is.	01
	How it is Known.	01
	The Method of Observation.	02
CHAPTER II.	GENERAL PRINCIPLES.	03
	The Three Great Truths.	03
	Corollaries.	04
	Advantages Gained from this Knowledge	04
CHAPTER III.	THE DEITY	05
	The Divine Scheme.	06
CHAPTER IV.	THE CONSTITUTION OF MAN.	08
	The True Man.	09
CHAPTER V.	REINCARNATION.	10
CHAPTER VI.	THE WIDER OUTLOOK.	12
CHAPTER VII.	DEATH.	13
CHAPTER VIII.	MAN'S PAST AND FUTURE.	16
CHAPTER IX.	CAUSE AND EFFECT.	18
CHAPTER X.	WHAT THEOSOPHY DOES FOR US.	20

A TEXTBOOK OF THEOSOPHY

CHAPTER I.	WHAT THEOSOPHY IS.	23
CHAPTER II.	FROM THE ABSOLUTE TO MAN.	25
CHAPTER III.	THE FORMATION OF A SOLAR SYSTEM.	28
CHAPTER IV.	THE EVOLUTION OF LIFE.	32
CHAPTER V.	THE CONSTITUTION OF MAN.	36
CHAPTER VI.	AFTER DEATH.	43
CHAPTER VII.	REINCARNATION.	54
CHAPTER VIII.	THE PURPOSE OF LIFE.	28
CHAPTER IX.	THE PLANETARY CHAINS.	62
CHAPTER X	THE RESULT OF THEOSOPHICAL STUDY.	66

DREAMS

CHAPTER I.	INTRODUCTORY.	72
CHAPTER II.	THE MECHANISM.	72
	1. Physical.	72
	2. Etheric.	73
	3. Astral.	75
CHAPTER III.	THE EGO	76
CHAPTER IV.	THE CONDITION OF SLEEP.	77
	1. The Brain.	77
	2. The Etheric Brain.	79
	3. The Astral Body.	80
	4. The Ego in Sleep.	80
	His Transcendental Measure of Time.	81

		PAGE
	Illustrative Examples of It.	81
	His Power of Dramatization.	82
	His Faculty of Prevision.	83
	Examples of Its Use.	84
	His Symbolic Thought.	85
	5. The Factors in the Production of Dreams.	85
CHAPTER V.	DREAMS.	86
	1. The True Vision.	86
	2. The Prophetic Dream.	86
	3. The Symbolic Dream.	86
	4. The Vivid and Connected Dream.	87
	5. The Confused Dream.	88
CHAPTER VI.	EXPERIMENTS ON THE DREAM-STATE.	88
CHAPTER VII.	CONCLUSION	90

INVISIBLE HELPERS

CHAPTER I.	THE UNIVERSAL BELIEF IN THEM.	92
CHAPTER II.	SOME MODERN INSTANCES.	93
CHAPTER III.	A PERSONAL EXPERIENCE.	95
CHAPTER IV.	THE HELPERS.	97
CHAPTER V.	THE REALITY OF SUPERPHYSICAL LIFE.	100
CHAPTER VI.	A TIMELY INTERVENTION.	101
CHAPTER VII.	THE "ANGEL" STORY.	102
CHAPTER VIII.	THE STORY OF A FIRE.	104
CHAPTER IX.	MATERIALIZATION AND REPERCUSSION.	106
CHAPTER X.	THE TWO BROTHERS.	106
CHAPTER XI.	WRECKS AND CATASTROPHES.	110
CHAPTER XII.	WORK AMONG THE DEAD.	112
CHAPTER XIII.	OTHER BRANCHES OF THE WORK.	116
CHAPTER XIV.	THE QUALIFICATIONS REQUIRED.	117
CHAPTER XV.	THE PROBATIONARY PATH.	120
CHAPTER XVI.	THE PATH PROPER.	123
CHAPTER XVII.	WHAT LIES BEYOND.	126

THE LIFE AFTER DEATH

CHAPTER I.	IS THERE ANY CERTAIN KNOWLEDGE?	129
CHAPTER II.	THE TRUE FACTS	130
CHAPTER III	PURGATORY	132
CHAPTER IV.	THE HEAVEN-WORLD	136
CHAPTER V.	MANY MANSIONS	139
CHAPTER VI.	OUR FRIENDS IN HEAVEN	142
CHAPTER VII.	GUARDIAN ANGELS	145
CHAPTER VIII.	HUMAN WORKERS IN THE UNSEEN	147
CHAPTER IX.	HELPING THE DEAD	150
CHAPTER X.	THOUGHTS ARE THINGS	151

The Astral Plane

	Page
Introduction	155

Scenery.—The Seven Subdivisions—Degrees of Materiality—Characteristics of Astral Vision—The Aura—The Etheric Double—Power of Magnifying Minute Objects—The "Summer-land"—Records of the Astral Light. — 158

Inhabitants.—I. Human. (1) *Living*:—The Adept or Chela in Mâyâvirûpa—The Psychically Developed Person—The Ordinary Person in Astral Body—The Black Magician. (2) *Dead*:—The Nirmânakâya—The Chela awaiting Reincarnation—The Ordinary Person after Death—The Shade—The Shell—The Vitalized Shell—The Suicide—The Victim of Sudden Death—The Vampire—The Werewolf—The Black Magician after Death. II. Non-human:—The Elemental Essence—The Kâmarûpas of Animals—Various Classes of Nature-Spirits, commonly called Fairies—Kâmadevas—Rûpadevas—Arûpadevas—The Devarâjahs. III. Artificial:—Elementals formed Unconsciously—Guardian Angels—Elementals formed Consciously—Human Artificials—The True Origin of Spiritualism. — 162

Phenomena.—Churchyard Ghosts.—Apparitions of the Dying—Haunted Localities—Family Ghosts—Bell-ringing, Stone-throwing, etc.—Fairies—Communicating Entities—Astral Resources—Clairvoyance—Prevision—Second-Sight—Astral Forces—Etheric Currents—Etheric Pressure—Latent Energy Sympathetic Vibration—Mantras—Disintegration Materialization—Why Darkness is required at a *Séance*—Spirit Photographs—Reduplication—Precipitation of Letters and Pictures—Slate-writing—Levitation—Spirit Lights—Handling Fire—Transmutation—Repercussion. — 187

Conclusion. — 193

The Devachanic Plane

Introduction.—The investigation—The place of Devachanin evolution—Difficulties of expression. — 195

Characteristics.—A beautiful description—The bliss of Devachan—Its intense vitality—The devachanic sense—Surroundings—The sea of light—The colour-language of the Devas—The great waves—The rûpa and arûpa planes—The action of thought—The formation of artificial elementals—Thought-forms—The sub-planes—The âkâshic records. — 196

Inhabitants.— — 205
   I. Human. The embodied—Adepts and initiates— Those in sleep or trance. — 205
      The disembodied—Their consciousness—Is the devachanic life an illusion?—The qualities necessary for devachanic life—How a man first gains Devachan. — 207
      The four rûpa levels, with examples on each. — 212
      The three arûpa levels. — 219
   II. Non-Human.—The elemental essence—What it is—The Veiling of Âtmâ—The four elemental kingdoms—How the essence evolves. — 222
      The Devas—Their divisions. — 226
   III. Artificial. — 227

Conclusion.—The still higher planes. — 227

Clairvoyance

Chapter I.	What Clairvoyance Is.	229
Chapter II.	Simple Clairvoyance: Full.	236
Chapter III.	Simple Clairvoyance: Partial.	242

		PAGE
CHAPTER IV.	CLAIRVOYANCE IN SPACE: INTENTIONAL.	244
CHAPTER V.	CLAIRVOYANCE IN SPACE: SEMI- INTENTIONAL.	251
CHAPTER VI.	CLAIRVOYANCE IN SPACE: UNINTENTIONAL.	253
CHAPTER VII.	CLAIRVOYANCE in Time: THE PAST.	255
CHAPTER VIII.	CLAIRVOYANCE in Time: THE FUTURE.	266
CHAPTER IX.	METHODS OF DEVELOPMENT.	275

THE MONAD

FORWARD		
CHAPTER I.	THE MONAD.	280
CHAPTER II.	HIGHER CONSCIOUSNESS.	288
CHAPTER III.	THE BUDDHIC CONSCIOUSNESS.	300
CHAPTER IV.	AN INSTANCE OF PSYCHIC DEVELOPMENT.	304
CHAPTER V.	TIME.	306
CHAPTER VI.	INSPIRATION.	307
CHAPTER VII.	PLAGIARISM.	313
CHAPTER VIII	EXAGGERATION.	316
CHAPTER IX.	MEDITATION.	319

An Outline of Theosophy

Chapter I.

Introductory.

What it is.

For many a year men have been discussing, arguing, enquiring about certain great basic truths—about the existence and the nature of God, about His relation to man, and about the past and future of humanity. So radically have they differed upon these points, and so bitterly have they assailed and ridiculed one another's beliefs, that there has come to be a firmly-rooted popular opinion that with regard to all these matters there is no certainty available—nothing but vague speculation amid a cloud of unsound deductions drawn from ill-established premises. And this in spite of the very definite, though frequently incredible, assertions made on these subjects on behalf of the various religions.

This popular opinion, though not unnatural under the circumstances, is entirely untrue. There are definite facts available—plenty of them. Theosophy gives them to us; but it offers them not (as the religions do) as matters of faith, but as subjects for study. It is not itself a religion, but it bears to the religions the same relation as did the ancient philosophies. It does not contradict them, but explains them. Whatever in any of them is unreasonable it rejects as necessarily unworthy of the Deity and derogatory to Him; whatever is reasonable in each and all of them it takes up, explains and emphasizes, and thus combines all into one harmonious whole.

It holds that truth on all these most important points is attainable—that there is a great body of knowledge about them already existing. It considers all the various religions as statements of that truth from different points of view; since, though they differ much as to nomenclature and as to articles of belief, they all agree as to the only matters which are of real importance—the kind of life which a good man should lead, the qualities which he must develope, the vices which he must avoid. On these practical points the teaching is identical in Hinduism and Buddhism, in Zoroastrianism and Muhammadanism, in Judaism and Christianity.

Theosophy may be described to the outside world as an intelligent theory of the universe. Yet for those who have studied it, it is not theory, but fact; for it is a definite science, capable of being studied, and its teachings are verifiable by investigation and experiment for those who are willing to take the trouble to qualify themselves for such enquiry. It is a statement of the great facts of Nature so far as they are known—an outline of the scheme of our corner of the universe.

How it is Known.

How did this scheme become known, some may ask; by whom was it discovered? We cannot speak of it as discovered, for in truth it has always been known to mankind, though sometimes temporarily forgotten in certain parts of the world. There has always existed a certain body of highly-developed men—men not of any one nation, but of all the advanced nations—who have held it in its fulness; and there have always been pupils of these men, who were specially studying it, while its broad principles have always been known in the outer world. This body of highly-developed men exists now, as in past ages, and Theosophical teaching is published to the Western world at their instigation, and through a few of their pupils.

Those who are ignorant have sometimes clamorously insisted that, if this be so, these truths ought to have been published long ago; and most unjustly they accuse the possessors of such knowledge of undue reticence in withholding them from the world at large. They forget that all who have really sought these truths have always been able to find them, and that it is only now that we in the Western world are truly beginning to seek. For many centuries Europe was content to live, for the most part, in the grossest superstition; and when a reaction at last set in from the just as conceited and bigoted in another direction. So that it is really only now that some of the humbler and more reasonable of our people are beginning to admit that they know nothing, and to enquire whether there is not real information available somewhere.

Though these reasonable enquirers are as yet but a small minority, the Theosophical Society has been founded in order to draw them together, and its books are put before the public so that those who will may read, mark, learn, and inwardly digest these great truths. Its mission is not to force its teaching upon reluctant minds, but simply to offer it, so that those may take it who feel the need for it. We are not in the least under the delusion of the poor arrogant missionary, who dares to condemn to an unpleasant eternity every one who will not pronounce his little provincial shibboleth; we are perfectly aware that all will at last be well for those who cannot as yet see their way to accept the truth, as well as for those who receive it with avidity. But the knowledge of this, truth has, for us and for thousands of others, made life easier to bear and death easier to face; and it is simply the wish to share these benefits with our fellowmen that urges us to devote ourselves to writing and lecturing on these subjects.

The broad outlines of the great truths have been widely known in the world for thousands of years, and are so known at the present day. It is only we in the West who, in our incredible self-sufficiency, have remained ignorant of them, and scoffed at any fragment of them which may have come in our way. As in the case of any other science, so in this science, of the soul, full details are known only to those who devote their lives to its pursuit. The men who fully know—those who are called Adepts—have patiently developed within themselves the powers necessary for perfect observation. For in this respect there is a difference between the methods of occult investigation and those of the more modern form of science; this latter ,devotes all its energy to the improvement of its instruments, while the former aims rather at the development of the observer.

The Method of Observation.

The detail of this development would take up more space than can be devoted to it in a preliminary manual such as this. The whole scheme will be found fully explained in other Theosophical works; for the moment let it suffice to say that it is entirely a question of vibration. All information which reaches a man from the world without reaches him by means of vibration of some sort, whether it be through the senses of sight, hearing, or touch. Consequently, if a man is able to make himself sensitive to additional vibrations he will acquire additional information; he will become what is commonly called "clairvoyant."

This word, as commonly used, means nothing more than a slight extension of normal vision; but it is possible for a man to become more and more sensitive to the subtler vibrations, until his consciousness, acting through many developed faculties, functions freely in new land higher ways. He will then find new worlds of subtler matter opening up before him, though in reality they are only new portions of the world he already knows. He learns in this way that a, vast unseen universe exists round him during his whole life, and that it is constantly affecting him in many ways, even though he remains blindly unconscious of it. But when he develops faculties whereby he can sense these other worlds it becomes possible for him to observe them scientifically, to repeat his observations many times, to compare them with those of others, to tabulate them, and draw deductions from them.

All this has been done—not once, but thousands of times. The Adepts of whom I spoke have done this to the fullest possible extent, but many efforts along the same line have been made by our own Theosophical students. The result of our investigations has been not only to verify much of the information given to us at the outset by those Adepts, but also to explain and amplify it very considerably.

The sight of this usually unseen portion of our world at once brings to our knowledge a vast body of entirely new facts which are of the very deepest interest. It gradually solves for us many of the most difficult problems of life; it clears up for us many mysteries, so that we now see them to have been mysteries to us for so long, only because heretofore we saw so small a part of the facts, because we were looking at the various matters from below, and as isolated and unconnected fragments, instead of rising above them to a standpoint whence they are comprehensible as parts of a mighty whole. It settles in a moment many questions which have been much disputed—such, for example, as that of the continued existence of man after death. It affords us the true explanation of all the wildly impossible statements made by the churches about heaven, hell, and purgatory; it dispels our ignorance and removes our fear of the unknown by supplying us with a rational and orderly scheme. What this scheme is I will now endeavour to explain.

Chapter II.

General Principles.

It is my desire to make this statement of Theosophy as clear and readily comprehensible as possible, and for this reason I shall at every point give broad principles only, referring those who wish for detailed information to larger books, or to monographs upon particular subjects. I hope at the end of each Chapter of this little treatise to give a list of such books as should be consulted by those who desire to go more deeply into this most fascinating system.

I shall begin, then, by a statement of the most striking of the broad general principles which emerge as a result of Theosophical study. There may be those who will find here matter which is incredible to them, or matter which runs entirely contrary to their preconceived ideas. If that be so, then I would ask such men to remember that I am not putting this forward as a theory—as a metaphysical speculation or a pious opinion of my own—but as a definite scientific fact proved and examined over and over again, not only by myself, but by many others also.

Furthermore, I claim that it is a fact which may be verified at first hand by any person who is willing to devote the time and trouble necessary to fit himself for the investigation. I am not offering to the reader a creed to be swallowed like a pill; I am trying to set before him a system to study, and, above all, a life to live. I ask no blind faith from him; I simply suggest to him the consideration of the Theosophical teaching as a hypothesis, though to me it is no hypothesis, but a living fact.

If he finds it more satisfactory than others which have been presented to him, if it seems to him to solve more of the problems of life, to answer a greater number of the questions which inevitably arise for the thinking man, then he will pursue its study further, and will find in it, I hope and believe, the same ever-increasing satisfaction and joy that I have myself found. If, on the other hand, he thinks some other system preferable, no harm is done; he has simply learnt something of the tenets of a body of men with whom he is as yet unable to agree. I have sufficient faith in it myself to believe that, sooner or later, a time will come when he *will* agree with them—when he also will know what we know.

The Three Great Truths.

In one of our earliest Theosophical books it was written that there are three truths which are absolute and cannot be but yet may remain silent for lack of speech. They are as great as life itself, and yet as simple as the simplest mind of man. I can hardly do better than paraphrase these for the greatest of my general principles.

I will then give some corollaries which follow naturally from them, and then, thirdly, some of the more prominent of the advantageous results which necessarily attend this definite knowledge. Having thus outlined the scheme in tabular form, I will take it up point by point, and endeavour to offer such elementary explanations as come within the scope of this little introductory book.

1. God exists, and He is good. He is the great lifegiver who dwells within us and without us, is undying and eternally beneficent. He is not heard, nor seen, nor touched, yet is perceived by the man who desires perception.

2. Man is immortal, and his future is one whose glory and splendour have no limit.

3. A Divine law of absolute justice rules the world, so that each man is in truth his own judge, the dispenser of glory or gloom to himself, the decreer of his life, his reward, his punishment.

COROLLARIES.

To each of these great truths are attached certain others, subsidiary and explanatory.
From the first of them it follows:

1. That, in spite of appearances, all' things are definitely and intelligently moving together for good; that all circumstances, however untoward they may seem, are in reality exactly what are needed; that everything around us, tends, not to hinder us, but to help us, if it is only understood.
2. That, since the whole scheme thus tends to man's benefit, clearly it is his duty to learn to understand it.
3. That when he thus understands if, it is also his duty intelligently to co-operate in this scheme.

From the second great truth it follows:

1. That the true man is a soul, and that this body is only an appanage.
2. That he must, therefore, regard everything from the standpoint of the soul, and that in every case when an internal struggle takes place he must realise his identity with the higher and not with the lower.
3. That what we commonly call his life is only one day in his true and larger life.
4. That death is a matter of far less importance than is usually supposed, since it is by no means the end of life, but merely the passage from one stage of it to another.
5. That man has an immense evolution behind him, the study of which is most fascinating, interesting, and instructive.
6. That he has also a splendid evolution before him, the study of which will be even more fascinating and instructive.
7. That there is an absolute certainty of final attainment for every human soul, no matter how far he may seem to have strayed from the path of evolution.

From the third great truth it follows:

1. That every thought, word, or action produces its definite result—not a reward or a punishment imposed from without, but a result inherent in the action itself, definitely connected with it in the relation of cause and effect, these being really but two inseparable parts of one whole.
2. That it is both the duty and interest of man to study this divine law closely, so that he may be able to adapt himself to it and to use it, as we use other great laws of nature.
3. That it is necessary for man to attain perfect control over himself, so that he may guide his life intelligently in accordance with this law.

ADVANTAGES GAINED FROM THIS KNOWLEDGE.

When this knowledge is fully assimilated, it changes the aspect of life so completely that it would be impossible for me to tabulate all the advantages which flow from it. I can only mention a few of the principal lines along which this change is produced, and the reader's own thought will, no doubt, supply some of the endless ramifications which are their necessary consequence.

But it must be understood that no vague knowledge will be sufficient. Such belief as most men accord to the assertions of their religions will be quite useless, since it produces no practical effect in their lives. But if we believe in these truths as we do in the other laws of nature—as we believe that fire burns and that water drowns—then the effect that they produce in our lives is enormous. For our belief in the laws of nature is sufficiently real to induce us to order our lives in accordance with it. Believing that fire burns, we take every precaution to avoid fire; believing that water drowns, we avoid going into water too deep for us unless we can swim.

Now these beliefs are so definite and real to us because they are founded on knowledge and illustrated by daily experience; and the beliefs of the Theosophical student are equally real and definite to him for exactly the same reason. And that is why we find following from them the results now to be described:

I. We gain a rational comprehension of life—we know how we should live and why, and we learn that life *is* worth living when properly understood.

2. We learn how to govern ourselves, and therefore how to develope ourselves.

3. We learn how best to help those whom we love, how to make ourselves useful to all with whom we come into contact, and ultimately to the whole human race.

4. We learn to view everything from the wider philosophical standpoint—never from the petty and purely personal side.

Consequently:

5. The troubles of life are no longer so large for us.

6. We have no sense of injustice in connection with our surroundings or our destiny.

7. We are altogether freed from the fear of death.

8. Our grief in connection with the death of those whom we love is very greatly mitigated.

9. We gain a totally different view of the life after death, and we understand its place in our evolution.

10. We are altogether free from religious fears or worry, either for ourselves or for our friends—fears as to the salvation of the soul, for example.

11. We are no longer troubled by uncertainty as to our future fate, but live in perfect serenity and perfect fearlessness.

Now let us take these points in detail, and endeavour briefly to explain them.

CHAPTER III.

THE DEITY.

When we lay down the existence of God as the first and greatest of our principles, it becomes necessary for us to define the sense in which we employ that much-abused, yet mighty word. We try to redeem it from the narrow limits imposed on it by the ignorance of undeveloped men, and to restore to it the splendid conception—splendid, though so infinitely below the reality—given to it by the founders of religions. And we distinguish between God as the Infinite Existence, and the manifestation of this Supreme Existence as a revealed God, evolving and guiding a universe. Only to this limited manifestation should the term "a personal God" be applied. God in Himself is beyond the bounds of personality, is "in all and through all" and indeed *is* all; and of the Infinite, the Absolute, the All, we can only say "He is."

For all practical purposes we need not go further than that marvellous and glorious manifestation of Him (a little less entirely beyond our comprehension) the great Guiding Force or Deity of our own solar system, whom philosophers have called the Logos. Of him is true all that we have ever heard predicated of God—all that is good, that is—not the blasphemous conceptions sometimes put forward, ascribing to Him human vices. But all that has ever been said of the love, the wisdom, the power, the patience and compassion, the omniscience, the omnipresence, the omnipotence—all of this, and much more, is true of the Logos of our system. Verily "in Him we live and move and have our being," not as a poetical expression, but (strange as it may seem) as a definite scientific fact; and so when we speak of the Deity our first thought is naturally of the Logos.

We do not vaguely hope that He may be; we do not even believe as a matter of faith that He is; we simply know it as we know that the sun shines, for to the trained and developed clairvoyant investigator this Mighty Existence is a definite certainty. Not that any merely human development can enable us directly to see Him, but that unmistakable evidence of His action and His purpose surrounds us on every side as we study the life of the unseen world, which is in reality only the higher part of this.

Here we meet the explanation of a dogma which is common to all religions—that of the Trinity. Incomprehensible as many of the statements made on this subject in our creeds may seem to the ordinary reader, they become significant and luminous when the truth is understood. As He shows Himself to us in His work, the Solar Logos is undoubtedly triple—three and yet one, as religion has long ago told us; and as much of the explanation of this apparent mystery as the intellect of man at its present stage can grasp will be found in the books presently to be mentioned.

That He is within us as well as without us, or, in other words, that man himself is in essence divine, is another great truth which, though those who are blind to all but the outer and lower world may still argue about it, is an absolute certainty to the student of the higher side of life. Of the constitution of man's soul and its various vehicles we shall speak under the heading of the second of the truths; suffice it for the moment to note that the inherent divinity is a fact, and that in it resides the assurance of the ultimate return of every human being to the divine level.

THE DIVINE SCHEME.

Perhaps none of our postulates will present greater difficulty to the average mind than the first corollary to this first great truth. Looking round us in daily life we see so much of the storm and stress, the sorrow and the suffering, so much that looks like the triumph of evil over good, that it seems almost impossible to suppose that all this apparent confusion is in reality part of an ordered progress. Yet this is the truth, and can be seen to be the truth so soon as we escape from the dust-cloud raised by the struggle in this outer world, and look upon it all from the vantage ground of the fuller knowledge and the inner peace.

Then the real motion of the complex machinery becomes apparent. Then it is seen that what have seemed to be counter-currents of evil prevailing against the stream of progress are merely trifling eddies into which for the moment a little water may turn aside, or tiny whirlpools on the surface, in which part of the water appears for the moment to be running backwards. But all the time the mighty river is sweeping steadily on its appointed course, bearing the superficial whirlpools along with it. Just so the great stream of evolution is moving evenly on its way, and what seems to us so terrible a tempest is the merest ruffling of its surface. Another analogy, very beautifully worked out, is given in Mr. C. H. Hinton's *Scientific Romances, vol. i.,* pp. 18 to 24.

Truly, as our third great truth tells us, absolute justice is meted out to all, and so, in whatever circumstances a man finds himself, he knows that he himself and none other has provided them; but he may also know much more than this. He may rest assured that under the action of evolutionary law matters are so arranged as to give him the best possible opportunity for developing within himself those qualities which he most needs. His circumstances are by no means necessarily those that he would have chosen for himself, but they are exactly what he has deserved; and, subject only to that consideration of his deserts (which frequently impose serious limitations), they are those best adapted for his progress. They may provide him with all sorts of difficulties, but these are offered only in order that he may learn to surmount them, and thereby develope within himself courage, determination, patience, perseverance, or whatever other quality he may lack. Men often speak as though the forces of Nature were conspiring against them, whereas as a matter of fact, if they would but understand it, everything about them is carefully calculated to assist them on their upward way.

That, since there is a Divine scheme, it is man's part to try to understand it, is a proposition which surely needs no argument. Even were it only from motives of self-interest, those who have to live under a certain set of conditions would do well to familiarize themselves with them; and when a man's objects in life become altruistic it is still more necessary for him to comprehend, in order that he may help the more effectually.

It is undoubtedly part of this plan for man's evolution that he himself should intelligently co-operate in it as soon as he has developed sufficient intelligence to grasp it and sufficient good feeling to wish to aid. But indeed this Divine scheme is so wonderful and so beautiful that, when once a man sees it, nothing else is possible for him than to throw all his energies into the effort to become a worker in it, no matter how humble may be the part which he has to sustain.

For fuller information on the subjects of this chapter the reader is referred to Mrs. Besant's *Esoteric Christianity* and *Ancient Wisdom,* and to my own little book on *The Christian Creed.* Much light is also thrown on these conceptions from the Greek standpoint in Mr. G. R. S. Mead's *Orpheus,* and from the Gnostic-Christian in his *Fragments of a Faith Forgotten.*

> I know, as my life grows older
> And mine eyes have clearer sight,
> That under each rank wrong somewhere
> There lies the root of right;
> That each sorrow has its purpose,
> By the sorrowing oft unguessed;
> That, as sure as the sun brings morning,
> Whatever is, is best.
>
> I know that each sinful action,
> As sure as the night brings shade,
> Is somewhere, some time punished,
> Though the hour be long delayed.
> I know that the soul is aided
> Sometimes by the heart's unrest,
> And to grow means oft to suffer;
> But whatever is, is best.
>
> I know that there are no errors
> In the great eternal plan,
> And that all things work together
> For the final good of man.
> And I know when my soul speeds onward
> In its grand eternal quest
> I shall say, as I look back earthward,
> Whatever is, is best.

[The above appeared anonymously in an American newspaper.]

Chapter IV.

The Constitution of Man.

The astounding practical materialism to which we have been reduced in this country can hardly be more clearly shown than it is by the expressions that we employ in common life. We speak quite ordinarily of man as having a soul, of "saving" our souls, and so on, evidently regarding the physical body as the real man and the soul as a mere appanage, a vague something to be considered as the property of the body. With an idea so little defined as this, it can hardly be a matter of surprise that many people go a little further along the same lines, and doubt whether this vague something exists at all. So it would seem that the ordinary man is very often quite uncertain whether he possesses a soul or not; still less does he know that that soul is immortal. That he should remain in this pitiable condition of ignorance seems strange, for there is a very great deal of evidence available, even in the outer world, to show that man has an existence quite apart from his body, capable of being carried on at a distance from it while it is living, and entirely without it when it is dead.

Until we have entirely rid ourselves of this extraordinary delusion that the body is the man, it is quite impossible that we should at all appreciate the real facts of the case. A little investigation immediately shows us that the body is only a vehicle by means of which the man manifests himself in connection with this particular type of gross matter out of which our visible world is built.

Furthermore, it shows that other and subtler types of matter exist—not only the ether admitted by modern science as interpenetrating all known substances, but other types of matter which interpenetrate ether in turn, and are as much finer than ether as it is than solid matter.

The question will naturally occur to the reader as to how it will be possible for man to become conscious of the existence of types of matter so wonderfully fine, so minutely subdivided. The answer is that he can become conscious of them in the same way as he becomes conscious of the lower matter—by receiving vibrations from them. And he is enabled to receive vibrations from them by reason of the fact that he possesses matter of these finer types as part of himself—that just as his body of dense matter is his vehicle for perceiving and communicating with the world of dense matter, so does the finer matter within him constitute for him a vehicle by means of which he can perceive and communicate with the world of finer matter which is imperceptible to the grosser physical senses.

This is by no means a new idea. It will be remembered that St. Paul remarks that "there is a natural body, and there is a spiritual body," and that he furthermore refers to both the soul and the spirit in man, by no means employing the two words synonymously, as is so often ignorantly done at the present day. It speedily becomes evident that man is a far more complex being than is ordinarily supposed; that not only is he a spirit within a soul, but that this soul has various vehicles of different degrees of density, the physical body being only one, and the lowest of them. These various vehicles may all be described as bodies in relation to their respective levels of matter. It might be said that there exist around us a series of worlds one within the other (by interpenetration), and that man possesses a body for each of these worlds, by means of which he may observe it and live in it.

He learns by degrees how to use these various bodies, and in that way gains a much more complete idea of, the great complex world in which he lives; for all these other inner worlds are in reality still part of it. In this way he comes to understand very many things which before seemed mysterious to him; he ceases to identify himself with his bodies, and learns that they are only vestures which he may put off and resume or change without being himself in the least affected thereby. Once more we must repeat that all this is by no means metaphysical speculation or pious opinion, but definite scientific fact, thoroughly well known experimentally to those who have studied Theosophy. Strange as it may seem to many to find precise statements taking the place of hypothesis upon questions such as these, I am speaking here of nothing that is not known by direct and constantly-repeated observation to a large number of students. Assuredly "we know whereof we speak," not by faith but by experiment, and therefore we speak with confidence.

To these inner worlds or different levels of nature we usually give the name of planes. We speak of the visible world as "the physical plane," though under that name we include also the gases and the various grades of ether. To the next stage of materiality the name of "the astral plane" was given by the mediæval alchemists (who were well aware of its existence), and we have adopted their title. Within this exists yet another world of still finer matter, of which we speak as "the mental plane," because of its matter is composed what is commonly called the mind in man. There are other still higher planes, but I need not trouble the reader with designations for them, since we are at present dealing only with man's manifestation in the lower worlds.

It must always be borne in mind that all these worlds are in no way removed from us in space. In fact, they all occupy exactly the same space, and are all equally about us always. At the moment our consciousness is focused in and working through our physical brain, and thus we are conscious only of the physical world, and not even of the whole of that. But we have only to learn to focus that consciousness in one of these higher vehicles, and at once the physical fades from our view, and we see instead the world of matter which corresponds to the vehicle used.

Recollect that all matter is in essence the same. Astral matter does not differ in its nature from physical matter any more than ice differs in its nature from steam. It is simply the same thing in a different condition. Physical matter may become astral, or astral may become mental, if only it be sufficiently subdivided, and caused to vibrate with the proper degree of rapidity.

THE TRUE MAN.

What, then, is the true man? He is in truth an emanation from the Logos, a spark of the Divine fire. The spirit within him is of the very essence of the Deity, and that spirit wears his soul as a vesture—a vesture which encloses and individualizes it and seems to our limited vision to separate it for a time from the rest of the Divine Life. The story of the original formation of the soul of man, and of the enfolding of the spirit within it, is a beautiful and interesting one, but too long for inclusion in a merely elementary work like this. It may be found in full detail in those of our books which deal with this part of the doctrine. Suffice it here to say that all three aspects of the Divine Life have their part in its inception, and that its formation is the culmination of that mighty sacrifice of the Logos in descending into matter, which has been called the Incarnation.

Thus the baby soul is born; and just as it is "made in the image of God"—threefold in aspect, as He is, and threefold in manifestation, as He is also—so is its method of evolution also a reflection of His descent into matter. The Divine Spark contains within it all potentiality, but it is only through long ages of evolution that all its possibilities can be realised. The appointed method for the evolution of the man's latent qualities seems to be by learning to vibrate in response to impacts from without. But at the level where he finds himself (that of the higher mental plane) the vibrations are far too fine to awaken this response at present; he must begin with those that are coarser and stronger, and having awakened his dormant sensibilities by their means he will gradually grow more and more sensitive until he is capable of perfect response at all levels to all possible rates of vibration.

That is the material aspect of his progress; but regarded subjectively, to be able to respond to all vibrations means to be perfect in sympathy and compassion. And that is exactly the condition of the developed man—the adept, the spiritual teacher, the Christ. It needs the development within him of all the qualities which go to make up the perfect man; and this is the real work of his long life in matter.

In this chapter we have brushed the surface of many subjects of extreme importance. Those who wish to study them further will find many Theosophical books to help them. On the constitution of man we would refer readers to Mrs. Besant's works, *Man and his Bodies, The Self and its Sheaths,* and *The Seven Principles of Man,* and also to my own book, *Man*

Visible and Invisible, in which will be found many illustrations of the different vehicles of man as they appear to clairvoyant sight.

On the use of the inner faculties refer to *Clairvoyance*.

On the formation and evolution of the soul to Mrs. Besant's *Birth and Evolution of the Soul*, Mr. Sinnett's *Growth of the Soul*, and my own *Christian Creed* and *Man, Visible and Invisible*.

On the spiritual evolution of man, Mrs. Besant's *In the Outer Court* and *The Path of Discipleship*, and the concluding chapters of my own little book, *Invisible Helpers*.

CHAPTER V.

REINCARNATION.

Since the finer movements cannot at first affect the soul, he has to draw round him vestures of grosser matter through which the heavier vibrations can play; and so he takes upon himself successively the mental body, the astral body, and the physical body. This is a birth or incarnation—the commencement of a physical life. During that life all kinds of experiences come to him through his physical body, and from them he should learn some lessons and develope some qualities within himself.

After a time he begins to withdraw again into himself, and puts off by degrees the vestures which he has assumed. The first of these to drop is the physical body, and his withdrawal from that is what we call death. It is not the end of his activities, as we so ignorantly suppose; nothing could be further from the fact. He is simply withdrawing from one effort, bearing back with him its results; and after a certain period of comparative repose he will make another effort of the same kind.

Thus, as has been said, what we ordinarily call his life is only one day in the real and wider life—a day at school, during which he learns certain lessons. But inasmuch as one short life of seventy or eighty years at most is not enough to give him an opportunity of learning all the lessons which this wonderful and beautiful world has to teach, and inasmuch as God means him to learn them all in His own good time, it is necessary that he should come back again many times, and live through many of these school-days that we call lives, in different classes and under different circumstances, until all the lessons are learnt; and then this lower school-work will be over, and he will pass to something higher and more glorious—the true divine life-work for which all this earthly school-life is fitting him.

This is what is called the doctrine of reincarnation or rebirth—a doctrine which was widely known in the ancient civilizations, and is even to-day held by the majority of the human race. Of it Hume has written:

"What is incorruptible must also be ungenerable. The soul, therefore, if immortal, existed before our birth. . . The metempsychosis is, therefore, the only system of this kind that Philosophy can hearken to."[1]

Writing of the theories of metempsychosis in India and Greece, Max Muller says:—"There is something underlying them which, if expressed in less mythological language, may stand the severest test of philosophical examination."[2] In his last and posthumous work this great Orientalist again refers to this doctrine, and expresses his personal belief in it.

And Huxley writes:—"Like the doctrine of evolution itself, that of transmigration has its roots in the world of reality; and it may claim such support as the great argument from analogy is capable of supplying."[3]

So it will be seen that modern as well as ancient writers recognize this hypothesis as one deserving of the most serious consideration.

---

[1] Hume, "Essay on Immortality," London, 1875.
[2] Max Muller, "Theosophy or Psychological Religion," p. 22, 1895 edition.
[3] Huxley, "Evolution and Ethics," p. 61, 1895 edition.

It must not for a moment be confounded with a theory held by the ignorant, that it was possible for a soul which had reached humanity in its evolution to re-become that of an animal. No such retrogression is within the limits of possibility; when once man comes into existence—a human soul, inhabiting what we call in our books a causal body —he can never again fall back into what is in truth a lower kingdom of nature, whatever mistakes he may make or however he may fail to take advantage of his opportunities. If he is idle in the school of life, he may need to take the same lesson over and over again before he has really learnt it, but still on the whole progress is steady, even though it may often be slow. A few years ago the essence of this doctrine was prettily put thus in one of the magazines:

"A boy went to school. He was very little. All that he knew he had drawn in with his mother's milk. His teacher (who was God) placed him in the lowest class, and gave him these lessons to learn: Thou shalt not kill. Thou shalt do no hurt to any living thing. Thou shalt not steal. So the man did not kill; but he was cruel, and he stole. At the end of the day (when his beard was gray—when the night was come) his teacher (who was God) said: Thou hast learned not to kill. But the other lessons thou hast not learned. Come back to-morrow.

"On the morrow he came back, a little boy. And his teacher (who was God) put him in a class a little higher, and gave him these lessons to learn: Thou shalt do no hurt to any living thing. Thou shalt not steal. Thou shalt not cheat. So the man did no hurt to any living thing; but he stole and he cheated. And at the end of the day (when his beard was gray—when the night was come) his teacher (who was God) said: Thou hast learned to be merciful. But the other lessons thou hast not learned. Come back to-morrow.

"Again, on the morrow, he came back, a little boy. And his teacher (who was God) put him in a class yet a little higher, and gave him these lessons to learn: Thou shalt not steal. Thou shalt not cheat. Thou shalt not covet. So the man did not steal; but he cheated, and he coveted. And at the end of the day (when his beard was gray—when the night was come) his teacher (who was God) said: Thou hast learned not to steal. But the other lessons thou hast not learned. Come back, my child, to-morrow.

"This is what I have read in the faces of men and women, in the book of the world, and in the scroll of the heavens, which is writ with stars." (Berry Benson, in *The Century Magazine*, May, 1894.)

I must not fill my pages with the many unanswerable arguments in favour of this doctrine of reincarnation; they are set forth very fully in our literature by a far abler pen than mine. Here I will say only this. Life presents us with many problems which, on any other hypothesis than this of reincarnation, seem utterly insoluble; this great truth does explain them, and therefore holds the field until another and more satisfactory hypothesis can be found. Like the rest of the teaching, this is not a hypothesis, but a matter of direct knowledge for many of us; but naturally our knowledge, is not proof to others.

Yet good men and true have been sorrowfully forced to admit that they were unable to reconcile the state of affairs which exists in the world around us with the theory that God was both almighty and all-loving.They felt, when they looked upon all the heart-breaking sorrow and suffering, that either He was not almighty, and could not prevent it, or He was not all-loving, and did not care. In Theosophy we hold with determined conviction that He is both almighty and all-loving, and we reconcile with that certainty the existing facts of life by means of this basic doctrine of reincarnation. Surely the only hypothesis which allows us reasonably to recognise the perfection of power and love in the Deity is one which is worthy of careful examination.

For we understand that our present life is not our first, but that we each have behind us a long line of lives, by means of the experiences of which we have evolved from the condition of primitive man to our present position. Assuredly in these past lives we shall have done both good and evil, and from every one of our actions a definite proportion of result must have followed under the inexorable law of justice. From the good follows always happiness and further opportunity; from the evil follows always sorrow and limitation.

So if we find ourselves limited in any way, the limitation is of our own making, or is merely due to the youth of the soul; if we have sorrow and suffering to endure, we ourselves alone are responsible. The manifold and complex destinies of men answer with rigid exactitude to the balance between the good and evil of their previous actions; and all is moving onward under the divine order towards the final consummation of glory.

There is, perhaps, no Theosophical teaching to which more violent objection is made than this great truth of reincarnation; yet it is in reality a most comforting doctrine For it gives us tine for the progress which lies before—time and opportunity to become "perfect, even as our Father in Heaven is perfect." Objectors chiefly found their protest on the fact that they have had so much trouble and sorrow in this life that they will not listen to any suggestion that it may be necessary to go through it all again. But this is obviously not argument; we are in search of truth, and when it is found we must not shrink from it, whether it be pleasant or unpleasant, though, as a matter of fact, as said above, reincarnation rightly understood is profoundly comforting.

Again, people often inquire why, if we have had so many previous lives, we do not remember any of them. Put very briefly, the answer to this is that some people do remember them; and the reason why the majority do not is because their consciousness is still focused in one or other of the lower Sheaths. That sheath cannot be expected to recollect previous incarnations, because it has not had any; and the soul, which *has,* is not yet fully conscious on its own plane. But the memory of all the past is stored within that soul, and expresses itself here in the innate qualities with which the child is born; and when the man has evolved sufficiently to be able to focus his consciousness there instead of only in lower vehicles the entire history of that real and wider life will be open before him like a book.

The whole of this question is fully and beautifully worked out in Mrs. Besant's manual on *Reincarnation,* Dr. Jerome Anderson's *Reincarnation,* and in the chapters on that subject in *The Ancient Wisdom,* to which the attention of the reader is specially directed.

CHAPTER VI.

THE WIDER OUTLOOK.

A little thought will soon show us what a radical change is introduced into the life of the man who realises that his physical life is nothing but a day at school, and that his physical body is merely a temporary vesture assumed for the purpose of learning through it. He sees at once that this purpose of "learning the lesson" is the only one of any importance, and that the man who allows himself to be diverted from that purpose by any consideration is acting with inconceivable stupidity.

To him who knows the truth, the life of the ordinary person devoted exclusively to physical objects, to the pursuit of wealth or fame, appears the merest child's play—a senseless sacrifice of all that is really worth having for a few moments' gratification of the lower part of man's nature. The student "sets his affection on things above, and not on things of the earth," not only because he sees this to be the right course of action, but because he realises very clearly the valuelessness of these things of earth. He always tries to take the higher point of view, for, he sees that the lower is utterly unreliable—that the lower desires and feelings gather round him like a dense fog, and make it impossible for him to see anything clearly from that level.

Yet even when he is thoroughly convinced that the higher course is always the right one, and when he is fully determined to follow it, he will nevertheless sometimes encounter very strong temptations to take the lower course, and will be sensible of a great struggle within him. He will discover that there is "a law of the members warring against the law of the mind," as St Paul says, so that "those things that I would I do not, and the thing which I would not, that I do."

Now good religious people often make the most serious mistakes about this interior struggle which we have all felt to a greater or less extent. They usually accept one of two theories on the subject. Either they suppose that the lower promptings come from exterior tempting demons, or else they mourn over the terrible wickedness and blackness of their hearts, in that such fathomless evil still exists within them. Indeed, many of the best of men and women go through a vast amount of totally unnecessary suffering on this account.

The first point to have clearly in mind if one wishes to understand this matter is that the lower desire is not in truth *our* desire at all. Nor is the work of some demon trying to destroy our souls. It is true that there sometimes are evil entities which are attracted by the base thought in man, and intensify it by their action; but such entities are man-made, everyone of them, and impermanent. They are merely the artificial forms called into existence by the thought of other evil men, and they have a period of what seems almost like life, proportioned to the strength of the thought that created them.

But the undesirable prompting within us usually comes from quite another source. It has been mentioned how man draws round him vestures of matter at different levels, in order that he may descend into incarnation. But this matter is not dead matter (indeed, occult science teaches us that there is no such thing as dead matter anywhere), but it is instinct with life; though it is life at a stage of evolution much earlier than our own—so much earlier that it is still moving on a downward course into lower matter, instead of rising again out of lower matter into higher. Consequently its tendency is always to press downwards toward the grosser material and the coarser vibrations which mean progress for it, but retrogression for us; and so it happens that the interest of the true man sometimes comes into collision with that of the living matter in some of his vehicles.

That is a very rough outline of the explanation of the curious internal strife that we sometimes feel—a strife which has suggested to poetic minds the idea of good and evil angels in conflict over the soul of man. A more detailed account will be found in *The Astral Plane*, p.40. and also in *the Other Side of Death.* But in the meantime it is important that the man should realise that *he is* the higher force, always moving towards and battling for good, while this lower force is not he at all, but only an uncontrolled fragment of one of his lower vehicles. He must learn to control it, to dominate it absolutely, and to keep it in order; but he should not, therefore, think of it as evil, but as an outpouring of the Divine power moving on its orderly course, though that course in this instance happens to be downwards into matter, instead of upwards and away from it, as ours is.

CHAPTER VII.

DEATH.

One of the most important practical results of a thorough comprehension of Theosophical truth is the entire change which it necessarily brings about in our attitude towards death. It is impossible for us to calculate the vast amount of utterly unnecessary sorrow and terror and misery which mankind in the aggregate has suffered simply from its ignorance and superstition with regard to this one matter of death. There is among us a mass of false and foolish belief along this line which has worked untold evil in the past and is causing indescribable suffering in the present, and its eradication would be one of the greatest benefits that could be conferred upon the human race.

This benefit the Theosophical teaching at once confers on those who, from their study of philosophy in past lives, now find themselves able to accept it. It robs death forthwith of all its terror and much of its sorrow, and enables us to see it in its true proportions and to understand its place in the scheme of our evolution.

While death is considered as the end of life, as a gateway into a dim but fearful unknown country, it is not unnaturally regarded with much misgiving, if not with positive terror. Since, in spite of all religious teaching to the contrary, this has been the view universally taken in the western world, many grisly horrors have sprung up around it, and have become matters of custom, thoughtlessly obeyed by many who should know better. All the ghastly paraphernalia of woe—the mutes, the plumes, the black velvet, the crape, the mourning garments, the black-edged notepaper—all these are nothing more than advertisements of ignorance on the part of those who employ them. The man who begins to understand what death is at once puts aside all this masquerade as childish folly, seeing that to mourn over the good fortune of his friend merely because it involves for himself the pain of an apparent separation from that friend, becomes, as soon as it is recognized, a display of selfishness. He cannot avoid feeling the wrench of the temporary separation, but he can avoid allowing his own pain to become a hindrance to the friend who has passed on.

He knows that there can be no need to fear or to mourn over death, whether it comes to himself or to those whom he loves. It has come to them all often before, so that there is nothing unfamiliar about it. Instead of representing it as a ghastly king of terrors, it would be more accurate and more sensible to symbolize it as an angel bearing a golden key to admit us to the glorious realms of the higher life.

He realises very definitely that life is continuous and that the loss of the physical body is nothing more than the casting aside of a garment, which in no way changes the real man who is the wearer of the garment. He sees that death is simply a promotion from a life which is more than half-physical to one which is wholly astral, and therefore very much superior. So for himself he unfeignedly welcomes it, and when it comes to those whom he loves he recognizes at once the great advantage for them, even though he cannot but feel a certain amount of selfish regret that *he* should be temporarily separated from them. But he knows also that this separation is in fact only apparent, and not real. He knows that the so-called dead are near him still, and that he has only to cast off temporarily his physical body in sleep, in order to stand side by side with them and commune with them as before.

He sees clearly that the world is one, and that the same Divine laws rule the whole of it, whether it be visible or invisible to physical sight. Consequently he has no feeling of nervousness or strangeness in passing from one part of it to the other, and no sort of uncertainty as to what he will find on the other side of the veil. The whole of the unseen world is so clearly and fully mapped out for him through the work of the Theosophical investigators that it is as well known to him as the physical life, and thus he is prepared to enter upon it without hesitation whenever it may be best for his evolution.

For full details of the various stages of this higher life we must refer the reader to the books specially devoted to this subject. It is sufficient here to say that the conditions into which the man passes are precisely those which he has made for himself. The thoughts and desires which he has encouraged within himself during earth-life take form as definite living entities hovering round him and reacting upon him until the energy which he poured into them is exhausted. When such thoughts and desires have been powerful and persistently evil, the companions so created may indeed be terrible; but happily such cases form a very small minority among the dwellers in the astral world. The worst that the ordinary man of the world usually provides for himself after death is a useless and unutterably wearisome existence, void of all rational interests—the natural sequence of a life wasted in self-indulgence, triviality, and gossip here on earth.

To this weariness active suffering may under certain conditions be added. If a man during earth-life has allowed strong Physical desire to obtain a mastery over him—if, for example, he has become a slave to such a vice as avarice, sensuality, or drunkenness—he has laid up for himself much purgatorial suffering after death. For in losing the physical body he in no way loses these and passions; they remain vivid as ever—nay, they are even more active when they have no longer the heavy particles of dense matter to set in motion. What he does lose is the power to gratify these passions; so that they remain as torturing, gnawing desires, unsatisfied and unsatisfiable. It will be seen that this makes a very real hell for the unfortunate man, though of course only a temporary one, since in process of time such desires must burn themselves out, expending their energy in the very suffering which they produce.

A terrible fate, truly; yet there are two points which we should bear in mind with regard to it. First, that the man has not only brought it upon himself, but has determined its intensity and its duration for himself. He has allowed this desire to reach a certain strength during earth-life, and now he has to meet it and control it. If during physical life he has made efforts to repress or check it, he will have just so much the less difficulty in conquering it now. He has created for himself the monster with which now he has to struggle; whatever strength his antagonist possesses is just what he has given it. Therefore, his fate is not imposed upon him from without, but is simply of his own making.

Secondly, the suffering which he thus brings upon himself is the only way of escape for him. If it were possible for him to avoid it, and to pass through the astral life without this gradual wearing away of the lower desires, what would be the result? Obviously that he would enter upon his next physical life entirely under the domination of these passions. He would be a born drunkard, a sensualist, a miser; and long before it would be possible to teach him that he ought to try to control such passions they would have grown far too strong for control—they would have enslaved him, body and soul, and so another live would be thrown away, another opportunity would be lost. He would enter thus upon a vicious circle from which there appears no escape, and his evolution would be indefinitely delayed.

The Divine scheme is not thus defective. The passion exhausts it elf during the astral life, and the man returns to physical existence without it. True, the weakness of mind which allowed passion to dominate him is still there; true also, he has made for himself for this new life an astral body capable of expressing exactly the same passions as before, so that it would not be difficult for him to resume his old evil life. But the ego, the real man, has had a terrible lesson, and assuredly he will make every effort to prevent his lower manifestation from repeating that mistake, from falling again under the sway of that passion. He has still the germs of it within him, but if he has deserved good and wise parents they will help to develope the good in him and check the evil, the germs will remain unfructified and will atrophy, and so in the next life after that they will not appear at all. So by slow degrees man conquers his evil qualities, and evolves virtues to replace them.

On the other hand, the man who is intelligent and helpful, who understands the conditions of this non-physical existence and takes the trouble to adapt himself to them and make the most of them, finds opening before him a splendid vista of opportunities both for acquiring fresh knowledge and for doing useful work. He discovers that life away from this dense body has a vividness and brilliancy to which all earthly enjoyment is as moonlight unto sunlight, and that through his clear knowledge and calm confidence the power of the endless life shines out upon all those around him. He may become a centre of peace and joy unspeakable to hundreds of his fellow-men, and may do more good in a few years of that astral existence than ever he could have done in the longest physical life.

He is well aware, too, that there lies before him another and still grander stage of this wonderful *post-mortem* life. Just as by his desires and his lower thoughts he has made for himself the surroundings of his astral life, so has he by his higher thought and his nobler aspirations made for himself a life in the heaven-world. For heaven is not a dream, but a living and glorious reality. Not a city far away beyond the stars, with gates of pearl and streets of gold, reserved for the habitation of a favoured few, but a state of consciousness into which every man will pass during the interval between his lives on earth. Not an eternal abiding-place truly, but a condition of bliss indescribable lasting through many centuries. Not even that alone, for although it contains the reality which underlies all the best and most spiritual ideas of Heaven which have been propounded in various religions, yet it must by no means be considered from that point of view only.

It is a realm of nature which is of exceeding importance to us—a vast and splendid world of vivid life in which we are living now, as well as in the periods intervening between physical incarnations.It is only our lack of development, only the limitation imposed upon us by this robe of flesh, that prevents us from fully realising that all the glory of the highest heaven is about us here and now, and that influences flowing from that world are ever playing upon us, if we will only understand and receive them. Impossible as this may seem to the man of the world, it is the plainest of realities to the occultist; and to those who have not yet grasped this fundamental truth we can gloat repeat the advice given by the Buddhist teacher:—"Do not complain and cry and pray, but open your eyes and see. The light is all about you, if you would only cast the bandage from your eyes and look. It is so wonderful, so beautiful, so far beyond what any man has dreamt of or prayed for, and it is for ever and for ever." *(The Soul of a People,"* p. 163.)

When the astral body, which is the vehicle of the lower thought and desire, has gradually been worn away and left behind, the man finds himself inhabiting that higher vehicle of finer matter which we have called the mental body. In this vehicle he is able to respond to the vibrations which reach him from the corresponding matter in the external world—the matter of the mental plane. His time of purgatory is over, the lower part of his nature has burnt itself away, and now there remain only the higher thoughts and aspirations which he has poured forth during earth-life. These cluster round him, and make a sort of shell about him, through the medium of which he is able to respond to certain types of vibration in this refined matter. These thoughts which surround him are the powers by which he draws upon the wealth of the heaven-world. This mental plane is a reflection of the Divine Mind—a storehouse of infinite extent from which the person enjoying heaven is able to draw just according to the power of his own thoughts and aspirations generated during the physical and astral life.

All religions have spoken of the bliss of Heaven, yet few of them have put before us with sufficient clearness this leading idea which alone explains rationally how for all alike such bliss is possible—Which is, indeed, the keynote of the conception—the fact that each man makes his own heaven by selection from the ineffable splendours of the Thought of God Himself. A man decides for himself both the length and the character of his heaven-life by the causes which he himself generates during his earth-life; therefore, he cannot but have exactly the amount which he has deserved and exactly the quality of joy which is best suited to his idiosyncrasies. This is a world in which every being must, from the very fact of his consciousness there, be enjoying the highest spiritual bliss of which he is capable—a world whose power of response to his aspirations is limited only by his capacity to aspire.

Further details as to the astral life will be found in *The Astral Plane;* the heaven-life is described in *The Devachanic Plane,* and information about both is also given in *Death and After,* and in *The Other Side of Death.*

CHAPTER VIII.

MAN'S PAST AND FUTURE.

When we have once grasped the fact that man has reached his present position through a long and varied series of lives, a question naturally arises in our minds as to how far we can obtain any information about this earlier evolution, which would obviously be of absorbing interest to us. Fortunately such information is available, not only by tradition, but also in another and much more certain way. I have no space here to dilate upon the marvels of psychometry, but must simply say that there is abundant evidence to show that nothing can happen without indelibly recording itself—that there exists a kind of memory of Nature from which can be recovered with absolute accuracy a true, full, and perfect picture of any scene or event since the world began. Those to whom this subject is entirely new, and who consequently seek for evidence, should consult Dr. Buchanan's *Psychometry* or Professor Denton's *Soul of Things;* but all occult students are familiar with the possibility, and most of them with the method, of reading these records of the past.

In essence this memory of Nature must be the Divine Memory, far away beyond human reach; but it is assuredly reflected into lower planes so that, as far as events on these lower planes are concerned, it is recoverable by the trained intelligence of man. All that passes before a mirror, for instance, is reflected on its surface, and to our dim eyes it seems that the images make no impression upon that surface, but that each passes away and leaves no trace. Yet that may not be so; it is not difficult to imagine that an impression *may* be left, somewhat as the impression of every sound is left upon the 'sensitive cylinder of a phonograph; and it may be possible to recover the impression from the mirror just as it is recoverable from the phonograph.

The higher psychometry shows us that this not only may be so, but *is* so; and that not a mirror only, but any physical object, retains the impression of all that has happened within its sight, as it were. We have thus at our disposal a faultlessly accurate method of arriving at the earlier history of our world and of mankind, and in this way much that is of the most entrancing interest can be observed in every detail, as though the scenes were being specially rehearsed for our benefit. (See *Clairvoyance,* p. 88.)

Investigations into the past conducted by these methods show a long process of gradual evolution, slow but never-ceasing. They show the development of man under the action of two great laws—first the law of evolution, which steadily presses him onward and upward; and secondly the law of divine justice, or cause and effect, which brings him inevitably the result of his every action, and thus gradually teaches him to live intelligently in harmony with the first law.

This long process of evolution has been carried out not only on this earth, but on other globes connected with it; but the subject is much too vast to be fully treated in an elementary book, such as this. It forms the principal theme of Madame Blavatsky's monumental work, *The Secret Doctrine;* but before commencing that students are advised to read the chapters on this subject in Mrs. Besant's *Ancient Wisdom* and Mr. Sinnett's *Growth of the Soul.*

The books just mentioned will afford the fullest available information not only as to man's past, but as to his future; and though the glory that awaits him is such as no tongue can tell, something at least may be understood of the earlier stages which lead towards it. That man is divine even now, and that he will presently unfold within himself the potentialities of divinity, is an idea which appears to shock some good people, and to be considered by them to savour of blasphemy. Why it should be so is not easy to see, for Jesus himself reminds the Jews around Him of the saying in their Scriptures, "I said, ye are Gods," and the doctrine of the deification of man was quite commonly held by the Fathers of the Church. But in these later days much of the earlier and purer doctrine has been forgotten and misunderstood; and the truth now seems to be held in its fulness only by the student of occultism.

Sometimes men ask why, if man was at the first a spark of the Divine, it should be necessary for him to go through all these eons of evolution, involving so much sorrow and suffering, only in order to be still Divine at the end of it all. But those who make this objection have not yet comprehended the scheme. That which came forth from the Divine was not yet man—not yet even a spark, for there was no developed individualization in it. It was simply a great cloud of Divine essence, though capable of condensing eventually into many sparks.

The difference between its condition when issuing forth and when returning is exactly like that between a great mass of shining nebulous matter, and the solar system which is eventually formed out of it. The nebula is beautiful, no doubt, but vague and useless; the suns formed from it by slow evolution pour life and heat and light upon many worlds and their inhabitants.

Or we may take another analogy. The human body is composed of countless millions of tiny particles, and some of them are constantly being thrown off from it. Suppose that it were possible for each of these particles to go through some kind of evolution by means of which it would in time become a human being, we should not say that because it had been in a certain sense human at the beginning of that evolution it had, therefore, not gained anything when it reached the end. The essence comes forth as a mere outpouring of force, even though it be Divine force; it returns in the form of thousands of millions of mighty adepts, each capable of himself developing into a Logos.

Thus it will be seen that we are abundantly justified in the statement that the future of man is a future to whose glory and splendour there is no limit. And a most important point to remember is that this magnificent future is for all without exception. He whom we call the good man—that is, the man whose will moves with the Divine Will, whose actions are such as to help the march of evolution—makes rapid progress on the upward path; while the man who unintelligently opposes himself to the great current by striving to pursue selfish aims instead of working for the good of the whole, will be able to progress only very slowly and erratically. But the Divine Will is infinitely stronger than any human will, and the working of the great scheme is perfect. The man who does not learn his lesson the first time has simply to try over and over again until he does learn it; the Divine patience is infinite, and sooner or later every human being attains the goal appointed for him. There is no fear and no uncertainty, but only perfect peace for those who know the Law and tie Will.

CHAPTER IX.

CAUSE AND EFFECT.

In previous chapters we have constantly had to take into consideration this mighty law of action and reaction under which every man necessarily receives his just desert; for without this law the rest of the Divine scheme would be incomprehensible to us. It is well worth our while to try to obtain a true appreciation of this law, and the first step towards doing that is to disabuse our minds entirely of the ecclesiastical idea of reward and punishment as following upon human action. It is inevitable that we should connect with that idea the thought of a judge administering such reward or punishment, and then at once follows the further possibility that the judge may be more lenient in one case than in another, that he may be swayed by circumstances, that an appeal may be made to him, and that in that way the incidence of the law may be modified or even escaped altogether.

Every one of these suggestions is in the highest degree misleading, and the whole body of thought to which they belong must be exorcised and utterly cast out before we can arrive at any real understanding of the facts. If a man put his hand upon a bar of red-hot iron, under ordinary circumstances he would be badly burnt; yet it would not occur to him to say that God had punished him for putting his hand on the bar. He would realise that what had happened was precisely what might have been expected under the action of the laws of Nature, and that one who understood what heat is and how it acts could explain exactly the production of the burn.

It is to be observed that the man's intention in no way affects the physical result; whether he seized that bar in order to do some harm with it or in order to save someone else from injury, he would be burnt just the same. Of course, in other and higher ways the results would be quite different; in the one case he would have done a noble deed, and would have the approval of his conscience, while in the other he could feel only remorse. But the physical burn would be there in one case just as much as in the other.

To obtain a true conception of the working of this law of cause and effect we must think of it as acting automatically, in exactly the same way. If we have a heavy weight hanging from the ceiling by a rope, and I exert a certain amount of force in pushing against that weight, we know by the laws of mechanics that that weight will press back against my hand with exactly the same amount of force; and this reaction will operate without the slightest reference to my reason for disturbing its equilibrium. Similarly the man who commits an evil action disturbs the equilibrium of the great current of evolution; and that mighty current invariably adjusts that equilibrium at his expense.

It must not be therefore supposed for a moment that the intention of the action makes no difference; on the contrary it is the most important factor connected with it, even though it does not affect the result upon the physical plane. We are apt to forget that the intention is itself a force, and a force acting upon the mental plane, where the matter is so much finer and vibrates so much more rapidly than on our lower level, that the same amount of energy will produce enormously greater effect. The physical action will produce its result on the physical plane, but the mental energy of the intention will works; out its own result simultaneously in the matter of the mental plane, totally irrespective of the other; and its effect is certain to be very much the more important of the two. In this way it will be seen that an absolutely perfect adjustment is always achieved; for however mixed the motives may be, and however good and evil may be mingled in the physical results, the equilibrium will always be perfectly readjusted, and along every line perfect justice must be done.

We must not forget that it is the man himself and no other who builds his future character as well as produces his future circumstances. Speaking very generally, it may be said that, while his actions in one life produce his environment in the next, his thoughts in the one life are the chief factors in the evolution of his character for the next. The method by which all this works is an exceedingly interesting study, but it would take us far too long to detail it here; it may be found very fully elaborated in Mrs. Besant's manual on *Karma,* and also in the chapter referring to this subject in her *Ancient Wisdom,* and in Mr. Sinnett's *Esoteric Buddhism,* to which the reader may be referred.

It is obvious that all these facts furnish us with exceedingly good reasons for many of our ethical precepts. If thought be a mighty power capable of producing upon its own plane results far more important than any that can be achieved in physical life, then the necessity that man should control that force immediately becomes apparent. Not only is the man building his own future character by means of his thought, but he is also constantly and inevitably affecting those around him by its means.

Hence there lies upon him a very serious responsibility as to the use which he makes of this power. If the feeling of annoyance or hatred arises in the heart of the ordinary man, his natural impulse is to express it in some way either in word or in action. The ordinary rules of civilized society, however, forbid him to do that, and dictate that he should as far as possible repress all outward sign of his feelings. If he succeeds in doing this he is apt to congratulate himself, and to consider that he has done the whole of his duty. The occult student, however, knows that it is necessary for him to carry his self-control a great deal further than that, and that he must absolutely repress the *thought* of irritation as well as its outward expression. For he knows that his feelings set in motion tremendous forces upon the astral plane, that these will act against the object of his irritation just as surely as a blow struck upon the physical plane, and that in many cases the results produced will be far more serious and lasting.

It is true in a very real sense that thoughts are things. To clairvoyant sight thoughts take definite, form and colour, the latter, of course, depending upon the rate of vibration connected with them. The study of these forms and colours is of great interest. A description of them illustrated with coloured drawings will be found in an article in *Lucifer* for September, 1896.

These considerations open up to us possibilities in various directions. Since it is easily possible to do harm by thought, it is also possible to do good by it. Currents may be set in motion which will carry mental help and comfort to many a suffering friend, and in this way a whole new world of usefulness opens before us. Many a grateful soul has been oppressed by a feeling that for want of physical wealth he was usable to do anything in return for the kindness lavished upon him by another; but here is a method by which he can be of the greatest service to him in a realm where physical wealth or its absence makes no difference.

All who can think can help others; and all who can help others ought to help. In this case, as in every other, knowledge is power, and those who understand the law can use the law. Knowing what effects upon themselves and upon others will be produced by certain thoughts, they can deliberately arrange to produce these results. In this way a man can not only steadily mould his character in his present life, but can decide exactly what it shall be in the next. For a thought is a vibration in the matter of the mental body, and the same thought persistently repeated evokes corresponding vibrations (an octave higher, as it were) in the matter of the causal body. In this way qualities are gradually built into the soul itself, and they will certainly reappear as part of the stock-in-trade with which he commences his next incarnation. It is in this way, by working from below upwards, that the faculties and qualities of the soul are gradually evolved, and thus man takes his evolution largely into his own hands and begins to co-operate intelligently in the great scheme of the Deity.

For further information on this subject the best book to study is Mrs. Besant's upon *Thought Power, its Control and Culture.*

CHAPTER X.

WHAT THEOSOPHY DOES FOR US.

It must already be obvious to the careful reader how utterly these Theosophical conceptions change the man's entire view of life when he once becomes fully convinced of them; and the direction of many of these changes, and the reasons on which they are based, will have been seen from what has already been written.

We gain from Theosophy a rational comprehension of that life which was before for so many of us a mere unsolved problem—a riddle without an answer. From it we know why we are here, what we are expected to do, and how we ought to set to work to do it. We see that, however little life may seem worth living for the sake of any pleasures or profits belonging exclusively to the physical plane, it is very emphatically worth living when regarded merely as a school to prepare us for the indescribable glories and the infinite possibilities of the higher planes.

In the light of the information which we acquire, we see not only how to evolve ourselves, but also how to help others to evolve—how by thought and action to make ourselves most useful, first of all to the small circle of those most closely associated with us or those whom we especially love, and then gradually by degrees, as our power increases, to the entire human race. By feelings and thoughts such as these we find ourselves lifted altogether to a higher platform, and we see how narrow and despicable is the petty and personal thought which has so often occupied us in the past. We inevitably begin to regard everything not merely as it affects our infinitesimal selves, but from the wider stand-point of its influence upon humanity as a whole.

The various troubles and sorrows which come to us are so often seen out of all proportion because they are so near to us; they seem to obscure the whole horizon, as a plate held near the eyes will shut out the sun, so that we often forget that "the heart of being is celestial rest." But Theosophical teaching brings all these things into due perspective, and enables us to rise above these clouds, to look down and see things as they are, and not merely as they appear when looked at from below by very limited vision. We learn to sink altogether the lower personality, with its mass of delusions and prejudices and its inability to see anything truly; we learn to rise to an impersonal and unselfish standpoint, where to do right for right's sake seems to us the only rule of life, and to help our fellow-man the greatest of our joys.

For it *is* a life of joy that now opens before us. As the man evolves, his sympathy and compassion increase, so that he becomes more and more sensitive to the sin and sorrow and suffering of the world. Yet at the same time he sees more and more clearly the cause of that suffering, and understands ever more and more fully that, in spite of it all, all things are working together for the final good of all. And so there comes to him not only the deep content and absolute security which is born of the certainty that all is well, but also the definite and radiant joy derived from the contemplation of the magnificent plan of the Logos, and of the steady unfailing success with which that mighty scheme moves to its appointed end. He learns that God means us to be happy, and that it is definitely our duty to be so, in order that we may spread around us vibrations of happiness upon others, since that is one of the methods by which we may lighten the sorrow of the world.

In ordinary life a great part of the annoyance which men feel in connection with their various troubles is often caused by a feeling that they come to them unjustly. A man will say: "Why should all this come to me? There is my neighbour, who is in no way a better man than I, yet *he* does not suffer from sickness, from loss of friends, or loss of wealth; why then should I?"

Theosophy saves its students from this mistake, since it makes it absolutely clear to them that no undeserved suffering can ever come to any man. Whatever trouble we may encounter is simply of the nature of a debt that we have incurred; since it has to be paid, the sooner it is cleared off the better. Nor is this all; for every such trouble is an opportunity for development. If we bear it patiently and bravely, not allowing it to crush us, but meeting it and making the best of it, we thereby evolve within ourselves the valuable qualities of courage, perseverance, determination; and so out of the result of our sins of long ago we bring good instead of evil.

As has before been stated, all fear of death is entirely removed for the Theosophical student, because he understands fully what death is. He no longer mourns for those who have gone before, because they are still present with him, and he knows that to give way to selfish grief would be to cause sadness and depression to *them*. Since they are very near to him, and since the sympathy between them and himself is closer than ever before, he is well aware that uncontrolled grief in him will assuredly reflect itself upon them.

Not that Theosophy counsels him to forget the dead; on the contrary, it encourages him to remember them as often as possible, but never with selfish sorrow, never with a longing to bring them back to earth, never with thought of *his* apparent loss, but only of their great gain. It assures him that a strong loving thought will be a potent factor in their evolution, and that if he will but think rightly and reasonably about them he may render them the greatest assistance in their upward progress.

A careful study of the life of man in the period between his incarnations shows how small a proportion this physical life bears to the whole. In the case of the average educated and cultured man of any of the higher races, the period of one life—that is to say of one day in the real life—would average about fifteen hundred years. Of this period perhaps seventy or eighty years would be spent in physical life, some fifteen or twenty upon the astral plane, and all the rest in the heaven-world, which is therefore by very far the most important part of man's existence. Naturally these proportions vary considerably for different types of men, and when we come to consider the younger souls, born either in inferior races or in the lower ranks of our own, we find that these proportions are entirely changed, for the astral life is likely to be much longer and the heaven-life much shorter. In the case of the absolute savage there is scarcely any heaven-life at all, because he has not yet developed within himself the qualities which alone enable the man to attain that life.

The knowledge of all these facts gives a clearness and certainty to our anticipations of the future which is a welcome relief from the vagueness and indecision of ordinary thought on these subjects. It would be impossible for a Theosophist to have any fears about his "salvation," for he knows that there is nothing for man to be saved from except his own ignorance, and he would consider it the grossest blasphemy to doubt that the will of the Logos will assuredly be fulfilled in the case of every one of his children.

No vague "eternal hope" is his, but utter certainty, born of his knowledge of the eternal law. He cannot fear the future, because he knows the future; so his only anxiety is to make himself worthy to bear his part in the mighty work of evolution. It may well be that there is very little that he can do as yet; yet there is none but can do something, just where he stands, in the circle around him, however lowly that may be.

Every man has his opportunities, for every connection is an opportunity. Every one with whom we are brought into contact is a soul who may be helped —whether it be a child born into the family, a friend who comes into our circle, a servant who joins our household—everyone gives in some way or other an opportunity. It is not for a moment suggested that we should make ourselves nuisances by thrusting our opinions and ideas upon every one with whom we come into contact, as the more ignorant and tactless of our religious friends sometimes do; but we should; be in an attitude of continual readiness to help.

Indeed, we should ever be eagerly watching for an opportunity to help, either with material aid, so far as that may be within our power, or with the benefit of our advice or our knowledge, whenever those may be asked for. Often cases arise in which help by word or deed is impossible for us; but there can never be a case in which friendly and helpful thought cannot be poured forth, and none who understands the power of thought will doubt as to its result, even though it may not be immediately visible upon the physical plane.

The student of Theosophy should be distinguishable from the rest of the world by his perennial cheerfulness, his undaunted courage under difficulties, and his ready sympathy and helpfulness. Assuredly, in spite of his cheerfulness, he will be one who takes life seriously—one who realises that there is much for each to do in the world, and no time to waste. He will see the necessity for gaining perfect control of himself and his various vehicles, because only in that way can he be thoroughly fitted to help others when the opportunity comes to him. He will range himself ever on the side of the higher rather than the lower thought, the nobler rather than the baser; his toleration will be perfect, because he sees the good in all. He will deliberately take the optimistic rather than the pessimistic view of everything, the hopeful rather than the cynical, because he knows that to be always fundamentally the true view—the evil in everything being necessarily the impermanent part, since in the end only the good can endure.

Thus he will look ever for the good in everything, that he may endeavour to strengthen it; he will watch for the working of the great law of evolution, in order that he may range himself on its side, and contribute to its energy his tiny stream of force. In this way, by striving always to help, and never to hinder, he will become, in his small sphere of influence, one of the beneficent powers of Nature; in however lowly a manner, at however unthinkable a distance, he is yet a fellow-worker together with God—and that is the highest honour and the greatest privilege that can ever fall to the lot of man.

A Textbook of Theosophy

Chapter I

What Theosophy Is

"There is a school of philosophy still in existence of which modern culture has lost sight." In these words Mr. A.P. Sinnett began his book, *The Occult World*, the first popular exposition of Theosophy, published thirty years ago. During the years that have passed since then, many thousands have learned wisdom in that school, yet to the majority its teachings are still unknown, and they can give only the vaguest of replies to the query, "What is Theosophy?"

Two books already exist which answer that question: Mr. Sinnett's *Esoteric Buddhism* and Dr. Besant's *The Ancient Wisdom*. I have no thought of entering into competition with those standard works; what I desire is to present a statement, as clear and simple as I can make it, which may be regarded as introductory to them.

We often speak of Theosophy as not in itself a religion, but the truth which lies behind all religions alike. That is so; yet, from another point of view, we may surely say that it is at once a philosophy, a religion and a science. It is a philosophy, because it puts plainly before us an explanation of the scheme of evolution of both the souls and the bodies contained in our solar system. It is a religion in so far as, having shown us the course of ordinary evolution, it also puts before us and advises a method of shortening that course, so that by conscious effort we may progress more directly towards the goal. It is a science, because it treats both these subjects as matters not of theological belief but of direct knowledge obtainable by study and investigation. It asserts that man has no need to trust to blind faith, because he has within him latent powers which, when aroused, enable him to see and examine for himself, and it proceeds to prove its case by showing how those powers may be awakened. It is itself a result of the awakening of such powers by men, for the teachings which it puts before us are founded upon direct observations made in the past, and rendered possible only by such development.

As a philosophy, it explains to us that the solar system is a carefully-ordered mechanism, a manifestation of a magnificent life, of which man is but a small part. Nevertheless, it takes up that small part which immediately concerns us, and treats it exhaustively under three heads—present, past and future.

It deals with the present by describing what man really is, as seen by means of developed faculties. It is customary to speak of man as having a soul. Theosophy, as the result of direct investigation, reverses that dictum, and states that man *is* a soul, and *has* a body—in fact several bodies, which are his vehicles and instruments in various worlds. These worlds are not separate in space; they are simultaneously present with us, here and now, and can be examined; they are the divisions of the material side of Nature—different degrees of density in the aggregation of matter, as will presently be explained in detail. Man has an existence in several of these, but is normally conscious only of the lowest, though sometimes in dreams and trances he has glimpses of some of the others. What is called death is the laying aside of the vehicle belonging to this lowest world, but the soul or real man in a higher world is no more changed or affected by this than the physical man is changed or affected when he removes his overcoat. All this is a matter, not of speculation, but of observation and experiment.

Theosophy has much to tell us of the past history of man—of how in the course of evolution he has come to be what he now is. This also is a matter of observation, because of the fact that there exists an indelible record of all that has taken place—a sort of memory of Nature—by examining which the scenes of earlier evolution may be made to pass before the eyes of the investigator as though they were happening at this moment. By thus studying the past we learn that man is divine in origin and that he has a long evolution behind him—a double evolution, that of the life or soul within, and that of the outer form. We learn, too, that the life of man as a soul is of, what to us seems, enormous length, and that what we have been in the habit of calling his life is in reality only one day of his real existence. He has already lived through many such days, and has many more of them yet before him; and if we wish to understand the real life and its object, we must consider it in relation not only to this one day of it, which begins with birth and ends with death, but also to the days which have gone before and those which are yet to come.

Of those that are yet to come there is also much to be said, and on this subject, too, a great deal of definite information is available. Such information is obtainable, first, from men who have already passed much further along the road of evolution than we, and have consequently direct experience of it; and, secondly, from inferences drawn from the obvious direction of the steps which we see to have been previously taken. The goal of this particular cycle is in sight, though still far above us but it would seem that, even when that has been attained, an infinity of progress still lies before everyone who is willing to undertake it.

One of the most striking advantages of Theosophy is that the light which it brings to us at once solves many of our problems, clears away many difficulties, accounts for the apparent injustices of life, and in all directions brings order out of seeming chaos. Thus, while some of its teaching is based upon the observation of forces whose direct working is somewhat beyond the ken of the ordinary man of the world, if the latter will accept it as a hypothesis he will very soon come to see that it must be a correct one, because it, and it alone, furnishes a coherent and reasonable explanation of the drama of life which is being played before him.

The existence of Perfected Men, and the possibility of coming into touch with Them and being taught by Them, are prominent among the great new truths which Theosophy brings to the western world. Another of them is the stupendous fact that the world is not drifting blindly into anarchy, but that its progress is under the control of a perfectly organized Hierarchy, so that final failure even for the tiniest of its units is of all impossibilities the most impossible. A glimpse of the working of that Hierarchy inevitably engenders the desire to co-operate with it, to serve under it, in however humble a capacity, and some time in the far-distant future to be worthy to join the outer fringes of its ranks.

This brings us to that aspect of Theosophy which we have called religious. Those who come to know and to understand these things are dissatisfied with the slow æons of evolution; they yearn to become more immediately useful, and so they demand and obtain knowledge of the shorter but steeper Path. There is no possibility of escaping the amount of work that has to be done. It is like carrying a load up a mountain; whether one carries it straight up a steep path or more gradually by a road of gentle slope, precisely the same number of foot-pounds must be exerted. Therefore to do the same work in a small fraction of the time means determined effort. It can be done, however, for it has been done; and those who have done it agree that it far more than repays the trouble. The limitations of the various vehicles are thereby gradually transcended, and the liberated man becomes an intelligent co-worker in the mighty plan for the evolution of all beings.

In its capacity as a religion, too, Theosophy gives its followers a rule of life, based not on alleged commands delivered at some remote period of the past, but on plain common sense as indicated by observed facts. The attitude of the student of Theosophy towards the rules which it prescribes resembles rather that which we adopt to hygienic regulations than obedience to religious commandments. We may say, if we wish, that this thing or that is in accordance with the divine Will, for the divine Will is expressed in what we know as the laws of Nature. Because that Will wisely ordereth all things, to infringe its laws means to disturb the smooth working of the scheme, to hold back for a moment that fragment or tiny part of evolution, and consequently to bring discomfort upon ourselves and others. It is for that reason that the wise man avoids infringing them—not to escape the imaginary wrath of some offended deity.

But if from a certain point of view we may think of Theosophy as a religion, we must note two great points of difference between it and what is ordinarily called religion in the West. First, it neither demands belief from its followers, nor does it even speak of belief in the sense in which that word is usually employed. The student of occult science either *knows* a thing or suspends his judgment about it; there is no place in his scheme for blind faith. Naturally, beginners in the study cannot yet *know* for themselves, so they are asked to read the results of the various observations and to deal with them as probable hypotheses—provisionally to accept and act upon them, until such time as they can prove them for themselves.

Secondly, Theosophy never endeavours to convert any man from whatever religion he already holds. On the contrary, it explains his religion to him, and enables him to see in it deeper meanings than he has ever known before. It teaches him to understand it and live it better than he did, and in many cases it gives back to him, on a higher and more intelligent level, the faith in it which he had previously all but lost.

Theosophy has its aspects as a science also; it is in very truth a science of life, a science of the soul. It applies to everything the scientific method of oft-repeated, painstaking observation, and then tabulates the results and makes deductions from them. In this way it has investigated the various planes of Nature, the conditions of man's consciousness during life and after what is commonly called death. It cannot be too often repeated that its statements on all these matters are not vague guesses or tenets of faith, but are based upon direct and oft-repeated *observation* of what happens. Its investigators have dealt also to a certain extent with subjects more in the range of ordinary science, as may be seen by those who read the book on *Occult Chemistry*.

Thus we see that Theosophy combines within itself some of the characteristics of philosophy, religion and science. What, it might be asked, is its gospel for this weary world? What are the main points which emerge from its investigations? What are the great facts which it has to lay before humanity?

They have been well summed up under three main heads.

"There are three truths which are absolute, and which cannot be lost, but yet may remain silent for lack of speech.

"The soul of man is immortal and its future is the future of a thing whose growth and splendour has no limit.

"The principle which gives life dwells in us and without us, is undying and eternally beneficent, is not heard or seen or smelt, but is perceived by the man who desires perception.

"Each man is his own absolute lawgiver, the dispenser of glory or gloom to himself, the decreer of his life, his reward, his punishment.

"These truths, which are as great as is life itself, are as simple as the simplest mind of man."

Put shortly, and in the language of the man of the street, this means that God is good, that man is immortal, and that as we sow so we must reap. There is a definite scheme of things; it is under intelligent direction and works under immutable laws. Man has his place in this scheme and is living under these laws. If he understands them and co-operates with them, he will advance rapidly and will be happy; if he does not understand them—if, wittingly or unwittingly, he breaks them, he will delay his progress and be miserable. These are not theories, but proved facts. Let him who doubts read on, and he will see.

CHAPTER II

FROM THE ABSOLUTE TO MAN

Of the Absolute, the Infinite, the All-embracing, we can at our present stage know nothing, except that It is; we can say nothing that is not a limitation, and therefore inaccurate.

In It are innumerable universes; in each universe countless solar systems. Each solar system is the expression of a mighty Being, whom we call the LOGOS, the Word of God, the Solar Deity. He is to it all that men mean by God. He permeates it; there is nothing in it which is not He; it is the manifestation of Him in such matter as we can see. Yet He exists above it and outside it, living a stupendous life of His own among His Peers. As is said in an Eastern Scripture: "Having permeated this whole universe with one fragment of Myself I remain."

Of that higher life of His we can know nothing. But of the fragment of His life which energises His system we may know something in the lower levels of its manifestation. We may not see Him, but we may see His power at work. No one who is clairvoyant can be atheistic; the evidence is too tremendous.

Out of Himself He has called this mighty system into being. We who are in it are evolving fragments of His life, Sparks of His divine Fire; from Him we all have come; into Him we shall all return.

Many have asked why He has done this; why He has emanated from Himself all this system; why He has sent us forth to face the storms of life. We cannot know, nor is the question practical; suffice it that we are here, and we must do our best. Yet many philosophers have speculated on this point and many suggestions have been made. The most beautiful that I know is that of a Gnostic philosopher:

"God is Love, but Love itself cannot be perfect unless it has those upon whom it can be lavished and by whom it can be returned. Therefore He put forth of Himself into matter, and He limited His glory, in order that through this natural and slow process of evolution we might come into being; and we in turn according to His Will are to develop until we reach even His own level, and then the very love of God itself will become more perfect, because it will then be lavished on those, His own children, who will fully understand and return it, and so His great scheme will be realized and His Will, be done."

At what stupendous elevation His consciousness abides we know not, nor can we know its true nature as it shows itself there. But when He puts Himself down into such conditions as are within our reach, His manifestation is ever threefold, and so all religions have imaged Him as a Trinity. Three, yet fundamentally One; Three Persons (for person means a mask) yet one God, showing Himself in those Three Aspects. Three to us, looking at Them from below, because Their functions are different; one to Him, because He knows Them to be but facets of Himself.

All Three of these Aspects are concerned in the evolution of the solar system; all Three are also concerned in the evolution of man. This evolution is His Will; the method of it is His plan.

Next below this Solar Deity, yet also in some mysterious manner part of Him, come His seven Ministers sometimes called the Planetary Spirits. Using an analogy drawn from the physiology of our own body, Their relation to Him is like that of the ganglia or the nerve centres to the brain. All evolution which comes forth from Him comes through one or other of Them.

Under Them in turn come vast hosts or orders of spiritual beings, whom we call Angels or Devas. We do not yet know all the functions which they fulfil in different parts of this wonderful scheme, but we find some of them intimately connected with the building of the system and the unfolding of life within it.

Here in our world there is a great Official who represents the Solar Deity and is in absolute control of all the evolution that takes place upon this planet. We may image Him as the true KING of this world and under Him are ministers in charge of different departments. One of these departments is concerned with the evolution of the different races of humanity so that for each great race there is a Head who founds it, differentiates it from all others, and watches over its development. Another department is that of religion and education, and it is from this that all the greatest teachers of history have come—that all religions have been sent forth. The great Official at the head of this department either comes Himself or sends one of His pupils to found a new religion when He decides that one is needed.

Therefore all religions, at the time of their first presentation to the world, have contained a definite statement of the Truth, and in its fundamentals this Truth has been always the same. The presentations of it have varied because of differences in the races to whom it was offered. The conditions of civilization and the degree of evolution obtained by various races have made it desirable to present this one Truth in divers forms. But the inner Truth is always the same, and the source from which it comes is the same, even though the external phases may appear to be different and even contradictory. It is foolish for men to wrangle over the question of the superiority of one teacher or one form of teaching to another, for the teacher is always one sent by the Great Brotherhood of Adepts, and in all its important points, in its ethical and moral principles, the teaching has always been the same.

There is in the world a body or Truth which lies at the back of all these religions, and represents the facts of nature as far as they are at present known to man. In the outer world, because of their ignorance of this, people are always disputing and arguing about whether there is a God; whether man survives death; whether definite progress is possible for him, and what is his relation to the universe. These questions are ever present in the mind of man as soon as intelligence is awakened. They are not unanswerable, as is frequently supposed; the answers to them are within the reach of anyone who will make proper efforts to find them. The truth is obtainable, and the conditions of its attainment are possible of achievement by anyone who will make the effort.

In the earlier stages of the development of humanity the great Officials of the Hierarchy are provided from outside, from other and more highly evolved parts of the system, but as soon as men can be trained to the necessary level of power and wisdom these offices are held by them. In order to be fit to hold such an office a man must raise himself to a very high level, and must become what is called an Adept—a being of goodness, power and wisdom so great that He towers above the rest of humanity, for He has already attained the summit of ordinary human evolution; He has achieved that which the plan of the Deity marked out for Him to achieve during this age or dispensation. But His evolution later on continues beyond that level—continues to divinity.

A large number of men have attained the Adept level—men not of one nation, but of all the leading nations of the world—rare souls who with indomitable courage have stormed the fortresses of nature, and captured her innermost secrets, and so have truly earned the right to be called Adepts. Among Them there are many degrees and many lines of activity; but always some of Them remain within touch of our earth as members of this Hierarchy which has in charge the administration of the affairs of our world and of the spiritual evolution of our humanity.

This august body is often called the Great White Brother-hood, but its members are not a community all living together. Each of Them, to a large extent, draws Himself apart from the world, and They are in constant communication with one another and with Their Head; but Their knowledge of higher forces is so great that this is achieved without any necessity for meeting in the physical world. In many cases They continue to live each in His own country, and Their power remains unsuspected among those who live near Them. Any man who will may attract Their attention, but he can do it only by showing himself worthy of Their notice. None need fear that his efforts will pass unnoticed; such oversight is impossible, for the man who is devoting himself to service such as this, stands out from the rest of humanity like a great flame in a dark night. A few of these great Adepts, who are thus working for the good of the world, are willing to take as apprentices those who have resolved to devote themselves utterly to the service of mankind; such Adepts are called Masters.

One of these apprentices was Helena Petrovna Blavatsky—a great soul who was sent out to offer knowledge to the world. With Colonel Henry Steel Olcott she founded The Theosophical Society for the spread of this knowledge which she had to give. Among those who came into contact with her in those early days was Mr. A.P. Sinnett, the editor of *The Pioneer*, and his keen intellect at once grasped the magnitude and the importance of the teaching which she put before him. Although Madame Blavatsky herself had previously written *Isis Unveiled*, it had attracted but little attention, and it was Mr. Sinnett who first made the teaching really available for western readers in his two books, *The Occult World* and *Esoteric Buddhism*.

It was through these works that I myself first came to know their author, and afterwards Madame Blavatsky herself; from both of them I learned much. When I asked Madame Blavatsky how one could learn still more, how one could make definite progress along the Path which she pointed out to us, she told me of the possibility that other students might be accepted as apprentices by the great Masters, even as she herself had been accepted, and that the only way to gain such acceptance was to show oneself worthy of it by earnest and altruistic work. She told me that to reach that goal a man must be absolutely one-pointed in his determination; that no one who tried to serve both God and Mammon could ever hope to succeed. One of these Masters Himself had said: "In order to succeed, a pupil must leave his own world and come into ours."

This means that he must cease to be one of the majority who live for wealth and power, and must join the tiny minority who care nothing for such things, but live only in order to devote themselves selflessly to the good of the world. She warned us clearly that the way was difficult to tread, that we should be misunderstood and reviled by those who still lived in the world, and that we had nothing to look forward to but the hardest of hard work; and though the result was sure, no one could foretell how long it would take to arrive at it. Some of us accepted these conditions joyfully, and we have never for a moment regretted the decision.

After some years of work I had the privilege of coming into contact with these great Masters of the Wisdom; from Them I learnt many things—among others, how to verify for myself at first hand most of the teachings which They had given. So that, in this matter, I write of what I know, and what I have seen for myself. Certain points are mentioned in the teaching, for the verification of which powers are required far beyond anything which I have gained so far. Of them, I can say only that they are consistent with what I do know, and in many cases are necessary as hypotheses to account for what I have seen. They came to me, along with the rest of the Theosophical system, upon the authority of these mighty Teachers. Since then I have learnt to examine for myself by far the greater part of what I was told, and I have found the information given to me to be correct in every particular; therefore I am justified in assuming the probability that that other part, which as yet I cannot verify, will also prove to be correct when I arrive at its level.

To attain the honour of being accepted as an apprentice of one of the Masters of the Wisdom is the object set before himself by every earnest Theosophical student. But it means a determined effort. There have always been men who were willing to make the necessary effort, and therefore there have always been men who knew. The knowledge is so transcendent that when a man grasps it fully he becomes more than man and he passes beyond our ken.

But there are stages in the acquirement of this knowledge, and we may learn much if we will, from those who themselves are still in process of learning; for all human beings stand on one or other of the rungs of the ladder of evolution. The primitive stand at its foot; we who are civilized beings have already climbed part of the way. But though we can look back and see rungs of the ladder below us which we have already passed, we may also look up and see many rungs above us to which we have not yet attained. Just as men are standing even now on each of the rungs below us, so that we can see the stages by which man has mounted, so also are there men standing on each of the rungs above us, so that from studying them we may see how man shall mount in the future. Precisely because we see men on every step of this ladder, which leads up to a glory which as yet we have no words to express, we know that the ascent to that glory is possible for us. Those who stand high above us, so high that They seem to us as gods in Their marvellous knowledge and power, tell us that They stood not long since where we are standing now, and They indicate to us clearly the steps which lie between, which we also must tread if we would be as They.

Chapter III

The Formation of a Solar System

The beginning of the universe (if ever it had a beginning) is beyond our ken. At the earliest point of history that we can reach, the two great opposites of spirit and matter, of life and form, are already in full activity. We find that the ordinary conception of matter needs a revision, for what are commonly called force and matter are in reality only two varieties of Spirit at different stages in evolution and the real matter or basis of everything lies in the background unperceived. A French scientist has recently said: "There is no matter; there are nothing but holes in the æther."

This also agrees with the celebrated theory of Professor Osborne Reynolds. Occult investigation shows this to be the correct view, and in that way explains what Oriental sacred books mean when they say that matter is an illusion.

The ultimate root-matter as seen at our level is what scientists call the æther of space.[1] To every physical sense the space occupied by it appears empty, yet in reality this æther is far denser than anything of which we can conceive. Its density is defined by Professor Reynolds as being ten thousand times greater than that of water, and its mean pressure as seven hundred and fifty thousand tons to the square inch.

This substance is perceptible only to highly developed clairvoyant power. We must assume a time (though we have no direct knowledge on this point) when this substance filled all space. We must also suppose that some great Being (not the Deity of a solar system, but some Being almost infinitely higher than that) changed this condition of rest by pouring out His spirit or force into a certain section of this matter, a section of the size of a whole universe. This effect of the introduction of this force is as that of the blowing of a mighty breath; it has formed within this æther an incalculable number of tiny spherical bubbles,[2] and these bubbles are the ultimate atoms of which what we call matter is composed. They are not the atoms of the chemist, nor even the ultimate atoms of the physical world. They stand at a far higher level, and what are usually called atoms are composed of vast aggregations of these bubbles, as will be seen later.

When the Solar Deity begins to make His system, He finds ready to His hand this material—this infinite mass of tiny bubbles which can be built up into various kinds of matter as we know it. He commences by defining the limit of His field of activity, a vast sphere whose circumference is far larger than the orbit of the outermost of His future planets. Within the limit of that sphere He sets up a kind of gigantic vortex—a motion which sweeps together all the bubbles into a vast central mass, the material of the nebula that is to be.

Into this vast revolving sphere He sends forth successive impulses of force, gathering together the bubbles into ever more and more complex aggregations, and producing in this way seven gigantic interpenetrating worlds of matter of different degrees of density, all concentric and all occupying the same space.

Acting through His Third Aspect He sends forth into this stupendous sphere the first of these impulses. It sets up all through the sphere a vast number of tiny vortices, each of which draws into itself forty-nine bubbles, and arranges them in a certain shape. These little groupings of bubbles so formed are the atoms of the second of the interpenetrating worlds. The whole number of the bubbles is not used in this way, sufficient being left in the dissociated state to act as atoms for the first and highest of these worlds. In due time comes the second impulse, which seizes upon nearly all these forty-nine bubble-atoms (leaving only enough to provide atoms for the second world), draws them back into itself and then, throwing them out again, sets up among them vortices, each of which holds within itself 2,401 bubbles (49^2). These form the atoms of the third world. Again after a time comes a third impulse, which in the same way seizes upon nearly all these 2,401 bubble-atoms, draws them back again into their original form, and again throws them outward once more as the atoms of the fourth world each atom containing this time 49^3 bubbles. This process is repeated until the sixth of these successive impulses has built the atom of the seventh or the lowest world—that atom containing 49^6 of the original bubbles.

This atom of the seventh world is the ultimate atom of the physical world—not any of the atoms of which chemists speak, but that ultimate out of which all their atoms are made. We have at this stage arrived at that condition of affairs in which the vast whirling sphere contains within itself seven types of matter, all one in essence, because all built of the same kind of bubbles, but differing in their degree of density. All these types are freely intermingled, so that

---

[1] This has been described in *Occult Chemistry* under the name of koilon.
[2] The bubbles are spoken of in *The Secret Doctrine* as the holes which Fohat digs in space.

specimens of each type would be found in a small portion of the sphere taken at random in any part of it, with, however, a general tendency of the heavier atoms to gravitate more and more towards the centre.

The seventh impulse sent out from the Third Aspect of the Deity does not, as before, draw back the physical atoms which were last made into the original dissociated bubbles, but draws them together into certain aggregations, thus making a number of different kinds of what may be called proto-elements, and these again are joined together into the various forms which are known to science as chemical elements. The making of these extends over a long period of ages, and they are made in a certain definite order by the interaction of several forces, as is correctly indicated in Sir William Crookes's paper, *The Genesis of the Elements*. Indeed the process of their making is not even now concluded; uranium is the latest and heaviest element so far as we know, but others still more complicated may perhaps be produced in the future.

As ages rolled on the condensation increased, and presently the stage of a vast glowing nebula was reached. As it cooled, still rapidly rotating, it flattened into a huge disc and gradually broke up into rings surrounding a central body—an arrangement not unlike that which Saturn exhibits at the present day, though on a far larger scale. As the time drew near when the planets would be required for the purposes of evolution, the Deity sets up somewhere in the thickness of each ring a subsidiary vortex into which a great deal of the matter of the ring was by degrees collected. The collisions of the gathered fragments caused a revival of the heat, and the resulting planet was for a long time a mass of glowing gas. Little by little it cooled once more, until it became fit to be the theatre of life such as ours. Thus were all the planets formed.

Almost all the matter of those interpenetrating worlds was by this time concentrated into the newly formed planets. Each of them was and is composed of all those different kinds of matter. The earth upon which we are now living is not merely a great ball of physical matter, built of the atoms of that lowest world, but has also attached to it an abundant supply of matter of the sixth, the fifth, the fourth and other worlds. It is well known to all students of science that particles of matter never actually touch one another, even in the hardest of substances. The spaces between them are always far greater in proportion than their own size—enormously greater. So there is ample room for all the other kinds of atoms of all those other worlds, not only to lie between the atoms of the denser matter, but to move quite freely among them and around them. Consequently, this globe upon which we live is not one world, but seven interpenetrating worlds, all occupying the same space, except that the finer types of matter extend further from the centre than does the denser matter.

We have given names to these interpenetrating worlds for convenience in speaking of them. No name is needed for the first, as man is not yet in direct connection with it; but when it is necessary to mention it, it may be called the divine world. The second is described as the monadic, because in it exist those Sparks of the divine Life which we call the human Monads; but neither of these can be touched by the highest clairvoyant investigations at present possible for us. The third sphere, whose atoms contain 2,401 bubbles, is called the spiritual world, because in it functions the highest Spirit in man as now constituted. The fourth is the intuitional world,[1] because from it come the highest intuitions. The fifth is the mental world, because from its matter is built the mind of man. The sixth is called the emotional or astral world, because the emotions of man cause undulations in its matter. (The name astral was given to it by mediæval alchemists, because its matter is starry or shining as compared to that of the denser world.) The seventh world, composed of the type of matter which we see all around us, is called the physical.

The matter of which all these interpenetrating worlds are built is essentially the same matter, but differently arranged and of different degrees of density. Therefore the rates at which these various types of matter normally vibrate differ also. They may be considered as a vast gamut of undulations consisting of many octaves. The physical matter uses a certain

---

[1] Previously called in Theosophical literature the buddhic plane.

number of the lowest of these octaves, the astral matter another group of octaves just above that, the mental matter a still further group, and so on.

Not only has each of these worlds its own type of matter; it has also its own set of aggregations of that matter—its own substances. In each world we arrange these substances in seven classes according to the rate at which their molecules vibrate. Usually, but not invariably, the slower oscillation involves also a larger molecule—a molecule, that is, built up by a special arrangement of the smaller molecules of the next higher subdivision. The application of heat increases the size of the molecules and also quickens and amplifies their undulation, so that they cover more ground, and the object, as a whole expands, until the point is reached where the aggregation of molecules breaks up, and the latter passes from one condition to that next above it. In the matter of the physical world the seven subdivisions are represented by seven degrees of density of matter, to which, beginning from below upwards, we give the names solid, liquid, gaseous, etheric, super-etheric, subatomic and atomic.

The atomic subdivision is one in which all forms are built by the compression into certain shapes of the physical atoms, without any previous collection of these atoms into blocks or molecules. Typifying the physical ultimate atom for the moment by a brick, any form in the atomic subdivision would be made by gathering together some of the bricks, and building them into a certain shape. In order to make matter for the next lower subdivision, a certain number of the bricks (atoms) would first be gathered together and cemented into small blocks of say four bricks each, five bricks each, six bricks or seven bricks; and then these blocks so made would be used as building stones. For the next subdivision several of the blocks of the second subdivision cemented together in certain shapes would form building-stones, and so on to the lowest.

To transfer any substance from the solid condition to the liquid (that is to say, to melt it) is to increase the vibration of its compound molecules until at last they are shaken apart into the simpler molecules of which they were built. This process can in all cases be repeated again and again until finally any and every physical substance can be reduced to the ultimate atoms of the physical world.

Each of these worlds has its inhabitants, whose senses are normally capable of responding to the undulations of their own world only. A man living (as we are all doing) in the physical world sees, hears, feels, by vibrations connected with the physical matter around him. He is equally surrounded by the astral and mental and other worlds which are interpenetrating his own denser world, but of them he is normally unconscious, because his senses cannot respond to the oscillations of their matter, just as our physical eyes cannot see by the vibrations of ultra-violet light, although scientific experiments show that they exist, and there are other consciousnesses with differently-formed organs who *can* see by them. A being living in the astral world might be occupying the very same space as a being living in the physical world, yet each would be entirely unconscious of the other and would in no way impede the free movement of the other. The same is true of all other worlds. We are at this moment surrounded by these worlds of finer matter, as close to us as the world we see, and their inhabitants are passing through us and about us, but we are entirely unconscious of them.

Since our evolution is centred at present upon this globe which we call the earth, it is in connection with it only that we shall be speaking of these higher worlds, so in future when I use the term "astral world" I shall mean by it the astral part of our own globe only, and not (as heretofore) the astral part of the whole solar system. This astral part of our own world is also a globe, but of astral matter. It occupies the same place as the globe which we see, but its matter (being so much lighter) extends out into space on all sides of us further than does the atmosphere of the earth—a great deal further. It stretches to a little less than the mean distance of the moon, so that though the two physical globes, the earth and the moon, are nearly 240,000 miles apart, the astral globes of these two bodies touch one another when the moon is in perigee, but not when she is in apogee. I shall apply the term "mental world" to the still larger globe of mental matter in the midst of which our physical earth exists. When we come to the still higher globes we have spheres large enough to touch the corresponding spheres of other planets in the system, though their matter also is just as much about us here on the surface of the solid earth as that of the others. All these globes of finer matter are a part of us, and are all revolving round the sun with their visible part. The student will do well to accustom himself to think of our earth as the whole of this mass of interpenetrating worlds—not only the comparatively small physical ball in the centre of it.

CHAPTER IV

THE EVOLUTION OF LIFE

All the impulses of life which I have described as building the interpenetrating worlds come forth from the Third Aspect of the Deity. Hence in the Christian scheme that Aspect is called "the Giver of Life", the Spirit who brooded over the face of the waters of space. In Theosophical literature these impulses are usually taken as a whole, and called the first outpouring.

When the worlds had been prepared to this extent, and most of the chemical elements already existed, the Second Outpouring of life took place, and this came from the Second Aspect of the Deity. It brought with it the power of combination. In all the worlds it found existing what may be thought of as elements corresponding to those worlds. It proceeded to combine those elements into organisms which it then ensouled, and in this way it built up the seven kingdoms of Nature. Theosophy recognizes seven kingdoms, because it regards man as separate from the animal kingdom and it takes into account several stages of evolution which are unseen by the physical eye, and gives to them the mediæval name of "elemental kingdoms".

The divine Life pours itself into matter from above, and its whole course may be thought of in two stages—the gradual assumption of grosser and grosser matter, and then the gradual casting off again of the vehicles which have been assumed. The earliest level upon which its vehicles can be scientifically observed is the mental—the fifth counting from the finer to the grosser, the first on which there are separated globes. In practical study it is found convenient to divide this mental world into two parts, which we call the higher and the lower according to the degree of density of their matter. The higher consists of the three finer subdivisions of mental matter; the lower part of the other four.

When the outpouring reaches the higher mental world it draws together the ethereal elements there, combines them into what at that level correspond to substances and of these substances builds forms which it inhabits. We call this the first elemental kingdom.

After a long period of evolution through different forms at that level, the wave of life, which is all the time pressing steadily downwards, learns to identify itself so fully with those forms that, instead of occupying them and withdrawing from them periodically, it is able to hold them permanently and make them part of itself, so that now from that level it can proceed to the temporary occupation of forms at a still lower level. When it reaches this stage we call it the second elemental kingdom, the ensouling life of which resides upon the higher mental levels, while the vehicles through which it manifests are on the lower.

After another vast period of similar length, it is found that the downward pressure has caused this process to repeat itself; once more the life has identified itself with its forms, and has taken up its residence upon the lower mental levels, so that it is capable of ensouling bodies in the astral world. At this stage we call it the third elemental kingdom.

We speak of all these forms as finer or grosser relatively to one another, but all of them are almost infinitely finer than any with which we are acquainted in the physical world. Each of these three is a kingdom of Nature, as varied in the manifestations of its different forms of life as is the animal or vegetable kingdom which we know. After a long period spent in ensouling the forms of the third of these elemental kingdoms it identifies itself with them in turn, and so is able to ensoul the etheric part of the mineral kingdom, and becomes the life which vivifies that—for there is a life in the mineral kingdom just as much as in the vegetable or the animal, although it is in conditions where it cannot manifest so freely. In the course of the mineral evolution the downward pressure causes it to identify itself in the same way with the etheric matter of the physical world, and from that to ensoul the denser matter of such minerals as are perceptible to our senses.

In the mineral kingdom we include not only what are usually called minerals, but also liquids, gases and many etheric substances the existence of which is unknown to western science. All the matter of which we know anything is living matter, and the life which it contains is always evolving. When it has reached the central point of the mineral stage the downward pressure ceases, and is replaced by an upward tendency; the outbreathing has ceased and the indrawing has begun.

When mineral evolution is completed, the life has withdrawn itself again into the astral world, but bearing with it all the results obtained through its experiences in the physical. At this stage it ensouls vegetable forms, and begins to show itself much more clearly as what we commonly call life—plant-life of all kinds; and at a yet later stage of its development it leaves the vegetable kingdom and ensouls the animal kingdom. The attainment of this level is the sign that it has withdrawn itself still further, and is now working from the lower mental world. In order to work in physical matter from that mental world it must operate through the intervening astral matter; and that astral matter is now no longer part of the garment of the group soul as a whole, but is the individual astral body of the animal concerned, as will be later explained.

In each of these kingdoms it not only passes a period of time which is to our ideas almost incredibly long, but it also goes through a definite course of evolution, beginning from the lower manifestations of that kingdom and ending with the highest. In the vegetable kingdom, for example, the life-force might commence its career by occupying grasses or mosses and end it by ensouling magnificent forest trees. In the animal kingdom it might commence with mosquitoes or with animalculæ, and might end with the finest specimens of the mammalia.

The whole process is one of steady evolution from lower forms to higher, from the simpler to the more complex. But what is evolving is not primarily the form, but the life within it. The forms also evolve and grow better as time passes; but this is in order that they may be appropriate vehicles for more and more advanced waves of life. When the life has reached the highest level possible in the animal kingdom, it may then pass on into the human kingdom, under conditions which will presently be explained.

The outpouring leaves one kingdom and passes to another, so that if we had to deal with only one wave of this outpouring we could have in existence only one kingdom at a time. But the Deity sends out a constant succession of these waves, so that at any given time we find a number of them simultaneously in operation. We ourselves represent one such wave; but we find evolving alongside us another wave which ensouls the animal kingdom—a wave which came out from the Deity one stage later than we did. We find also the vegetable kingdom, which represents a third wave, and the mineral kingdom, which represents a fourth; and occultists know of the existence all round us of three elemental kingdoms, which represent the fifth, sixth and seventh waves. All these, however, are successive ripples of the same great outpouring from the Second Aspect of the Deity.

We have here, then, a scheme of evolution in which the divine Life involves itself more and more deeply in matter, in order that through that matter it may receive vibrations which could not otherwise affect it—impacts from without, which by degrees arouse within it rates of undulation corresponding to their own, so that it learns to respond to them. Later on it learns of itself to generate these rates of undulation, and so becomes a being possessed of spiritual powers.

We may presume that when this outpouring of life originally came forth from the Deity, at some level altogether beyond our power of cognition, it may perhaps have been homogeneous; but when it first comes within practical cognizance, when it is itself in the intuitional world, but is ensouling bodies made of the matter of the higher mental world, it is already not one huge world-soul but many souls. Let us suppose a homogeneous outpouring, which may be considered as one vast soul, at one end of the scale; at the other, when humanity is reached, we find that one vast soul broken up into millions of the comparatively little souls of individual men. At any stage between these two extremes we find an intermediate condition, the immense world-soul already subdivided, but not to the utmost limit of possible subdivision.

Each man is a soul, but not each animal or each plant. Man, as a soul, can manifest through only one body at a time in the physical world, whereas one animal soul manifests simultaneously through a number of animal bodies, one plant-soul through a number of separate plants. A lion, for example, is not a permanently separate entity in the same way as a man is. When the man dies—that is, when he as a soul lays aside his physical body—he remains himself exactly as he was before, an entity separate from all other entities. When the lion dies, that which has been the separate soul of him is poured back into the mass from which it came—a mass which is at the same time providing the souls for many other lions. To such a mass we give the name of "group-soul".

To such a group-soul is attached a considerable number of lion bodies—let us say a hundred. Each of those bodies while it lives has its hundredth part of the group-soul attached to it, and for the time being this is apparently quite separate, so that the lion is as much an individual during his physical life as the man; but he is not a permanent individual. When he dies the soul of him flows back into the group-soul to which it belongs, and that identical lion-soul cannot be separated again from the group.

A useful analogy may help comprehension. Imagine the group-soul to be represented by the water in a bucket, and the hundred lion bodies by a hundred tumblers. As each tumbler is dipped into the bucket it takes out from it a tumblerful of water (the separate soul). That water for the time being takes the shape of the vehicle which it fills, and is temporarily separate from the water which remains in the bucket, and from the water in the other tumblers.

Now put into each of the hundred tumblers some kind of colouring matter or some kind of flavouring. That will represent the qualities developed by its experiences in the separate soul of the lion during its lifetime. Pour back the water from the tumbler into the bucket; that represents the death of the lion. The colouring matter or the flavouring will be distributed through the whole of the water in the bucket, but will be a much fainter colouring, a much less pronounced flavour when thus distributed than it was when confined in one tumbler. The qualities developed by the experience of one lion attached to that group-soul are therefore shared by the entire group-soul, but in a much lower degree.

We may take out another tumblerful of water from that bucket, but we can never again get exactly the same tumblerful after it has once been mingled with the rest. Every tumblerful taken from that bucket in the future will contain some traces of the colouring or flavouring put into each tumbler whose contents have been returned to the bucket. Just so the qualities developed by the experience of a single lion will become the common property of all lions who are in the future to be born from that group-soul, though in a lesser degree than that in which they existed in the individual lion who developed them.

That is the explanation of inherited instincts; that is why the duckling which has been hatched by a hen takes to the water instantly without needing to be shown how to swim; why the chicken just out of its shell will cower at the shadow of a hawk; why a bird which has been artificially hatched, and has never seen a nest, nevertheless knows how to make one, and makes it according to the traditions of its kind.

Lower down in the scale of animal life enormous numbers of bodies are attached to a single group-soul—countless millions, for example, in the case of some of the smaller insects; but as we rise in the animal kingdom the number of bodies attached to a single group-soul becomes smaller and smaller, and therefore the differences between individuals become greater.

Thus the group-souls gradually break up. Returning to the symbol of the bucket, as tumbler after tumbler of water is withdrawn from it, tinted with some sort of colouring matter and returned to it, the whole bucketful of water gradually becomes richer in colour. Suppose that by imperceptible degrees a kind of vertical film forms itself across the centre of the bucket, and gradually solidifies itself into a division, so that we have now a right half and a left half to the bucket, and each tumblerful of water which is taken out is returned always to the same section from which it came.

Then presently a difference will be set up, and the liquid in one half of the bucket will no longer be the same as that in the other. We have then practically two buckets, and when this stage is reached in a group-soul it splits into two, as a cell separates by fission. In this way, as the experience grows ever richer, the group-souls grow smaller but more numerous, until at the highest point we arrive at man with his single individual soul, which no longer returns into a group, but remains always separate.

One of the life-waves is vivifying the whole of a kingdom; but not every group-soul in that life-wave will pass through the whole of that kingdom from the bottom to the top. If in the vegetable kingdom a certain group-soul has ensouled forest trees, when it passes on into the animal kingdom it will omit all the lower stages—that is, it will never inhabit insects or reptiles, but will begin at once at the level of the lower mammalia. The insects and reptiles will be vivified by group-souls which have for some reason left the vegetable kingdom at a much lower level than the forest tree. In the same way the group-soul which has reached the highest levels of the animal kingdom will not individualize into primitive savages, but into men of somewhat higher type, the primitive savages being recruited from group-souls which have left the animal kingdom at a lower level.

Group-souls at any level or at all levels arrange themselves into seven great types, according to the Minister of the Deity through whom their life has poured forth. These types are clearly distinguishable in all the kingdoms, and the successive forms taken by any one of them form a connected series, so that animals, vegetables, minerals and the varieties of the elemental creatures may all be arranged into seven great groups, and the life coming along one of those lines will not diverge into any of the others.

No detailed list has yet been made of the animals, plants or minerals from this point of view; but it is certain that the life which is found ensouling a mineral of a particular type will never vivify a mineral of any other type than its own, though within that type it may vary. When it passes on to the vegetable and animal kingdoms it will inhabit vegetables and animals of that type and of no other; and when it eventually reaches humanity it will individualize into men of that type and of no other.

The method of individualization is the raising of the soul of a particular animal to a level so much higher than that attained by its group-soul that it can no longer return to the latter. This cannot be done with *any* animal, but only with those whose brain is developed to a certain level, and the method usually adopted to acquire such mental development is to bring the animal into close contact with man. Individualization, therefore, is possible only for domestic animals, and only for certain kinds even of those. At the head of each of the seven types stands one kind of domestic animal—the dog for one, the cat for another, the elephant for a third, the monkey for a fourth, and so on. The wild animals can all be arranged on seven lines leading up to the domestic animals; for example, the fox and the wolf are obviously on the same line with the dog, while the lion, the tiger and the leopard equally obviously lead up to the domestic cat; so that the group-soul animating a hundred lions mentioned some time ago might at a later stage of its evolution have divided into, let us say, five group-souls each animating twenty cats.

The life-wave spends a long period of time in each kingdom; we are now only a little past the middle of such an æon, and consequently the conditions are not favourable for the achievement of that individualization which normally comes only at the end of a period. Rare instances of such attainment may occasionally be observed on the part of some animal much in advance of the average. Close association with man is necessary to produce this result. The animal if kindly treated develops devoted affection for his human friend, and also unfolds his intellectual powers in trying to understand that friend and to anticipate his wishes. In addition to this, the emotions and the thoughts of the man act constantly upon those of the animal, and tend to raise him to a higher level both emotionally and intellectually. Under favourable circumstances this development may proceed so far as to raise the animal altogether out of touch with the group to which he belongs, so that his fragment of a group-soul becomes capable of responding to the outpouring which comes from the First Aspect of the Deity.

For this final outpouring is not like the others, a mighty outrush affecting thousands or millions simultaneously; it comes to each one individually as that one is ready to receive it. This outpouring has already descended as far as the intuitional world; but it comes no farther than that until this upward leap is made by the soul of the animal from below; but when that happens this Third Outpouring leaps down to meet it, and in the higher mental world is formed an ego, a permanent individuality—permanent, that is, until, far later in his evolution, the man transcends it and reaches back to the divine unity from which he came. To make this ego, the fragment of the group-soul (which has hitherto played the part always of ensouling force) becomes in its turn a vehicle, and is itself ensouled by that divine Spark which has fallen into it from on high. That Spark may be said to have been hovering in the monadic world over the group-soul through the whole of its previous evolution, unable to effect a junction with it until its corresponding fragment in the group-soul had developed sufficiently to permit it. It is this breaking away from the rest of the group-soul and developing a separate ego which marks the distinction between the highest animal and the lowest man.

CHAPTER V

THE CONSTITUTION OF MAN

Man is therefore in essence a Spark of the divine Fire, belonging to the monadic world.[1] To that Spark, dwelling all the time in that world, we give the name "Monad". For the purposes of human evolution the Monad manifests itself in lower worlds. When it descends one stage and enters the spiritual world, it shows itself there as the triple Spirit having itself three aspects (just as in worlds infinitely higher the Deity has His three Aspects). Of those three one remains always in that world, and we call that the Spirit in man. The second aspect manifests itself in the intuitional world, and we speak of it as the Intuition in man. The third shows itself in the higher mental world, and we call it the Intelligence in man. These three aspects taken together constitute the ego which ensouls the fragment from the group-soul. Thus man as we know him, though in reality a Monad residing in the monadic world, shows himself as an ego in the higher mental world, manifesting these three aspects of himself (Spirit, Intuition and Intelligence) through that vehicle of higher mental matter which we name the causal body.

This ego is the man during the human stage of evolution; he is the nearest correspondence, in fact, to the ordinary unscientific conception of the soul. He lives unchanged (except for his growth) from the moment of individualization until humanity is transcended and merged into divinity. He is in no way affected by what we call birth and death; what we commonly consider as his life is only a day in his life. The body which we can see, the body which is born and dies, is a garment which he puts on for the purposes of a certain part of his evolution.

Nor is it the only body which he assumes. Before he, the ego in the higher mental world, can take a vehicle belonging to the physical world, he must make a connection with it through the lower mental and astral worlds. When he wishes to descend he draws around himself a veil

---

[1] The President has now decided upon a set of names for the planes, so for the future these will be used instead of those previously employed. A table of them is given below for reference.

	NEW NAMES	OLD NAMES	
1.	Divine World	Âdi	Plane
2.	Monadic World	Anupâdaka	"
3.	Spiritual World	Âtmic or Nirvânic	"
4.	Intuitional World	Buddhic	"
5.	Mental World	Mental	"
6.	Emotional or Astral World	Astral	"
7.	Physical World	Physical	"

These will supersede the names given in Vol. II of *The Inner Life*.

of the matter of the lower mental world, which we call his mental body. This is the instrument by means of which he thinks all his concrete thoughts—abstract thought being a power of the ego himself in the higher mental world.

Next he draws round himself a veil of astral matter, which we call his astral body; and that is the instrument of his passions and emotions, and also (in conjunction with the lower part of his mental body) the instrument of all such thought as is tinged by selfishness and personal feeling. Only after having assumed these intermediate vehicles can he come into touch with a baby physical body, and be born into the world which we know. He lives through what we call his life, gaining certain qualities as the result of its experiences; and at its end, when the physical body is worn out, he reverses the process of descent and lays aside one by one the temporary vehicles which he has assumed. The first to go is the physical body, and when that is dropped, his life is centred in the astral world and he lives in his astral body.

The length of his stay in that world depends upon the amount of passion and emotion which he has developed within himself in his physical life. If there is much of these, the astral body is strongly vitalized, and will persist for a long time; if there is but little, the astral body has less vitality, and he will soon be able to cast that vehicle aside in turn. When that is done he finds himself living in his mental body. The strength of that depends upon the nature of the thoughts to which he has habituated himself, and usually his stay at this level is a long one. At last it comes to an end, and he casts aside the mental body in turn, and is once more the ego in his own world.

Owing to lack of development, he is as yet but partially conscious in that world; the vibrations of its matter are too rapid to make any impression upon him, just as the ultra-violet rays are too rapid to make any impression upon our eyes. After a rest there, he feels the desire to descend to a level where the undulations are perceptible to him, in order that he may feel himself to be fully alive; so he repeats the process of descent into denser matter, and assumes once more a mental, an astral and a physical body. As his previous bodies have all disintergrated, each in its tarn, these new vehicles are entirely distinct from them, and thus it happens that in his physical life he has no recollection whatever of other similar lives which have preceded it.

When functioning in this physical world he remembers by means of his mental body; but since that is a new one, assumed only for this birth, it naturally cannot contain the memory of previous births in which it had no part. The man himself, the ego, does remember them all when in his own world, and occasionally some partial recollection of them or influence from them filters through into his lower vehicles. He does not usually, in his physical life, remember the experiences of earlier lives, but he does manifest in physical life the qualities which those experiences have developed in him. Each man is therefore exactly what he has made himself during those past lives; if he has in them developed good qualities in himself, he possesses the good qualities now; if he neglected to train himself, and consequently left himself weak and of evil disposition, he finds himself precisely in that condition now. The qualities, good or evil, with which he is born are those which he has made for himself.

This development of the ego is the object of the whole process of materialization; he assumes those veils of matter precisely because through them he is able to receive vibrations to which he can respond, so that his latent faculties may thereby be unfolded. Though man descends from on high into these lower worlds, it is only through that descent that a full cognizance of the higher worlds is developed in him. Full consciousness in any given world involves the power to perceive and respond to all the undulations of that world: therefore the ordinary man has not yet perfect consciousness at any level—not even in this physical world which he thinks he knows. It is possible for him to unfold his percipience in all these worlds, and it is by means of such developed consciousness that we observe all these facts which I am now describing.

The causal body is the permanent vehicle of the ego in the higher mental world. It consists of matter of the first, second and third subdivisions of that world. In ordinary people it is not yet fully active, only that matter which belongs to the third subdivision being vivified. As the ego unfolds his latent possibilities through the long course of his evolution, the higher matter is gradually brought into action, but it is only in the perfected man whom we call the Adept that it is developed to its fullest extent. Such matter can be discerned by clairvoyant sight, but only by a seer who knows how to use the sight of the ego.

It is difficult to describe a causal body fully, because the senses belonging to its world are altogether different from and higher than ours at this level. Such memory of the appearance of a causal body as it is possible for a clairvoyant to bring into his physical brain represents it as ovoid, and as surrounding the physical body of the man, extending to a distance of about eighteen inches from the normal surface of that body. In the case of primitive man it resembles a bubble, and gives the impression of being empty. It is in reality filled with higher mental matter, but as this is not yet brought into activity it remains colourless and transparent. As advancement continues it is gradually stirred into alertness by vibrations which reach it from the lower bodies. This comes but slowly, because the activities of man in the earlier stages of his evolution are not of a character to obtain expression in matter so fine as that of the higher mental body; but when a man reaches the stage where he is capable either of abstract thought or of unselfish emotion the matter of the causal body is aroused into response.

When these rates of undulation are awakened within him they show themselves in his causal body as colours, so that instead of being a mere transparent bubble it gradually becomes a sphere filled with matter of the most lovely and delicate hues—an object beautiful beyond all conception. It is found by experience that these colours are significant. The vibration which denotes the power of unselfish affection shows itself as a pale rose-colour; that which indicates high intellectual power is yellow; that which expresses sympathy is green, while blue betokens devotional feeling, and a luminous lilac-blue typifies the higher spirituality. The same scheme of colour-significance applies to the bodies which are built of denser matter, but as we approach the physical world the hues are in every case by comparison grosser—not only less delicate but also less living.

In the course of evolution in the lower worlds man often introduces into his vehicles qualities which are undesirable and entirely inappropriate for his life as an ego—such, for example, as pride, irritability, sensuality. These, like the rest, are reducible to vibrations, but they are in all cases vibrations of the lower subdivisions of their respective worlds, and therefore they cannot reproduce themselves in the causal body, which is built exclusively of the matter of the three higher subdivisions of its world. For each section of the astral body acts strongly upon the corresponding section of the mental body, but only upon the corresponding section; it cannot influence any other part. So the causal body can be affected only by the three higher portions of the astral body; and the oscillations of those represent only good qualities.

The practical effect of this is that the man can build into the ego (that is, into his true self) nothing but good qualities; the evil qualities which he develops are in their nature transitory and must be thrown aside as he advances, because he has no longer within him matter which can express them. The difference between the causal bodies of the savage and the saint is that the first is empty and colourless, while the second is full of brilliant, coruscating tints. As the man passes beyond even saint-hood and becomes a great spiritual power, his causal body increases in size, because it has so much more to express, and it also begins to pour out from itself in all directions powerful rays of living light. In one who has attained Adeptship this body is of enormous dimensions.

The mental body is built of matter of the four lower subdivisions of the mental world, and expresses the concrete thoughts of the man. Here also we find the same colour-scheme as in the causal body. The hues are somewhat less delicate, and we notice one or two additions. For example, a thought of pride shows itself as orange, while irritability is manifested by a brilliant scarlet. We may see here sometimes the bright brown of avarice, the grey-brown of selfishness, and the grey-green of deceit. Here also we perceive the possibility of a mixture of colours; the affection, the intellect, the devotion may be tinged by selfishness, and in that case their distinctive colours are mingled with the brown of selfishness, and so we have an impure and muddy appearance. Although its particles are always in intensely rapid motion among themselves, this body has at the same time a kind of loose organization.

The size and shape of the mental body are determined by those of the causal vehicle.

There are in it certain striations which divide it more or less irregularly into segments, each of these corresponding to a certain department of the physical brain, so that every type of thought should function through its duly assigned portion. The mental body is as yet so imperfectly developed in ordinary men that there are many in whom a great number of special departments are not yet in activity, and any attempt at thought belonging to those departments has to travel round through some inappropriate channel which happens to be fully open. The result is that thought on those subjects is for those people clumsy and uncomprehending. This is why some people have a head for mathematics and others are unable to add correctly—why some people instinctively understand, appreciate and enjoy music, while others do not know one tune from another.

All the matter of the mental body should be circulating freely, but sometimes a man allows his thought upon a certain subject to set and solidify, and then the circulation is impeded, and there is a congestion which presently hardens into a kind of wart on the mental body. Such a wart appears to us down here as a prejudice; and until it is absorbed and free circulation restored, it is impossible for the man to think truly or to see clearly with regard to that particular department of his mind, as the congestion checks the free passage of undulations both outward and inward.

When a man uses any part of his mental body it not only vibrates for the time more rapidly, but it also temporarily swells out and increases in size. If there is prolonged thought upon a subject this increase becomes permanent, and it is thus open to any man to increase the size of his mental body either along desirable or undesirable lines.

Good thoughts produce vibrations of the finer matter of the body, which by its specific gravity tends to float in the upper part of the ovoid; whereas bad thoughts, such as selfishness and avarice, are always oscillations of the grosser matter, which tends to gravitate towards the lower part of the ovoid. Consequently the ordinary man, who yields himself not infrequently to selfish thoughts of various kinds, usually expands the lower part of his mental body, and presents roughly the appearance of an egg with its larger end downwards. The man who has repressed those lower thoughts, and devoted himself to higher ones, tends to expand the upper part of his mental body, and therefore presents the appearance of an egg standing on its smaller end. From a study of the colours and striations of a man's mental body the clairvoyant can perceive his character and the progress he has made in his present life. From similar features of the causal body he can see what progress the ego has made since its original formation, when the man left the animal kingdom.

When a man thinks of any concrete object—a book, a house, a landscape—he builds a tiny image of the object in the matter of his mental body. This image floats in the upper part of that body, usually in front of the face of the man and at about the level of the eyes. It remains there as long as the man is contemplating the object, and usually for a little time afterwards, the length of time depending upon the intensity and the clearness of the thought. This form is quite objective, and can be seen by another person, if that other has developed the sight of his own mental body. If a man thinks of another, he creates a tiny portrait in just the same way. If his thought is merely contemplative and involves no feeling (such as affection or dislike) or desire (such as a wish to see the person) the thought does not usually perceptibly affect the man of whom he thinks.

If coupled with the thought of the person there is a feeling, as for example of affection, another phenomenon occurs besides the forming of the image. The thought of affection takes a definite form, which it builds out of the matter of the thinker's mental body. Because of the emotion involved, it draws round it also matter of his astral body, and thus we have an astro-mental form which leaps out of the body in which it has been generated, and moves through space towards the object of the feeling of affection. If the thought is sufficiently strong, distance makes absolutely no difference to it; but the thought of an ordinary person is usually weak and diffused, and is therefore not effective outside a limited area.

When this thought-form reaches its object it discharges itself into his astral and mental bodies, communicating to them its own rate of vibration. Putting this in another way, a thought of love sent from one person to another involves the actual transference of a certain amount both of force and of matter from the sender to the recipient, and its effect upon the recipient is to arouse the feeling of affection in him, and slightly but permanently to increase his power of loving. But such a thought also strengthens the power of affection in the thinker, and therefore it does good simultaneously to both.

Every thought builds a form; if the thought be directed to another person it travels to him; if it be distinctly selfish it remains in the immediate neighbourhood of the thinker; if it belongs to neither of these categories it floats for awhile in space and then slowly disintegrates. Every man therefore is leaving behind him wherever he goes a trail of thought forms; as we go along the street we are walking all the time amidst a sea of other men's thoughts. If a man leaves his mind blank for a time, these residual thoughts of others drift through it, making in most cases but little impression upon him. Sometimes one arrives which attracts his attention, so that his mind seizes upon it and makes it its own, strengthens it by the addition of its force, and then casts it out again to affect somebody else. A man therefore, is not responsible for a thought which floats into his mind, because it may be not his, but someone else's; but he *is* responsible if he takes it up, dwells upon it and then sends it out strengthened.

Self-centred thought of any kind hangs about the thinker, and most men surround their mental bodies with a shell of such thoughts. Such a shell obscures the mental vision and facilitates the formation of prejudice.

Each thought-form is a temporary entity. It resembles a charged battery, awaiting an opportunity to discharge itself. Its tendency is always to reproduce its own rate of vibration in the mental body upon which it fastens itself, and so to arouse in it a like thought. If the person at whom it is aimed happens to be busy or already engaged in some definite train of thought, the particles of his mental body are already swinging at a certain determinate rate, and cannot for the moment be affected from without. In that case the thought-form bides its time, hanging about its object until he is sufficiently at rest to permit its entrance; then it discharges itself upon him, and in the act ceases to exist.

The self-centred thought behaves in exactly the same way with regard to its generator, and discharges itself upon him when opportunity offers. If it be an evil thought, he generally regards it as the suggestion of a tempting demon, whereas in truth he tempts himself. Usually each definite thought creates a new thought-form; but if a thought-form of the same nature is already hovering round the thinker, under certain circumstances a new thought on the same subject, instead of creating a new form, coalesces with and strengthens, the old one, so that by long brooding over the same subject a man may sometimes create a thought-form of tremendous power. If the thought be a wicked one, such a thought-form may become a veritable evil influence, lasting perhaps for many years, and having for a time all the appearance and powers of a real living entity.

All these which have been described are the ordinary unpremeditated thoughts of man. A man can make a thought-form intentionally, and aim it at another with the object of helping him. This is one of the lines of activity adopted by those who desire to serve humanity. A steady stream of powerful thought directed intelligently upon another person may be of the greatest assistance to him. A strong thought-form may be a real guardian angel, and protect its object from impurity, from irritability or from fear.

An interesting branch of the subject is the study of the various shapes and colours taken by thought-forms of different kinds. The colours indicate the nature of the thought, and are in agreement with those which we have already described as existing in the bodies. The shapes are of infinite variety, but are often in some way typical of the kind of thought which they express.

Every thought of definite character, such as a thought of affection or hatred, of devotion or suspicion, of anger or fear, of pride or jealousy, not only creates a form but also radiates an undulation. The fact that, each one of these thoughts is expressed by a certain colour indicates that the thought expresses itself as an oscillation of the matter of a certain part of the mental body. This rate of oscillation communicates itself to the surrounding mental matter precisely in the same way as the vibration of a bell communicates itself to the surrounding air.

This radiation travels out in all directions, and whenever it impinges upon another mental body in a passive or receptive condition it communicates to it something of its own vibration. This does not convey a definite complete idea, as does the thought-form, but it tends to produce a thought of the same character as itself. For example, if the thought be devotional its undulations will excite devotion, but the object of the worship may be different in the case of each person upon whose mental body they impinge. The thought-form, on the other hand, can reach only one person, but will convey to that person (if receptive) not only a general devotional feeling, but also a precise image of the Being for whom the adoration was originally felt.

Any person who habitually thinks pure, good and strong thoughts is utilizing for that purpose the higher part of his mental body—a part which is not used at all by the ordinary man, and is entirely undeveloped in him. Such an one is therefore a power for good in the world, and is being of great use to all those of his neighbours who are capable of any sort of response. For the vibration which he sends out tends to arouse a new and higher part of their mental bodies, and consequently to open before them altogether new fields of thought.

It may not be exactly the same thought as that sent out, but it is of the same nature. The undulations generated by a man thinking of Theosophy do not necessarily communicate Theosophical ideas to all those around him; but they do awaken in them more liberal and higher thought than that to which they have before been accustomed. On the other hand, the thought-forms generated under such circumstances, though more limited in their action than the radiation, are also more precise; they can affect only those who are to some extent open to them, but to them they will convey definite Theosophical ideas.

The colours of the astral body bear the same meaning as those of the higher vehicles, but are several octaves of colours below them, and much more nearly approaching to such hues as we see in the physical world. It is the vehicle of passion and emotion, and consequently it may exhibit additional colours, expressing man's less desirable feelings, which cannot show themselves at higher levels; for example, a lurid brownish-red indicates the presence of sensuality, while black clouds show malice and hatred. A curious livid grey betokens the presence of fear, and a much darker grey, usually arranged in heavy rings around the ovoid, indicates a condition of depression. Irritability is shown by the presence of a number of small scarlet flecks in the astral body, each representing a small angry impulse. Jealousy is shown by a peculiar brownish-green, generally studded with the same scarlet flecks. The astral body is in size and shape like those just described, and in the ordinary man its outline is usually clearly marked; but in the case of primitive man it is often exceedingly irregular, and resembles a rolling cloud composed of all the more unpleasant colours.

When the astral body is comparatively quiet (it is never actually at rest) the colours which are to be seen in it indicate those emotions to which the man is most in the habit of yielding himself. When the man experiences a rush of any particular feeling, the rate of vibration which expresses that feeling dominates for a time the entire astral body. If, for example, it be devotion, the whole of his astral body is flushed with, blue, and while the emotion remains at its strongest the normal colours do little more than modify the blue, or appear faintly through a veil of it; but presently the vehemence of the sentiment dies away, and the normal colours reassert themselves. But because of that spasm of emotion the part of the astral body which is normally blue has been increased in size. Thus a man who frequently feels high devotion soon comes to have a large area of the blue permanently existing in his astral body.

When the rush of devotional *feeling* comes over him, it is usually accompanied by *thoughts* of devotion. Although primarily formed in the mental body, these draw round themselves a large amount of astral matter as well, so that their action is in both worlds. In both worlds also is the radiation which was previously described, so that the devotional man is a centre of devotion, and will influence other people to share both his thoughts and his feelings. The same is true in the case of affection, anger, depression—and, indeed, of all other feelings.

The flood of emotion does not itself greatly affect the mental body, although for a time it may render it almost impossible for any activity from that mental body to come through into the physical brain. That is not because that body itself is affected, but because the astral body, which acts as a bridge between it and the physical brain, is vibrating so entirely at one rate as to be incapable of conveying any undulation which is not in harmony with that.

The permanent colours of the astral body react upon, the mental. They produce in it their correspondences, several octaves higher, in the same manner as a musical note produces overtones. The mental body in its turn reacts upon the causal in the same way, and thus all the good qualities expressed in the lower vehicles by degrees establish themselves permanently in the ego. The evil qualities cannot do so, as the rates of vibrations which express them are impossible for the higher mental matter of which the causal body is constructed.

So far, we have described vehicles which are the expression of the ego in their respective worlds—vehicles, which he provides for himself; in the physical world we come to a vehicle which is provided for him by Nature under laws which will be later explained—which though also in some sense an expression of him, is by no means a perfect manifestation. In ordinary life we see only a small part of this physical body—only that which is built of the solid and liquid subdivisions of physical matter. The body contains matter of all the seven subdivisions, and all of them play their part in its life and are of equal importance, to it.

We usually speak of the invisible part of the physical body as the etheric double; "double" because it exactly reproduces the size and shape of the part of the body that we can see, and "etheric" because it is built—of that finer kind of matter by the vibrations of which light is conveyed to the retina of the eye. (This must not be confused with the true æther of space—that of which matter is the negation.) This invisible part of the physical body is of great importance to us, since it is the vehicle through which flow the streams of vitality which keep the body alive, and without it, as a bridge to convey undulations of thought and feeling from the astral to the visible denser physical matter, the ego could make no use of the cells of his brain.

The life of a physical body is one of perpetual change and in order that it shall live, it needs constantly to be supplied from three distinct sources. It must have food for its digestion, air for its breathing, and vitality for its absorption. This vitality is essentially a force, but when clothed in matter it appears to us as a definite element, which exists in all the worlds of which we have spoken. At the moment we are concerned with that manifestation of it which we find in the highest subdivision of the physical world. Just as the blood circulates through the veins, so does the vitality circulate along the nerves; and precisely as any abnormality in the flow of the blood at once affects the physical body, so does the slightest irregularity in the absorption or flow of the vitality affect this higher part of the physical body.

Vitality is a force which comes originally from the sun. When an ultimate physical atom is charged with it, it draws round itself six other atoms, and makes itself into an etheric element. The original force of vitality is then subdivided into seven, each of the atoms carrying a separate charge. The element thus made is absorbed into the human body through the etheric part of the spleen. It is there split up into its component parts, which at once low to the various parts of the body assigned to them. The spleen is one of the seven force centres in the etheric part of the physical body. In each of our vehicles seven such centres should be in activity, and when they are thus active they are visible to clairvoyant sight. They appear usually as shallow vortices, for they are the points at which the force from the higher bodies enters the lower. In the physical body these centres are: (1) at the base of the spine, (2) at the solar plexus, (3) at the spleen, (4) over the heart, (5) at the throat, (6) between the eyebrows, and (7) at the top of the head. There are other dormant centres, but their awakening is undesirable.

The shape of all the higher bodies as seen by the clairvoyant is ovoid, but the matter composing them is not equally distributed throughout the egg. In the midst of this ovoid is the physical body. The physical body strongly attracts astral matter, and in its turn the astral matter strongly attracts mental matter. Therefore by far the greater part of the matter of the astral body is gathered within the physical frame; and the same is true of the mental vehicle. If we see the astral body of a man in its own world, apart from the physical body we shall still perceive the astral matter aggregated in exactly the shape of the physical, although, as the matter is more fluidic in its nature, what we see is a body built of dense mist, in the midst of an ovoid of much finer mist. The same is true for the mental body. Therefore, if in the astral or the mental world we should meet an acquaintance, we should recognise him by his appearance just as instantly as in the physical world.

This, then, is the true constitution of man. In the first place he is a Monad, a Spark of the Divine. Of that Monad the ego is a partial expression, formed in order that he may enter evolution, and may return to the Monad with joy, bringing his sheaves with him in the shape of qualities developed by garnered experience. The ego in his turn puts down part of himself for the same purpose into lower worlds, and we call that part a personality, because the Latin word *persona* means a mask, and this personality is the mask which the ego puts upon himself when he manifests in worlds lower than his own. Just as the ego is a small part and an imperfect expression of the Monad, so is the personality a small part and an imperfect expression of the ego; so that what we usually think of as the man is only in truth a fragment of a fragment.

The personality wears three bodies or vehicles, the mental, the astral and the physical. While the man is what we call alive and awake on the physical earth he is limited by his physical body, for he uses the astral and mental bodies only as bridges to connect himself with his lowest vehicle. One of the limitations of the physical body is that it quickly becomes fatigued and needs periodical rest. Each night the man leaves it to sleep, and withdraws into his astral vehicle, which does not become fatigued, and therefore needs no sleep. During this sleep of the physical body the man is free to move about in the astral world; but the extent to which he does this depends upon his development. The primitive savage usually does not move more than a few miles away from his sleeping physical form—often not as much as that; and he has only the vaguest consciousness.

The educated man is generally able to travel in his astral vehicle wherever he will, and has much more consciousness in the astral world, though he has not often the faculty of bringing into his waking life any memory of what he has seen and done while his physical body was asleep. Sometimes he does remember some incident which he has seen, some experience which he has had, and then he calls it a vivid dream. More often his recollections are hopelessly entangled with vague memories of waking life, and with impressions made from without upon the etheric part of his brain. Thus we arrive at the confused and often absurd dreams of ordinary life. The developed man becomes as fully conscious and active in the astral world as in the physical, and brings through into the latter full remembrance of what he has been doing in the former—that is, he has a continuous life without any loss of consciousness throughout the whole twenty-four hours, and thus throughout the whole of his physical life, and even through death itself.

Chapter VI

After Death

Death is the laying aside of the physical body; but it makes no more difference to the ego than does the laying aside of an overcoat to the physical man. Having put off his physical body, the ego continues to live in his astral body until the force has become exhausted which has been generated by such emotions and passions as he has allowed himself to feel during earth-life. When that has happened, the second death takes place; the astral body also falls away from him, and he finds himself living in the mental body and in the lower mental world. In that condition he remains until the thought-forces generated during his physical and astral lives have worn themselves out; then he drops the third vehicle in its turn and remains once more an ego in his own world, inhabiting his causal body.

There is, then, no such thing as death as it is ordinarily understood. There is only a succession of stages in a continuous life—stages lived in the three worlds one after another. The apportionment of time between these three worlds varies much as man advances. The primitive man lives almost exclusively in the physical world, spending only a few years in the astral at the end of each of his physical lives. As he develops, the astral life becomes longer, and as intellect unfolds in him, and he becomes able to think, he begins to spend a little time in the mental world as well. The ordinary man of civilized races remains longer in the mental world than in the physical and astral; indeed, the more a man evolves the longer becomes his mental, life and the shorter his life in the astral world.

The astral life is the result of all feelings which have in them the element of self. If they have been directly selfish, they bring him into conditions of great unpleasantness in the astral world; if, though tinged with thoughts of self, they have been good and kindly, they bring him a comparatively pleasant though still limited astral life. Such of his thoughts and feelings as have been entirely unselfish produce their results in his life in the mental world; therefore that life in the mental, world cannot be other than blissful. The astral life, which the man has made for himself either miserable or comparatively joyous, corresponds to what Christians call purgatory; the lower mental life, which is always entirely happy, is what is called heaven.

Man makes for himself his own purgatory and heaven, and these are not planes, but states of consciousness. Hell does not exist; it is only a figment of the theological imagination; but a man who lives foolishly may make for himself a very unpleasant and long enduring purgatory. Neither purgatory nor heaven can ever be eternal, for a finite cause cannot produce an infinite result. The variations in individual cases are so wide that to give actual figures is somewhat misleading. If we take the average man of what is called the lower middle class, the typical specimen of which would be a small shopkeeper or shop-assistant, his average life in the astral world would be perhaps about forty years, and the life in the mental world about two hundred. The man of spirituality and culture, on the other hand, may have perhaps twenty years of life in the astral world and a thousand in the heaven life. One who is specially developed may reduce the astral life to a few days or hours and spend fifteen hundred years in heaven.

Not only does the length of these periods vary greatly, but the conditions in both worlds also differ widely. The matter of which all these bodies are built is not dead matter but living, and that fact has to be taken into consideration. The physical body is built up of cells, each of which is a tiny separate life animated by the Second Outpouring, which comes forth from the Second Aspect of the Deity. These cells are of varying kinds and fulfil various functions, and all these facts must be taken into account if the man wishes to understand the work of his physical body and to live a healthy life in it.

The same thing applies to the astral and mental bodies. In the cell-life which permeates them there is as yet nothing in the way of intelligence, but there is a strong instinct always pressing in the direction of what is for its development. The life animating the matter of which such bodies are built is upon the outward arc of evolution, moving downwards or outwards into matter, so that progress for it means to descend into denser forms of matter, and to learn to express itself through them. Unfoldment for the man is just the opposite of this; he has already sunk deeply into matter and is now rising out of that towards his source. There is consequently a constant conflict of interests between the man within and the life inhabiting the matter of his vehicles, inasmuch as its tendency is downward, while his is upward.

The matter of the astral body (or rather the life animating its molecules) desires for its evolution such undulations as it can get, of as many different kinds as possible, and as coarse as possible. The next step in its evolution will be to ensoul physical matter and become used to its still slower oscillations; and as a step on the way to that, it desires the grossest of the astral vibrations. It has not the intelligence definitely to plan for these; but its instinct helps it to discover how most easily to procure them.

The molecules of the astral body are constantly changing, as are those of the physical body, but nevertheless the life in the mass of those astral molecules has a sense, though a very vague sense, of itself as a whole—as a kind of temporary entity. It does not know that it is part of a man's astral body; it is quite incapable of understanding what a man is; but it realizes in a blind way that under its present conditions it receives many more waves, and much stronger ones, than it would receive if floating at large in the atmosphere. It would then only occasionally catch, as from a distance, the radiation of man's passions and emotions; now it is in the very heart of them, it can miss none, and it gets them at their strongest. Therefore it feels itself in a good position, and it makes an effort to retain that position. It finds itself in contact with something finer than itself—the matter of the man's mental body; and it comes to feel that if it can contrive to involve that finer something in its own undulations, they will be greatly intensified and prolonged.

Since astral matter is the vehicle of desire and mental matter is the vehicle of thought, this instinct, when translated into our language, means that if the astral body can induce us to think that *we* want what *it* wants, it is much more likely to get it. Thus it exercises a slow steady pressure upon the man—a kind of hunger on its side, but for him a temptation to what is coarse and undesirable. If he be a passionate man there is a gentle but ceaseless pressure in the direction of irritability; if he be a sensual man, an equally steady pressure in the direction of impurity.

A man who does not understand this usually makes one of two mistakes with regard to it: either he supposes it to be the prompting of his own nature, and therefore regards that nature as inherently evil, or he thinks of the pressure as coming from outside—as a temptation of an imaginary devil. The truth lies between the two. The pressure is natural, not to the man but to the vehicle which he is using; its desire is natural and right for it, but harmful to the man, and therefore it is necessary that he should resist it. If he does so resist, if he declines to yield himself to the feelings suggested to him, the particles within him which need those vibrations become apathetic for lack of nourishment, and eventually atrophy and fall out from his astral body, and are replaced by other particles, whose natural wave-rate is more nearly in accordance with that which the man habitually permits within his astral body.

This gives the reason for what are called promptings of the lower nature during life. If the man yields himself to them, such promptings grow stronger and stronger until at last he feels as though he could not resist them, and identifies himself with them—which is exactly what this curious half-life in the particles of the astral body wants him to do.

At the death of the physical body this vague astral consciousness is alarmed. It realizes that its existence as a separated mass is menaced, and it takes instinctive steps to defend itself and to maintain its position as long as possible. The matter of the astral body is far more fluidic than that of the physical, and this consciousness seizes upon its particles and disposes them so as to resist encroachment. It puts the grossest and densest upon the outside as a kind of shell, and arranges the others in concentric layers, so that the body as a whole may become as resistant to friction as its constitution permits, and may therefore retain its shape as long as possible.

For the man this produces various unpleasant effects. The physiology of the astral body is quite different from that of the physical; the latter acquires its information from without by means of certain organs which are specialized as the instruments of its senses, but the astral body has no separated senses in our meaning of the word. That which for the astral body corresponds to sight is the power of its molecules to respond to impacts from without, which come to them by means of similar molecules. For example, a man has within his astral body matter belonging to all the subdivisions of the astral world, and it is because of that that he is capable of "seeing" objects built of the matter of any of these subdivisions.

Supposing an astral object to be made of the matter of the second and third subdivisions mixed, a man living in the astral world could perceive that object only if on the surface of his astral body there were particles belonging to the second and third subdivisions of that world which were capable of receiving and recording the vibrations which that object set up. A man who from the arrangement of his body by the vague consciousness of which we have spoken, had on the outside of that vehicle only the denser matter of the lowest subdivision, could no more be conscious of the object which we have mentioned than we are ourselves conscious in the physical body of the gases which move about us in the atmosphere or of objects built exclusively of etheric matter.

During physical life the matter of the man's astral body is in constant motion, and its particles pass among one another much as do those of boiling water. Consequently at any given moment it is practically certain that particles of all varieties will be represented on the surface of his astral body, and that therefore when he is using his astral body during sleep he will be able to "see" by its means any astral object which approaches him.

After death, if he has allowed the rearrangement to be made (as from ignorance, all ordinary persons do) his condition in this respect will be different. Having on the surface of his astral body only the lowest and grossest particles, he can receive impressions only from corresponding particles outside; so that instead of seeing the whole of the astral world about him, he will see only one-seventh of it, and that the densest and most impure. The vibrations of this heavier matter are the expressions only of objectionable feelings and emotions, and of the least refined class of astral entities. Therefore it emerges that a man in this condition can see only the undesirable inhabitants of the astral world, and can feel only its most unpleasant and vulgar influences.

He is surrounded by other men, whose astral bodies are probably of quite ordinary character; but since he can see and feel only that which is lowest and coarsest in them, they appear to him to be monsters of vice with no redeeming features. Even his friends seem not at all what they used to be, because he is now incapable of appreciating any of their better qualities. Under these circumstances it is little wonder that he considers the astral world a hell; yet the fault is in no way with the astral world, but with himself—first, for allowing within himself so much of that cruder type of matter, and, secondly, for letting that vague astral consciousness dominate him and dispose it in that particular way.

The man who has studied these matters declines absolutely to yield to the pressure during life or to permit the rearrangement after death, and consequently he retains his power of seeing the astral world as a whole, and not merely the cruder and baser part of it.

The astral world has many points in common with the physical; just like the physical, it presents different appearances to different people, and even to the same person at different periods of his career. It is the home of emotions and of lower thoughts; and emotions are much stronger in that world than in this. When a person is awake we cannot see that larger part of his emotion at all; its strength goes in setting in motion the gross physical matter of the brain. So if we see a man show affection here, what we can see is not the whole of his affection, but only such part of it as is left after all this other work has been done. Emotions therefore bulk far more largely in the astral life than in the physical. They in no way exclude higher thought if they are controlled, so in the astral world as in the physical a man may devote himself to study and to helping his fellows, or he may waste his time and drift about aimlessly.

The astral world extends nearly to the mean distance of the orbit of the moon; but though the whole of this realm is open to any of its inhabitants who have not permitted the redistribution of their matter, the great majority remain much nearer to the surface of the earth. The matter of the different subdivisions of that world interpenetrates with perfect freedom, but there is on the whole a general tendency for the denser matter to settle towards the centre. The conditions are much like those which obtain in a bucket of water which contains in suspension a number of kinds of matter of different degrees of density. Since the water is kept in perpetual motion, the different kinds of matter are diffused through it; but in spite of that, the densest matter is found in greatest quantity nearest to the bottom. So that though we must not at all think of the various subdivisions of the astral world as lying above one another as do the coats of an onion, it is nevertheless true that the average arrangement of the matter of those subdivisions partakes somewhat of that general character.

Astral matter interpenetrates physical matter precisely as though it were not there, but each subdivision of physical matter has a strong attraction for astral matter of the corresponding subdivision. Hence it arises that every physical body has its astral counterpart. If I have a glass of water standing upon a table, the glass and the table, being of physical matter in the solid state, are interpenetrated by astral matter of the lowest subdivision. The water in the glass, being liquid, is interpenetrated by what we may call astral liquid—that is, by astral matter of the sixth subdivision; whereas the air surrounding both, being physical matter in the gaseous condition, is entirely interpenetrated by astral gaseous matter—that is, astral matter of the fifth subdivision.

But just as air, water, glass and table are alike interpenetrated all the time by the finer physical matter which we have called etheric, so are all the astral counterparts interpenetrated by the finer astral matter of the higher subdivisions which correspond to the etheric. But even the astral solid is less dense than the finest of the physical ethers.

The man who finds himself in the astral world after death, if he has not submitted to the rearrangement of the matter of his body, will notice but little difference from physical life. He can float about in any direction at will, but in actual fact he usually stays in the neighbourhood to which he is accustomed. He is still able to perceive his house, his room, his furniture, his relations, his friends. The living, when ignorant of the higher worlds, suppose themselves to have "lost" those who have laid aside their physical bodies; but the dead are never for a moment under the impression that they have lost the living.

Functioning as they are in the astral body, the dead can no longer see the physical bodies of those whom they have left behind; but they do see their astral bodies, and as those are exactly the same in outline as the physical, they are perfectly aware of the presence of their friends. They see each one surrounded by a faint ovoid of luminous mist, and if they happen to be observant, they may notice various other small changes in their surroundings; but it is at least quite clear to them that they have not gone away to some distant heaven or hell, but still remain in touch with the world which they know, although they see it at a somewhat different angle.

The dead man has the astral body of his living friend obviously before him, so he cannot think of him as lost; but while the friend is awake, the dead man will not be able to make any impression upon him, for the consciousness of the friend is then in the physical world, and his astral body is being used only as a bridge. The dead man cannot therefore communicate with his friend, nor can he read his friend's higher thoughts; but he will see by the change in colour in the astral body any emotion which that friend may feel, and with a little practice and observation he may easily learn to read all those thoughts of his friend which have in them anything of self or of desire.

When the friend falls asleep the whole position is changed. He is then also conscious in the astral world side by side with the dead man, and they can communicate in every respect as freely as they could during physical life. The emotions felt by the living react strongly upon the dead who love them. If the former give way to grief, the latter cannot but suffer severely.

The conditions of life after death are almost infinite in their variety, but they can be calculated without difficulty by any one who will take the trouble to understand the astral world and to consider the character of the person concerned. That character is not in the slightest degree changed by death; the man's thoughts, emotions and desires are exactly the same as before. He is in every way the same man, minus his physical body; and his happiness or misery depends upon the extent to which this loss of the physical body affects him.

If his longings have been such as need a physical body for their gratification, he is likely to suffer considerably. Such a craving manifests itself as a vibration in the astral body, and while we are still in this world most of its strength is employed in setting in motion the heavy physical particles. Desire is therefore a far greater force in the astral life than in the physical, and if the man has not been in the habit of controlling it, and if in this new life it cannot be satisfied, it may cause him great and long-continued trouble.

Take as an illustration the extreme case of a drunkard or a sensualist. Here we have a lust which has been strong enough during physical life to overpower reason, common sense and all the feelings of decency and of family affection. After death the man finds himself in the astral world feeling the appetite perhaps a hundred times more strongly, yet absolutely unable to satisfy it because he has lost the physical body. Such a life is a very real hell—the only hell there is; yet no one is punishing him; he is reaping the perfectly natural result of his own action. Gradually as time passes this force of desire wears out, but only at the cost of terrible suffering for the man, because to him every day seems as a thousand years. He has no measure of time such as we have in the physical world. He can measure it only by his sensations. From a distortion of this fact has come the blasphemous idea of eternal damnation.

Many other cases less extreme than this will readily suggest themselves, in which a hankering which cannot be fulfilled may prove itself a torture. A more ordinary case is that of a man who has no particular vices, such as drink or sensuality, but yet has been attached entirely to things of the physical world, and has lived a life devoted to business or to aimless social functions. For him the astral world is a place of weariness; the only thing for which he craves are no longer possible for him, for in the astral world there is no business to be done, and, though he may have as much companionship as he wishes, society is now for him a very different matter, because all the pretences upon which it is usually based in this world are no longer possible.

These cases, however, are only the few, and for most people the state after death is much happier than life upon earth. The first feeling of which the dead man is usually conscious is one of the most wonderful and delightful freedom. He has absolutely nothing to worry about, and no duties rest upon him, except those which he chooses to impose upon himself. For all but a very small minority, physical life is spent in doing what the man would much rather not do; but he has to do it in order to support himself or his wife and family. In the astral world no support is necessary; food is no longer needed, shelter is not required, since he is entirely unaffected by heat or cold; and each man by the mere exercise of his thought clothes himself as he wishes. For the first time since early childhood the man is entirely free to spend the whole of his time in doing just exactly what he likes.

His capacity for every kind of enjoyment is greatly enhanced, if only that enjoyment does not need a physical body for its expression. If he loves the beauties of Nature, it is now within his power to travel with great rapidity and without fatigue over the whole world, to contemplate all its loveliest spots, and to explore its most secret recesses. If he delights in art, all the world's masterpieces are at his disposal. If he loves music, he can go where he will to hear it, and it will now mean much more to him than it has ever meant before; for though he can no longer hear the physical sounds, he can receive the whole effect of the music into himself in far fuller measure than in this lower world. If he is a student of science, he can not only visit the great scientific men of the world, and catch from them such thoughts and ideas as may be within his comprehension, but also he can undertake researches of his own into the science of this higher world, seeing much more of what he is doing than has ever before been possible to him. Best of all, he whose great delight in this world has been to help his fellow men will still find ample scope for his philanthropic efforts.

Men are no longer hungry, cold, or suffering from disease in this astral world; but there are vast numbers who, being ignorant, desire knowledge—who, being still in the grip of desire for earthly things, need the explanation which will turn their thought to higher levels—who have entangled themselves in a web of their own imaginings, and can be set free only by one who understands these new surroundings and can help them to distinguish the facts of the world from their own ignorant misrepresentation of them. All these can be helped by the man of intelligence and of kindly heart. Many men arrive in the astral world in utter ignorance of its conditions, not realizing at first that they are dead, and when they do realize it fearing the fate that may be in store for them, because of false and wicked theological teaching. All of these need the cheer and comfort which can only be given to them by a man of common sense who possesses some knowledge of the facts of Nature.

There is thus no lack of the most profitable occupation for any man whose interests during his physical life have been rational; nor is there any lack of companionship. Men whose tastes and pursuits are similar drift naturally together there just as they do here; and many realms of Nature, which during our physical life are concealed by the dense veil of matter, now lie open for the detailed study of those who care to examine them.

To a large extent people make their own surroundings. We have already referred to the seven sub-divisions of this astral world. Numbering these from the highest and least material downwards, we find that they fall naturally into three classes—divisions one, two and three forming one such class, and four, five and six another; while the seventh and lowest of all stands alone. As I have said, although they all interpenetrate, their substance has a general tendency to arrange itself according to its specific gravity, so that most of the matter belonging to the higher subdivisions is found at a greater elevation above the surface of the earth than the bulk of the matter of the lower portions.

Hence, although any person inhabiting the astral world can move into any part of it, his natural tendency is to float at the level which corresponds with the specific gravity of the heaviest matter in his astral body. The man who has not permitted the rearrangement of the matter of his astral body after death is entirely free of the whole astral world; but the majority, who do permit it, are not equally free—not because there is anything to prevent them from rising to the highest level or sinking to the lowest, but because they are able to sense clearly only a certain part of that world.

I have described something of the fate of a man who is on the lowest level, shut in by a strong shell of coarse matter. Because of the extreme comparative density of that matter he is conscious of less outside of his own subdivision than a man at any other level. The general specific gravity of his own astral body tends to make him float below the surface of the earth. The physical matter of the earth is absolutely non-existent to his astral senses, and his natural attraction is to that least delicate form of astral matter which is the counterpart of that solid earth. A man who has confined himself to that lowest subdivision will therefore usually find himself floating in darkness and cut off to a great extent from others of the dead, whose lives have been such as to keep them on a higher level.

Divisions four, five and six of the astral world (to which most people are attracted) have for their background the astral counterpart of the physical world in which we live, and all its familiar accessories. Life in the sixth subdivision is simply like our ordinary life on this earth minus the physical body and its necessities while as it ascends through the fifth and fourth divisions it becomes less and less material and is more and more withdrawn from our lower world and its interests.

The first, second and third sections, though occupying the same space, yet give the impression of being much further removed from the physical, and correspondingly less material. Men who inhabit these levels lose sight of the earth and its belongings; they are usually deeply self-absorbed, and to a large extent create their own surroundings, though these are sufficiently objective to be perceptible to other men of their level, and also to clairvoyant vision.

This region is the summerland of which we hear in spiritualistic circles—the world in which, by the exercise of their thought, the dead call into temporary existence their houses and schools and cities. These surroundings, though fanciful from our point of view, are to the dead as real as houses, temples or churches built of stone are to us, and many people live very contentedly there for a number of years in the midst of all these thought creations.

Some of the scenery thus produced is very beautiful; it includes lovely lakes, magnificent mountains, pleasant flower-gardens, decidedly superior to anything in the physical world; though on the other hand it also contains much which to the trained clairvoyant (who has learned to see things as they are) appears ridiculous—as, for example, the endeavours of the unlearned to make a thought-form of some of the curious symbolic descriptions contained in their various scriptures. An ignorant peasant's thought-image of a beast full of eyes within, or of a sea of glass mingled with fire, is naturally often grotesque, although to its maker it is perfectly satisfactory. This astral world is full of thought-created figures and landscapes. Men of all religions image here their deities and their respective conceptions of paradise, and enjoy themselves greatly among these dream-forms until they pass into the mental world and come into touch with something nearer to reality.

Every one after death—any ordinary person, that is, in whose case the rearrangement of the matter of the astral body has been made—has to pass through all these subdivisions in turn. It does not follow that every one is conscious in all of them. The ordinarily decent person has in his astral body but little of the matter of its lowest portion—by no means enough to construct a heavy shell. The redistribution puts on the outside of the body its densest matter; in the ordinary man this is usually matter of the sixth subdivision, mixed with a little of the seventh, and so he finds himself viewing the counterpart of the physical world.

The ego is steadily withdrawing into himself, and as he withdraws he leaves behind him level after level of this astral matter. So the length of the man's detention in any section of the astral world is precisely in proportion to the amount of its matter which is found in his astral body, and that in turn depends upon the life he has lived, the desires he has indulged, and the class of matter which by so doing he has attracted towards him and built into himself. Finding himself then in the sixth section, still hovering about the places and persons with which he was most closely connected while on earth, the average man, as time passes on, finds the earthly surroundings gradually growing dimmer and becoming of less and less importance to him, and he tends more and more to mould his entourage into agreement with the more persistent of his thoughts. By the time that he reaches the third level he finds that this characteristic has entirely superseded the vision of the realities of the astral world.

The second subdivision is a shade less material than the third, for if the latter is the summerland of the spiritualists, the former is the material heaven of the more ignorantly orthodox; while the first or highest level appears to be the special home of those who during life have devoted themselves to materialistic but intellectual pursuits, following them not for the sake of benefiting their fellow men, but either from motives of selfish ambition or simply for the sake of intellectual exercise. All these people are perfectly happy. Later on they will reach a stage when they can appreciate something much higher, and when that stage comes they will find the higher ready for them.

In this astral life people of the same nation and of the same interest tend to keep together, precisely as they do here. The religious people, for example, who imagine for themselves a material heaven, do not at all interfere with men of other faiths whose ideas of celestial joy are different. There is nothing to prevent a Christian from drifting into the heaven of the Hindu or the Muhammadan, but he is little likely to do so, because his interests and attractions are all in the heaven of his own faith, along with friends who have shared that faith with him. This is by no means the true heaven described by any of the religions, but only a gross and material misrepresentation of it; the real thing will be found when we come to consider the mental world.

The dead man who has not permitted the rearrangement of the matter of his astral body is free of the entire world, and can wander all over it at will, seeing the whole of whatever he examines, instead of only a part of it as the others do. He does not find it inconveniently crowded, for the astral world is much larger than the surface of the physical earth, while its population is somewhat smaller, because the average life of humanity in the astral world is shorter than the average in the physical.

Not only the dead, however, are the inhabitants of this astral world, but always about one-third of the living as well, who have temporarily left their physical bodies behind them in sleep. The astral world has also a great number of non-human inhabitants, some of them far below the level of man, and some considerably above him. The nature-spirits form an enormous kingdom, some of whose members exist in the astral world, and make a large part of its population. This vast kingdom exists in the physical world also, for many of its orders wear etheric bodies and are only just beyond the range of ordinary physical sight. Indeed, circumstances not infrequently occur under which they can be seen, and in many lonely mountain districts these appearances are traditional among the peasants, by whom they are commonly spoken of as fairies, good people, pixies or brownies.

They are protean, but usually prefer to wear a miniature human form. Since they are not yet individualized, they may be thought of almost as etheric and astral animals; yet many of them are intellectually quite equal to average humanity. They have their nations and types just as we have, and they are often grouped into four great classes, and called the spirits of earth, water, fire and air. Only the members of the last of these four divisions normally confine their manifestation to the astral world, but their numbers are so prodigious that they are everywhere present in it.

Another great kingdom has its representatives here—the kingdom of the angels (called in India the devas). This is a body of beings who stand far higher in evolution than man, and only the lowest fringe of their hosts touches the astral world—a fringe whose constituent members are perhaps at about the level of development of what we should call a distinctly good man.

We are neither the only nor even the principal inhabitants of our solar system; there are other lines of evolution running parallel with our own which do not pass through humanity at all, though they must all pass through a level corresponding to that of humanity. On one of these other lines of evolution are the nature-spirits above described, and at a higher level of that line comes this great kingdom of the angels. At our present level of evolution they come into obvious contact with us only very rarely, but as we develop we shall be likely to see more of them—especially as the cyclic progress of the world is now bringing it more and more under the influence of the Seventh Ray. This Seventh Ray has ceremonial for one of its characteristics, and it is through ceremonial such as that of the Church or of Freemasonry that we come most easily into touch with the angelic kingdom.

When all the man's lower emotions have worn themselves out—all emotions, I mean, which have in them any thought of self—his life in the astral world is over, and the ego passes on into the mental world. This is not in any sense a movement in space; it is simply that the steady process of withdrawal has now passed beyond even the finest kind of astral matter; so that the man's consciousness is focussed in the mental world. His astral body has not entirely disintegrated, though it is in process of doing so, and he leaves behind him an astral corpse, just as at a previous stage of the withdrawal he left behind him a physical corpse. There is a certain difference between the two which should be noticed, because of the consequences which ensue from it.

When the man leaves his physical body his separation from it should be complete, and generally is so; but this is not the case with the much finer matter of the astral body. In the course of his physical life the ordinary man usually entangles himself so much in astral matter (which, from another point of view, means that he identifies himself so closely with his lower desires) that the indrawing force of the ego cannot entirely separate him from it again. Consequently, when he finally breaks away from the astral body and transfers his activities to the mental, he loses a little of himself he leaves some of himself behind imprisoned in the matter of the astral body.

This gives a certain remnant of vitality to the astral, corpse, so that it still moves freely in the astral world, and may easily be mistaken by the ignorant for the man himself—the more so as such fragmentary consciousness as still remains to it is part of the man, and therefore it naturally regards itself and speaks of itself as the man. It retains his memories, but is only a partial and unsatisfactory representation of him. Sometimes in spiritualistic séances one comes into contact with an entity of this description, and wonders how it is that one's friend has deteriorated so much since his death. To this fragmentary entity we give the name "shade".

At a later stage even this fragment of consciousness dies out of the astral body, but does not return to the ego to whom it originally belonged. Even then the astral corpse still remains, but when it is quite without any trace of its former life we call it a "shell". Of itself a shell cannot communicate at a séance, or take any action of any sort; but such shells are frequently seized upon by sportive nature-spirits and used as temporary habitations. A shell so occupied *can* communicate at a séance and masquerade as its original owner, since some of his characteristics and certain portions of his memory can be evoked by the nature-spirit from his astral corpse.

When a man falls asleep, he withdraws in his astral body, leaving the whole of the physical vehicle behind him. When he dies, he draws out with him the etheric part of the physical body, and consequently has usually at least a moment of unconsciousness while he is freeing himself from it. The etheric double is not a vehicle and cannot be used as such; so when the man is surrounded by it, he is for the moment able to function neither in the physical world nor the astral. Some men succeed in shaking themselves free of this etheric envelope in a few moments; others rest within it for hours, days or even weeks.

Nor is it certain that, when the man is free from this, he will at once become conscious of the astral world. For there is in him a good deal of the lowest kind of astral matter, so that a shell of this may be made around him. But he may be quite unable to use that matter. If he has lived a reasonably decent life he is little in the habit of employing it or responding to its vibrations, and he cannot instantly acquire this habit. For that reason, he may remain unconscious until that matter gradually wears away, and some matter which he *is* in the habit of using comes on the surface. Such an occlusion, however, is scarcely ever complete, for even in the most carefully made shell some particles of the finer matter occasionally find their way to the surface, and give him fleeting glimpses of his surroundings.

There are some men who cling so desperately to their physical vehicles that they will not relax their hold upon the etheric double, but strive with all their might to retain it. They may be successful in doing so for a considerable time, but only at the cost of great discomfort to themselves. They are shut out from both worlds, and find themselves surrounded by a dense grey mist, through which they see very dimly the things of the physical world, but with all the colour gone from them. It is a terrible struggle for them to maintain their position in this miserable condition, and yet they will not relax their hold upon the etheric double, feeling that that is at least some sort of link with the only world that they know. Thus they drift about in a condition of loneliness and misery until from sheer fatigue their hold fails them, and they slip into the comparative happiness of astral life. Sometimes in their desperation they grasp blindly at other bodies, and try to enter into them, and occasionally they are successful in such an attempt. They may seize upon a baby body, ousting the feeble personality for whom it was intended, or sometimes they grasp even the body of an animal. All this trouble arises entirely from ignorance, and it can never happen to anyone who understands the laws of life and death.

When the astral life is over, the man dies to that world in turn, and awakens in the mental world. With him it is not at all what it is to the trained clairvoyant, who ranges through it and lives amidst the surroundings which he finds there, precisely as he would in the physical or astral worlds. The ordinary man has all through his life been encompassing himself with a mass of thought-forms. Some which are transitory, to which he pays little attention, have fallen away from him long ago, but those which represent the main interests of his life are always with him, and grow ever stronger and stronger. If some of these have been selfish, their force pours down into astral matter, and he has exhausted them during his life in the astral world. But those which are entirely unselfish belong purely to his mental body, and so when he finds himself in the mental world it is through these special thoughts that he is able to appreciate it.

His mental body is by no means fully developed; only those parts of it are really in action to their fullest extent which he has used in this altruistic manner. When he awakens again after the second death, his first sense is one of indescribable bliss and vitality—a feeling of such utter joy in living that he needs for the time nothing but just to live. Such bliss is of the essence of life in all the higher worlds of the system. Even astral life has possibilities of happiness far greater than anything that we can know in the dense body; but the heaven-life in the mental world is out of all proportion more blissful than the astral. In each higher world the same experience is repeated. Merely to live in any one of them seems the uttermost conceivable bliss; and yet, when the next one is reached, it is seen that it far surpasses the last.

Just as the bliss increases, so does the wisdom and the breadth of view. A man fusses about in the physical world and thinks himself so busy and so wise; but when he touches even the astral, he realizes at once that he has been all the time only a caterpillar crawling about and seeing nothing but his own leaf, whereas now he has spread his wings like the butterfly and flown away into the sunshine of a wider world. Yet, impossible as it may seem, the same experience is repeated when he passes into the mental world, for this life is in turn so much fuller and wider and more intense than the astral that once more no comparison is possible. And yet beyond all these there is still another life, that of the intuitional world, unto which even this is but as moonlight unto sunlight.

The man's position in the mental world differs widely from that in the astral. There he was using a body to which he was thoroughly accustomed, a body which he had been in the habit of employing every night during sleep. Here he finds himself living in a vehicle which he has never used before—a vehicle furthermore which is very far from being fully developed—a vehicle which shuts him out to a great extent from the world about him, instead of enabling him to see it. The lower part of his nature burnt itself away during his purgatorial life, and now there remain to him only his higher and more refined thoughts, the noble and unselfish aspirations which he poured out during earth-life. These cluster round him, and make a sort of shell about him, through the medium of which he is able to respond to certain types of vibrations in this refined matter.

These thoughts which surround him are the powers by which he draws upon the wealth of the heaven-world, and he finds it to be a storehouse of infinite extent, upon which he is able to draw just according to the power of those thoughts and aspirations; for in this world is existing the infinite fullness of the Divine Mind, open in all its limitless affluence to every soul, just in proportion as that soul has qualified itself to receive. A man who has already completed his human evolution, who has fully realized and unfolded the divinity whose germ is within him, finds the whole of this glory within his reach; but since none of us has yet done that, since we are only gradually rising towards that splendid consummation, it follows that none of us as yet can grasp that entirety.

But each draws from it and cognizes so much of it as he has by previous effort prepared himself to take. Different individuals bring very different capacities; they tell us in the East that each man brings his own cup, and some of the cups are large and some are small, but small or large every cup is filled to its utmost capacity; the sea of bliss holds far more than enough for all.

A man can look out upon all this glory and beauty only through the windows which he himself has made. Every one of these thought-forms is such a window, through which response may come to him from the forces without. If during his earth-life he has chiefly regarded physical things, then he has made for himself but few windows through which this higher glory can shine in upon him. Yet every man who is above the lowest savage must have had some touch of pure unselfish feeling, even if it were but once in all his life, and that will be a window for him now.

The ordinary man is not capable of any great activity in this mental world; his condition is chiefly receptive, and his vision of anything outside his own shell of thought is of the most limited character. He is surrounded by living forces, mighty angelic inhabitants of this glorious world, and many of their orders are very sensitive to certain aspirations of man and readily respond to them. But a man can take advantage of these only in so far as he has already prepared himself to profit by them, for his thoughts and aspirations are only along certain lines, and he cannot suddenly form new lines. There are many directions which the higher thought may take—some of them personal and some impersonal. Among the latter are art, music and philosophy; and a man whose interest lay along any one of these lines finds both measureless enjoyment and unlimited instruction waiting for him—that is, the amount of enjoyment and instruction is limited only by his power of perception.

We find a large number of people whose only higher thoughts are those connected with affection and devotion. If a man loves another deeply or if he feels strong devotion to a personal deity, he makes a strong mental image of that friend or of the deity, and the object of his feeling is often present in his mind. Inevitably he takes that mental image into the heaven-world with him, because it is to that level of matter that it naturally belongs.

Take first the case of affection. The love which forms and retains such an image is a very powerful force—a force which is strong enough to reach and to act upon the ego of his friend in the higher part of the mental world. It is that ego that is the real man whom he loves—not the physical body which is so partial a representation of him. The ego of the friend, feeling this vibration, at once and eagerly responds to it, and pours himself into the thought-form, which has been made for him; so that the man's friend is truly present with him more vividly than ever before. To this result it makes no difference whatever whether the friend is what we call living or dead; the appeal is made not to the fragment of the friend which is sometimes imprisoned in a physical body, but to the man himself on his own true level; and he always responds. A man who has a hundred friends can simultaneously and fully respond to the affection of every one of them, for no number of representations on a lower level can exhaust the infinity of the ego.

Thus every man in his heaven-life has around him all the friends for whose company he wishes, and they are for him always at their best, because he himself makes for them the thought-form through which they manifest to him. In our limited physical world we are so accustomed to thinking of our friend as only the limited manifestation which we know in the physical world, that it is at first difficult for us to realize the grandeur of the conception; when we can realize it, we shall see how much nearer we are in truth to our friends in the heaven-life than we ever were on earth. The same is true in the case of devotion. The man in the heaven-world is two great stages nearer to the object of his devotion than he was during physical life, and so his experiences are of a far more transcendent character.

In this mental world, as in the astral, there are seven subdivisions. The first, second and third are the habitat of the ego in his causal body, so the mental body contains matter of the remaining four only, and it is in those sections that his heaven-life is passed. Man does not, however, pass from one to the other of these, as is the case in the astral world, for there is nothing in this life corresponding to the rearrangement. Rather is the man drawn to the level which best corresponds to the degree of his development, and on that level he spends the whole of his life in the mental body. Each man makes his own conditions, so that the number of varieties is infinite.

Speaking broadly, we may say that the dominant characteristic observed in the lowest portion is unselfish family affection. Unselfish it must be, or it would find no place here; all selfish tinges, if there were any, worked out their results in the astral world. The dominant characteristic of the sixth level may be said to be anthropomorphical religious devotion; while that of the fifth section is devotion expressing itself in active work of some sort. All these—the fifth, sixth and seventh subdivisions—are concerned with the working out of devotion to personalities (either to one's family and friends or to a personal deity) rather than the wider devotion to humanity for its own sake, which finds its expression in the next section. The activities of this fourth stage are varied. They can best be arranged in four main divisions: unselfish pursuit of spiritual knowledge; high philosophy or scientific thought; literary or artistic ability exercised for unselfish purposes; and service for the sake of service.

Even to this glorious heaven-life there comes an end, and then the mental body in its turn drops away as the others have done, and the man's life in his causal body begins. Here the man needs no windows, for this is his true home and all his walls have fallen away. The majority of men have as yet but very little consciousness at such a height as this; they rest dreamily unobservant and scarcely awake, but such vision as they have is true, however limited it may be by their lack of development. Still, every time they return, these limitations will be smaller, and they themselves will be greater; so that this truest life will be wider and fuller for them.

As this improvement continues, this causal life grows, longer and longer, assuming an ever larger proportion as compared to the existence at lower levels. And as he grows, the man becomes capable not only of receiving but also of giving. Then indeed is his triumph approaching, for he is learning the lesson of the Christ, learning the crowning glory of sacrifice, the supreme delight of pouring out all his life for the helping of his fellow-men, the devotion of the self to the all, of celestial strength to human service, of all those splendid heavenly forces to the aid of the struggling sons of earth. That is part of the life that lies before us; these are some of the steps which even we who are still so near the bottom of the golden ladder may see rising above us, so that we may report them to those who have not seen as yet, in order that they too may open their eyes to the unimaginable splendour which surrounds them here and now in this dull daily life. This is part of the gospel of Theosophy—the certainty of this sublime future for all. It is certain because it is here already, because to inherit it we have only to fit ourselves for it.

CHAPTER VII

REINCARNATION

This life of the ego in his own world, which is so glorious and so fully satisfying for the developed man, plays but a very small part in the life of the ordinary person, for in his case the ego has not yet reached a sufficient stage of development to be awake in his causal body. In obedience to the law of Nature he has withdrawn into it, but in doing so he has lost the sensation of vivid life, and his restless desire to feel this once more pushes him in the direction of another descent into matter.

This is the scheme of evolution appointed for man at the present stage—that he shall develop by descending into grosser matter, and then ascend to carry back into himself the result of the experiences so obtained. His real life, therefore, covers millions of years, and what we are in the habit of calling a life is only one day of this greater existence. Indeed, it is in reality only a small part of one day; for a life of seventy years in the physical world is often succeeded by a period of twenty times that length spent in higher spheres.

Every one of us has a long line of these physical lives behind him, and the ordinary man has a fairly long line still in front of him. Each of such lives is a day at school. The ego puts upon himself his garment of flesh and goes forth into the school of the physical world to learn certain lessons. He learns them, or does not learn them, or partially learns them, as the case may be, during his school-day of earth-life; then he lays aside the vesture of the flesh and returns home to his own level for rest and refreshment. In the morning of each new life he takes up again his lesson at the point where he left it the night before. Some lessons he may be able to learn in one day, while others may take him many days.

If he is an apt pupil and learns quickly what is needed, if he obtains an intelligent grasp of the rules of the school, and takes the trouble to adapt his conduct to them, his school-life is comparatively short, and when it is over he goes forth fully equipped into the real life of the higher worlds for which all this is only a preparation. Other egos are duller boys who do not learn so quickly; some of them do not understand the rules of the school, and through that ignorance are constantly breaking them; others are wayward, and even when they see the rules they cannot at once bring themselves to act in harmony with them. All of these have a longer school-life, and by their own actions they delay their entry upon the real life of the higher worlds.

For this is a school in which no pupil ever fails; every one must go on to the end. He has no choice as to that; but the length of time which he will take in qualifying himself for the higher examinations is left entirely to his own discretion. The wise pupil, seeing that school-life is not a thing in itself, but only a preparation for a more glorious and far wider life, endeavours to comprehend as fully as possible the rules of his school, and shapes his life in accordance with them as closely as he can, so that no time may be lost in the learning of whatever lessons are necessary. He co-operates intelligently with the Teachers, and sets himself to do the maximum of work which is possible for him, in order that as soon as he can he may come of age and enter into his kingdom as a glorified ego.

Theosophy explains to us the laws under which this school-life must be lived, and in that way gives a great advantage to its students. The first great law is that of evolution. Every man has to become a perfect man, to unfold to the fullest degree the divine possibilities which lie latent within him, for that unfoldment is the object of the entire scheme so far as he is concerned. This law of evolution steadily presses him onward to higher and higher achievements. The wise man tries to anticipate its demands—to run ahead of the necessary curriculum, for in that way he not only avoids all collision with it, but he obtains the maximum of assistance from its action. The man who lags behind in the race of life finds its steady pressure constantly constraining him—a pressure which, if resisted, rapidly becomes painful. Thus the laggard on the path of evolution has always the sense of being hunted and driven by his fate, while the man who intelligently co-operates is left perfectly free to choose the direction in which he shall move, so long as it is onward and upward.

The second great law under which this evolution is taking place is the law of cause and effect. There can be no effect without its cause, and every cause must produce its effect. They are in fact not two but one, for the effect is really part of the cause, and he who sets one in motion sets the other also. There is in Nature no such idea as that of reward or punishment, but only of cause and effect. Anyone can see this in connection with mechanics or chemistry; the clairvoyant sees it equally clearly with regard to the problems of evolution. The same law obtains in the higher as in the lower worlds; there, as here, the angle of reflection is always equal to the angle of incidence. It is a law of mechanics that action and reaction are equal and opposite. In the almost infinitely finer matter of the higher worlds the reaction is by no means always instantaneous; it may sometimes be spread over long periods of time, but it returns inevitably and exactly.

Just as certain in its working as the mechanical law in the physical world is the higher law, according to which the man who sends out a good thought or does a good action receives good in return, while the man who sends out an evil thought or does an evil action, receives evil in return with equal accuracy—once more, not in the least a reward or punishment administered by some external will, but simply as the definite and mechanical result of his own activity. Man has learnt to appreciate a mechanical result in the physical world, because the reaction is usually almost immediate and can be seen by him. He does not invariably understand the reaction in the higher worlds because that takes a wider sweep, and often returns not in this physical life, but in some future one.

The action of this law affords the explanation of a number of the problems of ordinary life. It accounts for the different destinies imposed upon people, and also for the differences in the people themselves. If one man is clever in a certain direction and another is stupid, it is because in a previous life the clever man has devoted much effort to practise in that particular direction, while the stupid man is trying it for the first time. The genius and the precocious child are examples not of the favouritism of some deity but of the result produced by previous lives of application. All the varied circumstances which surrounded us are the result of our own actions in the past, precisely as are the qualities of which we find ourselves in possession. We are what we have made ourselves, and our circumstances are such as we have deserved.

There is, however, a certain adjustment or apportionment of these effects. Though the law is a natural law and mechanical in its operation, there are nevertheless certain great Angels who are concerned with its administration. They cannot change by one feather-weight the amount of the result which follows upon any given thought or act, but they can within certain limits expedite or delay its action, and decide what form it shall take.

If this were not done there would be at least a possibility that in his earlier stages the man might blunder so seriously that the results of his blundering might be more than he could bear. The plan of the Deity is to give man a limited amount of free-will; if he uses that small amount well, he earns the right to a little more next time; if he uses it badly, suffering comes upon him as the result of such evil use, and he finds himself restrained by the result of his previous actions. As the man learns how to use his free-will, more and more of it is entrusted to him, so that he can acquire for himself practically unbounded freedom in the direction of good, but his power to do wrong is strictly restricted. He can progress as rapidly as he will, but he cannot wreck his life in his ignorance. In the earlier stages of the savage life of primitive man it is natural that there should be on the whole more of evil than of good, and if the entire result of his actions came at once upon a man as yet so little developed, it might well crush the newly evolved powers which are still so feeble.

Besides this, the effects of his actions are varied in character. While some of them produce immediate results, others need much more time for their action, and so it comes to pass that as the man develops he has above him a hovering cloud of undischarged results, some of them good, some of them bad. Out of this mass (which we may regard for purposes of analogy much as though it were a debt owing to the powers of Nature) a certain amount falls due in each of his successive births; and that amount, so assigned, may be thought of as the man's destiny for that particular life.

All that it means is that a certain amount of joy and a certain amount of suffering are due to him, and will unavoidably happen to him; how he will meet this destiny and what use he will make of it, that is left entirely to his own option. It is a certain amount of force which has to work itself out. Nothing can prevent the action of that force, but its action may always be modified by the application of a new force in another direction, just as is the case in mechanics. The result of past evil is like any other debt; it may be paid in one large cheque upon the bank of life—by some one supreme catastrophe; or it may be paid in a number of smaller notes, in minor troubles and worries; in some cases it may even be paid in the small change of a great number of petty annoyances. But one thing is quite certain—that, in some form or other, paid it will have to be.

The conditions of our present life, then, are absolutely the result of our own action in the past; and the other side of that statement is that our actions in this life are building up conditions for the next one. A man who finds himself limited either in powers or in outer circumstances may not always be able to make himself or his conditions all that he would wish in this life; but he can certainly secure for the next one whatever he chooses.

Man's every action ends not with himself, but invariably affects others around him. In some cases this effect may be comparatively trivial, while in others it may be of the most serious character. The trivial results, whether good or bad, are simply small debits or credits in our account with Nature; but the greater effects, whether good or bad, make a personal account which is to be settled with the individual concerned.

A man who gives a meal to a hungry beggar, or cheers him by a kindly word, will receive the result of his good action as part of a kind of general fund of Nature's benefits; but one who by some good action changes the whole current of another man's life will assuredly have to meet that same man again in a future life, in order that he who has been benefited may have the opportunity of repaying the kindness that has been done to him. One who causes annoyance to another will suffer proportionately for it somewhere, somehow, in the future, though he may never meet again the man whom he has troubled; but one who does serious harm to another, one who wrecks his life or retards his evolution, must certainly meet his victim again at some later point in the course of their lives, so that he may have the opportunity, by kindly and self-sacrificing service, of counter-balancing the wrong which he has done. In short, large debts must be paid personally, but small ones go into the general fund.

These then are the principal factors which determine the next birth of the man. First acts the great law of evolution, and its tendency is to press the man into that position in which he can most easily develop the qualities which he most needs. For the purposes of the general scheme, humanity is divided into great races, called root-races, which rule and occupy the world successively. The great Aryan or Indo-Caucasian race, which at the present moment includes the most advanced of Earth's inhabitants, is one of these. That which came before it in the order of evolution was the Mongolian race, usually called in Theosophical books Atlantean because the continent from which it ruled the world lay where now roll the waters of the Atlantic ocean. Before that came the Negroid race, some of whose descendants still exist, though by this time much mingled with offshoots of later races. From each of these great root-races there are many offshoots which we call sub-races—such, for example, as the Roman races or the Teutonic; and each of the sub-races in turn divides itself into branch-races, such as the French and the Italians, the English and the Germans.

These arrangements are made in order that for each ego there may be a wide choice of varying conditions and surroundings. Each race is especially adapted to develop within its people one or other of the qualities which are needed in the course of evolution. In every nation there exist an almost infinite number of diverse conditions, riches and poverty, a wide field of opportunities or a total lack of them, facilities for development or conditions under which development is difficult or well-nigh impossible. Amidst all these infinite possibilities the pressure of the law of evolution tends to guide the man to precisely those which best suit his needs at the stage at which he happens to be.

But the action of this law is limited by that other law of which we spoke, the law of cause and effect. The man's actions in the past may not have been such as to deserve (if we may put it so) the best possible opportunities; he may have set in motion in his past certain forces the inevitable result of which will be to produce limitations; and these limitations may operate to prevent his receiving that best possible of opportunities, and so as the result of his own actions in the past he may have to put up with the second best. So we may say that the action of the law of evolution, which if left to itself would do the very best possible for every man, is restrained by the man's own previous actions.

An important feature in that limitation—one which may act most powerfully for good or for evil—is the influence of the group of egos with which the man has made definite links in the past—those with whom he has formed strong ties of love or hate, of helping or of injury—those souls whom he must meet again because of connections made with them in days of long ago. His relation with them is a factor which must be taken into consideration before it can be determined where and how he shall be reborn.

The Will of the Deity is man's evolution. The effort of that nature which is an expression of the Deity is to give the man whatever is most suitable for that evolution; but this is conditioned by the man's deserts in the past and by the links which he has already formed. It may be assumed that a man descending into incarnation could learn the lessons necessary for that life in any one of a hundred positions. From half of these or more than half he may be debarred by the consequences of some of his many and varied actions in the past. Among the few possibilities which remain open to him, the choice of one possibility in particular may be determined by the presence in that family or in that neighbourhood of other egos upon whom he has a claim for services rendered, or to whom he in his turn owes a debt of love.

Chapter VIII

The Purpose of Life

To fulfil our duty in the divine scheme we must try to understand not only that scheme as a whole, but the special part that man is intended to play in it. The divine outbreathing reached its deepest immersion in matter in the mineral kingdom, but it reaches its ultimate point of differentiation not at the lowest level of materiality, but at the entrance into the human kingdom on the upward arc of evolution. We have thus to realize three stages in the course of this evolution.

(a) The downward arc in which the tendency is towards differentiation and also towards greater materiality. In this stage spirit is involving itself in matter, in order that it may learn to receive impressions through it.

(b) The earlier part of the upward arc, in which the tendency is still towards greater differentiation, but at the same time towards spiritualization and escape from materiality. In this stage the spirit is learning to dominate matter and to see it as an expression of itself.

(c) The later part of the upward arc, when differentiation has been finally accomplished, and the tendency is towards unity as well as towards greater spirituality. In this stage the spirit, having learnt perfectly how to receive impression through matter and how to express itself through it, and having awakened its dormant powers, learns to use these powers rightly in the service of the Deity.

The object of the whole previous evolution has been to produce the ego as a manifestation of the Monad. Then the ego in its turn evolves by putting itself down into a succession of personalities. Men who do not understand this look upon the personality as the self, and consequently live for it alone, and try to regulate their lives for what appears to be its temporary advantage. The man who understands realizes that the only important thing is the life of the ego, and that its progress is the object for which the temporary personality must be used. Therefore when he has to decide between two possible courses he thinks not, as the ordinary man might: "Which will bring the greater pleasure and profit to me as a personality?" but "Which will bring greater progress to me as an ego?" Experience soon teaches him that nothing can ever be really good for him, or for anyone, which is not good for all, and so presently he learns to forget himself altogether, and to ask only what will be best for humanity as a whole.

Clearly then at this stage of evolution whatever tends to unity, whatever tends to spirituality, is in accord with the plan of the Deity for us, and is therefore right for us, while whatever tends to separateness or to materiality is equally certainly wrong for us. There are thoughts and emotions which tend to unity, such as love, sympathy, reverence, benevolence; there are others which tend to disunion, such as hatred, jealousy, envy, pride, cruelty, fear. Obviously the former group are for us the right, the latter group are for us the wrong.

In all these thoughts and feelings which are clearly wrong, we recognize one dominant note, the thought of self; while in all those which are clearly right we recognize that the thought is turned toward others, and that the personal self is forgotten. Wherefore we see that selfishness is the one great wrong, and that perfect unselfishness is the crown of all virtue. This gives us at once a rule of life. The man who wishes intelligently to co-operate with the Divine Will must lay aside all thought of the advantage or pleasure of the personal self, and must devote himself exclusively to carrying out that Will by working for the welfare and happiness of others.

This is a high ideal, and difficult of attainment, because there lies behind us such a long history of selfishness. Most of us are as yet far from the purely altruistic attitude; how are we to go to work to attain it, lacking as we do the necessary intensity in so many of the good qualities, and possessing so many which are undesirable?

Here comes into operation the great law of cause and effect to which I have already referred. Just as we can confidently appeal to the laws of Nature in the physical world, so may we also appeal to these laws of the higher world. If we find evil qualities within us, they have grown up by slow degrees through ignorance and through self-indulgence. Now that the ignorance is dispelled by knowledge, now that in consequence we recognize the quality as an evil, the method of getting rid of it lies obviously before us.

For each of these vices there is a contrary virtue; if we find one of them rearing its head within us, let us immediately determine deliberately to develop within ourselves the contrary virtue. If a man realizes that in the past he has been selfish, that means that he has set up within himself the habit of thinking of himself first and pleasing himself, of consulting his own convenience or his pleasure without due thought of the effect upon others; let him set to work purposefully to form the exactly opposite habit, to make a practice before doing anything of thinking how it will affect all those around him; let him set himself habitually to please others, even though it be at the cost of trouble or privation for himself. This also in time will become a habit, and by developing it he will have killed out the other.

If a man finds himself full of suspicion, ready always to assign evil motives to the actions of those about him, let him set himself steadily to cultivate trust in his fellows, to give them credit always for the highest possible motives. It may be said that a man who does this will lay himself open to be deceived, and that in many cases his confidence will be misplaced. That is a small matter; it is far better for him that he should sometimes be deceived as a result of his trust in his fellows than that he should save himself from such deception by maintaining a constant attitude of suspicion. Besides, confidence begets faithfulness. A man who is trusted will generally prove himself worthy of the trust, whereas a man who is suspected is likely presently to justify the suspicion.

If a man finds in himself the tendency towards avarice, let him go out of his way to be especially generous; if he finds himself irritable, let him definitely train himself in calmness; if he finds himself devoured by curiosity, let him deliberately refuse again and again to gratify that curiosity; if he is liable to fits of depression, let him persistently cultivate cheerfulness, even under the most adverse circumstances.

In every case the existence of an evil quality in the personality means a lack of the corresponding good quality in the ego. The shortest way to get rid of that evil and to prevent its reappearance is to fill the gap in the ego, and the good quality which is thus developed will show itself as an integral part of the man's character through all his future lives. An ego cannot be evil, but he can be imperfect. The qualities which he develops cannot be other than good qualities, and when they are well defined they show themselves in each of all his numerous personalities, and consequently those personalities can never be guilty of the vices opposite to these qualities; but where there is a gap in the ego, where there is a quality undeveloped, there is nothing inherent in the personality to check the growth of the opposite vice; and since others in the world about him already possess that vice, and man is an imitative animal, it is quite probable that it will speedily manifest itself in him. This vice, however, belongs to the vehicles only and not to the man inside. In these vehicles its repetition may set up a momentum which is hard to conquer; but if the ego bestirs himself to create in himself the opposite virtue, the vice is cut off at its root, and can no longer exist—neither in this life nor in all the lives that are to come.

A man who is trying to evolve these qualities in himself will find certain obstacles in his way—obstacles which he must learn to surmount. One of these is the critical spirit of the age—the disposition to find fault with a thing, to belittle everything, to look for faults in everything and everyone. The exact opposite of this is what is needed for progress. He who wishes to move rapidly along the path of evolution must learn to see good in everything—to see the latent Deity in everything and in everyone. Only so can he help those other people—only so can he get the best out of those other things.

Another obstacle is the lack of perseverance. We tend in these days to be impatient; if we try any plan we expect immediate results from it, and if we do not get them, we give up that plan and try something else. That is not the way to make progress in occultism. The effort which we are making is to compress into one or two lives the evolution which would naturally take perhaps a hundred lives. That is not the sort of undertaking in which immediate results are to be expected. We attempt to uproot an evil habit, and we find it hard work; why? Because we have indulged in that practice for, perhaps, twenty thousand years; one cannot shake off the custom of twenty thousand years in a day or two. We have allowed that habit to gain an enormous momentum, and before we can set up a force in the opposite direction we have to overcome that momentum. That cannot be done in a moment, but it is absolutely certain that it *will* be done eventually, if we persevere, because the momentum, however strong it may be, is a finite quantity, whereas the power that we can bring to bear against it is the infinite power of the human will, which can make renewed efforts day after day, year after year, even life after life if necessary.

Another great difficulty in our way is the lack of clearness in our thought. People in the West are little used to clear thought with regard to religious matters. Everything is vague and nebulous. For occult development vagueness and nebulosity will not do. Our conceptions must be clear-cut and our thought-images definite. Other necessary characteristics are calmness and cheerfulness; these are rare in modern life, but are absolute essentials for the work which we are here undertaking.

The process of building a character is as scientific as that of developing one's muscles. Many a man, finding himself with certain muscles flabby and powerless takes that as his natural condition, and regards their weakness as a kind of destiny imposed upon him; but anyone who understands a little of the human body is aware that by continued exercise those muscles can be brought into a state of health and the whole body eventually put in order. In exactly the same way, many a man finds himself possessed of a bad temper or a tendency to avarice or suspicion or self-indulgence, and when in consequence of any of these vices he commits some great mistake or does some great harm he offers it as an excuse that he is a hasty-tempered man, or that he possesses this or that quality by nature—implying that therefore he cannot help it.

In this case just as in the other the remedy is in his own hands. Regular exercise of the right kind will develop a certain muscle, and regular mental exercise of the right kind will develop a missing quality in a man's character. The ordinary man does not realize that he can do this, and even if he sees that he can do it, he does not see why he should, for it means much effort and much self-repression. He knows of no adequate motive for undertaking a task so laborious and painful.

The motive is supplied by the knowledge of the truth. One who gains an intelligent comprehension of the direction of evolution feels it not only his interest but his privilege and his delight to co-operate with it. One who wills the end wills also the means; in order to be able to do good work for the world he must develop within himself the necessary strength and the necessary qualities. Therefore he who wishes to reform the world must first of all reform himself. He must learn to give up altogether the attitude of insisting upon rights, and must devote himself utterly to the most earnest performance of his duties. He must learn to regard every connection with his fellow-man as an opportunity to help that fellow-man, or in some way to do him good.

One who studies these subjects intelligently cannot but realize the tremendous power of thought, and the necessity for its efficient control. All action springs from thought, for even when it is done (as we say) without thought, it is the instinctive expression of the thoughts, desires and feelings which the man has allowed to grow luxuriantly within himself in earlier days.

The wise man, therefore, will watch his thought with the greatest of care, for in it he possesses a powerful instrument, for the right use of which he is responsible. It is his duty to govern his thought, lest it should be allowed to run riot and to do evil to himself, and to others; it is his duty also to develop his thought-power, because by means of it a vast amount of actual and active good can be done. Thus controlling his thought and his action, thus eliminating from himself all evil and unfolding in himself all good qualities, the man presently raises himself far above the level of his fellows, and stands out conspicuously among them as one who is working on the side of good as against evil, of evolution as against stagnation.

The Members of the great Hierarchy, in whose hands is the evolution of the world, are watching always for such men in order that They may train them to help in the great work. Such a man inevitably attracts Their attention, and They begin to use him as an instrument in Their work. If he proves himself a good and efficient instrument, presently They will offer him definite training as an apprentice, that by helping Them in the world-business which They have to do he may some day become even as They are, and join the mighty Brotherhood to which They belong.

But for an honour so great as this mere ordinary goodness will not suffice. True, a man must be good first of all, or it would be hopeless to think of using him, but in addition to being good he must be wise and strong. What is needed is not merely a good man, but a great spiritual power. Not only must the candidate have cast aside all ordinary weaknesses but he must have acquired strong positive qualities before he can offer himself to Them with any hope that he will be accepted. He must live no longer as a blundering and selfish personality, but as an intelligent ego who comprehends the part which he has to play in the great scheme of the universe. He must have forgotten himself utterly; he must have resigned all thought of worldly profit or pleasure or advancement; he must be willing to sacrifice everything, and himself first of all, for the sake of the work that has to be done. He may be *in* the world, but he must not be *of* the world. He must be careless utterly of its opinion. For the sake of helping man he must make himself something more than man. Radiant, rejoicing, strong, he must live but for the sake of others and to be an expression of the love of God in the world. A high ideal, yet not too high; possible, because there are men who have achieved it.

When a man has succeeded in unfolding his latent possibilities so far that he attracts the attention of the Masters of the Wisdom, one of Them will probably receive him as an apprentice upon probation. The period of probation is usually seven years, but may be either shortened or lengthened at the discretion of the Master. At the end of that time, if his work has been satisfactory, he becomes what it commonly called the accepted pupil. This brings him into close relations with his Master, so that the vibrations of the latter constantly play upon him, and he gradually learns to look at everything as the Master looks at it. After yet another interval, if he proves himself entirely worthy, he may be drawn into a still closer relationship, when he is called the son of the Master.

These three stages mark his relationship to his own Master only, not to the Brotherhood as a whole. The Brotherhood admits a man to its ranks only when he has fitted himself to pass the first of the great Initiations.

This entry into the Brotherhood of Those who rule the world may be thought of as the third of the great critical points in man's evolution. The first of these is when he becomes man—when he individualizes out of the animal kingdom and obtains a causal body. The second is what is called by the Christian "conversion", by the Hindu "the acquirement of discrimination", and by the Buddhist "the opening of the doors of the mind". That is the point at which he realizes the great facts of life, and turns away from the pursuit of selfish ends in order to move intentionally along with the great current of evolution in obedience to the divine Will. The third point is the most important of all, for the Initiation which admits him to the ranks of the Brotherhood also insures him against the possibility of failure to fulfil the divine purpose in the time appointed for it. Hence those who have reached this point are called in the

Christian system the "elect", the "saved" or the "safe", and in the Buddhist scheme "those who have entered on the stream". For those who have reached this point have made themselves absolutely certain of reaching a further point also—that of Adeptship, at which they pass into a type of evolution which is definitely Superhuman.

The man who has become an Adept has fulfilled the divine Will so far as this chain of worlds is concerned. He has reached, even already at the midmost point of the æon of evolution, the stage prescribed for man's attainment at the end of it. Therefore he is at liberty to spend the remainder of that time either in helping his fellow-men or in even more splendid work in connection with other and higher evolutions. He who has not yet been initiated is still in danger of being left behind by our present wave of evolution, and dropping into the next one—the "æonian condemnation" of which the Christ spoke, which has been mistranslated "eternal damnation". It is from this fate of possible æonian failure—that is, failure for this age, or dispensation, or life-wave—that the man who attains Initiation is "safe". He has "entered upon the stream" which now *must* bear him on to Adeptship in this present age, though it is still possible for him by his actions to hasten or delay his progress along the Path which he is treading.

That first Initiation corresponds to the matriculation which admits a man to a University, and the attainment of Adeptship to the taking of a degree at the end of a course. Continuing the simile, there are three intermediate examinations, which are usually spoken of as the second, third, and fourth Initiations, Adeptship being the fifth. A general idea of the line of this higher evolution may be obtained by studying the list of what are called in Buddhist books "the fetters" which must be cast off—the qualities of which a man must rid himself as he treads this Path. These are: the delusion of separateness; doubt or uncertainty; superstition; attachment to enjoyment; the possibility of hatred; desire for life, either in this or the higher worlds; pride; agitation or irritability; and ignorance. The man who reaches the Adept level has exhausted all the possibilities of moral development, and so the future evolution which still lies before him can only mean still wider knowledge and still more wonderful spiritual powers.

CHAPTER IX

THE PLANETARY CHAINS

The scheme of evolution of which our Earth forms a part is not the only one in our solar system, for ten separate chains of globes exist in that system which are all of them theatres of somewhat similar progress. Each of these schemes of evolution is taking place upon a chain of globes, and in the course of each scheme its chain of globes goes through seven incarnations. The plan, alike of each scheme as a whole and of the successive incarnation of its chain of globes, is to dip step by step more deeply into matter, and then to rise step by step out of it again.

Each chain consists of seven globes, and both globes and chains observe the rule of descending into matter and then rising out of it again. In order to make this comprehensible let us take as an example the chain to which our Earth belongs. At the present time it is in its fourth or most material incarnation, and therefore three of its globes belong to the physical world, two to the astral world, and two to the lower part of the mental world. The wave of divine Life passes in succession from globe to globe of this chain, beginning with one of the highest, descending gradually to the lowest and then climbing again to the same level as that at which it began.

Let us for convenience of reference label the seven globes by the earlier letters of the alphabet, and number the incarnations in order. Thus, as this is the fourth incarnation of our chain, the first globe in this incarnation will be 4A, the second 4B, the third 4C, the fourth (which is our Earth) 4D, and so on.

These globes are not all composed of physical matter. 4A contains no matter lower than that of the mental world; it has its counterpart in all the worlds higher than that, but nothing below it. 4B exists in the astral world; but 4C is a physical globe, visible to our telescopes, and is in fact the planet which we know as Mars. Globe 4D is our own Earth, on which the life-wave of the chain is at present in action. Globe 4E is the planet which we call Mercury—also in the physical world. Globe 4F is in the astral world, corresponding on the ascending arc to globe 4B in the descent; while globe 4G corresponds to globe 4A in having its lowest manifestation in the lower part of the mental world. Thus it will be seen that we have a scheme of globes starting in the lower mental world, dipping through the astral into the physical and then rising into the lower mental through the astral again.

Just as the succession of the globes in a chain constitutes a descent into matter and an ascent from it again, so do the successive incarnations of a chain. We have described the condition of affairs in the fourth incarnation; looking back at the third, we find that that commences not on the lower level of the mental world but on the higher. Globes 3A and 3G, then, are both of higher mental matter, while globes 3B and 3F are at the lower mental level. Globes 3C and 3E belong to the astral world, and only globe 3D is visible in the physical world. Although this third incarnation of our chain is long past, the corpse of this physical globe 3D is still visible to us in the shape of that dead planet the Moon, whence that third incarnation is usually called the lunar chain.

The fifth incarnation of our chain, which still lies very far in the future, will correspond to the third. In that, globes 5A and 5G will be built of higher mental matter, globes 5B and 5F of lower mental, globes 5C and 5E of astral matter, and only globe 5D will be in the physical world. This planet 5D is of course not yet in existence.

The other incarnations of the chain follow the same general rule of gradually decreasing materiality; 2A, 2G, 6A and 6G are all in the intuitional world; 2B, 2F, 6B and 6F are all in the higher part of the mental world; 2C, 2E, 6C and 6E are in the lower part of the mental world; 2D and 6D are in the astral world. In the same way 1A, 1G, 7A and 7G belong to the spiritual world; 1B, 1F, 7B and 7F are in the intuitional world; 1C, 1E, 7C and 7E are in the higher part of the mental world; 1D and 7D are in the lower part of the mental world.

Thus it will be seen that not only does the life-wave in passing through one chain of globes dip down into matter and rise out of it again, but the chain itself in its successive incarnations does exactly the same thing.

There are ten schemes of evolution at present existing in our solar system, but only seven of them are at the stage where they have planets in the physical world. These are: (1) that of an unrecognized planet Vulcan, very near the sun, about which we have very little definite information. It was seen by the astronomer Herschel, but is now said to have disappeared. We at first understood that it was in its third incarnation; but it is now regarded as possible that it has recently passed from its fifth to its sixth chain, which would account for its alleged disappearance; (2) that of Venus, which is in its fifth incarnation, and also therefore, has only one visible globe; (3) that of the Earth, Mars and Mercury, which has three visible planets because it is in its fourth incarnation; (4) that of Jupiter, (5) that of Saturn, (6) that of Uranus, all in their third incarnations; and (7) that of Neptune and the two unnamed planets beyond its orbit, which is in its fourth incarnation, and therefore has three physical planets as we have.

In each incarnation of a chain (commonly called a chain-period) the wave of divine Life moves seven times round the chain of seven planets, and each such movement is spoken of as a round. The time that the life-wave stays upon each planet is known as a world-period, and in the course of a world-period there are seven great root-races. As has been previously explained, these are subdivided into sub-races, and those again into branch-races. For convenience of reference we may state this in tabular form:

7	Branch-Races	make	1	Sub-Race
7	Sub-Races	"	1	Root-Race
7	Root-Races	"	1	World-Period
7	World-Periods	"	1	Round
7	Rounds	"	1	Chain-Period
7	Chain-Periods	"	1	Schemes of Evolution
10	Scheme of Evolution	"		Our Solar System

It is clear that the fourth root-race of the fourth globe of the fourth round of a fourth chain-period would be the central point of a whole scheme of evolution, and we find ourselves at the present moment only a little past that point. The Aryan race, to which we belong, is the fifth root-race of the fourth globe, so that the actual middle point fell in the time of the last great root-race, the Atlantean. Consequently the human race as a whole is very little more than half-way through its evolution, and those few souls who are already nearing Adeptship, which is the end and crown of this evolution, are very far in advance of their fellows.

How do they come to be so far in advance? Partly and in some cases because they have worked harder, but usually because they are older egos—because they were individualized out of the animal kingdom at an earlier date, and so have had more time for the human part of their evolution.

Any given wave of life sent forth from the Deity usually spends a chain-period in each of the great kingdoms of Nature. That which in our first chain was ensouling the first elemental kingdom must have ensouled the second of those kingdoms in the second chain, in the third of them in the Moon-chain, and is now in the mineral kingdom in the fourth chain. In the future fifth chain it will ensoul the vegetable kingdom, in the sixth the animal, and in the seventh it will attain humanity.

From this it follows that we ourselves represented the mineral kingdom on the first chain, the vegetable on the second, and the animal on the lunar chain. There some of us attained our individualization, and so we were enabled to enter this Earth-chain as men. Others who were a little more backward did not succeed in attaining it, and so had to be born into this chain as animals for a while before they could reach humanity.

Not all of mankind, however, entered this chain together. When the lunar chain came to its end the humanity upon it stood at various levels. Not Adeptship, but what is now for us the fourth step on the Path, was the goal appointed for that chain. Those who had attained it (commonly called in Theosophical literature the Lords of the Moon) had, as is usual, seven choices before them as to the way in which they would serve. Only one of those choices brought them, or rather a few of them, over into this Earth-chain to act as guides and teachers to the earlier races. A considerable proportion—a vast proportion, indeed—of the Moon-men had not attained that level, and consequently had to reappear in this Earth-chain as humanity. Besides this, a great mass of the animal kingdom of the Moon-chain was surging up to the level of the individualization, and some of its members had already reached it, while many others had not. These latter needed further animal incarnations upon the Earth-chain, and for the moment may be put aside.

There were many classes even among the humanity, and the manner in which these distributed themselves over the Earth-chain needs some explanation. It is the general rule that those who have attained the highest possible in any chain on any globe, in any root-race, are not born into the beginning of the next chain, globe or race, respectively. The earlier stages are always for the backward entities, and only when they have already passed through a good deal of evolution and are beginning to approach the level of those others who had done better, do the latter descend into incarnation and join them once more. That is to say, almost the earlier half of any period of evolution, whether it be a race, a globe or a chain, seems to be devoted to bringing the backward people up to nearly the level of those who have got on better; then these latter also (who, in the meantime, have been resting in great enjoyment in the mental world) descend into incarnation along with the others, and they press on together until the end of the period.

Thus the first of the egos from the Moon who entered the Earth-chain were by no means the most advanced. Indeed they may be described as the least advanced of those who had succeeded in attaining humanity—the animal-men. Coming as they did into a chain of new globes, freshly aggregated, they had to establish the forms in all the different kingdoms of Nature. This needs to be done at the beginning of the first round in a new chain, but never after that; for though the life-wave is centred only upon one of the seven globes of a chain at any given time, yet life has not entirely departed from the other globes. At the present moment, for example, the life-wave of our chain is centred on this Earth, but on the other two physical globes of our chain, Mars and Mercury, life still exists. There is still a population, human, animal and vegetable, and consequently when the life-wave goes round again to either of those planets there will be no necessity for the creation of new forms. The old types are already there, and all that will happen will be a sudden marvellous fecundity, so that the various kingdoms will quickly increase and multiply, and make a rapidly increasing population instead of a stationary one.

It was, then, the animal-men, the lowest class of human beings of the Moon-chain, who established the forms in the first round of the Earth-chain. Pressing closely after them were the highest of the lunar animal kingdom, who were soon ready to occupy the forms which had just been made. In the second journey round the seven globes of the Earth-chain, the animal-men who had been the most backward of the lunar humanity were leaders of this terrene humanity, the highest of the moon-animals making its less developed grades. The same thing went on in the third round of the Earth-chain, more and more of the lunar animals attaining individualization and joining the human rank, until in the middle of that round on this very globe D which we call the Earth, a higher class of human beings—the Second Order of Moon-men—descended into incarnation and at once took the lead.

When we come to the fourth, our present round, we find the First Order of the Moon-men pouring in upon us—all the highest and the best of the lunar humanity who had only just fallen short of success. Some of those who had already, even on the Moon, entered upon the Path soon attained its end, became Adepts and passed away from the Earth. Some few others who had not been quite so far advanced have attained Adeptship only comparatively recently—that is, within the last few thousand years, and these are the Adepts of the present day. We, who find ourselves in the higher races of humanity now, were several stages behind Them, but the opportunity lies before us of following in Their steps if we will.

The evolution of which we have been speaking is that of the Ego himself, of what might be called the soul of man; but at the same time there has been also an evolution to the body. The forms built in the first round were very different from any of which we know anything now. Properly speaking, those which were made on our physical earth can scarcely be called forms at all, for they were constructed of etheric matter only, and resembled vague, drifting and almost shapeless clouds. In the second round they were definitely physical, but still shapeless and light enough to float about in currents of wind.

Only in the third round did they begin to bear any kind of resemblance to man as we know him today. The very methods of reproduction of those primitive forms differed from those of humanity today, and far more resembled those which we now find only in very much lower types of life. Man in those early days was androgynous, and a definite separation into sexes took place only about the middle of the third round. From that time onward until now the shape of man has been steadily evolving along definitely human lines, becoming smaller and more compact than it was, learning to stand upright instead of stooping and crawling, and generally differentiating itself from the animal forms out of which it had been evolved.

One curious break in the regularity of this evolution deserves mention. On this globe, in this fourth round, there was a departure from the straightforward scheme of evolution. This being the middle globe of a middle round, the midmost point of evolution upon it marked the last moment at which it was possible for members of what had been the lunar animal kingdom to attain individualization. Consequently a sort of strong effort was made—a special scheme was arranged to give a final chance to as many as possible. The conditions of the first and second rounds were specially reproduced in place of the first and second races—conditions of which in the earlier rounds these backward egos had not been able fully to take advantage. Now, with the additional evolution, which they had undergone during the third round, some of them were able to take such advantage, and so they rushed in at the very last moment before the door was shut, and became just human. Naturally they will not reach any high level of human development, but at least when they try again in some future chain it will be some advantage to them to have had even this slight experience of human life.

Our terrestrial evolution received a most valuable stimulus from the assistance given to us by our sister globe, Venus. Venus is at present in the fifth incarnation of its chain, and in the seventh round of that incarnation, so that its inhabitants are a whole chain-period and a half in front of us in evolution. Since, therefore, its people are so much more developed than ours, it was thought desirable that certain Adepts from the Venus evolution should be transferred to our Earth in order to assist in the specially busy time just before the closing of the door, in the middle of the fourth root-race.

These august Beings have been called the Lords of the Flame and the Children of the Fire-mist, and They have produced a wonderful effect upon our evolution. The intellect of which we are so proud is almost entirely due to Their presence, for in the natural course of events the next round, the fifth, should be that of intellectual advancement, and in this our present fourth round we should be devoting ourselves chiefly to the cultivation of the emotions. We are therefore in reality a long way in advance of the programme marked out for us; and such advance is entirely due to the assistance given by these great Lords of the Flame. Most of Them stayed with us only through that critical period of our history; a few still remain to hold the highest offices of the Great White Brotherhood until the time when men of our own evolution shall have risen to such a height as to be capable of relieving their august Visitors.

The evolution lying before us is both of the life and of the form; for in future rounds, while the egos will be steadily growing in power, wisdom and love, the physical forms also will be more beautiful and more perfect than they have ever yet been. We have in this world at the present time men at widely differing stages of evolution, and it is clear that there are vast hosts of savages who are far behind the great civilized races of the world—so far behind that it is quite impossible that they can overtake them. Later on in the course of our evolution a point will be reached at which it is no longer possible for those undeveloped souls to advance side by side with the others, so that it will be necessary that a division should be made.

The proceeding is exactly analogous to the sorting out by a schoolmaster of the boys in his class. During the school year he has to prepare his boys for a certain examination, and by perhaps the middle of that school year he knows quite well which of them will pass it. If he should have in his class some who are hopelessly behind the rest, he might reasonably say to them when the middle period was reached:

"It is quite useless for you to continue with your fellows, for the more difficult lessons which I shall now have to give will be entirely unintelligible to you. It is impossible that you can learn enough in the time to pass the examination, so that the effort would only be a useless strain for you, and meantime you would be a hindrance to the rest of the class. It is therefore far better for you to give up striving after the impossible, and to take up again the work of the lower class which you did not do perfectly, and then to offer yourselves for this examination along with next year's class, for what is now impossible for you will then be easy."

This is in effect exactly what is said at a certain stage in our future evolution, to the most backward egos. They drop out of this year's class and come along with the next one. This is the "æonian condemnation" to which reference was made a little while ago. It is computed that about two-fifths of humanity will drop out of the class in this way, leaving the remaining three-fifths to go on with far greater rapidity to the glorious destinies which lie before them.

CHAPTER X

THE RESULT OF THEOSOPHICAL STUDY

"Members of the Theosophical Society study these truths and Theosophists endeavour to live them." What manner of man then is the true Theosophist in consequence of his knowledge? What is the result in his daily life of all this study?

Finding that there is a Supreme Power who is directing the course of evolution, and that He is all-wise and all-loving, the Theosophist sees that everything which exists within this scheme must be intended to further its progress. He realizes that the scripture which tells us that all things are working together for good, is not indulging in a flight of poetic fancy or voicing a pious hope, but stating a scientific fact. The final attainment of unspeakable glory is an absolute certainty for every son of man, whatever may be his present condition; but that is by no means all. Here and at this present moment he is on his way towards the glory; and all the circumstances surrounding him are intended to help and not to hinder him, if only they are rightly understood. It is sadly true that in the world there is much of evil and of sorrow and of suffering; yet from the higher point of view the Theosophist sees that terrible though this be, it is only temporary and superficial, and is all being utilized as a factor in the progress.

When in the days of his ignorance he looked at it from its own level it was almost impossible to see this; while he looked from beneath at the under side of life, with his eyes fixed all the time upon some apparent evil, he could never gain a true grasp of its meaning. Now he raises himself above it to the higher levels of thought and consciousness, and looks down upon it with the eye of the spirit and understands it in its entirety, so he can see that in very truth all is well—not that all will be well at some remote period, but that even now at this moment, in the midst of incessant striving and apparent evil, the mighty current of evolution is still flowing, and so all is well because all is moving on in perfect order towards the final goal.

Raising his consciousness thus above the storm and stress of worldly life, he recognizes what used to seem to be evil, and notes how it is apparently pressing backwards against the great stream of progress; but he also sees that the onward sweep of the divine law of evolution bears the same relation to this superficial evil as does the tremendous torrent of Niagara to the fleckings of foam upon its surface. So while he sympathizes deeply with all who suffer, he yet realizes what will be the end of that suffering, and so for him despair or hopelessness is impossible. He applies this consideration to his own sorrows and troubles, as well as to those of the world, and therefore one great result of his Theosophy is a perfect serenity—even more than that, a perpetual cheerfulness and joy.

For him there is an utter absence of worry, because in truth there is nothing left to worry about, since he knows that all must be well. His higher Science makes him a confirmed optimist, for it shows him that whatever of evil there may be in any person or in any movement, it is of necessity temporary, because it is opposed to the resistless stream of evolution; whereas whatever is good in any person or in any movement must necessarily be persistent and useful, because it has behind it the omnipotence of that current, and therefore it must abide and it must prevail.

Yet it must not for a moment be supposed that because he is so fully assured of the final triumph of good he remains careless or unmoved by the evils which exist in the world around him. He knows that it is his duty to combat these to the utmost of his power, because in doing this he is working upon the side of the great evolutionary force, and is bringing nearer the time of its ultimate victory. None will be more active than he in labouring for the good, even though he is absolutely free from the feeling of helplessness and hopelessness which so often oppresses those who are striving to help their fellow-men.

Another most valuable result of his Theosophical study is the absence of fear. Many people are constantly anxious or worried about something or other; they are fearing lest this or that should happen to them, lest this or that combination may fail, and so all the while they are in a condition of unrest; and most serious of all for many is the fear of death. For the Theosophist the whole of this feeling is entirely swept away. He realizes the great truth of reincarnation. He knows that he has often before laid aside physical bodies, and so he sees that death is no more than sleep—that just as sleep comes in between our days of work and gives us rest and refreshment, so between these days of labour here on earth, which we call lives, there comes a long night of astral and of heavenly life to give us rest and refreshment and to help us on our way.

To the Theosophist death is simply the laying aside for a time of this robe of flesh. He knows that it is his duty to preserve the bodily vesture as long as possible, and gain through it all the experience he can; but when the time comes for him to lay it down he will do so thankfully, because he knows that the next stage will be a much pleasanter one than this. Thus he will have no fear of death, although he realizes that he must live his life to the appointed end, because he is here for the purpose of progress, and that progress is the one truly momentous matter. His whole conception of life is different; the object is not to earn so much money, not to obtain such and such a position; the one important thing is to carry out the divine plan. He knows that for this he is here, and that everything else must give way to it.

Utterly free also is he from any religious fears or worries or troubles. All such things are swept aside for him, because he sees clearly that progress towards the highest is the divine Will for us, that we cannot escape from that progress, and that whatever comes in our way and whatever happens to us is meant to help us along that line; that we ourselves are absolutely the only people who can delay our advance. No longer does he trouble and fear about himself. He simply goes on and does the duty which comes nearest in the best way that he can, confident that if he does this all will be well for him without his perpetual worrying. He is satisfied quietly to do his work and to try to help his fellows in the race, knowing that the great divine Power behind will press him onward slowly and steadily, and do for him all that can be done, so long as his face is set steadfastly in the right direction, so long as he does all that he reasonably can.

Since he knows that we are all part of one great evolution and all literally the children of one Father, he sees that the universal brotherhood of humanity is no mere poetical conception, but a definite fact; not a dream of something which is to be in the dim distance of Utopia, but a condition existing here and now. The certainty of this all-embracing fraternity gives him a wider outlook upon life and a broad impersonal point of view from which to regard everything. He realizes that the true interests of all are in fact identical, and that no man can ever make real gain for himself at the cost of loss or suffering to some one else. This is not to him an article of religious belief, but a scientific fact proved to him by his study. He sees that since humanity is literally a whole, nothing which injures one man can ever be really for the good of any other, for the harm done influences not only the doer but also those who are about him.

He knows that the only true advantage for him is that benefit which he shares with all. He sees that any advance which he is able to make in the way of spiritual progress or development is something secured not for himself alone but for others. If he gains knowledge or self-control, he assuredly acquires much for himself, yet he takes nothing away from anyone else, but on the contrary he helps and strengthens others. Cognizant as he is of the absolute spiritual unity of humanity, he knows that, even in this lower world, no true profit can be made by one man which is not made in the name of and for the sake of humanity; that one man's progress must be a lifting of the burden of all the others; that one man's advance in spiritual things means a very slight yet not imperceptible advance to humanity as a whole; that every one who bears suffering and sorrow nobly in his struggle towards the light is lifting a little of the heavy load of the sorrow and suffering of his brothers as well.

Because he recognizes this brotherhood not merely as a hope cherished by despairing men, but as a definite fact following in scientific series from all other facts; because he sees this as an absolute certainty, his attitude towards all those around him changes radically. It becomes a posture ever of helpfulness, ever of the deepest sympathy, for he sees that nothing which clashes with their higher interests can be the right thing for him to do, or can be good for him in any way.

It naturally follows that he becomes filled with the widest possible tolerance and charity. He cannot but be always tolerant, because his philosophy shows him that it matters little what a man believes, so long as he is a good man and true. Charitable also he must be, because his wider knowledge enables him to make allowances for many things which the ordinary man does not understand. The standard of the Theosophist as to right and wrong is always higher than that of the less instructed man, yet he is far gentler than the latter in his feeling towards the sinner, because he comprehends more of human nature. He realizes how the sin appeared to the sinner at the moment of its commission, and so he makes more allowances than is ever made by the man who is ignorant of all this.

He goes further than tolerance, charity, sympathy; he feels positive love towards mankind, and that leads him to adopt a position of watchful helpfulness. He feels that every contact with others is for him an opportunity, and the additional knowledge which his study has brought to him enables him to give advice or help in almost any case which comes before him. Not that he is perpetually thrusting his opinions upon other people. On the contrary, he observes that to do this is one of the commonest mistakes made by the uninstructed. He knows that argument is a foolish waste of energy, and therefore he declines to argue. If anyone desires from him explanation or advice he is more than willing to give it, yet he has no sort of wish to convert anyone else to his own way of thinking.

In every relation of life this idea of helpfulness comes into play, not only with regard to his fellow-men but also in connection with the vast animal kingdom which surrounds him. Units of this kingdom are often brought into close relation with man, and this is for him an opportunity of doing something for them. The Theosophist recognizes that these are also his brothers, even though they may be younger brothers, and that he owes a fraternal duty to them also—so to act and so to think that his relation with them shall be always for their good and never for their harm.

Pre-eminently and above all, this Theosophy is to him a doctrine of common sense. It puts before him, as far as he can at present know them, the facts about God and man and the relations between them; then he proceeds to take these facts into account and to act in relation to them with ordinary reason and common sense. He regulates his life according to the laws of evolution which it has taught him, and this gives him a totally different standpoint, and a touchstone by which to try everything—his own thoughts and feelings, and his own actions first of all, and then those things which come before him in the world outside himself.

Always he applies this criterion: Is the thing right or wrong, does it help evolution or does it hinder it? If a thought or a feeling arises within himself, he sees at once by this test whether it is one he ought to encourage. If it be for the greatest good of the greatest number then all is well; if it may hinder or cause harm to any being in its progress, then it is evil and to be avoided. Exactly the same reason holds good if he is called upon to decide with regard to anything outside himself. If from that point of view a thing be a good thing, then he can conscientiously support it; if not, then it is not for him.

For him the question of personal interest does not come into the case at all. He thinks simply of the good of evolution as a whole. This gives him a definite foothold and the clear criterion, and removes from him altogether the pain of indecision and hesitation. The Will of the Deity is man's evolution; whatever therefore helps on that evolution must be good; whatever stands in the way of it and delays it, that thing must be wrong, even though it may have on its side all the weight of public opinion and immemorial tradition.

Knowing that the true man is the ego and not the body, he sees that it is the life of the ego only which is really of moment, and that everything connected with the body must unhesitatingly be subordinated to those higher interests. He recognizes that this earth-life is given to him for the purpose of progress, and that that progress is the one important thing. The real purpose of his life is the unfoldment of his powers as an ego, the development of his character. He knows that there must be evolvement not only of the physical body but also of the mental nature, of the mind and of the spiritual perceptions. He sees that nothing short of absolute perfection is expected of him in connection with this development; that all power with regard to it is in his own hands; that he has everlasting time before him in which to attain this perfection, but that the sooner it is gained the happier and more useful will he be.

He recognizes his life as nothing but a day at school, and his physical body as a temporary vesture assumed for the purpose of learning through it. He knows at once that this purpose of learning lessons is the only one of any real importance, and that the man who allows himself to be diverted from that purpose by any consideration whatever is acting with inconceivable stupidity. To him the life devoted exclusively to physical objects, to the acquisition of wealth or fame, appears the merest child's-play—a senseless sacrifice of all that is really worth having for the sake of a few moments' gratification of the lower part of his nature. He "sets his affection on things above and not on things of the earth", not only because he sees this to be the right course of action, but because he realizes so clearly the valuelessness of these things of earth. He always tries to take the higher point of view, for he knows that the lower is utterly unreliable—that the lower desires and feelings gather round him like a dense fog, and make it impossible for him to see anything clearly from that level.

Whenever he finds a struggle going on within him he remembers that he himself is the higher, and that this which is the lower is not the real self, but merely an uncontrolled part of one of its vehicles. He knows that though he may fall a thousand times on the way towards his goal, his reason for trying to reach it remains just as strong after the thousandth fall as it was in the beginning, so that it would not only be useless but unwise and wrong to give way to despondency and hopelessness.

He begins his journey upon the road of progress at once—not only because he knows that it is far easier for him now than it will be if he leaves the effort until later, but chiefly because if he makes the endeavour now and succeeds in achieving some progress, if he rises thereby to some higher level, he is in a position to hold out a helping hand to those who have not yet reached even that step on the ladder which he has gained. In that way he takes a part, however humble it may be, in the great divine work of evolution.

He knows that he has arrived at his present position only by a slow process of growth, and so he does not expect instantaneous attainment of perfection. He sees how inevitable is the great law of cause and effect, and that when he once grasps the working of that law he can use it intelligently in regard to mental and moral development, just as in the physical world we can employ for our own assistance those laws of Nature the action of which we have learnt to understand.

Understanding what death is, he knows that there can be no need to fear it or to mourn over it, whether it comes to himself or to those whom he loves. It has come to them all often before, so there is nothing unfamiliar about it. He sees death simply as a promotion from a life which is more than half physical to one which is wholly superior, so for himself he unfeignedly welcomes it; and even when it comes to those whom he loves, he recognizes at once the advantage for them, even though he cannot but feel a pang of regret that he should be temporarily separated from them so far as the physical world is concerned. But he knows that the so-called dead are near him still, and that he has only to cast off for a time his physical body in sleep in order to stand side by side with them as before.

He sees clearly that the world is one, and that the same divine laws rule the whole of it, whether it be visible or invisible to physical sight. So he has no feeling of nervousness or strangeness in passing from one part of it to another, and no feeling of uncertainty as to what he will find on the other side of the veil. He knows that in that higher life there opens before him a splendid vista of opportunities both for acquiring fresh knowledge and for doing useful work; that life away from this dense body has a vividness and a brilliancy to which all earthly enjoyment is as nothing; and so through his clear knowledge and calm confidence the power of the endless life shines out upon all those round him.

Doubt as to his future is for him impossible, for just as by looking back on the savage he realizes that which he was in the past, so by looking to the greatest and wisest of mankind he knows what he will be in the future. He sees an unbroken chain of development, a ladder of perfection rising steadily before him, yet with human beings upon every step of it, so that he knows, that those steps are possible for him to climb. It is just because of the unchangeableness of the great law of cause and effect that he finds himself able to climb that ladder, because since the law works always in the same way, he can depend upon it and he can use it, just as he uses the laws of Nature in the physical worlds. His knowledge of this law brings to him a sense of perspective and shows him that if something comes to him, it comes because he has deserved it as a consequence of actions which he has committed, of words which he has spoken, of thought to which he has given harbour in previous days or in earlier lives. He comprehends that all affliction is of the nature of the payment of a debt, and therefore when he has to meet with the troubles of life he takes them and uses them as a lesson, because he understands why they have come and is glad of the opportunity which they give him to pay off something of his obligation.

Again, and in yet another way, does he take them as an opportunity, for he sees that there is another side to them if he meets them in the right way. He spends no time in bearing prospective burdens. When trouble comes to him he does not aggravate it by foolish repining but sets himself to endure so much of it as is inevitable, with patience and with fortitude. Not that he submits himself to it as a fatalist might, for he takes adverse circumstances as an incentive to such development as may enable him to transcend them, and thus out of long-past evil he brings forth a seed of future growth. For in the very act of paying the outstanding debt he develops qualities of courage and resolution that will stand him in good stead through all the ages that are to come.

He is distinguishable from the rest of the world by his perennial cheerfulness, his undaunted courage under difficulties, and his ready sympathy and helpfulness; yet he is at the same time emphatically a man who takes life seriously, who recognizes that there is much for everyone to do in the world, and that there is no time to waste. He knows with utter certainty that he not only makes his own destiny but also gravely affects that of others around him, and thus he perceives how weighty a responsibility attends the use of his power.

He knows that thoughts are things and that it is easily possible to do great harm or great good by their means. He knows that no man liveth to himself, for his every thought acts upon others as well; that the vibrations which he sends forth from his mind and from his mental nature are reproducing themselves in the minds and the mental natures of other men, so that he is a source either of mental health or of mental ill to all with whom he comes in contact.

This at once imposes upon him a far higher code of social ethics than that which is known to the outer world, for he knows that he must control not only his acts and his words, but also his thoughts, since they may produce effects more serious and more far-reaching than their outward expression in the physical world. He knows that even when a man is not in the least thinking of others, he yet inevitably affects them for good or for evil. In addition to this unconscious action of his thought upon others he also employs it consciously for good. He sets currents in motion to carry mental help and comfort to many a suffering friend, and in this way he finds a whole new world of usefulness opening before him.

He ranges himself ever on the side of the higher rather than the lower thought, the nobler rather than the baser. He deliberately takes the optimistic rather than the pessimistic view of everything, the helpful, rather than the cynical, because he knows that to be fundamentally the true view. By looking continually for the good in everything that he may endeavour to strengthen it, by striving always to help and never to hinder, he becomes ever of greater use to his fellow-men, and is thus in his small way a co-worker with the splendid scheme of evolution. He forgets himself utterly and lives but for the sake of others, realizing himself as a part of that scheme; he also realizes the God within him, and learns to become ever a truer expression of Him, and thus in fulfilling God's Will, he is not only blessed himself, but becomes a blessing to all.

DREAMS

WHAT THEY ARE AND HOW THEY ARE CAUSED

CHAPTER I.

INTRODUCTORY

MANY of the subjects with which our Theosophical studies bring us into contact are so far removed from the experiences and interests of everyday life, that while we feel drawn towards them by an attraction which increases in geometrical progression as we come to know more of them and understand them better, we are yet conscious, at the back of our minds, as it were, of a faint sense of unreality, or at least unpracticality, while we are dealing with them. When we read of the formation of the solar system, or even of the rings and rounds of our own planetary chain, we cannot but feel that, interesting though this is as an abstract study, useful as it is in showing us how man has become what we find him to be, it nevertheless associates itself only indirectly with the life we are living here and now.

No such objection as this, however, can be taken to our present subject: all readers of these lines have dreamed—probably many of them are in the habit of dreaming frequently; and they may therefore be interested in an endeavor to account for dream phenomena by the aid of the light thrown upon them by investigation along Theosophic lines.

The most convenient method in which we can arrange the various branches of our subject will perhaps be the following: first, to consider rather carefully the mechanism—physical, etheric and astral—by means of which impressions are conveyed to our consciousness; secondly, to see how the consciousness in its turn affects and uses this mechanism; thirdly, to note the condition both of the consciousness and its mechanism during sleep; and fourthly, to enquire how the various kinds of dreams which men experience are thereby produced.

As I am writing in the main for students of theosophy, I shall feel myself at liberty to use, without detailed explanation, the ordinary Theosophical terms, with which I may safely assume them to be familiar, since otherwise my little book would far exceed its allotted limits. Should it, however, fall into the hands of any to whom the occasional use of such terms constitutes a difficulty, I can only apologize to them, and refer them for these preliminary explanations to any elementary Theosophical work, such as Mrs. Besant's *Ancient Wisdom*, or *Man and his Bodies*.

CHAPTER II.

THE MECHANISM

1. PHYSICAL

FIRST, then, as to the physical part of the mechanism. We have in our bodies a great central axis of nervous matter, ending in the brain, and from this a network of nerve-threads radiates in every direction through the body. It is these nerve-threads, according to modern scientific theory, which by their vibrations convey all impressions from without to the brain, and the latter, upon receipts of these impressions, translates them into sensations or perceptions; so that if I put my hand upon some object and find it to be hot, it is really not my hand that feels, but my brain, which is acting upon information transmitted to it by the vibrations running along its telegraph wires, the nerve-threads.

It is important also to bear in mind that all the nerve-threads of the body are the same in constitution, and that the special bundle of them that we call the optic nerve—which conveys to the brain impressions made upon the retina of the eye, and so enables us to see—differs from the nerve-threads of the hand or foot only in the fact that through long ages of evolution it has been specialized to receive and transmit most readily one particular small set of rapid vibrations which thus become visible to us as light. The same remark holds good with reference to our other sense organs; the auditory, the olfactory, or the gustatory nerves differ from one another and from the rest only in this specialization: they are essentially the same, and they all do their respective work in exactly the same manner, by the transmission of vibrations to the brain.

Now this brain of ours, which is thus the great centre of our nervous system, is very readily affected by slight variations in our general health, and most especially by any which involve a change in the circulation of the blood through it. When the flow of blood through the vessels of the head is normal and regular, the brain (and, therefore, the whole nervous system) is at liberty to function in an orderly and efficient manner; but any alteration in this normal circulation, either as to quantity, quality, or speed, immediately produces a corresponding effect on the brain, and through it on the nerves throughout the body.

If, for example, too much blood is supplied to the brain, congestion of the vessels takes place, and irregularity in its action is at once produced; if too little, the brain (and, therefore, the nervous system) becomes first irritable and then lethargic. The quality of the blood supplied is also of great importance. As it courses through the body it has two principal functions to perform—to supply oxygen and to provide nutrition to the different organs of the body; and if it be unable adequately to fulfil either of these functions, a certain disorganization will follow.

If the supply of oxygen to the brain be deficient, it becomes overcharged with carbon dioxide, and heaviness and lethargy very shortly supervene. A common example of this is the feeling of dullness and sleepiness which frequently overtakes one in a crowded and ill-ventilated room; owing to the exhaustion of the oxygen in the room by the continued respiration of so large a number of people, the brain does not receive its due modicum, and therefore is unable to do its work properly.

Again, the speed with which the blood flows through the vessels affects the action of the brain; if it be too great, it produces fever; if too slow, then again lethargy is caused. It is obvious, therefore, that our brain (through which, be it remembered, all physical impressions must pass) may very easily be disturbed and more or less hindered in the due performance of its functions by causes apparently trivial—causes to which we should probably often pay no attention whatever even during waking hours—of which we should almost certainly be entirely ignorant during sleep.

Before we pass on, one other peculiarity of this physical mechanism must be noted, and that is its remarkable tendency to repeat automatically vibrations to which it is accustomed to respond. It is to this property of the brain that are to be attributed all those bodily habits and tricks of manner which are entirely independent of the will, and are often so difficult to conquer; and, as will presently be seen, it plays an even more important part during sleep than it does in our waking life.

2. ETHERIC

It is not alone through the brain to which we have hitherto been referring, however, that impressions may be received by the man. Almost exactly co-extensive with and interpenetrating its visible form is his etheric double (formerly called in Theosophical literature the *linga sharîra*), and that also has a brain which is really no less physical than the other, though composed of matter in a condition finer than the gaseous.

If we examine with psychic faculty the body of a newly-born child, we shall find it permeated not only by astral matter of every degree of density, but also by the different grades of etheric matter; and if we take the trouble to trace these inner bodies backwards to their origin, we find that it is of the latter that the etheric double—the mould upon which the physical body is built up—is formed by the agents of the Lords of Karma: while the astral matter has been gathered together by the descending ego—not of course consciously, but automatically—as he passed through the astral plane, and is, in fact, merely the development in that plane of tendencies whose seeds have been lying dormant in him during his experiences in the heaven-world, because on that level it was impossible that they could germinate for want of the grade of matter necessary for their expression.

Now this etheric double has often been called the vehicle of the human life-ether or vital force (called in Sanskrit prâna), and anyone who has developed the psychic faculties can see exactly how this is so. He will see the solar life-principle almost colorless, though intensely luminous and active, which is constantly poured into the earth's atmosphere by the sun; he will see how the etheric part of his spleen in the exercise of its wonderful function absorbs this universal life, and specializes it into prâna, so that it may be more readily assimilable by his body; how it then courses all over that body, running along every nerve-thread in tiny globules of lovely rosy light, causing the glow of life and health and activity to penetrate every atom of the etheric double; and how, when the rose-colored particles have been absorbed, the superfluous life-ether finally radiates from the body in every direction as bluish white light.

If he examines further into the action of this life-ether, he will soon see reason to believe that the transmission of impression to the brain depends rather upon its regular flow along the etheric portion of the nerve-threads than upon the mere vibration of the particles of their denser and visible portion, as is commonly supposed. It would take too much of our space to detail all the experiments by which this theory is established, but the indication of one or two of the simplest will suffice to show the lines upon which they run.

When a finger becomes entirely numbed with cold, it is incapable of feeling; and the same phenomenon of insensibility may readily be produced at will by a mesmerizer, who by a few passes over the arm of his subject will bring it into a condition in which it may be pricked with a needle or burnt by the flame of a candle without the slightest sensation of pain being experienced. Now *why* does the subject feel nothing in either of these two cases? The nerve-threads are still there, and though in the first case it might be contended that their action was paralyzed by cold and by the absence of blood from the vessels, this certainly cannot be the reason in the second case, where the arm retains its normal temperature and the blood circulates as usual.

If we call in the aid of the clairvoyant, we shall be able to get somewhat nearer to a real explanation, for he will tell us that the reason why the frozen finger seems dead, and the blood is unable to circulate through its vessels, is because the rosy life-ether is no longer coursing along the nerve-threads; for we must remember that though matter in the etheric condition is invisible to ordinary sight, it is still purely physical, and, therefore, can be affected by the action of cold or heat.

In the second case he will tell us that when the mesmerizer makes the passes by which he renders the subject's arm insensible, what he really does is to pour his own nerve-ether (or magnetism, as it is often called) into the arm, thereby driving back for the time that of the subject. The arm is still warm and living, because there is still life-ether coursing through it, but since it is no longer the subject's own specialized life-ether, and is therefore not *en rapport* with his brain, it conveys no information to that brain, and consequently there is no sense of feeling in the arm. From this it seems evident that though it is not absolutely the life-ether itself which does the work of conveying impressions from without to a man's brain, its presence as specialized by the man himself is certainly necessary for their due transmission along the nerve-threads.

Now just as any change in the circulation of the blood affects the receptivity of the denser brain-matter, and thus modifies the reliability of the impressions derived through it, so the condition of the etheric portion of the brain is affected by any change in the volume or the velocity of these life-currents.

For example, when the quantity of nerve-ether specialized by the spleen falls for any reason below the average, physical weakness and weariness are immediately felt, and if, under these circumstances, it also happens that the speed of its circulation is increased, the man becomes supersensitive, highly irritable, nervous, and perhaps even hysterical, while in such a condition he is often more sensitive to physical impressions than he would normally be, and so it often occurs that a person suffering from ill-health sees visions or apparitions which are imperceptible to his more robust neighbor. If, on the other hand, the volume and velocity of the life-ether are both reduced at the same time, the man experiences intense languor, becomes less sensitive to outside influences, and has a general feeling of being too weak to care much about what happens to him.

It must be remembered also that the etheric matter of which we have spoken and the denser matter ordinarily recognized as belonging to the brain are really both parts of one and the same physical organism, and that, therefore, neither can be affected without instantly producing some reaction on the other. Consequently there can be no certainty that impressions will be correctly transmitted through this mechanism unless both portions of it are functioning quite normally; any irregularity in either part may very readily so dull or disturb its receptivity as to produce blurred or distorted images of whatever is presented to it. Furthermore, as will presently be explained, it is infinitely more liable to such aberrations during sleep than when in the waking state.

3. ASTRAL

Still another mechanism that we have to take into account is the astral body, often called the desire-body. As its name implies, this vehicle is composed exclusively of astral matter, and is, in fact, the expression of the man on the astral plane, just as his physical body is the expression of him on the lower levels of the physical plane.

Indeed, it will save the Theosophical student much trouble if he will learn to regard these different vehicles simply as the actual manifestation of the ego on their respective planes—if he understands, for example, that it is the causal body (sometimes called the auric egg) which is the real vehicle of the reincarnating ego, and is inhabited by him as long as he remains upon the plane which is his true home, the higher levels of the mental world: but that when he descends into the lower levels he must, in order to be able to function upon them, clothe himself in their matter, and that the matter which he thus attracts to himself furnishes his mind-body. Similarly, descending into the astral plane, he forms his astral or desire-body out of its matter, though, of course, still retaining all the other bodies; and on his still further descent to this lowest plane of all, the physical body is formed in the midst of the auric egg, which thus contains the entire man.

This astral vehicle is even more sensitive to external impressions than the gross and etheric bodies, for it is itself the seat of all desires and emotions—the connecting link through which alone the ego can collect experiences from physical life. It is peculiarly susceptible to the influence of passing thought-currents, and when the mind is not actively controlling it, it is perpetually receiving these stimuli from without, and eagerly responding to them.

This mechanism also, like the others, is more readily influenced during the sleep of the physical body. That this is so is shown by many observations, a fair example of them being a case recently reported to the writer, in which a man who had been a drunkard was describing the difficulties in the way of his reformation. He declared that after a long period of total abstinence he had succeeded in entirely destroying the physical desire for alcohol, so that in his waking condition he felt an absolute repulsion for it; yet he stated that he still frequently *dreamed* that he was drinking, and in that dream state he felt the old horrible pleasure in such degradation.

Apparently, therefore, during the day his desire was kept under control by the will, and casual thought-forms or passing elementals were unable to make any impression upon it; but when the astral body was liberated in sleep it escaped to some extent from the domination of the ego, and its extreme natural susceptibility so far reasserted itself that it again responded readily to these baneful influences, and imagined itself experiencing once more the disgraceful delights of debauchery.

Chapter III.
The Ego

ALL these different portions of the mechanism are in reality merely instruments of the ego, though his control of them is as yet often very imperfect; for it must always be remembered that the ego is himself a developing entity, and that in the case of most of us he is scarcely more than a germ of what he is to be one day.

A stanza in the *Book of Dzyan* tells us: "Those who received but a spark remained destitute of knowledge: the spark burned low"; and Madame Blavatsky explains that "those who receive but a spark constitute the average humanity which have to acquire their intellectuality during the present manvantaric evolution". (*Secret Doctrine*, ii, 777.) In the case of most of them that spark is still smouldering, and it will be many an age before its slow increase brings it to the stage of steady and brilliant flame.

No doubt there are some passages in Theosophical literature which seem to imply that our higher ego needs no evolution, being already perfect, and godlike on his own plane; but wherever such expressions are used, whatever may be the terminology employed, they must be taken to apply only to the âtmâ, the true god within us, which is certainly far beyond the necessity of any kind of evolution of which we can know anything.

The reincarnating ego most undoubtedly does evolve, and the process of his evolution can be very clearly seen by those who have developed clairvoyant vision to the extent necessary for the perception of that which exists on the higher levels of the mental plane. As before remarked, it is of the matter of that plane (if we may venture still to call it matter) that the comparatively permanent causal body, which he carries with him from birth to birth until the end of the human stage of his evolution, is composed. But though every individualized being must necessarily have such a body—since it is the possession of it which constitutes individualization—its appearance is by no means similar in all cases. In fact, in the average unevolved man it is barely distinguishable at all, even by those who have the sight which unlocks for them the secrets of that plane, for it is a mere colorless film — just sufficient, apparently, to hold itself together and make a reincarnating individuality, but no more. (See *Man, Visible and Invisible*, Plates V and VIII).

As soon, however, as the man begins to develop in spirituality, or even higher intellect, a change takes place. The real individual then begins to have a persisting character of his own, apart from that moulded in each of his personalities in turn by training and surrounding circumstances: and this character shows itself in the size, color, luminosity, and definiteness of the causal body just as that of the personality shows itself in the mind-body, except that this higher vehicle is naturally subtler and more beautiful. (See *ibid.,* Plate XXI).

In one other respect, also, it happily differs from the bodies below it, and that is that in any ordinary circumstances no evil of any kind can manifest through it. The worst of men can commonly show himself on that plane only as an entirely undeveloped entity; his vices, even though continued through life after life, cannot soil that higher sheath; they can only make it more and more difficult to develop in it the opposite virtues.

On the other hand, perseverance along right lines soon tells upon the causal body, and in the case of a pupil who has made some progress on the Path of Holiness, it is a sight wonderful and lovely beyond all earthly conception (See *ibid.,* Plate XXVI); while that of an Adept is a magnificent sphere of living light, whose radiant glory no words can ever tell. He who has even once seen so sublime a spectacle as this, and can also see around him individuals at all stages of development between that and the colorless film of the ordinary person, can never feel any doubt as to the evolution of the reincarnating ego.

The grasp which the ego has of his various instruments, and, therefore, his influence over them, is naturally small in his earlier stages. Neither his mind nor his passions are thoroughly under his control; indeed, the average man makes almost no effort to control them, but allows himself to be swept hither and thither just as his lower thoughts or desires suggest. Consequently, in sleep the different parts of the mechanism which we have mentioned are very apt to act almost entirely on their own account without reference to him, and the stage of his spiritual advancement is one of the factors that we have to take into account in considering the question of dreams.

It is also important for us to realize the part which this ego takes in the formation of our conceptions of external objects. We must remember that what the vibrations of the nerve-threads present to the brain are merely impressions, and it is the work of the ego, acting through the mind, to classify, combine, and rearrange them.

For example, when I look out of the window and see a house and a tree, I instantly recognize them for what they are, yet the information really conveyed to me by my eyes falls very far short of such recognition. What actually happens is that certain rays of light—that is, currents of ether vibrating at certain definite rates—are reflected from those objects and strike the retina of my eye, and the sensitive nerve-threads duly report those vibrations to the brain.

But what is the tale they have to tell? All the information they really transmit is that in a particular direction there are certain varied patches of color bounded by more or less definite outlines. It is the mind which from its past experience is able to decide that one particular square white object is a house, and another rounded green one is a tree, and that they are both probably of such and such a size, and at such and such a distance from me.

A person who, having been born blind, obtains his sight by means of an operation, does not for some time know what are the objects he sees, nor can he judge their distance from him. The same is true of a baby, for it may often be seen grasping at attractive objects (such as the moon, for example) which are far out of its reach; but as it grows up it unconsciously learns, by repeated experience, to judge instinctively the probable distance and size of the form it sees. Yet even grown-up people may very readily be deceived as to the distance and therefore the size of any unfamiliar object, especially if seen in a dim or uncertain light.

We see, therefore, that mere vision is by no means sufficient for accurate perception, but that the discrimination of the ego acting through the mind must be brought to bear upon what is seen; and furthermore we see that this discrimination is not an inherent instinct of the mind, perfect from the first, but is the result of the unconscious comparison of a number of experiences—points which must be carefully borne in mind when we come to the next division of our subject.

CHAPTER IV.

THE CONDITION OF SLEEP

CLAIRVOYANT observation bears abundant testimony to the fact that when a man falls into a deep slumber the higher principles in their astral vehicle almost invariably withdraw from the body and hover in its immediate neighborhood. Indeed, it is the process of this withdrawal which we commonly call "going to sleep". In considering the phenomena of dreams, therefore, we have to bear in mind this rearrangement, and see how it affects both the ego and his various mechanisms.

In the case we are to examine, then, we assume that our subject is in deep sleep, the physical body (including that finer portion of it which is often called the etheric double) lying quietly on the bed, while the ego, in its astral body, floats with equal tranquility just above it. What, under these circumstances, will be the condition and the consciousness of these several principles?

1. THE BRAIN

When the ego has thus for the time resigned the control of his brain, it does not therefore become entirely unconscious, as one would perhaps expect. It is evident from various experiments that the physical body has a certain dim consciousness of its own, quite apart from that of the real self, and apart also from the mere aggregate of the consciousness of its individual cells.

The writer has several times observed an effect of this consciousness when watching the extraction of a tooth under the influence of gas. The body uttered a confused cry, and raised its hands vaguely towards the mouth, clearly showing that it to some extent felt the wrench; yet when the ego resumed possession twenty seconds later, he declared that *he* had felt absolutely nothing of the operation. Of course I am aware that such movements are ordinarily attributed to "reflex action", and that people are in the habit of accepting that statement as though it were a real explanation—not seeing that as employed here it is a mere phrase and explains nothing whatever.

This consciousness then, such as it is, is still working in the physical brain although the ego floats above it, but its grasp is, of course, far feebler than that of the man himself, and consequently all those causes which were mentioned above as likely to affect the action of the brain are now capable of influencing it to a very much greater extent. The slightest alteration in the supply or circulation of the blood now produces grave irregularities of action, and this is why indigestion, as affecting the flow of the blood, so frequently causes troubled sleep or bad dreams.

But even when undisturbed, this strange, dim consciousness has many remarkable peculiarities. Its action seems to be to a great extent automatic, and the results are usually incoherent, senseless, and hopelessly confused. It seems unable to apprehend an idea except in the form of a scene in which it is itself an actor, and therefore all stimuli, whether from within or without, are forthwith translated into perceptual images. It is incapable of grasping abstract ideas or memories as such; they immediately become imaginary percepts. If, for example, the idea of glory could be suggested to that consciousness, it could take shape only as a vision of some glorious being appearing before the dreamer; if a thought of hatred somehow came across it, it could be appreciated only as a scene in which some imaginary actor showed violent hatred towards the sleeper.

Again, every local direction of thought becomes for it an absolute spatial transportation. If during our waking hours we think of China or Japan, our thought is at once, as it were, in those countries; but nevertheless we are perfectly aware that our physical bodies are exactly where they were a moment before. In the condition of consciousness which we are considering, however, there is no discriminating ego to balance the cruder impressions, and consequently any passing thought suggesting China and Japan could image itself only as an actual, instantaneous transportation to those countries, and the dreamer would suddenly find himself there, surrounded by as much of the appropriate circumstance as he happened to be able to remember.

It has often been noted that while startling transitions of this sort are extremely frequent in dreams, the sleeper never seems at the time to feel any surprise at their suddenness. This phenomenon is easily explicable when examined by the light of such observations as we are considering, for in the mere consciousness of the physical brain there is nothing capable of such a feeling as surprise—it simply perceives the pictures as they appear before it; it has no power to judge either of their sequence or of their lack of that quality.

Another source of the extraordinary confusion visible in this half-consciousness is the manner in which the law of the association of ideas works in it. We are all familiar with the wonderful instantaneous action of this law in waking life; we know how a chance word—a strain of music—even the scent of a flower—may be sufficient to bring back to the mind a chain of long-forgotten memories.

Now in the sleeping brain this law is as active as ever, but it acts under curious limitations; every such association of ideas, whether abstract or concrete, becomes a mere combination of images; and as our association of ideas is often merely by synchronism, as of events which, though really entirely unconnected, happened to us in succession, it may readily be imagined that the most inextricable confusion of these images is of frequent occurrence, while their number is practically infinite, as whatever can be dragged from the immense stores of memory appears in pictorial form. Naturally enough a succession of such pictures is rarely perfectly recoverable by memory, since there is no order to help in recovery—just as it may be easy enough to remember in waking life a connected sentence or a verse of poetry, even when heard only once, whereas without some system of mnemonics it would be almost impossible to recollect accurately a mere jumble of meaningless words under similar circumstances.

Another peculiarity of this curious consciousness of the brain is, that while singularly sensitive to the slightest external influences, such as sounds or touches, it yet magnifies and distorts them to an almost incredible degree. All writers on dreams give examples of this, and, indeed, some will probably be within the knowledge of everyone who has paid any attention to the subject.

Among the stories most commonly told is one of a man who had a painful dream of being hanged because his shirt-collar was too tight; another man magnified the prick of a pin into a fatal stab received in a duel; another translated a slight pinch into the bite of a wild beast. Maury relates that part of the rail at the head of his bed once became detached and fell across his neck, so as just to touch it lightly; yet this trifling contact produced a terrible dream of the French Revolution, in which he seemed to himself to perish by the guillotine.

Another writer tells us that he frequently awoke from sleep with a confused remembrance of dreams full of noise, of loud voices and thunderous sounds, and was entirely unable for a long time to discover their origin; but at last he succeeded in tracing them to the murmurous sound made in the ear (perhaps by the circulation of the blood) when it is laid on the pillow, much as a similar but louder murmur may be heard by holding a shell to the ear.

It must by this time be evident that even from this bodily brain alone there comes enough confusion and exaggeration to account for many of the dream phenomena; but this is only one of the factors that we have to take into consideration.

2. The Etheric Brain

It will be obvious that this part of the organism, so sensitive to every influence even during our waking life, must be still more susceptible when in the condition of sleep. When examined under these circumstances by a clairvoyant, streams of thought are seen to be constantly sweeping through it—not its own thoughts in the least, for it has of itself no power to think—but the casual thoughts of others which are always floating round us.

Students of occultism are well aware that it is indeed true that "thoughts are things", for every thought impresses itself upon the plastic elemental essence and generates a temporary living entity, the duration of whose life depends upon the energy of the thought-impulse given to it. We are therefore living in the midst of an ocean of other men's thoughts, and whether we are awake or asleep, these are constantly presenting themselves to the etheric part of our brain.

So long as we ourselves are actively thinking and therefore keeping our brain fully employed, it is practically impervious to this continual impingement of thought from without; but the moment that we leave it idle, the stream of inconsequent chaos begins to pour through it. Most of the thoughts sweep through unassimilated and almost unnoticed, but now and then one comes along which reawakens some vibrations to which the etheric part of the brain is accustomed; at once that brain seizes upon it, intensifies it, and makes it its own; that thought in turn suggests another; and so a whole train of ideas is started, until eventually it also fades away, and the disconnected, purposeless stream begins flowing through the brain again.

The vast majority of people, if they will watch closely what they are in the habit of calling their thoughts will find that they are very largely made up of a casual stream of this sort—that in truth they are not *their* thoughts at all, but simply the castoff fragments of other people's. For, the ordinary man seems to have no control whatever over his mind; he hardly ever knows exactly of what he is thinking at any particular moment, or why is he thinking of it; instead of directing his mind to some definite point, he allows it to run riot at its own sweet will, or lets it lie fallow, so that any casual seed cast into it by the wind may germinate and come to fruition there.

The result of this is that even when he, the ego, really wishes for once to think consecutively on any particular subject, he finds himself practically unable to do so; all sorts of stray thoughts rush in unbidden from every side, and since he is quite unused to controlling his mind, he is powerless to stem the torrent. Such a person does not know what real concentrated thought is; and it is this utter lack of concentration, this feebleness of mind and will, that makes the early stages of occult development so difficult to the average man. Again, since in the present state of the world's evolution there are likely to be more evil thoughts than good ones floating around him, this weakness lays him open to all sorts of temptations which a little care and effort might have avoided altogether.

In sleep, then, the etheric part of the brain is even more than usually at the mercy of these thought-currents, since the ego is, for the time, in less close association with it. A curious fact brought out in some recent experiments is that when by any means these currents are shut out from this part of the brain, it does not remain absolutely passive, but begins very slowly and dreamily to evolve pictures for itself from its store of past memories. An example of this will be given later, when some of these experiments are described.

3. THE ASTRAL BODY

As before mentioned, it is in this vehicle that the ego is functioning during sleep, and it is usually to be seen (by anyone whose inner sight is opened) hovering over the physical body on the bed. Its appearance, however, differs very greatly according to the stage of development which the ego to which it belongs has reached. In the case of the entirely uncultured and undeveloped person it is simply a floating wreath of mist, roughly ovoid in shape, but very irregular and indefinite in outline, while the figure within the mist (the denser astral counterpart of the physical body) is also vague, though generally recognizable.

It is receptive only of the coarser and more violent vibrations of desire, and unable to move more than a few yards away from its physical body; but as evolution progresses, the ovoid mist becomes more and more definite in outline, and the figure within it more and more nearly a perfect image of the physical body beneath it. Its receptivity simultaneously increases, until it is instantly responsive to all the vibrations of its plane, the finer as well as the more ignoble; though in the astral body of a highly-developed person there would naturally be practically no matter left coarse enough to respond to the latter.

Its power of locomotion also becomes much greater; it can travel without discomfort to considerable distances from its physical encasement, and can bring back more or less definite impressions as to places which it may have visited and people whom it may have met. In every case this astral body is, as ever, intensely impressionable by any thought or suggestion involving desire, though in some the desires which most readily awaken a response in it may be somewhat higher than in others.

4. THE EGO IN SLEEP

Though the condition in which the astral body is to be found during sleep changes largely as evolution takes place, that of the ego inhabiting it changes still more. Where the former is in the stage of the floating wreath of mist, the ego is practically almost as much asleep as the body lying below him; he is blind to the sights and deaf to the voices of his own higher plane, and even if some idea belonging to it should by chance reach him, since he has no control over his mechanism, he will be quite unable to impress it upon his physical brain so that it may be remembered upon waking. If a man in this primitive condition recollects anything at all of what happens to him during sleep, it will almost invariably be the result of purely physical impressions made upon the brain either from within or from without—any experience which his real ego may have had being forgotten.

Sleepers may be observed at all stages, from this condition of all but blank oblivion, up to full and perfect consciousness on the astral plane, though this latter is naturally comparatively rare. Even a man who is sufficiently awake to meet not infrequently with important experiences in this higher life, may yet be (and often is) unable so far to dominate his brain as to check its current of inconsequent thought-pictures and impress upon it instead what he wishes it to recollect; and thus when his physical body awakes he may have only the most confused memory, or no memory at all, of what has really happened to him. And this is a pity, for he may meet with much that is of the greatest interest and importance to him.

Not only may he visit distant scenes of surpassing beauty, but he may meet and exchange ideas with friends, either living or departed, who happen to be equally awake on the astral plane. He may be fortunate enough to encounter those who know far more than he does, and may receive warning or instruction from them, he may, on the other hand, be privileged to help and comfort some who know less than himself. He may come into contact with non-human entities of various kinds—with nature-spirits, artificial elementals, or even, though very rarely, with Devas; he will be subject to all kinds of influences, good or evil, strengthening or terrifying.

HIS TRANSCENDENTAL MEASURE OF TIME.

But whether he remembers anything when physically awake or not, the ego who is fully or even partially conscious of his surroundings on the astral plane is beginning to enter into his heritage of powers which far transcend those he possesses down here; for his consciousness when thus liberated from the physical body has very remarkable possibilities. His measure of time and space is so entirely different from that which we use in waking life, that from our view it seems as though neither time nor space existed for him.

I do not wish here to discuss the question, intensely interesting though it be, as to whether time can be said really to exist, or whether it is but a limitation of this lower consciousness, and all that we call time—past, present and future alike—is "but one eternal Now"; I wish only to show that when the ego is freed from physical trammels, either during sleep, trance or death, he appears to employ some transcendental measure of time which has nothing in common with our ordinary physiological one. A hundred stories might be told to prove this fact; it will be sufficient if I give two—the first a very old one (related, I think, by Addison in *The Spectator*), the other an account of an event which happened but a short time ago, and has never before appeared in print.

ILLUSTRATIVE EXAMPLES OF IT.

It seems that in the Koran there is a wonderful narrative concerning a visit paid one morning by the prophet Mohammed to heaven, during which he saw many different regions there, had them all very fully explained to him, and also had numerous lengthy conferences with various angels; yet when he returned to his body, the bed from which he had risen was still warm, and he found that but a few seconds had passed—in fact, I believe the water had not yet all run out from a jug which he had accidentally overturned as he started on the expedition!

Now Addison's story runs that a certain sultan of Egypt felt it impossible to believe this, and even went to the impolitic length of bluntly declaring to his religious teacher that the tale was a falsehood. The teacher, who was a great doctor learned in the law, and credited with miraculous powers, undertook to prove on the spot to the doubting monarch that the story was, at any rate, not impossible. He had a large basin of water brought, and begged the sultan just to dip his head into the water and withdraw it as quickly as he could.

The king accordingly plunged his head into the basin, and to his intense surprise found himself at once in a place entirely unknown to him—on a lonely shore, near the foot of a great mountain. After the first stupefaction was over, what was probably the most natural idea for an oriental monarch came into his head—he thought he was bewitched, and at once began to execrate the doctor for such abominable treachery. However, time passed on; he began to get hungry, and realized that there was nothing for it but to find some means of livelihood in this strange country.

After wandering about for some time, he found some men at work felling trees in a wood, and applied to them for assistance. They set him to help them, and eventually took him with them to the town where they lived. Here he resided and worked for some years, gradually amassing money, and at length contrived to marry a rich wife. With her he spent many happy years of wedded life, bringing up a family of no less than fourteen children, but after her death he met with so many misfortunes that he at last fell into want again, and once more, in his old age, became a wood-porter.

One day, walking by the sea-side, he threw off his clothes and plunged into the sea for a bath; and as he raised his head and shook the water from his eyes, he was astounded to find himself standing among his old courtiers, with his teacher of long ago at his side, and a basin of water before him. It was long—and no wonder—before he could be brought to believe that all those years of incident and adventure had been nothing but one moment's dream, caused by the hypnotic suggestion of his teacher, and that really he had done nothing but dip his head quickly into the basin of water and draw it out again.

This is a good story, and illustrates our point well, but, of course, we have no proof whatever as to its truth. It is quite different, however, with regard to an event that happened only the other day to a well-known man of science. He unfortunately had to have two teeth removed, and took gas in the ordinary way for that purpose. Being interested in such problems as these, he had resolved to note very carefully his sensations all through the operation, but as he inhaled the gas, such a drowsy contentment stole over him that he soon forgot his intention and seemed to sink into sleep.

He rose next morning, as he supposed, and went on with his regular round of scientific experiment, lecturing before various learned bodies, etc., but all with a singular sense of enhanced power and pleasure—every lecture being a remarkable achievement, every experiment leading to new and magnificent discoveries. This went on day after day, week after week, for a very considerable period, though the exact time is uncertain; until at last one day, when he was delivering a lecture before the Royal Society, he was annoyed by the unmannerly behavior of some one present, who disturbed him by remarking, "It's all over now"; and as he turned round to see what this meant, another voice observed, "They are both out". Then he realized that he was still sitting in the dentist's chair, and that he had lived through that period of intensified life in just forty seconds!

Neither of these cases, it may be said, was exactly an ordinary dream. But the same thing occurs constantly in ordinary dreams, and there is again abundant testimony to show it.

Steffens, one of the German writers on the subject, relates how when a boy he was sleeping with his brother, and dreamed that he was in a lonely street, pursued by some dreadful wild beast. He ran on in great terror, though unable to cry out, until he came to a staircase, up which he turned, but being exhausted with fright and hard running, was overtaken by the animal, and severely bitten in the thigh. He awoke with a start, and found that his brother had pinched him on the thigh.

Richers, another German writer, tells the story of a man who was awakened by the firing of a shot, which yet came in as the *conclusion* of a long dream, in which he had become a soldier, had deserted and suffered terrible hardship, had been captured, tried, condemned, and finally shot—the whole long drama being lived through in the moment of being awakened by the sound of the shot. Again, we have the tale of the man who fell asleep in an armchair while smoking a cigar, and after dreaming through an eventful life of many years, awoke to find his cigar still alight. One might multiply authenticated cases to any extent.

HIS POWER OF DRAMATIZATION.

Another remarkable peculiarity of the ego, in addition to his transcendental measure of time, is suggested by some of these stories, and that is his faculty, or, perhaps, we should rather say his habit, of instantaneous dramatization. It will be noticed in the cases of the shot and the pinch which have just been narrated, that the physical effect which awakened the person came as the climax to a dream apparently extending over a considerable space of time, though obviously suggested in reality entirely by that physical effect itself.

Now the news, so to speak, of this physical effect, whether it be a sound or a touch, has to be conveyed to the brain by the nerve-threads, and this transmission takes a certain space of time—only a minute fraction of a second, of course, but still a definite amount which is calculable and measurable by the exceedingly delicate instruments used in modern scientific research. The ego, when out of the body, is able to perceive with absolute instantaneity without the use of the nerves, and consequently is aware of what happens just that minute fraction of a second before the information reaches his physical brain.

In that barely-appreciable space of time he appears to compose a kind of drama or series of scenes, leading up to and culminating in the event which awakens the physical body; and when after waking he is limited by the organs of that body, he becomes incapable of distinguishing in memory between the subjective and the objective, and therefore imagines himself to have really acted through his own drama in a dream state.

This habit, however, seems to be peculiar to the ego which, as far as spirituality goes, is still comparatively undeveloped; as evolution takes place, and the real man slowly comes to understand his position and his responsibilities, he rises beyond these graceful sports of his childhood. It would seem that just as primitive man casts every natural phenomenon into the form of a myth, so the unadvanced ego dramatizes every event that comes under his notice; but the man who has attained continuous consciousness finds himself so fully occupied in the work of the higher planes that he devotes no energy to such matters, and therefore he dreams no more.

HIS FACULTY OF PREVISION.

Another result which follows from the ego's supernormal method of time-measurement is that in some degree prevision is possible to him. The present, the past, and, to a certain extent, the future lie open before him if he knows how to read them; and he undoubtedly thus foresees at times events that will be of interest or importance to his lower personality, and makes more or less successful endeavors to impress them upon it.

When we take into account the stupendous difficulties in his way in the case of an ordinary person—the fact that he is himself probably not yet even half awake, that he has hardly any control over his various vehicles, and cannot, therefore, prevent his message from being distorted or altogether overpowered by the surgings of desire, by the casual thought-currents in the etheric part of his brain, or by some slight physical disturbance affecting his denser body—we shall not wonder that he so rarely fully succeeds in his attempt. Once, now and again, a complete and perfect forecast of some event is vividly brought back from the realms of sleep; far more often the picture is distorted or unrecognizable, while sometimes all that comes through is a vague sense of some impending misfortune, and still more frequently nothing at all penetrates the body.

It has sometimes been argued that when this prevision occurs it must be mere coincidence, since if events could really be foreseen they must be fore-ordained, in which case there can be no free-will for man. Man, however, undoubtedly *does* possess free-will; and therefore, as remarked above, prevision is possible only to a certain extent. In the affairs of the average man it is probably possible to a very large extent, since he has developed no will of his own worth speaking of, and is consequently very largely the creature of circumstances; his karma places him amid certain surroundings, and their action upon him is so much the most important factor in his history that his future course may be foreseen with almost mathematical certainty.

When we consider the vast number of events which can be but little affected by human action, and also the effects, it will scarcely seem wonderful to us that on the plane where the result of all causes at present in action is visible, a very large portion of the future may be foretold with considerable accuracy even as to detail. That this can be done has been proved again and again, not only by prophetic dreams, but by the second-sight of the Highlanders and the predictions of clairvoyants; and it is on this forecasting of effects from the causes already in existence that the whole scheme of astrology is based.

But when we come to deal with a developed individual—a man with knowledge and will—then prophecy fails us, for he is no longer the creature of circumstances but to a great extent their master. True, the main events of his life are arranged beforehand by his past karma; but the way in which he will allow them to affect him, the method by which he will deal with them, and perhaps triumph over them—these are his own, and they cannot be foreseen except as probabilities. Such actions of his in their turn become causes, and thus chains of effects are produced in his life which were not provided for by the original arrangement, and, therefore, could not have been foretold with any exactitude.

An analogy may be taken from a simple experiment in mechanics: if a certain amount of force be employed to set a ball rolling, we cannot in any way destroy or decrease that force when once the ball has started, but we can counteract or modify its actions by the application of a fresh force in a different direction. An equal force applied to the ball in exactly the opposite direction will stop it entirely; a lesser force so applied will reduce its speed; any force applied from either side will alter both its speed and its direction.

So with the working out of destiny. It is clear that at any given moment, a body of causes is in action which, if not interfered with, will inevitably produce certain results—results which on higher planes would seem already present, and could therefore be exactly described. But it is also clear that a man of strong will can, by setting up new forces, largely modify these results; and these modifications could not be foreseen by any ordinary clairvoyance until after the new forces had been set in motion.

EXAMPLES OF ITS USE.

Two incidents which recently came to the knowledge of the writer will serve as excellent illustrations both of the possibility of prevision and also of its modification by a determined will. A gentleman whose hand is often used for automatic writing one day received in that way a communication professing to come from a person whom he knew slightly, in which she informed him that she was in a great state of indignation and annoyance because, having arranged to give a certain lecture, she found no one in the hall at the appointed time, and was consequently unable to deliver her discourse.

Meeting the lady in question a few days later and supposing the letter to refer to a past event, he condoled with her on the disappointment, and she remarked with great surprise that what he told her was certainly very odd, as, though she had not yet delivered her lecture, she was to do so the following week, and she hoped the letter might not prove a prophecy. Unlikely as such an event seemed, the account written *did* prove to be a prophecy; no one attended at the hall, the lecture was not delivered, and the lecturer was much annoyed and distressed, exactly as the automatic writing had foretold. What kind of entity inspired the writing does not appear, but it was evidently one who moved on a plane where prevision was possible; and it may really have been, as it professed to be, the ego of the lecturer, anxious to break the disappointment to her by preparing her mind for it on this lower plane.

If it were so, it will be said, why should he not have influenced her directly? He may very well have been quite unable to do this, and the sensitivity of her friend may have been the only possible channel through which he could convey his warning. Roundabout as this method may seem, students of these subjects are well aware that there are many examples in which it is evident that means of communication such as are here employed are absolutely the only ones available.

On another occasion the same gentleman received in the same way what purported to be a letter from another feminine friend, relating a long and sad story from her recent life. She explained that she was in very great trouble, and that all the difficulty had originally arisen from a conversation (which she gave in detail) with a certain person, by means of which she was persuaded, much against her own feeling, to adopt a particular course of action. She went on to describe how, a year or so later, a series of events directly attributable to her adoption of this course of action ensued, culminating in the commission of a horrible crime, which had for ever darkened her life.

As in the previous case, when next the gentleman met the friend from whom the letter was supposed to come, he told her what it had contained. She knew nothing whatever of any such story, and though she was greatly impressed by its circumstantiality, they eventually decided that there was nothing in it. Some time later, to her intense surprise, the conversation foretold in the letter actually took place, and she found herself being implored to take the very course of action to which so disastrous an ending had been foreshadowed. She would certainly have yielded, distrusting her own judgement, but for the memory of the prophecy; having that in mind, however, she resisted in the most determined manner, even though her attitude caused surprise and pain to the friend with whom she was talking. The course of action indicated in the letter not being followed, the time of the predicted catastrophe naturally arrived and passed without any unusual incident.

So it might have done in any case, it may be said. Perhaps so; and yet, remembering how exactly that other prediction was fulfilled, one cannot but feel that the warning conveyed by this writing probably prevented the commission of a crime. If that be so, then here is a good example of the way in which our future may be altered by the exercise of a determined will.

HIS SYMBOLIC THOUGHT.

Another point worth notice in relation to the condition of the ego when out of the body during sleep is that he appears to think in symbols—that is to say, that what down here would be an idea requiring many words to express, is perfectly conveyed to him by a single symbolical image. Now when such a thought as this is impressed upon the brain, and so remembered in the waking consciousness, it of course needs translation. Often the mind duly performs this function, but sometimes the symbol is recollected without its key—comes through untranslated, as it were; and then confusion arises.

Many people, however, are quite in the habit of bringing the symbols through in this manner, and trying to invent an interpretation down here. In such cases, each person seems usually to have a system of symbology of his own. Mrs. Crowe mentions, in her *Night Side of Nature* (p.54), "a lady who, whenever a misfortune was impending, dreamt that she saw a large fish. One night she dreamt that this fish had bitten two of her little boy's fingers. Immediately afterwards a school-fellow of the child's injured those two very fingers by striking him with a hatchet. I have met with several persons who have learnt by experience to consider one particular dream as a certain prognostic of misfortune." There are, however, a few points upon which most of these dreamers agree—as, for example, that to dream of deep water signifies approaching trouble, and that pearls are a sign of tears.

5. THE FACTORS IN THE PRODUCTION OF DREAMS

Having thus examined the condition of man during sleep, we see that the factors which may be concerned in the production of dreams are:

1. The ego, who may be in any state of consciousness from almost utter insensibility to perfect command of his faculties, and as he approximates to the latter condition, enters more and more fully into possession of certain powers transcending any that most of us possess in our ordinary waking state.

2. The astral body, ever palpitating with the wild surgings of emotion and desire.

3. The etheric part of the brain, with a ceaseless procession of disconnected pictures sweeping through it.

4. The lower physical brain, with its infantile semi consciousness and its habit of expressing every stimulus in pictorial form.

When we go to sleep our ego withdraws further within himself, and leaves his various encasements freer to go their own way than they usually are; but it must be remembered that the separate consciousness of these vehicles, when they are thus allowed to show it, is of a very rudimentary character. When we add that each of these factors is then infinitely more susceptible of impression from without even than it ordinarily is, we shall see small cause to wonder that the recollection on waking, which is a sort of synthesis of all the different activities which have been going on, should generally be somewhat confused. Let us now, with these thoughts in our minds, see how the different kinds of dreams usually experienced are to be accounted for.

CHAPTER V.

DREAMS

1. THE TRUE VISION

THIS, which cannot properly be classified as a dream at all, is a case where the ego either sees for himself some fact upon a higher plane of nature, or else has it impressed upon him by a more advanced entity; at any rate he is made aware of some fact which it is important for him to know, or perhaps sees some glorious and ennobling vision which encourages and strengthens him. Happy is the man to whom such vision comes with sufficient clearness to make its way through all obstacles and fix itself firmly in his waking memory.

2. THE PROPHETIC DREAM

This also we must attribute exclusively to the action of the ego, who either foresees for himself or is told of some future event for which he wishes to prepare his lower consciousness. This may be of any degree of clearness and accuracy, according to the power of the ego to assimilate it himself and, having done so, to impress it upon his waking brain.

Sometimes the event is one of serious moment, such as death or disaster, so that the motive of the ego in endeavoring to impress it is obvious. On other occasions, however, the fact foretold is apparently unimportant, and it is difficult for us to comprehend why the ego should take any trouble about it. Of course it is always possible that in such a case the fact remembered may be only a trifling detail of some far larger vision, the rest of which has not come through to the physical brain.

Often the prophecy is evidently intended as a warning, and instances are not wanting in which that warning has been taken, and so the dreamer has been saved from injury or death. In most cases the hint is neglected, or its true signification not understood until the fulfillment comes. In others an attempt is made to act upon the suggestion, but nevertheless circumstances over which the dreamer has no control bring him in spite of himself into the position foretold.

Stories of such prophetic dreams are so common that the reader may easily find some in almost any of the books on such subjects. I quote a recent example from Mr. W. T. Stead's *Real Ghost Stories* (p. 77).

The hero of the tale was a blacksmith at a manufacturing mill, which was driven by a water-wheel. He knew the wheel to be out of repair, and one night he dreamed that at the close of the next day's work the manager detained him to repair it, that his foot slipped and became entangled between the two wheels, and was injured and afterwards amputated. He told his wife the dream in the morning, and made up his mind to be out of the way that evening if he was wanted to repair the wheel.

During the day the manager announced that the wheel must be repaired when the workpeople left that evening, but the blacksmith determined to make himself scarce before the hour arrived. He fled to a wood in the vicinity, and thought to hide himself there in its recesses. He came to a spot where lay some timber which belonged to the mill, and detected a lad stealing some pieces of wood from the heap. On this he pursued him in order to rescue the stolen property, and became so excited that he forgot all about his resolution, and ere he was aware of it, found himself back at the mill just as the workmen were being dismissed.

He could not escape notice, and as he was principal smith he had to go upon the wheel, but he resolved to be unusually careful. In spite of all his care, however, his foot slipped and got entangled between the two wheels, just as he had dreamed. It was crushed so badly that he had to be carried to the Bradford Infirmary, where the leg was amputated above the knee; so the prophetic dream was fulfilled throughout.

3. THE SYMBOLIC DREAM

This, too, is the work of the ego, and, indeed, it might almost be defined as a less successful variant of the preceding class, for it is, after all, an imperfectly translated effort on his part to convey information as to the future.

A good example of this kind of dream was described by Sir Noel Paton in a letter to Mrs. Crowe, published by the latter in *The Night Side of Nature* (p. 54). The great artist writes:

"That dream of my mother's was as follows. She stood in a long, dark, empty gallery; on one side was my father, on the other my eldest sister, then myself and. the rest of the family according to their ages. . . . We all stood silent and motionless. At last it entered—the unimagined *something* that, casting its grim shadow before, had enveloped all the trivialities of the preceding dream in the stifling atmosphere of terror. It entered, stealthily descending the three steps that led from the entrance down into the chamber of horror; and my mother felt that it was Death.

"He carried on his shoulder a heavy axe, and had come, she thought, to destroy all her little ones at one fell swoop. On the entrance of the shape my sister Alexes leapt out of the rank, interposing herself between him and my mother. He raised his axe and aimed a blow at my sister Catherine—a blow which, to her horror, my mother could not intercept, though she had snatched up a three-legged stool for that purpose. She could not, she felt, fling the stool at the figure without destroying Alexes, who kept shooting out and in between her and the ghastly thing. . . .

"Down came the axe, and poor Catherine fell. . . . Again the axe was lifted by the inexorable shape over the head of my brother, who stood next in the line, but now Alexes had disappeared somewhere behind the ghastly visitant, and with a scream my mother flung the stool at his head. He vanished and she awoke. . . .

"Three months had elapsed when we children were all of us seized with scarlet fever. My sister Catherine, died almost immediately—sacrificed, as my mother in her misery thought, to her (my mother's) over-anxiety for Alexes, whose danger seemed more imminent. The dream prophecy was in part fulfilled.

"I also was at death's door—given up by the doctors, but not by my mother; she was confident of my recovery. But for my brother, who was scarcely considered in danger at all, but over whose head she had seen the visionary axe impending, her fears were great; for she could not recollect whether the blow had or had not descended when the spectre vanished. My brother recovered, but relapsed and barely escaped with life; but Alexes did not. For a year and ten months the poor child lingered . . . and I held her little hand as she died. . . . Thus the dream was fulfilled."

It is very curious to notice here how accurately the details of the symbolism work themselves out, even to the supposed sacrifice of Catherine for the sake of Alexes, and the difference in the manner of their deaths.

4. THE VIVID AND CONNECTED DREAM

This is sometimes a remembrance, more or less accurate of a real astral experience which has occurred to the ego while wandering away from his sleeping physical body; more frequently, perhaps, it is the dramatization by that ego either of the impression produced by some trifling physical sound or touch, or of some casual idea which happens to strike him.

Examples of this latter kind have already been given, and there are many to be found of the former also. We may take as an instance an anecdote quoted by Mr. Andrew Lang, in *Dreams and Ghosts* (p. 35), from the distinguished French physician Dr Brierre de Boismont, who describes it as occurring within his own intimate knowledge.

"Miss C., a lady of excellent sense, lived before her marriage in the house of her uncle D., a celebrated physician and member of the Institute. Her mother at this time was seriously ill in the country. One night the girl dreamed that she saw her mother, pale and dying, and especially grieved at the absence of two of her children—one a cure in Spain, and the other (herself) in Paris.

"Next she heard her own Christian name called, "Charlotte!" and in her dream saw the people about her mother bring in her own little niece and godchild Charlotte from the next room. The patient intimated by a sign that she did not want *this* Charlotte, but her daughter in Paris. She displayed the deepest regret; her countenance changed, she fell back and died.

"Next day the melancholy of Miss C., attracted the attention of her uncle. She told him her dream, and he admitted that her mother was dead. Some months later, when her uncle was absent, she arranged his papers, which he did not like anyone to touch. Among these was a letter containing the story of her mother's death and giving all the details of her own dream, which D. had kept concealed lest they should impress her too painfully."

Sometimes the clairvoyant dream refers to a matter of much less importance than a death, as in the following case, which is given by Dr. F.G. Lee in *Glimpses in the Twilight* (p. 108). A mother dreams that she sees her son on a boat of strange shape, standing at the foot of a ladder which leads to an upper deck. He looks extremely pale and worn, and says to her earnestly, "Mother, I have nowhere to sleep." In due course a letter arrives from the son, in which he encloses a sketch of the curious boat, showing the ladder leading to the upper deck; he also explained that on a certain day (that of his mother's dream) a storm nearly wrecked their boat and hopelessly soaked his bed, and the account ends with the words, "I had nowhere to sleep."

It is quite clear that in both these cases the dreamers, drawn by thoughts of love or anxiety, had really travelled in the astral body during sleep to those in whose fate they were so keenly interested, and simply witnessed the various occurrences as they took place.

5. THE CONFUSED DREAM

This, which is by far the commonest of all, may be caused, as has already been pointed out, in various ways. It may be simply a more or less perfect recollection of a series of the disconnected pictures and impossible transformations produced by the senseless automatic action of the lower physical brain; it may be a reproduction of the stream of casual thought which has been pouring through the etheric part of the brain; if sensual images of any kind enter into it, it is due to the ever-restless tide of earthly desire, probably stimulated by some unholy influence of the astral world; it may be due to an imperfect attempt at dramatization on the part of an undeveloped ego; or it may be (and most often is) due to an inextricable mingling of several or all of these influences. The way in which such mingling takes place will perhaps be made clearer by a short account of some of the experiments on the dream state recently made by the London Lodge of the Theosophical Society, with the aid of some clairvoyant investigators among its members.

CHAPTER VI.
EXPERIMENTS ON THE DREAM-STATE

THE object specially in view in the investigation, part of which I am about to describe, was to discover whether it was possible to impress the ego of an ordinary person during sleep sufficiently to enable him to recollect the circumstance when he awoke; and it was also desired, as far as possible, to find out what are the obstacles that usually stand in the way of such recollection. The first experiment tried was with an average man of small education and rough exterior—a man of the Australian shepherd type—whose astral form, as seen floating above his body, was externally little more than a shapeless wreath of mist.

It was found that the consciousness of the body on the bed was dull and heavy, both as regards the grosser and the etheric parts of the frame. The former responded to some extent to external stimuli—for example, the sprinkling of two or three drops of water on the face called up in the brain (though somewhat tardily) a picture of a heavy shower of rain; while the etheric part of the brain was as usual a passive channel for an endless stream of disconnected thoughts, it rarely responded to any of the vibrations they produced, and even when it did it seemed somewhat sluggish in its action. The ego floating above was in an undeveloped and semi-unconscious condition, but the astral envelope, though shapeless and ill-defined, showed considerable activity.

The floating astral can at any time be acted upon, with an ease that can scarcely be imagined, by the conscious thought of another person; and in this case the experiment was made withdrawing it to some little distance from the physical body on the bed, with the result, however, that as soon as it was more than a few yards away considerable uneasiness was manifested in both the vehicles, and it became necessary to desist from the attempt, as evidently any further withdrawal would have caused the man to awake, probably in a state of great terror.

A certain scene was chosen—a view of the most magnificent character from the summit of a mountain in the tropics—and a vivid picture of it was projected by the operator into the dreamy consciousness of the ego, which assimilated and examined it, though in a dull, apathetic, and unappreciative kind of way. After this scene had been held before his view for some time the man was awakened, the object being, of course, to see whether he recollected it as a dream. His mind, however, was an absolute blank on the subject, and except for some vague yearnings of the most animal description, he had brought back no memory whatever from the state of sleep.

It was suggested that possibly the constant stream of thought-forms from outside, which flowed through his brain, might constitute an obstacle by so distracting it as to make it unreceptive to influences from its higher principles; so after the man had again fallen asleep, a magnetic shell was formed around his body to prevent the entrance of this stream, arid the experiment was tried again.

When thus deprived of its ordinary pabulum, his brain began very slowly and dreamily to evolve out of itself scenes of the man's past life; but when he was again aroused, the result was precisely the same—his memory was absolutely blank as to the scene put before him, though he had some vague idea of having dreamed of some event in his past. This subject was then for the time resigned as hopeless, it being fairly evident that his ego was too little developed, and his kârmic principle too strong, to give any reasonable probability of success.

Another effort made with the same man at a later period was not quite so utter a failure, the scene put before him in this case being a very exciting incident from the battle-field, which was chosen as being probably more likely to appeal to his type of mind than the landscape. This picture was undoubtedly received by this undeveloped ego with more interest than the other, but still, when the man was awakened the memory was gone, all that remained being an indistinct idea that *he* had been fighting, but where or why he had quite forgotten.

The next subject taken was a person of much higher type—a man of good moral life, educated and intellectual, with broad philanthropic ideas and exalted ambitions. In his case the denser body responded instantaneously to the water test by a very respectable picture of a tremendous thunder-storm, and that in turn, reacting on the etheric part of the brain, called up by association a whole series of vividly-represented scenes. When this disturbance was over, the usual stream of thoughts began to flow through, but it was observable that a far greater proportion of them awoke a response in this brain—also that the responsive vibrations were much stronger, and that in each case a train of associations was started which sometimes excluded the stream from outside for quite a considerable time.

The astral vehicle in this subject was far more definite in its ovoid outline, and the body of denser astral matter within it was a very fair reproduction of his physical form; and while desire was decidedly less active, the ego itself possessed a much higher grade of consciousness. The astral body in this case could be drawn away to a distance of several miles from the physical without apparently producing the slightest sense of disquiet in either of them.

When the tropical landscape was submitted to this ego, he at once seized upon it with the greatest appreciation, admiring and dwelling upon its beauties in the most enthusiastic manner. After letting him admire it for awhile the man was aroused, but the result was somewhat disappointing. He knew that he had had a beautiful dream, but was quite unable to recall any details, the few elusive fragments that were uppermost in his mind being remnants of the ramblings of his own brain.

With him, as with the other man, the experiment was then repeated with the addition of a magnetic shell thrown round the body, and in this case, as in the other, the brain at once began to evolve pictures of its own. The ego received the landscape with even greater enthusiasm than at first, recognizing it at once as the view he had seen before, and surveying it point by point with quite ecstatic admiration of its many beauties.

But while he was thus engaged in contemplation of it, the etheric brain down below was amusing itself by recalling pictures of his school-life, the most prominent being a scene on a winter day, when the ground was covered with snow, and he and a number of his playmates were snowballing one another in the school playground.

When the man was aroused as usual, the effect was exceedingly curious. He had a most vivid remembrance of standing upon the summit of a mountain, admiring a magnificent view, and he even had the main features of the scenery quite clearly in his mind; but instead of the gorgeous tropical verdure which lent such richness to the real prospect, he saw the surrounding country entirely covered with a mantle of snow! And it seemed to him that even while he was drinking in with deep delight the loveliness of the panorama spread out before him, he suddenly found himself, by one of the rapid transitions so frequent in dreams, snowballing with boyhood's long-forgotten companions in the old school-yard, of which he had not thought for years.

CHAPTER VII.

CONCLUSION

SURELY these experiments show very clearly how the remembrance of our dreams becomes so chaotic and inconsequent as it frequently is. Incidentally they also explain why some people—in whom the ego is undeveloped and earthly desires of various kinds are strong—never dream at all, and why many others are only now and then, under a collocation of favorable circumstances, able to bring back a confused memory of nocturnal adventure; and we see, further, from them that if a man wishes to reap in his waking consciousness the benefit of what his ego may learn during sleep, it is absolutely necessary for him to acquire control over his thoughts, to subdue all lower passions, and to attune his mind to higher things.

If he will take the trouble to form during waking life the habit of sustained and concentrated thought, he will soon find that the advantage he gains thereby is not limited to the daytime in its action. Let him learn to hold his mind in check—to show that he is master of that also, as well as of his lower passions; let him patiently labor to acquire absolute control of his thoughts, so that he will always know exactly what he is thinking about, and why, and he will find that his brain, thus trained to listen only to the promptings of the ego, will remain quiescent when not in use, and will decline to receive and respond to casual currents from the surrounding ocean of thought, so that he will no longer be impervious to influences from the less material planes, where insight is keener and judgment truer than they can ever be down here.

The performance of a very elementary act of magic may be of assistance to some people in this training of the etheric part of the brain. The pictures which it evolves for itself (when the thought-stream from outside is shut off) are certainly less likely altogether to prevent the recollection of the ego's experiences, than is the tumultuous rush of that thought-stream itself; so the exclusion of this turbid current, which contains so much more evil than good, is of itself no inconsiderable step towards the desired end. And that much may be accomplished without serious difficulty. Let a man when he lies down to sleep think of the aura which surrounds him; let him will strongly that the outer surface of that aura shall become a shell to protect him from the impingement of influences from without, and the auric matter will obey his thought; a shell will really be formed around him, and the thought-stream will be excluded.

Another point very strongly brought out in our further investigations is the immense importance of the last thought in a man's mind as he sinks to sleep. This is a consideration which never occurs to the vast majority of people at all, yet it affects them physically, mentally, and morally.

We have seen how passive and how easily influenced man is during sleep; if he enters that state with his thought fixed upon high and holy things, he thereby draws round him the elementals created by like thought in others; his rest is peaceful, his mind open to impressions from above and closed to those from below, for he has set it working in the right direction. If, on the contrary, he falls asleep with impure and earthly thoughts floating through his brain, he attracts to himself all the gross and evil creatures who come near him, while his sleep is troubled by the wild surgings of passion and desire which render him blind to the sights, deaf to the sounds, that come from higher planes.

All earnest Theosophists should therefore make a special point of raising their thoughts to the loftiest level of which they are capable before allowing themselves to sink into slumber. For remember, through what seem at first but the portals of dream, entrance may perchance presently be gained into those grander realms where alone true vision is possible.

If one guides his soul persistently upward, its inner senses will at last begin to unfold; the light within the shrine will burn brighter and brighter, until at last the full continuous consciousness comes, and then he will dream no more. To lie down to sleep will no longer mean for him to sink into oblivion, but simply to step forth radiant, rejoicing, strong, into that fuller, nobler life where fatigue can never come—where the soul is always learning, even though all his time be spent in service; for the service is that of the great Masters of Wisdom, and the glorious task They set before him is to help ever to the fullest limit of his power in Their never-ceasing work for the aiding and the guidance of the evolution of humanity.

INVISIBLE HELPERS

CHAPTER I.

THE UNIVERSAL BELIEF IN THEM.

It is one of the most beautiful characteristics of Theosophy that it gives back to people in a more rational form everything which was really useful and helpful to them in the religions which they have outgrown. Many who have broken through the chrysalis of blind faith, and mounted on the wings of reason and intuition to the freer, nobler mental life of more exalted levels, nevertheless feel that in the process of this glorious gain a something has been lost—that in giving up the beliefs of their childhood they have also cast aside much of the beauty and the poetry of life.

If, however, their lives in the past have been sufficiently good to earn for them the opportunity of coming under the benign influence of Theosophy, they very soon discover that even in this particular there has been no loss at all, but an exceeding great gain—that the glory and the beauty and the poetry are there in fuller measure than they had ever hoped before, and no longer as a mere pleasant dream from which the cold light of commonsense may at any time rudely awaken them, but as truths of nature which will bear investigation—which become only brighter, fuller and more perfect as they are more accurately understood.

A marked instance of this beneficent action of Theosophy is the way in which the invisible world (which, before the great wave of materialism engulfed us, used to be regarded as the source of all living help) has been restored by it to modern life. All the charming folk-lore of the elf, the brownie and the gnome, of the spirits of air and water, of the forest, the mountain and the mine, is shown by it to be no more meaningless superstition, but to have a basis of actual and scientific fact behind it. Its answer to the great fundamental question "If a man die, shall he live again?" is equally definite and scientific, and its teaching on the nature and conditions of the life after death throws a flood of light upon much that, for the Western world at least, was previously wrapped in impenetrable darkness.

It cannot be too often repeated that in this teaching as to the immortality of the soul and the life after death, Theosophy stands in a position totally different from that of ordinary religion. It does not put forward these great truths merely on the authority of some sacred book of long ago; in speaking of these subjects it is not dealing with pious opinions, or metaphysical speculations, but with solid, definite facts, as real and as close to us as the air we breathe or the houses we live in—facts of which many among us have constant experience—facts among which lies the daily work of some of our students, as will presently be seen.

Among the beautiful conceptions which Theosophy has restored to us stands pre-eminent that of the great helpful agencies of nature. The belief in these has been world-wide from the earliest dawn of history, and is universal even now outside the narrow domains of protestantism, which has emptied and darkened the world for its votaries by its attempt to do away with the natural and perfectly true idea of intermediate agents, and reduce everything to the two factors of man and deity—a device whereby the conception of deity has been infinitely degraded, and man has remained unhelped.

A moment's thought will show that the ordinary view of providence—the conception of an erratic interference by the central power of the universe with the result of his own decrees—would imply the introduction of partiality into the scheme, and therefore of the whole train of evils which must necessarily follow upon its heels. The Theosophical teaching, that a man can be thus specially helped only when his past actions have been such as to deserve this assistance, and that even then the help will be given through those who are comparatively near his own level, is free from this serious objection; and it furthermore brings back to us the older and far grander conception of an unbroken ladder of living beings extending down from the Logos Himself to the very dust beneath our feet.

In the East the existence of the invisible helpers has always been recognized, though the names given and the characteristics attributed to them naturally vary in different countries; and even in Europe we have had the old Greek stories of the constant interference of the gods in human affairs, and the Roman legend that Castor and Pollux led the legions of the infant republic in the battle of Lake Regillus. Nor did such a conception die out when the classical period ended, for these stories have their legitimate successors in mediaeval tales of saints who appeared at critical moments and turned the fortune of war in favour of the Christian hosts, or of guardian angels who sometimes stepped in and saved a pious traveller from what would otherwise have been certain destruction.

Chapter II.

Some Modern Instances.

EVEN in this incredulous age, and amidst the full whirl of our nineteenth-century civilization, in spite of the dogmatism of our science and the deadly dullness of our protestantism, instances of intervention inexplicable from the materialistic standpoint may still be found by anyone who will take the trouble to look for them; and in order to demonstrate this to the reader I will briefly epitomize a few of the examples given in one or other of the recent collections of such stories, adding thereto one or two that have come within my own notice.

One very remarkable feature of these more recent examples is that the intervention seems nearly always to have been directed towards the helping or saving of children.

An interesting case which occurred in London only a few years ago was connected with the preservation of a child's life in the midst of a terrible fire, which broke out in a street near Holborn, and entirely destroyed two of the houses there. The flames had obtained such hold before they were discovered that the firemen were unable to save the houses, but they succeeded in rescuing all the inmates except two—an old woman who was suffocated by the smoke before they could reach her, and a child about five years old, whose presence in the house had been forgotton in the hurry and excitement of the moment.

The mother of the child, it seems, was a friend or relative of the landlady of the house, and had left the little creature in her charge for the night, because she was herself obliged to go down to Colchester on business. It was not until everyone else had been rescued, and the whole house was wrapped in flame, that the landlady remembered with a terrible pang the trust that had been confided to her. It seemed hopeless then to attempt to get at the garret where the child had been put to bed, but one of the firemen heroically resolved to make the desperate effort, and, after receiving minute directions as to the exact situation of the room, plunged in among the smoke and flame.

He found the child, and brought him forth entirely unharmed; but when he rejoined his comrades he had a very singular story to tell. He declared that when he reached the room he found it in flames, and most of the floor already fallen; but the fire had curved round the room towards the window in an unnatural and unaccountable manner, the like of which in all his experience he had never seen before, so that the corner in which the child lay was wholly untouched, although the very rafters of the fragment of floor on which his little crib stood were half burnt away. The child was naturally very much terrified, but the fireman distinctly and repeatedly declared that as at great risk he made his way towards him he saw a form like an angel—here his exact words are given—a something "all gloriously white and silvery, bending over the bed and smoothing down the counterpane." He could not possibly have been mistaken about it, he said, for it was visible in a glare of light for some moments, and in fact disappeared only when he was within a few feet of it.

Another curious feature of this story is that the child's mother found herself unable to sleep that night down at Colchester, but was constantly harrassed by a strong feeling that something was wrong with her child, insomuch that at last she was compelled to rise and spend some time in earnest prayer that the little one might be protected from the danger which she instinctively felt to be hanging over him. The intervention was thus evidently what a Christian would call an answer to prayer; a Theosophist, putting the same idea in more scientific phraseology, would say that her intense outpouring of love constituted a force which one of our invisible helpers was able to use for the rescue of her child from a terrible death.

A remarkable case in which children were abnormally protected occurred on the banks of the Thames near Maidenhead a few years earlier than our last example. This time the danger from which they were saved arose not from fire but from water. Three little ones, who lived, if I recollect rightly, in or near the village of Shottesbrook, were taken out for a walk along the towing-path by their nurse. They rushed suddenly round a corner upon a horse which was drawing a barge, and in the confusion two of them got on the wrong side of the tow-rope and were thrown into the water.

The boatman, who saw the accident, sprang forward to try to save them, and he noticed that they were floating high in the water "in quite an unnatural way, like," as he said, and moving quietly towards the bank. This was all that he and the nurse saw, but the children each declared that "a beautiful person, all white and shining," stood beside them in the water, held them up and guided them to the shore. Nor was their story without corroboration, for the bargeman's little daughter, who ran up from the cabin when she heard the screams of the nurse, also affirmed that she saw a lovely lady in the water dragging the two children to the bank.

Without fuller particulars than the story gives us, it is impossible to say with certainty from what class of helpers this "angel" was drawn; but the probabilities are in favour of its having been a developed human being functioning in the astral body, as will be seen when later on we deal with this subject from the other side, as it were—from the point of view of the helpers rather than the helped.

A case in which the agency is somewhat more definitely distinguishable is related by the well-known clergyman, Dr. John Mason Neale. He states that a man who had recently lost his wife was on a visit with his little children at the country house of a friend. It was an old, rambling mansion, and in the lower part of it there were long, dark passages, in which the children played about with great delight. But presently they came upstairs very gravely, and two of them related that as they were running down one of these passages they were met by their mother, who told them to go back again, and then disappeared. Investigation revealed the fact that if the children had run but a few steps farther they would have fallen down a deep uncovered well which yawned full in their path, so that the apparition of their mother had saved them from almost certain death.

In this instance there seems no reason to doubt that the mother herself was still keeping a loving watch over her children from the astral plane, and that (as has happened in some other cases) her intense desire to warn them of the danger into which they were so heedlessly rushing gave her the power to make herself visible and audible to them for the moment—or perhaps merely to impress their minds with the idea that they saw and heard her. It is possible, of course, that the helper may have been someone else, who took the familiar form of the mother in order not to alarm the children; but the simplest hypothesis is to attribute the intervention to the action of the ever-wakeful mother-love itself, undimmed by the passage through the gates of death.

This mother-love, being one of the holiest and most unselfish of human feelings, is also one of the most persistent on higher planes. Not only does the mother who finds herself upon the lower levels of the astral plane, and consequently still within touch of the earth, maintain her interest in and her care for her children as long as she is able to see them; even after her entry into the heaven-world these little ones are still the most prominent objects in her thought, and the wealth of love that she lavishes upon the images which she there makes of them is a great outpouring of spiritual force which flows down upon her offspring who are still struggling in this lower world, and surrounds them with living centres of beneficent energy which may not inaptly be described as veritable guardian angels. An illustration of this will be found in the sixth of our Theosophical manuals, p. 38.

Not long ago the little daughter of one of our English bishops was out walking with her mother in the town where they lived, and in running heedlessly across a street the child was knocked down by the horses of a carriage which came quickly upon her round a corner. Seeing her among the horses' feet, the mother rushed forward, expecting to find her very badly injured, but she sprang up quite merrily, saying, "Oh, mamma, I am not at all hurt, for something all in white kept the horses from treading upon me, and told me not to be afraid."

A case which occurred in Buckinghamshire, somewhere in the neighbourhood of Burnham Beeches, is remarkable on account of the length of time through which the physical manifestation of the succouring agency seems to have maintained itself. It will have been seen that in the instances hitherto given the intervention was a matter of but a few moments, whereas in this a phenomenon was produced which appears to have persisted for more than half an hour.

Two of the little children of a small farmer were left to amuse themselves while their parents and their entire household were engaged in the work of harvesting. The little ones started for a walk in the woods, wandered far from home, and then managed to lose their way. When the weary parents returned at dusk it was discovered that the children were missing, and after enquiring at some of the neighbours' houses the father sent servants and labourers in various directions to seek for them.

Their efforts were, however, unsuccessful, and their shouts unanswered; and they had reassembled at the farm in a somewhat despondent frame of mind, when they all saw a curious light some distance away moving slowly across some fields towards the road. It was described as a large globular mass of rich golden glow, quite unlike ordinary lamplight; and as it drew nearer it was seen that the two missing children were walking steadily along in the midst of it. The father and some others immediately set off running towards it; the appearance persisted until they were close to it, but just as they grasped the children it vanished, leaving them in the darkness.

The children's story was that after night came on they had wandered about crying in the woods for some time, and had at last lain down under a tree to sleep. They had been roused, they said, by a beautiful lady with a lamp, who took them by the hand and led them home; when they questioned her she smiled at them, but never spoke a word. To this strange tale they both steadily adhered, nor was it possible in any way to shake their faith in what they had seen. It is noteworthy, however, that though all present saw the light, and noticed that it lit up the trees and hedges which came within its sphere precisely as an ordinary light would, yet the form of the lady was visible to none but the children.

CHAPTER III.

A Personal Experience.

ALL the above stories are comparatively well-known, and may be found in some of the books which contain collections of such accounts—most of them in Dr. Lee's *More Glimpses of the World Unseen;* but the two instances which I am now about to give have never been in print before, and both occurred within the last ten years—one to myself, and the other to a very dear friend of mine, a prominent member of the Theosophical Society, whose accuracy of observation is beyond all shadow of doubt.

My own story is a simple one enough, though not unimportant to me, since the interposition undoubtedly saved my life. I was walking one exceedingly wet and stormy night down a quiet back street near Westbourne Grove, struggling with scant success to hold up an umbrella against the savage gusts of wind that threatened every moment to tear it from my grasp, and trying as I laboured along to think out the details of some work upon which I was just then engaged.

With startling suddenness a voice which I know well—the voice of an Indian teacher—cried in my ear "Spring back!" and in mechanical obedience I started violently backwards almost before I had time to think. As I did so my umbrella, which had swung forward with the sudden movement, was struck from my hand, and a huge metal chimney-pot crashed upon the pavement less than a yard in front of my face. The great weight of this article, and the tremendous force with which it fell, make it absolutely certain that but for the warning voice I should have been killed on the spot; yet the street was empty, and the voice was that of one whom I knew to be seven thousand miles away from me, as far as the physical body was concerned.

Nor was this the only occasion upon which I received assistance of this supernormal kind, for in early life, long before the foundation of the Theosophical Society, the apparition of a dear one who had recently died prevented me from committing what I now see would have been a serious crime, although by the light of such knowledge as I then had it appeared not only a justifiable but even a laudable act of retaliation. Again, at a later date, though still before the foundation of this Society, a warning conveyed to me from a higher plane amid most impressive surroundings enabled me to prevent another man from entering upon a course which I now know would have ended disastrously, though I had no reason to suppose so at the time. So it will be seen that I have a certain amount of personal experience to strengthen my belief in the doctrine of invisible helpers, even apart from my knowledge of the help that is constantly being given at the present time.

The other case is a very much more striking one. One of our members, who gives me permission to publish her story, but does not wish her name mentioned, once found herself in very serious physical peril. Owing to circumstances which need not be detailed here, she was in the very centre of a dangerous street fracas, and seeing several men struck down and evidently badly hurt close to her, was in momentary expectation of a similar fate, since escape from the crush seemed quite impossible.

Suddenly she experienced a curious sensation of being whirled out of the crowd, and found herself standing quite uninjured and entirely alone in a small bye-street parallel with the one in which the disturbance had taken place. She still heard the noise of the struggle, and while she stood wondering what on earth had happened to her, two or three men who had escaped from the crowd came running round the corner of the street, and on seeing her expressed great astonishment and pleasure, saying that when the brave lady so suddenly disappeared from the midst of the fight they had felt certain that she had been struck down.

At the time no sort of explanation was forthcoming, and she returned home in a very mystified condition; but when at a later period she mentioned this strange occurrence to Madame Blavatsky she was informed that, her karma being such as to enable her to be saved from her exceedingly dangerous position, one of the Masters had specially sent some One to protect her in view of the fact that her life was needed for the work.

Nevertheless the case remains a very extraordinary one, both with regard to the great amount of power exercised and the unusually public nature of its manifestation. It is not difficult to imagine the *modus operandi;* she must have been lifted bodily over the intervening block of houses, and simply set down in the next street; but since her physical body was not visible floating in the air, it is also evident that a veil of some sort (probably of etheric matter) must have been thrown round her while in transit.

If it be objected that whatever can hide physical matter must itself be physical, and therefore visible, it may be replied that by a process familiar to all occult students it is possible to bend rays of light (which, under all conditions at present known to science, travel only in straight lines unless refracted) so that after passing round an object they may resume exactly their former course; and it will at once be seen that if this were done such an object would to all physical eyes be absolutely invisible until the rays were allowed to resume their normal course. I am fully aware that this one statement alone is sufficient to brand my remarks as nonsense in the eyes of the scientist of the present day, but I cannot help that; I am merely stating a possibility in nature which the science of the future will no doubt one day discover, and for those who are not students of occultism the remark must wait until then for its justification.

The process, as I say, is comprehensible enough to anyone who understands a little about the more occult forces of nature; but the phenomenon still remains an exceedingly dramatic one, while the name of the heroine of the story, were I permitted to give it, would be a guarantee of its accuracy to all my readers.

Another recent instance of interposition, less striking, perhaps, but entirely successful, has been reported to me since the publication of the first edition of this book. A lady, being obliged to undertake a long railway journey alone, had taken the precaution to secure an empty compartment; but just as the train was leaving the station, a man of forbidding and villainous appearance sprang in and seated himself at the other end of the carriage. The lady was much alarmed, thus to be left alone with so doubtful-looking a character, but it was too late to call for help, so she sat still and commended herself earnestly to the care of her patron saint.

Soon her fears were redoubled, for the man arose and turned toward her with an evil grin, but he had hardly taken one step when he started back with a look of the most intense astonishment and terror. Following the direction of his glance, she was startled to see a gentleman seated directly opposite'to her, gazing quietly but firmly at the baffled robber—a gentleman who certainly could not have entered the carriage by any ordinary means. Too much awed to speak, she watched him as though fascinated for a full half-hour; he uttered no word, and did not even look at her, but kept his eyes steadily upon the villain, who cowered trembling in the furthest corner of the compartment. The moment that the train reached the next station, and even before it came to a standstill, the would-be thief tore open the door and sprang hurriedly out. The lady, deeply thankful to be rid of him, turned to express her gratitude to the gentleman, but found only an empty seat, though it would have been impossible for any physical body to have left the carriage in the time.

The materialization was in this case maintained for a longer period than usual, but on the other hand it expended no force in action of any kind—nor indeed was it necessary that it should do so, as its mere appearance was sufficient to effect its purpose.

But these stories, all referring as they do to what would commonly be called angelic intervention, illustrate only one small part of the activities of our invisible helpers. Before, however, we can profitably consider the other departments of their work it will be well that we should have clearly in our minds the various classes of entities to which it is possible that these helpers may belong. Let that, then, be the portion of our subject to be next treated.

CHAPTER IV.

THE HELPERS.

HELP, then, may be given by several of the many classes of inhabitants of the astral plane. It may come from devas, from nature-spirits, or from those whom we call dead, as well as from those who function consciously upon the astral plane during life—chiefly the adepts and their pupils. But if we examine the matter a little more closely we shall see that though all the classes mentioned may, and some times do, take a part in this work, yet their shares in it are so unequal that it is practically left almost entirely to one class.

The very fact that so much of this work of helping has to be done either upon or from the astral plane goes far in itself towards explaining this. To anyone who has even a faint idea of what the powers at the command of an adept really are, it will be at once obvious that for him to work upon the astral plane would be a far greater waste of energy than for our leading physicians or scientists to spend their time in breaking stones upon the road.

The work of the adept lies in higher regions—chiefly upon the arupa levels of the devachanic plane or heaven-world, where he may direct his energies to the influencing of the true individuality of man, and not the mere personality which is all that can be reached in the astral or physical world. The strength which he puts forth in that more exalted realm produces results greater, more far-reaching and more lasting than any which can be attained by the expenditure of even ten times the force down here; and the work up there is such as he alone can fully accomplish, while that on lower planes may be at any rate to some extent achieved by/ those whose feet are yet upon the earlier steps of the great stairway which will one day lead them to the position where he stands.

The same remarks apply also in the case of the devas. Belonging as they do to a higher kingdom of nature than ours, their work seems for the most part entirely unconnected with humanity; and even those of their orders—and there are some such—which do sometimes respond to our higher yearnings or appeals, do so on the mental plane rather than on the physical or astral, and more frequently in the periods between our incarnations than during our earthly lives.

It may be remembered that some instances of such help were observed in the course of investigations into the subdivisions of the devachanic plane which were undertaken when the Theosophical manual on the subject was in preparation. In one case a deva was found teaching the most wonderful celestial music to a chorister; and in another one of a different class was giving instruction and guidance to an astronomer who was seeking to comprehend the form and structure of the universe.

These two were but examples of many instances in which the great deva kingdom was found to be helping onward the evolution and responding to the higher aspirations of man after death; and there are methods by which, even during earth-life, these great ones may be approached, and an infinity of knowledge acquired from them, though even then such intercourse is gained rather by rising to their plane than by invoking them to descend to ours.

In the ordinary events of our physical life the deva very rarely interferes—indeed, he is so fully occupied with the far grander work of his own plane that he is probably scarcely conscious of this; and though it may occasionally happen that he becomes aware of some human sorrow or difficulty which excites his pity and moves him to endeavour to help in some way, his wider vision undoubtedly recognizes that at the present stage of evolution such interpositions would in the vast majority of cases be productive of infinitely more harm than good.

There was indubitably a period in the past—in the infancy of the human race—when it was much more largely assisted from outside than is at present the case. At the time when all its Buddhas and Manus, and even its more ordinary leaders and teachers, were drawn either from the ranks of the deva evolution or from the perfected humanity of a more advanced planet, any such assistance as we are considering in this treatise must also have been given by these exalted beings. But as man progresses he becomes himself qualified to act as a helper, first on the physical plane and then on higher levels; and we have now reached a stage at which humanity ought to be able to provide, and to some slight extent does provide, invisible helpers for itself, thus setting free for still more useful and elevated work those beings who are capable of it.

It becomes obvious then that such assistance as that to which we are here referring may most fitly be given by men and women at a particular stage of their evolution; not by the adepts, since they are capable of doing far grander and more widely useful work, and not by the ordinary person of no special spiritual development, for he would be unable to be of any use. Just as these considerations would lead us to expect, we find that this work of helping on the astral and lower mental planes is chiefly in the hands of the pupils of the Masters—men who, though yet far from the attainment of adeptship, have evolved themselves to the extent of being able to function consciously upon the planes in question.

Some of these have taken the further step of completing the links between the physical consciousness and that of the higher levels, and they therefore have the undoubted advantage of recollecting in waking life what they have done and what they have learnt in those other worlds; but there are many others who, though as yet unable to carry their consciousness through unbroken, are nevertheless by no means wasting the hours when they think they are asleep, but spending them in noble and unselfish labour for their fellow-men.

What this labour is we will proceed to consider, but before we enter upon that part of the subject we will first refer to an objection which is very frequently brought forward with regard to such work, and we will also dispose of the comparatively rare cases in which the agents are either nature-spirits or men who have cast off the physical body.

People whose grasp of Theosophical ideas is as yet imperfect are often in doubt as to whether it is allowable for them to try to help some one whom they find in sorrow or difficulty, lest they should interfere with the fate which has been decreed for him by the absolute justice of the eternal law of karma. "The man is in his present position," they say in effect, "because he has deserved it; he is now working out the perfectly natural result of some evil which he has committed in the past; what right have I to interfere with the action of the great cosmic law by trying to ameliorate his condition, either on the astral plane or the physical?"

Now the good people who make such suggestions are really, however unconsciously to themselves, exhibiting the most colossal conceit, for their position implies two astounding assumptions; first, that they know exactly what another man's karma has been, and how long it has decreed that his sufferings shall last; and secondly, that they—the insects of a day—could absolutely override the cosmic law and prevent the due working-out of karma by any action of theirs. We may be well assured that the great karmic deities are perfectly well able to manage their business without our assistance, and we need have no fear that any steps we may take can by any possibility cause them the slightest difficulty or uneasiness.

If a man's karma is such that he cannot be helped, then all our well-meant efforts in that direction will fail, though we shall nevertheless have gained good karma for ourselves by making them. What the man's karma has been is no business of ours; our duty is to give help to the utmost of our power, and our right is only to the act; the result is in other and higher hands. How can we tell how a man's account stands? For all we know he may just have exhausted his evil karma, and be at this moment at the very point where a helping hand is needed to give relief and raise him out of his trouble or depression; why should not we have the pleasure and privilege of doing that good deed as well as another? If we *can* help him, then that fact of itself shows that he has deserved to be helped; but we can never know unless we try. In any case the law of karma will take care of itself, and we need not trouble ourselves about it.

The cases in which assistance is given to mankind by nature-spirits are few. The majority of such creatures shun the haunts of man, and retire before him, disliking his emanations and the perpetual bustle and unrest which he creates all around him. Also, except some of their higher orders, they are generally inconsequent and thoughtless—more like happy children at play under exceedingly favourable physical conditions than like grave and responsible entities. Still it sometimes happens that one of them will become attached to a human being, and do him many a good turn; but at the present stage of its evolution this department of nature cannot be relied upon for anything like steady co-operation in the work of invisible helpers. For a fuller account of the nature-spirits the reader is referred to the fifth of our Theosophical manuals.

Again, help is sometimes given by those recently departed—those who are still lingering on the astral plane, and still in close touch with earthly affairs, as (probably) in the above-mentioned case of the mother who saved her children from falling down a well. But it will readily be seen that the amount of such help available must naturally be exceedingly limited. The more unselfish and helpful a person is, the less likely is he to be found after death lingering in full consciousness on the lower levels of the astral plane, from which the earth is most readily accessible. In any case, unless he were an exceptionally bad man, his stay within the realm whence alone any interference would be possible would be comparatively short; and although from the heaven-world he may still shed benign influence upon those whom he has loved on earth, it will usually be rather of the nature of a general benediction than a force capable of bringing about definite results in a specific case, such as those which we have been considering.

Again, many of the departed who wish to help those whom they left behind, find themselves quite unable to influence them in any way, since to work from one plane upon an entity on another requires either very great sensitiveness on the part of that entity, or a certain amount of knowledge and skill on the part of the operator. Therefore, although instances of apparitions shortly after death are by no means uncommon, it is rare to find one in which the departed person has really done anything useful, or succeeded in impressing what he wished upon the friend or relation whom he visited. There are such cases, of course—a good many of them when we come to put them all together; but they are not numerous compared to the great number of ghosts who have succeeded in showing themselves. So that but little help is usually given by the dead—indeed, as will presently be explained, it is far more common for them to be themselves in need of assistance than to be able to accord it to others.

At present, therefore, the main bulk of the work which has to be done along these lines falls to the share of those living persons who are able to function consciously on the astral plane.

Chapter V.

The Reality of Superphysical Life.

It seems difficult for those who are accustomed only to the ordinary and somewhat materialistic lines of thought of the nineteenth century, to believe in and realize fully a condition of perfect consciousness apart from the physical body. Every Christian, at any rate, is bound by the very foundations of his creed to believe that he possesses a soul; but if you suggest to him the possibility that that soul may be a sufficiently real thing to become visible under certain conditions apart from the body either during life or after death, the chances are ten to one that he will scornfully tell you that he does not believe in ghosts, and that such an idea is nothing but an anachronistic survival of an exploded mediaeval superstition.

If, therefore, we are at all to comprehend the work of the band of invisible helpers, and perchance ourselves to learn to assist in it, we must shake ourselves free from the trammels of contemporary thought on these subjects, and endeavour to grasp the great truth (now a demonstrated fact to many among us) that the physical body is in simple truth nothing but a vehicle or vesture of the real man. It is put off permanently at death, but it is also put off temporarily every night when we go to sleep—indeed the process of falling asleep consists in this very action of the real man in his astral vehicle slipping out of the physical body.

Again I repeat, this is no mere hypothesis or ingenious supposition. There are many among us who are able to perform (and *do* perform every day of their lives) this elementary act of magic in full consciousness—who pass from one plane to the other at will; and if that is clearly realized, it will become apparent how grotesquely absurd to them must appear the ordinary unreasoning assertion that such *a* thing is utterly impossible. It is like telling a man that it is impossible for him to fall asleep, and that if he thinks he has ever done so he is under a hallucination.

Now the man who has not yet developed the link between the astral and physical consciousness is unable to leave his denser body at will, or to recollect most of what happens to him while away from it; but the fact nevertheless remains that he leaves it every time he sleeps, and may be seen by any trained clairvoyant either hovering over it or wandering about at a greater or less distance from it, as the case may be.

The entirely undeveloped person usually floats close above his physical body, scarcely less asleep than it is, and comparatively shapeless and inchoate, and it is found that he cannot be drawn away from the immediate neighbourhood of that physical body without causing serious discomfort which would in fact awaken it. As the man evolves, however, his astral body grows more definite and more conscious, and so becomes a fitter vehicle for him. In the case of the majority of intelligent and cultured people the degree of consciousness is already very considerable, and a man who is at all spiritually developed is as fully himself in that vehicle as in this denser body.

But though he may be fully conscious on the astral plane during sleep, and able to move about on it freely if he wishes to do so, it does not yet follow that he is ready to join the band of helpers. Most people at this stage are so wrapped up in their own train of thought—usually a continuation of some line taken up in waking hours—that they are like a man in a brown study, so much absorbed as to be practically entirely heedless of all that is going on about them. And in many ways it is well that this is so, for there is much upon the astral plane which might be unnerving and terrifying to one who had not the courage born of full knowledge as to the real nature of all that he would see.

Sometimes a man gradually rouses himself out of this condition—wakes up to the astral world around him, as it were; but more often he remains in that state until someone who is already active there takes him in hand and wakens him. This is, however, not a responsibility to be lightly undertaken, for while it is comparatively easy thus to wake a man up on the astral plane, it is practically impossible, except by a most undesirable exercise of mesmeric influence, to put him to sleep again. So that before a member of the band of workers will thus awaken a dreamer, he must fully satisfy himself that the man's disposition is such that he will make good use of the additional powers that will then be put into his hands, and also that his knowledge and his courage are sufficient to make it reasonably certain that no harm will come to him as a result of the action.

Such awakening so performed will put a man in a position to join if he will the band of those who help mankind. But it must be clearly understood that this does not necessarily or even usually bring with it the power of remembering in the waking consciousness anything which has been done. That capacity has to be attained by the man for himself, and in most cases it does not come for years afterwards—perhaps not even in the same life. But happily this lack of memory in the body in no way impedes the work out of the body; so that, except for the satisfaction to a man of knowing during his waking hours upon what work he has been engaged during his sleep, it is not a matter of importance. What really matters is that the work should be done—not that we should remember who did it.

CHAPTER VI.

A TIMELY INTERVENTION.

VARIED as is this work on the astral plane, it is all directed to one great end—the furtherance, in however humble a degree, of the processes of evolution, Occasionally it is connected with the development of the lower kingdoms, which it is possible slightly to accelerate under certain conditions. A duty towards these lower kingdoms, elemental as well as animal and vegetable, is distinctly recognized by our adept leaders, since it is in some cases only through connection with or use by man that their progress takes place.

But naturally by far the largest and most important part of the work is connected with humanity in some way or other. The services rendered are of many and various kinds, but chiefly concerned with man's spiritual development, such physical interventions as are recounted in the earlier part of this book being exceedingly rare. They do, however, occasionally take place, and though it is my wish to emphasize rather the possibility of extending mental and moral help to our fellow-men, it will perhaps be well to give two or three instances in which friends personally known to me have rendered physical assistance to those in sore need of it, in order that it may be seen how these examples from the experience of the helpers gear in with the accounts given by those who have received the supernormal aid—such stories, I mean, as those which are to be found in the literature of so-called "supernatural occurrences."

In the course of the recent rebellion in Matabeleland one of our members was sent upon an errand of mercy which may serve as an illustration of the way in which help upon this lower plane has occasionally been given. It seems that one night a certain farmer and his family in that country were sleeping tranquilly in fancied security, quite unaware that only a few miles away relentless hordes of savage foes were lying in ambush maturing fiendish plots of murder and rapine. Our member's business was in some way or other to arouse the sleeping family to a sense of the terrible danger which so unexpectedly menaced them, and she found this by no means an easy matter.

An attempt to impress the idea of imminent peril upon the brain of the farmer failed utterly, and as the urgency of the case seemed to demand strong measures, our friend decided to materialize herself sufficiently to shake the housewife by the shoulder and adjure her to get up and look about her. The moment she saw that she had been successful in attracting attention she vanished, and the farmer's wife has never from that day to this been able to find out *which* of her neighbours it was who roused her so opportunely, and thus saved the lives of the entire family, who but for this mysterious intervention would undoubtedly have been massacred in their beds half an hour later; nor can she even now understand how this friend in need contrived to make her way in, when all the windows and doors were found so securely barred.

Being thus abruptly awakened, the housewife was half inclined to consider the warning as a mere dream; however, she arose and looked round just to see that all was right, and fortunate it was that she did so, for though she found nothing amiss indoors she had no sooner thrown open a shutter than she saw the sky red with a distant conflagration. She at once roused her husband and the rest of her family, and owing to this timely notice they were able to escape to a place of concealment near at hand just before the arrival of the horde of savages, who destroyed the house and ravaged the fields indeed, but were disappointed of the human prey which they had expected. The feelings of the rescuer may be imagined when she read in the newspaper some time afterwards an account of the providential deliverance of this family.

CHAPTER VII.

THE "ANGEL STORY."

ANOTHER instance of intervention on the physical plane which occurred a short time ago makes a very beautiful little story, though this time only one life was saved. It needs, however, a few words of preliminary explanation. Among our band of helpers here in Europe are two who were brothers long ago in ancient Egypt, and are still warmly attached to one another. In this present incarnation there is a wide difference in age between them, one being advanced in middle life, while the other was at that time a mere child in the physical body, though an ego of considerable advancement and promise. Naturally it falls to the lot of the elder to train and guide the younger in the occult work to which they are so heartily devoted, and as both are fully conscious and active on the astral plane they spend most of the time during which their grosser bodies are asleep in labouring together under the direction of their common Master, and giving to both living and dead such help as is within their power.

I will quote the story of the particular incident which I wish to relate from a letter written by the elder of the two helpers immediately after its occurrence, as the description there given is more vivid and picturesque than any account in the third person could possibly be.

"We were going about quite other business, when Cyril suddenly cried, 'What's that?' for we heard a terrible scream of pain or fright. In a moment we were on the spot, and found that a boy of about eleven or twelve had fallen over a cliff on to some rocks below, and was very badly hurt. He had broken a leg and an arm, poor fellow, but what was still worse was a dreadful cut in the thigh, from which blood was pouring in a torrent. Cyril cried, 'Let us help him quick, or he'll die!'

"In emergencies of this kind one has to think quickly. There were clearly two things to be done; that bleeding must be stopped, and physical help must be procured. I was obliged to materialize either Cyril or myself, for we wanted physical hands at once to tie a bandage, and besides it seemed better that the poor boy should *see* someone standing by him in his trouble. I felt that while undoubtedly he would be more at home with Cyril than with me, I should probably be more readily able to procure help than Cyril would, so the division of labour was obvious.

"The plan worked capitally. I materialized Cyril instantly (he does not know yet how to do it for himself), and told him to take the boy's neckerchief and tie it round the thigh, and twist a stick through it. 'Won't it hurt him terribly?' said Cyril; but he *did* it, and the blood stopped flowing. The injured boy seemed half unconscious, and could scarcely speak, but he looked up at the shining little form bending so anxiously over him, and asked, 'Be you an angel, master?' Cyril smiled so prettily, and replied, 'No, I'm only a boy, but I've come to help you;' and then I left him to comfort the sufferer while I rushed off for the boy's mother, who lived about a mile away.

"The trouble I had to force into that woman's head the conviction that something was wrong, and that she must go and see about it, you would never believe; but at last she threw down the pan she was cleaning, and said aloud, 'Well, I don't know what's come over me, but I must go and find the boy.' When she once started I was able to guide her without much difficulty, though all the time I was holding Cyril together by will-power, lest the poor child's angel should suddenly vanish from before his eyes.

"You see, when you materialize a form you are changing matter from its natural state into another—temporarily opposing the cosmic will, as it were; and if you take your mind off it for one half-second, back it flies into its original condition like a flash of lightning. So I could not give more than half my attention to that woman, but still I got her along somehow, and as soon as she came round the corner of the cliff I let Cyril disappear; but she had seen him, and now that village has one of the best-attested stories of angelic intervention on record!

"The accident happened in the early morning, and the same evening I looked in (astrally) upon the family to see how matters were going on. The poor boy's' leg and arm had been set, and the great cut bandaged, and he lay in bed looking very pale and weak, but evidently *going* to recover in time. The mother had a couple of neighbours in, and was telling them the story; and a curious tale it sounded to one who knew the real facts.

"She explained, in very many, words, how she couldn't tell what it was, but something came over her all in a minute like, making her feel something had happened to the boy, and she *must* go out and see after him; how at first she thought it was nonsense, and tried to throw off the feeling, 'but it warn't no use—she just had to go.' She told how she didn't know what made her go round by that cliff more than any other way, but it just happened so, and as she turned round the corner there she saw him lying propped up against a rock, and kneeling beside him was the 'beautifullest child ever she saw, dressed all in white and shining, with rosy cheeks and lovely brown eyes;' and how he smiled at her 'so heavenly like,' and then all in a moment he was not there, and at first she was so startled she didn't know what to think; and then all at once she felt what it was, and fell on her knees and thanked God for sending one of his angels to help her poor boy.

"Then she told how when she lifted him to carry him home she wanted to take off the handkerchief that was cutting into his poor leg so, but he would not let her, because he said the angel had tied it and said he was not to touch it; and how when she told the doctor this afterwards he explained to her that if she *had* unfastened it the boy would certainly have died.

"Then she repeated the boy's part of the tale—how the moment after he fell this lovely little angel came to him (he knew it *was* an angel because he knew there had been nobody in sight for half a mile round when he was at the top of the cliff just before—only he could not understand why it hadn't any wings, and why it said it was only a boy)—how it lifted him against the rock and tied up his leg, and then began to talk to him and tell him he need not be frightened, because somebody was gone to fetch mother, and she would be there directly; how it kissed him and tried to make him comfortable, and how its soft, warm, little hand held his all the time, while it told him strange, beautiful stories which he could not clearly remember, but he knew they were very good, because he had almost forgotten he was hurt until he saw mother coming; and how then it assured him he would soon be well again, and smiled and squeezed his hand, and then somehow it was gone.

"Since then there has been quite a religious revival in that village! Their minister has told them that so signal an interposition of divine providence must have been meant as a sign to them, to rebuke scoffers and to prove the truth of holy scripture and of the Christian religion—and nobody seems to see the colossal conceit involved in such an astonishing proposition.

"But the effect on the boy has been undoubtedly good, morally as well as physically; by all accounts he was a careless enough young scamp before, but now he feels 'his angel' may be near him at any time, and he will never do or say anything rough or coarse or angry, lest it should see or hear. The one great desire of his life is that some day he may see it again, and he knows that when he dies its lovely face will be the first to greet him on the other side."

A beautiful and pathetic little story, truly. The moral drawn from the occurrence by the village and its minister is perhaps somewhat of a *non sequitur;* yet the testimony to the existence of at least something beyond this material plane must surely do the people more good than harm, and after all the mother's conclusion from what she saw was a perfectly correct one, though more accurate knowledge would probably have led her to express it a little differently.

An interesting fact afterwards discovered by the investigations of the writer of the letter throws a curious side-light upon the reasons underlying such incidents. It was found that the two boys had met before, and that some thousands of years ago the one who fell from the cliff had been the slave of the other, and had once saved his young master's life at the risk of his own, and had been liberated in consequence; and now, long afterwards, the master not only repays the debt in kind, but also gives his former slave a high ideal and an inducement to morality of life which will probably change the whole course of his future evolution. So true is it that no good deed ever goes unrewarded by karma, however tardy it may seem in its action—that

> Though the mills of God grind slowly,
> Yet they grind exceeding small;
> Though with patience stands He waiting,
> With exactness grinds He all.

CHAPTER VIII.

THE STORY OF A FIRE.

ANOTHER piece of work done by the same boy Cyril furnishes an almost exact parallel to some of the stories from the books which I have given in earlier pages. He and his older friend, it seems, were passing along in the prosecution of their usual work one night, when they noticed the fierce glare of a big fire below them, and promptly dived down to see if they could be of any use.

It was a great hotel which was in flames, a huge caravanserai on the edge of a great lake. The house, many stories in height, formed three sides of a square round a sort of garden, planted with trees and flowers, while the lake formed the fourth side. The two wings ran right down to the lake, the big bay windows which terminated them almost projecting over the water, so as to leave only quite a narrow passage-way under them at the two sides.

The front and wings were built round inside wells, which contained also the lattice-work shafts of the lifts, so that when once the fire broke out, it spread with almost incredible rapidity, and before our friends saw it on their astral journey all the middle floors in each of the three great blocks were in flames. Fortunately the inmates—except one little boy—had already been rescued, though some of them had sustained very serious burns and other injuries.

This little fellow had been forgotten in one of the upper rooms of the left wing, for his parents were out at a ball, and knew nothing of the fire, while naturally enough no one else thought of the lad till it was far too late. The fire had gained such a hold on the middle floors of that wing that nothing could have been done, even if anyone had remembered him, as his room faced on to the inner garden which has been mentioned, so that he was completely cut off from all outside help. Besides, he was not even aware of his danger, for the dense, suffocating smoke had so gradually filled the room that his sleep had grown deeper and deeper, till he was all but stupefied.

In this state he was discovered by Cyril, who seems to be specially attracted towards children in need or danger. He first tried to make some of the people remember the boy, but in vain; and in any case it seemed scarcely possible that they could have helped him, so that it was soon evident that this was merely a waste of time. The older helper then materialized Cyril, as before, in the room, and set him to work to awaken and rouse up the more than half-stupefied child. After a good deal of difficulty this was accomplished to some extent, but the boy remained in a half-dazed, semi-conscious condition through all that followed, so that he needed to be pushed and pulled about, guided and helped at every turn.

The two boys first crept out of the room into the central passage which ran through the wing, and then, finding that the smoke and the flames beginning to come through the floor made it impassable for a physical body, Cyril got the other boy back into the room again and out of the window on to a stone ledge, about a foot wide, which ran right along the block just below the windows. Along this he managed to guide his companion, half balancing himself on the extreme edge of the ledge, and half floating on air, but always placing himself outside of the other, so as to keep him from dizziness and prevent him from feeling afraid of a fall.

Towards the end of the block nearest the lake, in which direction the fire seemed less developed, they climbed in through an open window and again reached the passage, hoping to find the staircase at that end still passable. But it, too, was full of flame and smoke; so they crawled back along the passage, Cyril advising his companion to keep his mouth close to the ground, till they reached the latticed cage of the lift running down the long well in the centre of the block.

The lift of course was at the bottom, but they managed to clamber down the lattice work inside the cage till they stood on the roof of the elevator itself. Here they found themselves blocked, but luckily Cyril discovered a doorway opening from the cage of the lift on to a sort of *entresol* just above the ground floor. Through this they reached a passage, which they crossed, the little boy being half-stifled by the smoke; then they made their way through one of the rooms opposite, and finally, clambering out of the window, found themselves on the top of the veranda which ran along in front of the ground floor, between it and the garden.

Thence it was easy enough to swarm down one of the pillars and reach the garden itself; but even there the heat was intense, and the danger, when the walls should fall, very considerable. So Cyril tried to conduct his charge round the end first of one, then of the other wing; but in both cases the flames had burst through, and the narrow, overhung passages were quite impassable. Finally they took refuge in one of the pleasure boats which were moored to the steps of the quay at the side of the garden next the lake, and, casting loose, rowed out on to the water.

Cyril intended to row round past the burning wing and land the boy whom he had saved; but when they got some little way out, they fell in with a passing lake steamer, and were seen—for the whole scene was lit up by the glare of the burning hotel, till everything was as plain as in broad daylight. The steamer came alongside the boat to take them off; but instead of the two boys they had seen, the crew found only one—for his older friend had promptly allowed Cyril to slip back into his astral form, dissipating the denser matter which had made for the time a material body, and he was therefore now invisible.

A careful search was made, of course, but no trace of the second boy could be found, and so it was concluded that he must have fallen overboard and been drowned just as they came alongside. The child who had been rescued fell into a dead faint as soon as he was safe on board, so they could get no information from him, and when he did recover, all he could say was that he had seen the other boy the moment before they came alongside, and then knew nothing more.

The steamer was bound down the lake to a place some two days' sail distant, and it was a week or so before the rescued boy could be restored to his parents, who of course thought that he had perished in the flames, for though an effort was made to impress on their minds the fact that their son had been saved, it was found impossible to convey the idea to them, so it may be imagined how great was the joy of the meeting.

The boy is still well and happy, and is never weary of relating his wonderful adventure. Many a time he has regretted that the kind friend who saved him should have perished so mysteriously at the very moment when all the danger seemed over at last. Indeed, he has even ventured to suggest that perhaps he *didn't* perish after all—that perhaps he was a fairy prince; but of course this idea elicits nothing but tolerant smiles of superiority from his elders. The kârmic link between him and his preserver has not yet been traced, but no doubt there must be one somewhere.

CHAPTER IX.
MATERIALIZATION AND REPERCUSSION.

ON meeting with a story such as this, students often enquire whether the invisible helper is perfectly safe amidst these scenes of deadly peril—whether, for example, this boy who was materialized in order to save another from a burning house was not himself in some danger— whether his physical body would not have suffered in any way by repercussion if his materialized form had passed through the flames, or fallen from the high ledge on the edge of which he walked so unconcernedly. In fact, since we know that in many cases the connection between a materialized form and a physical body is sufficiently close to produce repercussion, might it not have occurred in this case?

Now this subject of repercussion is an exceedingly abstruse and difficult one, and we are by no means yet in a position fully to explain its very remarkable phenomena; indeed, in order to understand the matter perfectly, it would probably be necessary to comprehend the laws of sympathetic vibration on more planes than one. Still, we do know by observation some of the conditions which permit its action, and some which definitely exclude it, and I think we are warranted in saying that it was absolutely impossible here.

To see why this is so we must first remember that there are at least three well-defined varieties of materialization, as anyone who has at all an extended experience of spiritualism will be aware. I am not concerned at the moment to enter upon any explanation as to how these three varieties are respectively produced, but am merely stating the indubitable fact of their existence.

1. There is the materialization which, though tangible, is not visible to ordinary physical sight. Of this nature are the unseen hands which so often clasp one's arm or stroke one's face at a *séance*, which sometimes carry physical objects through the air or make raps upon the table—though of course both these latter phenomena may easily be produced without a materialized hand at all.

2. There is the materialization which though visible is not tangible—the spirit-form through which one's hand passes as through empty air. In some cases this variety is obviously misty and impalpable, but in others its appearance is so entirely normal that its solidity is never doubted until some one endeavours to grasp it.

3. There is the perfect materialization which is both visible and tangible—which not only bears the outward semblance of your departed friend, but shakes you cordially by the hand with the very clasp that you know so well.

Now while there is a good deal of evidence to show that repercussion takes place under certain conditions in the case of this third kind of materialization, it is by no means so certain that it can occur with the first or second class. In the case of the boy-helper it is probable that the materialization would not be of the third type, since the greatest care is always taken not to expend more force than is absolutely necessary to produce whatever result may be required, and it is obvious that less energy would be used in the production of the more partial forms which we have called the first and second classes. The probability is that only the arm with which the boy held his little companion would be solid to the touch, and that the rest of his body, though looking perfectly natural, would have proved far less palpable if it had been tested.

But, apart from this probability, there is another point to be considered. When a full materialization takes place, whether the subject be living or dead, physical matter of some sort has to be gathered together for the purpose. At a spiritualistic *séance* this matter is obtained by drawing largely upon the etheric double of the medium—and sometimes even upon his physical body also, since cases are on record in which his weight has been very considerably decreased while manifestations of this character were taking place.

This method is employed by the directing entities of the *séance* simply because when an available medium is within reach it is very much the easiest way in which a materialization can be brought about; and the consequence is that the very closest connection is thus set up between that medium and the materialized body, so that the phenomenon which (although very imperfectly understanding it) we call repercussion, occurs in its clearest form. If, for example, the hands of the materialized body be rubbed with chalk, that chalk will afterwards be found on the hands of the medium, even though he may have been all the time carefully locked up in a cabinet under circumstances which absolutely preclude any suspicion of fraud. If any injury be inflicted upon the materialized form, that injury will be accurately reproduced upon the corresponding part of the medium's body; while sometimes food of which the spirit-form has partaken will be found to have passed into the body of the medium—at least that happened in one case at any rate within my own experience.

It would be far otherwise, however, in the case which we have been describing. Cyril was thousands of miles from his sleeping physical body, and it would therefore be quite impossible for his friend to draw etheric matter from it, while the regulations under which all pupils of the great Masters of Wisdom perform their work of helping man would assuredly prevent him, even form the noblest purpose, from putting such a strain upon any one else's body. Besides, it would be quite unnecessary, for the far less dangerous method invariably employed by the helpers when materialization seems desirable would be ready to his hand—the condensation from the circumambient ether, or even from the physical air, of such an amount of matter as may be requisite. This feat, though no doubt beyond the power of the average entity manifesting at a *séance,* presents no difficulty to a student of occult chemistry.

But mark the difference in the result obtained. In the case of the medium we have a materialized form in the closest possible connection with the physical body, made out of its very substance, and therefore capable of producing all the phenomena of repercussion. In the case of the helper we have indeed an exact reproduction of the physical body, but it is created by a mental effort out of matter entirely foreign to that body, and is no more capable of acting upon it by repercussion than an ordinary marble statue of the man would be.

Thus it is that a passage through the flames or a fall from a high window-ledge would have had no terrors for the boy-helper, and that on another occasion a member of the band, though materialized, was able without any inconvenience to the physical body to go down in a sinking vessel.

In both the incidents of his work that have been described above, it will have been noticed that the boy Cyril was unable to materialize himself, and that the operation had to be performed for him by an older friend. One more of his experiences is worth relating, for it gives us a case in which by intensity of pity and determination of will he *was* able to show himself—a case somewhat parallel to that previously related of the mother whose love enabled her somehow to manifest herself in order to save her children's lives.

Inexplicable as it may seem, there is no doubt whatever of the existence in nature of this stupendous power of will over matter of all planes, so that if only the power be great enough, practically *any* result may be produced by its direct action, without any knowledge or even thought on the part of the man exercising that will as to *how* it is to do its work. We have had plenty of evidence that this power holds good in the case of materialization, although ordinarily it is an art which must be learnt just like any other. Assuredly an average man on the astral plane could no more materialize himself without having previously learnt how to do it than the average man on this plane could play the violin without having previously learnt it; but there are exceptional cases, as will be seen from the following narrative.

CHAPTER X.

THE TWO BROTHERS.

THIS story has been told by a pen of far greater dramatic capability than mine, and with a wealth of detail for which I have here no space, in *The Theosophical Review* of November, 1897, p. 229. To that account I would refer the reader, since my own description of the case will be a mere outline, as brief as is consistent with clearness. The names given are of course fictitious, but the incidents are related with scrupulous accuracy.

Our *dramatis personae are* two brothers, the sons of a country gentleman—Lancelot, aged fourteen, and Walter, aged eleven—very good boys of the ordinary healthy, manly type, like hundreds of others in this fair realm, with no obvious psychic qualifications of any sort, except the possession of a good deal of Celtic blood. Perhaps the most remarkable feature about them was the intensity of the affection that existed between them, for they were simply inseparable—neither would go anywhere without the other, and the younger idolized the elder as only a younger boy can.

One unlucky day Lancelot was thrown from his pony and killed, and for Walter the world became empty. The child's grief was so real and terrible that he could neither eat nor sleep, and his mother and nurse were at their wits' end as to what to do for him. He seemed deaf alike to persuasion and blame; when they told him that grief was wicked, and that his brother was in heaven, he simply answered that he could not be certain of that, and that even if it were true, he knew that Lancelot could no more be happy in heaven without him than he could on earth without Lancelot.

Incredible as it may sound, the poor child was actually dying of grief, and what made the case even more pathetic was the fact that, all unknown to him, his brother stood at his side all the time, fully conscious of his misery, and himself half-distracted at the failure of his repeated attempts to touch him or speak to him.

Affairs were still in this most pitiable condition on the third evening after the accident, when Cyril's attention was drawn to the two brothers—he cannot tell how. "He just happened to be passing," he says; yet surely the will of the Lords of Compassion guided him to the scene. Poor Walter lay exhausted yet sleepless—alone in his desolation, so far as he knew, though all the time his sorrowing brother stood beside him. Lancelot, free from the chains of the flesh, could see and hear Cyril, so obviously the first thing to do was to soothe his pain with a promise of friendship and help in communicating with his brother.

As soon as the dead boy's mind was thus cheered with hope, Cyril turned to the living one, and tried with all his strength to impress upon his brain the knowledge that his brother stood beside him, not dead, but living and loving as of yore. But all his efforts were in vain; the dull apathy of grief so filled poor Walter's mind that no suggestion from without could enter, and Cyril knew not what to do. Yet so deeply was he moved by the sad sight, so intense was his sympathy and so firm his determination to help in some way or other at any cost of strength to himself, that somehow (even to this day he cannot tell how) he found himself able to touch and speak to the heart-broken child.

Putting aside Walter's questions as to who he was and how he came there, he went straight to the point, telling him that his brother stood beside him, trying hard to make him hear his constantly repeated assurances that he was not dead, but living and yearning to help and comfort him. Little Walter longed to believe, yet hardly dared to hope; but Cyril's eager insistence vanquished his doubts at last, and he said,

"Oh! I do believe you, because you're so kind; but if I could only see him, then I should *know,* then I should be quite sure; and if I could only hear his voice telling me he was happy, I shouldn't mind a bit his going away again afterwards."

Young though he was at the work, Cyril knew enough to be aware that Walter's wish was one not ordinarily granted, and was beginning regretfully to tell him so, when suddenly he felt a Presence that all the helpers know, and though no word was spoken it was borne in upon his mind that instead of what he had meant to say, he was to promise Walter the boon his heart desired. "Wait till I come back," he said, "and you shall see him then." And then—he vanished.

That one touch from the Master had shown him what to do and how to do it, and he rushed to fetch the older friend who had so often helped him before. This older man had not yet retired for the night, but on hearing Cyril's hurried summons, he lost no time in accompanying him, and in a few minutes they were back at Walter's bedside. The poor child was just beginning to believe it all a lovely dream, and his delight and relief when Cyril reappeared were beautiful to see. Yet how much more beautiful was the scene a moment later, when, in obedience to a word from the Master, the elder man materialized the eager Lancelot, and the living and the dead stood hand in hand once more!

Now in very truth for both the brothers had sorrow been turned into joy unspeakable, and again and again they both declared that now they should never feel sad any more, because they knew that death had no power to part them. Nor was their gladness damped even when Cyril explained carefully to them, at his older friend's suggestion, that this strange physical reunion would not be repeated, but that all day long Lancelot would be near Walter, even though the latter could not see him, and every night Walter would slip out of his body and be consciously with his brother once more.

Hearing this, poor weary Walter sank to sleep at once and proved its truth, and was amazed to find with what hitherto unknown rapidity he and his brother could fly together from one to another of their old familiar haunts. Cyril thoughtfully warned him that he would probably forget most of his freer life when he awoke next day; but by rare good fortune he did *not* forget, as so many of us do. Perhaps the shock of the great joy had somewhat aroused the latent psychic faculty which belongs to the Celtic blood; at any rate he forgot no single detail of all that had happened, and next morning he burst upon the house of mourning with a wondrous tale which suited it but ill.

His parents thought that grief had turned his brain, and, since he is now the heir, they have been watching long and anxiously for further symptoms of insanity, which happily they have not found. They still think him a monomaniac on this point, though they fully recognize that his "delusion" has saved his life; but his old nurse (who is a Catholic) is firm in her belief that all he says is true—that the Lord Jesus, who was once a child himself, took pity on that other child as he lay dying of grief, and sent one of His angels to bring his brother back to him from the dead as a reward for a love which was stronger than death. Sometimes popular superstition gets a good deal nearer to the heart of things than does educated scepticism!

Nor does the story end here, for the good work begun that night is still progressing, and none can say how far the influence of that one act may ramify. Walter's astral consciousness, once having been thus thoroughly awakened, remains in activity; every morning he brings back into his physical brain the memory of his night's adventures with his brother; every night they meet their dear friend Cyril, from whom they have learned so much about the wonderful new world that has opened before them, and the other worlds to come that lie higher yet. Under Cyril's guidance they also—the living and the dead alike have become eager and earnest. members of the band of helpers; and probably for years to come—until Lancelot's vigorous young astral body disintegrates—many a dying child will have cause to be grateful to these three who are trying to pass on to others something of the joy that they have themselves received.

Nor is it to the dead alone that these new converts have been of use, for they have sought and found some other living children who show consciousness on the astral plane during sleep; and one at least of those whom they have thus brought to Cyril has already proved a valuable little recruit to the children's band, as well as a very kind little friend down here on the physical plane.

Those to whom all these ideas are new sometimes find it very difficult to understand how children can be of any use in the astral world. Seeing, they would say, that the astral body of a child must be undeveloped, and the ego thus limited by childhood on the astral as well as the physical plane, in what way could such an ego be of use, or be able to help towards the spiritual, mental and moral evolution of humanity, which we are told is the chief concern of the helpers?

When first such a question was asked, shortly after the publication of one of these stories in our magazine, I sent it to Cyril himself, to see what he would say to it, and his answer was this:

"It is quite true, as the writer says, that I am only a boy, and know very little yet, and that I shall be much more useful when I have learnt more. But I am able to do a little even now, because there are so many people who have learnt nothing about Theosophy yet, though they may know very much more than I do about everything else. And you see when you want to get to a certain place, a little boy who knows the way can do more for you than a hundred wise men who don't know it."

It may be added that when even a child had been awakened upon the astral plane the development of the astral body would proceed so rapidly that he would very soon be in a position upon that plane but little inferior to that of the awakened adult, and would of course be much in advance, so far as usefulness is concerned, of the wisest man who was as yet unawakened. But unless the ego expressing himself through that child-body possessed the necessary qualification of a determined yet loving disposition, and had clearly manifested it in his previous lives, no occultist would take the very serious responsibility of awakening him upon the astral plane. When, however, their karma is such that it is possible for them to be thus aroused, children often prove most efficient helpers, and throw themselves into their work with a whole-souled devotion which is very beautiful to see. And so is fulfilled once more the ancient prophecy "a little child shall lead them."

Another question that suggests itself to one's mind in reading this last story of the two brothers is this Since Cyril was somehow able to materialize himself by sheer force of love and pity and strength of will, is it not strange that Lancelot, who had been trying so much longer to communicate, had not succeeded in doing the same thing?

Well, there is of course no difficulty in seeing why poor Lancelot was unable to communicate with his brother, for that inability is simply the normal condition of affairs; the wonder is that Cyril *was* able to materialize himself, not that Lancelot was *not*. Not only, however, was the feeling probably stronger in Cyril's case, but he also knew exactly what he wanted to do—knew that such a thing as materialization was a possibility, and had some general idea as to how it was done—while Lancelot naturally knew nothing of all this then, though he does now.

Chapter XI.

Wrecks and Catastrophes.

Sometimes it is possible for members of the band of helpers to avert impending catastrophes of a somewhat larger order. In more than one case when the captain of a vessel has been carried unsuspecting far out of his course by some unknown current or through some mistaken reckoning, and has thereby run into serious danger, it has been possible to prevent shipwreck by repeatedly impressing upon his mind a feeling that something was wrong; and although this generally comes through into the captain's brain merely as a vaguely warning intuition, yet if it occurs again and again he is almost certain to give it some attention and take such precautions as suggest themselves to him.

In one case, for example, in which the master of a barque was much nearer in to the land than he supposed, he was again and again pressed to heave the lead, and though he resisted this suggestion for some time as being unnecessary and absurd, he at last gave the order in a somewhat hesitating way. The result astounded him, and he at once put his vessel about and stood off from the coast, though it was not until morning came that he realized how very close he had been to an appalling disaster.

Often, however, a catastrophe is karmic in its nature, and consequently cannot be averted; but it must not therefore be supposed that in such cases no help can be given. It may be that the people concerned are destined to die, and therefore cannot be saved from death; but in many cases they may still be to some extent prepared for it, and may certainly be helped upon the other side after it is over. Indeed, it may be definitely stated that wherever a great catastrophe of any kind takes place, there is also a special sending of help.

Two recent cases in which such help was given were the sinking of the *Drummond Castle* off Cape Ushant, and the terrible cyclone which devastated the city of St. Louis in America. On both these occasions a few minutes' notice was given, and the helpers did their best to calm and raise men's minds, so that when the shock came upon them it would be less disturbing than it might otherwise have been. Naturally, however, the greater part of the work done with the victims in both these calamities was done upon the astral plane after they had left their physical bodies; but of this we shall speak later.

It is sad to relate how often when some catastrophe is impending the helpers are hindered in their kindly offices by wild panic among those whom the danger threatens—or sometimes, worse still, by a mad outburst of drunkenness among those whom they are trying to assist. Many a ship has gone to her doom with almost every soul on board mad with drink, and therefore utterly incapable of profiting by any assistance offered either before death or for a very long time afterwards.

If it should ever happen to any of us to find ourselves in a position of imminent danger which we can do nothing to avert, we should try to remember that help is certainly near us, and that it rests entirely with ourselves to make the helper's work easy or difficult. If we face the danger calmly and bravely, recognizing that the true ego can in no way be affected by it, our minds will then be open to receive the guidance which the helpers are trying to give, and this cannot but be best for us, whether its object be to save us from death or, when that is impossible, to conduct us safely through it.

Assistance of this latter kind has not infrequently been given in cases of accidents to individuals, as well as of more general catastrophes. It will be sufficient to mention one example as an illustration of what is meant. In one of the great storms which did so much damage around our coasts a few years ago, it happened that a fishing boat was capsized far out at sea. The only people on board were an old fisherman and a boy, and the former contrived to cling for a few minutes to the overturned boat. There was no physical help at hand, and even if there had been in such a raging storm it would have been impossible for anything to be done, so that the fisherman knew well enough that there was no hope of escape, and that death could only be a question of a few moments. He felt great terror at the prospect, being especially impressed by the awful loneliness of that vast waste of waters, and he was also much troubled with thoughts of his wife and family, and the difficulties in which they would be left by his sudden decease.

A passing helper seeing all this endeavoured to comfort him, but finding his mind too much disturbed to be impressionable, she thought it advisable to show herself to him in order to assist him the better. In relating the story afterwards she said that the change which came over the fisherman's face at sight of her was wonderful and beautiful to see; with the shining form standing upon the boat above him he could not but think that an angel had been sent to comfort him in his trouble, and therefore he felt that not only would he himself be carried safely through the gates of death, but his family would assuredly be looked after also. So, when death came to him a few moments later, he was in a frame of mind very different from the terror and preplexity which had previously overcome him; and naturally when he recovered consciousness upon the astral plane and found the "angel" still beside him he felt himself at home with her, and was prepared to accept her advice as regards the new life upon which he had entered.

Some time later the same helper was engaged in another piece of work of very similar character, the story of which she has since told as follows:

"You remember that steamer that went down in the cyclone at the end of last November; I betook myself to the cabin where about a dozen women had been shut in, and found them wailing in the most pitiful manner, sobbing and moaning with fear. The ship had to founder— no aid was possible—and to go out of the world in this state of frantic terror is the worst possible way to enter the next. So in order to calm them I materialized myself, and of course they thought I was an angel, poor souls; they all fell on their knees and prayed me to save them, and one poor mother pushed her baby into my arms imploring me to save that at least. They soon grew quiet and composed as we talked, and the wee baby went to sleep smiling, and presently they all fell asleep peacefully, and I filled their minds with thoughts of the heaven-world, so that they did not wake up when the ship made her final plunge downwards. I went down with them to ensure their sleeping through the last moments, and they never stirred as their sleep became death."

Evidently in this case, too, those who were thus helped had not only the enormous advantage of being enabled to meet death calmly and reasonably, but also the still greater one of being received on its farther shore by one whom they were already disposed to love and trust—one who thoroughly understood the new world in which they found themselves, and could not only reassure them as to their safety, but advise them how to order their lives under these much altered circumstances. And this brings us to the consideration of one of the largest and most important departments of the work of invisible helpers—the guidance and assistance which they are able to give to the dead.

CHAPTER XII.

Work Among the Dead.

It is one of the many evils resulting from the absurdly erroneous teaching as to conditions after death which is unfortunately current in our western world, that those who have recently shaken off this mortal coil are usually much puzzled and often very seriously frightened at finding everything so different from what their religion had led them to expect. The mental attitude of a large number of such people was pithily voiced the other day by an English general, who three days after his death met one of the band of helpers whom he had known in physical life. After expressing his great relief that he at last found someone with whom he was able to communicate, his first remark was: "But if I am dead, where am I? For if this is heaven I don't think much of it; and if it is hell, it is better than I expected."

But unfortunately a far greater number take things less philosophically. They have been taught that all men are destined to eternal flames except a favoured few who are superhumanly good; and since a very small amount of self-examination convinces them that they do not belong to *that* category, they are but too often in a condition of panic terror, dreading every moment that the new world in which they find themselves may dissolve and drop them into the clutches of the devil, in whom they have been sedulously taught to believe. In many cases they spend long periods of acute mental suffering before they can free themselves from the fatal influence of this blasphemous doctrine of everlasting punishment—before they can realize that the world is governed, not according to the caprice of a hideous demon who gloats over human anguish, but according to a benevolent and wonderfully patient law of evolution, which is absolutely just indeed, but yet again and again offers to man opportunities of progress, if he will but take them, at every stage of his career.

It ought in fairness to be mentioned that it is only among what are called protestant communities that this terrible evil assumes its most aggravated form. The great Roman Catholic Church, with its doctrine of purgatory, approaches much more nearly to a conception of the astral plane, and its devout members at any rate realize that the state in which they find themselves shortly after death is merely a temporary one, and that it is their business to endeavour to raise themselves out of it as soon as may be by intense spiritual aspiration, while they accept any suffering which may come to them as necessary for the wearing away of the imperfections in their character before they can pass to higher and brighter regions.

It will thus be seen that there is plenty of work for the helpers to do among the newly dead, for in the vast majority of cases they need to be calmed and reassured, to be comforted and instructed. In the astral, just as in the physical world, there are many who are but little disposed to take advice from those who know better than they; yet the very strangeness of the conditions surrounding them renders many of the dead willing to accept the guidance of those to whom these conditions are obviously familiar; and many a man's stay on that plane has been considerably shortened by the earnest efforts of this band of energetic workers.

Not, be it understood, that the karma of the dead man can in any way be interfered with; he has built for himself during life an astral body of a certain degree of density, and until that body is sufficiently dissolved he cannot pass on into the heaven-world beyond; but he need not lengthen the period necessary for that process by adopting an improper attitude.

All students ought clearly to grasp the truth that the length of a man's astral life after he has put off his physical body depends mainly upon two factors—the nature of his past physical life, and his attitude of mind after what we call death. During his earth-life he is constantly influencing the building of matter into his astral body. He affects it directly by the passions, emotions, and desires which he allows to hold sway over him; he affects it indirectly by the action upon it of his thoughts from above, and of the details of his physical life—his continence or his debauchery, his cleanliness or his uncleanliness, his food and his drink—from below.

If by persistence in perversity along any of these lines he is so stupid as to build for himself a coarse and gross astral vehicle, habituated to responding only to the lower vibrations of the plane, he will find himself after death bound to that plane during and long and slow process of that body's disintegration. On the other hand if by decent and careful living he gives himself a vehicle mainly composed of finer material, he will have very much less *post-mortem* trouble and discomfort, and his evolution will proceed much more rapidly and easily.

This much is generally understood, but the second great factor—his attitude of mind after death—seems often to be forgotten. The desirable thing is for him to realize his position on this particular little arc of his evolution—to learn that he is at this stage withdrawing steadily inward towards the plane of the true ego, and that consequently it is his business to disengage his thoughts as far as may be from things physical, and to fix his attention more and more upon those spiritual matters which will occupy him during his life in the heaven-world. By doing this he will greatly facilitate the natural astral disintegration, and will avoid the sadly common mistake of unnecessarily delaying himself upon the lower levels of what should be so temporary a residence.

But many of the dead very considerably retard the process of dissolution by clinging passionately to the earth which they have left; they simply will not turn their thoughts and desires upward, but spend their time in struggling with all their might to keep in full touch with the physical plane, thus causing great trouble to any one who may be trying to help them. Earthly matters are the only ones in which they have ever had any living interest, and they cling to them with desperate tenacity even after death. Naturally as time passes on they find it increasingly difficult to keep hold of things down here, but instead of welcoming and encouraging this process of gradual refinement and spiritualization they resist it vigorously by every means in their power.

Of course the mighty force of evolution is eventually too strong for them, and they are swept on in its beneficent current, yet they fight every step of the way, thereby not only causing themselves a vast amount of entirely unnecessary pain and sorrow, but also very seriously delaying their upward progress and prolonging their stay in astral regions to an almost indefinite extent. In convincing them that this ignorant and disastrous opposition to the cosmic will is contrary to the laws of nature, and persuading them to adopt an attitude of mind which is the exact reversal of it, lies a great part of the work of those who are trying to help.

It happens occasionally that the dead are earthbound by anxiety—anxiety sometimes about duties unperformed or debts undischarged, but more often on account of wife or children left unprovided for. In such cases as this it has more than once been necessary, before the dead man was satisfied to pursue his upward path in peace, that the helper should to some extent act as his representative upon the physical plane, and attend on his behalf to the settlement of the business which was troubling him. An illustration taken from our recent experience will perhaps make this clearer.

One of the band of pupils was trying to assist a poor man who had died in one of our western cities, but found it impossible to withdraw his mind from earthly things because of his anxiety about two young children whom his death had left without means of support. He had been a working man of some sort, and had been unable to lay by any money for them; his wife had died some two years previously and his landlady, though exceedingly kindhearted and very willing to do anything in her power for them, was herself far too poor to be able to adopt them, and very reluctantly came to the conclusion that she would be obliged to hand them over to the parish authorities. This was a great grief to the dead father, though he could not blame the landlady, and was himself unable to suggest any other course.

Our friend asked him whether he had no relative to whom he could entrust them, but the father knew of none. He had a younger brother, he said, who would certainly have done something for him in this extremity, but he had lost sight of him for fifteen years, and did not even know whether he was living or dead. When last heard of he had been apprenticed to a carpenter in the north, and he was then described as a steady young fellow who, if he lived, would surely get on.

The clues at hand were certainly very slight, but since there seemed no other prospect of help for the children, our friend thought it worth while to make a special effort to follow them up. Taking the dead man with him he commenced a patient search after the brother in the town indicated; and after a great deal of trouble they were actually successful in finding him. He was now a master carpenter in a fairly flourishing way of business—married, but without children though earnestly desiring them, and therefore apparently just the man for the emergency.

The question now was how the information could best be conveyed to this brother. Fortunately he was found to be so far impressionable that the circumstances of his brother's death and the destitution of his children could be put vividly before him in a dream, and this was repeated three times, the place and even the name of the landlady being clearly indicated to him. He was immensely impressed by this recurring vision, and discussed it earnestly with his wife, who advised him to write to the address given. This he did not like to do, but was strongly inclined to travel down into the west country, find out whether there was such a house as that which he had seen, and if so make some excuse to call there. He was a busy man, however, and he finally decided that he could not afford to lose a day's work for what after all might well prove to be nothing but the baseless fabric of a dream.

The attempt along these lines having apparently failed, it was determined to try another method, so one of the helpers wrote a letter to the man detailing the circumstances of his brother's death and the position of the children, exactly as he had seen them in his dream. On receipt of this confirmation he no longer hesitated, but set off the very next day for the town indicated, and was received with open arms by the kind-hearted landlady. It had been easy enough for the helpers to persuade her, good soul that she was, to keep the children with her for a few days on the chance that something or other would turn up for them, and she has ever since congratulated herself that she did so. The carpenter of course took the children back with him and provided them with a happy home, and the dead father, now no longer anxious, passed rejoicing on his upward way.

Since some Theosophical writers have felt it their duty to insist in vigorous terms upon the evils so frequently attendant upon the holding of spiritualistic séances, it is only fair to admit that on several occasions good work similar to that of the helper in the case just described has been done through the agency of a medium or of some one present at a circle. Thus, though spiritualism has too often detained souls who but for it would have attained speedier liberation, it must be set to the credit of its account that it has also furnished the means of escape to others, and thus opened up the path of advancement for them. There have been instances in which the defunct has been able to appear unassisted to his relatives or friends and explain his wishes to them; but these are naturally rare, and most souls who are earth-bound by anxieties of the kind indicated can satisfy themselves only by means of the services of the medium or the conscious helper.

Another case very frequently encountered on the astral plane is that of the man who cannot believe that he is dead at all, Indeed, most people consider the very fact that they are still conscious to be an absolute proof that they have not passed through the portals of death; somewhat of a satire this, if one thinks of it, on the practical value of our much-vaunted belief in the immortality of the soul! However they may have labelled themselves during life, the great majority of those who die, in this country at any rate, show themselves by their subsequent attitude to have been to all intents and purposes materialists at heart; and those who on earth have honestly called themselves so are often no more difficult to deal with than others who would have been shocked at the very name.

A very recent instance was that of a scientific man who, finding himself fully conscious, and yet under conditions differing radically from any that he had ever experienced before, had persuaded himself that he was still alive, and merely the victim of a prolonged and unpleasant dream. Fortunately for him there happened to be among the band of those able to function upon the astral plane a son of an old friend of his, a young man whose father had commissioned him to search for the departed scientist and endeavour to render him some assistance. When after some trouble the youth found and accosted him, he frankly admitted that he was in a condition of great bewilderment and discomfort, but still clung desperately to his dream hypothesis as on the whole the most probable explanation of what he saw, and even went so far as to suggest that his visitor was nothing but a dream-figure himself!

At last, however, he so far gave way as to propose a kind of test, and said to the young man, "If you are, as you assert, a living person, and the son of my old friend, bring me from him some message that shall prove to me your objective reality." Now although under all ordinary conditions of the physical plane the giving of any kind of phenomenal proof is strictly forbidden to the pupils of the Masters, it seemed as though a case of this kind hardly came under the rules; and therefore, when it had been ascertained that there was no objection on the part of higher authorities, an application was made to the father, who at once sent a message referring to a series of events which had occurred before the son's birth. This convinced the dead man of the real existence of his young friend, and therefore of the plane upon which they were both functioning; and as soon as he felt this established, his scientific training at once reasserted itself, and he became exceeding eager to acquire all possible information about this new region.

Of course the message which he so readily accepted as evidence was in reality no proof at all, since the facts to which it referred might have been read from his own mind or from the records of the past by any creature possessed of astral senses! But his ignorance of these possibilities enabled this definite impression to be made upon him, and the Theosophical instruction which his young friend is now nightly giving to him will undoubtedly have a stupendous effect upon his future, for it cannot but greatly modify not only the heaven-state which lies immediately before him, but also his next incarnation upon earth.

The main work, then, done for the newly dead by our helpers is that of soothing and comforting them—of delivering them when possible from the terrible though unreasoning fear which but too often seizes them, and not only causes them much unnecessary suffering, but retards their progress to higher spheres—and of enabling them as far as may be to comprehend the future that lies before them.

Others who have been longer on the astral plane may also receive much help, if they will but accept it, from explanations and advice as to their course through its different stages. They may, for example, be warned of the danger and delay caused by attempting to communicate with the living through a medium, and sometimes (though rarely) an entity already drawn into a spiritualistic circle may be guided into higher and healthier life. Teaching thus given to persons on this plane is by no means lost, for though the memory of it cannot of course be directly carried over to the next incarnation, there always remains the real inner knowledge, and therefore the strong predisposition to accept it immediately when heard again in the new life.

A rather remarkable instance of service rendered to the dead was the first achievement of a very recent recruit to the band of helpers—one who is hardly as yet a fully-fledged member. This young aspirant had not long before lost an aged relation, for whom he had felt an especially warm affection; and his earliest request was to be taken by a more experienced friend to visit her in the hope that he might be of some service to her. This was done and the effect of the meeting of the living and the dead was very beautiful and touching. The older person's astral life was already approaching its end, but a condition of apathy, dullness and uncertainty prevented her from making any immediate progress.

But when the boy, who had been so much to her in earth-life, stood once more before her and dissolved by the sunlight of his love the grey mist of depression which had gathered around her, she was aroused from her stupor; and soon she understood that he had come in order to explain to her her situation, and to tell her of the glories of the higher life toward which her thoughts and aspirations ought now to be directed. But when this was fully realized, there was such an awakening of dormant feeling in her and such an outrush of devoted affection towards her earnest young helper, that the last fetters which bound her to the astral life were broken, and that one great outburst of love and gratitude swept her forthwith into the higher consciousness of the heaven-world. Truly there is no greater and more beneficent power in the universe than that of pure, unselfish love.

CHAPTER XIII.

OTHER BRANCHES OF THE WORK.

BUT turning back again now from the all-important work among the dead to the consideration of the work among the living, we must briefly indicate a great branch of it, without a notice of which our account of the labours of our invisible helpers would indeed be incomplete, and that is the immense amount which is done by suggestion—by simply putting good thoughts into the minds of those who are ready to receive them.

Let there be no mistake as to what is meant here. It would be perfectly easy—easy to a degree which would be quite incredible to those who do not understand the subject practically—for a helper to dominate the mind of any average man, and make him think just as he pleased, and that without arousing the faintest suspicion of any outside influence in the mind of the subject. But, however admirable the result might be, such a proceeding would be entirely inadmissible. All that may be done is to throw the good thought into the person's mind as one among the hundreds that are constantly sweeping through it; whether the man takes it up, makes it his own, and acts upon it, depends upon himself entirely. Were it otherwise, it is obvious that all the good karma of the action would accrue to the helper only, for the subject would have been a mere tool, and not an actor—which is not what is desired.

The assistance given in this way is exceedingly varied in character. The consolation of those who are suffering or in sorrow at once suggests itself, as does also the endeavour to guide toward the truth those who are earnestly seeking it. When a person is spending much anxious thought upon some spiritual or metaphysical problem, it is often possible to put the solution into his mind without his being at all aware that it comes from external agency.

A pupil too may often be employed as an agent in what can hardly be described otherwise than as the answering of prayer; for though it is true that any earnest spiritual desire, such as might be supposed to find its expression in prayer, is itself a force which automatically brings about certain results, it is also a fact that such a spiritual effort offers an opportunity of influence to the Powers of Good, of which they are not slow to take advantage; and it is sometimes the privilege of a willing helper to be made the channel through which their energy is poured forth. What is said of prayers is true to an even greater extent of meditation, for those to whom this higher exercise is a possibility.

Besides these more general methods of help there are also special lines open only to the few. Again and again such pupils as are fitted for the work have been employed to suggest true and beautiful thoughts to authors, poets, artists and musicians; but obviously it is not every helper who is capable of being used in this way.

Sometimes, though more rarely, it is possible to warn persons of the danger to their moral development of some course which they are pursuing, to clear away evil influences from about some person or place, or to counteract the machinations of black magicians. It is not often that direct instruction in the great truths of nature can be given to people outside the circle of occult students, but occasionally it is possible to do something in that way by putting before the minds of preachers and teachers a wider range of thought or a more liberal view of some question than they would otherwise have taken.

Naturally as an occult student progresses on the Path he attains a wider sphere of usefulness. Instead of assisting individuals only, he learns how classes, nations and races are dealt with, and he is entrusted with a gradually increasing share of the higher and more important work done by the adepts themselves. As he acquires the requisite power and knowledge he begins to wield the greater forces of the mental and the astral planes and is shown how to make the utmost possible use of each favourable cyclic influence. He is brought into relation with those great Nirmânakâyas who are sometimes symbolized as the Stones of the Guardian Wall, and he becomes—at first of course in the very humblest capacity—one of the band of their almoners, and learns how those forces are dispersed which are the fruit of their sublime self-sacrifice. Thus he rises gradually higher and higher until, blossoming at length into adeptship, he is able to take his full share of the responsibility which lies upon the Masters of Wisdom, and to help others along the road which he has trodden.

On the mental plane the work differs somewhat, since teaching can be both given and received in a much more direct, rapid and perfect manner, while the influences set in motion are infinitely more powerful, because acting on so much higher a level. But (though it is useless to speak of it in detail at present, since so few of us are yet able to function consciously upon this plane during life) here also—and even higher still—there is always plenty of work to be done, as soon as ever we can make ourselves capable of doing it; and there is certainly no fear that for countless aeons we shall ever find ourselves without a career of unselfish usefulness open before us.

CHAPTER XIV.

THE QUALIFICATIONS REQUIRED.

How, it may be asked, are we to make ourselves capable of sharing in this great work? Well, there is no mystery as to the qualifications which are needed by one who aspires to be a helper; the difficulty is not in learning what they are, but in developing them in oneself. To some extent they have been already incidentally described, but it is nevertheless as well that they should be set out fully and categorically.

1. *Single-mindedness.* The first requisite is that we shall have recognized the great work which the Masters would have us do, and that it shall be for us the one great interest of our lives. We must learn to distinguish not only between useful and useless work, but between the different kinds of useful work, so that we may each devote ourselves to the very highest of which we are capable, and not fritter away our time in labouring at something which, however good it may be for the man who cannot yet do anything better, is unworthy of the knowledge and capacity which should be ours as Theosophists. A man who wishes to be considered eligible for employment on higher planes must begin by doing the utmost that lies in his power in the way of definite work for Theosophy down here.

Of course I do not for a moment mean that we are to neglect the ordinary duties of life. We should certainly do well to undertake no new worldly duties of any sort, but those which we have already bound upon our shoulders have become a karmic obligation which we have no right to neglect. Unless we have done to the full the duties which karma has laid upon us we are not free for the higher work. But this higher work must nevertheless be to us the one thing really worth living for—the constant background of a life which is consecrated to the service of the Masters of Compassion.

2. *Perfect self-control.* Before we can be safely trusted with the wider powers of the astral

life, we must have ourselves perfectly in hand. Our temper, for example, must be thoroughly under control, so that nothing that we may see or hear can cause real irritation in us, for the consequences of such irritation would be far more serious on that plane than on this. The force of thought is always an enormous power, but down here it is reduced and deadened by the heavy physical brain-particles which it has to set in motion. In the astral world it is far freer and more potent, and for a man with fully-awakened faculty to feel anger against a person there would be to do him serious and perhaps even fatal injury.

Not only do we need control of temper, but control of nerve, so that none of the fantastic or terrible sights that we may encounter may be able to shake our dauntless courage. It must be remembered that the pupil who awakens a man upon the astral plane incurs thereby a certain amount of responsibility for his actions and for his safety, so that unless his neophyte had courage to stand alone the whole of the older worker's time would be wasted in hovering round to protect him, which it would be manifestly unreasonable to expect.

It is to make sure of this control of nerve, and to fit them for the work that has to be done, that candidates are always made, now as in days of old, to pass what are called the tests of earth, water, air and fire.

In other words, they have to learn with that absolute certainty that comes not by theory, but by practical experience, that in their astral bodies none of these elements can by any possibility be hurtful to them—that none can oppose any obstacle in the way of the work which they have to do.

In this physical body we are fully convinced that fire will burn us, that water will drown us, that the solid rock forms an impassable barrier to our progress, that we cannot with safety launch ourselves unsupported into the ambient air. So deeply is this conviction engrained in us that it costs most men a good deal of effort to overcome the instinctive action which follows from it, and to realize that in the astral body the densest rock offers no 'impediment to their freedom of motion, that they may leap with impunity from the highest cliff, and plunge with the most absolute confidence into the heart of the raging volcano or the deepest abysses of the fathomless ocean.

Yet until a man *knows* this—knows it sufficiently to act upon his knowledge instinctively and confidently—he is comparatively useless for astral work, since in emergencies that are constantly arising he would be perpetually paralyzed by imaginary disabilities. So he has to go through his tests, and through many another strange experience—to meet face to face with calm courage the most terrifying apparitions amid the most loathsome surroundings—to show in fact that his nerve may be thoroughly trusted under any and all of the varied groups of circumstances in which he may at any moment find himself.

Further, we need control of mind and of desire; of mind, because without the power of concentration it would be impossible to do good work amid all the distracting currents of the astral plane; of desire, because in that strange world to desire is very often to have, and unless this part of our nature were well controlled we might perchance find ourselves face to face with creations of our own of which we should be heartily ashamed.

3. *Calmness.* This is another most important point—the absence of all worry and depression. Much of the work consists in soothing those who are disturbed, and cheering those who are in sorrow; and how can a helper do that work if his own aura is vibrating with constant fuss and worry, or grey with the deadly gloom that comes from perpetual depression? Nothing is more hopelessly fatal to occult progress or usefulness than our nineteenth century habit of ceaselessly worrying over trifles—of eternally making mountains out of molehills. Many of us simply spend our lives in magnifying the most absurd trivialities—in solemnly and elaborately going to work to make ourselves miserable about nothing.

Surely we who are Theosophists ought, at any rate, to have got beyond this stage of irrational worry and causeless depression; surely we, who are trying to acquire some definite knowledge of the cosmic order, ought by this time to have realized that the optimistic view of everything is always nearest to the divine view, and therefore to the truth, because only that in any person which is good and beautiful can by any possibility be permanent, while the evil must by its very nature be temporary. In fact, as Browning said, "the evil is null, is naught, is silence implying sound," while above and beyond it all "the soul of things is sweet, the Heart of Being is celestial rest." So They who know maintain unruffled calm, and with Their perfect sympathy combine the joyous serenity which comes from the certainty that all will at last be well; and those who wish to help must learn to follow Their example.

4. *Knowledge.* To be of use the man must at least have some knowledge of the nature of the plane on which he has to work, and the more knowledge he has in any and every direction the more useful he will be. He must fit himself for this task by carefully studying Theosophical literature; for he cannot expect those whose time is already so fully occupied to waste some of it in explaining to him what he might have learnt down here by taking the trouble to read the books. No one who is not already as earnest a student as his capacities and opportunities permit, need begin to think of himself as a candidate for astral work.

5. *Unselfishness.* It would seem scarcely needful to insist upon this as a qualification, for surely everyone who has made the least study of Theosophy must know that while the slightest taint of selfishness remains in a man, he is not yet fit to be entrusted with higher powers, not yet fit to enter upon a work of whose very essence it is that the worker should forget himself but to remember the good of others. He who is still capable of selfish thought, whose personality is still so strong in him that he can allow himself to be turned aside from his work by feelings of petty pride or suggestions of wounded dignity—that man is not yet ready to show the selfless devotion of the helper.

6. *Love.* This, the last and greatest of the qualifications, is also the most misunderstood. Most emphatically it is *not* the cheap, namby-pamby backboneless sentimentalism which is always overflowing into vague platitudes and gushing generalities, yet fears to stand firm for the right lest it should be branded by the ignorant as "unbrotherly." What is wanted is the love which is strong enough *not* to boast itself, but to act without talking about it—the intense desire for service which is ever on the watch for an opportunity to render it, even though it prefers to do so anonymously—the feeling which springs up in the heart of him who has realized the great work of the Logos, and, having once seen it, knows that for him there can be in the three worlds no other. course but to identify himself with it to the utmost limit of his power—to become, in however humble a way, and at however great a distance, a tiny channel of that wondrous love of God which, like the peace of God, passeth man's understanding.

These are the qualities toward the possession of which the helper must ceaselessly strive, and of which some considerable measure at least must be his before he can hope that the Great Ones who stand behind will deem him fit for full awakening. The ideal is in truth a high one, yet none need therefore turn away disheartened, nor think that while he is still but struggling toward it he must necessarily remain entirely useless on the astral plane, for short of the responsibilities and dangers of that full awakening there is much that may safely and usefully be done.

There is hardly one among us who would not be capable of performing at least one definite act of mercy and good will each night while we are away from our bodies. Our condition when asleep is usually one of absorption in thought, be it remembered—a carrying on of the thoughts that have principally occupied us during the day, and especially of the last thought in the mind when sinking into sleep. Now if we make that last thought a strong intention to go and give help to some one whom we know to be in need of it, the soul when freed from the body will undoubtedly carry out that intention, and the help will be given. There are several cases on record in which, when this attempt has been made, the person thought of has been fully conscious of the effort of the would-be helper, and has even seen his astral body in the act of carrying out the instructions impressed upon it.

Indeed, no one need sadden himself with the thought that he can have no part nor lot in this glorious work. Such a feeling would be entirely untrue, for every one who can think can help. Nor need such useful action be confined to our hours of sleep. If you know (and who does not?) of some one who is in sorrow or suffering, though you may not be able consciously to stand in astral form by their bedside, you can nevertheless send them loving thoughts and earnest good wishes; and be well assured that such thoughts and wishes are real and living and strong—that when you so send them they do actually go and work your will in proportion to the strength which you have put into them.

Thoughts are things, intensely real things, visible enough to those whose eyes have been opened to see, and by their means the poorest man may bear his part in the good work of the world as fully as the richest. In this way at least, whether we can yet function consciously upon the astral plane or not, we all can join, and we all ought to join, the army of invisible helpers.

But the aspirant, who definitely desires to become one of the band of astral helpers who are working under the direction of the great Masters of Wisdom, will make his preparation part of a far wider scheme of development. Instead of merely endeavouring to fit himself for this particular branch of their service, he will undertake with high resolution the far greater task of training himself to follow in their footsteps, of bending all the energies of his soul to attain even as they have attained, so that his power of helping the world may not be confined to the astral plane, but may extend to those higher levels which are the true home of the divine self of man.

For him the path has been marked out long ago by the wisdom of those who have trodden it in days of old—a path of self-development which sooner or later all must follow, whether they choose to adopt it of their own free will, or to wait until, after many lives and an infinity of suffering, the slow, resistless force of evolution drives them along it among the laggards of the human family. But the wise man is he who eagerly enters upon it immediately, setting his face resolutely toward the goal of adeptship, in order that, being safe for ever from all doubt and fear and sorrow himself, he may help others into safety and happiness also. What are the steps of this Path of Holiness, as the Buddhists call it, and in what order they are arranged, let us see in our next chapter.

CHAPTER XV.

THE PROBATIONARY PATH.

EASTERN books tell us that there are four means by which a man may be brought to the beginning of the path of spiritual advancement: I. By the companionship of those who have already entered upon it. 2. By the hearing or reading of definite teaching on occult philosophy. 3. By enlightened reflection; that is to say, that by sheer force of hard thinking and close reasoning he may arrive at the truth, or some portion of it, for himself. 4. By the practice of virtue, which means that a long series of virtuous lives, though it does not necessarily involve any increase of intellectuality, does eventually develope in a man sufficient intuition to enable him to grasp the necessity of entering upon the path, and show him in what direction it lies.

When, by one or another of these means, he has arrived at this point, the way to the highest adept-ship lies straight before him, if he chooses to take it. In writing for students of occultism it is hardly necessary to say that at our present stage of development we cannot expect to learn all, or nearly all, about any but the lowest steps of this path; whilst of the highest we know little but the names, though we may get occasional glimpses of the indescribable glory which surrounds them.

According to the esoteric teachings these steps are grouped in three great divisions:

1. The probationary period, before any definite pledges are taken, or initiations (in the full sense of the word) are given. This carries a man to the level necessary to pass successfully through what in Theosophical books is usually called the critical period of the fifth round.

2. The period of pledged discipleship, or the path proper, whose four stages are often spoken of in Oriental books as the four paths of holiness. At the end of this the pupil obtains adeptship—the level which humanity should reach at the close of the seventh round.

3. What we may venture to call the official period, in which the adept takes a definite part (under the great Cosmic Law) in the government of the world, and holds a special office connected therewith. Of course every adept—every pupil even, when once definitely accepted, as we have seen in the earlier chapters—takes a part in the great work of helping forward the

evolution of man; but those standing on the higher levels take charge of special departments, and correspond in the cosmic scheme to the ministers of the crown in a well-ordered earthly state. It is not proposed to make any attempt in this book to treat of this official period; no information about it has ever been made public, and the whole subject is too far above our comprehension to be profitably dealt with in print. We will confine ourselves therefore to the two earlier divisions.

Before going into details of the probationary period it is well to mention that in most of the Eastern sacred books this stage is regarded as merely preliminary, and scarcely as part of the path at all, for they consider that the latter is really entered upon only when definite pledges have been given. Considerable confusion has been created by the fact that the numbering of the stages occasionally commences at this point, though more often at the beginning of the second great division; sometimes the stages themselves are counted, and sometimes the initiations leading into or out of them, so that in studying the books one has to be perpetually on one's guard to avoid misunderstanding.

This probationary period, however, differs considerably in character from the others; the divisions between its stages are less decidedly marked than are those of the higher groups, and the requirements are not so definite or so exacting. But it will be easier to explain this last point after giving a list of the five stages of this period, with their respective qualifications. The first four were very ably described by Mr. Mohini Mohun Chatterji in the first Transaction of the London Lodge, to which readers may be referred for fuller definitions of them than can be given here. Much exceedingly valuable information about them is also given by Mrs. Besant in her books *The Path of Discipleship* and In *the Outer Court.*

The names given to the stages will differ somewhat, for in those books the Hindu Sanskrit terminology was employed, whereas the Pâli nomenclature used here is that of the Buddhist system; but although the subject is thus approached from a different side as it were, the qualifications exacted will be found to be precisely the same in effect even when the outward form varies. In the case of each word the mere dictionary meaning will first be given in parentheses, and the explanation of it which is usually given by the teacher will follow. The first stage, then, is called among Buddhists.

1. Manodvâravajjana (the opening of the doors of the mind, or perhaps escaping by the door of the mind)—and in it the candidate acquires a firm intellectual conviction of the impermanence and worthlessness of mere earthly aims. This is often described as learning the difference between the real and the unreal; and to learn it often takes a long time and many hard lessons. Yet it is obvious that it must be the first step toward anything like real progress, for no man can enter whole-heartedly upon the path until he has definitely decided to "set his affection upon things above, not on things on the earth," and that decision comes from the certainty that nothing on earth has any value as compared with the higher life. This step is called by the Hindus the acquirement of Viveka or discrimination, and Mr. Sinnett speaks of it as the giving allegiance to the higher self.

2. Parikamma (preparation for action)—the stage in which the candidate learns to do the .right merely because it is right, without considering his own gain or loss either in this world or the future, and acquires, as the Eastern books put it, perfect indifference to the enjoyment of the fruit of his own actions. This indifference is the natural result of the previous step; for when the neophyte has once grasped the unreal and impermanent character of all earthly rewards, he ceases to crave for them; when once the radiance of the real has shone upon the soul, nothing below that can any longer be an object of desire. This higher indifference is called by the Hindus Vairâgya.

3. Upachâro (attention or conduct)—the stage in which what are called "the six qualifications" (the Shatsampatti of the Hindus) must be acquired. These are called in Pâli:

(*a*). Samo (quietude)—that purity and calmness of thought which comes from perfect control of the mind—a qualification exceedingly difficult of attainment, and yet most necessary, for unless the mind moves only in obedience to the guidance of the will it cannot be a perfect instrument for the Master's work in the future. This qualification is a very comprehensive one, and includes within itself both the; self-control and the calmness which were described in chapter xiv. as necessary for astral work.

(*b*). Damo (subjugation)—a similar mastery over, and therefore purity in, one's actions and words—a quality which again follows necessarily from its predecessor.

(*c*). Uparati (cessation)—explained as cessation from bigotry or from belief in the necessity of any act or ceremony prescribed by a particular religion—so leading the aspirant to independence of thought and to a wide and generous tolerence.

(*d*). Titikkhâ (endurance or forbearance)—by which is meant the readiness to bear with cheerfulness whatever one's karma may bring upon one, and to part with anything and everything worldly whenever it may be necessary. It also includes the idea of complete absence of resentment for wrong, the man knowing that those who do him wrong are but the instruments of his own karma.

(*e*). Samâdhâna (intentness)—one-pointedness involving the incapability of being turned aside from one's path by temptation. This corresponds very closely with the single-mindness spoken of in the previous chapter.

(*f*). Saddhâ (faith)—confidence in one's Master and oneself: confidence, that is, that the Master is a competent teacher, and that, however diffident the pupil may feel as to his own powers, he has yet within him that divine spark which when fanned into a flame will one day enable him to achieve even as his Master has done.

(4). Anuloma (direct order or succession, signifying that its attainment follows as a natural consequence from the other three)—the stage in which is acquired that intense desire for liberation from earthly life, and for union with the highest, which is called by the Hindus Mumukshatva.

5. Gotrabhû (the condition of fitness for initiation); in this stage the candidate gathers up, as it were, his previous acquisitions, and strengthens them to the degree necessary for the next great step, which will set his feet upon the path proper as an accepted pupil. The attainment of this level is followed very rapidly by initiation into the next grade. In answer to the question, "Who is the Gotrabhû?" Buddha says, "The man who is in possession of those conditions upon which the commencement of sanctification immediately ensues—he is the Gotrabhû."

The wisdom necessary for the reception of the path of holiness is called Gotrabhû-gñâna.

Now that we have hastily glanced at the steps of the probationary period, we must emphasize the point to which reference was made at the commencement—that the *perfect* attainment of these accomplishments and qualifications is not expected at this early stage. As Mr. Mohini says, "If all these are equally strong, adeptship is attained in the same incarnation." But such a result is of course extremely rare. It is in the direction of these acquirements that the candidate must easelessly strive, but it would be an error to suppose that no one has been admitted to the next step without possessing all of them in the fullest possible degree. Nor do they necessarily follow one another in the same definite order as the later steps; in fact, in many cases a man would be developing the various qualifications all at the same time—rather side by side than in regular succession.

It is obvious that a man might easily be working along a great part of this path even though he was quite unaware of its very existence, and no doubt many a good Christian, many an earnest freethinker is already far on the road that will eventually lead him to initiation, though he may never have heard the word occultism in his life. I mention these two classes especially, because in every other religion occult development is recognized as a possibility, and would certainly therefore be intentionally sought by those who felt yearnings for something more satisfactory than the exoteric faiths.

We must also note that the steps of this probationary period are not separated by initiations in the full sense of the word, though they will certainly be studded with tests and trials of all sorts and on all planes, and may be relieved by encouraging experiences, and by hints and help whenever these may safely be given. We are apt sometimes to use the word initiation somewhat loosely, as for example when it is applied to such tests as have just been mentioned; properly speaking it refers only to the solemn ceremony at which a pupil is formally admitted to a higher grade by an appointed official, who in the name of the One Initiator receives his plighted vow, and puts into his hands the new key of knowledge which he is to use on the level to which he has now attained. Such an initiation is taken at the entrance to the division which we shall next consider, and also at each passage from any one of its steps to the next.

CHAPTER XVI.
THE PATH PROPER.

IT is in the four stages of this division of the path that the ten Saṁyojana, or fetters which bind man to the circle of rebirth and hold him back from Nirvâṇa, must be cast off. And here comes the difference between this period of pledged discipleship and the previous probation. No partial success in getting rid of these fetters is sufficient now; before a candidate can pass on from one of the steps to the next he must be *entirely* free from certain of these clogs; and when they are enumerated it will be seen how far-reaching this requirement is, and there will be little cause to wonder at the statement made in the sacred books that seven incarnations are sometimes required to pass through this division of the path.

Each of these four steps or stages is again divided into four: for each has (1) its Maggo, or way, during which the student is striving to cast off the fetters; (2) its Phala (result or fruit) when he finds the results of his action in so doing showing themselves more and more; (3) its Bhavagga or consummation, the period when, the result having culminated, he is able to full satisfactorily the work belonging to the step on which he now firmly stands; and (4) its Gotrabhû, meaning, as before, the time when he arrives at a fit state to receive the next initiation. The first stage is:

I. Sotâpatti or Sohan. The pupil who has attained this level is spoken of as the Sowani or Sotâpanna—"he who has entered the stream,"—because from this period, though he may linger, though he may succumb to more refined temptations and turn aside from his course for a time, he can no longer fall back altogether from spirituality and become a mere worldling. He has entered upon the stream of definite higher human evolution, upon which all humanity must enter by the middle of the next round, unless they are to be left behind as temporary failures by the great life-wave, to wait for further progress until the next chain of worlds.

The pupil who is able to take this initiation has therefore already outstripped the majority of humanity to the extent of an entire round of all our seven planets, and in doing so has definitely secured himself against the possibility of falling out of the stream in the fifth round. He is consequently sometimes spoken of as "the saved" or "the safe one." It is from a misunderstanding of this idea that there arises the curious theory of salvation promulgated by a certain section of the Christian community. The "æonian salvation" of which some of its documents speak is not, as has been blasphemously supposed by the ignorant, from eternal torture, but simply from wasting the rest of this æon or dispensation by falling out of its line of progress. This also is the meaning, naturally, of the celebrated clause in the Athanasian Creed, "Whosoever will be saved, before all things it is necessary that he hold the catholic faith" (See *The Christian Creed,* p. 91). The fetters which he must cast off before he can pass into the next stage are:

1. Sakkâyadiṭṭhi—the delusion of self.
2. Vichikichchhâ—doubt or uncertainty.
3. Sîlabbataparâmâsa—superstition.

The first of these is the "I am I" consciousness, which as connected with the *personality* is nothing but an illusion, and must be got rid of at the very first step of the real upward path. But to cast off this fetter completely means even more than this, for it involves the realization of the fact that the individuality also is in very truth one with the All, that it can therefore never have any interests opposed to those of its brethren, and that it is most truly progressing when it most assists the progress of others.

For the very sign and seal of the attainment of the Sotâpatti level is the first entrance of the pupil into the plane next above the mental—that which we usually call the buddhic. It may be—nay, it will be—the merest touch of the lowest sub-plane of that stupendously exalted condition that the pupil can as yet experience, even with his Master's help; but even that touch is something that can never be forgotten—something that opens a new world before him, and entirely revolutionizes his feelings and conceptions. Then for the first time, by means of the extended consciousness of that plane, he truly realizes the underlying unity of all, not as an intellectual conception merely, but as a definite fact that is patent to his opened eyes; then first he really knows something of the world in which he lives—then first he gets some slight glimpse of what the love and compassion of the great Masters must be.

As to the second letter, a word of caution is necessary. We who have been trained in European habits of thought are unhappily so familiar with the idea that a blind unreasoning adhesion to certain dogmas may be claimed from a disciple, that on hearing that occultism considers *doubt* as an obstacle to progress, we are likely to suppose that it also re-requires the same unquestioning faith from its followers as modern superstitions do. No idea could be more entirely false.

It is true that doubt (or rather uncertainty) on certain questions is a bar to spiritual progress, but the antidote to that doubt is not blind faith (which is itself considered as a fetter, as will presently be seen) but the certainty of conviction founded on individual experiment or mathematical reasoning. While a child doubted the accuracy of the multiplication table he would hardly acquire proficiency in the higher mathematics; but his doubts could be satisfactorily cleared up only by his attaining a comprehension, founded on reasoning or experiment, that the statements contained in the table are true. He believes that twice two are four, not merely because he has been told so, but because it has become to him a self-evident fact. And this is exactly the method, and the only method, of resolving doubt known to occultism.

Vichikichchhâ has been defined as doubt of the doctrines of karma and reincarnation, and of the efficacy of the method of attaining the highest good by this path of holiness; and the casting off of this Saṃyojana is the arriving at absolute certainty, based either upon personal first-hand knowledge or upon reason, that the occult teaching upon these points is true.

The third fetter to be got rid of comprehends all kinds of unreasoning or mistaken belief, all dependence on the efficacy of outward rites and ceremonies to purify the heart. He who would cast it off must learn to depend upon himself alone, not upon others, nor upon the outer husk of any religion.

The first three fetters are in a coherent series. The difference between individuality and personality being fully realized, it is then possible to some extent to appreciate the actual course of reincarnation, and so as to dispel all doubt on that head. This done, the knowledge of the spiritual permanence of the true ego gives rise to reliance on one's own spiritual strength, and so dispels superstition.

II. Sakadâgâmî. The pupil who has entered upon this second stage is spoken of as a Sakridâgâmin—"the man who returns but once"—signifying that a man who has reached this level should need but one more incarnation before attaining arahatship. At this step no additional fetters are cast off, but the pupil is occupied in reducing to a minimum those which still enchain him. It is, however, usually a period of considerable psychic and intellectual advancement.

If what are commonly called psychic faculties have not been previously acquired, they must be developed at this stage, as without them it would be impossible to assimilate the knowledge which must now be given, or to do the higher work for humanity in which the pupil is now privileged to assist. He must have the astral consciousness at his command during his physical waking life, and during sleep the heaven-world will be open before him—for the consciousness of a man when away from his physical body is always one stage higher than it is while he is still burdened with the house of flesh.

III. Anâgâmî. The Anâgâmin (he who does not return) is so called because, having reached this stage, he ought to be able to attain the next one in the life he is then living. He enjoys, while moving through the round of his daily work, all the splendid possibilities of progress given by the full possession of the priceless faculties of the heaven-world, and when he leaves his physical vehicle at night he enters once more into the wonderfully-widened consciousness that belongs to the buddhi. In this step he finally gets rid of any lingering remains of the two fetters of

4. Kâmarâga—attachment to the enjoyment of sensation, typified by earthly love, and
5. Patigha—all possibility of anger or hatred.

The student who has cast off these fetters can no longer be swayed by the influence of his senses either in the direction of love or hatred, and is free from either attachment to or impatience of physical plane conditions.

Here again we must guard against a possible misconception—one with which we frequently meet. The purest and noblest human love *never* dies away—is *never* in any way diminished by occult training; on the contrary, it is increased and widened until it embraces all with the same fervor which at first was lavished on one or two. But the student does in time rise above all considerations connected with the mere *personality* of those around him, and so is free from all the injustice and partiality which ordinary love so often brings in its train.

Nor should it for a moment be supposed that in gaining this wide affection for all he loses the especial love for his closer friends. The unusually perfect link between Ânanda and the Buddha, as between S. John and Jesus, is on record to prove that on the contrary this is enormously intensified; and the tie between a Master and his pupils is stronger far than any earthly bond. For the affection which flourishes upon the path of holiness is an affection between egos, and not merely between personalities; therefore it is strong and permanent, without fear of diminution or fluctuation, for it is that "perfect love which casteth out fear."

IV. Arahat (the venerable, the perfect). On attaining this level the aspirant constantly enjoys the consciousness of the buddhic plane, and is able to use its powers and faculties while still in the physical body; and when he leaves that body in sleep or trance he passes at once into the unutterable glory of the nirvâṇic plane. In this stage the occultist must cast off the last remnants of the five remaining fetters, which are:

6. Rûparâga—desire for beauty of form or for physical existence in a form, even including that in the heaven-world.
7. Arûparâga—desire for formless life.
8. Mâno—pride.
9. Uddhachcha—agitation or irritability.
10. Avijjâ—ignorance.

On this we may remark that the casting off of Rûparâga involves not only getting rid of desire for earthly life, however grand or noble that life may be, and astral or devachanic life, however glorious, but also of all liability to be unduly influenced or repelled by the external beauty or ugliness of any person or thing.

Arûparâga—desire for life either in the highest and formless planes of the heaven-world or in the still more exalted buddhic plane—would be merely a higher and less sensual form of selfishness, and must be cast off just as much as the lower. Uddhachcha really means "liability to be disturbed in mind," and a man who had finally cast off this fetter would be absolutely unruffled by anything whatever that might happen to him—perfectly impervious to any kind of attack upon his dignified serenity.

The getting rid of ignorance of course implies the acquisition of perfect knowledge—practical omniscience as regards our planetary chain. When all the fetters are finally cast off the advancing ego reaches the fifth stage—the stage of full adeptship—and becomes

V. Asekha, "the one who has no more to learn," again as regards our planetary chain. It is quite impossible for us to realize at our present level what this attainment means. All the splendor of the nirvâṇic plane lies open before the waking eyes of the adept, while when he chooses to leave his body he has the power to enter upon something higher still—a plane which to us is the merest name. As Professor Rhys Davids explains, "He is now free from all sin; he sees and values all things in this life at their true value; all evil being rooted from his mind, he experiences only righteous desires for himself, and tender pity and regard and exalted love for others."

To show how little he has lost the sentiment of love, we read in the Metta Sutta of the state of mind of one who stands at this level: "As a mother loves, who even at the risk of her own life protects her only son, such love let there be toward all beings. Let goodwill without measure prevail in the whole world, above, below, around, unstinted, unmixed with any feeling of differing or opposing interests. When a man remains steadfastly in this state of mind all the while, whether he be standing or walking, sitting or lying down, then is come to pass the saying which is written, 'Even in this life has holiness been found.'"

CHAPTER XVII.

WHAT LIES BEYOND.

BEYOND this period it is obvious that we can know nothing of the new qualifications required for the still higher levels which yet lie before the perfect man. It is abundantly clear, however, that when a man has become Asekha he has exhausted all the possibilities of moral development, so that further advancement for him can only mean still wider knowledge and still more wonderful spiritual powers. We are told that when man has thus attained his spiritual majority, whether in the slow course of evolution or by the shorter path of self-development, he assumes the fullest control of his own destinies, and makes choice of his future line of evolution among seven possible paths which he sees opening before him.

Naturally at our present level we cannot expect to understand much about these, and the faint outline of some of them which is all that can be sketched in for us conveys very little to the mind, except that most of them take the adept altogether away from our earth-chain, which no longer affords sufficient scope for his evolution.

One path is that of those who, as the technical phrase goes, "accept Nirvâṇa." Through what incalculable æons they remain in that sublime condition, for what work they are preparing themselves what will be their future line of evolution, are questions upon which we know nothing; and indeed if information upon such points could be given it is more than likely that it would prove quite incomprehensible to us at our present stage.

But this much at least we may grasp—that the blessed state of Nirvâṇa is not, as some have ignorantly supposed, a condition of blank nothingness, but on the contrary of far more intense and beneficent activity; and that ever as man rises higher in the scale of nature his possibilities become greater, his work for others ever grander and more far-reaching and that infinite wisdom and infinite power mean for him only infinite capacity for service, because they are directed by infinite love.

Another class chooses a spiritual evolution not quite so far removed from humanity, for though not directly connected with the next chain of our system it extends through two long periods corresponding to its first and second rounds, at the end of which time they also appear to "accept Nirvâṇa," but at a higher stage than those previously mentioned.

Others join the deva evolution, whose progress lies along a grand chain consisting of seven chains like ours, each of which to them is as one world. This line of evolution is spoken of as the most gradual and therefore the least arduous of the seven courses; but though it is sometimes referred to in the books as "yielding to the temptation to become a god," it is only in comparison with the sublime height of renunciation of the Nirmânakâya that it can be spoken of in this half-disparaging manner, for the adept who chooses this course has indeed a glorious career before him, and though the path which he selects is not the shortest, it is nevertheless a very noble one.

Yet another group are the Nirmânakâyas—those who, declining all these easier methods, choose the shortest but steepest path to the heights which still lie before them. They form what is poetically termed the "guardian wall," and, as *The Voice of the Silence* tells us, "protect the world from further and far greater misery and sorrow," not indeed by warding off from it external evil influences, but by devoting all their strength to the work of pouring down upon it a flood of spiritual force and assistance, without which it would assuredly be in far more hopeless case than now.

Yet again there are those who remain even more directly in association with humanity, and continue to incarnate among it, choosing the path which leads through the four stages of what we have called above the official period ; and among these are the Masters of Wisdom—those from whom we who study Theosophy have learnt such fragments as we know of the mighty harmony of evolving Nature. But it would seem that only a certain comparatively small number adopt this course—probably only so many as are necessary for the carrying on of this physical side of the work.

In hearing of these different possibilities, people sometimes exclaim rashly that there could of course be no thought in a Master's mind of choosing any but that course which most helps humanity—a remark which greater knowledge would have prevented them from making. We should never forget that there are other evolutions in the solar system besides our own, and no doubt it is necessary for the carrying out of the vast plan of the Logos that there should be adepts working on all the seven lines to which we have referred. Surely the choice of the Master would be to go wherever his work was most needed—to place his services with absolute selflessness at the disposal of the Powers in charge of this part of the great scheme of evolution.

This then is the path which lies before us, the path which each one of us should be beginning to tread. Stupendous though its heights appear we should remember that they are attained but gradually and step by step, and that those who now stand near the summit once toiled in the mire of the valleys, even as we are doing. Although this path may at first seem hard and toilsome, yet ever as we rise our footing becomes firmer and our outlook wider, and thus we find ourselves better able to help those who are climbing beside us.

Because it is at first thus hard and toilsome to the lower self, it has sometimes been called by the very misleading title of "the path of woe;" but, as Mrs. Besant has beautifully written, "through all such suffering there is a deep and abiding joy, for the suffering is of the lower nature, and the joy of the higher. When the last shred of the personality is gone all that can thus suffer has passed away, and in the perfected Adept there is unruffled peace and everlasting joy. He sees the end toward which all is working, and rejoices in that end, knowing that earth's sorrow is but a passing phase in human evolution.

"That of which little has been said is the profound content which comes from being on the path, from realizing the goal and the way to it, from knowing that the power to be useful is increasing, and that the lower nature is being gradually extirpated. And little has been said of the rays of joy which fall upon the path from loftier levels, the dazzling glimpses of the glory to be revealed, the serenity which the storms of earth cannot ruffle. To any one who has entered on the path all other ways have lost their charm, and its sorrows have a deeper bliss than the best joys of the lower world." (Vâhan, vol. v., No. 12.)

Let no man therefore despair because he thinks the task too great for him; what man has done man can do, and just in proportion as we extend our aid to those whom we can help, so will those who have already attained be able in their turn to help us. So from the lowest to the highest we who are treading the steps of the path are bound together by one long chain of mutual service, and none need feel neglected or alone, for though sometimes the lower flights of the great staircase may be wreathed in mist, we know that it leads up to happier regions and purer air, where the light is always shining.

The Life After Death,
and how Theosophy unveils it

Fig. 1.

CHAPTER I.

IS THERE ANY CERTAIN KNOWLEDGE?

THIS subject of life after death is one of great interest to all of us, not only because we ourselves must certainly one day die, but far more because there can scarcely be any one among us, except perhaps the very young, who has not lost (as we call it) by death some one or more of those who are near and dear to us. So if there be any information available with regard to the life after death, we are naturally very anxious to have it.

But the first thought which arises in the mind of the man who sees such a title as this is usually "Can anything be certainly known as to life after death?" We have all had various theories put before us on the subject by the various religious bodies, and yet even the most devoted followers of these sects seem hardly to believe their teachings about this matter, for they still speak of death as "the king of terrors," and seem to regard the whole question as surrounded by mystery and horror. They may use the term "falling asleep in Jesus," but they still employ the black dresses and plumes, the horrible crape and the odious black-edged notepaper, they still surround death with all the trappings of woe, and with everything calculated to make it seem darker and more terrible. We have an evil heredity behind us in this matter; we have inherited these funereal horrors from our forefathers, and so we are used to them, and do not see the absurdity and monstrosity of it all. The ancients were in this respect wiser than we, for they did not associate all these nightmares of gloom with the death of the body—partly perhaps because they had a so much more rational method of disposing of the body—a method which was not only infinitely better for the dead man and more healthy for the living, but was also free from the gruesome suggestions connected with slow decay. They knew much more about death in those days, and because they knew more they mourned less.

The first thing that we must realise about death is that it is a perfectly natural incident in the course of our life. That ought to be obvious to us from the first, because if we believe at all in a God who is a loving Father we should know that a fate which, like death, comes to all alike, cannot have in it aught of evil to any, and that whether we are in this world or the next we must be equally safe in His hands. This consideration alone should have shown us that death is not something to be dreaded, but simply a necessary step in our evolution. It ought not to be necessary for Theosophy to come among Christian nations and teach that death is a friend and not an enemy, and it would not be necessary if Christianity had not so largely forgotten its own best traditions. It has come to regard the grave as "the bourne from which no traveller returns," and the passage of it as a leap in the dark, into some awful unknown void. On this point, as on many others, Theosophy has a gospel for the Western world; it has to announce that there is no gloomy impenetrable abyss beyond the grave, but instead a world of light and life, which may be known to us as clearly and fully and accurately as the streets of our own city. We have created the gloom and the horror for ourselves, like children who frighten themselves with ghastly stories, and we have only to study the facts of the case, and all these artificial clouds will roll away at once. Death is no darksome king of terrors, no skeleton with a scythe to cut short the thread of life, but rather an angel bearing a golden key, with which he unlocks for us the door into a fuller and higher life than this.

But men will naturally say "This is very beautiful and poetical, but how can we certainly know that it is really so?" You may know it in many ways; there is plenty of evidence ready to the hand of any one who will take the trouble to gather it together. Shakespeare's statement is really a remarkable one when we consider that ever since the dawn of history, and in every country of which we know anything, travellers have always been returning from that bourne, and showing themselves to their fellowmen. There is any amount of evidence for such apparitions, as they have been called. At one time it was fashionable to ridicule all such stories; now it is no longer so, since scientific men like Sir William Crookes, the discoverer of the metal thallium and the inventor of Crookes's radiometer, and Sir Oliver Lodge, the great electrician, and eminent public men like Mr. Balfour, the late Premier of England, have joined and actively worked with a society instituted for the investigation of such phenomena. Read the reports of the work of that Society for Psychical Research, and you will see something of the testimony which exists as to the return of the dead. Read books like Mr. Stead's "Real Ghost Stories," or Camille Flammarion's "L'Inconnu," and you will find there plenty of accounts of apparitions, showing themselves not centuries ago in some far-away land, but here and now among ourselves, to persons still living, who can be questioned and can testify to the reality of their experiences.

Another line of testimony to the life after death is the study of Modern Spiritualism. I know that many people think that there is nothing to be found along that line but fraud and deception; but I can myself bear personal witness that this is not so. Fraud and deception there may have been—nay, there has been—in certain cases; but nevertheless I fearlessly assert that there are great truths behind, which may be discovered by any man who is willing to devote the necessary time and patience to their unfolding. Here again there is a vast literature to be studied, or the man who prefers it may make his investigations for himself at first-hand as I did. Many men may not be willing to take that trouble or to devote so much time; very well, that is their affair, but unless they will examine, they have no right to scoff at those who have seen, and therefore know that these things are true.

A third line of evidence, which is the one most commending itself to Theosophical students, is that of direct investigation. Every man has within himself latent faculties, undeveloped senses, by means of which the unseen world can be directly cognised, and to any one who will take the trouble to evolve these powers the whole world beyond the grave will lie open as the day. A good many Theosophical students have already unfolded these inner senses, and it is the evidence thus obtained that I wish to lay before you. I know very well that this is a considerable claim to make—a claim which would not be made by any minister of any church when he gave you his version of the states after death. He will say, "The Church teaches this," or "The Bible tells us so," but he will never say, "I who speak to you, I myself have seen this, and know it to be true." But in Theosophy we are able to say to you quite definitely that many of us know personally that of which we speak, for we are dealing with a definite series of facts which we have investigated, and which you yourselves may investigate in turn. We offer you what we know, yet we say to you "Unless this commends itself to you as utterly reasonable, do not rest contented with our assertion; look into these things for yourselves as fully as you can, and then you will be in a position to speak to others as authoritatively as we do." But what are the facts which are disclosed to us by these investigations?

CHAPTER II.

THE TRUE FACTS.

THE state of affairs found as actually existing is much more rational than most of the current theories. It is not found that any sudden change takes place in man at death, or that he is spirited away to some heaven beyond the stars. On the contrary, man remains after death exactly what he was before it—the same in intellect, the same in his qualities and powers; and the conditions in which he finds himself are those which his own thoughts and desires have already created for him. There is no reward or punishment from outside, but only the actual result of what the man himself has done and said and thought while here on earth. In fact, the man makes his bed during earth life and afterwards he has to lie on it.

This is the first and most prominent fact—that we have not here a strange new life, but a continuation of the present one. We are not separated from the dead, for they are here about us all the time. The only separation is the limitation of our consciousness, so that we have lost, not our loved ones, but the power to see them. It is quite possible for us to raise our consciousness, that we can see them and talk with them as before, and all of us constantly do that, though we only rarely remember it fully. A man may learn to focus his consciousness in his astral body while his physical body is still awake, but that needs special development, and in the case of the average man would take much time. But during the sleep of his physical body every man uses his astral vehicle to a greater or lesser extent, and in that way we are daily with our departed friends. Sometimes we have a partial remembrance of meeting them, and then we say we have dreamt of them; more frequently we have no recollection of such encounters and remain ignorant that they have taken place. Yet it is a definite fact that the ties of affection are still as strong as ever, and so the moment the man is freed from the chains of his physical encasement he naturally seeks the company of those whom he loves. So that in truth the only change is that he spends the night with them instead of the day, and he is conscious of them astrally instead of physically.

The bringing through of the memory from the astral plane to the physical is another and quite separate consideration, which in no way affects our consciousness on that other plane, nor our ability to function upon it with perfect ease and freedom. Whether you recollect them or not, they are still living their life close to you, and the only difference is that they have taken off this robe of flesh which we call the body. That makes no change in them, any more than it makes a change in your personality when you remove your overcoat. You are somewhat freer, indeed, because you have less weight to carry, and precisely the same is the case with them. The man's passions, affections, emotions, and intellect are not in the least affected when he dies, for none of these belong to the physical body which he has laid aside. He has dropped this vesture, and is living in another, but he is still able to think and to feel just as before.

I know how difficult it is for the average mind to grasp the reality of that which we cannot see with our physical eyes. It is very hard for us to realise how very partial our sight is—to understand that we are living in a vast world of which we see only a tiny part. Yet science tell us with no uncertain voice that this is so, for it describes to us whole worlds of minute life of whose very existence we should be entirely ignorant as far as our senses are concerned. Nor are the creatures of those worlds unimportant because minute, for upon a knowledge of the condition and habits of some of those microbes depends our ability to preserve health, and in many cases life itself. But our senses are limited in another direction. We cannot see the very air that surrounds us; our senses would give us no indication of its existence, except that when it is in motion we are aware of it by the sense of touch. Yet in it there is a force that can wreck our mightiest vessels and throw down our strongest buildings. You see how all about us there are mighty forces which yet elude our poor and partial senses; so obviously we must beware of falling into the fatally common error of supposing that what we see is all there is to see.

We are, as it were, shut up in a tower, and our senses are tiny windows opening out in certain directions. In many other directions we are entirely shut in, but clairvoyance or astral sight opens for us one or two additional windows, and so enlarges our prospect, and spreads before us a new and wider world, which is yet part of the old one, though before we did not know of it.

Looking out into this new world, what should we first see? Supposing that one of us transferred his consciousness to the astral plane, what changes would be the first to strike him? To the first glance there would probably be very little difference, and he would suppose himself to be looking upon the same world as before. Let me explain to you why this is so—partially at least, for to explain fully would need a whole treatise upon astral physics.[1] Just as we have different conditions of matter here, the solid, the liquid, the gaseous, so are there different conditions or degrees of density of astral matter, and each degree is attracted by and corresponds to that which is similar to it on the physical plane. So that your friend would still see the walls and the furniture to which he was accustomed, for though the physical matter of which they are composed would no longer be visible to him, the densest type of astral matter would still outline them for him as clearly as ever. True, if he, examined the object closely he would perceive that all the particles were visibly in rapid motion, instead of only invisibly, as is the case on this plane; but very few men do observe closely, and so a man who dies often does not know at first that any change has come over him.

He looks about him, and sees the same rooms with which he is familiar, peopled still by

---

[1] Fuller details on this may be found in my "The Other Side of Death."

those whom he has known and loved—for they also have astral bodies, which are within the range of his new vision. Only by degrees does he realise that in some ways there is a difference. For example, he soon finds that for him all pain and fatigue have passed away. If you can at all realise what that means, you will begin to have some idea of what the higher life truly is. Think of it, you who have scarcely ever a comfortable moment, you who in the stress of your busy life can hardly remember when you last felt free from fatigue; what would it be to you never again to know the meaning of the words weariness and pain? We have so mismanaged our teaching in these Western countries on the subject of immortality that usually a dead man finds it difficult to believe that he is dead, simply because he still sees and hears, thinks and feels. "I am not dead," he will often say, "I am alive as much as ever, and better than I ever was before." Of course he is; but that is exactly what he ought to have expected, if he had been properly taught.

Realisation may perhaps come to him in this way. He sees his friends about him, but he soon discovers that he cannot always communicate with them. Sometimes he speaks to them, and they do not seem to hear; he tries to touch them, and finds that he can make no impression upon them. Even then, for some time, he persuades himself that he is dreaming, and will presently awake, for at other times (when they are what we call asleep) his friends are perfectly conscious of him, and talk with him as of old. But gradually he discovers the fact that he is after all dead, and then he usually begins to become uneasy. Why? Again because of the defective teaching which he has received. He does not understand where he is, or what has happened, since his situation is not what he expected from the orthodox standpoint. As an English general once said on this occasion, "But if I am dead, where am I? If this is heaven I don't think much of it; and if it is hell, it is better than I expected I"

CHAPTER III.

PURGATORY.

A GREAT deal of totally unnecessary uneasiness and even acute suffering has been caused by those who still continue to teach the world silly fables about non-existent bugbears instead of using reason and common sense. The baseless and blasphemous hellfire theory has done more harm than even its promoters know, for it has worked evil beyond the grave as well as on this side. But presently the "dead" man will meet with some other dead person who has been more sensibly instructed, and will learn from him that there is no cause for fear, and that there is a rational life to be lived in this new world, just as there was in the old one.

He will find by degrees that there is very much that is new as well as much that is a counterpart of that which he already knows; for in this astral world thoughts and desires express themselves in visible forms, though these are composed mostly of the finer matter of the plane. As his astral life proceeds, these become more and more prominent, for we must remember that he is all the while steadily withdrawing further and further into himself. The entire period of an incarnation is in reality occupied by the ego in first putting himself forth into matter, and then in drawing back again with the results of his effort. If the ordinary man were asked to draw a line symbolical of life, he would probably make it a straight one, beginning at birth and ending at death; but the Theosophical student should rather represent the life as a great ellipse, starting from the ego on the higher mental level and returning to him. The line would descend into the lower part of the mental plane, and then into the astral. A very small portion, comparatively, at the bottom of the ellipse, would be upon the physical plane, and the line would very soon reascend into the astral and mental planes. The physical life would therefore be represented only by that small portion of the curve which lay below the line which indicated the boundary between the astral and physical planes, and birth and death would simply be the points at which the curve crossed that line—obviously by no means the most important points of the whole.

The real central point would clearly be that furthest removed from the ego—the turning point, as it were—what in astronomy we should call the aphelion. That is neither birth nor death, but should be a middle point in the physical life, when the force from the ego has expended its outward rush, and turns to begin the long process of withdrawal. Gradually his thoughts should turn upward, he cares less and less for merely physical matters, and presently he drops the dense body altogether. His life on the astral plane commences, but during the whole of it the process of withdrawal continues. The result of this is that as time passes he pays less and less attention to the lower matter of which counterparts of physical objects are composed, and is more and more occupied with that higher matter of which thought-forms are built—so far, that is, as thought-forms appear on the astral plane at all. So his Life becomes more and more a life in a world of thought, and the counterpart of the world which he has left fades from his view, not that he has changed his location in space, but that his interest is shifting its centre. His desires still persist, and the forms surrounding him will be very largely the expression of these desires, and whether his life is one of happiness or discomfort will depend chiefly upon the nature of these.

A study of this astral life shows us very clearly the reason for many ethical precepts. Most men recognise that sins which injure others are definitely and obviously wrong; but they sometimes wonder why it should be said to be wrong for them to feel jealousy, or hatred, or ambition, so long as they do not allow themselves to manifest these feelings outwardly in deed or in speech. A glimpse at this after-world shows us exactly how such feelings injure the man who harbours them, and how they would cause him suffering of the most acute character after his death. We shall understand this better if we examine a few typical cases of astral life, and see what their principal characteristics will be.

Let us think first of the ordinary colourless man, who is neither specially good, nor specially bad, nor, indeed specially anything in particular. The man is in no way changed, so colourlessness will remain his principal characteristic (if we can call it one) after his death. He will have no special suffering and no special joy, and may very probably find astral life rather dull, because he has not during his time on earth developed any rational interests. If he has had no ideas beyond gossip or what is called sport, or nothing beyond his business or his dress, he is likely to find time hang heavy on his hands when all such things are no longer possible. But the case of a man who has had strong desires of a low material type, such as could be satisfied only on the physical plane, is an even worse one. Think of the case of the drunkard or the sensualist. He has been the slave of overmastering craving during earth-life, and it still remains undiminished after death—rather, it is stronger than ever, since its vibrations have no longer the heavy physical particles to set in motion. But the possibility of gratifying this terrible thirst is for ever removed, because the body, through which alone it could be satisfied, is gone. We see that the fires of purgatory are no inapt symbols for the vibrations of such a torturing desire as this. It may endure for quite a long time, since it passes only by gradually wearing itself out, and the man's fate is undoubtedly a terrible one. Yet there are two points that we should bear in mind in considering it. First, the man has made it absolutely for himself, and determined the exact degree of its power and its duration. If he had controlled that desire during life there would have been just so much the less of it to trouble him after death. Secondly, it is the only way in which he can get rid of the vice. If he could pass from a life of sensuality and drunkenness directly into his next incarnation, he would be born a slave to his vice—it would dominate him from the beginning, and there would be for him no possibility of escape. But now that the desire has worn itself out, he will begin his new career without that burden, and the soul, having had so severe a lesson, will make every possible effort to restrain its lower vehicles from repeating such a mistake.

All this was known to the world even as lately as classical times. We see it clearly imaged for us in the myth of Tantalus, who suffered always with raging thirst, yet was doomed for ever to see the water recede just as it was about to touch his lips. Many another sin produces its result in a manner just as gruesome, although each is peculiar to itself. See how the miser will suffer when he can no longer hoard his gold, when he perhaps knows that it is being spent by alien hands. Think how the jealous man will continue to suffer from his jealousy, knowing that he has now no power to interfere upon the physical plane, yet feeling more strongly than ever. Rem-

Fig. 2.

Fig. 3.

ember the fate of Sisyphus in Greek myth—how he was condemned for ever to roll a heavy rock up to the summit of a mountain, only to see it roll down again the moment that success seemed within his reach. See how exactly this typifies the after-life of the man of worldly ambition. He has all his life been in the habit of forming selfish plans, and therefore he continues to do so in the astral world; he carefully builds up his plot until it is perfect in his mind, and only then realises that he has lost the physical body which is necessary for its achievement. Down fall his hopes; yet so ingrained is the habit that he continues again and again to roll the same stone up the same mountain of ambition, until the vice is worn out. Then at last he realises that he need not roll his rock, and lets it rest in peace at the bottom of the hill.

We have considered the case of the ordinary man, and of the man who differs from the ordinary because of his gross and selfish desires. Now let us examine the case of the man who differs from the ordinary in the other direction—who has some interests of a rational nature. In order to understand how the after-life appears to him, we must bear in mind that the majority of men spend the greater part of their waking life and most of their strength in work that they do not really like, that they would not do at all if it were not necessary in order to earn their living, or support those who are dependent upon them. Realise the condition of the man when all necessity for this grinding toil is over, when it is no longer needful to earn a living, since the astral body requires no food nor clothing nor lodging. Then for the first time since earliest childhood that man is free to do precisely what he likes, and can devote his whole time to whatever may be his chosen occupation—so long, that is, as it is of such a nature as to be capable of realisation without physical matter. Suppose that a man's greatest delight is in music; upon the astral plane he has the opportunity of listening to all the grandest music that earth can produce, and is even able under these new conditions to hear far more in it than before, since here other and fuller harmonies than our dull ears can grasp are now within his reach. The man whose delight is in art, who loves beauty in form and colour, has all the loveliness of this higher world before him from which to choose. If his delight is in beauty in Nature, he has unequalled possibilities for indulging it; for he can readily and rapidly move from place to place, and enjoy in quick succession wonders of Nature which the physical man would need years to visit. If his fancy turns towards science or history, the libraries and the laboratories of the world are at his disposal, and his comprehension of processes in chemistry and biology would be far fuller than ever before, for now he could see the inner as well as the outer workings, and many of the causes as well as the effects. And in all these cases there is the wonderful additional delight that no fatigue is possible. Here we know how constantly, when we are making some progress in our studies or our experiments, we are unable to carry them on because our brain will not bear more than a certain amount of strain; outside of the physical no fatigue seems to exist, for it is in reality the brain and not the mind that tires.

All this time I have been speaking of mere selfish gratification, even though it be of the rational and intellectual kind. But there are those among us who would not be satisfied without something higher than this—whose greatest joy in any life would consist in serving their fellow-men. What has the astral life in store for them? They will pursue their philanthropy more vigorously than ever, and under better conditions than on this lower plane. There are thousands whom they can help, and with far greater certainty of really being able to do good than we usually attain in this life. Some devote themselves thus to the general good; some are especially occupied with cases among their own family or friends, either living or dead. It is a strange inversion of the facts, this employment of those words living and dead; for surely we are the dead, we who are buried in these gross, cramping physical bodies; and they are truly the living, who are so much freer and more capable, because less hampered. Often the mother who has passed into that higher life will still watch over her child, and be to him a veritable guardian angel; often the "dead" husband still remains within reach, and in touch with his sorrowing wife, thankful if even now and then he is able to make her feel that he lives in strength and love beside her as of yore.

If all this be so, you may think, then surely the sooner we die the better; such knowledge seems almost to place a premium on suicide! If you are thinking solely of yourself and of your pleasure, then emphatically that would be so. But if you think of your duty towards God and towards your fellows, then you will at once see that this consideration is negatived. You are here for a purpose—a purpose which can only be attained upon this physical plane. The soul has to take much trouble, to go through much limitation, in order to gain this earthly incarnation, and therefore its efforts must not be thrown away unnecessarily. The instinct of self-preservation is divinely implanted in our breasts, and it is our duty to make the most of this earthly life which is ours, and to retain it as long as circumstances permit. There are lessons to be learnt on this plane which cannot be learnt anywhere else, and the sooner we learn them the sooner we shall be free for ever from the need of return to this lower and more limited life. So none must dare to die until his time comes, though when it does come he may well rejoice, for indeed he is about to pass from labour to refreshment. Yet all this which I have told you now is insignificant beside the glory of the life which follows it—the life of the heaven-world. This is the purgatory—that is the endless bliss of which monks have dreamed and poets sung—not a dream after all, but a living and glorious reality. The astral life is happy for some, unhappy for others, according to the preparation they have made for it; but what follows it is perfect happiness for all, and exactly suited to the needs of each.

Before closing this chapter let us consider one or two questions which are perpetually recurring to the minds of those who seek information about the next life. Shall we be able to make progress there, some will ask? Undoubtedly, for progress is the rule of the Divine Scheme. It is possible to us just in proportion to our development. The man who is a slave to desire can only progress by wearing out his desire; still, that is the best that is possible at his stage. But the man who is kindly and helpful learns much in many ways through the work which he is able to do in that astral life; he will return to earth with many additional powers and qualities because of the practice he has had in unselfish effort. So we need have no fear as to this question of progress.

Another point often raised is, shall we recognise our loved ones who have passed on before us? Assuredly we shall, for neither they nor we shall be changed; why, then, should we not recognise them? The attraction is still there, and will act as a magnet to draw together those who feel it, more readily and more surely there than here. True, that if the loved one has left this earth very long ago, he may have already passed beyond the astral plane, and entered the heaven-life; that case we must wait until we also reach that level before we can rejoin him, but when that is gained we shall possess our friend more perfectly than in this prison-house we can ever realise. But of this be sure, that those whom you have loved are not lost; if they have died recently, then you will find them on the astral plane; if they have died long ago, you will find them in the heaven-life, but in any case the reunion is sure where the affection exists. For love is one of the mightiest powers of the universe, whether it be in life or in death.

There is an infinity of interesting information to be given about this higher life. You should read the literature; read Mrs. Besant's "Death and After," and my own books on "The Astral Plane" and "The Other Side of Death." It is very well worth your while to study this subject, for the knowledge of the truth takes away all fear of death, and makes life easier to live, because we understand its object and its end. Death brings no suffering, but only joy, for those who live the true, the unselfish life. The old Latin saying is literally true—*Mors janua vitæ*—death is the gate of life. That is exactly what it is—a gate into a fuller and higher life. On the other side of the grave, as well as on this, prevails the great law of Divine Justice, and we can trust as implicitly there as here to the action of that law, with regard both to ourselves and to those we love.

CHAPTER IV.

THE HEAVEN-WORLD.

ALL religions agree in declaring the existence of heaven and in stating that the enjoyment of its bliss follows upon a well-spent earthly life. Christianity and Mohammedanism speak of it as a reward assigned by God to those who have pleased Him, but most other faiths describe it rather as the necessary result of the good life, exactly as we should from the Theosophical point of view. Yet though all religions agree in painting this happy life in glowing terms, none of them have succeeded in producing an impression of reality in their descriptions. All that is written about heaven is so absolutely unlike anything that we have known, that many of the descriptions seem almost grotesque to us. We should hesitate to admit this with regard to the legends familiar to us from our infancy, but if the stories of one of the other great religions were read to us, we should see it readily enough. In Buddhist or Hindu books you will find magniloquent accounts of interminable gardens, in which the trees are all of gold and silver, and their fruits of various kinds of jewels, and you might be tempted to smile, unless the thought occurred to you that after all, to the Buddhist or Hindu our tales of streets of gold and gates of pearl might in truth seem quite as improbable. The fact is that the ridiculous element is imported into these accounts only when we take them literally, and fail to realise that each scribe is trying the same task from his point of view, and that all alike are failing because the great truth behind it all is utterly indescribable. The Hindu writer had no doubt seen some of the gorgeous gardens of the Indian kings, where just such decorations as he describes are commonly employed. The Jewish scribe had no familiarity with such things, but he dwelt in a great and magnificent city—probably Alexandria; and so his conception of splendour was a city, but made unlike anything on earth by the costliness of its material and its decorations. So each is trying to paint a truth which is too grand for words by employing such similes as are familiar to his mind.

There have been those since that day who have seen the glory of heaven, and have tried in their feeble way to describe it. Some of our own students have been among these, and in the Theosophical Manual No. 6[1] you may find an effort of my own in that direction. We do not speak now of gold and silver, of rubies and diamonds, when we wish to convey the idea of the greatest possible refinement and beauty of colour and form; we draw our similes rather from the colours of the sunset, and from all the glories of sea and sky, because to us these are the more heavenly. Yet those of us who have seen the truth know well that in all our attempts at description we have failed as utterly as the Oriental scribes to convey any idea of a reality which no words can ever picture, though every man one day shall see it and know it for himself.

For this heaven is not a dream; it is a radiant reality; but to comprehend anything of it we must first change one of our initial ideas on the subject. Heaven is not a place, but a state of consciousness. If you ask me "Where is heaven?" I must answer you that it is here—round you at this very moment, near to you as the air you breathe. The light is all about you, as the Buddha said so long ago; you have only to cast the bandage from your eyes and look. But what is this casting away of a bandage? Of what is it symbolical? It is simply a question of raising the consciousness to a higher level, of learning to focus it in the vehicle of finer matter. I have already spoken of the possibility of doing this with regard to the astral body, thereby seeing the astral world; this needs simply a further stage of the same process, the raising of the consciousness to the mental plane, for man has a body for that level also, through which he may receive its vibrations, and so live in the glowing splendour of heaven while still possessing a physical body—though indeed after such an experience he will have little relish for the return to the latter.

The ordinary man reaches this state of bliss only after death, and not immediately after it except in very rare cases. I have explained how after death the Ego steadily withdrew into himself. The whole astral life is in fact a constant process of withdrawal, and when in course of time the soul reaches the limit of that plane, he dies to it in just the same way as he did to the physical plane. That is to say, he casts off the body of that plane, and leaves it behind him while he passes on to higher and still fuller life. No pain or suffering of any kind precedes this second death, but just as with the first, there is usually a period of unconsciousness, from which the man awakes gradually. Some years ago I wrote a book called "The Devachanic Plane," in which I endeavoured to some extent to describe what he would see, and to tabulate as far as I could the various subdivisions of this glorious Land of Light, giving instances which had been observed in the course of our investigations in connection with this heaven-life. For the moment I shall try to put the matter before you from another point of view, and those who wish may supplement the information by reading the book as well.

Perhaps the most comprehensive opening statement is that this is the plane of the Divine Mind, that here we are in the very realm of thought itself, and that everything that man

---

[1] "The Devachanic Plane, or the Heaven-World."

possibly could think is here in vivid living reality. We labour under a great disadvantage from our habit of regarding material things as real, and those which are not material as dream-like and therefore unreal; whereas the fact is that everything which is material is buried and hidden in this matter, and so whatever of reality it may possess is far less obvious and recognisable than it would be when regarded from a higher standpoint. So that when we hear of a world of thought, we immediately think of an unreal world, built out of "such stuff as dreams are made of," as the poet says.

Try to realise that when a man leaves his physical body and opens his consciousness to astral life, his first sensation is of the intense vividness and reality of that life, so that he thinks "Now for the first time I know what it is to live." But when in turn he leaves that life for the higher one, he exactly repeats the same experience, for this life is in turn so much fuller and wider and more intense than the astral that once more no comparison is possible. And yet there is another life yet, beyond all this, unto which even this is but as moonlight unto sunlight; but it is useless at present to think of that.

There may be many to whom it sounds absurd that a realm of thought should be more real than the physical world; well, it must remain so for them until they have some experience of a life higher than this, and then in one moment they will know far more than any words can ever tell them.

On this plane, then, we find existing the infinite fulness of the Divine Mind, open in all its limitless affluence to every soul, just in proportion as that soul has qualified himself to receive. If man had already completed his destined evolution, if he had fully realised and, unfolded the divinity whose germ is within him, the whole of this glory would be within his reach; but since none of us has yet done that, since we are only gradually rising towards that splendid consummation, it comes that none as yet can grasp that entirely, but each draws from it and cognises only so much as he has by previous effort prepared himself to take. Different individuals bring very different capabilities; as the Eastern simile has it, each man brings his own cup, and some of the cups are large and some are small, but, small or large, every cup is filled to its utmost capacity; the sea of bliss holds far more than enough for all.

All religions have spoken of this bliss of heaven, yet few of them have put before us with sufficient clearness and precision this leading idea which alone explains rationally how for all alike such bliss is possible—which is, indeed, the key-note of the conception—the fact that each man makes his own heaven by selection from the ineffable splendours of the Thought of God Himself. A man decides for himself both the length and character of his heaven-life by the causes which he himself generates during his earth-life; therefore he cannot but have exactly the amount which he has deserved, and exactly the quality of joy which is best suited to his idiosyncrasies, for this is a world in which every being must, from the very fact of his consciousness there, be enjoying the highest spiritual bliss of which he is capable—a world whose power of response to his aspirations is limited only by his capacity to aspire.

He had made himself an astral body by his desires and passions during earth-life, and he had to live in it during his astral existence, and that time was happy or miserable for him according to its character. Now this time of purgatory is over, for that lower part of his nature has burnt itself away; now there remain only the higher and more refined thoughts, the noble and unselfish aspirations that he poured out during earth-life. These cluster round him, and make a sort of shell about him, through the medium of which he is able to respond to certain types of vibration in this refined matter. These thoughts which surround him are the powers by which he draws upon the wealth of the heaven-world, and he finds it to be a storehouse of infinite extent upon which he is able to draw just according to the power of those thoughts and aspirations which he generated in the physical and astral life. All the highest of his affection and his devotion is now producing its results, for there is nothing else left; all that was selfish or grasping has been left behind in the plane of desire.

For there are two kinds of affection. There is one, hardly worthy of so sublime a name, which thinks always of how much love it is receiving, in return for its investment of attachment, which is ever worrying as to the exact amount of affection which the other person is showing for it, and so is constantly entangled in the evil meshes of jealousy and suspicion.

Such feeling, grasping and full of greed, will work out its results of doubt and misery upon the plane of desire, to which it so clearly belongs. But there is another kind of love, which never stays to think how much it is loved, but has only the one object of pouring itself out unreservedly at the feet of the object of its affection, and considers only how best it can express in action the feeling which fills its heart so utterly. Here there is no limitation, because there is no grasping, no drawing towards the self, no thought of return, and just because of that there is a tremendous outpouring of force, which no astral matter could express, nor could the dimensions of the astral plane contain it. It needs the finer matter and the wider space of the higher level, and so the energy generated belongs to the mental world. Just so there is a religious devotion which thinks mainly of what it will get for its prayers, and lowers its worship into a species of bargaining; while there is also a genuine devotion, which forgets itself absolutely in the contemplation of its deity. We all know well that in our highest devotion there is something which has never yet been satisfied, that our grandest aspirations have never yet been realised, that when we really love unselfishly, our feeling is far beyond all power of expression on this physical plane, that the profound emotion stirred within our hearts by the noblest music or the most perfect art reaches to heights and depths unknown to this dull earth. Yet all of this is a wondrous force of power beyond our calculation, and it must produce its result somewhere, somehow, for the law of the conservation of energy holds good upon the higher planes of thought and aspiration just as surely as in ordinary mechanics. But since it must react upon him who set it in motion, and yet it cannot work upon the physical plane because of its narrowness and comparative grossness of matter, how and when can it produce its inevitable result? It simply waits for the man until it reaches its level; it remains as so much stored-up energy until its opportunity arrives. While his consciousness is focussed upon the physical and astral planes it cannot react upon him, but as soon as he transfers himself entirely to the mental it is ready for him, its floodgates are opened, and its action commences. So perfect justice is done, and nothing is ever lost, even though to us in this lower world it seems to have missed its aim and come to nothing.

CHAPTER V.

MANY MANSIONS.

THE key-note of the conception is the comprehension of how man makes his own heaven. Here Upon this plane of the Divine Mind exists, as we have said, all beauty and glory conceivable; but the man can look out upon it all only through the windows he himself has made. Every one of his thought-forms is such a window, through which response may come to him from the forces without. If he has chiefly regarded physical things during his earth-life, then he has made for himself but few windows through which this higher glory can shine in upon him. Yet every man will have had some touch of pure, unselfish feeling, even if it were but once in all his life, and that will be a window for him now. Every man, except the utter savage at a very early stage, will surely have something of this wonderful time of bliss. Instead of saying, as orthodoxy does, that some men will go to heaven and some to hell, it would be far more correct to say that all men will have their share of both states (if we arc to call even the lowest astral life by so horrible a name as hell), and it is only their relative proportions which differ, It must be borne in mind that the soul of the ordinary man is as yet but at an early stage of his development. He has learnt to use his physical vehicle with comparative ease, and he can also function tolerably freely in his astral body, though he is rarely able to carry through the memory of its activities to his physical brain; but his mental body is not yet in any true sense a vehicle at all, since he cannot utilise it as he does those lower bodies, cannot travel about in it, nor employ its senses for the reception of information in the normal way.

We must not think of him, therefore, as in a condition of any great activity, or as able to move about freely, as he did upon the astral levels. His condition here is chiefly receptive, and his communication with the world outside him is only through his own windows, and therefore exceedingly limited. The man who can put forth full activity there is already almost more than man, for he must be a glorified spirit, a great and highly-evolved entity. He would have full consciousness there, and would use his mental vehicle as freely as the ordinary man employs his physical body, and through it vast fields of higher knowledge would lie open to him.

But we are thinking of one as yet less developed than this—one who has his windows, and sees only through them. In order to understand his heaven we must consider two points: His relation to the plane itself, and his relation to his friends. The question of his relation to his surroundings upon the plane divides itself into two parts, for we have to think first of the matter of the plane as moulded by his thought, and secondly of the forces of the plane as evoked in answer to his aspirations.

I have mentioned how man surrounds himself with thought-forms; here on this plane we are in the very home of thought, so naturally those forms are all-important in connection with both these considerations. There are living forces about him, mighty angelic inhabitants of the plane, and many of their orders are very sensitive to certain aspirations of man, and readily respond to them. But naturally both his thoughts and his aspirations are only along the lines which he has already prepared during earth-life. It might seem that when he was transferred to a plane of such transcendent force and vitality he might well be stirred up to entirely new activities along hitherto unwonted lines; but this is not possible. His mind-body is not in by any means the same order as his lower vehicles, and is by no means so fully under his control. All through a past of many lives it has been accustomed to receive its impressions and incitements to action from below, through the lower vehicles, chiefly from the physical body, and sometimes from the astral; it has done very little in the way of receiving direct mental vibrations at its own level, and it cannot suddenly begin to accept and respond to them. Practically, then, the man does not initiate any new thoughts, but those which he has already form the windows through which he looks out on his new world.

With regard to these windows there are two possibilities of variation—the direction in which they look, and the kind of glass of which they are composed. There are very many directions which the higher thought may take. Some of these; such as affection and devotion, are so generally of a personal character that it is perhaps better to consider them in connection with the man's relation to other people; let us rather take first an example where that element does not come in—where we have to deal only with the influence of his surroundings. Suppose that one of his windows into heaven is that of music. Here we have a very mighty force; you know how wonderfully music can uplift a man, can make him for the time a new being in a new world; if you have ever experienced its effect you will realise that here we are in the presence of a stupendous power. The man that has no music in his soul has no window open in that direction; but a man who has a musical window will receive through it three entirely distinct sets of impressions, all of which, however, will be modified by the kind of glass he has in his window. It is obvious that his gloss may be a great limitation to his view; it may be coloured, and so admit only certain rays of light, or it may be of poor material, and so distort and darken all the rays as they enter. For example, one man may have been able while on earth to appreciate only one class of music, and so on. But suppose his musical window to be a good one, what will he receive through it?

First, he will sense that music which is the expression of the ordered movement of the forces of the plane. There was a definite fact behind the poetic idea of the music of the spheres, for on these higher planes all movement and action of any kind produces glorious harmonies both of sound and colour. All thought expresses itself in this way—his own as well as that of others—in a lovely yet indescribable series of ever-changing chords, as of a thousand Æolian harps. This musical manifestation of the vivid and glowing life of heaven would be for him a kind of ever-present and ever-delightful background to all his other experiences.

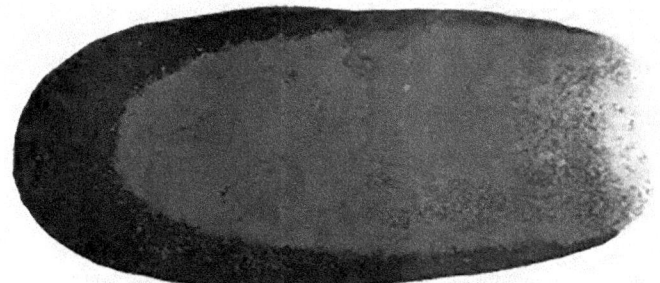

Fig. 4.

Fig. 5.

Secondly, there is among the inhabitants of the plane one class of entities—one great order of angels, as our Christian friends would call them, who are specially devoted to music, and habitually express themselves by its means to a far fuller extent than the rest. They are spoken of in old Hindu books under the name of Gandharvas. The man whose soul is in tune with music will certainly attract their attention, and will draw himself into connection with some of them, and so will learn with ever-increasing enjoyment all the marvellous new combinations which they employ. Thirdly, he will be a keenly appreciative listener to the music made by his fellow-men in the heaven-world. Think how many great composers have preceded him: Bach, Beethoven, Mendelssohn, Handel, Mozart, Rossini—all are there, not dead but full of vigorous life, and ever pouring forth far grander strains, far more glorious harmonies, than any which they knew on earth. Each of these is indeed a fountain of wondrous melody, and many an inspiration of our earthly musicians is in reality but a faint and far-off echo of the sweetness of their song. Very far more than we realise of the genius of this lower world is naught but a reflection of the untrammelled powers of those who have gone before, us; oftener than we think the man who is receptive here can catch some thought from them, and reproduce it, so far as may be possible, in this lower sphere. Great masters of music have told us how they sometimes hear the whole of some grand oratorio, some stately march, some noble chorus in one resounding chord; how it is in this way that the inspiration comes to them, though when they try to write it down in notes, many pages of music may be necessary to express it. That exactly expresses the manner in which the heavenly music differs from that which we know here; one mighty chord there will convey what here would, take hours to render far less effectively.

Very similar would be the experiences of the man whose window was art. He also would have the same three possibilities of delight, for the order of the plane expresses itself in colour as well as in sound, and all Theosophical students are familiar with the fact that there is a colour language of the Devas—an order of spirits whose very communication one with another is by flashings of splendid colour. Again, all the great artists of mediaeval times are working still—not with brush and canvas, but with the far easier, yet infinitely more satisfactory, moulding of mental matter by the power of thought. Every artist knows how far below the conception in his mind is the most successful expression of it upon paper or canvas; but here to think is to realise, and disappointment is impossible. The same thing is true of all directions of thought, so that there is in truth an infinity to enjoy and to learn, far beyond all that, our limited minds can grasp down here.

CHAPTER VI.

OUR FRIENDS IN HEAVEN.

BUT let us turn to the second part of our subject, the question of the man's relations with persons whom he loves, or with those for whom he feels devotion or adoration. Again and again people ask us whether they will meet and know their loved ones in this grander life, whether amid all this unimaginable splendour they will look in vain for the familiar faces without which all would for them seem vanity. Happily to this question the answer is clear and unqualified; the friends will be there without the least shadow of doubt, and far more fully, far more really, than ever they have been with us yet.

Yet again, men often ask "what of our friends already in the enjoyment of the heaven-life; can they see us here below? Are they watching us and waiting for us?" Hardly; for there would be difficulties in the way of either of these theories. How could the dead be happy if he looked back and saw those whom he loved in sorrow or suffering, or, far worse still, in the commission of sin? And if we adopt the other alternative, that he does not see, but is waiting, the case is scarcely better. For then the man will have a long and wearisome period of waiting, a painful time of suspense, often extending over many years, while the friend would in many cases arrive so much changed as to be no longer sympathetic. On the system so wisely provided for us by Nature all these difficulties are avoided; those whom the man loves most he has ever with him, and always at their noblest and best, while no shadow of discord or change can ever come between them, since he receives from them all the time exactly what he wishes. The arrangement is infinitely superior to anything which the imagination of man has been able to offer us in its place—as indeed we might have expected—for all those speculations were man's idea of what is best, but the truth is God's idea. Let me try to explain it.

Whenever we love a person very deeply we form a strong mental image of him, and he is often present in our mind. Inevitably we take his mental image into the heaven-world with us, because it is to that level of matter that it naturally belongs. But the love which forms and retains such an image is a very powerful force—a force which is strong enough to reach and act upon the soul of that friend, the real man whom we love. That soul at once and eagerly responds, and pours himself into the thought-form which we have made for him, and in that way we find our friend truly present with us, more vividly than ever before. Remember, it is the soul we love, not the body; and it is the soul that we have with us here. It may be said, "Yes, that would be so if the friend were also dead; but suppose he is still alive; he cannot be in two places at once." The fact is that, as far as this is concerned, he can be in two places at once, and often many more than two; and whether he is what we commonly call living, or what we commonly call dead, makes not the slightest difference. Let us try to understand what a soul really is, and we shall see better how this may be.

The soul belongs to a higher plane, and is a much greater and grander thing than any manifestation of it can be. Its relation to its manifestations is that of one dimension to another—that of a line to square, or a square to a cube. No number of squares could ever make a cube, because the square has only two dimensions, while the cube has three. So no number of expressions on any lower plane can eve] exhaust the fulness of the soul, since he stands upon an altogether higher level. He puts down a small portion of himself into a physical body in order to acquire experience which can only be had on this plane; he can take only one such body at a time, for that is the law; but if he could take a thousand, they would not be sufficient to express what he really is. He may have only one physical body, but if he has evoked such love from a friend, that that friend has a strong mental image of him always present in his thought, then he is able to respond to that love by pouring into that thought-form his own life, and so vivifying it into a real expression of him on this level, which is two whole planes higher than the physical, and therefore so much the better able to express his qualities.

If it still seems difficult to realise how his consciousness can be active in that manifestation as well as in this, compare with this an ordinary physical experience. Each of us, as he sits in his chair, is conscious at the same instant of several physical contacts. He touches the seat of the chair, his feet rest on the ground, his hands feel the arms of the chair, or perhaps hold a book; and yet his brain had no difficulty in realising all these contacts at once; why, then, should it be harder for the soul, which is so much greater than the mere physical consciousness, to be conscious simultaneously in more than one of these manifestations on planes so entirely below him? It is really the one man who feels all those different contacts; it is really the one man who feels all these different thought-images, and is real, living and loving in all of them. You have hind there always at his best, for this is a far fuller expression than the physical plane could ever give, even under the best of circumstances.

Will this affect the evolution of the friend in any way, it may be asked? Certainly it will, for it allows him an additional opportunity of manifestation. If he has a physical body he is already learning physical lessons through it, but this enables him at the very same time to develop the quality of affection much more rapidly through the form on the mental plan which you have given him. So your love for him is doing great things for him. As we have said, the soul may manifest in many images if he is fortunate enough to have them made for him. One who is much loved by many people may have part in many heavens simultaneously, and so may evolve with far greater rapidity; but this vast additional opportunity is the direct result and reward of those lovable qualities which drew towards him the affectionate regard of so many of his fellow-men. So not only does he receive love from all these, but through that receiving he himself grows in love, whether these friends be living or dead.

We should observe, however, that there are two possible limitations to the perfection of this intercourse. First, your image of your friend may be partial and imperfect, so that many of his higher qualities may not be represented, and may therefore be unable to show themselves forth through it. Then, secondly, there may be some difficulty from your friend's side. You may have formed a conception somewhat inaccurately; if your friend be as yet not a highly evolved soul, it is possible that you may even have overrated him in some direction, and in that case there might be some aspect of your thought imago which he could not completely fill. This, however, is unlikely, and could only take place when a quite unworthy object had been unwisely idolised. Even then the man who made the image would not find any change or lack in his friend, for the latter is at least better able to fulfil his ideal than he has ever been during physical life. Being undeveloped, he may not be perfect, but at least he is better than ever before, so nothing is wanting to the joy of the dweller in heaven. Your friend can fill hundreds of images with those qualities which he possesses, but when a quality is as yet undeveloped in him, he does not suddenly evolve it because you have supposed him already to have attained it. Here is the enormous advantage which those have who form images only of those who cannot disappoint them—or, since there could be no disappointment, we should rather say, of those capable of rising above even the highest conception that the lower mind can form of them. The Theosophist who forms in his mind the image of the Master knows that all the inadequacy will be on his own side, for he is drawing there upon a depth of love and power which his mental plummet can never sound.

But, it may be asked, since the soul spends so large a proportion of his time in the enjoyment of the bliss of this heaven-world, what are his opportunities of development during his stay there? They may be divided into three classes, though of each there may be many varieties. First, through certain qualities in himself he has opened certain windows into this heaven-world; by the continued exercise of those qualities through so long a time he will greatly strengthen them, and will return to earth for his next incarnation very richly dowered in that respect. All thoughts are intensified by reiteration, and the man who spends a thousand years principally in pouring forth unselfish affection will assuredly at the end of that period "mow how to love strongly and well.

Secondly, if through his window he pours forth an aspiration which brings him into contact with one of the great orders of spirits, he will certainly acquire much from his intercourse with them. In music they will use all kinds of overtones and variants which were previously unknown to him; in art they are familiar with a thousand types of which he has had no conception. But all of these will gradually impress themselves upon him, and in this way also he will come out of that glorious heaven-life richer far than he entered it.

Thirdly, he will gain additional information through the mental images which he has made, if these people themselves are sufficiently developed to be able to teach him. Once more, the Theosophist who has made the image of a Master will obtain very definite teaching and help through it, and in a lesser degree this is possible with lesser people.

Above and beyond all this comes the life of the soul or ego in his own causal body—the vehicle which he carries on with him from life to life, unchanging except for its gradual evolution. There comes an end even to that glorious heaven-life, and then the mental body in its turn drops away as the others have done, and the life in the causal begins. Here the soul needs no windows, for this is his true home, and here all his walls have fallen away. The majority of men have as yet but very little consciousness at such a height as this: they rest, dreamily unobservant and scarcely awake, but such vision as they have is true, however limited by their lack of development. Still, every time they return these limitations will be smaller, and they themselves will be greater, so that this truest life will be wider and fuller for them. As the improvement continues, this causal life grows longer and longer, assuming an ever larger portion, as compared to the existence at lower levels. And as he grows the man becomes capable not only of receiving, but of giving. Then, indeed, is his triumph approaching, for he is learning the lesson of the Christ, learning the crowning glory of sacrifice, the supreme delight of pouring out all his life for the helping of his fellow-men, the devotion of the self to the all, of celestial strength to human service, of all these splendid heavenly forces to the aid of struggling sons of earth. That is part of the life that lies before us; these are some of the steps which even we, who are as yet at the very bottom of the golden ladder, may see rising above us, so that we may report them to you who have not seen them yet, in order that you, too, may open your eyes to the unimaginable splendour which surrounds you here and now in this dull daily life. This is part of the gospel which Theosophy brings to you—the certainty of this sublime future for all. It is certain because it is here already, because to inherit it we have only to fit ourselves for it.

CHAPTER VII.

GUARDIAN ANGELS.

To my mind it is one of the most beautiful points about our Theosophical teaching that it gives back to a man all the most useful and helpful beliefs of the religions which he has outgrown. There are many who, though they feel that they cannot bring themselves to accept much that they used to take as a matter of course, nevertheless look back with a certain amount of regret to some of the prettier ideas of their mental childhood. They have come up out of the twilight into fuller light, and they are thankful for the fact, and they could not return into their former attitude if they would; yet some of the dreams of the twilight were lovely, and the fuller light seems sometimes a little hard in comparison with its softer tints. Theosophy comes to their rescue here, and shows them that all the glory and the beauty and the poetry, glimpses of which they used dimly to catch in their twilight, exists as a living reality, and that instead of disappearing before the noonday glow, its splendour will be only the more vividly displayed thereby. But our teaching gives them back their poetry on quite a new basis—a basis of scientific fact instead of uncertain tradition. A very good example of such belief is to be found under our title of "Guardian Angels." There are many graceful traditions of spiritual guardianship and angelic intervention which we should all very much like to believe if we could only see our way to accept them rationally, and I hope to explain that to a very large extent we may do this.

The belief in such intervention is a very old one. Among the earliest Indian legends we find accounts of the occasional appearances of minor deities at critical points in human affairs; the Greek epics are full of similar stories, and in the history of Rome itself we read how the heavenly twins, Castor and Pollux, led the armies of the infant republic at the battle of Lake Regillus. In mediæval days St. James is recorded to have led the Spanish troops to victory, and there are many tales of angels who watched over the pious wayfarer, or interfered at the right moment to protect him from harm. "Merely a popular superstition," the superior person will say; perhaps, but wherever we encounter a popular superstition which is widely-spread and persistent, we almost invariably find some kernel of truth behind it—distorted and exaggerated often, yet a truth still. And this is a case in point.

Most religions speak to men of guardian angels, who stand by them in times of sorrow and trouble; and Christianity was no exception to this rule. But for its sins there came upon Christendom the blight which by an extraordinary inversion of truth was called the Reformation, and in that ghastly upheaval very much was lost that for the majority of us has not even yet been regained. That terrible abuses existed, and that a reform was needed in the church I should be the last to deny: yet surely the Reformation was a very heavy judgment for the sins which had preceded it. What is called Protestantism has emptied and darkened the world for its votaries, for among many strange and gloomy falsehoods it has endeavoured to propagate the theory that nothing exists to occupy the infinity of stages between the Divine and the human. It offers us the amazing conception of a constant capricious interference by the Ruler of the universe with the working of His own laws and the result of His own decrees, and this usually at the request of His creatures, who are apparently supposed to know better than He what is good for them. It would be impossible, if one could ever come to believe this, to divest one's mind of the idea that such interference might be, and indeed must be, partial and unjust. In Theosophy we have no such thought, for we hold the belief in perfect Divine justice, and therefore we recognise that there can be no intervention unless the person involved has deserved such help. Even then, it would come to him through agents, and never by direct Divine interposition. We know from our study, and many of us from our experience also, that many intermediate stages exist between the human and the Divine. The old belief in angels and archangels is justified by the facts, for just as there are various kingdoms below humanity, so there are also kingdoms above it in evolution. We find next above us, holding much the same position with regard to us that we in turn hold to the animal kingdom, the great kingdom of the devas or angels, and above them again an evolution which has been called that of the

Dhyan Chohans, or archangels (though the names given to these orders matter little), and so onward and upward to the very feet of Divinity. All is one graduated life, from God Himself to the very dust beneath our feet—one long ladder, of which humanity occupies only one of the steps. There are many steps below and above us, and every one of them is occupied. It would indeed be absurd for us to suppose that we constitute the highest possible form of development—the ultimate achievement of evolution. The occasional appearance among humanity of men much further advanced shows us our next stage, and furnishes us with an example to follow. Men such as the Buddha and the Christ, and many other lesser teachers, exhibit before our eyes a grand ideal towards which we may work, however far from its attainment we may find ourselves at the present moment.

If special interventions in human affairs occasionally take place, is it then to the angelic hosts that we may look as the probable agents employed in them? Perhaps sometimes, but very rarely, for these higher beings have their own work to do, connected with their place in the mighty scheme of things, and they are little likely either to notice or to interfere with us. Man is unconsciously so extraordinarily conceited that he is prone to think that all the greater powers in the universe ought to be watching over him, and ready to help him whenever he suffers through his own folly or ignorance. He forgets that he is not engaged in acting as a beneficent providence to the kingdoms below him, or going out of his way to look after and help the wild animals. Sometimes he plays to them the part of the orthodox devil, and breaks into their innocent and harmless lives with torture and wanton destruction, merely to gratify his own degraded lust of cruelty, which he chooses to denominate "sport"; sometimes he holds animals in bondage, and takes a certain amount of care of them, but it is only that they may work for him—not that he may forward their evolution in the abstract. How can he expect from those above him a type of supervision which he is so very far from giving to those below him? It may well be that the angelic kingdom goes about its own business, taking little more notice of us than we take of the sparrows in the trees. It may now and then happen that an angel becomes aware of some human sorrow or difficulty which moves his pity, and he may try to help us, just as we might try to assist an animal in distress; but certainly his wider vision would recognise the fact that at the present stage of evolution such interpositions would in the vast majority of cases be productive of infinitely more harm than good. In the far-distant past man was frequently assisted by these non-human agencies because then there were none as yet among our infant humanity capable of taking the lead as teachers; but now that we are attaining our adolescence, we are supposed to have arrived at a stage when we can provide leaders and helpers from among our own ranks.

There is another kingdom of Nature of which little is known—that of Nature-spirits or fairies. Here again popular tradition has preserved a trace of the existence of an order of beings unknown to science. They have been spoken of under many names—pixies, gnomes, kobolds, brownies, sylphs, undines, good people, etc., and there are few lands in whose folklore they do not play a part. They are beings possessing either astral or etheric bodies, and consequently it is only rarely and under peculiar circumstances that they become visible to man. They usually avoid his neighbourhood, for they dislike his wild outbursts of passion and desire, so that when they are seen it is generally in some lonely spot, and by some mountaineer or shepherd whose work takes him far from the busy haunts of the crowd. It has sometimes happened that one of these creatures has become attached to some human being and devoted himself to his service as will be found in stories of the Scottish Highlands; but as a rule intelligent assistance is hardly to be expected from entities of this class.

Then there are the great Adepts, the Masters of Wisdom—men like ourselves, yet so much more highly evolved that to us they seem as gods in power, in wisdom and in compassion. Their whole life is devoted to the work of helping evolution; would they therefore be likely to intervene sometimes in human affairs? Possibly occasionally, but only very rarely, because they have other and far greater work to do. The ignorant sometimes have suggested that the Adepts ought to come down into our great towns and succour the poor—the ignorant, I say, because only one who is exceedingly ignorant and incredibly presumptuous ever ventures to criticise thus the action of those so infinitely wiser and greater than himself. The sensible and modest man realises that what they do they must have good reason for doing, and that for him to blame them would be the height of stupidity and ingratitude. They have their own work on planes far higher than we can reach; they deal directly with the souls of men, and shine upon them as sunlight upon a flower, drawing them upwards and onwards, and filling them with power and life; and that is a grander work by far than healing or caring for or feeding their bodies, good though this also may be in its place. To employ them in working on the physical plane would be a waste of force infinitely greater than it would be to set our most learned men of science to the labour of breaking stones upon the road, upon the plea that that was a physical work for the good of all, while scientific work was not immediately profitable to the poor! It is not from the Adept that physical intervention is likely to come, for he is far more usefully employed.

Chapter VIII.

Human Workers in the Unseen.

THERE are two classes from whom intervention in human affairs may come, and in both cases they are men like ourselves, and not far removed from our own level. The first class consists of those whom we call the dead. We think of them as far away, but that is a delusion; they are very near us, and though in their new life they cannot usually see our physical bodies, they can and do see our astral vehicles, and therefore they know all our feelings and emotions. So they know when we are in trouble, and when we need help, and it sometimes happens that they are able to give it. Here, then, we have an enormous number of possible helpers, who may occasionally intervene in human affairs. Occasionally, but not very often; for the dead man is all the while steadily withdrawing into himself, and therefore passing rapidly out of touch with earthly things; and the most highly developed, and therefore the most helpful of men, are precisely those who must pass away from earth most quickly. Still there are undoubted cases in which the dead have intervened in human affairs; indeed, perhaps such cases are more numerous than we imagine, for in very many of them the work done is only the putting of a suggestion into the mind of some person still living on the physical plane, and he often remains unconscious of the source of his happy inspiration. Sometimes it is necessary for the dead man's purpose that he should show himself, and it is only then that we who are so blind are aware of his loving thought for us. Besides, he cannot always show himself at will; there may be many times when he tries to help, but is unable to do so, and we all the time know nothing of his offer. Still there are such cases, and some of them will be found recounted in my book on "The Other Side of Death."

The second class among which helpers may be found consists of those who are able to function consciously upon the astral plane while still living—or perhaps we had better say, while still in the physical body, for the words "living" and "dead" are in reality ludicrously misapplied in ordinary parlance.

It is we, immeshed as we are in this physical matter, buried in the dark and noisome mist of earth-life, blinded by the heavy veil that shuts out from us so much of the light and the glory that are shining around us—it is surely we who are the dead; not those who, having cast off for the time the burden of the flesh, stand amongst us radiant, rejoicing, strong, so much freer, so much more capable than we.

These who, while still in the physical world, have learnt to use their astral bodies, and in some cases their mental bodies also, are usually the pupils of the great Adepts before-mentioned. They cannot do the work which the Master does, for their powers are not developed; they cannot yet function freely on those lofty planes where He can produce such magnificent results; but they can do something at lower levels, and they are thankful to serve in whatever way He thinks best for them, and to undertake such work as is within their power. So sometimes it happens that they see some human trouble or suffering which they are able to alleviate, and they gladly try to do what they can. They are often able to help both the living

Fig. 6.

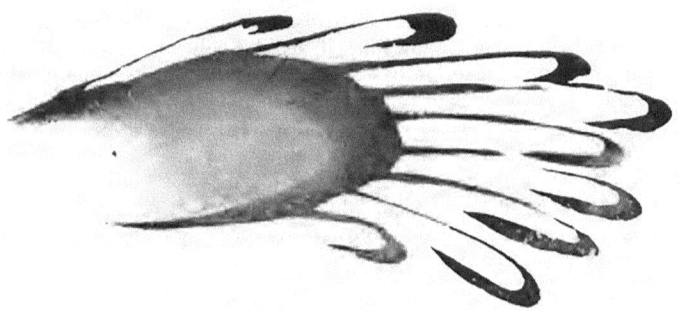

Fig. 7.

and the dead, but it must always be remembered that they work under conditions. When such power and such training are given to a man, they are given to him under restrictions. He must never use them selfishly, never display them to gratify curiosity, never employ them to pry into the business of others, never give what at Spiritualistic seances are called tests—that is to say, he must never do anything which can be proved as a phenomenon on the physical plane. He might if he chose take a message to a dead man, but it would be beyond his province to bring back a reply from the dead to the living, unless it were under direct instructions from the

Master. Thus the band of invisible helpers does not constitute itself into a detective office, nor into an astral information bureau, but it simply and quietly does such work as is given to it to do, or as comes in its way.

Let us see how a man is able to do such work and give such help as we have described, so that we may understand what are the limits of this power, and see how we ourselves may to some extent attain it. We must first think how a man leaves his body in sleep. He abandons the physical body, in order that it may have complete rest; but he himself, the soul, needs no rest, for he feels no fatigue. It is only the physical body that ever becomes tired. When we speak of mental fatigue, it is in reality a misnomer, for it is the brain and not the mind that is tired. In sleep, then, the man is simply using his astral body instead of his physical, and it is only that body. that is asleep, not the man himself. If we examine a sleeping savage with clairvoyant sight, indeed, we shall probably find that he is nearly as much asleep as his body—that he has very little definite consciousness in the astral vehicle which he is inhabiting. He is unable to move away from the immediate neighbourhood of the sleeping physical body, and if an attempt were made to draw him away he would wake in terror.

If we examine a more civilised man, as for example one of ourselves, we shall find a very great difference. In this case the man in his astral body is by no means unconscious, but quite actively thinking. Nevertheless, he may be taking very little more notice of his surroundings than the savage, though not at all for the same reason. The savage is incapable of seeing; the civilised man is so wrapped up in his own thoughts that he does not see, though he could. He has behind him the immemorial custom of a long series of lives in which the astral faculties have not been used, for these faculties have been gradually growing inside a shell, something as a chicken grows inside the egg. The shell is composed of the great mass of self-centred thought in which the ordinary man is so hopelessly entombed. Whatever may have been the thoughts chiefly engaging his mind during the past day, he usually continues them when falling asleep, and he is thus surrounded by so dense a wall of his own making that he practically knows nothing of what is going on outside. Occasionally some violent impact from without, or some strong desire of his own from within, may tear aside this curtain of mist for the moment and permit him to receive some definite impression ; but even then the fog closes in again almost immediately, and he dreams on unobservantly as before.

Can he be awakened, you will say? Yes, that may happen to him in four different ways. First, in the far-distant future the slow, but sure, evolution of the man will undoubtedly gradually dissipate the curtain of the mist. Secondly, the man himself, having learnt the facts of the case, may by steady and persistent effort clear away the mist from within, and by degrees overcome the inertia resulting from ages of inactivity. He may resolve before going to sleep to try when he leaves his body to awaken himself and see something. This is merely a hastening of the natural process, and there will be no harm in it if the man has previously developed common sense and the moral qualities. If these are defective, he may come very sadly to grief, for he runs the double danger of misusing such powers as he may acquire, and of being overwhelmed by fear in the presence of forces which he can neither understand nor control. Thirdly, it has sometimes happened that some accident, or some unlawful use of magical ceremonies, has so rent the veil that it can never wholly be closed again. In such a case the man may be left in the terrible condition so well described by Madame Blavatsky in her story of "A Bewitched Life," or by Lord Lytton in his powerful novel, "Zanoni." Fourthly, some friend who knows the man thoroughly, and believes him capable of facing the dangers of the astral plane and doing good, unselfish work there, may act upon this cloud-shell from without and gradually arouse the man to his higher possibilities. But he will never do this unless he feels absolutely sure of him, of his courage and devotion, and of his possession of the necessary qualifications for good work. If in all these ways he is judged satisfactory, he may thus be invited and enabled to join the band of helpers.

Now, as to the work such helpers can do. I have given many illustrations of this in the little book which I have written, bearing the title of "Invisible Helpers," so I will not repeat those stories now, but rather give you a few leading ideas as to the different types of work which are most usually done. Naturally it is of varied kinds, and most of it is not in any way physical; perhaps it may best be divided into work with the living and work with the dead.

The giving of comfort and consolation in sorrow or sickness at once suggests itself as a comparatively easy task, and one that can constantly be performed without any one knowing who does it.

Often efforts are made to patch up quarrels—to effect a reconciliation between those who long have been separated by some difference of opinions or of interests. Sometimes it has been possible to warn men of some great danger which impended over their heads, and thus to avert an accident. There have been cases in which this has been clone even with regard to a purely physical matter, though more generally it is against moral danger that such warnings are given. Occasionally it has been permissible to offer a solemn warning to one who was leading an immoral life, and so to help him back into the path of rectitude. If the helpers happen to know of a time of special trouble for a friend, they will endeavour to stand by him through it, and to give him strength and comfort.

In great catastrophes, too, there is often much that can be done by those whose work is unrecognised by the outer world. Sometimes it may be permitted that some one or two persons may be saved; and so it comes that in accounts of terrible wholesale destruction we hear now and then of escapes which are esteemed miraculous. But this is only when among those who are in danger there is one who is not to die in that way—one who owes to the Divine law no debt that can be paid in that fashion. In the great majority of cases all that can be done is to make some effort to impart strength and courage to face what must happen, and then afterwards to meet the souls as they arrive upon the astral plane, and welcome and assist them there.

CHAPTER IX.

HELPING THE DEAD.

THIS brings us to the consideration of what is by far the greatest and most important part of the work —the helping of the dead. Before we can understand this we must throw aside altogether the ordinary clumsy and erroneous ideas about death and the condition of the dead. They are not far away from us, they are not suddenly entirely changed, they have not become angels or demons. They are just human r beings, exactly such as they were before, neither better nor worse, and they stand close by us still, sensitive to our feelings and our thoughts even more than of yore. That is why uncontrolled grief for the dead is so wrong as well as so selfish. The dead man feels every emotion which passes through the heart of his loved ones, and if they uncomprehendingly give way to sorrow, that throws a corresponding cloud of depression over him, and makes his way harder than it need be if his friends had been better taught.

So there is much help that may be given to the dead in very many ways. First of all, many of them—indeed, most of them—need much explanation with regard to the new world in which they find themselves. Their religion ought to have taught them what to expect, and how to live amid these new conditions; but in most cases it has not done anything of the kind. So it comes that very many of them are in a condition of considerable uneasiness, and others of positive terror. They need to be soothed and comforted, for when they encounter the dreadful thought-forms which they and their kind have been making for centuries—thoughts of a personal devil and an angry and cruel Deity—they are often reduced to a pitiable state of fear, which is not only exceedingly unpleasant, but very bad for their evolution; and it often costs the helper much time and trouble to bring them into a more reasonable frame of mind.

There are men to whom this entry into a new life seems to give for the first time an opportunity to see themselves as they really are, and some of them are therefore filled with remorse. Here again the helper's services are needed to explain that what is past is past, and that the only effective repentance is the resolve to do this thing no more—that whatever the dead man may have done, he is not a lost soul, but that he must simply begin from where he finds himself, and try to live the true life for the future. Some of them cling passionately to earth, where all their thoughts and interests have been fixed, and they suffer much when they find themselves losing hold and sight of it. Others are earth-bound by the thoughts of crimes that they have committed, or duties that they have left undone, while others in turn are worried about the condition of those whom they have left behind. All these are cases which need explanation, and sometimes it is also necessary for the helper to take steps on the physical plane in order to carry out the wishes of the dead man, and so leave him free and untroubled to pass on to higher matters. People are inclined to look at the dark side of Spiritualism; but we must never forget that it has done an enormous amount of good in this sort of work—in giving to the dead an opportunity to arrange their affairs after a sudden and unexpected departure.

It is surely a happy thought that the time of much-needed repose for the body is not necessarily a period of inactivity for the true man within. I used at one time to feel that the time given to sleep was sadly wasted time; now I understand that Nature does not so mismanage her affairs as to lose one-third of the man's life. Of course there are qualifications required for this work; but I have given them so carefully and at length in my little book on the subject[1] that I need only just mention them here. First, he must be one-pointed, and the work of helping others must be ever the first and highest duty for him. Secondly, he must have perfect self-control—control over his temper and his nerves. He must never allow his emotions to interfere with his work in the slightest degree • he must be above anger, and above fear. Thirdly, he must have perfect calmness, serenity and joyousness. Men subject to depression and worry are useless, for one great part of the work is to soothe and to calm others, and how can they do that if they are all the time in a whirl of excitement or worry themselves? Fourthly, the man must have knowledge; he must have already learnt down here on this plane all that he can about the other, for he cannot expect that men there will waste valuable time in teaching him what he might have acquired for himself. Fifthly, he must be perfectly unselfish. He must be above the foolishness of wounded feelings, and must think not of himself but of the work that he has to do, so that he will be glad to take the humblest duty or the greatest duty without envy on the one hand or conceit on the other. Sixthly, he must have a heart filled with love—not sentimentalism, but the intense desire to serve, to become a channel for that love of God which, like the peace of God, passeth man's understanding.

You may think that this is an impossible standard; on the contrary, it is attainable by every man. It will take time to reach it, but assuredly it will be time well spent. Do not turn away disheartened, but set to work here and now, and strive to become fit for this glorious task, and while we are striving, do not let us wait idly, but try to undertake some little piece of work along the same lines. Every one knows some case of sorrow or distress, whether among the living or the dead does not matter; if you know such a case, take it into your mind when you lie down to sleep, and resolve as soon as you are free from this body to go to that person and endeavour to comfort him. You may not be conscious of the result, you may not remember anything of it in the morning; but be well assured that your resolve will not be fruitless, and that whether you remember what you have done or not, you will be quite sure to have done something. Some day, sooner or later, you will find evidence that you have been successful. Remember that as we help, we can be helped; remember that from the lowest to the highest we are bound together by one long chain of mutual service, and that although we stand on the lower steps of the ladder, it reaches up above these earthly mists to where the light of God is always shining.

CHAPTER X.

THOUGHTS ARE THINGS.

REFERENCE has been made to the fact that thought and emotion, besides the effect which they produce upon the physical body, cause vibration in the subtler bodies appropriate to them—the

---

[1] "Invisible Helpers."

astral and mental bodies by which each human being is surrounded. The following passages from an article by Mrs. Besant, which appeared in 1896, will help to make the matter clearer, when read in conjunction with the illustrations reproduced in this booklet.[1]

The pictures of thought-forms herewith presented were obtained as follows: two clairvoyant Theosophists observed the forms caused by definite thoughts thrown out by one of them, and also watched the forms projected by other persons under the influence of various emotions. They described these as fully and accurately as they could to an artist who sat with them, and he made sketches and mixed colours, till some approximation to the objects was made. Unfortunately the clairvoyants could not draw and the artist could not see, so the arrangement was a little like that of the blind and lame men—the blind men having good legs carried the lame ones, and the lame men having good eyes guided the blind. The artist at his leisure painted the forms, and then another committee was held and sat upon the paintings, and in the light of the criticisms then made our long suffering brother painted an almost entirely new set—the most successful attempt that has hitherto been made to present these elusive shapes in the dull pigments of earth.

All students know that what is called the Aura, of man is the outer part of the cloud-like substance of his higher bodies, interpenetrating each other, and extending beyond the confines of his physical body, the smallest of all. They know also that two of these bodies, the mental and desire bodies, are those chiefly concerned with the appearance of what are called thought-forms. But in order that the matter may be made clear for all, and not only for students already acquainted with Theosophical teachings, a recapitulation of the main facts will not be out of place.

Man, the Thinker, is clothed in a body composed of innumerable combinations of the subtle matter of the mental plane, this body being more or less refined in its constituents and organised more or less fully for its functions, according to the stage of intellectual development at which the man himself has arrived. The mental body is an object of great beauty, the delicacy and rapid motion of its particles giving it an aspect of living iridescent light, and this beauty becomes an extraordinarily radiant and entrancing loveliness as the intellect becomes more highly evolved and is employed chiefly on pure and sublime topics. Every thought gives rise to a set of correlated vibrations in the matter of this body, accompanied with a marvellous play of colour, like that in the spray of a waterfall as the sunlight strikes it, raised to the nth degree of colour and vivid delicacy. The body under this impulse throws off a vibrating portion of itself, shaped by the nature of the vibrations—as figures are made by sand on a disk vibrating to a musical note—and this gathers from the surrounding atmosphere matter like itself in fineness from the elemental essence of the mental world. We have then a thought-form pure and simple, and it is a living entity of intense activity animated by the one idea that generated it. If made of the finer kinds of matter, it will be of great power and energy, and may be used as a most potent agent when directed by a strong and steady will. Into the details of such use we will enter later. Such a thought-form, if directed to affect any object or person on the astral world, will take to itself a covering of astral materials, of fineness correlated to its own, from the elemental essence of the astral world.

When the man's energy flows outwards towards external objects of desire, or is occupied in passional and emotional activities, this energy works in a less subtle order of matter than the mental, in that of the astral world. What is called his desire-body is composed of this matter, and it forms the most prominent part of the aura in the undeveloped man. Where the man is of a gross type, the desire-body is of the denser matter of the astral plane, and is dull in hue, browns and dirty greens and reds playing a great part in it. Through this will flash various characteristic colours as his passions are excited. A man of higher type has his desire-body composed of the finer qualities of astral matter, with the colours rippling over and flashing through it fine and clear in hue. While less delicate and less radiant than the mental body it forms a beautiful object, and as selfishness is eliminated all the duller and heavier shades

---

[1] For a fuller account of these researches see "Thought Forms," by Annie Besant and C. W. Leadbeater, with 30 full-page coloured plates. Price 10s 6d, net.

disappear.

Three general principles underlie the production of all thought-forms:

1: Quality of thought determines colour.
2: Nature of thought determines form.
3: Definiteness of thought determines clearness of outline.

Colour. Colours depend on the number of vibrations that take place in a second, and this is true in the astral and mental worlds as well as in the physical. If the astral and mental bodies are vibrating under the influence of devotion, the aura will be suffused with blue, more or less intense, beautiful and pure according to the depth, elevation and purity of the feeling. In a church, such thought-forms may be seen rising, for the most part not very definitely outlined, but rolling masses of blue clouds* (Fig. 2). Too often the colour is dulled by the intermixture of selfish feelings, when the blue is mixed with browns, and thus loses its pure brilliancy. But the devotional thought of an unselfish heart is very lovely in colour, like the deep blue of a summer sky. Through such clouds of blue will often shine out golden stars of great brilliancy, darting upwards like a shower of sparks.

Anger gives rise to red, of all shades from lurid brick-red to brilliant scarlet; brutal anger will show as flashes of lurid dull red from dark-brown clouds, while the anger of "noble indignation" is a vivid scarlet, by no means unbeautiful to look at, though it gives an unpleasant thrill.

Affection, love, sends out clouds of rosy hue varying from dull crimson, where the love is animal in its nature, rose-red mingled with brown when selfish, or with dull green when jealous, to the most exquisite shades of delicate rose like the early flushes of the dawning, as the love becomes more purified from all selfish elements, and flows out in wider and wider circles of generous impersonal tenderness and compassion to all who are in need.

Intellect produces yellow thought-forms (Fig. 6), the pure reason directed to spiritual ends giving rise to a very beautiful delicate yellow, while used for more selfish ends or mingled with ambition it yields deep shades of orange, clear and intense (Fig. 7).

Form. According to the nature of the thought will be the form it generates. In the thought-forms of devotion the flower which is figured was a thought of pure devotion offered to One worshipped by the thinker, a thought of self-surrender, of sacrifice (Fig. 3).

Such thoughts constantly assume flower-like forms, exceedingly beautiful, varying much in outline but characterised by curved upward-pointing petals like azure flames. It is this flower-like characteristic of devotion that may have led to the direction, by those who saw, of offering flowers as part of religious worship, figuring in suggestive material forms that which was visible in the astral world, hinting at things unseen by things seen, and influencing the mind by an appropriate symbology. A beam of blue light, like a pencil of rays, shot upwards towards the sky, was a thought of loving devotion to the Christ from the mind of a Christian. The five-pointed star (Fig. 1, Frontispiece) was a thought directed towards the Deity, a devotional aspiration to be in harmony with cosmic law, as the expression of His nature, and it was these latter elements which gave it its geometrical form, while the mental constituents added the yellow rays. Thoughts which assume geometrical shapes, such as the circle, cube, pyramid, triangle, pentacle, double triangle, and the like, are thoughts concerned with cosmic order, or they are metaphysical concepts. Thus if this star were yellow, it would be a thought directed intellectually to the working of law, in connection with the Deity or with rational man.

Among the thought-forms of affection, Fig. 4 is very good—a thought of love, clearly defined and definitely directed towards its object. Fig. 5 is a thought which is loving but appropriate, seeking to draw to itself and to hold.

Fig. 7 is a characteristic form of a strong and ambitious thought; it was taken from the aura of a man of keen intellect and noble character, who was ambitious (and worthy) to wield power, and whose thoughts were turned to the public good. The ambitious element contributes

---

* Editor: As this book is published in black and white, the colours cannot truly be represented. I do apologise for that.

the hooked extensions, just as the grasping love in Fig. 5 causes similar protrusions

Clearness of outline. This depends entirely on the definiteness of the thought, and is a comparatively rare thing. Contrast Figs. 1, 2 and 8. Vague, dreamy devotion yields the cloudy mass of Fig. 2 and comparatively few worshippers show anything but this So the great majority of people when thinking sense out such clouds as Fig. 6. The creator of Fig. 3 knew knit what he meant, and so did the creator of Fig. 1. There was no drifting, no "wobbling," clear, pure and strong were the thoughts of these devotees. So again the person who generated the form represented by Fig. 4 had a very clear and definite love directed towards a specific object, and the maker of Fig. 7 meant to carry out the thought there outlined.

A thought of love and of desire to protect directed strongly towards some beloved object creates a form which goes to the person thought of and remains in his aura as a shielding and protecting agent; it will seek all opportunities to serve; and all opportunities to defend, not by a conscious and deliberate action, but by a blind following out of the impulse impressed upon it, and it will strengthen friendly forces that impinge on the aura and weaken unfriendly ones. Thus may we create and maintain veritable guardian angels round those we love, and many a mother's prayer for a distant child thus circles round him, though she knows not the method by which her "prayer is answered."

THE ASTRAL PLANE

IT'S SCENERY, INHABITANTS AND PHENOMENA

PREFACE.

Few words are needed in sending this little book out into the world. It is the fifth of a series of Manuals designed to meet the public demand for a simple exposition of Theosophical teachings. Some have complained that our literature is at once too abstruse, too technical, and too expensive for the ordinary reader, and it is our hope that the present series may succeed in supplying what is a very real want. Theosophy is not only for the learned; it is for all. Perhaps among those who in these little books catch their first glimpse of its teachings, there may be a few who will be led by them to penetrate more deeply into its philosophy, its science and its religion, facing its abstruser problems with the student's zeal and the neophyte's ardour. But these Manuals are not written for the eager student, whom no initial difficulties can daunt; they are written for the busy men and women of the work-a-day world, and seek to make plain some of the great truths that render life easier to bear and death easier to face. Written by servants of the Masters who are the Elder Brothers of our race, they can have no other object than to serve our fellow-men.

INTRODUCTION

REFERENCE to the astral plane, or Kâmaloka as it is called in Sanskrit, has frequently been made by Theosophical writers, and a good deal of information on the subject of this realm of nature is to be found scattered here and there in our books; but there is not, so far as I am aware, any single volume to which one can turn for a complete summary of the facts at present known to us about this interesting region. The object of this manual is to collect and make some attempt to arrange this scattered information, and also to supplement it slightly in cases where new facts have come to our knowledge. It must be understood that any such additions are only the result of the investigations of a few explorers, and must not, therefore, be taken as in any way authoritative, but are given simply for what they are worth. On the other hand every precaution in our power has been taken to ensure accuracy, no fact, old or new, being admitted to this manual unless it has been confirmed by the testimony of at least two independent trained investigators among ourselves, and has also been passed as correct by older students whose knowledge on these points is necessarily much greater than ours. It is hoped, therefore, that this account of the astral plane, though it cannot be considered as quite complete, may yet be found reliable as far as it goes.

The first point which it is necessary to make clear in describing this astral plane is its absolute *reality*. Of course in using that word I am not speaking from that metaphysical standpoint from which all but the One Unmanifested is unreal because impermanent; I am using the word in its plain, every-day sense, and I mean by it that the objects and inhabitants of the astral plane are real in exactly the same way as our own bodies, our furniture, our houses or monuments are real—as real as Charing Cross, to quote an expressive remark from one of the earliest Theosophical works. They will no more endure for ever than will objects on the physical plane, but they are nevertheless realities from our point of view while they last—realities which we cannot afford to ignore merely because the majority of mankind is as yet unconscious, or but vaguely conscious, of their existence.

There appears to be considerable misunderstanding even among Theosophical students upon this question of the reality of the various planes of the universe. This may perhaps be partly due to the fact that the word "plane" has occasionally been very loosely used in our literature—writers speaking vaguely of the mental plane, the moral plane, and so on; and this vagueness has led many people to suppose that the information on the subject which is to be found in Theosophical books is inexact and speculative—a mere hypothesis incapable of definite proof. No one can get a clear conception of the teachings of the Wisdom-Religion until he has at any rate an intellectual grasp of the fact that in our solar system there exist perfectly definite planes, each with its own matter of different degrees of density, and that some of these planes can be visited and observed by persons who have qualified themselves for the work, exactly as a foreign country might be visited and observed; and that, by comparison of the observations of those who are constantly working on these planes, evidence can be obtained of their existence and nature at least as satisfactory as that which most of us have for the existence of Greenland or Spitzbergen. The names usually given to these planes, taking them in order of materiality, rising from the denser to the finer, are the physical, the astral, the devachanic, the sushuptic, and the nirvânic. Higher than this last are two others, but they are so far above our present power of conception that for the moment they may be left out of consideration. Now it should be understood that the matter of each of these planes differs from that of the one below it in the same way as, though to a much greater degree than, vapour differs from solid matter; in fact, the states of matter which we call solid, liquid, and gaseous are merely the three lowest subdivisions of the matter belonging to this one physical plane.

The astral region which I am to attempt to describe is the second of these great planes of nature—the next above (or within) that physical world with which we are all familiar. It has often been called the realm of illusion—not that it is itself any more illusory than the physical world, but because of the extreme unreliability of the impressions brought back from it by the untrained seer. This is to be accounted for mainly by two remarkable characteristics of the astral world—first, that many of its inhabitants have a marvellous power of changing their forms with Protean rapidity, and also of casting practically unlimited glamour over those with whom they choose to sport; and secondly, that sight on that plane is a faculty very different from and much more extended than physical vision. An object is seen, as it were, from all sides at once, the inside of a solid being as plainly open to the view as the outside; it is therefore obvious that an inexperienced visitor to this new world may well find considerable difficulty in understanding what he really does see, and still more in translating his vision into the very inadequate language of ordinary speech. A good example of the sort of mistake that is likely to occur is the frequent reversal of any number which the seer has to read from the astral light, so that he would be liable to render, say, 139 as 931, and so on. In the case of a student of occultism trained by a capable Master such a mistake would be impossible except through great hurry or carelessness, since such a pupil has to go through a long and varied course of instruction in this art of seeing correctly, the Master, or perhaps some more advanced pupil, bringing before him again and again all possible forms of illusion, and asking him "What do you see?" Any errors in his answers are then corrected and their reasons explained, until by degrees the neophyte acquires a certainty and confidence in dealing with the phenomena of the astral plane which far exceeds anything possible in physical life. But he has to learn not only to see correctly but to translate the memory of what he has seen accurately from one plane to the other; and to assist him in this he is trained to carry his consciousness without break from the physical plane to the astral or devachanic and back again, for until that can be done there is always a possibility that his recollections may be partially lost or distorted during the blank interval which separates his periods of consciousness on the various planes. When the power of bringing over the consciousness is perfectly acquired the pupil will have the advantage of the use of all the astral faculties, not only while out of his body during sleep or trance, but also while fully awake in ordinary physical life.

It has been the custom of some Theosophists to speak with scorn of the astral plane, and treat it as entirely unworthy of attention; but that seems to me a somewhat mistaken view. Most assuredly that at which we have to aim is the purely spiritual plane, and it would be most disastrous for any student to neglect that higher development and rest satisfied with the attainment of astral consciousness. There are some whose Karma is such as to enable them to develop the purely spiritual faculties first of all—to over-leap the astral plane for the time, as it were; and when afterwards they make its acquaintance they have, if their spiritual development has been perfect, the immense advantage of dipping into it from above, with the aid of a spiritual insight which cannot be deceived and a spiritual strength which nothing can resist. It is, however, a mistake to suppose, as some writers have done, that this is the only, or even the ordinary method adopted by the Masters of Wisdom with their pupils. Where it is possible it saves much trouble, but for most of us such progress by leaps and bounds has been forbidden by our own faults or follies in the past: all that we can hope for is to win our way slowly step by step, and since this astral plane lies next to our world of denser matter, it is usually in connection with it that our earliest superphysical experiences take place. It is therefore by no means without interest to those of us who are but beginners in these studies, and a clear comprehension of its mysteries may often be of the greatest importance to us, not only by enabling us to understand many of the phenomena of the *séance*-room, of haunted houses, etc., which would otherwise be inexplicable, but also to guard ourselves and others from possible dangers.

The first introduction to this remarkable region comes to people in various ways. Some only once in their whole lives under some unusual influence become sensitive enough to recognize the presence of one of its inhabitants, and perhaps, because the experience does not repeat itself, come in time to believe that on that occasion they must have been the victims of hallucination: others find themselves with increasing frequency seeing and hearing something to which those around them are blind and deaf; others again—and perhaps this is the commonest experience of all—begin to recollect with greater and greater clearness that which they have seen or heard on that other plane during sleep. Among those who make a study of these subjects, some try to develop the astral sight by crystal-gazing or other methods, while those who have the inestimable advantage of the direct guidance of a qualified teacher will probably be placed upon that plane for the first time under his special protection, which will be continued until, by the application of various tests, he has satisfied himself that the pupil is proof against any danger or terror that he is likely to encounter. But, however it may occur, the first actual realization that we are all the while in the midst of a great world full of active life, of which most of us are nevertheless entirely unconscious, cannot but be to some extent a memorable epoch in a man's existence.

So abundant and so manifold is this life of the astral plane that at first it is absolutely bewildering to the neophyte; and even for the more practised investigator it is no easy task to attempt to classify and to catalogue it. If the explorer of some unknown tropical forest were asked not only to give a full account of the country through which he had passed, with accurate details of its vegetable and mineral productions, but also to state the genus and species of every one of the myriad insects, birds, beasts, and reptiles which he had seen, he might well shrink appalled at the magnitude of the undertaking: yet even this affords no parallel to the embarrassments of the psychic investigator, for in his case matters are further complicated, first by the difficulty of correctly translating from that plane to this the recollection of what he has seen, and secondly by the utter inadequacy of ordinary language to express much of what he has to report. However, just as the explorer on the physical plane would probably commence his account of a country by some sort of general description of its scenery and characteristics, so it will be well to begin this slight sketch of the astral plane by endeavouring to give some idea of the scenery which forms the background of its marvellous and ever-changing activities. Yet here at the outset an almost insuperable difficulty confronts us in the extreme complexity of the matter. All who see fully on that plane agree that to attempt to call up before those whose eyes are as yet unopened a vivid picture of this astral scenery is like speaking to a blind man of the exquisite variety of tints in a sunset sky—however detailed and elaborate the description may be, there is no certainty that the idea presented before the hearer's mind will be an adequate representation of the truth.

Scenery.

First of all, then, it must be understood that the astral plane has seven subdivisions, each of which has its corresponding degree of materiality and its corresponding condition of matter. Now numbering these from the highest and least material downwards, we find that they naturally fall into three classes, divisions 1, 2 and 3 forming one such class, and 4, 5 and 6 another, while the seventh and lowest of all stands alone. The difference between the matter of one of these classes and the next would be commensurable with that between a solid and a liquid, while the difference between the matter of the subdivisions of a class would rather resemble that between two kinds of solid, such as, say, steel and sand. Putting aside for the moment the seventh, we may say that divisions 4, 5 and 6 of the astral plane have for their background the physical world we live in and all its familiar accessories. Life on the sixth division is simply our ordinary life on this earth, minus the physical body and its necessities; while as it ascends through the fifth and fourth divisions it becomes less and less material, and is more and more withdrawn from our lower world and its interests.

The scenery of these lower divisions, then, is that of the earth as we know it: but it is also very much more; for when looked at from this different standpoint, with the assistance of the astral senses, even purely physical objects present a very different appearance. As has already been mentioned, they are seen by one whose eyes are fully opened, not as usual from one point of view, but from all sides at once—an idea in itself sufficiently confusing; and when we add to this that every particle in the interior of a solid body is as fully and clearly visible as those on the outside, it will be comprehended that under such conditions even the most familiar objects may at first be totally unrecognizable. Yet a moment's consideration will show that such vision approximates much more closely to true perception than does physical sight. Looked at on the astral plane, for example, the sides of a glass cube would all appear equal, as they really are, while on the physical plane we see the further side in perspective—that is, it appears smaller than the nearer side, which is, of course, a mere illusion. It is this characteristic of astral vision which has led to its sometimes being spoken of as sight in the fourth dimension—a very suggestive and expressive phrase. But in addition to these possible sources of error matters are further complicated by the fact that astral sight cognizes forms of matter which, while still purely physical, are nevertheless invisible under ordinary conditions. Such, for example, are the particles composing the atmosphere, all the various emanations which are always being given out by everything that has life, and also four grades of a still finer order of physical matter which, for want of more distinctive names, must all he described as etheric. The latter form a kind of system by themselves, freely interpenetrating all other physical matter; and the investigation of their vibrations and the manner in which various higher forces affect them would in itself constitute a vast field of deeply interesting study for any man of science who possessed the requisite sight for its examination.

Even when our imagination has fully grasped all that is comprehended in what has already been said, we do not yet understand half the complexity of the problem; for besides all these new forms of physical matter we have to deal with the still more numerous and perplexing subdivisions of astral matter. We must note first that every material object, every particle even, has its astral counterpart; and this counterpart is itself not a simple body, but is usually extremely complex, being composed of various kinds of astral matter. In addition to this each living creature is surrounded with an atmosphere of its own, usually called its aura, and in the case of human beings this aura forms of itself a very fascinating branch of study. It is seen as an oval mass of luminous mist of highly complex structure, and from its shape has sometimes been called the auric egg. Theosophical readers will hear with pleasure that even at the early stage of his development at which the pupil begins to acquire this astral sight, he is able to assure himself by direct observation of the accuracy of the teaching given through our great founder, Madame Blavatsky, on the subject of some at least of the seven principles of man. In regarding his fellow-man he no longer sees only his outer appearance; exactly co-extensive with that physical body he clearly distinguishes the etheric double, which in Theosophical literature has usually been called the Linga Sharîra; while the Jîva, as it is absorbed and specialized into Prâna, as it circulates in rosy light throughout the body, as it eventually radiates from the healthy person in its altered form, is also perfectly obvious. Most brilliant and most easily seen of all, perhaps, though belonging to quite a different order of matter—the astral—is the kâmic aura, which expresses by its vivid and ever-changing flashes of colour the different desires which sweep across the man's mind from moment to moment. This is the true astral body. Behind that, and consisting of a finer grade of matter—that of the rûpa levels of Devachan—lies the devachanic body or aura of the lower Manas, whose colours, changing only by slow degrees as the man lives his life, show the disposition and character of the personality; while still higher and infinitely more beautiful, where at all clearly developed, is the living light of the Kârana Sharîra, the aura or vehicle of the higher Manas, which shows the stage of development of the real Ego in its passage from birth to birth. But to see these the pupil must have developed something more than mere astral vision.

It will save the student much trouble if he learns at once to regard these auras not as mere emanations, but as the actual manifestation of the Ego on their respective planes—if he understands that it is the auric egg which is the real man, not the physical body which on this plane crystallizes in the middle of it. So long as the reincarnating Ego remains upon the plane which is his true home in the arûpa levels of Devachan, the body which he inhabits is the Kârana Sharîra, but when he descends into the rûpa levels he must, in order to be able to function upon them, clothe himself in their matter; and the matter that he thus attracts to himself furnishes his devachanic or mind-body. Similarly, descending into the astral plane he forms his astral or kâmic body out of its matter, though of course still retaining all the other bodies, and on his still further descent to this lowest plane of all the physical body is formed in the midst of the auric egg, which thus contains the entire man. Fuller accounts of these auras will be found in *Transaction* No. 18 of the London Lodge, and in a recent article of mine in *The Theosophist*, but enough has been said here to show that as they all occupy the same space (which by the way they share also with the physical health-aura), the finer interpenetrating the grosser, it needs careful study and much practice to enable the neophyte to distinguish clearly at a glance the one from the other. Nevertheless the human aura, or more usually some one part of it only, is not infrequently one of the first purely astral objects seen by the untrained, though in such a case its indications are naturally very likely to be misunderstood.

Though the kâmic aura from the brilliancy of its flashes of colour may often be more conspicuous, the nerve-ether and the etheric double are really of a much denser order of matter, being strictly speaking within the limits of the physical plane, though invisible to ordinary sight. It has been the custom in Theosophical literature to describe the Linga Sharîra as the astral counterpart of the human body, the word "astral" having been usually applied to everything beyond the cognition of our physical senses. As closer investigation enables us to be more precise in the use of our terms, however, we find ourselves compelled to admit much of this invisible matter as purely physical, and therefore to define the Linga Sharîra no longer as the astral, but as the etheric double. This seems an appropriate name for it, since it consists of various grades of that matter which scientists call "ether," though this proves on examination to be not a separate substance, as has been generally supposed, but a condition of finer subdivision than the gaseous, to which any kind of physical matter may be reduced by the application of the appropriate forces. The name "etheric double" will therefore for the future be used in Theosophic writings instead of "Linga Sharîra": and this change will not only give us the advantage of an English name which is clearly indicative of the character of the body to which it is applied, but will also relieve us from the frequent misunderstandings which have arisen from the fact that an entirely different signification is attached in all the Oriental books to the name we have hitherto been using. It must not however be supposed that in making this alteration in nomenclature we are in any way putting forward a new conception; we are simply altering, for the sake of greater accuracy, the labels previously attached to certain facts in nature. If we examine with psychic faculty the body of a newly-born child, we shall find it permeated not only by astral matter of every degree of density, but also by the several grades of etheric matter; and if we take the trouble to trace these inner bodies backwards to their origin, we find that it is of the latter that the etheric double—the mould upon which the physical body is built up—is formed by the agents of the LORDS of Karma; while the astral matter has been gathered together by the descending Ego—not of course consciously, but automatically—as he passes through the astral plane. (See *Manual* No. IV., p. 44.)

Into the composition of the etheric double must enter something of all the different grades of etheric matter; but the proportions may vary greatly, and are determined by several factors, such as the race, sub-race, and type of a man, as well as by his individual Karma. When it is remembered that these four subdivisions of matter are made up of numerous combinations, which, in their turn, form aggregations that enter into the composition of the "atom" of the so-called "element" of the chemist, it will be seen that this second principle of man is highly complex, and the number of its possible variations practically infinite, so that, however complicated and unusual a man's Karma may be, the LIPIKA are able to give a mould in accordance with which a body exactly suiting it can be formed.

One other point deserves mention in connection with the appearance of physical matter when looked at from the astral plane, and that is that the astral vision possesses the power of magnifying at will the minutest physical particle to any desired size, as though by a microscope, though its magnifying power is enormously greater than that of any microscope ever made or ever likely to be made. The hypothetical molecule and atom postulated by science are therefore visible realities to the occult student, though the latter recognizes them as much more complex in their nature than the scientific man has yet discovered them to be. Here again is a vast field of study of absorbing interest to which a whole volume might readily be devoted; and a scientific investigator who should acquire this astral sight in perfection, would not only find his experiments with ordinary and known phenomena immensely facilitated, but would also see stretching before him entirely new vistas of knowledge needing more than a lifetime for their thorough examination. For example, one curious and very beautiful novelty brought to his notice by the development of this vision would be the existence of other and entirely different colours beyond the limits of the ordinarily visible spectrum, the ultra-red and ultra-violet rays which science has discovered by other means being plainly perceptible to astral sight. We must not, however, allow ourselves to follow these fascinating bye-paths, but must resume our endeavour to give a general idea of the appearance of the astral plane.

It will by this time be obvious that though, as above stated, the ordinary objects of the physical world form the background to life on certain levels of the astral plane, yet so much more is seen of their real appearance and characteristics that the general effect differs widely from that with which we are familiar. For the sake of illustration take a rock as an example of the simpler class of objects. When regarded with trained sight it is no mere inert mass of stone. First of all, the whole of the physical matter of the rock is seen instead of a very small part of it; secondly, the vibrations of its physical particles are perceptible; thirdly, it is seen to possess an astral counterpart composed of various grades of astral matter, whose particles are also in constant motion; fourthly, the Jîva or universal life is seen to be circulating through it and radiating from it; fifthly, an aura will be seen surrounding it, though this is, of course, much less extended and varied than in the case of the higher kingdoms; sixthly, its appropriate elemental essence is seen permeating it, ever active but ever fluctuating. In the case of the vegetable, animal and human kingdoms, the complications are naturally much more numerous.

It may be objected by some readers that no such complexities as these are described by most of the psychics who occasionally get glimpses of the astral world, nor are they reported at *séances* by the entities that manifest there; but this is readily accounted for. Few untrained persons on that plane, whether living or dead, see things as they really are until after very long experience; even those who do see fully are often too dazed and confused to understand or remember: and among the very small minority who both see and remember there are hardly any who can translate the recollection into language on our lower plane. Many untrained psychics never examine their visions scientifically at all: they simply obtain an impression which may be quite correct, but may also be half false, or even wholly misleading.

All the more probable does the latter hypothesis become when we take into consideration the frequent tricks played by sportive denizens of the other world, against which the untrained person is usually absolutely defenceless. It must also be remembered that the regular inhabitant of the astral plane, whether he be human or elemental, is under ordinary circumstances conscious only of the objects of that plane, physical matter being to him as entirely invisible as is astral matter to the majority of mankind. Since, as before remarked, every physical object has its astral counterpart, which *would* be visible to him, it may be thought that the distinction is a trivial one, yet it is an essential part of the symmetrical conception of the subject. If, however, an astral entity constantly works through a medium, these finer astral senses may gradually be so coarsened as to become insensible to the higher grades of matter on their own plane, and to include in their purview the physical world as we see it instead; but only the trained visitor from this life, who is fully conscious on both planes, can depend upon seeing both clearly and simultaneously. Be it understood, then, that the complexity exists, and that only when it is fully perceived and scientifically unravelled is there perfect security against deception or mistake.

For the seventh or lowest subdivision of the astral plane also this physical world of ours may be said to be the background, though what is seen is only a distorted and partial view of it, since all that is light and good and beautiful seems invisible. It was thus described four thousand years ago in the Egyptian papyrus of the Scribe Ani: "What manner of place is this unto which I have come? It hath no water, it hath no air; it is deep, unfathomable; it is black as the blackest night, and men wander helplessly about therein; in it a man may not live in quietness of heart." For the unfortunate entity on that level it is indeed true that "all the earth is full of darkness and cruel habitations," but it is darkness which radiates from within himself and causes his existence to be passed in a perpetual night of evil and horror—a very real hell, though, like all other hells, entirely of man's own creation.

Most students find the investigation of this section an extremely unpleasant task, for there appears to be a sense of density and gross materiality about it which is indescribably loathsome to the liberated astral body, causing it the sense of pushing its way through some black, viscous fluid, while the inhabitants and influences encountered there are also usually exceedingly undesirable.

The first, second, and third subdivisions seem much further removed from this physical world, and correspondingly less material. Entities inhabiting these levels lose sight of the earth and its belongings; they are usually deeply self-absorbed, and to a large extent create their own surroundings, though these are not purely subjective, as in Devachan, but on the contrary sufficiently objective to be perceptible to other entities and also to clairvoyant vision. This region is beyond doubt the "summerland" of which we hear so much at spiritualistic *séances*, and the entities who descend from and describe it are probably often speaking the truth as far as their knowledge extends. It is on these planes that "spirits" call into temporary existence their houses, schools, and cities, for these objects are often real enough for the time, though to a clearer sight they may sometimes be pitiably unlike what their delighted creators suppose them to be. Nevertheless, many of the imaginations that take form there are of real though temporary beauty, and a visitor who knew of nothing higher might wander contentedly enough there among forests and mountains, lovely lakes and pleasant flower-gardens, or might even construct such surroundings to suit his own fancies.

It may be said in passing that communication is limited on the astral plane by the knowledge of the entity, just as it is here. While a person able to function freely on that plane can communicate with any of the human entities there present more readily and rapidly than on earth, by means of mental impressions, the inhabitants themselves do not usually seem able to exercise this power, but appear to be restricted by limitations similar to those that prevail on earth, though perhaps less rigid. The result of this is that they are found associating, there as here in groups drawn together by common sympathies, beliefs, and language.

An account of the scenery of the astral plane would be incomplete without mention of what are commonly called the Records of the Astral Light, the photographic representation of all that has ever happened. These records are really and permanently impressed upon that higher medium called the Âkâsha, and are only reflected in a more or less spasmodic manner in the astral light, so that one whose power of vision does not rise above this plane will be likely to obtain only occasional and disconnected pictures of the past instead of a coherent narrative. But nevertheless pictures of all kinds of past events are constantly being reproduced on the astral plane, and form an important part of the surroundings of the investigator there.

INHABITANTS.

Having sketched in, however slightly, the background of our picture, we must now attempt to fill in the figures—to describe the inhabitants of the astral plane. The immense variety of these entities makes it exceedingly difficult to arrange and tabulate them. Perhaps the most convenient method will be to divide them into three great classes, the human, the non-human, and the artificial.

I. HUMAN.

The human denizens of Kâmaloka fall naturally into two groups, the living and the dead, or, to speak more accurately, those who have still a physical body, and those who have not.

I. LIVING.

The entities which manifest on the astral plane during physical life may be subdivided into four classes:

1. *The Adept or Chela in the Mâyâvirûpa.* This body is the artificial vehicle used on the four lower or rûpa divisions of the devachanic plane by those capable of functioning there during earth-life, and is formed out of the substance of the mind-body. The pupil is at first unable to construct this for himself, and has therefore to be content with his ordinary astral body composed of the less refined matter of the kâmic aura; but at a certain stage of his progress the Master Himself forms his Mâyâvirûpa for him for the first time, and afterwards instructs and assists him until he can make it for himself easily and expeditiously. When this facility is attained this vehicle is habitually used in place of the grosser astral body, since it permits of instant passage from the astral to the devachanic plane and back again at will, and allows of the use at all times of the higher powers belonging to its own plane. It must be noted, however, that a person travelling in the Mâyâvirûpa is not perceptible to merely astral vision unless he chooses to make himself so by gathering around him particles of astral matter and so creating for himself a temporary body suitable to that plane, though such a temporary creation would resemble the ordinary astral body only as a materialization resembles the physical body; in each case it is a manifestation of a higher entity on a lower plane in order to make himself visible to those whose senses cannot yet transcend that plane. But whether he be in the Mâyâvirûpa or the astral body, the pupil who is introduced to the astral plane under the guidance of a competent teacher has always the fullest possible consciousness there, and is in fact himself, exactly as his friends know him on earth, minus only the four lower principles in the former case and the three lower in the latter, and plus the additional powers and faculties of this higher condition, which enable him to carry on far more easily and far more efficiently on that plane during sleep the Theosophical work which occupies so much of his thought in his waking hours. Whether he will remember fully and accurately on the physical plane what he has done or learnt on the other depends largely, as before stated, upon whether he is able to carry his consciousness without intermission from the one state to the other.

2. *The Psychically-developed Person who is not under the guidance of a Master.* Such a person may or may not be spiritually developed, for the two forms of advancement do not necessarily go together, and when a man is born with psychic powers it is simply the result of efforts made during a previous incarnation, which may have been of the noblest and most unselfish character, or on the other hand may have been ignorant and ill-directed or even entirely unworthy. Such an one will usually be perfectly conscious when out of the body, but for want of proper training is liable to be greatly deceived as to what he sees. He will often be able to range through the different subdivisions of the astral plane almost as fully as persons belonging to the last class; but sometimes he is especially attracted to some one division and

rarely travels beyond its influences. His recollection of what he has seen may vary according to the degree of his development through all the stages from perfect clearness to utter distortion or blank oblivion. He will appear always in the astral body, since by the hypothesis he does not know how to form the Mâyâvirûpa.

3. *The Ordinary Person*—that is, the person without any psychic development—floating about in his astral body in a more or less unconscious condition. In deep slumber the higher principles in their astral vehicle almost invariably withdraw from the body, and hover in its immediate neighbourhood, practically almost as much asleep as the latter. In some cases, however, this astral vehicle is less lethargic, and floats dreamily about on the various astral currents, occasionally recognizing other people in a similar condition, and meeting with experiences of all sorts, pleasant and unpleasant, the memory of which, hopelessly confused and often travestied into a grotesque caricature of what really happened, will cause the man to think next morning what a remarkable dream he has had. These extruded astral bodies are almost shapeless and very indefinite in outline in the case of the more backward races and individuals, but as the man develops in intellect and spirituality his floating astral becomes better defined and more closely resembles his physical encasement. Since the psychical faculties of mankind are in course of evolution, and individuals are at all stages of their development, this class naturally melts by imperceptible gradations into the former one.

4. *The Black Magician or his pupil.* This class corresponds closely to the first, except that the development has been for evil instead of good, and the powers acquired are used for purely selfish purposes instead of for the benefit of humanity. Among its lower ranks come members of the negro race who practise the ghastly rites of the Obeah or Voodoo schools, and the medicine-men of many a savage tribe; while higher in intellect, and therefore the more blameworthy, stand the Tibetan black magicians, who are often, though incorrectly, called by Europeans Dûgpas—a title properly belonging, as is quite correctly explained by Surgeon-Major Waddell in his recent work on *The Buddhism of Tibet*, only to the Bhotanese subdivision of the great Kargyu sect, which is part of what may be called the semi-reformed school of Tibetan Buddhism. The Dûgpas no doubt deal in Tântrik magic to a considerable extent, but the real red-hatted entirely unreformed sect is that of the Ñin-mâ-pa, though far beyond them in a still lower depth lie the Bön-pa—the votaries of the aboriginal religion, who have never accepted any form of Buddhism at all. It must not, however, be supposed that all Tibetan sects except the Gelûgpa are necessarily and altogether evil; a truer view would be that as the rules of other sects permit considerably greater laxity of life and practice, the proportion of self-seekers among them is likely to be much larger than among the stricter reformers. The investigator will occasionally meet on the astral plane students of occultism from all parts of the world (belonging to lodges quite unconnected with the Masters of whom Theosophists know most) who are in many cases most earnest and self-sacrificing seekers after truth. It is noteworthy, however, that all such lodges are at least aware of the existence of the great Himalayan Brotherhood, and acknowledge it as containing among its members the highest Adepts now known on earth.

2. Dead.

To begin with, of course this very word "dead" is an absurd misnomer, as most of the entities classified under this heading are as fully alive as we are ourselves; the term must be understood as meaning those who are for the time unattached to a physical body. They may be subdivided into nine principal classes as follows:—

1. *The Nirmânakâya.* This class is just mentioned in order to make the catalogue complete, but it is of course very rarely indeed that so exalted a being manifests himself upon so low a plane as this. When for any reason connected with his sublime work he found it desirable to do so, he would probably create a temporary astral body for the purpose, just as the Adept in the Mâyâvirûpa would do, since the more refined vesture would be invisible to astral sight. Further information about the position and work of the Nirmânakâyas may be found in Madame Blavatsky's *Theosophical Glossary* and *The Voice of the Silence.*

2. *The Chela awaiting reincarnation.* It has frequently been stated in Theosophical literature that when the pupil reaches a certain stage he is able with the assistance of his Master to escape from the action of what is in ordinary cases the law of nature which carries a human being into the devachanic condition after death, there to receive his due reward in the full working out of all the spiritual forces which his highest aspirations have set in motion while on earth. As the pupil must by the hypothesis be a man of pure life and high thought, it is probable that in his case these spiritual forces will be of abnormal strength, and therefore if he, to use the technical expression, "takes his Devachan," it is likely to be an extremely long one; but if instead of taking it he chooses the Path of Renunciation (thus even at his low level and in his humble way beginning to follow in the footsteps of the Great Master of Renunciation, Gautama Buddha Himself), he is able to expend that reserve of force in quite another direction—to use it for the benefit of mankind, and so, infinitesimal though his offering may be, to take his tiny part in the great work of the Nirmânakâyas. By taking this course he no doubt sacrifices centuries of intense bliss, but on the other hand he gains the enormous advantage of being able to continue his life of work and progress without a break. When a pupil who has decided to do this dies, he simply steps out of his body, as he has often done before, and waits upon the astral plane until a suitable reincarnation can be arranged for him by his Master. This being a marked departure from the usual course of procedure, the permission of a very high authority has to be obtained before the attempt can be made; yet, even when this is granted, so strong is the force of natural law, that it is said the pupil must be careful to confine himself strictly to the Kâmaloka while the matter is being arranged, lest if he once, even for a moment, touched the devachanic plane, he might be swept as by an irresistible current into the line of normal evolution again. In some cases, though these are rare, he is enabled to avoid the trouble of a new birth by being placed directly in an adult body whose previous tenant has no further use for it, but naturally it is not often that a suitable body is available. Far more frequently he has to wait on the astral plane, as mentioned before, until the opportunity of a fitting birth presents itself. In the meantime, however, he is losing no time, for he is just as fully himself as ever he was, and is able to go on with the work given him by his Master even more quickly and efficiently than when in the physical body, since he is no longer hampered by the possibility of fatigue. His consciousness is of course quite complete, and he roams at will through all the divisions of the Kâmaloka with equal facility. The chela awaiting reincarnation is by no means one of the common objects of the astral plane, but still he may be met with occasionally, and therefore he forms one of our classes. No doubt as the evolution of humanity proceeds, and an ever-increasing proportion enter upon the Path of Holiness, this class will become more numerous.

3. *The Ordinary Person after death.* Needless to say, this class is millions of times larger than those of which we have spoken, and the character and condition of its members vary within extremely wide limits. Within similarly wide limits may vary also the length of their lives upon the astral plane, for while there are those who pass only a few days or hours there, others remain upon this level for many years and even centuries. A man who has led a good and pure life, whose strongest feelings and aspirations have been unselfish and spiritual, will have no attraction to this plane, and will, if entirely left alone, find little to keep him upon it, or to awaken him into activity even during the comparatively short period of his stay. For it must be understood that after death the true man is withdrawing into himself, and just as at the first step of that process he casts off the physical body, and almost directly afterwards the etheric double and the Prâna, so it is intended that he should as soon as possible cast off also the astral or kâmic body, and pass into the devachanic condition, where alone his spiritual aspirations can find their full fruition. The noble and pure-minded man will be able to do this, for he has subdued all earthly passions during life; the force of his will has been directed into higher channels, and there is therefore but little energy of lower desire to be worked out in Kâmaloka. His stay there will consequently be very short, and most probably he will have little more than a dreamy half-consciousness of existence until he sinks into the sleep during which his higher principles finally free themselves from the kâmic envelope and enter upon the blissful rest of Devachan.

For the person who has not as yet entered upon the path of occult development, what has been described is the ideal state of affairs, but naturally it is not attained by all, or even by the majority. The average man has by no means freed himself from the lower desires before death, and it takes a long period of more or less fully conscious life on the astral plane to allow the forces he has generated to work themselves out, and thus release the higher Ego. The body which he occupies during this period is the Kâmarûpa which may be described as a rearrangement of the matter of his astral body; but it is much more defined in outline, and there is also this important difference between the two that while the astral body, if sufficiently awakened during life to function at all freely, would probably be able to visit all, or at any rate most, of the subdivisions of its plane, the Kâmarûpa has not that liberty, but is strictly confined to that level to which its affinities have drawn it. It has, however, a certain kind of progress connected with it, for it generally happens that the forces a man has set in motion during earth-life need for their appropriate working out a sojourn on more divisions than one of the Kâmaloka, and when this is the case a regular sequence is observed, commencing with the lowest; so that when the Kâmarûpa has exhausted its attractions to one level, the greater part of its grosser particles fall away, and it finds itself in affinity with a somewhat higher state of existence. Its specific gravity, as it were, is constantly decreasing, and so it steadily rises from the denser to the lighter strata, pausing only when it is exactly balanced for a time. This is evidently the explanation of a remark frequently made by the entities which appear at *séances* to the effect that they are about to rise to a higher sphere, from which it will be impossible, or not so easy, to "communicate" through a medium; and it is as a matter of fact true that a person upon the highest subdivision of this plane would find it almost impossible to deal with any ordinary medium.

It ought perhaps to be explained here that the definiteness of outline which distinguishes the Kâmarûpa from the astral body is of an entirely different character from that definiteness which was described as a sign of progress in the astral of the man before death. There can never be any possibility of confusion between the two entities, for while in the case of the man attached to a physical body the different orders of astral particles are all inextricably mingled and ceaselessly changing their position, after death their activity is much more circumscribed, since they then sort themselves according to their degree of materiality, and become, as it were, a series of sheaths or shells surrounding him, the grossest being always outside and so dissipating before the others. This dissipation is not necessarily complete, the extent to which it is carried being governed by the power of Manas to free itself from its connection with any given level; and on this also, as will be seen later, the nature of the "shade" depends.

The poetic idea of death as a universal leveller is a mere absurdity born of ignorance, for, as a matter of fact, in the vast majority of cases the loss of the physical body makes no difference whatever in the character or intellect of the person, and there are therefore as many different varieties of intelligence among those whom we usually call the dead as among the living. The popular religious teaching of the West as to man's *post-mortem* adventures has long been so wildly inaccurate that even intelligent people are often terribly puzzled when they recover consciousness in Kâmaloka after death. The condition in which the new arrival finds himself differs so radically from what he has been led to expect that it is no uncommon case for him to refuse at first to believe that he has passed through the portals of death at all; indeed, of so little practical value is our much-vaunted belief in the immortality of the soul that most people consider the very fact that they are still conscious an absolute proof that they have not died. The horrible doctrine of eternal punishment, too, is responsible for a vast amount of most pitiable and entirely groundless terror among those newly arrived in Kâmaloka who in many cases spend long periods of acute mental suffering before they can free themselves from the fatal influence of that hideous blasphemy, and realize that the world is governed not according to the caprice of some demon who gloats over human anguish, but according to a benevolent and wonderfully patient law of evolution. Many members of the class we are considering do not really attain an intelligent appreciation of this fact at all, but drift through their astral interlude in the same aimless manner in which they have spent the physical portion of their lives. Thus in Kâmaloka, exactly as on earth, there are the few who comprehend something of their position and know how to make the best of it, and the many who have not yet acquired that knowledge; and there, just as here, the ignorant are rarely ready to profit by the advice or example of the wise.

But of whatever grade the entity's intellect may be, it is always a fluctuating and on the whole a gradually diminishing quantity, for the lower Manas is being drawn in opposite directions by the higher Triad which acts on it from above its level and the Kâma which operates from below; and therefore it oscillates between the two attractions, with an ever-increasing tendency towards the former as the kâmic forces wear themselves out. And here comes in the evil of what is called at *séances* the "development" of a spirit through a medium—a process the object of which is to intensify the downward pull of the Kâma, to awaken the lower portion of the entity (that being all that can be reached) from the natural and desirable unconsciousness into which it is passing, and thus to prolong unnaturally its existence in the Kâmaloka. The peculiar danger of this will be seen when it is recollected that the real man is all the while steadily withdrawing into himself, and is therefore as time goes on less and less able to influence or guide this lower portion, which nevertheless, until the separation is complete, has the power to generate Karma, and under the circumstances is obviously far more likely to add evil than good to its record. Thus the harm done is threefold: first, the retardation of the separation between Manas and Kâma, and the consequent waste of time and prolongation of the interval between two incarnations; secondly, the extreme probability (almost amounting to certainty) that a large addition will be made to the individual's evil Karma, which will have to be worked out in future births; thirdly, the terrible danger that this abnormal intensification of the force of Kâma may eventually enable the latter to entangle the whole of the lower Manas inextricably, and so cause the entire loss of an incarnation. Though such a result as this last-mentioned is happily uncommon, it is a thing that has happened more than once; and in very many cases where the evil has fallen short of this ultimate possibility, the individual has nevertheless lost much more of his lower Manas by this additional entanglement with Kâma than he would have done if left to withdraw into himself quietly as nature intended. It is not denied that a certain amount of good may occasionally be done to very degraded entities at spiritualistic circles; but the intention of nature obviously is that such assistance should be given, as it frequently is, by occult students who are able to visit the astral plane during earth-life, and have been trained by competent teachers to deal by whatever methods may be most helpful with the various cases which they encounter. It will be readily seen that such a scheme of help, carrying with it as it does the possibility of instant reference to higher authorities in any doubtful case, is infinitely safer than any casual assistance obtained through a medium who may be (and indeed generally is) entirely ignorant of the laws governing spiritual evolution, and who is as liable to the domination of evil or mischievous influences as of good ones.

Apart altogether from any question of development through a medium, there is another and much more frequently exercised influence which may seriously retard a disembodied entity on his way to Devachan, and that is the intense and uncontrolled grief of his surviving friends or relatives. It is one among many melancholy results of the terribly inaccurate and even irreligious view that we in the West have for centuries been taking of death, that we not only cause ourselves an immense amount of wholly unnecessary pain over this temporary parting from our loved ones, but we often also do serious injury to those for whom we bear so deep an affection by means of this very regret which we feel so acutely. As one of our ablest writers has recently told us, when our departed brother is sinking peacefully and naturally into pre-devachanic unconsciousness "an awakening may be caused by the passionate sorrow and desires of friends left on earth, and these, violently vibrating the kâmic elements in the embodied persons, may set up vibrations in the Kâmarûpa of the disembodied, and so reach and rouse the lower Manas not yet withdrawn to and reunited with its parent, the spiritual intelligence. Thus it may be roused from its dreamy state to vivid remembrance of the earth-life so lately left. This awakening is often accompanied by acute suffering, and even if this be avoided the natural process of the Triad freeing itself is rudely disturbed, and the completion of its freedom is delayed." (*Death and After*, p. 32.) It would be well if those whose loved ones have passed on before them would learn from these undoubted facts the duty of restraining for the sake of those dear ones a grief which, however natural it may be, is yet in its essence selfish. Not that occult teaching counsels forgetfulness of the dead—far from it; but it does suggest that a man's affectionate remembrance of his departed friend is a force which, if properly directed into the channel of earnest good wishes for his progress towards Devachan and his quiet passage through Kâmaloka might be of real value to him, whereas when wasted in mourning for him and longing to have him back again it is not only useless but harmful. It is with a true instinct that the Hindu religion prescribes its Shrâddha ceremonies and the Catholic Church its prayers for the dead.

It sometimes happens, however, that the desire for communication is from the other side, and that an entity of the class we are considering has something which it specially desires to say to those whom it has left behind. Occasionally this message is an important one, such as, for example, an indication of the place where a missing will is concealed; but more often it seems to us quite trivial. Still, whatever it may be, if it is firmly impressed upon the mind of the dead person, it is undoubtedly desirable that he should be enabled to deliver it, as otherwise the anxiety to do so would perpetually draw his consciousness back into the earth-life, and prevent him from passing to higher spheres. In such a case a psychic who can understand him, or a medium through whom he can write or speak, is of real service to him. It should be observed that the reason why he cannot usually write or speak without a medium is that one state of matter can ordinarily act only upon the state next below it, and, as he has now no denser matter in his organism than that of which the Kâmarûpa is composed, he finds it impossible to set up vibrations in the physical substance of the air or to move the physical pencil without borrowing living matter of the intermediate order contained in the etheric double, by means of which an impulse can readily be transferred from the one plane to the other. Now he would be unable to borrow this material from an ordinary person, because such a man's principles would be too closely linked together to be separated by any means likely to be at his command, but the very essence of mediumship is the ready separability of the principles, so from a medium he can draw without difficulty the matter he needs for his manifestation, whatever it may be. When he cannot find a medium or does not understand how to use one he sometimes makes clumsy and blundering endeavours to communicate on his own account, and by the strength of his will he sets elemental forces blindly working, perhaps producing such apparently aimless manifestations as stone-throwing, bell-ringing, etc. It consequently frequently happens that a psychic or medium going to a house where such manifestations are taking place may be able to discover what the entity who produces them is attempting to say or do, and may thus put an end to the disturbance. This would not, however, invariably be the case, as these elemental forces are occasionally set in motion by entirely different causes.

But for one entity who is earth-bound by the desire to communicate with his surviving friends, there are thousands who, if left alone, would never think of doing so, although when the idea is suggested to them through a medium they will respond to it readily enough, for since during earth-life their interests were probably centred less in spiritual than in worldly affairs, it is not difficult to re-awaken in them vibrations sympathetic to matters connected with the existence they have so lately left; and this undesirable intensification of earthly thoughts is frequently brought about by the interference of well-meaning but ignorant friends, who endeavour to get communications from the departed through a medium, with the result that just in proportion to their success he is subjected to the various dangers mentioned above. It should also be remembered that the possible injury to the entity itself is by no means all the harm that may accrue from such a practice, for those who habitually attend *séances* during life are almost certain to develop a tendency to haunt them after death, and so themselves in turn run the risks into which they have so often brought their predecessors. Besides, it is well known that the vital energy necessary to produce physical manifestations is frequently drawn from the sitters as well as from the medium, and the eventual effect on the latter is invariably evil, as is evinced by the large number of such sensitives who have gone either morally or psychically to the bad—some becoming epileptic, some taking to drink, others falling under influences which induced them to stoop to fraud and trickery of all kinds.

4. *The Shade.* When the separation of the principles is complete, the Kâmaloka life of the person is over, and, as before stated, he passes into the devachanic condition. But just as when he dies to this plane he leaves his physical body behind him, so when he dies to the astral plane he leaves his Kâmarûpa behind him. If he has purged himself from all earthly desires during life, and directed all his energies into the channels of unselfish spiritual aspiration, his higher Ego will be able to draw back into itself the whole of the lower Manas which it put forth into incarnation; in that case the Kâmarûpa left behind on the astral plane will be a mere corpse like the abandoned physical body, and it will then come not into this class but into the next. Even in the case of a man of somewhat less perfect life almost the same result may be attained if the forces of lower desire are allowed to work themselves out undisturbed in Kâmaloka but the majority of mankind make but very trifling and perfunctory efforts while on earth to rid themselves of the less elevated impulses of their nature, and consequently doom themselves not only to a greatly prolonged sojourn on the astral plane, but also to what cannot be described otherwise than as a loss of a portion of the lower Manas. This is, no doubt, a very material method of expressing the great mystery of the reflection of the higher Manas in the lower, but since only those who have passed the portals of initiation can fully comprehend this, we must content ourselves with the nearest approximation to exactitude which is possible to us; and as a matter of fact, a very fairly accurate idea of what actually takes place will be obtained by adopting the hypothesis that the mânasic principle sends down a portion of itself into the lower world of physical life at each incarnation, and expects to be able to withdraw it again at the end of the life, enriched by all its varied experiences. The ordinary man, however, usually allows himself to be so pitiably enslaved by all sorts of base desires that a certain portion of this lower Manas becomes very closely interwoven with Kâma, and when the separation takes place, his life in Kâmaloka being over, the mânasic principle has, as it were, to be torn apart, the degraded portion remaining within the Kâmarûpa.

This Kâmarûpa then consists of the particles of astral matter from which the lower Manas has not been able to disengage itself, and which therefore retain it captive; for when Manas passes into Devachan these clinging fragments adhere to a portion of it and as it were wrench it away. The proportion of the matter of each level present in the Kâmarûpa will therefore depend on the extent to which Manas has become inextricably entangled with the lower passions. It will be obvious that as Manas in passing from level to level is unable to free itself completely from the matter of each, the Kâmarûpa will show the presence of each grosser kind which has succeeded in retaining its connection with it.

Thus comes into existence the class of entity which has been called "The Shade"—an entity, be it observed, which is not in any sense the real individual at all (for he has passed away into Devachan), but nevertheless, not only bears his exact personal appearance, but possesses his memory and all his little idiosyncrasies, and may, therefore, very readily personate him, as indeed it frequently does at *séances*. It is not, of course, conscious of any act of impersonation, for as far as its intellect goes it must necessarily suppose itself to be the individual, but one can imagine the horror and disgust of the friends of the departed, if they could only realize that they had been deceived into accepting as their loved one a mere soulless bundle of all his worst qualities. Its length of life varies according to the amount of the lower Manas which animates it, but as this is all the while in process of fading out, its intellect is a steadily diminishing quantity, though it may possess a great deal of a certain sort of animal cunning; and even quite towards the end of its career it is still able to communicate by borrowing temporary intelligence from the medium. From its very nature it is exceedingly liable to be swayed by all kinds of evil influences, and, having separated from its higher Ego, it has nothing in its constitution capable of responding to good ones. It therefore lends itself readily to various minor purposes of some of the baser sort of black magicians. So much of the matter of the mânasic nature as it possesses gradually disintegrates and returns to its own plane, though not to any individual mind, and thus the shade fades by almost imperceptible gradations into a member of our next class.

5. *The Shell.* This is absolutely the mere astral corpse in process of disintegration, every

particle of the lower Manas having left it. It is entirely without any kind of consciousness or intelligence, and is drifted passively about upon the astral currents just as a cloud might be swept in any direction by a passing breeze; but even yet it may be galvanized for a few moments into a ghastly burlesque of life if it happens to come within reach of a medium's aura. Under such circumstances it will still exactly resemble its departed personality in appearance, and may even reproduce to some extent his familiar expressions or handwriting, but it does so merely by the automatic action of the cells of which it is composed, which tend under stimulation to repeat the form of action to which they are most accustomed, and whatever amount of intelligence may lie behind any such manifestation has most assuredly no connection with the original entity, but is lent by the medium or his "guides" for the occasion. It is, however, more frequently temporarily vitalized in quite another manner, which will be described under the next head. It has also the quality of being still blindly responsive to such vibrations—usually of the lowest order—as were frequently set up in it during its last stage of existence as a shade, and consequently persons in whom evil desires or passions are predominant will be very likely, when they attend physical *séances*, to find these intensified and as it were thrown back upon them by the unconscious shells.

There is also another variety of corpse which it is necessary to mention under this head, though it belongs to a much earlier stage of man's *post-mortem* history. It has been stated above that after the death of the physical body the Kâmarûpa is comparatively quickly formed, and the etheric double cast off—this latter body being destined to slow disintegration, precisely as is the kâmarûpic shell at a later stage of the proceedings. This etheric shell, however, is not to be met with drifting aimlessly about, as is the variety with which we have hitherto been dealing; on the contrary, it remains within a few yards of the decaying physical body, and since it is readily visible to any one even slightly sensitive, it is accountable for many of the commonly current stories of churchyard ghosts. A psychically developed person passing one of our great cemeteries will see hundreds of these bluish-white, misty forms hovering over the graves where are laid the physical vestures which they have recently left; and as they, like their lower counterparts, are in various stages of disintegration, the sight is by no means a pleasant one. This also, like the other kind of shell, is entirely devoid of consciousness and intelligence; and though it may under certain circumstances be galvanized into a very horrible form of temporary life, this is possible only by means of some of the most loathsome rites of one of the worst forms of black magic, about which the less said the better. It will thus be seen that in the successive stages of his progress from earth-life to Devachan, man casts off and leaves to slow disintegration no less than three corpses—the physical body, the etheric double and the Kâmarûpa—all of which are by degrees resolved into their constituent elements and utilized anew on their respective planes by the wonderful chemistry of nature.

6. *The Vitalized Shell.* This entity ought not, strictly speaking, to be classified under the head "human" at all, since it is only its outer vesture, the passive, senseless shell, that was once an appanage of humanity; such life, intelligence, desire and will as it may possess are those of the artificial elemental animating it, and that, though in terrible truth a creation of man's evil thought, is not itself human. It will therefore perhaps be better to deal with it more fully under its appropriate class among the artificial entities, as its nature and genesis will be more readily comprehensible by the time that part of our subject is reached. Let it suffice here to mention that it is always a malevolent being—a true tempting demon, whose evil influence is limited only by the extent of its power. Like the shade, it is frequently used to further the horrible purposes of the Voodoo and Obeah forms of magic. Some writers have spoken of it under the name "elementary," but as that title has at one time or other been used for almost every variety of *post-mortem* entity, it has become so vague and meaningless that it is perhaps better to avoid it.

7. *The Suicide, or victim of sudden death.* It will be readily understood that a man who is torn from physical life hurriedly while in full health and strength, whether by accident or suicide, finds himself upon the astral plane under conditions differing considerably from those which surround one who dies either from old age or from disease. In the latter case the hold of

earthly desires upon the entity is more or less weakened, and probably the very grossest particles are already got rid of, so that the Kâmarûpa will most likely form itself on the sixth or fifth subdivision of the Kâmaloka, or perhaps even higher; the principles have been gradually prepared for separation, and the shock is therefore not so great. In the case of the accidental death or suicide none of these preparations have taken place, and the withdrawal of the principles from their physical encasement has been very aptly compared to the tearing of the stone out of an unripe fruit; a great deal of the grossest kind of astral matter still clings around the personality, which is consequently held in the seventh or lowest subdivision of the Kâmaloka. This has already been described as anything but a pleasant abiding-place, yet it is by no means the same for all those who are compelled for a time to inhabit it. Those victims of sudden death whose earth-lives have been pure and noble have no affinity for this plane, and the time of their sojourn upon it is passed, to quote from an early Letter on this subject, either "in happy ignorance and full oblivion, or in a state of quiet slumber, a sleep full of rosy dreams". But on the other hand, if their earth-lives have been low and brutal, selfish and sensual, they will, like the suicides, be conscious to the fullest extent in this undesirable region; and they are liable to develop into terribly evil entities. Inflamed with all kinds of horrible appetites which they can no longer satisfy directly now they are without a physical body, they gratify their loathsome passions vicariously through a medium or any sensitive person whom they can obsess; and they take a devilish delight in using all the arts of delusion which the astral plane puts in their power in order to lead others into the same excesses which have proved so fatal to themselves. Quoting again from the same letter:—"These are the Pisâchas the *incubi* and *succubæ* of mediæval writers—demons of thirst and gluttony, of lust and avarice, of intensified craft, wickedness and cruelty, provoking their victims to horrible crimes, and revelling in their commission". From this class and the last are drawn the tempters—the devils of ecclesiastical literature; but their power fails utterly before purity of mind and purpose; they can do nothing with a man unless he has first encouraged in himself the vices into which they seek to draw him.

One whose psychic sight has been opened will often see crowds of these unfortunate creatures hanging round butchers' shops, public-houses, or other even more disreputable places—wherever the gross influences in which they delight are to be found, and where they encounter men and women still in the flesh who are like-minded with themselves. For such an entity as one of these to meet with a medium with whom he is in affinity is indeed a terrible misfortune; not only does it enable him to prolong enormously his dreadful life in Kâmaloka but it renews for perhaps an indefinite period his power to generate evil Karma, and so prepare for himself a future incarnation of the most degraded character, besides running the risk of losing a large portion or even the whole of the lower Manas. On this lowest level of the astral plane he must stay at least as long as his earthly life would have lasted if it had not been prematurely cut short; and if he is fortunate enough *not* to meet with a sensitive through whom his passions can be vicariously gratified, the unfulfilled desires will gradually burn themselves out, and the suffering caused in the process will probably go far towards working off the evil Karma of the past life.

The position of the suicide is further complicated by the fact that his rash act has so enormously diminished the power of the higher Ego to withdraw its lower portion into itself, and therefore has exposed him to manifold and great additional dangers: but it must be remembered that the guilt of suicide differs considerably according to its circumstances, from the morally blameless act of Seneca or Socrates through all degrees down to the heinous crime of the wretch who takes his own life in order to escape from the entanglements into which his villainy has brought him, and of course the position after death varies accordingly.

It should be noted that this class, as well as the shades and the vitalized shells, are all what may be called minor vampires; that is to say, whenever they have the opportunity they prolong their existence by draining away the vitality from human beings whom they find themselves able to influence. This is why both medium and sitters are often so weak and exhausted after a physical *séance*. A student of occultism is taught how to guard himself from their attempts, but without that knowledge it is difficult for one who puts himself in their way to avoid being more or less laid under contribution by them.

8. *The Vampire and Werewolf.* There remain two even more awful but happily very rare possibilities to be mentioned before this part of our subject is completed, and though they differ very widely in many ways we may yet perhaps group them together, since they have in common the qualities of unearthly horror and of extreme rarity—the latter arising from the fact that they are really relics of earlier races. We of the fifth root race ought to have evolved beyond the possibility of meeting such a ghastly fate as is indicated by either of the two headings of this sub-section, and we have so nearly done it that these creatures are commonly regarded as mere mediæval fables; yet there *are* examples to be found occasionally even now, though chiefly in countries where there is a considerable strain of fourth-race blood, such as Russia or Hungary. The popular legends about them are probably often considerably exaggerated, but there is nevertheless a terribly serious sub-stratum of truth beneath the eerie stories which pass from mouth to mouth among the peasantry of Central Europe. The general characteristics of such tales are too well known to need more than a passing reference; a fairly typical specimen of the vampire story, though it does not profess to be more than the merest fiction, is Sheridan le Fanu's *Carmilla*, while a very remarkable account of an unusual form of this creature is to be found in *Isis Unveiled*, vol. i., p. 454. All readers of Theosophical literature are familiar with the idea that it is possible for a man to live a life so absolutely degraded and selfish, so utterly wicked and brutal, that the whole of his lower Manas may become entirely immeshed in Kâma, and finally separated from its spiritual source in the higher Ego. Some students even seem to think that such an occurrence is quite a common one, and that we may meet scores of such "soulless men," as they have been called, in the street every day of our lives, but this, happily, is untrue. To attain the appalling pre-eminence in evil which thus involves the entire loss of a personality and the weakening of the developing individuality behind, a man must stifle every gleam of unselfishness or spirituality, and must have absolutely no redeeming point whatever; and when we remember how often, even in the worst of villains, there is to be found something not wholly bad, we shall realize that the abandoned personalities must always be a very small minority. Still, comparatively few though they be, they do exist, and it is from their ranks that the still rarer vampire is drawn. The lost entity would very soon after death find himself unable to stay in Kâmaloka, and would be irresistibly drawn in full consciousness into "his own place," the mysterious eighth sphere, there slowly to disintegrate after experiences best left undescribed. If, however, he perishes by suicide or sudden death, he may under certain circumstances, especially if he knows something of black magic, hold himself back from that awful fate by a death in life scarcely less awful—the ghastly existence of the vampire. Since the eighth sphere cannot claim him until after the death of the body, he preserves it in a kind of cataleptic trance by the horrible expedient of the transfusion into it of blood drawn from other human beings by his semi-materialized Kâmarûpa, and thus postpones his final destiny by the commission of wholesale murder. As popular "superstition" again quite rightly supposes, the easiest and most effectual remedy in such a case is to exhume and burn the body, thus depriving the creature of his *point d'appui*. When the grave is opened the body usually appears quite fresh and healthy, and the coffin is not infrequently filled with blood. Of course in countries where cremation is the custom vampirism of this sort is impossible.

The Werewolf, though equally horrible, is the product of a somewhat different Karma, and indeed ought perhaps to have found a place under the first instead of the second division of the human inhabitants of Kâmaloka, since it is always during a man's lifetime that he first manifests under this form. It invariably implies some knowledge of magical arts—sufficient at any rate to be able to project the astral body. When a perfectly cruel and brutal man does this, there are certain circumstances under which the body may be seized upon by other astral entities and materialized, not into the human form, but into that of some wild animal—usually the wolf; and in that condition it will range the surrounding country killing other animals, and even human beings, thus satisfying not only its own craving for blood, but that of the fiends who drive it on. In this case, as so often with the ordinary astral body, any wound inflicted upon the animal materialization will be reproduced upon the human physical body by the extraordinary phenomenon of repercussion; though after the death of that physical body the Kâmarûpa, which will probably continue to appear in the same form, will be less vulnerable. It will then, however, he also less dangerous, as unless it can find a suitable medium it will be unable to materialize fully.

It has been the fashion of this century to scoff at what are called the foolish superstitions of the ignorant peasantry; but, as in the above cases, so in many others the occult student finds on careful examination that obscure or forgotten truths of nature lie behind what at first sight appears mere nonsense, and he learns to be cautious in rejecting as well as cautious in accepting. Intending explorers of the astral plane need have little fear of encountering the very unpleasant creatures described under this head, for, as before stated, they are even now extremely rare, and as time goes on their number will happily steadily diminish. In any case their manifestations are usually restricted to the immediate neighbourhood of their physical bodies, as might be supposed from their extremely material nature.

9. *The Black Magician or his pupil.* This person corresponds at the other extremity of the scale to our second class of departed entities, the chela awaiting reincarnation, but in this case, instead of obtaining permission to adopt an unusual method of progress, the man is defying the natural process of evolution by maintaining himself in Kâmaloka by magical arts—sometimes of the most horrible nature. It would be easy to make various subdivisions of this class, according to their objects, their methods, and the possible duration of their existence on this plane, but as they are by no means fascinating objects of study, and all that an occult student wishes to know about them is how to avoid them, it will probably be more interesting to pass on to the examination of another part of our subject. It may, however, be just mentioned that every such human entity which prolongs its life thus on the astral plane beyond its natural limit invariably does so at the expense of others, and by the absorption of their life in some form or another.

II. NON-HUMAN.

Though it might have been thought fairly obvious even to the most casual glance that many of the terrestrial arrangements of nature which affect us most nearly have not been designed exclusively with a view to our comfort or even our ultimate advantage, it was yet probably unavoidable that the human race, at least in its childhood, should imagine that this world and everything it contains existed solely for its own use and benefit. Undoubtedly we ought by this time to have grown out of that infantile delusion and realized our proper position and the duties that attach to it; that most of us have not yet done so is shown in a dozen ways in our daily life notably by the atrocious cruelty habitually displayed towards the animal kingdom under the name of sport by many who probably consider themselves highly civilized people. Of course the veriest tyro in the holy science of occultism knows that all life is sacred, and that without universal compassion there is no true progress; but it is only as he advances in his studies that he discovers how manifold evolution is, and how comparatively small a place humanity really fills in the economy of nature. It becomes clear to him that just as earth, air and water support myriads of forms of life which, though invisible to the ordinary eye, are revealed to us by the microscope, so the higher planes connected with our earth have an equally dense population of whose existence we are ordinarily completely unconscious. As his knowledge increases he becomes more and more certain that in one way or another the utmost use is being made of every possibility of evolution, and that wherever it seems to us that in nature force or opportunity is being wasted or neglected, it is not the scheme of the universe that is in fault, but our ignorance of its method and intention.

For the purposes of our present consideration of the non-human inhabitants of the astral plane it will be best to leave out of consideration those very early forms of the universal life which are evolving, in a manner of which we can have little comprehension, through the successive encasement of atoms, molecules and cells: for if we commence at the lowest of what are usually called the elemental kingdoms, we shall even then have to group together under this general heading an enormous number of inhabitants of the astral plane upon whom it will be possible to touch only very slightly, as anything like a detailed account of them would swell this manual to the dimensions of an encyclopædia.

The most convenient method of arranging the non-human entities will perhaps be in four classes it being understood that in this case the class is not, as previously, a comparatively small subdivision, but usually a great kingdom of nature at least as large and varied as, say, the animal or vegetable kingdom. Some of these rank considerably below humanity, some are our equals, and others again rise far above us in goodness and power. Some belong to our scheme of evolution—that is to say, they either have been or will be men like ourselves; others are evolving on entirely distinct lines of their own. Before proceeding to consider them it is necessary, in order to avoid the charge of incompleteness, to mention that in this branch of the subject two reservations have been made. First, no reference is made to the occasional appearances of very high Adepts from other planets of the solar system and of even more august Visitors from a still greater distance, since such matters cannot fitly be described in an essay for general reading; and besides it is practically inconceivable, though of course theoretically possible, that such glorified Beings should ever need to manifest Themselves on a plane so low as the astral. If for any reason They should wish to do so, the body appropriate to the plane would be temporarily created out of astral matter belonging to this planet, just as in the case of the Nirmânakâya. Secondly, quite outside of and entirely unconnected with the four classes into which we are dividing this section, there are two other great evolutions which at present share the use of this planet with humanity; but about them it is forbidden to give any particulars at this stage of the proceedings, as it is not apparently intended under ordinary circumstances either that they should be conscious of man's existence or man of theirs. If we ever do come into contact with them it will most probably be on the purely physical plane, for in any case their connection with our astral plane is of the slightest, since the only possibility of their appearance there depends upon an extremely improbable accident in an act of ceremonial magic, which fortunately only a few of the most advanced sorcerers know how to perform. Nevertheless, that improbable accident has happened at least once, and may happen again, so that but for the prohibition above mentioned it would have been necessary to include them in our list.

1. *The Elemental Essence belonging to our own evolution.* Just as the name "elementary" has been given indiscriminately by various writers to any or all of man's possible *post-mortem* conditions, so this word "elemental" has been used at different times to mean any or all non-human spirits, from the most godlike of the Devas down through every variety of nature-spirit to the formless essence which pervades the kingdoms lying behind the mineral, until after reading several books the student becomes absolutely bewildered by the contradictory statements made on the subject. For the purposes of this treatise it will perhaps simplify matters to restrict its meaning to the last-mentioned class only, and use it to denote the three great kingdoms which precede the mineral in the order of our evolution. It may be remembered that in one of the earlier letters from an Adept teacher these elemental kingdoms are referred to, and the statement is made that the first and second cannot readily be comprehended except by an Initiate. Fortunately this, the most incomprehensible part of the vast subject, does not come within the province of this manual, as those first and second elemental kingdoms exist and function respectively upon the arûpa and rûpa levels of the devachanic plane. We have consequently to deal for the moment only with kingdom No. 3—the one next before the mineral; though even that will be found quite sufficiently complicated, as will be understood when it is stated that it contains just over two thousand four hundred perfectly distinct varieties of elemental essence, each of which the pupil who wishes to attain perfect control of the astral forces must learn not only to distinguish instantly at sight, but to deal with in its own special method and no other. Of course phenomena of various sorts may be, and constantly are, produced by those who are able to wield only one or two of these forces, but the Adept prefers to take the additional trouble requisite to understand all of them thoroughly, and uses in every case precisely the most appropriate force or combination of forces, so that his object may be attained with scientific accuracy and with the least possible expenditure of energy.

To speak, as we so often do, of *an* elemental in connection with the group we are now considering is somewhat misleading, for strictly speaking there is no such thing. What we find is a vast store of elemental essence, wonderfully sensitive to the most fleeting human thought, responding with inconceivable delicacy in an infinitesimal fraction of a second to a vibration set up in it even by an entirely unconscious exercise of human will or desire. But the moment that by the influence of such thought or exercise of will it is moulded into a living force—into something that may correctly be described as *an* elemental—it at once ceases to belong to the category we are discussing, and becomes a member of the artificial class. Even then its separate existence is usually of the most evanescent character, and as soon as its impulse has worked itself out it sinks back into the undifferentiated mass of that particular subdivision of elemental essence from which it came. It would be tedious to attempt to catalogue these subdivisions, and indeed even if a list of them were made it would be unintelligible except to the practical student who can call them up before him and compare them. Some idea of the leading lines of classification can, however, be grasped without much trouble, and may prove of interest. First comes the broad division which has given the elementals their name—the classification according to the kind of matter which they inhabit. Here, as usual, the septenary character of our evolution shows itself, for there are seven such chief groups, related respectively to the seven states of physical matter—to "earth, water, air and fire," or to translate from mediæval symbolism to modern accuracy of expression, to the solid, liquid, gaseous and etheric conditions. It has long been the custom to pity and despise the ignorance of the alchemists of the middle ages, because they gave the title of "elements" to substances which modern chemistry has discovered to be compounds; but in speaking of them thus slightingly we have done them great injustice, for their knowledge on this subject was really wider, not narrower, than ours. They may or may not have catalogued all the sixty or seventy substances which we now call elements; but they certainly did not apply that name to them, for their occult studies had taught them that in that sense of the word there was but one element, Âkâsha itself, of which these and all other forms of matter were but modifications—a truth which some of the greatest chemists of the present day are just beginning to suspect.

The fact is that in this particular case our despised forefathers' analysis went several steps deeper than our own. They understood and were able to observe the ether, which modern science can only postulate as a necessity for its theories; they were aware that it consists of physical matter in four entirely distinct states above the gaseous—a fact which has not yet been re-discovered. They knew that all physical objects consisted of matter in one or other of these seven states, and that into the composition of every organic body all seven entered in a greater or lesser degree; hence all their talk of fiery and watery humours, or "elements," which seems so grotesque to us. It is obvious that they used the latter word simply as a synonym for "constituent parts," without in the least degree intending it to connote the idea of substances which could not be further reduced. They knew also that each of these orders of matter served as an Upâdhi or basis of manifestation for a great class of evolving monadic essence, and so they christened the essence "elemental".

What we have to try to realize, then, is that in every particle of solid matter, so long as it remains in that condition, there resides, to use the picturesque phraseology of mediæval students, an earth elemental—that is, a certain amount of the living elemental essence appropriate to it, while equally in every particle of matter in the liquid, gaseous, or etheric states, the water, air, and fire "elementals" respectively inhere. It will be observed that this first broad division of the third of the elemental kingdoms is, so to speak, a horizontal one—that is to say, its respective classes stand in the relation of steps, each somewhat less material than the one below it, which ascends into it by almost imperceptible degrees; and it is easy to understand how each of these classes may again be divided horizontally into seven, since there are obviously many degrees of density among solids, liquids and gases. There is, however, what may be described as a perpendicular division also, and this is somewhat more difficult to comprehend, especially as great reserve is always maintained by occultists as to some of the facts which would be involved in a fuller explanation of it. Perhaps the clearest way to put what it is permissible to say on the subject will be to state that in each of the horizontal classes and subclasses will be found seven perfectly distinct types of elemental, the difference between them being no longer a question of degree of materiality, but rather of character and affinities. Each of these types so reacts upon the others that, though it is impossible for them ever to interchange their essence, in each of them seven sub-types will be found to exist, distinguished by the colouring given to their original peculiarity by the influence which sways them most readily. It will at once be seen that this perpendicular division and subdivision differs entirely in its character from the horizontal, in that it is far more permanent and fundamental; for while it is the evolution of the elemental kingdom to pass with almost infinite slowness through its various horizontal classes and subclasses in succession, and thus to belong to them all in turn, this is not so with regard to the types and sub-types, which remain unchangeable all the way through. A point which must never be lost sight of in endeavouring to understand this elemental evolution is that it is taking place on what is sometimes called the downward curve of the arc; that is to say, it is progressing *towards* the complete entanglement in matter which we witness in the mineral kingdom, instead of *away* from it, as is most other evolution of which we know anything; and this fact sometimes gives it a curiously inverted appearance in our eyes until we thoroughly grasp its object.

In spite of these manifold subdivisions, there are certain properties which are possessed in common by all varieties of this strange living essence; but even these are so entirely different from any with which we are familiar on the physical plane that it is exceedingly difficult to explain them to those who cannot themselves see it in action. Let it be premised, then, that when any portion of this essence remains for a few moments entirely unaffected by any outside influence (a condition, by the way, which is hardly ever realized) it is absolutely without any definite form of its own, though even then its motion is rapid and ceaseless; but on the slightest disturbance, set up perhaps by some passing thought-current, it flashes into a bewildering confusion of restless, ever-changing shapes, which form, rush about, and disappear with the rapidity of the bubbles on the surface of boiling water. These evanescent shapes, though generally those of living creatures of some sort, human or otherwise, no more express the existence of separate entities in the essence than do the equally changeful and multiform waves raised in a few moments on a previously smooth lake by a sudden squall. They seem to be mere reflections from the vast storehouse of the astral light, yet they have usually a certain appropriateness to the character of the thought-stream which calls them into existence, though nearly always with some grotesque distortion, some terrifying or unpleasant aspect about them. A question naturally arises in the mind here as to what intelligence it is that is exerted in the selection of an appropriate shape or its distortion when selected. We are not dealing with the more powerful and longer-lived artificial elemental created by a strong definite thought, but simply with the result produced by the stream of half-conscious, involuntary thoughts which the majority of mankind allow to flow idly through their brains, so that the intelligence is obviously not derived from the mind of the thinker; and we certainly cannot credit the elemental essence itself, which belongs to a kingdom further from individualization even than the mineral, with any sort of awakening of the mânasic quality. Yet it does possess a marvellous adaptability which often seems to come very near it, and it is no doubt this property that caused elementals to be described in one of our early books as "the semi-intelligent creatures of the astral light". We shall find further evidence of this power when we come to consider the case of the artificial class. When we read of a good or evil elemental, it must always be either an artificial entity or one of the many varieties of nature spirits that is meant, for the elemental kingdoms proper do not admit of any such conceptions as good and evil, though there is undoubtedly a sort of bias or tendency permeating nearly all their subdivisions which operates to render them rather hostile than friendly towards man, as every neophyte knows, for in most cases his very first impression of the astral plane is of the presence all around him of vast hosts of Protean spectres who advance upon him in threatening guise, but always retire or dissipate harmlessly if boldly faced. It is to this curious tendency that the distorted or unpleasant aspect above mentioned must be referred, and mediæval writers tell us that man has only himself to thank for its existence. In the golden age before this Kaliyuga men were on the whole less selfish and more spiritual, and then the "elementals" were friendly, though now they are no longer so because of man's indifference to, and want of sympathy with, other living beings. From the wonderful delicacy with which the essence responds to the faintest action of our minds or desires it seems clear that this elemental kingdom as a whole is very much what the collective thought of humanity makes it. Any one who will think for a moment how far from elevating the action of that collective thought is likely to be at the present time will see little reason to wonder that we reap as we have sown, and that this essence, which has no power of perception, but only blindly receives and reflects what is projected upon it, should usually exhibit unfriendly characteristics. There can be no doubt that in later races or rounds, when mankind as a whole has evolved to a much higher level, the elemental kingdoms will be influenced by the changed thought which continually impinges upon them, and we shall find them no longer hostile, but docile and helpful, as we are told that the animal kingdom will also be. Whatever may have happened in the past, it is evident that we may look forward to a very passable "golden age" in the future, if we can arrive at a time when the majority of men will be noble and unselfish, and the forces of nature will co-operate willingly with them.

The fact that we are so readily able to influence the elemental kingdoms at once shows us that we have a responsibility towards them for the manner in which we use that influence; indeed, when we consider the conditions under which they exist, it is obvious that the effect produced upon them by the thoughts and desires of all intelligent creatures inhabiting the same world with them must have been calculated upon in the scheme of our system as a factor in their evolution. In spite of the consistent teaching of all the great religions, the mass of mankind is still utterly regardless of its responsibility on the thought-plane; if a man can flatter himself that his words and deeds have been harmless to others, he believes that he has done all that can be required of him, quite oblivious of the fact that he may for years have been exercising a narrowing and debasing influence on the minds of those about him, and filling surrounding space with the unlovely creations of a sordid mind. A still more serious aspect of this question will come before us when we discuss the artificial elemental; but in regard to the essence it will be sufficient to state that we undoubtedly have the power to accelerate or delay its evolution according to the use which consciously or unconsciously we are continually making of it.

It would be hopeless within the limits of such a treatise as this to attempt to explain the different uses to which the forces inherent in the manifold varieties of this elemental essence can be put by one who has been trained in their management. The vast majority of magical ceremonies depend almost entirely upon its manipulation, either directly by the will of the magician, or by some more definite astral entity evoked by him for that purpose. By its means nearly all the physical phenomena of the *séance*-room are produced, and it is also the agent in most cases of stone-throwing or bell-ringing in haunted houses, such results as these latter being brought about either by blundering efforts to attract attention made by some earth-bound human entity, or by the mere mischievous pranks of some of the minor nature-spirits belonging to our third class. But the "elemental" must never be thought of as itself a prime mover; it is simply a latent force, which needs an external power to set it in motion. It may be noted that although all classes of the essence have the power of reflecting images from the astral light as described above, there are varieties which receive certain impressions much more readily than others—which have, as it were, favourite forms of their own into which upon disturbance they would naturally flow unless absolutely forced into some other, and such shapes tend to be a trifle less evanescent than usual.

Before leaving this branch of the subject it may be well to warn the student against the confusion of thought into which some have fallen through failing to distinguish this elemental essence which we have been considering from the monadic essence manifesting through the mineral kingdom. It must be borne in mind that monadic essence at one stage of its evolution towards humanity manifests through the elemental kingdom, while at a later stage it manifests through the mineral kingdom: but the fact that two bodies of monadic essence at these different stages are in manifestation at the same moment, and that one of these manifestations (the earth elemental) occupies the same space as and inhabits the other (say a rock), in no way interferes with the evolution either of one or the other, nor does it imply any relation between the bodies of monadic essence lying within both. The rock will also be permeated by its appropriate variety of the omnipresent Jîva or life principle, but that of course is again totally distinct from either of the essences above mentioned.

2. *The Kâmarûpas of Animals.* This is an extremely large class, yet it does not occupy a particularly important position on the astral plane, since its members usually stay there but a very short time. The vast majority of animals have not as yet acquired permanent individualization, and when one of them dies the monadic essence which has been manifesting through it flows back again into the particular stratum whence it came, bearing with it such advancement or experience as has been attained during that life. It is not, however, able to do this quite immediately; the kâmic aura of the animal forms itself into a Kâmarûpa, just as in man's case, and the animal has a real existence on the astral plane, the length of which, though never great, varies according to the intelligence which it has developed. In most cases it does not seem to be more than dreamily conscious, but appears perfectly happy. The comparatively few domestic animals who have already attained individuality, and will therefore be reborn no more as animals in this world, have a much longer and much more vivid life in Kâmaloka than their less advanced fellows, and at the end of it sink gradually into a subjective condition, which is likely to last for a very considerable period. One interesting subdivision of this class consists of the Kâmarûpas of those anthropoid apes mentioned in *The Secret Doctrine* (vol. i, p. 184) who are already individualized, and will be ready to take human incarnation in the next round, or perhaps some of them even sooner.

3. *Nature-Spirits of all Kinds.* So many and so varied are the subdivisions of this class that to do them anything like justice one would need to devote a separate treatise to this subject alone. Some characteristics, however, they all have in common, and it will be sufficient here to try to give some idea of those. To begin with, we have to realize that we are here dealing with entities which differ radically from all that we have hitherto considered. Though we may rightly classify the elemental essence and the animal Kâmarûpa as non-human, the monadic essence which manifests itself through them will, nevertheless, in the fulness of time, evolve to the level of manifesting itself through some future humanity comparable to our own, and if we were able to look back through countless ages on our own evolution in previous manvantaras, we should find that that which is now ourselves has passed on its upward path through similar stages. That, however, is not the case with the vast kingdom of nature-spirits; they neither have been, nor ever will be, members of a humanity such as ours; their line of evolution is entirely different, and their only connection with us consists in our temporary occupancy of the same planet. Of course since we are neighbours for the time being we owe neighbourly kindness to one another when we happen to meet, but our lines of development differ so widely that each can do but little for the other.

Many writers have included these spirits among the elementals, and indeed they are the elementals (or perhaps, to speak more accurately, the animals) of a higher evolution. Though much more highly developed than our elemental essence, they have yet certain characteristics in common with it; for example, they also are divided into seven great classes, inhabiting respectively the same seven states of matter already mentioned as permeated by the corresponding varieties of the essence. Thus, to take those which are most readily comprehensible to us, there are spirits of the earth, water, air, and fire (or ether) definite intelligent astral entities residing and functioning in each of those media. It may be asked how it is possible for any kind of creature to inhabit the solid substance of a rock, or of the crust of the earth. The answer is that since the nature-spirits are formed of astral matter, the substance of the rock is no hindrance to their motion or their vision, and furthermore physical matter in its solid state is their natural element—the only one to which they are accustomed and in which they feel at home. The same is of course true of those who live in water, air or ether. In mediæval literature, these earth-spirits are often called gnomes, while the water-spirits are spoken of as ûndinés, the air-spirits as sylphs, and the ether-spirits as salamanders. In popular language they are known by many names—fairies, pixies, elves, brownies, peris, djinns, trolls, satyrs, fauns, kobolds, imps, goblins, good people, etc.—some of these titles being applied only to one variety, and others indiscriminately to all. Their forms are many and various, but most frequently human in shape and somewhat diminutive in size. Like almost all inhabitants of the astral plane, they are able to assume any appearance at will, but they undoubtedly have definite forms of their own, or perhaps we should rather say favourite forms, which they wear when they have no special object in taking any other. Of course under ordinary conditions they are not visible to physical sight at all, but they have the power of making themselves so by materialization when they wish to be seen.

There are an immense number of subdivisions or races among them, and individuals of these subdivisions differ in intelligence and disposition precisely as human beings do. The great majority of them apparently prefer to avoid man altogether; his habits and emanations are distasteful to them, and the constant rush of astral currents set up by his restless, ill-regulated desires disturbs and annoys them. On the other hand instances are not wanting in which nature-spirits have as it were made friends with human beings and offered them such assistance as lay in their power, as in the well-known stories told of the Scotch brownies or of the fire-lighting fairies mentioned in spiritualistic literature. This helpful attitude, however, is comparatively rare, and in most cases when they come in contact with man they either show indifference or dislike, or else take an impish delight in deceiving him and playing childish tricks upon him. Many a story illustrative of this curious characteristic may be found among the village gossip of the peasantry in almost any lonely mountainous district, and any one who has been in the habit of attending *séances* for physical phenomena will recollect instances of practical joking and silly though usually good-natured horseplay, which always indicate the presence of some of the lower orders of the nature-spirits. They are greatly assisted in their tricks by the wonderful power which they possess of casting a glamour over those who yield themselves to their influence, so that such victims for the time see and hear only what these fairies impress upon them, exactly as the mesmerized subject sees, hears, feels and believes whatever the magnetizer wishes. The nature-spirits, however, have not the mesmerizer's power of dominating the human will, except in the case of quite unusually weak-minded people, or of those who allow themselves to fall into such a condition of helpless terror that their will is temporarily in abeyance; they cannot go beyond deception of the senses, but of that art they are undoubted masters, and cases are not wanting in which they have cast their glamour over a considerable number of people at once. It is by invoking their aid in the exercise of this peculiar power that some of the most wonderful feats of the Indian jugglers are performed—the entire audience being in fact hallucinated and made to imagine that they see and hear a whole series of events which have not really taken place at all.

We might almost look upon the nature-spirits as a kind of astral humanity, but for the fact that none of them—not even the highest possess a permanent reincarnating individuality. Apparently therefore one point in which their line of evolution differs from ours is that a much greater proportion of intelligence is developed before permanent individualization takes place; but of the stages through which they have passed, and those through which they have yet to pass, we can know little. The life-periods of the different subdivisions vary greatly, some being quite short, others much longer than our human lifetime. We stand so entirely outside such a life as theirs that it is impossible for us to understand much about its conditions; but it appears on the whole to be a simple, joyous, irresponsible kind of existence, much such as a party of happy children might lead among exceptionally favourable physical surroundings. Though tricky and mischievous, they are rarely malicious unless provoked by some unwarrantable intrusion or annoyance; but as a body they also partake to some extent of the universal feeling of distrust for man, and they generally seem inclined to resent somewhat the first appearance of a neophyte on the astral plane, so that he usually makes their acquaintance under some unpleasant or terrifying form. If, however, he declines to be frightened by any of their freaks, they soon accept him as a necessary evil and take no further notice of him, while some among them may even after a time become friendly and manifest pleasure on meeting him.

Some among the many subdivisions of this class are much less childlike and more dignified than those we have been describing, and it is from these sections that the entities who have sometimes been reverenced under the name of wood-gods, or local village-gods, have been drawn. Such entities would be quite sensible of the flattery involved in the reverence shown to them, would enjoy it, and would no doubt be quite ready to do any small service they could in return. (The village-god is also often an artificial entity, but that variety will be considered in its appropriate place.) The Adept knows how to make use of the services of the nature-spirits when he requires them, but the ordinary magician can obtain their assistance only by processes either of invocation or evocation—that is, either by attracting their attention as a suppliant and making some kind of bargain with them, or by endeavouring to set in motion influences which would compel their obedience. Both methods are extremely undesirable, and the latter is also excessively dangerous, as the operator would arouse a determined hostility which might prove fatal to him. Needless to say, no one studying occultism under a qualified Master would ever be permitted to attempt anything of the kind at all.

4. *The Devas.* The highest system of evolution connected with this earth, so far as we know, is that of the beings whom Hindus call the Devas, and who have elsewhere been spoken of as angels, sons of God, etc. They may, in fact, be regarded as a kingdom lying next above humanity, in the same way as humanity in turn lies next above the animal kingdom, but with this important difference, that while for an animal there is no possibility of evolution through any kingdom but the human, man, when he attains a certain high level, finds various paths of advancement opening before him, of which this great Deva evolution is only one. In comparison with the sublime renunciation of the Nirmânakâya, the acceptance of this line of evolution is sometimes spoken of in the books as "yielding to the temptation to become a god," but it must not be inferred from this expression that any shadow of blame attaches to the man who makes this choice. The path he selects is not the shortest, but it is nevertheless a very noble one, and if his developed intuition impels him towards it, it is probably the one best suited for his capacities. We must never forget that in spiritual as in physical climbing it is not every one who can bear the strain of the steeper path; there may be many for whom what seems the slower way is the only one possible, and we should indeed be unworthy followers of the great Teachers if we allowed our ignorance to betray us into the slightest thought of despisal towards those whose choice differs from our own. However confident that ignorance of the difficulties of the future may allow us to feel now, it is impossible for us to tell at this stage what we shall find ourselves able to do when, after many lives of patient striving, we have earned the right to choose our own future; and indeed, even those who "yield to the temptation to become gods," have a sufficiently glorious career before them, as will presently be seen. To avoid possible misunderstanding it may be mentioned *par parenthèse* that there is another and entirely evil sense sometimes attached in the books to this phrase of "becoming a god," but in that form it certainly could never be any kind of "temptation" to the developed man, and in any case it is altogether foreign to our present subject.

In oriental literature this word "Deva" is frequently used vaguely to mean almost any kind of non-human entity, so that it would often include DHYÂN CHOHANS on the one hand and nature-spirits and artificial elementals on the other. Here, however, its use will be restricted to the magnificent evolution which we are now considering. Though connected with this earth, the Devas are by no means confined to it, for the whole of our present chain of seven worlds is as one world to them, their evolution being through a grand system of seven chains. Their hosts have hitherto been recruited chiefly from other humanities in the solar system, some lower and some higher than ours, since but a very small portion of our own has as yet reached the level at which for us it is possible to join them; but it seems certain that some of their very numerous classes have not passed in their upward progress through any humanity at all comparable to ours. It is not possible for us at present to understand very much about them, but it is clear that what may be described as the aim of their evolution is considerably higher than ours; that is to say, while the object of our human evolution is to raise the successful portion of humanity to a certain degree of occult development by the end of the seventh round, the object of the Deva evolution is to raise their foremost rank to a very much higher level in the corresponding period. For them, as for us, a steeper but shorter path to still more sublime heights lies open to earnest endeavour; but what those heights may be in their case we can only conjecture.

It is of course only the lower fringe of this august body that need be mentioned in connection with our subject of the astral plane. Their three lower great divisions (beginning from the bottom) are generally called Kâmadevas, Rûpadevas, and Arûpadevas respectively. Just as our ordinary body here—the lowest body possible for us—is the physical, so the ordinary body of a Kâmadeva is the astral; so that he stands in somewhat the same position as humanity will do when it reaches planet F, and he, living ordinarily in an astral body, would go out of it to higher spheres in a Mâyâvirûpa just as we might in an astral body, while to enter the Kârana Sharîra would be to him (when sufficiently developed) no greater effort than to form a Mâyâvirûpa is to us. In the same way the Rûpadeva's ordinary body would be the Mâyâvirûpa, since his habitat is on the four lower or rûpa levels of that spiritual state which we usually call Devachan: while the Arûpadeva belongs to the three higher levels of that plane, and owns no nearer approach to a body than the Kârana Sharîra. But for Rûpa and Arûpadevas to manifest on the astral plane is an occurrence at least as rare as it is for astral entities to materialize on this physical plane, so we need do no more than mention them now. As regards the lowest division—the Kâmadevas—it would be quite a mistake to think of all of them as immeasurably superior to ourselves, since some have entered their ranks from a humanity in some respects less advanced than our own; of course the general average among them is much higher than among us, for all that is actively or wilfully evil has long been weeded out from their ranks; but they differ widely in disposition, and a really noble, unselfish, spiritually-minded man may well stand higher in the scale of evolution than some of them. Their attention can be attracted by certain magical evocations, but the only human will which can dominate theirs is that of a certain high class of Adepts. As a rule they seem scarcely conscious of us on our physical plane, but it does now and then happen that one of them becomes aware of some human difficulty which excites his pity, and he perhaps renders some assistance, just as any of us would try to help an animal that we saw in trouble. But it is well understood among them that any interference in human affairs at the present stage is likely to do far more harm than good. Above the Arûpadevas there are four other great divisions, and again, above and beyond the Deva kingdom altogether, stand the great hosts of the Dhyân Chohans, but the consideration of such glorified Beings would be out of place in an essay on the astral plane.

Though we cannot claim them as belonging exactly to any of our classes, this is perhaps the best place in which to mention those wonderful and important Beings, the four Devarâjahs. In this name the word Deva must not, however, be taken in the sense in which we have been using it, for it is not over the Deva kingdom but over the four "elements" of earth, water, air, and fire, with their indwelling nature-spirits and essences, that these four Kings rule. What the evolution has been through which they rose to their present height of power and wisdom we cannot tell, save only that it has certainly not passed through anything corresponding to our own humanity. They are often spoken of as the Regents of the Earth, or Angels of the four cardinal points, and the Hindu books call them the Chatur Mahârâjahs, giving their names as Dhritarāshtra, Virūdhaka, Virūpaksha, and Vaishrāvana. In the same books their hosts are called Gandharvas, Kumbhandas, Nâgas, and Yakshas respectively, the points of the compass appropriated to each being in corresponding order east, south, west, and north, and their symbolical colours white, blue, red, and gold. They are mentioned in *The Secret Doctrine* as "winged globes and fiery wheels"; and in the Christian bible Ezekiel makes a very remarkable attempt at a description of them in which very similar words are used. References to them are to be found in the symbology of every religion, and they have always been held in the highest reverence as the protectors of mankind. It is they who are the agents of man's Karma during his life on earth, and they thus play an extremely important part in human destiny. THE LIPIKA, the great karmic deities of the Kosmos, weigh the deeds of each personality when the final separation of its principles takes place in Kâmaloka and give as it were the mould of an etheric double exactly suitable to its Karma for the man's next birth; but it is the Devarâjahs who, having command of the "elements" of which that etheric double must be composed, arrange their proportion so as to fulfil accurately the intention of the LIPIKA. It is they also who constantly watch all through life to counter-balance the changes perpetually being introduced into man's condition by his own free will and that of those around him, so that no injustice may be done, and Karma may be accurately worked out, if not in one way then in another. A learned dissertation upon these marvellous beings will be found in *The Secret Doctrine*, vol. i., pp. 122-126. They are able to take human material forms at will, and several cases are recorded when they have done so. All the higher nature-spirits and hosts of artificial elementals act as their agents in the stupendous work they carry out, yet all the threads are in their hands, and the whole responsibility rests upon them alone. It is not often that they manifest upon the astral plane, but when they do they are certainly the most remarkable of its non-human inhabitants. A student of occultism will not need to be told that as there are seven great classes both of nature-spirits and elemental essence there must really be seven and not four Devarâjahs but outside the circle of initiation little is known and less may be said of the higher three.

III. ARTIFICIAL.

This, the largest class of astral entities, is also much the most important to man. Being entirely his own creation, it is inter-related with him by the closest karmic bonds, and its action upon him is direct and incessant. It is an enormous inchoate mass of semi-intelligent entities, differing among themselves as human thoughts differ, and practically incapable of anything like classification or arrangement. The only division which can be usefully made is that which distinguishes between the artificial elementals made by the majority of mankind unconsciously, and those made by magicians with definite intent; while we may relegate to a third class the very small number of artificially arranged entities which are not elementals at all.

1. *Elementals formed unconsciously.* It has already been explained that the elemental essence which surrounds us on every side is in all its numberless varieties singularly susceptible to the influence of human thought. The action of the mere casual wandering thought upon it, causing it to burst into a cloud of rapidly-moving, evanescent forms, has already been described; we have now to note how it is affected when the human mind formulates a definite, purposeful thought or wish. The effect produced is of the most striking nature. The thought seizes upon the plastic essence, and moulds it instantly into a living being of appropriate form—a being which when once thus created is in no way under the control of its creator, but lives out a life of its own, the length of which is proportionate to the intensity of the thought or wish which called it into existence. It lasts, in fact, just as long as the thought-force holds it together. Most people's thoughts are so fleeting and indecisive that the elementals created by them last only a few minutes or a few hours, but an often-repeated thought or an earnest wish will form an elemental whose existence may extend to many days. Since the ordinary man's thoughts refer very largely to himself, the elementals they form remain hovering about him, and constantly tend to provoke a repetition of the idea they represent, since such repetitions, instead of forming new elementals, would strengthen the old one, and give it a fresh lease of life. A man, therefore, who frequently dwells upon one wish often forms for himself an astral attendant which, constantly fed by fresh thought, may haunt him for years, ever gaining more and more strength and influence over him; and it will easily be seen that if the desire be an evil one the effect upon his moral nature may be of the most disastrous character.

Still more pregnant of result for good or evil are a man's thoughts about other people, for in that case they hover not about the thinker, but about the object of the thought. A kindly thought about any person or an earnest wish for his good will form and project towards him a friendly artificial elemental; if the wish be a definite one, as, for example, that he may recover from some sickness, then the elemental will be a force ever hovering over him to promote his recovery, or to ward off any influence that might tend to hinder it, and in doing this it will display what appears like a very considerable amount of intelligence and adaptability, though really it is simply a force acting along the line of least resistance—pressing steadily in one direction all the time, and taking advantage of any channel that it can find, just as the water in a cistern would in a moment find the one open pipe among a dozen closed ones, and proceed to empty itself through that. If the wish be merely an indefinite one for his general good, the elemental essence in its wonderful plasticity will respond exactly to that less distinct idea also, and the creature formed will expend its force in the direction of whatever action for the man's advantage comes most readily to hand. Of course in all cases the amount of such force it has to expend, and the length of time that it will live to expend it, depend entirely upon the strength of the original wish or thought which gave it birth; though it must be remembered that it can be, as it were, fed and strengthened, and its life-period protracted by other good wishes or friendly thoughts projected in the same direction.

Furthermore, it appears to be actuated, like most other beings, by an instinctive desire to prolong its life, and thus reacts on its creator as a force constantly tending to provoke the renewal of the feeling which called it into existence. It also influences in a similar manner others with whom it comes into contact, though its *rapport* with them is naturally not so perfect.

All that has been said as to the effect of good wishes and friendly thoughts is also true in the opposite direction of evil wishes and angry thoughts; and considering the amount of envy, hatred, malice and all uncharitableness that exists in the world, it will be readily understood that among the artificial elementals many terrible creatures are to be seen. A man whose thoughts or desires are spiteful, brutal, sensual, avaricious, moves through the world carrying with him everywhere a pestiferous atmosphere of his own, peopled with the loathsome beings he has created to be his companions, and thus is not only in sadly evil case himself, but is a dangerous nuisance to his fellow-men, subjecting all who have the misfortune to come into contact with him to the risk of moral contagion from the influence of the abominations with which he chooses to surround himself. A feeling of envious or jealous hatred towards another person will send an evil elemental to hover over him and seek for a weak point through which it can operate; and if the feeling be a persistent one, such a creature may be continually nourished by it and thereby enabled to protract its undesirable activity for a very long period. It can, however, produce no effect upon the person towards whom it is directed unless he has himself some tendency which it can foster—some fulcrum for its lever, as it were; from the aura of a man of pure thought and good life all such influences at once rebound, finding nothing upon which they can fasten, and in that case, by a very curious law, they react in all their force upon their original creator. In him by the hypothesis they find a very congenial sphere of action, and thus the Karma of his evil wish works itself out at once by means of the very entity which he himself has called into existence. It occasionally happens, however, that an artificial elemental of this description is for various reasons unable to expend its force either upon its object or its creator, and in such cases it becomes a kind of wandering demon, readily attracted by any person who indulges feelings similar to that which gave it birth, and equally prepared either to stimulate such feelings in him for the sake of the strength it may gain from them, or to pour out its store of evil influence upon him through any opening which he may offer it. If it is sufficiently powerful to seize upon and inhabit some passing shell it frequently does so, as the possession of such a temporary home enables it to husband its dreadful resources more carefully. In this form it may manifest through a medium, and by masquerading as some well-known friend may sometimes obtain an influence over people upon whom it would otherwise have little hold.

What has been written above will serve to enforce the statement already made as to the importance of maintaining a strict control over our thoughts. Many a well-meaning man, who is scrupulously careful to do his duty towards his neighbour in word and deed, is apt to consider that his thoughts at least are nobody's business but his own, and so lets them run riot in various directions, utterly unconscious of the swarms of baleful creatures he is launching upon the world. To such a man an accurate comprehension of the effect of thought and desire in producing artificial elementals would come as a horrifying revelation; on the other hand, it would be the greatest consolation to many devoted and grateful souls who are oppressed with the feeling that they are unable to do anything in return for the kindness lavished upon them by their benefactors. For friendly thoughts and earnest good wishes are as easily and as effectually formulated by the poorest as by the richest, and it is within the power of almost any man, if he will take the trouble, to maintain what is practically a good angel always at the side of the brother or sister, the friend or the child whom he loves best, no matter in what part of the world he may be. Many a time a mother's loving thoughts and prayers have formed themselves into an angel guardian for the child, and except in the almost impossible case that the child had in him no instinct responsive to a good influence, have undoubtedly given him assistance and protection. Such guardians may often be seen by clairvoyant vision, and there have even been cases where one of them has had sufficient strength to materialize and become for the moment visible to physical sight. A curious fact which deserves mention here is that even after the passage of the mother into the devachanic condition the love which she pours out upon the children she thinks of as surrounding her will react upon the real children still living in this world, and will often support the guardian elemental which she created while on earth, until her dear ones themselves pass away in turn. As Madame Blavatsky remarks, "her love will always be felt by the children in the flesh; it will manifest in their dreams and often in various events, in providential protections and escapes—for love is a strong shield, and is not limited by space or time" (*Key to Theosophy*, p. 150). All the stories of the intervention of guardian angels must not, however, be attributed to the action of artificial elementals, for in many cases such "angels" have been the souls of either living or recently departed human beings, and they have also occasionally, though rarely, been Devas.

This power of an earnest desire, especially if frequently repeated, to create an active elemental which ever presses forcefully in the direction of its own fulfilment, is the scientific explanation of what devout but unphilosophical people describe as answers to prayer. There are occasions, though at present these are rare, when the Karma of the person so praying is such as to permit of assistance being directly rendered to him by an Adept or his pupil, and there is also the still rarer possibility of the intervention of a Deva or some friendly nature-spirit; but in all these cases the easiest and most obvious form for such assistance to take would be the strengthening and the intelligent direction of the elemental already formed by the wish.

A very curious and instructive instance of the extreme persistence of these artificial elementals under favourable circumstances came under the notice of one of our investigators quite recently. All readers of the literature of such subjects are aware that many of our ancient families are supposed to have associated with them a traditional death-warning—a phenomenon of one kind or another which foretells, usually some days beforehand, the approaching decease of the head of the house. A picturesque example of this is the well-known story of the white bird of the Oxenhams, whose appearance has ever since the time of Queen Elizabeth been recognized as a sure presage of the death of some member of the family; while another is the spectral coach which is reported to drive up to the door of a certain castle in the north when a similar calamity is impending. A phenomenon of this order occurs in connection with the family of one of our members, but it is of a much commoner and less striking type than either of the above, consisting only of a solemn and impressive strain of dirge-like music, which is heard apparently floating in the air three days before the death takes place. Our member, having himself twice heard this mystic sound, finding its warning in both cases quite accurate, and knowing also that according to family tradition the same thing had been happening for several centuries, set himself to seek by occult methods for the cause underlying so strange a phenomenon. The result was unexpected but interesting. It appeared that somewhere in the twelfth century the head of the family went to the crusades, like many another valiant man, and took with him to win his spurs in the sacred cause his youngest and favourite son, a promising youth whose success in life was the dearest wish of his father's heart. Unhappily, however, the young man was killed in battle, and the father was plunged into the depths of despair, lamenting not only the loss of his son, but still more the fact that he was cut off so suddenly in the full flush of careless and not altogether blameless youth. So poignant, indeed, were the old man's feelings that he cast off his knightly armour and joined one of the great monastic orders, vowing to devote all the remainder of his life to prayer, first for the soul of his son, and secondly that henceforward no descendant of his might ever again encounter what seemed to his simple and pious mind the terrible danger of meeting death unprepared. Day after day for many a year he poured all the energy of his soul into the channel of that one intense wish, firmly believing that somehow or other the result he so earnestly desired would be brought about. A student of occultism will have little difficulty in deciding what would be the effect of such a definite and long-continued stream of thought; our knightly monk created an artificial elemental of immense power and resourcefulness for its own particular object, and accumulated within it a store of force which would enable it to carry out his wishes for an indefinite period. An elemental is a perfect storage-battery—one from which there is practically no leakage; and when we remember what its original strength must have been, and how comparatively rarely it would be called upon to put it forth, we shall scarcely wonder that even now it exhibits unimpaired vitality, and still warns the direct descendants of the old crusader of their approaching doom by repeating in their ears the strange wailing music which was the dirge of a young and valiant soldier seven hundred years ago in Palestine.

2. *Elementals formed consciously.* Since such results as have been described above have been achieved by the thought-force of men who were entirely in the dark as to what they were doing, it will readily be imagined that a magician who understands the subject, and can see exactly what effect he is producing, may wield immense power along these lines. As a matter of fact occultists of both the white and dark schools frequently use artificial elementals in their work, and few tasks are beyond the powers of such creatures when scientifically prepared and directed with knowledge and skill; for one who knows how to do so can maintain a connection with his elemental and guide it, no matter at what distance it may be working, so that it will practically act as though endowed with the full intelligence of its master. Very definite and very efficient guardian angels have sometimes been supplied in this way, though it is probably very rarely that Karma permits such a decided interference in a person's life as that would be. In such a case, however, as that of a pupil of the Adepts, who might have in the course of his work for them to run the risk of attack from forces with which his unaided strength would be entirely insufficient to cope, guardians of this description have been given, and have fully proved their sleepless vigilance and their tremendous power. By some of the more advanced processes of black magic, also, artificial elementals of great power may be called into existence, and much evil has been worked in various ways by such entities. But it is true of them, as of the previous class, that if they are aimed at a person whom by reason of his purity of character they are unable to influence they react with terrible force upon their creator; so that the mediæval story of the magician being torn to pieces by the fiends he himself had raised is no mere fable, but may well have an awful foundation in fact.

Such creatures occasionally, for various reasons, escape from the control of those who are trying to make use of them, and become wandering and aimless demons, as do some of those mentioned under the previous heading under similar circumstances; but those that we are considering, having much more intelligence and power, and a much longer existence, are proportionately more dangerous. They invariably seek for means of prolonging their life either by feeding like vampires upon the vitality of human beings, or by influencing them to make offerings to them; and among simple half-savage tribes they have frequently succeeded by judicious management in getting themselves recognized as village or family gods. Any deity which demands sacrifices involving the shedding of blood may always be set down as belonging to the lowest and most loathsome class of this order; other less objectionable types are sometimes content with offerings of rice and cooked food of various kinds. There are parts of India where both these varieties may be found flourishing even at the present day, and in Africa they are probably comparatively numerous. By means of whatever nourishment they can obtain from the offerings, and still more by the vitality they draw from their devotees, they may continue to prolong their existence for many years, or even centuries, retaining sufficient strength to perform occasional phenomena of a mild type in order to stimulate the faith and zeal of their followers, and invariably making themselves unpleasant in some way or other if the accustomed sacrifices are neglected. For example, it was asserted recently that in one

Indian village the inhabitants had found that whenever for any reason the local deity did not get his or her regular meals, spontaneous fires began to break out with alarming frequency among the cottages, sometimes three or four simultaneously, in cases where they declared it was impossible to suspect human agency; and other stories of a more or less similar nature will no doubt recur to the memory of any reader who knows something of the out-of-the-way corners of that most wonderful of all countries.

The art of manufacturing artificial elementals of extreme virulence and power seems to have been one of the specialities of the magicians of Atlantis—"the lords of the dark face". One example of their capabilities in this line is given in *The Secret Doctrine* (vol. ii., p. 427), where we read of the wonderful speaking animals who had to be quieted by an offering of blood, lest they should awaken their masters and warn them of the impending destruction. But apart from these strange beasts they created other artificial entities of power and energy so tremendous, that it is darkly hinted that some of them have kept themselves in existence even to this day, though it is more than eleven thousand years since the cataclysm which overwhelmed their original masters. The terrible Indian goddess whose devotees were impelled to commit in her name the awful crimes of Thuggee—the ghastly Kâlî, worshipped even to this day with rites too abominable to be described—might well be a relic of a system which had to be swept away even at the cost of the submergence of a continent, and the loss of sixty-five million human lives.

3. *Human Artificials.* We have now to consider a class of entities which, though it contains but very few individuals, has acquired from its intimate connection with one of the great movements of modern times an importance entirely out of proportion to its numbers. It seems doubtful whether it should appear under the first or third of our main divisions; but, though certainly human, it is so far removed from the course of ordinary evolution, so entirely the product of a will outside of its own, that it perhaps falls most naturally into place among the artificial beings. The easiest way of describing it will be to commence with its history, and to do that we must once more look back to the great Atlantean race. In thinking of the Adepts and schools of occultism of that remarkable people our minds instinctively revert to the evil practices of which we hear so much in connection with their latter days; but we must not forget that before that age of selfishness and degradation the mighty civilization of Atlantis had brought forth much that was noble and worthy of admiration, and that among its leaders were some who now stand upon the loftiest pinnacles as yet attained by man. Among the lodges for occult study preliminary to initiation formed by the Adepts of the good Law was one in a certain part of America which was then tributary to one of the great Atlantean monarchs—"the Divine Rulers of the Golden Gate"; and though it has passed through many and strange vicissitudes, though it has had to move its head-quarters from country to country as each in turn was invaded by the jarring elements of a later civilization, that lodge still exists even at the present day, observing still the same old-world ritual even teaching as a sacred and hidden language the same Atlantean tongue which was used at its foundation so many thousands of years ago. It still remains what it was from the first—a lodge of occultists of pure and philanthropic aims, which can lead those students whom it finds worthy no inconsiderable distance on the road to knowledge, and confers such psychic powers as are in its gift only after the most searching tests as to the fitness of the candidate. Its teachers do not stand upon the Adept level, yet hundreds have learnt through it how to set their feet upon the Path which has led them to Adeptship in later lives; and though it is not in direct communication with the Brotherhood of the Himalayas, there are some among the latter who have themselves been connected with it in former incarnations, and therefore retain a more than ordinarily friendly interest in its proceedings.

The chiefs of this lodge, though they have always kept themselves and their society strictly in the background, have nevertheless done what they could from time to time to assist the progress of truth in the world, and some half-century ago, in despair at the rampant materialism which seemed to be stifling all spirituality in Europe and America, they determined to make an attempt to combat it by somewhat novel methods—in point of fact to offer opportunities by which any reasonable man could acquire absolute proof of that life apart from the physical body which it was the tendency of science to deny. The phenomena exhibited were not in themselves absolutely new, since in some form or other we may hear of them all through history; but their definite organization—their production as it were to order—these were features distinctly new to the modern world. The movement they thus set on foot gradually grew into the vast fabric of modern spiritualism, and though it would perhaps be unfair to hold the originators of the scheme directly responsible for many of the results which have followed, we must admit that they have achieved their purpose to the extent of converting vast numbers of people from a belief in nothing in particular to a firm faith in at any rate some kind of future life. This is undoubtedly a magnificent result, though, in the opinion of many of those whose power and knowledge enable them to take a wider view of such matters than we can, it has been attained at too great a cost, since it seems to them that on the whole the harm done outweighs the good. The method adopted was to take some ordinary person after death, arouse him thoroughly upon the astral plane, instruct him to a certain extent in the powers and possibilities belonging to it, and then put him in charge of a spiritualistic circle. He in his turn "developed" other departed personalities along the same line, they all acted upon those who sat at their *séances*, and "developed" them as mediums; and so spiritualism grew and flourished. No doubt living members of the original lodge occasionally manifested themselves in astral form at some of the circles—perhaps they may do so even now; but in most cases they simply gave such direction and guidance as they considered necessary to the persons they had put in charge. There is little doubt that the movement increased so much more rapidly than they had expected that it soon got quite beyond their control, so that, as has been said, for many of the later developments they can only be held indirectly responsible.

Of course the intensification of the astral-plane life in those persons who were thus put in charge of circles distinctly delayed their natural progress; and though the idea had been that anything lost in this way would be fully atoned for by the good Karma gained by helping to lead others to the truth, it was soon found that it was impossible to make use of a "spirit-guide" for any length of time without doing him serious and permanent injury. In some cases such "guides" were therefore withdrawn, and others substituted for them; in others it was considered for various reasons undesirable to make such a change, and then a very remarkable expedient was adopted which gave rise to the curious class of creatures we have called "human artificials". The higher principles of the original "guide" were allowed to pass on their long delayed evolution into the devachanic condition, but the shade he left behind him was taken possession of, sustained, and operated upon so that it might appear to its admiring circle practically just as before. This seems at first to have been done by members of the lodge themselves, but apparently that arrangement was found irksome or unsuitable, or perhaps was considered a waste of force, and the same objection applied to the use for this purpose of an artificial elemental; so it was eventually decided that the departed person who would have been appointed to succeed the late "spirit-guide" should still do so, but should take possession of the latter's shade or shell, and in fact simply wear his appearance. It is said that some members of the lodge objected to this on the ground that though the purpose might be entirely good a certain amount of deception was involved; but the general opinion seems to have been that as the shade really was the same, and contained something at any rate of the original lower Manas, there was nothing that could be called deception in the matter. This, then, was the genesis of the human artificial entity, and it is understood that in some cases more than one such change has been made without arousing suspicion, though on the other hand some investigators of spiritualism have remarked on the fact that after a considerable lapse of time certain differences suddenly became observable in the manner and disposition of a "spirit". It is needless to say that none of the Adept Brotherhood has ever approved of the formation of an artificial entity of this sort, though they could not interfere with any one who thought it right to take such a course. A weak point in the arrangement is that many others besides the original lodge may adopt this plan, and there is nothing whatever to prevent black magicians from supplying communicating "spirits"—as, indeed, they have been known to do.

With this class we conclude our survey of the inhabitants of the astral plane. With the reservations specially made some few pages back, the catalogue may be taken as a fairly complete one; but it must once more be emphasized that this treatise claims only to sketch the merest outline of a very vast subject, the detailed elaboration of which would need a lifetime of study and hard work.

Phenomena.

Though in the course of this paper various superphysical phenomena have been mentioned and to some extent explained, it will perhaps before concluding be desirable so far to recapitulate as to give a list of those which are most frequently met with by the student of these subjects, and to show by which of the agencies we have attempted to describe they are usually caused. The resources of the astral world, however, are so varied that almost any phenomenon with which we are acquainted can be produced in several different ways, so that it is only possible to lay down general rules in the matter.

Apparitions or ghosts furnish a very good instance of the remark just made, for in the loose manner in which the words are ordinarily used they may stand for almost any inhabitant of the astral plane. Of course psychically developed people are constantly seeing such things, but for an ordinary person to "see a ghost," as the common expression runs, one of two things must happen: either that ghost must materialize, or that person must have a temporary flash of psychic perception. But for the fact that neither of these events is a common one, ghosts would be met with in our streets as frequently as living people.

Churchyard Ghosts.   If the ghost is seen hovering about a grave it is probably the etheric shell of a newly-buried person, though it *may* be the astral body of a living man haunting in sleep the tomb of a friend; or again, it may be a materialized thought-form—that is, an artificial elemental created by the energy with which a man thinks of himself as present at that particular spot. These varieties would be easily distinguishable one from the other by any one accustomed to use astral vision, but an unpractised person would be quite likely to call them all vaguely "ghosts".

Apparitions of the Dying.   Apparitions at the time of death are by no means uncommon, and are very often really visits paid by the astral form of the dying man just before what we elect to call the moment of dissolution; though here again they are quite likely to be thought-forms called into being by his earnest wish to see some friend once more before he passes into an unfamiliar condition.

Haunted Localities.   Apparitions at the spot where some crime was committed are usually thought-forms projected by the criminal, who, whether living or dead, but most especially when dead, is perpetually thinking over again and again the circumstances of his action; and since these thoughts are naturally specially vivid in his mind on the anniversary of the original crime, it is often only on that occasion that the artificial elementals he creates are strong enough to materialize themselves to ordinary sight—a fact which accounts for the periodicity of some manifestations of this class. Another point in reference to such phenomena is, that wherever any tremendous mental disturbance has taken place, wherever overwhelming terror, pain, sorrow, hatred, or indeed any kind of intense passion has been felt, an impression of so very marked a character has been made upon the astral light that a person with even the faintest glimmer of psychic faculty cannot but be deeply impressed by it, and it would need but a slight temporary increase of sensibility to enable him to visualize the entire scene—to see the event in all its detail apparently taking place before his eyes—and in such a case he would of course report that the place was haunted, and that he had seen a ghost. Indeed, people who are as yet unable to see psychically under any circumstances are frequently very unpleasantly impressed when visiting such places as we have mentioned; there are many, for example, who feel uncomfortable when passing the site of Tyburn Tree, or cannot stay in the Chamber of Horrors at Madame Tussaud's, though they may not be in the least aware that their discomfort is due to the dreadful impressions in the astral light which surround places and objects redolent of horror and crime, and to the presence of the loathsome astral entities which always swarm about such centres.

Family Ghosts. The family ghost, whom we generally find in the stock stories of the supernatural as an appanage of the feudal castle, may be either a thought-form or an unusually vivid impression in the astral light, or again he may really be an earth-bound ancestor still haunting the scenes in which his thoughts and hopes centred during life.

Bell-ringing, stone-throwing, Another class of hauntings which take the form of bellringing, stone-throwing, or the breaking of crockery, has already been referred to, and is almost invariably the work of elemental forces, either set blindly in motion by the clumsy efforts of an ignorant person trying to attract the attention of his surviving friends, or intentionally employed by some childishly mischievous nature-spirit.

Fairies. The nature-spirits are also responsible for whatever of truth there may be in all the strange fairy stories which are so common in certain parts of the country. Sometimes a temporary accession of clairvoyance, which is by no means uncommon among the inhabitants of lonely mountainous regions, enables some belated wayfarer to watch their joyous gambols; sometimes strange tricks are played upon some terrified victim, and a glamour is cast over him, making him, for example, see houses and people where he knows none really exist. And this is frequently no mere momentary delusion, for a man will sometimes go through quite a long series of imaginary but most striking adventures, and then suddenly find that all his brilliant surroundings have vanished in a moment, leaving him standing in some lonely valley or on some wind-swept plain. On the other hand, it is by no means safe to accept as founded on fact all the popular legends on the subject, for the grossest superstition is often mingled with the theories of the peasantry about these beings, as was shown by a recent terrible murder case in Ireland.

To the same entities must be attributed a large portion of what are called physical phenomena at spiritualistic *séances*—indeed, many a *séance* has been given entirely by these mischievous creatures; and such a performance might easily include many very striking items, such as the answering of questions and delivery of pretended messages by raps or tilts, the exhibition of "spirit lights," the apport of objects from a distance, the reading of thoughts which were in the mind of any person present, the precipitation of writings or drawings, and even materializations. In fact, the nature-spirits alone, if any of them happened to be disposed to take the trouble, could give a *séance* equal to the most wonderful of which we read; for though there may be certain phenomena which they would not find it easy to reproduce, their marvellous power of glamour would enable them without difficulty to persuade the entire circle that these phenomena also had duly occurred, unless, indeed, there were present a trained observer who understood their arts and knew how to defeat them. As a general rule, whenever silly tricks or practical jokes are played at a *séance*, we may infer the presence either of low-class nature-spirits, or of human beings who were of a sufficiently degraded type to find pleasure in such idiotic performances during life.

Communicating Entities. As to the entities who may "communicate" at a *séance*, or may obsess and speak through an entranced medium, their name is simply legion; there is hardly a single class among all the varied inhabitants of the astral plane from whose ranks they may not be drawn, though after the explanations given it will be readily understood that the chances are very much against their coming from a high one. A manifesting "spirit" *may* be exactly what it professes to be, but on the whole the probabilities are that it is nothing of the kind; and for the ordinary sitter there is absolutely no means of distinguishing the true from the false, since the extent to which a being having all the resources of the astral plane at his command can delude a person on the physical plane is so great that no reliance can be placed even on what seems the most convincing proof. If something manifests which announces itself as a man's long-lost brother, he can have no certainty that its claim is a just one; if it tells him of some fact known only to that brother and to himself, he remains unconvinced, for he knows that it might easily have read the information from his own mind, or from his surroundings in the astral light; even if it goes still further and tells him something connected with his brother, of which he himself is unaware, but which he afterwards verifies, he still realizes that even this may have been read from the astral record, or that what he sees before him may be only the shade of his brother, and so possess his memory without in any way being himself. It is not for one moment denied that important communications have sometimes been made at *séances* by entities who in such cases have been precisely what they said they were; all that is claimed is that it is quite impossible for the ordinary person who visits a *séance* ever to be certain that he is not being cruelly deceived in one or other of half a dozen different ways.

There have been a few cases in which members of the lodge of occultists referred to above as originating the spiritualistic movement have themselves given, through a medium, a series of valuable teachings on deeply interesting subjects, but this has invariably been at strictly private family *séances*, not at public performances for which money has been paid.

To understand the methods by which a large class of physical phenomena are produced, it is necessary to have some comprehension of the various resources mentioned above, which a person functioning on the astral plane finds at his command; and this is a branch of the subject which it is by no means easy to make clear, especially as it is hedged about with certain obviously necessary restrictions. *Astral Resources.* It may perhaps help us if we remember that the astral plane may be regarded as in many ways only an extension of the physical, and the idea that matter may assume the etheric state (in which, though intangible to us, it is yet purely physical) may serve to show us how the one melts into the other. In fact, in the Hindu conception of Jagrat, or "the waking state," the physical and astral planes are combined, its seven subdivisions corresponding to the four conditions of physical matter, and the three broad divisions of astral matter explained above. With this thought in our minds it is easy to move a step further, and grasp the idea that astral vision, or rather astral perception, may from one point of view be defined as the capability of receiving an enormously increased number of different sets of vibrations. In our physical bodies one small set of slow vibrations is perceptible to us as sound; another small set of much more rapid vibrations affects us as light; and again another set as electric action: but there are immense numbers of intermediate vibrations which produce no result which our physical senses can cognize at all. Now it will readily be seen that if all, or even some only, of these intermediates, with all the complications producible by differences of wave-length, are perceptible on the astral plane, our comprehension of nature might be very greatly increased on that level, and we might be able to acquire much information which is now hidden from us.

It is admitted that some of these pass through solid matter with perfect ease, so that this enables us to account scientifically for some of the peculiarities of astral vision, though those minds to which the theory of the fourth dimension commends itself find in it a neater and more complete explanation. *Clairvoyance.* It is clear that the mere possession of this astral vision by a being would at once account for his capability to produce many results that seem very wonderful to us—such, for example, as the reading of a passage from a closed book; and when we remember, furthermore, that this faculty includes the power of thought-reading to the fullest extent, and also, when combined with the knowledge of the projection of currents in the astral light, that of observing a desired object in almost any part of the world, we see that a good many of the phenomena of clairvoyance are explicable even without rising above this level. Of course true, trained, and absolutely reliable clairvoyance calls .into operation an entirely different set of faculties, but as these belong to a higher plane than the astral, they form no part of our present subject. The faculty of accurate prevision, again, appertains altogether to that higher plane, yet flashes or reflections of it frequently show themselves to purely astral sight, more especially among simple-minded people who live under suitable *Prevision and Second-sight* conditions—what is called "second-sight" among the Highlanders of Scotland being a well-known example.

Another fact which must not be forgotten is that any intelligent inhabitant of the astral plane is not only able to perceive these etheric vibrations, but can also—if he has learnt how it is done—adapt them to his own ends or himself set them in motion.

It will be readily understood that superphysical forces and the methods of managing them are not subjects about which much can be written for publication at present, though there is reason to suppose that it may not be very long before at any rate some   Astral Forces. applications of one or two of them come to be known to the world at large: but it may perhaps be possible, without transgressing the limits of the permissible, to give so much of an idea of them as shall be sufficient to show in outline how certain phenomena are performed. All who have much experience of spiritualistic *séances* at which physical results are produced must at one time or another have seen evidence of the employment of practically resistless force in, for example, the instantaneous movement of enormous weights, and so on; and if of a scientific turn of mind, they may perhaps have wondered whence this force was obtained, and what was the leverage employed. As usual in connection with astral phenomena, there are several ways in which such work may have been done, but it will be enough for the moment to hint at four. First, there are great etheric currents constantly sweeping   Etheric over the surface of the earth from pole to pole in volume which makes their   Currents. power as irresistible as that of the rising tide, and there are methods by which this stupendous force may be safely utilized, though unskilful attempts to control it would be fraught with frightful danger. Secondly, there is what can best be described as   Etheric an etheric pressure, somewhat corresponding to, though immensely greater than,   Pressure. the atmospheric pressure. In ordinary life we are as little conscious of one of these pressures as we are of the other, but nevertheless they both exist, and if science were able to exhaust the ether from a given space, as it can exhaust the air, the one could be proved as readily as the other. The difficulty of doing that lies in the fact that matter in the etheric condition freely interpenetrates matter in all states below it, so that there is as yet no means within the knowledge of our physicists by which any given body of ether can be isolated from the rest. Practical Occultism, however, teaches how this can be done, and thus the tremendous force of etheric pressure can be brought into play. Thirdly, there is a vast store of potential energy which has become dormant in matter during the involution   Latent of the subtle into the gross, and by changing the condition of the matter some of   Energy. this may be liberated and utilized, somewhat as latent energy in the form of heat may be liberated by a change in the condition of visible matter. Fourthly, many   Sympathetic striking results, both great and small, may be produced by an extension of a   Vibration. principle which may be described as that of sympathetic vibration.

Illustrations taken from the physical plane seem generally to misrepresent rather than elucidate astral phenomena, because they can never be more than partially applicable; but the recollection of two simple facts of ordinary life may help to make this important branch of our subject clearer, if we are careful not to push the analogy further than it will hold good. It is well known that if one of the wires of a harp be made to vibrate vigorously, its movement will call forth sympathetic vibrations in the corresponding strings of any number of harps placed round it, if they are tuned to exactly the same pitch. It is also well known that when a large body of soldiers crosses a suspension bridge it is necessary for them to break step, since the perfect regularity of their ordinary march would set up a vibration in the bridge which would be intensified by every step they took, until the point of resistance of the iron was passed, when the whole structure would fly to pieces. With these two analogies in our minds (never forgetting that they are only partial ones) it may seem more comprehensible that one who knows exactly at what rate to start his vibrations—knows, so to speak, the keynote of the class of matter he wishes to affect—should be able by sounding that keynote to call forth an immense number of sympathetic vibrations. When this is done on the physical plane no additional energy is developed; but on the astral plane there is this difference, that the matter with which we are dealing is far less inert, and so when called into action by these sympathetic vibrations it adds its own living force to the original impulse, which may thus be multiplied many-fold; and then by further rhythmic repetition of the original impulse, as in the case of the soldiers marching over the bridge, the vibrations may be so intensified that the result is out of all apparent proportion to the cause. Indeed, it may be said that there is scarcely any limit to the conceivable achievements of this force in the hands of a great Adept Who fully comprehends its possibilities; for the very building of the Universe itself was but the result of the vibrations set up by the Spoken Word.

The class of mantras or spells which produce their result not by controlling some elemental, but merely by the repetition of certain sounds, also depend for their efficacy upon this action of sympathetic vibration. Mantras

The phenomenon of disintegration also may be brought about by the action of extremely rapid vibrations, which overcome the cohesion of the molecules of the object Disintegrati operated upon. A still higher rate of vibrations of a somewhat different type will separate these molecules into their constituent atoms. A body reduced by these means to the etheric condition can be moved by an astral current from one place to another with very great rapidity; and the moment that the force which has been exerted to put it into that condition is withdrawn it will be forced by the etheric pressure to resume its original form. It is in this way that objects are sometimes brought almost instantaneously from great distances at spiritualistic *séances*, and it is obvious that when disintegrated they could be passed with perfect ease through any solid substance, such, for example, as the wall of a house or the side of a locked box, so that what is commonly called "the passage of matter through matter" is seen, when properly understood, to be as simple as the passage of water through a sieve, or of a gas through a liquid in some chemical experiment.

Since it is possible by an alteration of vibrations to change matter from the solid to the etheric condition, it will be comprehended that it is also possible to reverse the process and to bring etheric matter into the solid state. As the one process explains the phenomenon of disintegration, so does the other that of materialization; and just as in the former case a continued effort of will is necessary to prevent the object Materialization from resuming its original form, so in exactly the same way in the latter phenomenon a continued effort is necessary to prevent the materialized matter from relapsing into the etheric condition. In the materializations seen at an ordinary *séance*, such matter as may be required is borrowed as far as possible from the medium's etheric double—an operation which is prejudicial to his health, and also undesirable in various other ways; and this explains the fact that the materialized form is usually strictly confined to the immediate neighbourhood of the medium, and is subject to an attraction which is constantly drawing it back to the body from which it came, so that if kept away from the medium too long the figure collapses, and the matter which composed it, returning to the etheric condition, rushes back instantly to its source.

The reason why the beings directing a *séance* find it easier to operate in darkness or in very subdued light will now be manifest, since their power would usually be insufficient to hold together a materialized form or even a "spirit hand" for more than a very few seconds amidst the intense vibrations set up by brilliant light. The *habitués* of *séances* will no doubt have noticed that materializations are of three kinds:—First, those which are tangible but not visible; second, those which are visible but not tangible; and third, those which are both visible and tangible. To the first kind, which is much the most common, belong the invisible spirit hands which so frequently stroke the faces of the sitters or carry small objects about the room, and the vocal organs from which the "direct voice" proceeds. In this case, an order of matter is being used which can neither reflect nor obstruct light, but which is capable under certain conditions of setting up vibrations in the atmosphere which affect us as sound. A variation of this class is that kind of partial materialization which, though incapable of reflecting any light that we can see, is yet able to affect some of the ultra-violet rays, and can therefore make a more or less Spirit definite impression upon the camera, and so provide us with what are known Photographs as "spirit photographs". When there is not sufficient power available to produce a perfect materialization we sometimes get the vaporous-looking form which constitutes our second class, and in such a case the "spirits" usually warn their sitters that the forms which appear must not be touched. In the rarer case of a full materialization there is sufficient power to hold together, at least for a few moments, a form which can be both seen and touched.

Why Darkness is required.

When an Adept or pupil finds it necessary for any purpose to materialize his Mâyâvirûpa or his astral body, he does not draw upon either his own etheric double or any one else's, since he has been taught how to extract the matter which he requires directly from the astral light or even from the Âkâsha.

Another phenomenon closely connected with this part of the subject is that of reduplication, which is produced by simply forming in the astral light a perfect mental image of the object to be copied, and then gathering about that mould the necessary physical matter. Of course for this purpose it is necessary that every particle, interior as well as exterior, of the object to be duplicated should be held accurately in view simultaneously, and consequently the phenomenon is one which requires considerable power of concentration to perform. Persons unable to reduce the matter required directly from the astral light have sometimes borrowed it from the material of the original article, which in this case would be correspondingly reduced in weight. *Reduplication.*

We read a good deal in Theosophical literature about the precipitation of letters or pictures. This result, like everything else, may be obtained in several ways. An Adept wishing to communicate with some one might place a sheet of paper before him, form an image of the writing which he wished to appear upon it, and draw from the astral light the matter wherewith to objectify that image; or if he preferred to do so it would be equally easy for him to produce the same result upon a sheet of paper lying before his correspondent, whatever might be the distance between them. A third method which, since it saves time, is much more frequently adopted, is to impress the whole substance of the letter on the mind of some pupil, and leave him to do the mechanical work of precipitation. That pupil would then take his sheet of paper, and, imagining he saw the letter written thereon in his Master's hand, would proceed to objectify the writing as before described. If he found it difficult to perform simultaneously the two operations of drawing his material from the astral light and precipitating the writing on the paper, he might have either ordinary ink or a small quantity of coloured powder on the table beside him, which, being already physical matter, could be drawn upon more readily. *Precipitatio*

It is of course obvious that the possession of this power would be a very dangerous weapon in the hands of an unscrupulous person, since it is just as easy to imitate one man's handwriting as another's, and it would be impossible to detect by any ordinary means a forgery committed in this manner. A pupil definitely connected with any Master has always an infallible test by which he knows whether any message really emanates from that Master or not, but for others the proof of its origin must always lie solely in the contents of the letter and the spirit breathing through it, as the handwriting, however cleverly imitated, is of absolutely no value as evidence.

As to speed, a pupil new to the work of precipitation would probably be able to image only a few words at a time, and would, therefore, get on hardly more rapidly than if he wrote his letter in the ordinary way, but a more experienced individual who could visualize a whole page or perhaps the entire letter at once would get through his work with greater facility. It is in this manner that quite long letters are sometimes produced in a few seconds at a *séance*.

When a picture has to be precipitated the method is precisely the same, except that here it is absolutely necessary that the entire scene should be visualized at once, and if many colours are required there is of course the additional complication of manufacturing them, keeping them separate, and reproducing accurately the exact tints of the scene to be represented. Evidently there is scope here for the exercise of the artistic faculty, and it must not be supposed that every inhabitant of the astral plane could by this method produce an equally good picture; a man who had been a great artist in life, and had therefore learnt how to see and what to look for, would certainly be very much more successful than the ordinary person if he attempted precipitation when on the astral plane after death.

The slate-writing, for the production of which under test conditions some of the greatest mediums have been so famous, is sometimes produced by precipitation, though more frequently the fragment of pencil enclosed between the slates is guided by a spirit hand, of which only just the tiny points sufficient to grasp it are materialized. *Slate-writing.*

Levitation An occurrence which occasionally takes place at *séances*, and more frequently among eastern Yôgîs, is what is called levitation—that is, the floating of a human body in the air. No doubt when this takes place in the case of a medium, he is often simply upborne by "spirit hands," but there is another and more scientific method of accomplishing this feat which is always used in the East, and occasionally here also. Occult science is acquainted with a means of neutralizing or even entirely reversing the attraction of gravity, and it is obvious that by the judicious use of this power all the phenomena of levitation may be easily produced. It was no doubt by a knowledge of this secret that some of the air-ships of ancient India and Atlantis were raised from the earth and made light enough to be readily moved and directed; and not improbably the same acquaintance with nature's finer forces greatly facilitated the labours of those who raised the enormous blocks of stone sometimes used in cyclopean architecture, or in the building of the Pyramids and Stonehenge.

With the knowledge of the forces of nature which the resources of the astral plane place at the command its inhabitants the production of what are called "spirit lights" is a very easy matter, whether they be of the mildly phosphorescent or the dazzling electrical variety, or those curious dancing globules of light into which a certain class of fire elementals so readily transform themselves. **Spirit Lights.** Since all light consists simply of vibrations of the ether, it is obvious that any one who knows how to set up these vibrations can readily produce any kind of light that he wishes.

It is by the aid of the etheric elemental essence also that the remarkable feat of handling fire unharmed is generally performed, though there are as usual other ways in which it can be done. The thinnest layer of etheric substance can be so manipulated as to be absolutely impervious to heat, and when the hand of a medium or sitter is covered with this he may pick up burning coal or red-hot iron with perfect safety. **Handling Fire.**

Most of the occurrences of the *séance*-room have now been referred to, but there are one or two of the rarer phenomena of the outer world which must not be left quite without mention in our list. The transmutation of metals is commonly supposed to be a mere dream of the mediæval alchemists, and no doubt in most cases the description of the phenomenon was merely a symbol of the purification of the soul; yet there seems to be some evidence that it was really accomplished by them on several occasions, and there are petty magicians in the East who profess to do it under test conditions even now. **Transmutation** Be that as it may, it is evident that since the ultimate atom is one and the same in all substances, and it is only the methods of its combination that differ, any one who possessed the power of reducing a piece of metal to the atomic condition and of re-arranging its atoms in some other form would have no difficulty in effecting transmutation to any extent that he wished.

The principle of sympathetic vibration mentioned above also provides the explanation of that strange and little-known phenomenon called repercussion, by means of which any injury done to, or any mark made upon, the astral body in the course of its wanderings will be reproduced in the physical body. **Repercussion.** We find traces of this in some of the evidence given at trials for witchcraft in the middle ages, in which it is not infrequently stated that some wound given to the witch when in the form of a dog or a wolf was found to have appeared in the corresponding part of her human body. The same strange law has sometimes led to an entirely unjust accusation of fraud against a medium, because, for example, some colouring matter rubbed upon the hand of a materialized "spirit" was afterwards found upon his hand—the explanation being that in that case, as so often happens, the "spirit" was simply the medium's astral body or perhaps even his etheric double, forced by the guiding influences to take some form other than his own. In fact the astral and physical bodies are so intimately connected that it is impossible to touch the keynote of one without immediately setting up exactly corresponding vibrations in the other.

CONCLUSION.

It is hoped that any reader who has been sufficiently interested to follow this treatise thus far, may by this time have a general idea of the astral plane and its possibilities, such as will enable him to understand and fit into their proper places in its scheme any facts in connection with it which he may pick up in his reading. Though only the roughest sketch has been given of a very great subject, enough has perhaps been said to show the extreme importance of astral perception in the study of biology, physics, chemistry, astronomy, medicine and history, and the great impulse which might be given by its development to all these sciences. Yet its attainment should never be regarded as an end in itself, since any means adopted with that object in view would inevitably lead to what is called in the East the *laukika* method of development—a system by which certain psychic powers are indeed acquired, but only for the present personality; and since their acquisition is surrounded by no safeguards, the student is extremely likely to misuse them. To this class belong all systems which involve the use of drugs, invocation of elementals, or the practices of Hatha Yoga. The other method, which is called the *lokottara*, consists of Raj Yoga or spiritual progress, and though it may be somewhat slower than the other, whatever is acquired along this line is gained for the permanent individuality, and never lost again, while the guiding care of a Master ensures perfect safety from misuse of power as long as his orders are scrupulously obeyed. The opening of astral vision must be regarded then only as a stage in the development of something infinitely nobler—merely as a step, and a very small step, on that great Upward Path which leads men to the sublime heights of Adeptship, and beyond even that through glorious vistas of wisdom and power such as our finite minds cannot now conceive.

Yet let no one think it an unmixed blessing to have the wider sight of the astral plane, for upon one in whom that vision is opened the sorrow and misery, the evil and the greed of the world press as an ever-present burden, until he often feels inclined to echo the passionate adjuration of Schiller: "Why hast thou cast me thus into the town of the ever-blind, to proclaim thine oracle with the opened sense? Take back this sad clear-sightedness; take from mine eyes this cruel light! Give me back my blindness—the happy darkness of my senses; take back thy dreadful gift!" This feeling is perhaps not an unnatural one in the earlier stages of the Path, yet higher sight and deeper knowledge soon bring to the student the perfect certainty that all things are working together for the eventual good of all—that

> Hour after hour, like an opening flower,
>   Shall truth after truth expand;
> For the sun may pale, and the stars may fail,
>   But the LAW of GOOD shall stand.
> Its splendour glows and its influence grows
>   As Nature's slow work appears,
> From the zoophyte small to the LORDS of all,
>   Through kalpas and crores of years.

THE DEVACHANIC PLANE

ITS CHARACTERISTICS AND INHABITANTS

PREFACE.

Few words are needed in sending this little book out into the world. It is the sixth of a series of Manuals designed to meet the public demand for a simple exposition of Theosophical teachings. Some have complained that our literature is at once too abstruse, too technical, and too expensive for the ordinary reader, and it is our hope that the present series may succeed in supplying what is a very real want. Theosophy is not only for the learned; it is for all. Perhaps among those who in these little books catch their first glimpse of its teachings, there may be a few who will be led by them to penetrate more deeply into its philosophy, its science and its religion, facing its abstruser problems with the student's zeal and the neophyte's ardour. But these Manuals are not written for the eager student, whom no initial difficulties can daunt; they are written for the busy men and women of the work-a-day world, and seek to make plain some of the great truths that render life easier to bear and death easier to face. Written by servants of the Masters who are the Elder Brothers of our race, they can have no other object than to serve our fellow-men.

INTRODUCTION.

IN the introduction to the manual recently issued on *The Astral Plane, I* remarked that "a good deal of information on the subject of this realm of nature is to be found scattered here and there in our books, but there is not, so far as I am aware, any single volume to which one can turn for a complete summary of the facts at present known to us about this interesting region." It seems evident that this remark applies with even greater force to the plane next above the astral—that of Devachan or Sukhâvatî. There is indeed a most instructive chapter on the subject in that indispensable text-book of every Theosophical student, Mr. Sinnett's *Esoteric Buddhism;* but though nothing which we have since learnt has in any way contradicted the lucid exposition of the devachanic state there given, it is nevertheless true that such investigations as we have been able to make during the thirteen years which have elapsed since it was written have placed us in possession of a considerable body of additional information as to details. It will be readily understood that there are many minor points about which Mr. Sinnett could not venture to trouble his Adept correspondent, which are nevertheless of the greatest interest to humanity, since by far the greater part of its existence is passed upon the plane under consideration—a plane which is in fact the true and permanent home of the reincarnating ego, each descent into incarnation being merely a short though all-important episode in its career. The object of this manual then is to present a summary of the facts about Devachan at present known to us; and, as previously in the case of the astral plane, I am requested by our investigators to say that, while they deprecate the ascription of anything like authority to their statements, they have felt it due to their fellow-students to take every precaution in their power to ensure accuracy. Indeed, I may say that in this case also "no fact, old or new, has been admitted to this treatise unless it has been confirmed by the testimony of at least two independent trained investigators among ourselves, and has also been passed as correct by older students whose knowledge on these points is necessarily much greater than ours. It is hoped therefore that this account, though it cannot be considered as complete, may yet be found reliable as far as it goes."

I will not here reproduce the remarks made in the previous manual as to the absolute necessity, to the student of Occultism, of a definite realization of the fact that nature is divided into various great planes, each with its own matter of different degrees of density, and each interpenetrating those below it—though these observations are quite as applicable to the study of the devachanic plane as to the astral: I will simply refer the enquirer on that matter to the introduction to Theosophical Manual No. V., and recapitulate here only so far as to remind the reader that Devachan is the third of the five great planes with which humanity is at present concerned, having below it the astral and the physical, and above it the buddhic (sometimes, though perhaps less appropriately, called the sushuptic) and the nirvânic. As just now remarked, it is the plane upon which man, unless at an exceedingly early stage of his progress, spends by far the greater part of his time during the process of evolution; for, except in the case of the entirely undeveloped, the proportion of the physical life to the devachanic is rarely much greater than one in twenty, and in the case of fairly good people it would sometimes fall as low as one in forty. It is therefore well worth our while to devote to its study such time and care as may be necessary to acquire as thorough a comprehension of it as is possible for us while encased in the physical body.

Unfortunately there are practically insuperable difficulties in the way of any attempt to put the facts of this third plane of nature into language—and not unnaturally, for we often find words insufficient to express our ideas and feelings even on this lowest plane. Readers of *The Astral Plane* will remember what was there stated as to the impossibility of conveying any adequate conception of the marvels of that region to those whose experience had not as yet transcended the physical world; one can but say that every observation there made to that effect applies with tenfold force to the effort which is before us in this sequel to that treatise. Not only is the matter which we must endeavour to describe much further removed than is astral matter from that to which we are accustomed, but the consciousness of that plane is so immensely wider than anything we can imagine down here, and its very conditions so entirely different, that when called upon to translate it all into mere ordinary words the explorer feels himself utterly at a loss, and can only trust that the intuition of his readers will supplement the inevitable imperfections of his description.

To take one only out of many possible examples, it would seem as though in Devachan space and time were non-existent, for events which here take place in succession and at widely-separated places, appear there to be occurring simultaneously and at the same point. That at least is the effect produced on the consciousness of the ego, though there are circumstances which favour the supposition that absolute simultaneity is the attribute of a still higher plane, and that the sensation of it in Devachan is simply the result of a succession so rapid that the infinitesimally minute spaces of time are indistinguishable, just as, in the well-known optical experiment of whirling round a stick the end of which is red-hot, the eye receives the impression of a continuous ring of fire if the stick be whirled more than ten times a second; not because a continuous ring really exists, but because the average human eye is incapable of distinguishing as separate any similar impressions which follow one another at intervals of less than the tenth part of a second.

However that may be, the reader will readily comprehend that in the endeavour to describe a condition of existence so totally unlike that of physical life as is the one which we have to consider, it will be impossible to avoid saying many things that will be partly unintelligible and may even seem wholly incredible to those who have not personally experienced the devachanic life. That this should be so is, as I have said, quite inevitable, so readers who find themselves unable to accept the report of our investigators must simply wait for a more satisfactory account of Devachan until they are able to examine it for themselves: I can only repeat the assurance that all reasonable precautions have been taken to ensure accuracy.

The general arrangement of the previous manual will as far as possible be followed in this one also, so that those who wish to do so will be able to compare the two planes stage by stage. The heading "Scenery" would however be inappropriate to Devachan, as will be seen later; we will therefore substitute for it the title which follows.

GENERAL CHARACTERISTICS.

Perhaps the least unsatisfactory method of approaching this exceedingly difficult subject will be to plunge *in medias res* and make the attempt (foredoomed to failure though it be) to depict what a pupil sees when first the devachanic plane opens before him. I use the word pupil advisedly, for unless a man stand in that relation to a qualified Master, there is but little likelihood of his being able to pass in full consciousness into that glorious land of bliss, and return to earth with clear remembrance of that which he has seen there. Thence no accommodating "spirit" ever comes to utter cheap platitudes through the mouth of the professional medium; thither no ordinary clairvoyant ever rises, though sometimes the best and purest have entered it when in deepest trance they slipped from the control of their Mesmerizers—yet even then they have rarely brought back more than a faint recollection of an intense but indescribable bliss, generally deeply coloured by their personal religious convictions.

When once the departed ego, withdrawing into himself after what we call death, has reached that plane, neither the yearning thoughts of his sorrowing friends nor the allurements of the spiritualistic circle can ever draw him back into communion with the physical earth until all the spiritual forces which he has set in motion in his recent life have worked themselves out to the full, and he once more stands ready to take upon himself new robes of flesh. Nor, even if he could so return, would his account of his experiences give any true idea of the plane, for, as will presently be, seen, it is only those who can enter it in full waking consciousness who are able to move about freely and drink in all the wondrous glory and beauty which Devachan has to show. But all this will be more fully explained later, when we come to deal with the inhabitants of this celestial realm.

A BEAUTIFUL DESCRIPTION.

In an early letter from an eminent occultist the following beautiful passage was given as a quotation from memory. I have never been able to discover whence it was taken, though what seems to be another version of it, considerably expanded, appears in Beal's *Catena of Buddhist Scriptures,* p. 378.

"Our Lord BUDDHA says: Many thousand myriads of systems of worlds beyond this is a region of bliss called Sukhâvatî. This region is encircled within seven rows of railings, seven rows of vast curtains, seven rows of waving trees. This holy abode of the Arhats is governed by the Tathâgatas and is possessed by the Bodhisattvas. It has seven precious lakes, in the midst of which flow crystalline waters having seven and yet one distinctive properties and qualities. This, O Sâriputra, is the Devachan. Its divine udambara flower casts a root in the shadow of every earth, and blossoms for all those who reach it. Those born in this blessed region—who have crossed the golden bridge and reached the seven golden mountains—they are truly felicitous; there is no more grief or sorrow in that cycle for them."

Veiled though they be under the gorgeous imagery of the Orient, we may easily trace in this passage some of the leading characteristics which have appeared most prominently in the accounts of our own modern investigators. The "seven golden mountains" can be but the seven subdivisions of the devachanic plane, separated from one another by barriers impalpable, yet real and effective there as "seven rows of railings, seven rows of vast curtains, seven rows of waving trees" might be here: the seven kinds of crystalline water, having each its distinctive properties and qualities, represent the different powers and conditions of mind belonging to them respectively, while the one quality which they all have in common is that of ensuring to those residing upon them the utmost intensity of bliss which they are capable of experiencing. Its flower indeed "casts a root in the shadow of every earth," for from every world man enters the corresponding Devachan, and happiness such as no tongue may tell is the blossom which burgeons forth for all who so live as to fit themselves to attain it. For they have "crossed the golden bridge" over the stream which divides this realm from Kâmaloka; for them the struggle between the higher and the lower is over, and for them, therefore, is "no more grief or sorrow in that cycle," until once more the ego puts himself forth into incarnation, and the celestial world is again left for a time behind.

THE BLISS OF DEVACHAN.

This intensity of bliss is the first great idea which must form a background to all our conceptions of Devachan. It is not only that we are dealing with a world in which, by its very constitution, evil and sorrow are impossible; it is not only a world in which every creature is happy: the facts of the case go far beyond all that. It is a world in which every being must, from the very fact of his presence there, be enjoying the highest spiritual bliss of which he is capable—a world whose power of response to his aspirations is limited only by his capacity to aspire. How this can be so we must endeavour to make clear later on; the point to be emphasized for the moment is that this radiant sense not only of the welcome absence of all evil and discord, but of the insistent, over-whelming presence of universal joy, is the first and most striking sensation experienced by him who enters upon the devachanic plane. And it never leaves him so long as he remains there; whatever work he may be doing, whatever still higher possibilities of spiritual exaltation may arise before him as he learns more of the capabilities of this new world in which he finds himself, the strange indescribable feeling of inexpressible delight in mere existence in such a realm underlies all else—this enjoyment of the abounding joy of others is ever present with him. Nothing on earth is like it, nothing can image it; if one could suppose the bounding life of childhood carried up into our spiritual experience and then intensified many thousandfold, perhaps some faint shadow of an idea of it might be suggested; yet even such a simile falls miserably short of that which lies beyond all words—the tremendous spiritual vitality of the devachanic plane.

One way in which this intense vitality manifests itself is the extreme rapidity of vibration of all particles and atoms of devachanic matter. As a theoretical proposition we are all aware that even here on the physical plane no particle of matter, though forming part of the densest of solid bodies, is ever for a moment at rest; nevertheless when by the opening of astral vision this becomes for us no longer a mere theory of the scientists, but an actual and ever-present fact, we realize the universality of life in a manner and to an extent that was quite impossible before; our mental horizon widens out and we begin even already to have glimpses of possibilities in nature which to those who cannot yet see must appear the wildest of dreams.

If this be the effect of acquiring the mere astral vision, and applying it to dense physical matter, try to imagine the result produced on the mind of the observer when, having left this lower plane behind and thoroughly studied the far more vivid life and infinitely more rapid vibrations of Kâmaloka, he finds a new and transcendent sense opening within him, which unfolds to his enraptured gaze yet another and a higher world, whose vibrations are as much quicker than those of our physical plane as vibrations of light are than those of sound—a world where the omnipresent life which pulsates ceaselessly around and within him is of a different order altogether, is as it were raised to an enormously higher power.

THE DEVACHANIC SENSE.

The very sense itself, by which he is enabled to cognize all this, is not the least of the marvels of this celestial world; no longer does he hear and see and feel by separate and limited organs, as he does down here, nor has he even the immensely extended capacity of sight and hearing which he possessed on the astral plane; instead of these he feels within him a strange new power which is not any of them, and yet includes them all and much more—a power which enables him the moment any person or thing comes before him not only to see it and feel it and hear it, but to know all about it instantly inside and out—its causes, its effects, and its possibilities, so far at least as that plane and all below it are concerned. He finds that for him to think is to realize; there is never any doubt, hesitation, or delay, about this direct action of the higher sense. If he thinks of a place, he is there; if of a friend, that friend is before him. No longer can misunderstandings arise, no longer can he be deceived or misled by any outward appearances, for every thought and feeling of his friend lies open as a book before him on that plane.

And if he is fortunate enough to have among his friends another whose higher sense is opened, their intercourse is perfect beyond all earthly conception. For them distance and separation do not exist; their feelings are no longer hidden or at best but half expressed by clumsy words; question and answer are unnecessary, for the thought-pictures are read as they are formed, and the interchange of ideas is as rapid as is their flashing into existence in the mind.

All knowledge is theirs for the searching—all, that is, which does not transcend even this lofty plane; the past of the world is as open to them as the present; the âkâshic records are ever at their disposal, and history, whether ancient or modern, unfolds itself before their eyes at their will. No longer are they at the mercy of the historian, who may be ill-informed, and must be more or less partial; they can study for themselves any incident in which they are interested, with the absolute certainty of seeing "the truth, the whole truth, and nothing but the truth." If they are able to stand upon the higher or arûpa levels of the plane the long line of their past lives unrolls itself before them like a scroll; they see the karmic causes which have made them what they are; they see what Karma still lies in front to be worked out before "the long sad count is closed," and thus they realize with unerring certainty their exact place in evolution.

If it be asked whether they can see the future clearly as the past, the answer must be in the negative, for though prevision is to a great extent possible to them, yet it is not perfect, because wherever in the web of destiny the hand of the developed man comes in, his powerful will may introduce new threads, and change the pattern of the life to come. The course of the ordinary undeveloped man, who has practically no will of his own worth speaking of, may often be foreseen clearly enough, but when the ego boldly takes his future into his own hands, exact prevision becomes impossible.

SURROUNDINGS.

The first impressions, then, of the pupil who enters the devachanic plane in full consciousness will probably be those of intense bliss, indescribable vitality, and enormously increased power. And when he makes use of his new sense to examine his surroundings, what does he see? He finds himself in the midst of what seems to him a whole universe of ever-changing light and colour and sound, such as it has never entered into his loftiest dreams to imagine. Verily it is true that down here "eye hath not seen, nor ear hath heard, neither hath it entered into the heart of man to conceive" the glories of the devachanic plane: and the man who has once experienced them in full consciousness will regard the world with widely different eyes for ever after. Yet this experience is so utterly unlike anything we know on the physical plane that in trying to put it into words one is troubled by a curious sense of helplessness—of absolute incapacity, not only to do it justice, for of *that* one resigns all hope from the very outset, but even to give any idea at all of it to those who have not themselves seen it.

Let a man imagine himself, with the feelings of intense bliss and enormously increased power already described, floating in a sea of living light, surrounded by every conceivable variety of loveliness in colour and form—the whole changing with every wave of thought that he sends out from his mind, and being indeed, as he presently discovers, only the expression of his thought in the matter of the plane and in its elemental essence. For that matter is of the very same order as that of which the mind-body is itself composed, and therefore when that vibration of the particles of the mind-body which we call a thought occurs, it immediately extends itself to this surrounding devachanic matter, and sets up corresponding vibrations in it, while in the elemental essence it images itself with absolute exactitude. Concrete thought naturally takes the shape of its objects, while abstract ideas usually represent themselves by all kinds of perfect and most beautiful geometrical forms; though in this connection it should be remembered that many thoughts which are little more than the merest abstractions to us down here become concrete facts on this loftier plane.

It will thus be seen that in Devachan anyone who wishes to devote himself for a time to quiet thought, and to abstract himself from his surroundings, may actually live in a world of his own without possibility of interruption, and with the additional advantage of seeing all his ideas and their consequences fully worked out passing in a sort of panorama before his eyes. If, however, he wishes instead to observe the plane upon which he finds himself, it will be necessary for him very carefully to suspend his thought for the time, so that its creations may not influence the readily impressible matter around him, and thus alter the entire conditions so far as he is concerned.

This holding of the mind in suspense must not be confounded with the blankness of mind towards the attainment of which so many of the Hatha Yoga practices are directed: in the latter case the mind is dulled down into absolute passivity in order that it may not by any thought of its own offer resistance to the entry of any external influence that may happen to approach it—a condition closely approximating to medium-ship; while in the former the mind is as keenly alert and positive as it can be, holding its thought in suspense for the moment merely to prevent the intrusion of a personal equation into the observation which it wishes to make.

When the visitor to the devachanic plane succeeds in putting himself in this position he finds that although he is no longer himself a centre of radiation of all that marvellous wealth of light and colour, form and sound, which I have so vainly endeavoured to picture, it has not therefore ceased to exist; on the contrary, its harmonies and its coruscations are but grander and fuller than ever. Casting about for an explanation of this phenomenon, he begins to realize that all this magnificence is not a mere idle or fortuitous display —a kind of devachanic aurora borealis; he finds that it all has a meaning—a meaning which he himself can understand; and presently he grasps the fact that what he is watching with such ecstasy of delight is simply the glorious colour-language of the Devas—the expression of the thought or the conversation of beings far higher than himself in the scale of evolution. By experiment and practice he discovers that he also can use this new and beautiful mode of expression, and by this very discovery he enters into possession of another great tract of his heritage in this celestial realm—the power to hold converse with, and to learn from, its loftier non-human inhabitants, with whom we shall deal more fully when we come to treat of that part of our subject.

By this time it will have become apparent why it was impossible to devote a section of this paper to the scenery of Devachan, as was done in the case of the astral plane; for in point of fact Devachan has *no* scenery except such as each individual chooses to make for himself by his thought—unless indeed we take into account the fact that the vast numbers of entities who are continually passing before him are themselves objects in many cases of the most transcendent beauty.

THE GREAT WAVES.

If the visitor wishes to carry his analysis of the plane still further, and discover what it would be when entirely undisturbed by the thought or conversation of any of its, inhabitants, he can do so by forming round himself a huge shell through which none of these influences can penetrate, and then (of course holding his own mind perfectly still as before) examining the conditions which exist inside his shell.

If he performs this experiment with sufficient care, he will find that the sea of light has become—not still, for its particles continue their intense and rapid vibration, but as it were homogeneous; that those wonderful coruscations of colour and constant changes of form are no longer taking place, but that he is now able to perceive another and entirely different series of regular pulsations which the other more artificial phenomena had previously obscured. These are evidently universal, and no shell which human power can make will check or turn them aside. They cause no change of colour, no assumption of form, but flow with resistless regularity through all the matter of the plane, outwards and in again, like the exhalations and inhalations of some great breath beyond our ken.

There are several sets of these, clearly distinguishable from one another by volume and by period of vibration, and grander than them all sweeps one great wave which seems the very heart-beat of the system—a wave which, welling up from unknown centres on far higher planes, pours out its life through all our world, and then draws back in its tremendous tide to That from which it came. In one long undulating curve it comes, and the sound of it is like the murmur of the sea; and yet in it and through it all the while there echoes a mighty ringing chant of triumph—the very music of the spheres. The man who once has heard that glorious song of nature never quite loses it again; even here on this dreary physical plane of illusion he hears it always as a kind of undertone, keeping ever before his mind the strength and light and splendour of the real life above.

If the visitor be pure in heart and mind, and has reached a certain degree of spiritual development, it is possible for him to identify his consciousness with the sweep of that wondrous wave—to merge his spirit in it, as it were, and let it bear him upward to its source. It is possible, I say; but it is not wise—unless, indeed, his Master stands beside him to draw him back at the right moment from its mighty embrace; for otherwise its irresistible force will carry him away onward and upward into still higher planes, whose far greater glories his ego is as yet unable to sustain; he will lose consciousness, and with no certainty as to when and where and how he will regain it. It is true that the ultimate object of man's evolution is the attainment of unity, but he must reach that final goal in full and perfect consciousness as a victorious king entering triumphantly upon his heritage, not drift into absorption in a state of blank unconsciousness but little removed from annihilation.

The Rûpa and Arûba Planes.

All that we have hitherto attempted to indicate in this description may be taken as applying to the lowest-subdivision of the devachanic plane; for this realm of nature, exactly like the astral or the physical, has its seven subdivisions. Of these four are called in the books the rûpa planes, while the other three are spoken of as arûpa or formless—the reason for these names being that on the rûpa planes every thought takes to itself a certain definite form, while on the arf.ipa subdivisions it expresses itself in an entirely different manner, as will presently be explained. The distinction between these two great divisions of the plane—the rûpa and the arûpa—is very marked; indeed, it even extends so far as to necessitate the use of different vehicles of consciousness.

The vehicle appropriate to the four rûpa levels is the mind-body, out of the matter of which the Adept forms his Mâyâvirûpa, while that of the three arûpa levels is the causal body—the vehicle of the reincarnating ego, in which he passes from life to life throughout the whole manvantara. Another enormous distinction is that on those four lower subdivisions illusion is still possible—not indeed for the entity who stands upon them in full consciousness during life, but for the person who passes there after the change which men call death. The higher thoughts and aspirations which he has poured forth during earth-life then cluster round him, and make a sort of shell about him—a kind of subjective world of his own; and in that he lives his devachanic life, seeing but very faintly or not at all the real glories of the plane which lie outside. On the three arûpa subdivisions no such self-deception is possible; it is true that even there many egos are only slightly and dreamily conscious of their surroundings, but in so far as they see, they see truly, for thought no longer assumes the same deceptive forms which it took upon itself lower down.

The Action of Thought.

The exact condition of mind of the human inhabitants of these various sub-planes will naturally be much more fully dealt with under its own appropriate heading; but a comprehension of the manner in which thought acts in the rûpa and arûpa levels respectively is so necessary to an accurate understanding of these great divisions that it will perhaps be worth while to recount in detail some of the experiments made by our explorers in the endeavour to throw light upon this subject.

At an early period of the investigation it became evident that on the devachanic as on the astral plane there was present an elemental essence quite distinct from the mere matter of the plane, and that it was, if possible, even more instantaneously sensitive to the action of thought here than it had been in that lower world. But here in Devachan *all* was thought-substance, and therefore not only the elemental essence, but the very matter of the plane was directly affected by the action of the mind; and hence it became necessary to make an attempt to discriminate between these two effects.

After various less conclusive experiments a method was adopted which gave a fairly clear idea of the different results produced, one investigator remaining on the lowest subdivision to send out the thought-forms, while others rose to the next higher level, so as to be able to observe what took place from above, and thus avoid many possibilities of confusion. Under these circumstances the experiment was tried of sending an affectionate and helpful thought to an absent friend. The result was very remarkable; a sort of vibrating shell, formed in the matter of the plane, issued in all directions round the operator, corresponding exactly to the circle which spreads out in still water from the spot where a stone has been thrown into it, except that this was a sphere of vibration extending itself in three (or perhaps four) dimensions instead of merely over a flat surface. These vibrations, like those on the physical plane, though very much more gradually, lost in intensity as they passed further away from their source, till at last at an enormous distance they seemed to be exhausted, or at least became so faint as to be imperceptible. Thus every one on the devachanic plane is a centre of radiant thought, and yet all the rays thrown out cross in all directions without interfering with one another in the slightest degree, just as rays of light do down here. This expanding sphere of vibrations was many coloured and opalescent, but its colours also grew gradually fainter and fainter as it spread away.

The effect on the elemental essence of the plane was, however, entirely different. In this the thought immediately called into existence a distinct form resembling the human, of one colour only, though exhibiting many shades of that colour. This form flashed across the ocean with the speed of thought to the friend to whom the good wish had been directed, and there took to itself elemental essence of the astral plane, and thus became an ordinary artificial elemental of that plane, waiting, as explained in Manual No. V., for an opportunity to pour out upon him its store of helpful influence. In taking on that astral form the devachanic elemental lost much of its brilliancy, though its glowing rose-colour was still plainly visible inside the shell of lower matter which it had assumed, showing that just as the original thought ensouled the elemental essence of its own plane, so that same thought, plus its form as a devachanic elemental, acted as soul to the astral elemental—thus following closely the method in which Âtmâ itself takes on sheath after sheath in its descent through the various planes and sub-planes of matter.

Further experiments along similar lines revealed the fact that the colour of the elemental sent forth varied with the character of the thought. As above stated, the thought of strong affection produced a creature of glowing rose-colour; an intense wish of healing, projected towards a sick friend, called into existence a most lovely silvery-white elemental; while an earnest mental effort to steady and strengthen the mind of a depressed and despairing person resulted in the production of a beautiful flashing golden-yellow messenger.

In all these cases it will be perceived that, besides the effect of radiating colours and vibrations produced in the matter of the plane, a definite force in the shape of an elemental was sent forth towards the person to whom the thought was directed; and this invariably happened, with one notable exception. One of the operators, while on the lower division of the plane, directed a thought of intense love and devotion towards the Adept who is his spiritual teacher, and it was at once noticed by the observers above that the result was in some sense a reversal of what had happened in the previous cases.

It should be premised that a pupil of any one of the great Adepts is always connected with his Master by a constant current of thought and influence, which expresses itself on the devachanic plane as a great ray or stream of dazzling light of all colours—violet and gold and blue; and it might perhaps have been expected that the pupil's earnest, loving thought would send a special vibration along this line. Instead of this, however, the result was a sudden intensification of the colours of this bar of light, and a very distinct flow of magnetic influence *towards the pupil;* so that it is evident that when a student turns his thought to the Master, what he really does is to vivify his connection with that Master, and thus to open a way for an additional out-pouring of strength and help to himself from higher planes. It would seem that the Adept is, as it were, so highly charged with the influences which sustain and strengthen, that any thought which brings into increased activity a channel of communication with him sends no current towards him, as it ordinarily would, but simply gives a wider opening through which the great ocean of his love finds vent.

On the arûpa levels the difference in the effect of thought is very marked, especially as regards the elemental essence. The disturbance set up in the mere matter of the plane is similar, though greatly intensified in this much more refined form of matter; but in the essence no form at all is now created, and the method of action is entirely changed. In all the experiments on lower planes it was found that the elemental produced hovered about the person thought of, and awaited a favourable opportunity of expending his energy either upon his mind-body, his astral, or even his physical body; here the result is a kind of lightning-flash of the essence from the causal body of the thinker direct to the causal body of the object of his thought; so that while the thought on those lower divisions is always directed to the mere personality, here you influence the reincarnating ego, the real man himself, and if your message has any reference to the personality it will reach it only from above, through the instrumentality of the Kârana Sharîra.

THOUGHT-FORMS.

Naturally the thoughts to be seen on this plane are not all definitely directed at some other person; many are simply thrown off to float vaguely about, and the diversity of form and colour shown among these is practically infinite, so that the study of them is a science in itself, and a very fascinating one. Anything like a detailed description even of the main classes among them would occupy far more space than we have to spare; but an idea of the principles upon. Which such classes might be formed may be gained from the following extract from a most illuminative paper on the subject written by Mrs. Besant in *Lucifer* for September, 1896. She there enunciates the three great principles underlying the production of thought-forms—that (*a*) the quality of a thought determines its colour, (*b*) the nature of a thought determines its form, (*c*) the definiteness of a thought determines the clearness of its outline. Giving instances of the way in which the colour is affected, she continues:

"If the astral and mental bodies are vibrating under the influence of devotion, the aura will be suffused with blue, more or less intense, beautiful and pure according to the depth, elevation and purity of the feeling. In a church such thought-forms may be seen rising, for the most part not very definitely outlined, but rolling masses of blue clouds. Too often the colour is dulled by the intermixture of selfish feelings, when the blue is mixed with browns and thus loses its pure brilliancy. But the devotional thought of an unselfish heart is very lovely in colour, like the deep blue of a summer sky. Through such clouds of blue will often shine out golden stars of great brilliancy, starting upwards like a shower of sparks.

"Anger gives rise to red, of all shades from brick-red to brilliant scarlet; brutal anger will show as flashes of lurid dull red from dark brown clouds, while the anger of 'noble indignation' is a vivid scarlet, by no means unbeautiful to look at though it gives an unpleasant thrill.

"Affection sends out clouds of rosy hue, varying from dull crimson, where the love is animal in its nature, rose-red mingled with brown when selfish, or with dull green when jealous, to the most exquisite shades of delicate rose like the early flushes of the dawning, as the love becomes purified from all selfish elements, and flows out in wider and wider circles of generous impersonal tenderness and compassion to all who are in need.

"Intellect produces yellow thought-forms, the pure reason directed to spiritual ends giving rise to a very delicate, beautiful yellow, while used for more selfish ends or mingled with ambition it yields deeper shades of orange, clear and intense" *(Lucifer,* vol. xix. p. 71).

It must of course be borne in mind that astral as well as mental thought-forms are described in the above quotation, some of the feelings mentioned needing matter of the lower plane as well as of the higher before they can find expression. Some examples are then given of the beautiful flower-like and shell-like forms sometimes taken by our nobler thoughts; and especial reference is made to the not infrequent case in which the thought, taking human form, is liable to be confounded with an apparition:

"A thought-form may assume the shape of its projector; if a person wills strongly to be present at a particular place, to visit a particular person, and be seen, such a thought-form may take his own shape, and a clairvoyant present at the desired spot would see what he would probably mistake for his friend in the astral body. Such a thought-form might convey a message, if that formed part of its content, setting up in the astral body of the person reached vibrations like its own, and these being passed on by that astral body to the brain, where they would be translated into a thought or a sentence. Such a thought-form, again, might convey to its projector, by the magnetic relation between them, vibrations impressed on itself" (p. 73).

The whole of the article from which these extracts are taken should be very carefully studied by those who wish to grasp this very complex branch of our subject, for, with the aid of the beautifully-executed coloured illustrations which accompany it, it enables those who cannot yet see for themselves to approach much more nearly to a realization of what thought-forms actually are than anything previously written.

THE SUB-PLANES.

If it be asked what is the real difference between the matter of the various sub-planes of Devachan, it is not easy to answer in other than very general terms, for the unfortunate scribe bankrupts himself of adjectives in an unsuccessful endeavour to describe the lowest plane, and then has nothing left to say about the others. What, indeed, can be said, except that ever as we ascend the material becomes finer, the harmonies fuller, the light more living and transparent? There are more over-tones in the sound, more delicate intershades in the colours as we rise, more and more new colours appear—hues entirely unknown to the physical sight; and it has been poetically yet truly said that the light of the lower plane is darkness on the one above it. Perhaps this idea is simpler if we start in thought from the top instead of the bottom, and try to realize that on that highest sub-plane we shall find its appropriate matter ensouled and vivified by an energy which still flows down like light from above—from a plane which lies away beyond Devachan altogether. Then if we descend to the second subdivision we shall find that the matter of our first sub-plane has become the energy of this—or, to put the thing more accurately, that the original energy, plus the garment of matter of the first sub-plane with which it has endued itself, is the energy of this second sub-plane. In the same way, in the third division we shall find that the original energy has twice veiled itself in the matter of these first and second sub-planes through which it has passed; so that by the time we get to our seventh subdivision we shall have our original energy six times enclosed or veiled, and therefore by so much the weaker and less active. This process is exactly analogous to the veiling of Âtmâ in its descent as monadic essence in order to energize the matter of the planes of the cosmos, and as it is one which frequently takes place in nature, it will save the student much trouble if he will try to familiarize himself with the idea.

THE ÂKÂSHIC RECORDS.

In speaking of the general characteristics of the plane we must not omit to mention the âkâshic records, which form what may be called the memory of nature, the only really reliable history of the world. Whether what we have on this plane is the absolute record itself or merely a devachanic reflection of something higher still, it is at any rate clear, accurate, and continuous, differing therein from the disconnected and spasmodic manifestation which is all that represents it in the astral world. It is, therefore, only when a clairvoyant possesses the vision of this devachanic plane that his pictures of the past can be relied upon; and even then, unless he has the power of passing in full consciousness from that plane to the physical we have to allow for the possibility of errors in bringing back the recollection of what he has seen.

But the student who has succeeded in developing the powers latent within himself so far as to enable him to use the devachanic sense while still in the physical body, has before him a field of historical research of most entrancing interest. Not only can he review at his leisure all history with which we are acquainted, correcting as he examines it the many errors and misconceptions which have crept into the accounts handed down to us; he can also range at will over the whole story of the world from its very beginning, watching the slow development of intellect in man, the descent of the Lords of the Flame, and the growth of the mighty civilizations which they founded.

Nor is his study confined to the progress of humanity alone; he has before him, as in a museum, all the strange animal and vegetable forms which occupied the stage in days when the world was young; he can follow all the wonderful geological changes which have taken place, and watch the course of the great cataclysms which have altered the whole face of the earth again and again.

Many and varied are the possibilities opened up. by access to the âkâshic records—so many and so varied indeed that even if this were the only advantage of the devachanic plane it would still transcend in interest all the lower worlds; but when to this we add the remarkable increase in the opportunities for the acquisition of knowledge given by its new and wider faculty—the privilege of direct untrammelled intercourse not only with the great Deva kingdom, but with the very Masters of Wisdom themselves—the rest and relief from the weary strain of physical life that is brought by the enjoyment of its deep unchanging bliss, and above all the enormously enhanced capability of the developed student for the service of his fellow-men—then we shall begin to have some faint conception of what a pupil gains when he wins the right to enter at will and in perfect consciousness upon his heritage in the bright realm of Sukhâvatî.

INHABITANTS.

In our endeavour to describe the inhabitants of Devachan it will perhaps be well for us to divide them into the same three great classes chosen in the manual on the astral plane—the human, the non-human, and the artificial—though the sub-divisions will naturally be less numerous in this case than in that, since the products of man's evil passions, which bulked so largely in Kâmaloka, can find no place here.

I. HUMAN.

Exactly as was the case when dealing with the lower world, it will be desirable to subdivide the human inhabitants of the devachanic plane into two classes—those who are still attached to a physical body, and those who are not—the living and the dead, as they are commonly but most erroneously called. Very little experience of these higher planes is needed to alter fundamentally the student's conception of the change which takes place at death; he realizes immediately on the opening of his consciousness even in the astral, and still more in the devachanic world, that the fulness of true life is something which can never be known down here, and that when we leave this physical earth we are passing *into* that true life, not out of it. We have not at present in the English language any convenient and at the same time accurate words to express these conditions; perhaps to call them respectively embodied and disembodied will be, on the whole, the least misleading of the various possible phrases. Let us therefore proceed to consider those inhabitants of Devachan who come under the head of

THE EMBODIED.

Those human beings who, while still attached to a physical body, are found moving in full consciousness and activity upon this plane are invariably either initiates or Adepts, for until a pupil has been taught by his Master how to form the Mâyâvirûpa he will be unable to move with freedom upon even the rûpa levels of Devachan. To function consciously during physical life upon the arûpa levels denotes still greater advancement, for it means the unification of the Manas, so that the man down here is no longer a mere personality, more or less influenced by the individuality above, but is himself that individuality—trammelled and confined by a body, certainly, but nevertheless having within him the power and knowledge of a highly developed ego.

Very magnificent objects are these Adepts and initiates to the vision which has learnt to see them—splendid globes of light and colour, driving away all evil influence wherever they go, and shedding around them a feeling of restfulness and happiness of which even those who do not see them are often conscious. It is in this celestial world that much of their most important work is done—more especially upon its higher levels, where the individuality can be acted upon directly. It is from this plane that they shower the grandest spiritual influences upon the world of thought; from it also they impel great and beneficent movements of all kinds. Here much of the spiritual force poured out by the glorious self-sacrifice of the Nirmânâkayas is distributed; here also direct teaching is given to those pupils who are sufficiently advanced to receive it in this way, since it can be imparted far more readily and completely than on the astral plane. In addition to all these activities they have a great field of work in connection with devachanees, but this will be more fitly explained under a later heading.

It is a pleasure to find that a class of inhabitants which obtruded itself painfully on our notice on the astral plane is entirely absent here. In a world whose characteristics are unselfishness and spirituality the black magician and his pupils can obviously find no place, since selfishness is of the essence of all the proceedings of the darker school. Not but that in many of them the intellect is very highly developed, and consequently the matter of the mind-body extremely active and sensitive along certain lines; but in every case those lines are connected with personal desire of some sort, and they can therefore find expression only through Kâma-Manas—that is, the part of the mind-body which has become almost inextricably entangled with Kama. As a necessary consequence of this limitation it follows that their activities are confined to the astral and physical planes, and thus is justified the grand old description of the heaven-world as the place "where the wicked cease from troubling, and the weary are at rest."

IN SLEEP OR TRANCE.

In thinking of the living inhabitants of Devachan, the question naturally suggests itself whether either ordinary people during sleep, or psychically developed persons in a trance condition, can ever penetrate to this plane. In both cases the answer must be that the occurrence is possible, though extremely rare. Purity of life and purpose would be an absolute pre-requisite, and even when the plane was reached there would be nothing that could be called real consciousness, but simply a capacity for receiving certain impressions.

As exemplifying the possibility of entering the devachanic state during sleep, an incident may be mentioned which occurred in connection with the experiments made by the London Lodge of the Theosophical Society on dream consciousness, an account of some of which was given in their Transaction on *Dreams*. It may be remembered by those who have read that Transaction that a thought-picture of a lovely tropical landscape was presented to the minds of various classes of sleepers, with a view of testing the extent to which it was afterwards recollected on awaking. One case which was not referred to in the account previously published, as it had no special connection with the phenomena of dreams, will serve as a useful illustration here.

It was that of a person of pure mind and considerable though untrained psychic capacity; and the effect of the presentation of the thought-picture to her mind was of a somewhat startling character. So intense was the feeling of reverent joy, so lofty and so spiritual were the thoughts evoked by the contemplation of this glorious scene, that the consciousness of the sleeper passed entirely into the mind-body—or to put the same idea into other words, rose on to the devachanic plane. It must not, however, he supposed from this that she became cognizant of her surroundings upon that plane, or of its real conditions; she was simply in the state of the ordinary devachanee after death, floating in the sea of light and colour indeed, but entirely absorbed in her own thought, and conscious of nothing beyond it—resting in ecstatic contemplation of the landscape and of all that it had suggested to her—yet contemplating it, be it understood, with the keener insight, the more perfect appreciation, and the enhanced vigour of thought peculiar to the devachanic plane, and enjoying all the while the intensity of bliss which has so often been spoken of before. The sleeper remained in that condition for several hours, though apparently entirely unconscious of the passage of time, and at last awoke with a sense of deep peace and inward joy for which, since she had brought back no recollection of what had happened, she was quite unable to account. There is no doubt, however, that such an experience as this, whether remembered in the physical body or not, would act as a distinct impulse to the spiritual evolution of the ego concerned.

Though in the absence of a sufficient number of experiments one hesitates to speak too positively, it seems almost certain that such a result as this just described would be possible only in the case of a person having already some amount of psychic development; and the same condition is even more definitely necessary in order that a mesmerized subject should touch the devachanic plane in trance. So decidedly is this the case, that probably not one in a thousand among ordinary clairvoyants ever reaches it at all; but on the rare occasions when it is so attained the clairvoyant, as before remarked, must be not only of exceptional development, but of perfect purity of life and purpose: and even when all these unusual characteristics are present there still remains the difficulty which an untrained psychic always finds in translating a vision accurately from the higher plane to the lower. All these considerations, of course, only emphasize what has been so often insisted upon before—the necessity of the careful training of all psychics under a qualified instructor before it is possible to attach much weight to their reports of what they see.

THE DISEMBODIED.

Before considering in detail the condition of the disembodied entities on the various sub-planes of Devachan, we must have very clearly in our minds the broad distinction between the rûpa and arûpa levels, of which mention has already been made. On the former the man lives entirely in the world of his own thoughts, still fully identifying himself with his personality in the life which he has recently quitted; on the latter he is simply the reincarnating ego, who (if he has developed sufficient consciousness on that level to know anything clearly at all) understands, at least to some extent, the evolution upon which he is engaged, and the work that he has to do. It should be remembered that every man passes through both these stages between death and birth, though the undeveloped majority have so-little consciousness in either of them as yet that they might more truly he said to dream through them. Nevertheless, whether consciously or unconsciously, every human being must touch his own ego on the arûpa level of Devachan before reincarnation can take place: and as his evolution proceeds this touch becomes more and more definite and real to him. Not only is he more conscious here as he progresses, but the period he passes in this world of reality becomes longer; for the fact is that his consciousness is slowly but steadily rising through the different planes of the system.

Primitive man, for example, would have comparatively little consciousness on any plane but the physical during life and the lower astral after death; and indeed the same may be said of the quite undeveloped man even in our own day. A person a little more advanced would perhaps begin to have a short devachanic period (on the rûpa levels, of course), but would still spend by far the greater part of his time, between incarnations, on the astral plane. As he progressed the astral life would grow shorter and the devachanic life longer, until when he became an intellectual and spiritually-minded person he would pass through Kâmaloka with hardly any delay at all, and would enjoy a long and happy sojourn on the higher of the rûpa levels. By this time, however, the consciousness in the true ego on the arûpa levels would have been awakened to a very considerable extent, and thus his conscious life in Devachan would divide itself into two parts—the later and shorter portion being spent on the higher sub-planes in the causal body.

The process previously described would then repeat itself, the life on the rûpa levels gradually shortening, while the higher life became steadily longer and fuller, till at last the time came when the consciousness was unified—when the higher and lower Manas were indissolubly united, and the man was no longer capable of wrapping himself up in his own cloud of thought, and mistaking that for the great heaven-world around him—when he realized the true possibilities of his life, and so for the first time truly began to live. But by the time that he attains these heights he will already be an initiate, and will have taken his future progress definitely into his own hands.

Is the Devachanic Life an Illusion.

It has frequently been urged, as an objection to the Theosophical teaching on the subject of the hereafter, that the life of the ordinary person in Devachan is nothing but a dream and an illusion—that when he imagines himself happy amidst his family and friends, or carrying out his plans with such fulness of joy and success, he is really only the victim of a cruel delusion: and this is sometimes unfavourably contrasted with what is called the solid objectivity of the heaven promised by Christianity. The reply to such an objection is twofold: first, that when we are studying the problems of the future life we are not concerned to know which of two hypotheses put before us would be the pleasanter (that being, after all, a matter of opinion), but rather which of them is the true one; and secondly, that when we enquire more fully into the facts of the case we shall see that those who maintain the illusion theory are looking at the matter from quite a wrong point of view.

As to the first point, the actual state of the facts is quite easily discoverable by those who have developed the power to pass consciously on to the devachanic plane during life; and when so investigated it is found to agree perfectly with the teaching given to us by the Masters of Wisdom through our great founder and teacher Madame Blavatsky. This, of course, disposes of the "solid objectivity" theory mentioned above. As to the second point, if the contention be that on the lower levels of Devachan truth in its fulness is not yet known to man, and that consequently illusion still exists there, we must frankly admit that that is so. But that is not what is usually meant by those who bring forward this objection; they are generally oppressed by a feeling that the devachanic life will be more illusory and useless than the physical—an idea which further consideration will, I think, show to be inaccurate.

Let it be clearly grasped first of all that such illusion as there is inheres in the personality, and that when that is for the time dissipated no illusion remains. (Of course I am using the word illusion in its ordinary everyday meaning—not in that metaphysical sense in which all is illusion until the absolute is attained.) It will be seen, as our account of the plane progresses, that this illusion differs very much on different levels, and that it steadily diminishes as the soul advances. Indeed, we may say that just as it is only the child down here who constantly "makes believe," so it is only the child-soul who surrounds himself again and again with an illusory world created by his own thoughts.

In point of fact, the Devachan of each person is exactly suited to him; as *he* becomes more real, *it* becomes more real also. And we ought in fairness to bear in mind, before inveighing against the unreality of Devachan, that we are, after all, at the present moment living a life which is still more unreal. Is it contended that on that plane we make our own surroundings, and that they have therefore no objective existence? But surely that argument cuts both ways: for even down here the world of which a person is sensible is never the *whole* of the outer world, but only so much of it as his senses, his intellect, his education, enable him to take in. It is obvious that during life the average person's conception of everything around him is really quite a wrong one—empty, imperfect, inaccurate in a dozen ways; for what does he know of the great forces—etheric, astral, devachanic—which lie behind everything he sees, and in fact form by far the most important part of it? What does he know, as a rule, even of the more recondite physical facts which surround him and meet him at every step that he takes? The truth is that here, as in Devachan, he lives in a world which is very largely of his own creation. He does not realize it, of course, either there or here, but that is only because of his ignorance—because he knows no better.

It may be thought that there is a difference in the case of our friends—that here we have them really with us, whereas in Devachan what we have is only an image of them which we ourselves make. This latter statement is true only of the lowest planes, and if the friend is an entirely undeveloped person; but, once more, is not the case exactly the same down here? Here also we see our friend only partly—we know only the part of him which is congenial to us, and the other sides of his character are practically nonexistent for us. If we were for the first time, and with the direct and perfect vision of the devachanic plane, to see the *whole* of our friend, the probability is that he would be quite unrecognizable: certainly he would not be at all the dear one whom we had known.

Not only is it true that as a man becomes more real himself his Devachan becomes more real; it is also a fact that, as the man evolves, the image of him in his friend's Devachan becomes more real too. This was very well illustrated by a simple case which recently came under the notice of our investigators. It was that of a mother who had died perhaps twenty years ago, leaving behind her two boys to whom she was deeply attached. Naturally they were the most prominent figures in her Devachan, and quite naturally, too, she thought of them as she had left them, as boys of fifteen or sixteen years of age. The love which she thus ceaselessly poured out upon these images in Devachan was really acting as a beneficent force showered down upon the grown-up men in this physical world, but it did not affect them both to the same extent—not that her love was stronger for one than the other, but because there was a great difference between the images themselves. Not a difference, be it understood, that the mother could see; to her both appeared equally with her and equally all that she could possibly desire: yet to the eyes of the investigators it was very evident that one of these images was a mere thought-form of the mother's, without anything that could be called a reality at the back of it, while the other was distinctly much more than a mere image, for it was instinct with living force. On tracing this very interesting phenomenon to its source, it was found that in the first case the son had grown up into an ordinary man of business—not specially evil in any way, but by no means spiritually-minded—while the second had become a man of high unselfish aspiration, and of considerable refinement and culture. His life had been such as to develope a much greater amount of consciousness in the ego than his brother's, and consequently his higher self was able to energize the image of himself as a boy which his mother had formed in her Devachan—to put something of himself into it, as it were.

A large number of similar instances were revealed by further research, and it was eventually clearly established that the more highly a man is developed along spiritual lines, the more truly is his image in his friend's Devachan informed by a ray from his higher ego, even though the personality down here in incarnation may often be entirely ignorant of its action. Thus as the man rises his image becomes more really himself, until in the case of an Adept that image is fully and consciously entered and used as a means of raising and instructing the pupil who has formed it. Of this more will be said later; but meantime it is abundantly evident that, as man evolves, the illusions which clung round his spiritual childhood drop away, and he draws ever nearer and nearer to the reality which lies behind them.

In this manner, and in this manner only, is communication possible between those who still live on earth and those who have passed into this celestial realm. A man's higher self may be informing his image in a friend's Devachan, and yet the living man here on earth may know nothing of it, and therefore remain quite unable to communicate with his departed friend; but if the living man has evolved his consciousness to the point of unification, and can therefore use the powers of the ego while still in the physical body, he can enter at will and in full consciousness into that image of his, and can speak once more face to face with his friend, as of yore: so that in such a case the "devachanic dream" is no longer an illusion, but a living reality.

Is it said that on the devachanic plane a man takes his thoughts for real things? He is quite right; they *are* real things, and on this, the thought-plane, nothing but thought *can* be real. There we recognize that great fact—here we do not; on which plane, then, is the delusion greater? Those thoughts of the devachanee are indeed realities, and are capable of producing the most striking results upon living men—results which can never be otherwise than beneficial, because upon that high plane there can be none but loving thought.

Another point worth bearing in mind is that this system upon which nature has arranged the life after death is the only imaginable one which could fulfil its object of making every one happy to the fullest extent of his capacity for happiness. If the joy of heaven were of one particular type only, as it is according to the orthodox Christian theory, there must always be some who would weary of it, some who would be incapable of participating in it, either from want of taste in that particular direction, or from lack of the necessary education—to say nothing of that other obvious fact, that if this condition of affairs were eternal the grossest injustice must be perpetrated by giving practically the same reward to all who enter, no matter what their respective deserts might be.

Again, what other arrangement with regard to relatives and friends could possibly be equally satisfactory? If the departed were able to follow the fluctuating fortunes of their friends on earth, happiness would be impossible for them; if, without knowing what was happening to them, they had to wait until the death of those friends before meeting them, there would he a painful period of suspense, often extending over many years, while the friend would in many cases arrive so much changed as to be no longer sympathetic.

On the system so wisely provided for us by nature every one of these difficulties is avoided; a man decides for himself both the length and the character of his Devachan by the causes which he himself generates during his earth-life; therefore he cannot but have exactly the amount which he has deserved, and exactly that quality of joy which is best suited to his idiosyncrasies. Those whom he loves most he has ever with him, and always at their noblest and best; while no shadow of discord or change can ever come between them, since he receives from them all the time exactly what he wishes. In point of fact, as we might have expected, the arrangement really made by nature is infinitely superior to anything which the imagination of man has been able to offer us in its place.

THE QUALITIES NECESSARY FOR DEVACHANIC LIFE.

The greater reality of the devachanic life as compared with that on earth is again evidenced when we consider what conditions are requisite for the attainment of this higher state of existence. For the very qualities which a man must develope during life, if he is to have any Devachan after death, are just those which all the best and noblest of our race have agreed in considering as really and permanently desirable. In order that an aspiration or a thought-force should result in existence on that plane, its dominant characteristic must be unselfishness.

Affection for family or friends takes many a man into Devachan, and so also does religious devotion; yet it would be a mistake to suppose that *all* affection or all devotion must therefore necessarily find its *post-mortem* expression there, for of each of these qualities there are obviously two varieties, the selfish and the unselfish—though it might perhaps reasonably be argued that it is only the latter kind in each case which is really worthy of the name.

There is the love which pours itself out upon its object, seeking for nothing in return—never even thinking of itself, but only of what it can do for the loved one and such a feeling as this generates a spiritual force which cannot work itself out except upon the devachanic plane. But there is also another emotion which is sometimes called love—an exacting, selfish kind of passion which desires mainly to *be* loved—which is thinking all the time of what it receives rather than of what it gives, and is quite likely to degenerate into the horrible vice of jealousy upon (or even without) the smallest provocation. Such affection as this has in it no seed of devachanic development; the forces which it sets in motion will never rise above the astral plane.

The same is true of the feeling of a certain very large class of religious devotees, whose one thought is, not the glory of their deity, but how they may save their own miserable souls—a position which forcibly suggests that they have not yet developed anything that really deserves the name of a soul at all.

On the other hand there is the real religious devotion, which thinks never of self, but only of love and gratitude towards the deity or leader, and is filled with ardent desire to do something for him or in his name; and such a feeling often leads to prolonged Devachan of a comparatively exalted type.

This would of course be the case whoever the deity or leader might be, and followers of Buddha, Krishna, Ormuzd, Allah and Christ would all equally attain their need of devachanic bliss—its length and quality depending upon the intensity and purity of the feeling, and not in the least upon its object, though this latter consideration would undoubtedly affect the possibility of receiving instruction during that higher life.

Most human devotion, however, like most human love, is neither wholly pure nor wholly selfish. That love must be low indeed into which no unselfish thought or impulse has entered; and on the other hand an affection which is usually and chiefly quite pure and noble may yet sometimes be clouded by a spasm of jealous feeling or a passing thought of self. In both these cases, as in all, Karma discriminates unerringly; and just as the momentary flash of nobler feeling in the less developed heart will receive its devachanic meed even though there be nought else in the life to raise the soul above the astral plane, so the baser thought which erstwhile dimmed the holy radiance of a real love will reap its due reward in Kâmaloka, interfering not at all with the magnificent celestial life which flows infallibly from years of deep affection here below.

HOW A MAN FIRST GAINS DEVACHAN.

It will be seen, therefore, that many undeveloped and backward egos never consciously attain the devachanic state at all, whilst a still larger number obtain only a comparatively slight touch of some of its lower planes. Every ego must of course withdraw into its true self upon the arûpa levels before reincarnation; but it does not at all follow that in that condition it will experience anything that we should call consciousness. This subject will be dealt with more fully when we come to treat of the arûpa planes; it seems better to begin with the lowest of the rûpa levels, and work steadily upwards, so we may for the moment leave on one side that portion of humanity whose conscious existence after death is practically confined to the astral plane, and proceed to consider the case of an entity who has just risen out of that position—who for the first time has a slight and fleeting consciousness in the lowest subdivision of Devachan.

There are evidently various methods by which this important step in the early development of the ego may be brought about, but it will be sufficient for our present purpose if we take as an illustration of one of them a somewhat pathetic little story from real life which came under the observation of our students when they were investigating this question. In this case the agent of the great evolutionary forces was a poor seamstress, living in one of the dreariest and most squalid of our terrible London slums—a foetid court in the East End into which light and air could scarcely struggle.

Naturally she was not highly educated, for her life had been one long round of the hardest work under the least favourable of conditions; but nevertheless she was a good-hearted, benevolent creature, overflowing with love and kindness towards all with whom she came into contact. Her rooms were as poor, perhaps, as any in the court, but at least they were cleaner and neater than the others. She had no money to give when sickness brought need even more dire than usual to some of her neighbours, yet on such an occasion she was always at hand as often as she could snatch a few moments from her work, offering with ready sympathy such service as was within her power.

Indeed, she was quite a providence to the rough, ignorant factory girls about her, and they gradually came to look upon her as a kind of angel of help and mercy, always at hand in time of trouble or illness. Often after toiling all day with scarcely a moment's intermission she sat up half the night, taking her turn at nursing some of the many sufferers who are always to be found in surroundings so fatal to health and happiness as those of a London slum; and in many cases the gratitude and affection which her unremitting kindness aroused in them were absolutely the only higher feelings that they had during the whole of their rough and sordid lives.

The conditions of existence in that court being such as they were, there is little wonder that some of her patients died, and then it became clear that she had done for them much more than she knew; she had given them not only a little kindly assistance in their temporal trouble, but a very important impulse on the course of spiritual evolution. For these were undeveloped egos—pitris of a very backward class—who' had never yet in any of their births set in motion the spiritual forces which alone could give them conscious existence on the devachanic plane; but now for the first time not only had an ideal towards which they could strive been put before them, but also really unselfish love had been evoked in them by her action, and the very fact of having so strong a feeling as this had raised them and given them more individuality, and so after their stay in Kâmaloka was ended they gained their first experience of the lowest subdivision of Devachan. A short experience, probably, and of by no means an advanced type, but still of far greater importance than appears at first sight; for when once the great spiritual energy of unselfishness has been awakened the very working-out of its results in Devachan gives it the tendency to repeat itself, and small in amount though this first outpouring may be, it yet builds into the ego a faint tinge of a quality which will certainly express itself again in the next life.

So the gentle benevolence of a poor seamstress has given to several less developed souls their introduction to a conscious spiritual life which incarnation after incarnation will grow steadily stronger, and react more and more upon the earth-lives of the future. This little incident perhaps suggests an explanation of the fact that in the various religions so much importance is attached to the personal element in charity—the direct association between donor and recipient.

Seventh Sub-Plane.

This lowest subdivision of Devachan, to which the action of our poor seamstress raised the objects of her kindly care, has for its principal characteristic that of affection for family or friends—unselfish, of course, but usually somewhat narrow. Here, however, we must guard ourselves against the possibility of misconception. When it is said that family affection takes a man to the seventh devachanic sub-plane, and religious devotion to the sixth, people sometimes very naturally imagine that a person having both these characteristics strongly developed in him would divide his devachanic period between these two subdivisions, first spending a long period of happiness in the midst of his family, and then passing upward to the next level, there to exhaust the spiritual forces engendered by his devotional aspirations.

This, however, is not what happens, for in such a case as we have supposed the man would awaken to consciousness in the sixth sub-division, where he would find himself engaged, together with those whom he had loved so much, in the highest form of devotion which he was able to realize. And when we think of it this is reasonable enough, for the man who is capable of religious devotion as well as mere family affection is naturally likely to be endowed with a higher and broader development of the latter virtue than one whose mind is susceptible to influence in one direction only. The same rule holds good all the way up; the higher plane may always include the qualities of the lower as well as those peculiar to itself, and when it does so its inhabitants almost invariably have these qualities in fuller measure than the souls on a lower plane.

When it is said that family affection is the characteristic of the seventh sub-plane, it must not therefore be supposed for a moment that love is confined to this plane, but rather that the man who will find himself here after death is one in whose character this affection was the highest quality—the only one, in fact, which entitled him to Devachan at all. But love of a far nobler and grander type than anything to be seen on this level may of course be found upon the higher sub-planes.

One of the first entities encountered by the investigators upon this sub-plane forms a very fair typical example of its inhabitants. The man during life had been a small grocer—not a person of intellectual development or of any particular religious feeling, but simply the ordinary honest and respectable small tradesman. No doubt he had gone to church regularly every Sunday, because it was the customary and proper thing to do; but religion had been to him a sort of dim cloud which he did not really understand, which had no connection with the business of everyday life, and was never taken into account in deciding its problems. He had therefore none of the depth of devotion which might have lifted him to the next sub-plane; but he had for his wife and family a warm affection in which there was a large element of unselfishness. They were constantly in his mind, and it was for them far more than for himself that he worked from morning to night in his tiny little shop; and so when, after a period of existence in Kâmaloka, he had at last shaken himself free from the decaying astral body, he found himself upon this lowest subdivision of Devachan with all his loved ones gathered round him.

He was no more an intellectual or highly spiritual man than he had been on earth, for death brings with it no sudden development of that kind; the surroundings in which he found himself with his family were not of a very refined type, for they represented only his own highest ideals of non-physical enjoyment during life; but nevertheless he was as intensely happy as he was capable of being, and since he was all the time thinking of his family rather than of himself he was undoubtedly developing unselfish characteristics, which would be built into the ego, and so would reappear in his next life on earth.

Another typical case was that of a man who had died while his only daughter was still young; here in Devachan he had her always with him and always at her best, and he was continually occupying himself in weaving all sorts of beautiful pictures of her future. Yet another was that of a young girl who was always absorbed in contemplating the manifold perfections of her father, and planning little surprises and fresh pleasures for him. Another was a Greek woman who was spending a marvellously happy time with her three children—one of them a beautiful boy, whom she delighted in imagining as the victor in the Olympic games.

A striking characteristic of this sub-plane for the last few centuries has been the very large number of Romans, Carthaginians and English-men to be found there—this being due to the fact that among men of these nations the principal unselfish activity found its outlet through family affection; while comparatively few Hindus and Buddhists are here, since in their case real religious feeling usually enters more immediately into their daily lives, and consequently takes them to a higher level.

There was, of course, an almost infinite variety among the cases observed, their different degrees of advancement being distinguishable by varying degrees of luminosity, while differences of colour indicated respectively the qualities which the persons in question had developed. Some were lovers who had died in the full strength of their affection, and so were always occupied with the one person they loved to the entire exclusion of all others; others there were who had been almost savages, one example being a Malay, a low third-class pitri, who obtained a slight experience of Devachan in connection with a daughter whom he had loved.

In all these cases it was the touch of unselfish affection which gave them their Devachan; indeed, apart from that, there was nothing in the activity of their personal lives which could have expressed itself on that plane. In most instances observed on this level the images of the loved ones have in them but the faintest glimmer of real vitality, owing to the fact that naturally in the vast majority of cases their individualities have not been developed into activity on this plane. Of course wherever such development has taken place the image would be vivified by a ray of the higher self of the person whom it represented, and much benefit might he derived by the devachanee from his intercourse with it.

Before passing on to consider the higher levels it would be well perhaps to refer to the way in which consciousness is recovered upon entering the devachanic plane. On the final separation of the mind-body from the astral a period of blank unconsciousness supervenes—varying in length between very wide limits—analogous to that which usually follows physical death. The awakening from this into active devachanic consciousness closely resembles what often occurs in waking from a night's sleep. Just as on first awakening in the morning one sometimes passes through a period of intensely delightful repose during which one is conscious of the sense of enjoyment, though the mind is as yet inactive and the body hardly under control, so the entity awakening on the devachanic plane first passes through a more or less prolonged period of intense and gradually increasing bliss before his full activity of consciousness on that plane is reached. When first this sense of wondrous joy dawns on him it fills the entire field of his consciousness, but gradually as he awakens he finds himself surrounded by a world of his own creation presenting the features appropriate to the sub-plane to which he has been drawn.

SIXTH SUB-PLANE.

The dominant characteristic of this subdivision appears to be anthropomorphic religious devotion. The distinction between such devotion and the religious feeling which finds its expression on the second sub-plane of the astral lies in the fact that the former is purely unselfish, and the man who feels it is totally unconcerned as to what the result of his devotion may be as regards himself, while the latter is always aroused by the hope and desire of gaining some advantage through it; so that on the second astral sub-plane such religious feeling as is there active invariably contains an element of selfish bargaining, while the devotion which raises a man to this sixth devachanic sub-plane is entirely free from any such taint.

On the other hand this phase of devotion, which consists essentially in the perpetual adoration of a personal deity, must be carefully distinguished from those still higher forms which find their expression in performing some definite work for the deity's sake. A few examples of the cases observed on this sub-plane will perhaps show these distinctions more clearly than any mere description can do.

A fairly large number of entities whose devachanic activities work themselves out on this level are drawn from the oriental religions; but only those are included who have the characteristic of pure but comparatively unreasoning and unintelligent devotion. Worshippers of Vishnu, both in his avatâr of Krishna and otherwise, as well as a few followers of Shiva, are to be found here, each wrapped up in the self-woven cocoon of his own thoughts, alone with his own god, and oblivious of the rest of mankind, except in so far as his affections may associate with him in his adoration those whom he loved on earth. A Vaishnavite, for example, was noticed wholly absorbed in the ecstatic worship of the very same image of Vishnu to which he had made offerings during life.

Some of the most characteristic examples of this plane are to be found among women, who indeed form a very large majority of its inhabitants. Among others there was a Hindu woman who had glorified her husband into a divine being, and also thought of the child Krishna as playing with her own children, but while these latter were thoroughly human and real the child Krishna was obviously nothing but the semblance of a blue wooden image galvanized into life. Krishna also appeared in her Devachan under another form—that of an effeminate young man playing on a flute; but she was not in the least confused or troubled by this double manifestation. Another woman, who was a worshipper of Shiva, had confounded the god with her husband, looking upon the latter as a manifestation of the former, so that the one seemed to be constantly changing into the other. Some Buddhists also are found upon this subdivision, but apparently exclusively those who regard the Buddha rather as an object of adoration than as a great teacher.

The Christian religion also contributes many of the inhabitants of this plane. The unintellectual devotion which is exemplified on the one hand by the illiterate Roman Catholic peasant, and on the other by the earnest and sincere "soldier" of the Salvation Army, seems to produce results very similar to those already described, for these people also are found wrapped up in contemplation of their ideas of Christ or his mother respectively. For instance, an Irish peasant was seen absorbed in the deepest adoration of the Virgin Mary, whom he imaged as standing on the moon after the fashion of Titian's "Assumption," but holding out her hands and' speaking to him. A mediæval monk was found in ecstatic contemplation of Christ crucified, and the intensity of his yearning love and pity was such that as he watched the blood dropping from the wounds of the figure of his Christ the stigmata reproduced themselves upon his own body.

Another man seemed to have forgotten the sad story of the crucifixion, and thought of his Christ only as glorified on his throne, with the crystal sea before him, and all around a vast multitude of worshippers, among whom he himself stood with his wife and family. His affection for these relatives was very deep, yet his thoughts were more occupied in adoration of the Christ, though his conception of his deity was so material that he imaged him as constantly changing kaleidoscopically backwards and forwards between the form of a man and that of the lamb bearing the flag which we often see represented in church windows.

A more interesting case was that of a Spanish nun who had died at about the age of nineteen or twenty. In her Devachan she carried herself back to the date of Christ's life upon earth, and imagined herself as accompanying him through the chain of events recounted in the gospels, and after his crucifixion taking care of his mother the Virgin Mary. Not unnaturally, perhaps, her pictures of the scenery and costumes of Palestine were entirely inaccurate, for the Saviour and his disciples wore the dress of Spanish peasants, while the hills round Jerusalem were mighty mountains clothed with vineyards, and the olive trees were hung with grey Spanish moss. She thought of herself as eventually martyred for her faith, and ascending into heaven, but yet only to live over and over again this life in which she so delighted.

A quaint and pretty little example of the Devachan of a child may conclude our list of instances from this sub-plane. He had died at the age of seven, and was occupied in re-enacting in the heaven-world the religious stories which his Irish nurse had told him down here; and best of all he loved to think of himself as playing with the infant Jesus, and helping him to make those clay sparrows which the power of the child-Christ is fabled to have brought to life and caused to fly.

It will be seen that the blind unreasoning devotion of which we have been speaking does not at any time raise its votaries to any great spiritual heights; but it must be remembered that in all cases they are entirely happy and most fully satisfied, for what they receive is always the highest which they are capable of appreciating. Nor is it without a very good effect on their future career, for although no amount of mere devotion such as this will ever develope intellect, yet it does produce an increased capacity for a higher form of devotion, and in most cases it leads also to purity of life. A person therefore who lives such a life and enjoys such a Devachan as we have been describing, though he is not likely to make rapid progress on the path of spiritual development, is at least guarded from many dangers, for it is very improbable that in his next birth he should fall into any of the grosser sins, or be drawn away from his devotional aspirations into a mere worldly life of avarice, ambition or dissipation. Nevertheless, a survey of this sub-plane distinctly emphasizes the necessity of following St. Peter's advice, "Add to your faith virtue, and to virtue *knowledge.*"

Fifth Sub-Plane.

The chief characteristic of this subdivision may be defined as devotion expressing itself in active work. The Christian on this plane, for example, instead of merely adoring his Saviour, would think of himself as going out into the world to work for him. It is especially the plane for the working out of great schemes and designs unrealized on earth—of great organizations inspired by religious devotion, and usually having for their object some philanthropic purpose. It must be borne in mind, however, that ever as we rise higher greater complexity and variety is introduced, so that though we may still be able to give a definite characteristic as on the whole dominating the plane, we shall yet be more and more liable to find variations and exceptions that do not so readily range themselves under the general heading.

A typical case, although somewhat above the average, was that of a man who was found working out a grand scheme for the amelioration of the condition of the lower classes. While a deeply religious man himself, he had felt that the first step necessary in dealing with the poor was to improve their physical condition; and the plan which he was now working out in Devachan, with triumphant success and loving attention to every detail, was one which had often crossed his mind while on earth, though he had been quite unable there to take any steps towards its realization.

His idea had been that, if possessed of enormous wealth, he would buy up and get into his own hands the whole of one of the smaller trades—one in which perhaps three or four large firms only were now engaged; and he thought that by so doing he could effect very large savings by doing away with competitive advertising and other wasteful forms of trade rivalry, and thus be able, while supplying goods to the public at the same price as now, to pay much better wages to his workmen. It was part of his scheme to buy a plot of land and erect upon it cottages for his workmen, each surrounded by its little garden; and after a certain number of years' service, each workman was to acquire a share in the profits of the business which would be sufficient to provide for him in his old age. By working out this system the devachanee had hoped to show to the world that there was an eminently practical side to Christianity, and also to win the souls of his men to his own faith out of gratitude for the material benefits they had received.

Another not dissimilar case was that of an Indian prince whose ideal on earth had been the divine hero-king, Râma, on whose example he had tried to model his life and methods of government. Naturally down here all sorts of untoward accidents had occurred, and many of his schemes had consequently failed, but in Devachan everything went well, and the greatest possible result followed every one of his well-meant efforts—Râma of course personally advising and directing his work, and receiving perpetual adoration from all his devoted subjects.

A curious and rather touching instance of personal religious work was that of a woman who had been a nun, belonging to one not of the contemplative but of the working orders. She had evidently based her life upon the text "Inasmuch as ye have done it unto one of the least of these my brethren, ye have done it unto me," and now in Devachan she was still carrying out to the fullest extent the injunctions of her Lord, and was constantly occupied in healing the sick, in feeding the hungry, and clothing and helping the poor—the peculiarity of the case being that each of those to whom she had ministered at once changed into the appearance of the Christ, whom she then worshipped with fervent devotion.

An instructive case was that of two sisters, both of whom had been intensely religious; one of them had been a crippled invalid, and the other had spent a long life in tending her. On earth they had often discussed and planned what religious and philanthropic work they would carry out if they were able, and now each is the most prominent figure in the other's Devachan, the cripple being well and strong, while each thinks of the other as joining her in carrying out the unrealized wishes of her earth-life; and in this case the image of each sister in the other's Devachan was at least to some extent vivified and real.

On this plane also the higher type of sincere and devoted missionary activity finds expression. Of course the ordinary ignorant fanatic never reaches this level, but a few of the noblest cases, such as Livingstone, might be found here engaged in the congenial occupation of converting multitudes of people to the particular religion which they happened to advocate. One of the most striking of such cases which came under notice was that of a Mohammedan, who imagined himself as working most zealously at the conversion of the world and its government according to the most approved principles of the faith of Islam.

It appears that under certain conditions artistic capacity may also bring its votaries to this sub-plane. But here a careful distinction must be drawn. The artist or musician whose only object is the selfish one of personal fame, or who habitually allows himself to be influenced by feelings of professional jealousy, of course generates no forces which will bring him to the devachanic plane at all. On the other hand that grandest type of art whose disciples regard it as a mighty power entrusted to them for the spiritual elevation of their fellows will express itself in even higher regions than this. But between these two extremes those devotees of art who follow it for its own sake or regard it as an offering to their deity, never thinking of its effect on their fellows, may in some cases find their appropriate Devachan on this sub-plane.

As an example of this may be mentioned a musician of very religious temperament who regarded all his labour of love simply as an offering to the Christ, and knew nothing of the magnificent arrangement of sound and colour which his soul-inspiring compositions were producing in the matter of the devachanic plane. Nor would all his enthusiasm be wasted and fruitless, for its result would certainly be to give him increased devotion and increased musical capacity in his next birth; but without the still wider aspiration to help humanity this kind of Devachan might repeat itself almost indefinitely. Indeed, glancing back at the three planes with which we have just been dealing we may notice that they are in all cases concerned with the working out of devotion to personalities—either to one's family and friends or to a personal deity—rather than the wider devotion to humanity for its own sake which finds its expression on the next sub-plane.

FOURTH SUB-PLANE.

So varied are the activities of this, the highest of the rûpa levels, that it is difficult to group them under a single characteristic. Perhaps they might best be arranged into four main divisions—unselfish pursuit of spiritual knowledge, high philosophic or scientific thought, literary or artistic ability exercised for unselfish purposes, and service for service's sake. The exact definition of each of these classes will be more readily comprehended when some examples of each have been given.

Naturally it is from those religions in which the necessity of obtaining spiritual knowledge is recognized that most of the population of this sub-plane is drawn. It will be remembered that on the sixth sub-plane we found many Buddhists whose religion had chiefly taken the form of devotion to their great leader as a person; here on the contrary we have those more intelligent followers whose supreme aspiration was to sit at his feet and learn—who looked upon him in the light of a teacher rather than as a being to be adored.

Now in their Devachan this highest wish is fulfilled; they find themselves in very truth learning from the Buddha, and the image which they have thus made of him is no mere empty form, but most assuredly has in it a ray which is really part of himself. They are therefore beyond doubt acquiring fresh knowledge and wider views; and the effect upon their next life cannot but be of the most marked character. They will not, of course, remember any individual facts that they may have learnt (though when such facts are presented to their minds in a subsequent life they will grasp them with avidity and intuitively recognize their truth), but the result of the teaching will be to build into the ego a strong tendency to take broader and more philosophical views on all such subjects. Thus it will be seen that the Devachan enjoyed on this higher subdivision very definitely and unmistakably hastens the evolution of the ego; and once more our attention is drawn to the enormous advantage gained by those who have in their Devachan the figures of real, living and powerful teachers.

A less developed type of this form of instruction is found in cases in which some really great and spiritual writer has become to a student a living personality, and has taken on the aspect of a friend, forming part of the student's mental life—an ideal figure in his musings. Such an one may enter into the pupil's Devachan, and by virtue of his own highly evolved ego may vivify the devachanic image of himself, and further illuminate the teachings in his own books, bringing out of them the more hidden meanings.

Many of the followers of the path of wisdom among the Hindus find their Devachan upon this plane—that is, if their Gurus have been men possessing any real knowledge. A few of the more advanced among the Sûfîs and Parsîs are also here, and we still find some of the early Gnostics whose spiritual development was such as to earn for them a prolonged stay in this celestial region. But except for this comparatively small number of Sûfîs and Gnostics neither Mohammedanism nor Christianity seems to raise its followers to this level, though of course some who nominally belong to these religions may be carried on to this sub-plane by the presence in their character of qualities which do not depend upon the teachings peculiar to their religion.

In this region we also find earnest and devoted students of Occultism who are not yet so far advanced as to have earned the right and the power to forego their Devachan for the good of the world. Among these was one who in life had been personally known to some of the investigators—a Buddhist monk who had been an earnest student of Theosophy, and had long cherished the hope of being one day privileged to receive instruction directly from its adept teachers. In his Devachan the Buddha was the dominant figure, while the two Masters who have been most closely concerned with the Theosophical Society appeared also as his lieutenants, expounding and illustrating his teaching. All three of these images were very fully vitalized and informed by the power and wisdom of the great beings whom they represented, and the monk was therefore definitely receiving real teaching upon occult subjects, the effect of which would almost certainly be to bring him actually on to the Path of Initiation in his next birth.

Another instance from our ranks which was encountered on this level illustrates the terrible effect of harbouring unfounded and uncharitable suspicions. It was the case of a devoted and self-sacrificing student who towards the end of her life had unfortunately fallen into an attitude of quite unworthy and unjustifiable distrust of the motives of her old friend and teacher, Madame Blavatsky; and it was sad to notice how this feeling had shut out to a considerable extent the higher influence and teaching which she might have enjoyed in her Devachan. It was not that the influence and teaching were in any way withheld from her, but that her own mental attitude rendered her to some extent unreceptive of them. She was of course quite unconscious of this, and seemed to herself to be enjoying the fullest and most perfect communion with the Masters, yet it was obvious to the investigators that but for this unfortunate self-limitation she would have reaped far greater advantage from her stay on this level.

It will be understood that since there are other Masters of wisdom besides those connected with our own movement, and other schools of occultism working along the same general lines as that to which they belong, students attached to some of these are also frequently met with upon this sub-plane.

Passing now to the next class, that of high philosophic and scientific thought, we find here many of those nobler and more unselfish thinkers who seek insight and knowledge only for the purpose of enlightening and helping their fellows. We are of course not including as students of philosophy those men, either in the east or the west, who waste their time in mere verbal argument and hair-splitting—a form of discussion which has its roots in selfishness and conceit, and can therefore never help towards a real understanding of the facts of the universe; for naturally such foolish superficiality as this produces no results that can work themselves out on the devachanic plane.

As an instance of a true student noticed on this sub-plane we may mention one of the later followers of the neo-platonic system, whose name has fortunately been preserved to us in the surviving records of that period. He had striven all through his earth-life really to master the teachings of that school, and now his Devachan was occupied in unravelling its mysteries and in endeavouring to understand its bearing upon human life and development.

Another case was that of an astronomer, who seemed to have begun life as a Christian, but had gradually under the influence of his studies widened out into Pantheism; in his Devachan he was still pursuing these studies with a mind full of reverence, and was undoubtedly gaining real knowledge, apparently from the Devas who are concerned on this plane with the distribution and administration of stellar influences. He was lost in contemplation of a vast panorama of whirling nebulae and gradually-forming systems and worlds, and he appeared to be groping after some dim idea as to the shape of the universe, which he imagined as some vast animal. His thoughts surrounded him as elemental forms shaped as stars, and one especial source of joy to him consisted in listening to the stately rhythm of the music that pealed out in mighty chorales from the moving orbs.

The third type of activity on this plane is that highest kind of artistic and literary effort which is chiefly inspired by a desire to elevate and spiritualize the race. Here we find all our greatest musicians; on this sub-plane Mozart, Beethoven, Bach, Wagner and others are still flooding the heaven-world with harmony far more glorious even than the grandest which they were able to produce when on earth. It seems as if a great stream of divine music poured into them from higher regions, and was, as it were, specialized by them and made their own, to be then sent forth through all the plane in a great tide of melody which adds to the bliss of all around. Those who are functioning in full consciousness on the devachanic plane will clearly hear and thoroughly appreciate this magnificent outpouring, but even the disembodied entities of this level, each of whom is wrapped up in his own thought-cloud, are affected also by the elevating and ennobling influence of its resonant melody.

The painter and the sculptor also, if they have followed their respective arts always with a grand, unselfish aim, are here constantly making and sending forth all kinds of lovely forms for the delight and encouragement of their fellow-men—the forms being, of course, artificial elementals created by their thought. And not only may these beautiful conceptions give pleasure to those living entirely upon this plane; they may also in many cases be grasped by the minds of artists still in the flesh—may act as inspirations to them, and so be reproduced down here for the elevating and ennobling of that portion of humanity which is struggling amid the turmoil of physical life.

One touching and beautiful figure seen upon this plane was that of a boy who had been a chorister, and had died at the age of fourteen. His whole soul was full of music and of boyish devotion to his art, deeply coloured with the thought that by it he was expressing the religious longings of the multitude who crowded a vast cathedral, and yet was at the same time pouring out to them celestial encouragement and inspiration. He had known little enough save for this one great gift of song, but he had used that gift worthily, trying to he the voice of the people to heaven and of heaven to the people, and ever longing to know more music and render it more worthily for the Church's sake. In his Devachan his wish was bearing fruit, and over him was bending a teacher in a form evidently made by his mind from the quaint angular figure of a mediæval St. Cecilia in a stained glass window, and this thought-image was vivified by a Deva, who through it taught him greater music than he had ever dreamed on earth.

Here also was one of earth's failures—for the tragedy of the earth-life leaves strange marks sometimes even in "the heavenly places." He was alone in Devachan; in the world where all thoughts of loved ones smile upon man as friends, he was thinking and writing in solitude. On earth he had striven to write a great book, and for the sake of it had refused to use his literary power in making mere sustenance from paltry hack-work ; but none would look at his book, and he walked the streets despairing, till sorrow and starvation closed his eyes to earth. He had been lonely all his life—in his youth friendless and shut out from family ties, and in his manhood able to work only in his own way, pushing aside hands that would have led him to a wider view of life's possibilities than the earthly paradise which he longed to make for all. Now, as he thought and wrote, though there were none he had loved as personal or ideal helpers who could make part of his devachanic life, he saw stretching before him the Utopia of which he had dreamed, for which he had tried to live, and the vast thronging impersonal multitudes whom he had longed to serve; and the joy of their joy surged back on him and made his solitude a heaven. When he is born again to earth he will surely return with power to achieve as well as to plan, and the devachanic vision will be partially bodied forth in happier terrene lives.

Many were found on this plane who during their earth-stay had devoted themselves to helping men because they felt the tie of brotherhood—who rendered service for service's sake rather than because they desired to please any particular deity. They were engaged in working out with full knowledge and calm wisdom vast schemes of beneficence, magnificent plans of world-improvement, and at the same time they were maturing powers with which to carry them out hereafter on the lower plane of physical life.

The Arûpa Levels.

We now pass from the four lower or rûpa levels of Devachan, on which the personality functions, to the three higher or arûpa levels, where the reincarnating ego has his home. Here, so far as he sees at all, he sees clearly, for he has risen above the illusions of personality and the refracting medium of the lower self, and though his consciousness may be dim, dreamily unobservant and scarcely awake, yet his vision is at least true, however limited. The conditions of consciousness are so far away from all with which we are familiar down here that all terms known to psychology are useless and misleading. This has been called the realm of the noumenal in contrast with the phenomenal, of the formless in contrast with the formed; but it is still a world of manifestation, however real when opposed to the unrealities of lower states, and it still has forms, however rare in their materials and subtle in their essence.

Third Sub-Plane.

This, the lowest of the arûpa sub-planes, is also by far the most populous of all the regions with which we are acquainted, for here are present almost all the sixty thousand millions of egos who are said to be engaged in the present human evolution—all, in fact, except the comparatively small number who are capable of functioning on the second and first sub-planes. Each ego is represented by an ovoid form, the auric egg—at first a mere film, colourless and almost invisible, of most tenuous consistency; but, as the ego developes, this body begins to show a shimmering iridescence like a soap-bubble, colours playing over its surface like the changing hues made by sunlight on the spray of a waterfall. Composed of matter inconceivably fine, delicate and ethereal, intensely alive and pulsating with living fire, it becomes as its evolution proceeds a radiant globe of flashing colours, its high vibrations sending ripples of changing hues over its surface—hues of which earth knows nothing—brilliant, soft and luminous beyond the power of language to describe. Take the colours of an Egyptian sunset and add to them the wonderful softness of an English sky at eventide—raise these as high above themselves in light and translucency and splendour as they are above the colours given by the cakes of a child's paint-box—and even then none who have not seen can image the beauty of these radiant orbs which flash into the field of the devachanic sight as it is lifted to the vision of this supernal world.

All these causal bodies are filled with living fire drawn from a higher plane, with which the globe appears to be connected by a quivering thread of intense light, vividly recalling to the mind the words of the Stanzas of Dzyân, "the Spark hangs from the Flame by the finest thread of Fohat;" and as the ego grows and is able to receive more and more from the inexhaustible ocean of Âtmâ-Buddhi which pours down through the thread as a channel, the latter expands and gives wider passage to the flood, till on the next sub-plane it might he imaged as a water-spout connecting earth and sky, and higher still as itself a great globe through which rushes the living spring, until the causal body seems to melt into the inpouring light. Once more the Stanza says it for us: "The thread between the Watcher and his shadow becomes more strong and radiant with every change. The morning sunlight has changed into noon-day glory. This is thy present wheel, said the Flame to the Spark. Thou art myself, my image and my shadow. I have clothed myself in thee, and thou art my vâhan to the day, 'Be-with-us, when thou shalt rebecome myself and others, thyself and me."

The egos who are connected with a physical body are distinguishable from those enjoying the disembodied state by a difference in the types of vibrations set up on the surface of the globes, and it is therefore easy to see at a glance whether an individual is or is not in incarnation at the time. The immense majority, whether in or out of the body, are but dreamily semiconscious, though few are now in the condition of mere colourless films; those who are fully awake are marked and brilliant exceptions, standing out amid the less radiant crowds like stars of the first magnitude, and between these and the least-developed are ranged every variety of size and beauty of colour—each thus representing the exact stage of evolution at which it has arrived.

The majority are not yet sufficiently definite, even in such consciousness as they possess, to understand the purpose or the laws of the evolution in which they are engaged; they seek incarnation in obedience to the impulse of the Cosmic Will, and also to *Tanhâ,* the blind thirst for manifested life—a desire to find some region in which they can feel and be conscious of living; they put forth as groping, waving tentacles into the ocean of existence the personalities which are themselves on the lower planes of life, but they are as yet in no sense aware that these personalities are the means whereby they are to be nourished and to grow. They see nothing of their past or their future, not being yet conscious on their own plane. Still, as they are slowly drawing in experience and assimilating it, there grows up a sense that certain things are good to do and others bad, and this expresses itself imperfectly in the connected personality as the beginning of a conscience, a feeling of right and wrong: and gradually as they develope, this sense more and more clearly formulates itself in the lower nature, and becomes a less inefficient guide of conduct.

When the personality belonging to an ego in this undeveloped condition has completed its Devachan on the rûpa levels, it yields up to the higher individuality whatever it has assimilated and transmuted, itself disintegrating and leaving the ego as the sole survivor, the real and enduring man. But at that moment, before it puts itself forth again into embodied existence, the ego has a flash of consciousness, showing the results of the life that is completed, and something of what will follow from that life in the next; for a moment all that there is of the man is in the arûpa world, and thence it again descends. These glimpses may be said to be the opportunities of the ego. At first it makes little of them, being so dimly conscious and so poorly fitted to apprehend facts and their interrelations; but gradually the power to appreciate what is seen increases, and later the ability comes to remember the flashes of the past and to compare them, and thus to mark out the road which is being traversed, and estimate the progress made and the direction in which it is going.

In this way the most advanced egos of this sub-plane develope to a point at which they are engaged in studying their past, tracing out the causes set going in it, and learning much from the retrospection, so that the impulses sent downwards become clearer and more definite, and translate themselves in the lower consciousness as firm convictions and imperative intuitions.

It is perhaps scarcely necessary to repeat that the thought-images of the rûpa levels are not carried into the arûpa world; if an ego conscious on this plane has been surrounded by the images of less developed individualities who were dear to him on earth, he comes into contact with them in this higher region as they really are, and will find them irresponsive to him here, because they have not yet developed their consciousness on this loftier plane. This, however, can be but an exceedingly rare case, and even when it occurs the ego experiences no sense of loss, for the ties that are only of the personality have no power over him; his true relations are with other individualities, and these endure when the personality vanishes, so that on the arûpa levels each ego knows his real kindred, sees them and is seen in his own royal nature, as the true immortal man that passes on from life to life, with all the ties intact that are knit to his real being.

SECOND SUB-PLANE.

From the densely-thronged region which we have been considering we pass into a more thinly-populated world, as out of a great city into a peaceful countryside; for at the present stage of human evolution only a small minority of individuals have risen to this loftier level where even the least advanced is definitely self-conscious, and also conscious of his surroundings. Able at least to some extent to review the past through which he has come, the ego on this level is aware of the purpose and method of evolution; he knows that he is engaged in a work of self-development, and recognizes the stages of physical and *post-mortem* life through which he passes in his lower vehicles. The personality with which he is connected is seen by him as part of himself, and he endeavours to guide it, using his knowledge of the past as a store of experience from which he formulates principles of conduct, clear and immutable convictions of right and wrong. These he sends down into his lower mind, super-intending and directing its activities. While he continually fails in the earlier part of his life on this sub-plane to make the lower mind understand logically the foundations of the principles he impresses on it, he yet very definitely succeeds in making the impression, and such abstract ideas as truth, justice and honour become unchallenged and ruling conceptions in the lower mental life.

There are rules of conduct enforced by social, national and religious sanctions, by which a man guides himself in daily life, and yet which may be swept away by some rush of temptation, some overmastering surge of passion and desire; but there are some things an evolved man *cannot* do—things which are against his very nature; he cannot lie, or betray, or do a dishonourable action. Into the inmost fibres of his being certain principles are wrought, and to act against them is an impossibility, no matter what may be the strain of circumstance or the torrent of temptation; for these things are of the life of the ego. While, however, he thus succeeds in guiding his lower vehicle, his knowledge of it and its doings is often far from precise and clear. He sees the lower planes but dimly, understanding their principles rather than their details, and part of his evolution on this plane consists of coming more and more consciously into direct touch with the personality which so imperfectly represents him below.

It will he understood from this that only such egos as are deliberately aiming at spiritual growth live on this plane, and they have in consequence become largely receptive of influences from the planes above them. The channel of communication grows and enlarges, and a fuller flood pours through. The thought under this influence takes on a singularly clear and piercing quality, even in the less developed, and the effect of this in the lower mind shows itself as a tendency to philosophic and abstract thinking. In the more highly evolved the vision is far-reaching: it ranges with clear insight over the past, recognizing the causes set up, their working out, and what remains still unexhausted of their effects.

The egos living on this plane have wide opportunities for growth when freed from the physical body, for here they may receive instructions from more advanced entities, coming into direct touch with their teachers. No longer by thought-pictures, but by a flashing luminousness impossible to describe, the very essence of the idea flies like a star from one ego to the other, its correlations expressing themselves as light waves pouring out from the central star, and needing no separate enunciation. A thought is like a light placed in a room; it shows all things round it, but requires no words to describe them.

First Sub-Plane.

This, the most glorious level of the devachanic world, has but few denizens from our humanity, for none but Masters and initiates dwell on its heights. Of the beauty of form and colour and sound here no words can speak, for mortal language has no terms in which those radiant splendours may find expression. Enough that they *are,* and that some of our race are wearing them, the earnest of what others shall be, the fruition of which the seed was sown on lowlier planes. These have accomplished the mânasic evolution, and have unified self-consciousness; from their eyes the illusion-veil of personality has been lifted, and they know and realize that they are not the lower nature, but only use it as a vehicle of experience. It may still have power in the less evolved of them to shackle and to hamper, but they can never fall into the blunder of confusing it with themselves. From this they are saved by carrying their consciousness through unbroken, not only from day to day but from life to life, so that past lives are not so much looked back upon as always present in the consciousness, the man feeling them as one life rather than as many.

From this highest level of the arûpa world come down most of the influences poured out by the Masters as they work for the evolution of the human race, acting on the individualities of men, shedding on them the inspiring energies which stimulate spiritual growth, which enlighten the intellect and purify the emotions. Hence genius receives its illumination; here all upward efforts find their guidance. As the sun-rays fall everywhere from one centre, and each body that receives them uses them after its nature, so from the Elder Brothers of the race fall on all egos the light and life which it is their function to dispense; and each uses as much as it can assimilate, and thereby grows and evolves. Thus, as everywhere else, the highest glory of the devachanic world is found in the glory of service, and they who have accomplished the mânasic evolution are the fountains from which flows strength for those who still are climbing.

II. Non-Human.

When we attempt to describe the non-human inhabitants of the devachanic plane, we at once find ourselves face to face with difficulties of the most insuperable character. For in touching the arûpa levels we come into contact for the first time with a plane which is cosmic in its extent—on which therefore may be met many an entity which mere human language has no words to portray. For the purposes of our present paper it will probably be best to put aside altogether those vast hosts of beings whose range is cosmic, and confine our remarks strictly to the inhabitants peculiar to the mânasic plane of our own chain of worlds. It may be remembered that in the manual on *The Astral Plane* the same course was adopted, no attempt being made to describe visitors from other planets and systems; and although such visitors as were there only occasional would here be very much more frequent, it is obviously desirable in an essay for general reading to adhere to the same rule. A few words, therefore, upon the elemental essence of the plane and the sections of the great Deva kingdom which are especially connected with it will be as much as it will be useful to give here; and the extreme difficulty of presenting even these comparatively simple ideas will conclusively show how impossible it would be to deal with others which could not but be far more complicated.

THE ELEMENTAL ESSENCE.

It may be remembered that in one of the earlier letters received from an Adept teacher the remark was made that to comprehend the condition of the first and second of the elemental kingdoms was impossible except to an initiate—an observation which shows how partial must be the success which can attend any effort to describe them down here upon the physical plane. It will be well first of all that we should endeavour to form as clear an idea in our minds as possible of what elemental essence really is, since this is a point upon which much confusion often seems to exist, even amongst those who have made considerable study of Theosophical literature.

WHAT IT IS.

Elemental essence, then, is merely a name applied during certain early stages of its evolution to monadic essence, which in its turn may be defined as the outpouring of Âtmâ-Buddhi into matter. We are all familiar with the fact that before this outpouring arrives at the stage of individualization at which it ensouls a man, it has passed through and ensouled in turn six lower phases of evolution—the animal, vegetable, mineral and three elemental kingdoms. When energizing through those respective stages it has sometimes been called the animal, vegetable or mineral monad—though this term is distinctly misleading, since long before it arrives at any of these kingdoms it has become not *one* but *many* monads. The name was however adopted to convey the idea that, though differentiation in the monadic essence had already long ago set in, it had not yet been carried to the extent of individualization. Now when this monadic essence is energizing through the three great elemental kingdoms which precede the mineral it is called by the name of "elemental essence."

THE VEILING OF ÂTMÂ.

Before, however, its nature and the manner in which it manifests itself on the various planes can be understood, the method in which Âtmâ enfolds itself in its descent into matter must be realized. We are not now dealing with the original formation of the matter of the planes by aggregation after a universal pralaya, but simply with the descent of a new wave of evolution into matter already existing.

Before the period of which we are speaking, this wave of life has spent countless ages evolving, in a manner of which we can have very little comprehension, through the successive encasements of atoms, molecules and cells: but we will leave all that earlier part of its stupendous history out of account for the moment, and consider only its descent into the matter of planes somewhat more within the grasp of human intellect, though still far above the merely physical level.

Be it understood then that when Âtmâ, resting on any plane (it matters not which), on its path downward into matter, is driven by the resistless force of its own evolution to pass onward to the plane next below, it must, in order to manifest itself there, enfold itself in the matter of that lower plane—draw round itself as a body a veil of that matter, to which it will act as soul or energizing force. Similarly, when it continues its descent to a third plane, it must draw round itself some of *its* matter, and we shall have then an entity whose body or outer covering consists of the matter of that third plane.

But the force energizing in it—its soul, so to speak—will not be Âtmâ in the condition in which it was upon the higher plane on which we first found it; it will be that Âtmâ *plus* the veil of the matter of the second plane through which it has passed. When a still further descent is made to a fourth plane, the entity becomes still more complex, for it will then have a body of the matter of that fourth plane, ensouled by Âtmâ already twice veiled, in the matter of the second and third planes. It will be seen that, since this process repeats itself for every sub-plane of each plane of the solar system, by the time the original force reaches our physical level it is so thoroughly veiled that it is small wonder that men often fail to recognize it as Âtmâ at all.

THE THREE ELEMENTAL KINGDOMS.

Now suppose that the monadic essence has carried on this process of veiling itself down to the atomic level of the devachanic plane, and that, instead of descending through the various subdivisions of that plane, it plunges down directly into the astral plane, ensouling or aggregating around it a body of atomic astral matter; such a combination would be the elemental essence of the astral plane, belonging to the third of the great elemental kingdoms—the one immediately preceding the mineral. In the course of its two thousand four hundred differentiations on the astral plane it draws to itself many and various combinations of the matter of its several subdivisions; but these are only temporary, and it still remains essentially one kingdom, whose characteristic is monadic essence involved down to the atomic level of the devachanic plane only, but manifesting primarily through the atomic matter of the astral plane.

The elemental essence which we find on the devachanic plane constitutes the first and second of the great elemental kingdoms, but the principle of its formation is the same as that described above. A mass of monadic essence (the expression is materialistic and misleading, but it is difficult to see how to avoid it) carries on the process of veiling itself down to the atomic level of the buddhic plane, and then plunges down directly into the devachanic plane, ensouling a body of atomic devachanic matter—that is, of the matter belonging to the highest of the arûpa levels—and so becomes the elemental essence of the first great kingdom. In this—its simplest or natural condition, be it understood—it does not combine the atoms of the plane into molecules in order to form a body for itself, but simply applies by its attraction an immense compressing force to them. In the course of its differentiations it aggregates around itself various combinations of the matter of the second and third sub-divisions, but it never loses the special and definite characteristics which mark it as the elemental essence of the arûpa levels.

The second great kingdom, whose habitat is the rûpa division of Devachan, is formed upon a very similar principle. The essence of the first kingdom, after evolving through various differentiations during ages whose length is unknown to us, returns to its simplest condition—not of course, as it was before that evolution, but bearing within it all that it has gained throughout its course; and it then puts itself down directly into the fourth sub-division of Devachan—the highest of the rûpa levels—drawing to itself as a body some of the matter of that sub-plane. That is the simplest condition of the elemental essence of the second kingdom, but as before, it takes on in the course of its evolution garbs many and various, composed of combinations of the matter of the lower sub-planes.

It might naturally be supposed that these elemental kingdoms which exist and function upon the devachanic plane must certainly, being so much higher, be further advanced in evolution than the third kingdom, which belongs exclusively to the astral plane. This however is not so; for it must be remembered that in speaking of this phase of evolution the word "higher" means not, as usual, more advanced, but *less* advanced, since here we are dealing with the monadic essence on the downward sweep of its arc, and progress for the elemental essence therefore means descent into matter instead of, as with us, ascent towards higher planes. Unless the student bears this fact constantly and clearly in mind, he will again and again find himself beset by perplexing anomalies, and his view of this side of evolution will be lacking in grasp and comprehensiveness.

The general characteristics of elemental essence were indicated at considerable length in the manual on *The Astral Plane,* and all that is there said as to the number of subdivisions in the kingdoms and their marvellous impressibility by human thought is equally true of these devachanic varieties. A few words should perhaps be said to explain how the seven horizontal subdivisions of each kingdom arrange themselves in connection with the sub-planes of Devachan. In the case of the first kingdom, its highest subdivision corresponds with the first sub-plane of Devachan, while the second and third sub-planes are each divided into three parts, each of which is the habitat of one of the elemental subdivisions. The second kingdom distributes itself over the rûpa levels, its highest subdivision corresponding to the fourth sub-plane, while the fifth, sixth and seventh sub-planes are each divided into two to accommodate the remainder.

HOW THE ESSENCE EVOLVES.

So much was written in the earlier part of this manual as to the effect of thought upon the devachanic elemental essence that it will be unnecessary to return to that branch of the subject now; but it must be borne in mind that it is, if possible, even more instantaneously sensitive to thought-action here than it is on the astral plane, the wonderful delicacy with which it responds to the faintest action of the mind being constantly and prominently brought before our investigators. We shall grasp this capability the more fully if we realize that it is in such response that its very life consists—that its progress is due to the use made of it in the process of thought by the more advanced entities whose evolution it shares.

If it could be imagined as entirely free for a moment from the action of thought, it would be but a formless conglomeration of dancing infinitesimal atoms—instinct indeed with a marvellous intensity of life, yet making no kind of progress on the downward path of its involution into matter. But when by the thoughts of the beings functioning on those respective planes it is thrown on the rûpa levels into all kinds of lovely forms, and on the arûpa levels into flashing streams, it receives a distinct additional impulse which, often repeated, helps it forward on its way. For whenever a thought is directed from those higher levels to the affairs of earth, it naturally sweeps downward and takes upon itself the matter of the lower planes. In doing so it brings into contact with that matter the elemental essence of which its first veil was formed, and so by degrees habituates it to answering to lower vibrations; thus, very gradually, proceeds its downward evolution into matter.

Very noticeably also is it affected by music—by the splendid floods of glorious sound of which we have previously spoken as poured forth upon these lofty planes by the great masters of melody who are carrying on there in far fuller measure the work which down here on this dull earth they had only commenced.

Another point which should be remembered is the vast difference between the grandeur and power of thought on this plane and the comparative feebleness of the efforts that we dignify with that name down here. Our ordinary thought begins in the mind-body on the rûpa levels and clothes itself as it descends with the appropriate astral elemental essence; but when a man has advanced so far as to have his consciousness active in the true ego upon the arûpa levels, then his thought commences there and clothes itself first in the elemental essence of the rûpa levels, and is consequently infinitely finer, more penetrating and in every way more effective. If the thought be directed exclusively to higher objects, its vibrations may be of too fine a character to find expression on the astral plane at all; but when they do affect this lower matter they will do so with much more far-reaching effect than those which are generated so much nearer to its own level.

Following this idea a stage further we see the thought of the initiate taking its rise upon the buddhic plane, above Devachan altogether, and clothing itself with the elemental essence of the arûpa levels for garment, while the thought of the Adept pours down from Nirvana itself, wielding the tremendous, the wholly incalculable powers of regions beyond the ken of mere ordinary humanity. Thus ever as our conceptions rise higher we see before us wider and wider fields of usefulness for our enormously increased capacities, and we realize how true is the saying that the work of one day on levels such as these may well surpass in efficiency the toil of a thousand years on the physical plane.

THE DEVAS.

So much of the little that can be expressed in human language about these wonderful and exalted beings was written in *The Astral Plane* that it is unnecessary to go at length into the subject here. For the information of those who have not that manual at hand I will repeat here somewhat of the general explanation there given with reference to these entities.

The highest system of evolution connected with this earth, so far as we know, is that of the beings whom Hindus call the Devas, and who have elsewhere been spoken of as angels, sons of God, etc. They may in fact be regarded as a kingdom lying next above humanity in the same way as humanity in turn lies next above the animal kingdom, but with this important difference, that while for an animal there is no possibility of evolution through any kingdom but the human, man, when he attains the level of the Asekha, or full Adept, finds various paths of advancement opening before him, of which this great Deva evolution is only one (see article on "The Steps of the Path," in *Lucifer* for October, 1896).

In Oriental literature this word "Deva" is frequently used vaguely to mean almost any kind of non-human entity, so that it would often include DHYÂN CHOHANS on the one hand and nature-spirits and artificial elementals on the other. Here, however, its use will be restricted to the magnificent evolution which we are now considering.

Though connected with this earth, the Devas are by no means confined to it, for the whole of our present chain of seven worlds is as one world to them, their evolution being through a grand system of seven chains. Their hosts have hitherto been recruited chiefly from other humanities in the solar system, some lower and some higher than ours, since but a very small portion of our own has as yet reached the level at which for us it is possible to join them: but it seems certain that some of their very numerous classes have not passed in their upward progress through any humanity at all comparable with ours.

It is not possible for us at present to understand very much about them, but it is clear that what may be described as the aim of their evolution is considerably higher than ours; that is to say, while the object of our human evolution is to raise the successful portion of humanity to the position of the Asekha Adept by the end of the seventh round, the object of the Deva evolution is to raise their foremost rank to a very much higher level in the corresponding period. For them, as for us, a steeper but shorter path to still more sublime heights lies open to earnest endeavour; but what those heights may be in their case we can only conjecture.

THEIR DIVISIONS.

Their three lower great divisions, beginning from the bottom, are generally called Kâmadevas, Rûpadevas, and Arûpadevas respectively. Just as our ordinary body here—the lowest body possible for us—is the physical, so the ordinary body of a Kâmadeva is the astral; so that he stands in somewhat the same position as humanity will do when it reaches planet F, and he, living ordinarily in an astral body, would go out of it to higher spheres in a Mâyâvirûpa just as we might in an astral body, while to enter the causal body would be to him (when sufficiently developed) no greater effort than to form a Mâyâvirûpa might be to us. In the same way the Rûpadeva's ordinary body would be the Mâyâvirûpa, since his habitat is the four rapa levels of the devachanic plane; while the Arûpadeva belongs to the three higher levels of that plane, and owns no nearer approach to a body than the Kârana Sharîra. Above the Arûpadevas there are four other great classes of this kingdom, inhabiting respectively the four higher planes of our solar system; and again above and beyond the Deva kingdom altogether stand the great hosts of the DHYÂN CHOHANS, but the consideration of such glorified beings would be out of place here.

Each of the two great divisions of this kingdom which have been mentioned as inhabiting the devachanic plane contains within itself many different classes; but their life is in every way so far removed from our own that it is useless to endeavour to give anything but the most general idea of it. I do not know that I can better indicate the impression produced upon the minds of our investigators on the subject than by reproducing the very words used by one of them at the time of the enquiry: "I get the effect of an intensely exalted consciousness—a consciousness glorious beyond all words; yet so very strange; so different—so entirely different from anything I have ever felt before, so unlike any possible kind of human experience, that it is absolutely hopeless to try to put it into words."

Equally hopeless is it on this physical plane to try to give any idea of the appearance of these mighty beings, for it changes with every line of thought which they follow. Some reference was made earlier in this paper to the magnificence and wonderful power of expression of their colour-language, and it will also have been realized from some passing remarks made in describing the human inhabitants that under certain conditions it is possible for men functioning upon this plane to learn much from them. It may be remembered how one of them had animated the angel-figure in the Devachan of a chorister, and was teaching him music grander far than any ever heard by earthly ears, and how in another case those connected with the wielding of certain planetary influences were helping forward the devachanic evolution of a certain astronomer.

Their relation to the nature-spirits (for an account of whom see Manual V.) might be described as somewhat resembling, though on a higher scale, that of men to the animal kingdom; for just as the animal can attain individualization only by association with man, so it appears that a permanent reincarnating individuality can normally be acquired by a nature-spirit only by an attachment of somewhat similar character to members of some of the orders of Devas.

Of course nothing that has been, or indeed can be, said of this great Deva evolution does more than brush the fringe of a very mighty subject, the fuller elaboration of which it must be left to each reader to make for himself when he develops the consciousness of these higher planes; yet what has been written, slight and unsatisfactory as it is and must be, may help to give some faint idea of the hosts of helpers with which man's advance in evolution will bring him into touch, and to show how every aspiration which his increased capacities make possible for him as he ascends is more than satisfied by the beneficent arrangements which nature has made for him.

III. Artificial.

Very few words need be said upon this branch of our subject. The devachanic plane is even more fully peopled than the astral by the artificial elementals called into temporary existence by the thoughts of its inhabitants; and when it is remembered how much grander and more powerful thought is upon this plane, and that its forces are being wielded not only by the human inhabitants, embodied and disembodied, but by the Devas and by visitors from higher planes, it will at once be seen that the importance and influence of such artificial entities can hardly be exaggerated. It is not necessary here to go over again the ground traversed in the previous manual as to the effect of men's thoughts and the necessity of guarding them carefully; and enough was said in describing the difference between the action of thought on the rûpa and arûpa levels to show how the artificial elemental of the devachanic plane is called into existence, and to give some idea of the infinite variety of temporary entities which might be so produced, and the immense importance of the work that might be, and constantly is, done by their means. Great use is made of them by Adepts and initiates, and it is needless to say that the artificial elemental formed by such powerful minds as these is a being of infinitely longer existence and proportionately greater power than any of those described in dealing with the astral plane.

Conclusion.

In glancing over what has been written, the prominent idea is not unnaturally a humiliating sense of the utter inadequacy of all the attempts at description—of the hopelessness of any effort to put into human words the ineffable glories of the heaven-world. Still, lamentably imperfect as such an essay as this must be, it is yet better than nothing, and it may serve to put into the mind of the reader some faint conception of what awaits him on the other side of the grave; and though when he reaches this bright realm of bliss he will certainly find infinitely more than he has been led to expect, he will not, it is hoped, have to unlearn any of the information that he has here acquired.

Man, as at present constituted, has within him principles belonging to two planes even higher than Devachan, for his Buddhi represents him upon what from that very fact we call the buddhic plane, and his Attila upon that third plane of the solar system which has usually been spoken of as the nirvânic. In the average man these highest principles are as yet almost entirely undeveloped, and in any case the planes to which they belong are still more beyond the reach of all description than was Devachan. It must suffice to say that on the buddhic plane all limitations begin to fall away, and the consciousness of man expands until he realizes, no longer in theory only, but by absolute experience, that the consciousness of his fellows is included within his own, and he feels and knows and experiences with an absolute perfection of sympathy all that is in them, because it is in reality a part of himself; while on the nirvânic plane he moves a step further, and realizes that his consciousness and theirs are one in a yet higher sense, because they are all in reality facets of the infinitely greater consciousness of the Locos, in Whom they all live and move and have their being; so that when "the dewdrop slips into the shining sea" the effect produced is rather as though the process had been reversed and the ocean poured into the drop, which now for the first time realizes that it *is* the ocean—not a part of it, but the whole. Paradoxical, utterly incomprehensible, apparently impossible; yet absolutely true.

But this much at least we may grasp—that the blessed state of Nirvâna is not, as some have ignorantly supposed, a condition of blank nothingness, but of far more intense and beneficent activity; and that ever as we rise higher in the scale of nature our possibilities become greater, our work for others ever grander and more far-reaching, and that infinite wisdom and infinite power mean only infinite capacity for service, because they are directed by infinite love.

CLAIRVOYANCE

CHAPTER I.

WHAT CLAIRVOYANCE IS.

CLAIRVOYANCE means literally nothing more than "clear-seeing," and it is a word which has been sorely misused, and even degraded so far as to be employed to describe the trickery of a mountebank in a variety show. Even in its more restricted sense it covers a wide range of phenomena, differing so greatly in character that it is not easy to give a definition of the word which shall be at once succinct and accurate. It has been called "spiritual vision," but no rendering could well be more misleading than that, for in the vast majority of cases there is no faculty connected with it which has the slightest claim to be honoured by so lofty a name.

For the purpose of this treatise we may, perhaps, define it as the power to see what is hidden from ordinary physical sight. It will be as well to premise that it is very frequently (though by no means always) accompanied by what is called clairaudience, or the power to hear what would be inaudible to the ordinary physical ear; and we will for the nonce take our title as covering this faculty also, in order to avoid the clumsiness of perpetually using two long words where one will suffice.

Let me make two points clear before I begin. First, I am not writing for those who do not believe that there is such a thing as clairvoyance, nor am I seeking to convince those who are in doubt about the matter. In so small a work as this I have no space for that; such people must study the many books containing lists of cases, or make experiments for themselves along mesmeric lines. I am addressing myself to the better-instructed class who know that clairvoyance exists, and are sufficiently interested in the subject to be glad of information as to its methods and possibilities; and I would assure them that what I write is the result of much careful study and experiment, and that though some of the powers which I shall have to describe may seem new and wonderful to them, I mention no single one of which I have not myself seen examples.

Secondly, though I shall endeavour to avoid technicalities as far as possible, yet as I am writing in the main for students of Theosophy, I shall feel myself at liberty sometimes to use, for brevity's sake and without detailed explanation, the ordinary Theosophical terms with which I may safely assume them to be familiar.

Should this little book fall into the hands of any to whom the occasional use of such terms constitutes a difficulty, I can only apologize to them and refer them for these preliminary explanations to any elementary Theosophical work, such as Mrs. Besant's *Ancient Wisdom* or *Man and His Bodies*. The truth is that the whole Theosophical system hangs together so closely, and its various parts are so interdependent, that to give a full explanation of every term used would necessitate an exhaustive treatise on Theosophy as a preface even to this short account of clairvoyance.

Before a detailed explanation of clairvoyance can usefully be attempted, however, it will be necessary for us to devote a little time to some preliminary considerations, in order that we may have clearly in mind a few broad facts as to the different planes on which clairvoyant vision may be exercised, and the conditions which render its exercise possible.

We are constantly assured in Theosophical literature that all these higher faculties are presently to be the heritage of mankind in general—that the capacity of clairvoyance, for example, lies latent in every one, and that those in whom it already manifests itself are simply in that one particular a little in advance of the rest of us. Now this statement is a true one, and yet it seems quite vague and unreal to the majority of people, simply because they regard such a faculty as something absolutely different from anything they have yet experienced, and feel fairly confident that they themselves, at any rate, are not within measurable distance of its development.

It may help to dispel this sense of unreality if we try to understand that clairvoyance, like so many other things in nature, is mainly a question of vibrations, and is in fact nothing but an extension of powers which we are all using every day of our lives. We are living all the while surrounded by a vast sea of mingled air and ether, the latter inter-penetrating the former, as it does all physical matter; and it is chiefly by means of vibrations in that vast sea of matter that impressions reach us from the outside. This much we all know, but it may perhaps never have occurred to many of us that the number of these vibrations to which we are capable of responding is in reality quite infinitesimal.

Up among the exceedingly rapid vibrations which affect the ether there is a certain small section—a *very* small section—to which the retina of the human eye is capable of responding, and these particular vibrations produce in us the sensation which we call light. That is to say, we are capable of seeing only those objects from which light of that particular kind can either issue or be reflected.

In exactly the same way the tympanum of the human ear is capable of responding to a certain very small range of comparatively slow vibrations—slow enough to affect the air which surrounds us; and so the only sounds which we can hear are those made by objects which are able to vibrate at some rate within that particular range.

In both cases it is a matter perfectly well known to science that there are large numbers of vibrations both above and below these two sections, and that consequently there is much light that we cannot see, and there are many sounds to which our ears are deaf. In the case of light the action of these higher and lower vibrations is easily perceptible in the effects produced by the actinic rays at one end of the spectrum and the heat rays at the other.

As a matter of fact there exist vibrations of every conceivable degree of rapidity, filling the whole vast space intervening between the slow sound waves and the swift light waves; nor is even that all, for there are undoubtedly vibrations slower than those of sound, and a whole infinity of them which are swifter than those known to us as light. So we begin to understand that the vibrations by which we see and hear are only like two tiny groups of a few strings selected from an enormous harp of practically infinite extent, and when we think how much we have been able to learn and infer from the use of those minute fragments, we see vaguely what possibilities might lie before us if we were enabled to utilize the vast and wonderful whole.

Another fact which needs to be considered in this connection is that different human beings vary considerably, though within relatively narrow limits, in their capacity of response even to the very few vibrations which are within reach of our physical senses. I am not referring to the keenness of sight or of hearing that enables one man to see a fainter object or hear a slighter sound than another; it is not in the least a question of strength of vision, but of extent of susceptibility.

For example, if anyone will take a good bisulphide of carbon prism, and by its means throw a clear spectrum on a sheet of white paper, and then get a number of people to mark upon the paper the extreme limits of the spectrum as it appears to them, he is fairly certain to find that their powers of vision differ appreciably. Some will see the violet extending much farther than the majority do; others will perhaps see rather less violet than most, while gaining a corresponding extension of vision at the red end. Some few there will perhaps be who can see farther than ordinary at both ends, and these will almost certainly be what we call sensitive people—susceptible in fact to a greater range of vibrations than are most men of the present day.

In hearing, the same difference can be tested by taking some sound which is just not too high to be audible—on the very verge of audibility as it were—and discovering how many among a given number of people are able to hear it. The squeak of a bat is a familiar instance of such a sound, and experiment will show that on a summer evening, when the whole air is full of the shrill, needle-like cries of these little animals, quite a large number of men will be absolutely unconscious of them, and unable to hear anything at all.

Now these examples clearly show that there is no hard-and-fast limit to man's power of response to either etheric or aerial vibrations, but that some among us already have that power to a wider extent than others; and it will even be found that the same man's capacity varies on different occasions. It is therefore not difficult for us to imagine that it might be possible for a man to develop this power, and thus in time to learn to see much that is invisible to his fellow-men, and hear much that is inaudible to them, since we know perfectly well that enormous numbers of these additional vibrations do exist, and are simply, as it were, awaiting recognition.

The experiments with the Röntgen rays give us an example of the startling results which are produced when even a very few of these additional vibrations are brought within human ken, and the transparency to these rays of many substances hitherto considered opaque at once shows us one way at least in which we may explain such elementary clairvoyance as is involved in reading a letter inside a closed box, or describing those present in an adjoining apartment. To learn to see by means of the Röntgen rays in addition to those ordinarily employed would be quite sufficient to enable anyone to perform a feat of magic of this order.

So far we have thought only of an extension of the purely physical senses of man; and when we remember that a man's etheric body is in reality merely the finer part of his physical frame, and that therefore all his sense organs contain a large amount of etheric matter of various degrees of density, the capacities of which are still practically latent in most of us, we shall see that even if we confine ourselves to this line of development alone there are enormous possibilities of all kinds already opening out before us.

But besides and beyond all this we know that man possesses an astral and a mental body, each of which can in process of time be aroused into activity, and will respond in turn to the vibrations of the matter of its own plane, thus opening up before the Ego, as he learns to function through these vehicles, two entirely new and far wider worlds of knowledge and power. Now these new worlds, though they are all around us and freely inter-penetrate one another, are not to be thought of as distinct and entirely unconnected in substance, but rather as melting the one into the other, the lowest astral forming a direct series with the highest physical, just as the lowest mental in its turn forms a direct series with the highest astral. We are not called upon in thinking of them to imagine some new and strange kind of matter, but simply to think of the ordinary physical kind as subdivided so very much more finely and vibrating so very much more rapidly as to introduce us to what are practically entirely new conditions and qualities.

It is not then difficult for us to grasp the possibility of a steady and progressive extension of our senses, so that both by sight and by hearing we may be able to appreciate vibrations far higher and far lower than those which are ordinarily recognised. A large section of these additional vibrations will still belong to the physical plane, and will merely enable us to obtain impressions from the etheric part of that plane, which is at present as a closed book to us. Such impressions will still be received through the retina of the eye; of course they will affect its etheric rather than its solid matter, but we may nevertheless regard them as still appealing only to an organ specialized to receive them, and not to the whole surface of the etheric body.

There are some abnormal cases, however, in which other parts of the etheric body respond to these additional vibrations as readily as, or even more readily than, the eye. Such vagaries are explicable in various ways, but principally as effects of some partial astral development, for it will be found that the sensitive parts of the body almost invariably correspond with one or other of the *chakrams*, or centres of vitality in the astral body. And though, if astral consciousness be not yet developed, these centres may not be available on their own plane, they are still strong enough to stimulate into keener activity the etheric matter which they inter-penetrate.

When we come to deal with the astral senses themselves the methods of working are very different. The astral body has no specialized sense-organs—a fact which perhaps needs some explanation, since many students who are trying to comprehend its physiology seem to find it difficult to reconcile with the statements that have been made as to the perfect inter-penetration of the physical body by astral matter, the exact correspondence between the two vehicles, and the fact that every physical object has necessarily its astral counterpart.

Now all these statements are true, and yet it is quite possible for people who do not normally see astrally to misunderstand them. Every order of physical matter has its corresponding order of astral matter in constant association with it—not to be separated from it except by a very considerable exertion of occult force, and even then only to be held apart from it as long as force is being definitely exerted to that end. But for all that the relation of the astral particles one to another is far looser than is the case with their physical correspondences.

In a bar of iron, for example, we have a mass of physical molecules in the solid condition—that is to say, capable of comparatively little change in their relative positions, though each vibrating with immense rapidity in its own sphere. The astral counterpart of this consists of what we often call solid astral matter—that is, matter of the lowest and densest sub-plane of the astral; but nevertheless its particles are constantly and rapidly changing their relative position, moving among one another as easily as those of a liquid on the physical plane might do. So that there is no permanent association between any one physical particle and that amount of astral matter which happens at any given moment to be acting as its counterpart.

This is equally true with respect to the astral body of man, which for our purpose at the moment we may regard as consisting of two parts—the denser aggregation which occupies the exact position of the physical body, and the cloud of rarer astral matter which surrounds that aggregation. In both these parts, and between them both, there is going on at every moment of time the rapid inter-circulation of the particles which has been described, so that as one watches the movement of the molecules in the astral body one is reminded of the appearance of those in fiercely boiling water.

This being so, it will be readily understood that though any given organ of the physical body must always have as its counterpart a certain amount of astral matter, it does not retain the same particles for more than a few seconds at a time, and consequently there is nothing corresponding to the specialization of physical nerve-matter into optic or auditory nerves, and so on. So that though the physical eye or ear has undoubtedly always its counterpart of astral matter, that particular fragment of astral matter is no more (and no less) capable of responding to the vibrations which produce astral sight or astral hearing than any other part of the vehicle.

It must never be forgotten that though we constantly have to speak of "astral sight" or "astral hearing" in order to make ourselves intelligible, all that we mean by those expressions is the faculty of responding to such vibrations as convey to the man's consciousness, when he is functioning in his astral body, information of the same character as that conveyed to him by his eyes and ears while he is in the physical body. But in the entirely different astral conditions, specialized organs are not necessary for the attainment of this result; there is matter in every part of the astral body which is capable of such response, and consequently the man functioning in that vehicle sees equally well objects behind him, beneath him, above him, without needing to turn his head.

There is, however, another point which it would hardly be fair to leave entirely out of account, and that is the question of the *chakrams* referred to above. Theosophical students are familiar with the idea of the existence in both the astral and the etheric bodies of man of certain centres of force which have to be vivified in turn by the sacred serpent-fire as the man advances in evolution. Though these cannot be described as organs in the ordinary sense of the word, since it is not through them that the man sees or hears, as he does in physical life through eyes and ears, yet it is apparently very largely upon their vivification that the power of exercising these astral senses depends, each of them as it is developed giving to the whole astral body the power of response to a new set of vibrations.

Neither have these centres, however, any permanent collection of astral matter connected with them. They are simply vortices in the matter of the body—vortices through which all the particles pass in turn—points, perhaps, at which the higher force from planes above impinges upon the astral body. Even this description gives but a very partial idea of their appearance, for they are in reality four-dimensional vortices, so that the force which comes through them and is the cause of their existence seems to well up from nowhere. But at any rate, since all particles in turn pass through each of them, it will be clear that it is thus possible for each in turn to evoke in all the particles of the body the power of receptivity to a certain set of vibrations, so that all the astral senses are equally active in all parts of the body.

The vision of the mental plane is again totally different, for in this case we can no longer speak of separate senses such as sight and hearing, but rather have to postulate one general sense which responds so fully to the vibrations reaching it that when any object comes within its cognition it at once comprehends it fully, and as it were sees it, hears it, feels it, and knows all there is to know about it by the one instantaneous operation. Yet even this wonderful faculty differs in degree only and not in kind from those which are at our command at the present time; on the mental plane, just as on the physical, impressions are still conveyed by means of vibrations travelling from the object seen to the seer.

On the buddhic plane we meet for the first time with a quite new faculty having nothing in common with those of which we have spoken, for there a man cognizes any object by an entirely different method, in which external vibrations play no part. The object becomes part of himself, and he studies it from the inside instead of from the outside. But with *this* power ordinary clairvoyance has nothing to do.

The development, either entire or partial, of any one of these faculties would come under our definition of clairvoyance—the power to see what is hidden from ordinary physical sight. But these faculties may be developed in various ways, and it will be well to say a few words as to these different lines.

We may presume that if it were possible for a man to be isolated during his evolution from all but the gentlest outside influences, and to unfold from the beginning in perfectly regular and normal fashion, he would probably develop his senses in regular order also. He would find his physical senses gradually extending their scope until they responded to all the physical vibrations, of etheric as well as of denser matter; then in orderly sequence would come sensibility to the coarser part of the astral plane, and presently the finer part also would be included, until in due course the faculty of the mental plane dawned in its turn.

In real life, however, development so regular as this is hardly ever known, and many a man has occasional flashes of astral consciousness without any awakening of etheric vision at all. And this irregularity of development is one of the principal causes of man's extraordinary liability to error in matters of clairvoyance—a liability from which there is no escape except by a long course of careful training under a qualified teacher.

Students of Theosophical literature are well aware that there are such teachers to be found—that even in this materialistic nineteenth century the old saying is still true, that "when the pupil is ready, the Master is ready also," and that "in the hall of learning, when he is capable of entering there, the disciple will always find his Master." They are well aware also that only under such guidance can a man develop his latent powers in safety and with certainty, since they know how fatally easy it is for the untrained clairvoyant to deceive himself as to the meaning and value of what he sees, or even absolutely to distort his vision completely in bringing it down into his physical consciousness.

It does not follow that even the pupil who is receiving regular instruction in the use of occult powers will find them unfolding themselves exactly in the regular order which was suggested above as probably ideal. His previous progress may not have been such as to make this for him the easiest or most desirable road; but at any rate he is in the hands of one who is perfectly competent to be his guide in spiritual development, and he rests in perfect contentment that the way along which he is taken will be that which is the best way for him.

Another great advantage which he gains is that whatever faculties he may acquire are definitely under his command and can be used fully and constantly when he needs them for his Theosophical work; whereas in the case of the untrained man such powers often manifest themselves only very partially and spasmodically, and appear to come and go, as it were, at their own sweet will.

It may reasonably be objected that if clairvoyant faculty is, as stated, a part of the occult development of man, and so a sign of a certain amount of progress along that line, it seems strange that it should often be possessed by primitive peoples, or by the ignorant and uncultured among our own race—persons who are obviously quite undeveloped, from whatever point of view one regards them. No doubt this does appear remarkable at first sight but the fact is that the sensitiveness of the savage or of the coarse and vulgar European ignoramus is not really at all the same thing as the faculty of his properly trained brother, nor is it arrived at in the same way.

An exact and detailed explanation of the difference would lead us into rather recondite technicalities, but perhaps the general idea of the distinction between the two may be caught from an example taken from the very lowest plane of clairvoyance, in close contact with the denser physical. The etheric double in man is in exceedingly close relation to his nervous system, and any kind of action upon one of them speedily reacts on the other. Now in the sporadic appearance of etheric sight in the savage, whether of Central Africa or of Western Europe, it has been observed that the corresponding nervous disturbance is almost entirely in the sympathetic system, and that the whole affair is practically beyond the man's control—is in fact a sort of massive sensation vaguely belonging to the whole etheric body, rather than an exact and definite sense-perception communicated through a specialized organ.

As in later races and amid higher development the strength of the man is more and more thrown into the evolution of the mental faculties, this vague sensitiveness usually disappears; but still later, when the spiritual man begins to unfold, he regains his clairvoyant power. This time, however, the faculty is a precise and exact one, under the control of the man's will, and exercised through a definite sense-organ; and it is noteworthy that any nervous action set up in sympathy with it is now almost exclusively in the cerebro-spinal system.

On this subject Mrs. Besant writes:—"The lower forms of psychism are more frequent in animals and in very unintelligent human beings than in men and women in whom the intellectual powers are well developed. They appear to be connected with the sympathetic system, not with the cerebro-spinal. The large nucleated ganglionic cells in this system contain a very large proportion of etheric matter, and are hence more easily affected by the coarser astral vibrations than are the cells in which the proportion is less. As the cerebro-spinal system develops, and the brain becomes more highly evolved, the sympathetic system subsides into a subordinate position, and the sensitiveness to psychic vibrations is dominated by the stronger and more active vibrations of the higher nervous system. It is true that at a later stage of evolution psychic sensitiveness reappears, but it is then developed in connection with the cerebro-spinal centres, and is brought under the control of the will. But the hysterical and ill-regulated psychism of which we see so many lamentable examples is due to the small development of the brain and the dominance of the sympathetic system."

Occasional flashes of clairvoyance do, however, sometimes come to the highly cultured and spiritual-minded man, even though he may never have heard of the possibility of training such a faculty. In his case such glimpses usually signify that he is approaching that stage in his evolution when these powers will naturally begin to manifest themselves, and their appearance should serve as an additional stimulus to him to strive to maintain that high standard of moral purity and mental balance without which clairvoyance is a curse and not a blessing to its possessor.

Between those who are entirely unimpressible and those who are in full possession of clairvoyant power there are many intermediate stages. One to which it will be worth while to give a passing glance is the stage in which a man, though he has no clairvoyant faculty in ordinary life, yet exhibits it more or less fully under the influence of mesmerism. This is a case in which the psychic nature is already sensitive, but the consciousness is not yet capable of functioning in it amidst the manifold distractions of physical life. It needs to be set free by the temporary suspension of the outer senses in the mesmeric trance before it can use the diviner faculties which are but just beginning to dawn within it. But of course even in the mesmeric trance there are innumerable degrees of lucidity, from the ordinary patient who is blankly unintelligent to the man whose power of sight is fully under the control of the operator, and can be directed whithersoever he wills, or to the more advanced stage in which, when the consciousness is once set free, it escapes altogether from the grasp of the magnetizer, and soars into fields of exalted vision where it is entirely beyond his reach.

Another step along the same path is that upon which such perfect suppression of the physical as that which occurs in the hypnotic trance is not necessary, but the power of supernormal sight, though still out of reach during waking life, becomes available when the body is held in the bonds of ordinary sleep. At this stage of development stood many of the prophets and seers of whom we read, who were "warned of God in a dream," or communed with beings far higher than themselves in the silent watches of the night.

Most cultured people of the higher races of the world have this development to some extent: that is to say, the senses of their astral bodies are in full working order, and perfectly capable of receiving impressions from objects and entities of their own plane. But to make that fact of any use to them down here in the physical body, two changes are usually necessary; first, that the Ego shall be awakened to the realities of the astral plane, and induced to emerge from the chrysalis formed by his own waking thoughts, and look round him to observe and to learn; and secondly, that the consciousness shall be so far retained during the return of the Ego into his physical body as to enable him to impress upon his physical brain the recollection of what he has seen or learnt.

If the first of these changes has taken place, the second is of little importance, since the Ego, the true man, will be able to profit by the information to be obtained upon that plane, even though he may not have the satisfaction of bringing through any remembrance of it into his waking life down here.

Students often ask how this clairvoyant faculty will first be manifested in themselves—how they may know when they have reached the stage at which its first faint foreshadowings are beginning to be visible. Cases differ so widely that it is impossible to give to this question any answer that will be universally applicable.

Some people begin by a plunge, as it were, and under some unusual stimulus become able just for once to see some striking vision; and very often in such a case, because the experience does not repeat itself, the seer comes in time to believe that on that occasion he must have been the victim of hallucination. Others begin by becoming intermittently conscious of the brilliant colours and vibrations of the human aura; yet others find themselves with increasing frequency seeing and hearing something to which those around them are blind and deaf; others, again, see faces, landscapes, or coloured clouds floating before their eyes in the dark before they sink to rest; while perhaps the commonest experience of all is that of those who begin to recollect with greater and greater clearness what they have seen and heard on the other planes during sleep.

Having now to some extent cleared our ground, we may proceed to consider the various phenomena of clairvoyance.

They differ so widely both in character and in degree that it is not very easy to decide how they can most satisfactorily be classified. We might, for example, arrange them according to the kind of sight employed—whether it were mental, astral, or merely etheric. We might divide them according to the capacity of the clairvoyant, taking into consideration whether he was trained or untrained; whether his vision was regular and under his command, or spasmodic and independent of his volition; whether he could exercise it only when under mesmeric influence, or whether that assistance was unnecessary for him; whether he was able to use his faculty when awake in the physical body, or whether it was available only when he was temporarily away from that body in sleep or trance.

All these distinctions are of importance, and we shall have to take them all into consideration as we go on, but perhaps on the whole the most useful classification will be one something on the lines of that adopted by Mr. Sinnett in his *Rationale of Mesmerism*—a book, by the way, which all students of clairvoyance ought to read. In dealing with the phenomena, then, we will arrange them rather according to the capacity of the sight employed than to the plane upon which it is exercised, so that we may group instances of clairvoyance under some such headings as these:

1. Simple clairvoyance—that is to say, a mere opening of sight, enabling its possessor to see whatever astral or etheric entities happen to be present around him, but not including the power of observing either distant places or scenes belonging to any other time than the present.

2. Clairvoyance in space—the capacity to see scenes or events removed from the seer in

space, and either too far distant for ordinary observation or concealed by intermediate objects.

3. Clairvoyance in time—that is to say, the capacity to see objects or events which are removed from the seer in time, or, in other words, the power of looking into the past or the future.

CHAPTER II.

SIMPLE CLAIRVOYANCE: FULL.

WE have defined this as a mere opening of etheric or astral sight, which enables the possessor to see whatever may be present around him on corresponding levels, but is not usually accompanied by the power of seeing anything at a great distance or of reading either the past or the future. It is hardly possible altogether to exclude these latter faculties, for astral sight necessarily has considerably greater extension than physical, and fragmentary pictures of both past and future are often casually visible even to clairvoyants who do not know how to seek specially for them; but there is nevertheless a very real distinction between such incidental glimpses and the definite power of projection of the sight either in space or time.

We find among sensitive people all degrees of this kind of clairvoyance, from that of the man who gets a vague impression which hardly deserves the name of sight at all, up to the full possession of etheric and astral vision respectively. Perhaps the simplest method will be for us to begin by describing what would be visible in the case of this fuller development of the power, as the cases of its partial possession will then be seen to fall naturally into their places.

Let us take the etheric vision first. This consists simply, as has already been said, in susceptibility to a far larger series of physical vibrations than ordinary, but nevertheless its possession brings into view a good deal to which the majority of the human race still remains blind. Let us consider what changes its acquisition produces in the aspect of familiar objects, animate and inanimate, and then see to what entirely new factors it introduces us. But it must be remembered that what I am about to describe is the result of the full and perfectly-controlled possession of the faculty only, and that most of the instances met with in real life will be likely to fall far short of it in one direction or another.

The most striking change produced in the appearance of inanimate objects by the acquisition of this faculty is that most of them become almost transparent, owing to the difference in wave-length of some of the vibrations to which the man has now become susceptible. He finds himself capable of performing with the utmost ease the proverbial feat of "seeing through a brick wall," for to his newly-acquired vision the brick wall seems to have a consistency no greater than that of a light mist. He therefore sees what is going on in an adjoining room almost as though no intervening wall existed; he can describe with accuracy the contents of a locked box, or read a sealed letter; with a little practice he can find a given passage in a closed book. This last feat, though perfectly easy to astral vision, presents considerable difficulty to one using etheric sight, because of the fact that each page has to be looked at *through* all those which happen to be superimposed upon it.

It is often asked whether under these circumstances a man sees always with this abnormal sight, or only when he wishes to do so. The answer is that if the faculty is perfectly developed it will be entirely under his control, and he can use that or his more ordinary vision at will. He changes from one to the other as readily and naturally as we now change the focus of our eyes when we look up from our book to follow the motions of some object a mile away. It is, as it were, a focussing of consciousness on the one or the other aspect of what is seen; and though the man would have quite clearly in his view the aspect upon which his attention was for the moment fixed, he would always be vaguely conscious of the other aspect too, just as when we focus our sight upon any object held in our hands we yet vaguely see the opposite wall of the room as a background.

Another curious change, which comes from the possession of this sight, is that the solid ground upon which the man walks becomes to a certain extent transparent to him, so that he is able to see down into it to a considerable depth, much as we can now see into fairly clear water. This enables him to watch a creature burrowing underground, to distinguish a vein of coal or of metal if not too far below the surface, and so on.

The limit of etheric sight when looking through solid matter appears to be analogous to that imposed upon us when looking through water or mist. We cannot see beyond a certain distance, because the medium through which we are looking is not perfectly transparent.

The appearance of animate objects is also considerably altered for the man who has increased his visual powers to this extent. The bodies of men and animals are for him in the main transparent, so that he can watch the action of the various internal organs, and to some extent diagnose some of their diseases.

The extended sight also enables him to perceive, more or less clearly, various classes of creatures, elemental and otherwise, whose bodies are not capable of reflecting any of the rays within the limit of the spectrum as ordinarily seen. Among the entities so seen will be some of the lower orders of nature-spirits—those whose bodies are composed of the denser etheric matter. To this class belong nearly all the fairies, gnomes, and brownies, about whom there are still so many stories remaining among Scotch and Irish mountains and in remote country places all over the world.

The vast kingdom of nature-spirits is in the main an astral kingdom, but still there is a large section of it which appertains to the etheric part of the physical plane, and this section, of course, is much more likely to come within the ken of ordinary people than the others. Indeed, in reading the common fairy stories one frequently comes across distinct indications that it is with this class that we are dealing. Any student of fairy lore will remember how often mention is made of some mysterious ointment or drug, which when applied to a man's eyes enables him to see the members of the fairy commonwealth whenever he happens to meet them.

The story of such an application and its results occurs so constantly and comes from so many different parts of the world that there must certainly be some truth behind it, as there always is behind really universal popular tradition. Now no such anointing of the eyes alone could by any possibility open a man's astral vision, though certain ointments rubbed over the whole body will very greatly assist the astral body to leave the physical in full consciousness—a fact the knowledge of which seems to have survived even to mediæval times, as will be seen from the evidence given at some of the trials for witchcraft. But the application to the physical eye might very easily so stimulate its sensitiveness as to make it susceptible to some of the etheric vibrations.

The story frequently goes on to relate how when the human being who has used this mystical ointment betrays his extended vision in some way to a fairy, the latter strikes or stabs him in the eye, thus depriving him not only of the etheric sight, but of that of the denser physical plane as well. (See *The Science of Fairy Tales*, by E. S. Hartland, in the "Contemporary Science" series—or indeed almost any extensive collection of fairy stories.) If the sight acquired had been astral, such a proceeding would have been entirely unavailing, for no injury to the physical apparatus would affect an astral faculty; but if the vision produced by the ointment were etheric, the destruction of the physical eye would in most cases at once extinguish it, since that is the mechanism by means of which it works.

Anyone possessing this sight of which we are speaking would also be able to perceive the etheric double of man; but since this is so nearly identical in size with the physical, it would hardly be likely to attract his attention unless it were partially projected in trance or under the influence of anæsthetics. After death, when it withdraws entirely from the dense body, it would be clearly visible to him, and he would frequently see it hovering over newly made graves as he passed through a churchyard or cemetery. If he were to attend a spiritualistic séance he would see the etheric matter oozing out from the side of the medium, and could observe the various ways in which the communicating entities make use of it.

Another fact which could hardly fail soon to thrust itself upon his notice would be the extension of his perception of colour. He would find himself able to see several entirely new colours, not in the least resembling any of those included in the spectrum as we at present know it, and therefore of course quite indescribable in any terms at our command. And not only would he see new objects that were wholly of these new colours, but he would also discover that modifications had been introduced into the colour of many objects with which he was quite familiar, according to whether they had or had not some tinge of these new hues intermingled with the old. So that two surfaces of colour which to ordinary eyes appeared to match perfectly would often present distinctly different shades to his keener sight.

We have now touched upon some of the principal changes which would be introduced into a man's world when he gained etheric sight; and it must always be remembered that in most cases a corresponding change would at the same time be brought about in his other senses also, so that he would be capable of hearing, and perhaps even of feeling, more than most of those around him. Now supposing that in addition to this he obtained the sight of the astral plane, what further changes would be observable?

Well, the changes would be many and great; in fact, a whole new world would open before his eyes. Let us consider its wonders briefly in the same order as before, and see first what difference there would be in the appearance of inanimate objects. On this point I may begin by quoting a recent quaint answer given in *The Vâhan*.

"There is a distinct difference between etheric sight and astral sight, and it is the latter which seems to correspond to the fourth dimension.

"The easiest way to understand the difference is to take an example. If you looked at a man with both the sights in turn, you would see the buttons at the back of his coat in both cases; only if you used etheric sight you would see them *through* him, and would see the shank-side as nearest to you, but if you looked astrally, you would see it not only like that, but just as if you were standing behind the man as well.

"Or if you were looking etherically at a wooden cube with writing on all its sides, it would be as though the cube were glass, so that you could see through it, and you would see the writing on the opposite side all backwards, while that on the right and left sides would not be clear to you at all unless you moved, because you would see it edgewise. But if you looked at it astrally you would see all the sides at once, and all the right way up, as though the whole cube had been flattened out before you, and you would see every particle of the inside as well—not *through* the others, but all flattened out. You would be looking at it from another direction, at right angles to all the directions that we know.

"If you look at the back of a watch etherically you see all the wheels through it, and the face *through them*, but backwards; if you look at it astrally, you see the face right way up and all the wheels lying separately, but nothing on the top of anything else."

Here we have at once the keynote, the principal factor of the change; the man is looking at everything from an absolutely new point of view, entirely outside of anything that he has ever imagined before. He has no longer the slightest difficulty in reading any page in a closed book, because he is not now looking at it through all the other pages before it or behind it, but is looking straight down upon it as though it were the only page to be seen. The depth at which a vein of metal or of coal may lie is no longer a barrier to his sight of it, because he is not now looking through the intervening depth of earth at all. The thickness of a wall, or the number of walls intervening between the observer and the object, would make a great deal of difference to the clearness of the etheric sight; they would make no difference whatever to the astral sight, because on the astral plane they would *not* intervene between the observer and the object. Of course that sounds paradoxical and impossible, and it *is* quite inexplicable to a mind not specially trained to grasp the idea; yet it is none the less absolutely true.

This carries us straight into the middle of the much-vexed question of the fourth dimension—a question of the deepest interest, though one that we cannot pretend to discuss in the space at our disposal. Those who wish to study it as it deserves are recommended to begin with Mr. C. H. Hinton's *Scientific Romances* or Dr. A. T. Schofield's *Another World*, and then follow on with the former author's larger work, *A New Era of Thought*. Mr. Hinton not only claims to be able himself to grasp mentally some of the simpler fourth-dimensional figures, but also states that anyone who will take the trouble to follow out his directions may with perseverance acquire that mental grasp likewise. I am not certain that the power to do this is within the reach of everyone, as he thinks, for it appears to me to require considerable mathematical ability; but I can at any rate bear witness that the tesseract or fourth-dimensional cube which he describes is a reality, for it is quite a familiar figure upon the astral plane. He has now perfected a new method of representing the several dimensions by colours instead of by arbitrary written symbols. He states that this will very much simplify the study, as the reader will be able to distinguish instantly by sight any part or feature of the tesseract. A full description of this new method, with plates, is said to be ready for the press, and is expected to appear within a year, so that intending students of this fascinating subject might do well to await its publication.

I know that Madame Blavatsky, in alluding to the theory of the fourth dimension, has expressed an opinion that it is only a clumsy way of stating the idea of the entire permeability of matter, and that Mr. W. T. Stead has followed along the same lines, presenting the conception to his readers under the name of *throughth*. Careful, oft-repeated and detailed investigation does, however, seem to show quite conclusively that this explanation does not cover all the facts. It is a perfect description of etheric vision, but the further and quite different idea of the fourth dimension as expounded by Mr. Hinton is the only one which gives any kind of explanation down here of the constantly-observed facts of astral vision. I would therefore venture deferentially to suggest that when Madame Blavatsky wrote as she did, she had in mind etheric vision and not astral, and that the extreme applicability of the phrase to this other and higher faculty, of which she was not at the moment thinking, did not occur to her.

The possession of this extraordinary and scarcely expressible power, then, must always be borne in mind through all that follows. It lays every point in the interior of every solid body absolutely open to the gaze of the seer, just as every point in the interior of a circle lies open to the gaze of a man looking down upon it.

But even this is by no means all that it gives to its possessor. He sees not only the inside as well as the outside of every object, but also its astral counterpart. Every atom and molecule of physical matter has its corresponding astral atoms and molecules, and the mass which is built up out of these is clearly visible to our clairvoyant. Usually the astral of any object projects somewhat beyond the physical part of it, and thus metals, stones and other things are seen surrounded by an astral aura.

It will be seen at once that even in the study of inorganic matter a man gains immensely by the acquisition of this vision. Not only does he see the astral part of the object at which he looks, which before was wholly hidden from him; not only does he see much more of its physical constitution than he did before, but even what was visible to him before is now seen much more clearly and truly. A moment's consideration will show that his new vision approximates much more closely to true perception than does physical sight. For example, if he looks astrally at a glass cube, its sides will all appear equal, as we know they really are, whereas on the physical plane he sees the further side in perspective—that is, it appears smaller than the nearer side, which is, of course, a mere allusion due to his physical limitations.

When we come to consider the additional facilities which it offers in the observation of animate objects we see still more clearly the advantages of the astral vision. It exhibits to the clairvoyant the aura of plants and animals, and thus in the case of the latter their desires and emotions, and whatever thoughts they may have, are all plainly shown before his eyes.

But it is in dealing with human beings that he will most appreciate the value of this faculty, for he will often be able to help them far more effectually when he guides himself by the information which it gives him.

He will be able to see the aura as far up as the astral body, and though that leaves all the higher part of a man still hidden from his gaze, he will nevertheless find it possible by careful observation to learn a good deal about the higher part from what is within his reach. His capacity of examining the etheric double will give him considerable advantage in locating and classifying any defects or diseases of the nervous system, while from the appearance of the astral body he will be at once aware of all the emotions, passions, desires and tendencies of the man before him, and even of very many of his thoughts also.

As he looks at a person he will see him surrounded by the luminous mist of the astral aura, flashing with all sorts of brilliant colours, and constantly changing in hue and brilliancy with every variation of the person's thoughts and feelings. He will see this aura flooded with the beautiful rose-colour of pure affection, the rich blue of devotional feeling, the hard, dull brown of selfishness, the deep scarlet of anger, the horrible lurid red of sensuality, the livid grey of fear, the black clouds of hatred and malice, or any of the other hundredfold indications so easily to be read in it by a practised eye; and thus it will be impossible for any persons to conceal from him the real state of their feelings on any subject.

These varied indications of the aura are of themselves a study of very deep interest, but I have no space to deal with them in detail here. A much fuller account of them, together with a large number of coloured illustrations, will be found in my work on the subject *Man Visible and Invisible*.

Not only does the astral aura show him the temporary result of the emotion passing through it at the moment, but it also gives him, by the arrangement and proportion of its colours when in a condition of comparative rest, a clue to the general disposition and character of its owner. For the astral body is the expression of as much of the man as can be manifested on that plane, so that from what is seen in it much more which belongs to higher planes may be inferred with considerable certainty.

In this judgment of character our clairvoyant will be much helped by so much of the person's thought as expresses itself on the astral plane, and consequently comes within his purview. The true home of thought is on the mental plane, and all thought first manifests itself there as a vibration of the mind-body. But if it be in any way a selfish thought, or if it be connected in any way with an emotion or a desire, it immediately descends into the astral plane, and takes to itself a visible form of astral matter.

In the case of the majority of men almost all thought would fall under one or other of these heads, so that practically the whole of their personality would lie clearly before our friend's astral vision, since their astral bodies and the thought-forms constantly radiating from them would be to him as an open book in which their characteristics were writ so largely that he who ran might read. Anyone wishing to gain some idea as to *how* the thought-forms present themselves to clairvoyant vision may satisfy themselves to some extent by examining the illustrations accompanying Mrs. Besant's valuable article on the subject in *Lucifer* for September 1896.

We have seen something of the alteration in the appearance of both animate and inanimate objects when viewed by one possessed of full clairvoyant sight as far as the astral plane is concerned; let us now consider what entirely new objects he will see. He will be conscious of a far greater fulness in nature in many directions, but chiefly his attention will be attracted by the living denizens of this new world. No detailed account of them can be attempted within the space at our disposal; for that the reader is referred to No. V. of the *Theosophical Manuals*. Here we can do no more than barely enumerate a few classes only of the vast hosts of astral inhabitants.

He will be impressed by the protean forms of the ceaseless tide of elemental essence, ever swirling around him, menacing often, yet always retiring before a determined effort of the will; he will marvel at the enormous army of entities temporarily called out of this ocean into separate existence by the thoughts and wishes of man, whether good or evil. He will watch the manifold tribes of the nature-spirits at their work or at their play; he will sometimes be able to study with ever-increasing delight the magnificent evolution of some of the lower orders of the glorious kingdom of the devas, which corresponds approximately to the angelic host of Christian terminology.

But perhaps of even keener interest to him than any of these will be the human denizens of the astral world, and he will find them divisible into two great classes—those whom we call the living, and those others, most of them infinitely more alive, whom we so foolishly misname the dead. Among the former he will find here and there one wide awake and fully conscious, perhaps sent to bring him some message, or examining him keenly to see what progress he is making; while the majority of his neighbours, when away from their physical bodies during sleep, will drift idly by, so wrapped up in their own cogitations as to be practically unconscious of what is going on around them.

Among the great host of the recently dead he will find all degrees of consciousness and intelligence, and all shades of character—for death, which seems to our limited vision so absolute a change, in reality alters nothing of the man himself. On the day after his death he is precisely the same man as he was the day before it, with the same disposition, the same qualities, the same virtues and vices, save only that he has cast aside his physical body; but the loss of that no more makes him in any way a different man than would the removal of an overcoat. So among the dead our student will find men intelligent and stupid, kind-hearted and morose, serious and frivolous, spiritually-minded and sensually-minded, just as among the living.

Since he can not only see the dead, but speak with them, he can often be of very great use to them, and give them information and guidance which is of the utmost value to them. Many of them are in a condition of great surprise and perplexity, and sometimes even of acute distress, because they find the facts of the next world so unlike the childish legends which are all that popular religion in the West has to offer with reference to this transcendently important subject; and therefore a man who understands this new world and can explain matters is distinctly a friend in need.

In many other ways a man who fully possesses this faculty may be of use to the living as well as to the dead; but of this side of the subject I have already written in my little book on *Invisible Helpers*. In addition to astral entities he will see astral corpses—shades and shells in all stages of decay; but these need only be just mentioned here, as the reader desiring a further account of them will find it in our third and fifth manuals.

Another wonderful result which the full enjoyment of astral clairvoyance brings to a man is that he has no longer any break in consciousness. When he lies down at night he leaves his physical body to the rest which it requires, while he goes about his business in the far more comfortable astral vehicle. In the morning he returns to and re-enters his physical body, but without any loss of consciousness or memory between the two states, and thus he is able to live, as it were, a double life which yet is one, and to be usefully employed during the whole of it, instead of losing one-third of his existence in blank unconsciousness.

Another strange power of which he may find himself in possession (though its full control belongs rather to the still higher devachanic faculty), is that of magnifying at will the minutest physical or astral particle to any desired size, as though by a microscope—though no microscope ever made or ever likely to be made possesses even a thousandth part of this psychic magnifying power. By its means the hypothetical molecule and atom postulated by science become visible and living realities to the occult student, and on this closer examination he finds them to be much more complex in their structure than the scientific man has yet realised them to be. It also enables him to follow with the closest attention and the most lively interest all kinds of electrical, magnetic, and other etheric action; and when some of the specialists in these branches of science are able to develop the power to see those things whereof they write so facilely, some very wonderful and beautiful revelations may be expected.

This is one of the *siddhis* or powers described in Oriental books as accruing to the man who devotes himself to spiritual development, though the name under which it is there mentioned might not be immediately recognizable. It is referred to as "the power of making oneself large or small at will," and the reason of a description which appears so oddly to reverse the fact is that in reality the method by which this feat is performed is precisely that indicated in these ancient books. It is by the use of temporary visual machinery of inconceivable minuteness that the world of the infinitely little is so clearly seen; and in the same way (or rather in the opposite way) it is by temporarily enormously increasing the size of the machinery used that it becomes possible to increase the breadth of one's view—in the physical sense as well as, let us hope, in the moral—far beyond anything that science has ever dreamt of as possible for man. So that the alteration in size is really in the vehicle of the student's consciousness, and not in anything outside of himself; and the old Oriental book has, after all, put the case more accurately than we.

Psychometry and second-sight *in excelsis* would also be among the faculties which our friend would find at his command; but those will be more fitly dealt with under a later heading, since in almost all their manifestations they involve clairvoyance either in space or in time.

I have now indicated, though only in the roughest outlines, what a trained student, possessed of full astral vision, would see in the immensely wider world to which that vision introduced him; but I have said nothing of the stupendous change in his mental attitude which comes from the experiential certainty as to the existence of the soul, its survival after death, the action of the law of karma, and other points of equally paramount importance. The difference between even the profoundest intellectual conviction and the precise knowledge gained by direct personal experience must be felt in order to be appreciated.

Chapter III.

Simple Clairvoyance: Partial.

The experiences of the untrained clairvoyant—and be it remembered that that class includes all European clairvoyants except a very few—will, however, usually fall very far short of what I have attempted to indicate; they will fall short in many different ways—in degree, in variety, or in permanence, and above all in precision.

Sometimes, for example, a man's clairvoyance will be permanent, but very partial, extending only perhaps to one or two classes of the phenomena observable; he will find himself endowed with some isolated fragment of higher vision, without apparently possessing other powers of sight which ought normally to accompany that fragment, or even to precede it. For example, one of my dearest friends has all his life had the power to see the atomic ether and atomic astral matter, and to recognize their structure, alike in darkness or in light, as interpenetrating everything else; yet he has only rarely seen entities whose bodies are composed of the much more obvious lower ethers or denser astral matter, and at any rate is certainly not permanently able to see them. He simply finds himself in possession of this special faculty, without any apparent reason to account for it, or any recognizable relation to anything else: and beyond proving to him the existence of these atomic planes and demonstrating their arrangement, it is difficult to see of what particular use it is to him at present. Still, there the thing is, and it is an earnest of greater things to come—of further powers still awaiting development.

There are many similar cases—similar, I mean, not in the possession of that particular form of sight (which is unique in my experience), but in showing the development of some one small part of the full and clear vision of the astral and etheric planes. In nine cases out of ten, however, such partial clairvoyance will at the same time lack precision also—that is to say, there will be a good deal of vague impression and inference about it, instead of the clear-cut definition and certainty of the trained man. Examples of this type are constantly to be found, especially among those who advertise themselves as "test and business clairvoyants."

Then, again, there are those who are only temporarily clairvoyant under certain special conditions. Among these there are various subdivisions, some being able to reproduce the state of clairvoyance at will by again setting up the same conditions, while with others it comes sporadically, without any observable reference to their surroundings, and with yet others the power shows itself only once or twice in the whole course of their lives.

To the first of these subdivisions belong those who are clairvoyant only when in the mesmeric trance—who when not so entranced are incapable of seeing or hearing anything abnormal. These may sometimes reach great heights of knowledge and be exceedingly precise in their indications, but when that is so they are usually undergoing a course of regular training, though for some reason unable as yet to set themselves free from the leaden weight of earthly life without assistance.

In the same class we may put those—chiefly Orientals—who gain some temporary sight only under the influence of certain drugs, or by means of the performance of certain ceremonies. The ceremonialist sometimes hypnotizes himself by his repetitions, and in that condition becomes to some extent clairvoyant; more often he simply reduces himself to a passive condition in which some other entity can obsess him and speak through him. Sometimes, again, his ceremonies are not intended to affect himself at all, but to invoke some astral entity who will give him the required information; but of course that is a case of magic, and not of clairvoyance. Both the drugs and the ceremonies are methods emphatically to be avoided by any one who wishes to approach clairvoyance from the higher side, and use it for his own progress and for the helping of others. The Central African medicine-man or witch-doctor and some of the Tartar Shamans are good examples of the type.

Those to whom a certain amount of clairvoyant power has come occasionally only, and without any reference to their own wish, have often been hysterical or highly nervous persons, with whom the faculty was to a large extent one of the symptoms of a disease. Its appearance showed that the physical vehicle was weakened to such a degree that it no longer presented any obstacle in the way of a certain modicum of etheric or astral vision. An extreme example of this class is the man who drinks himself into delirium tremens, and in the condition of absolute physical ruin and impure psychic excitation brought about by the ravages of that fell disease, is able to see for the time some of the loathsome elemental and other entities which he has drawn round himself by his long course of degraded and bestial indulgence. There are, however, other cases where the power of sight has appeared and disappeared without apparent reference to the state of the physical health; but it seems probable that even in those, if they could have been observed closely enough, some alteration in the condition of the etheric double would have been noticed.

Those who have only one instance of clairvoyance to report in the whole of their lives are a difficult band to classify at all exhaustively, because of the great variety of the contributory circumstances. There are many among them to whom the experience has come at some supreme moment of their lives, when it is comprehensible that there might have been a temporary exaltation of faculty which would be sufficient to account for it.

In the case of another subdivision of them the solitary case has been the seeing of an apparition, most commonly of some friend or relative at the point of death. Two possibilities are then offered for our choice, and in each of them the strong wish of the dying man is the impelling force. That force may have enabled him to materialize himself for a moment, in which case of course no clairvoyance was needed or more probably it may have acted mesmerically upon the percipient, and momentarily dulled his physical and stimulated his higher sensitiveness. In either case the vision is the product of the emergency, and is not repeated simply because the necessary conditions are not repeated.

There remains, however, an irresolvable residuum of cases in which a solitary instance occurs of the exercise of undoubted clairvoyance, while yet the occasion seems to us wholly trivial and unimportant. About these we can only frame hypotheses; the governing conditions are evidently not on the physical plane, and a separate investigation of each case would be necessary before we could speak with any certainty as to its causes. In some such it has appeared that an astral entity was endeavouring to make some communication, and was able to impress only some unimportant detail on its subject—all the useful or significant part of what it had to say failing to get through into the subject's consciousness.

In the investigation of the phenomena of clairvoyance all these varied types and many others will be encountered, and a certain number of cases of mere hallucination will be almost sure to appear also, and will have to be carefully weeded out from the list of examples. The student of such a subject needs an inexhaustible fund of patience and steady perseverance, but if he goes on long enough he will begin dimly to discern order behind the chaos, and will gradually get some idea of the great laws under which the whole evolution is working.

It will help him greatly in his efforts if he will adopt the order which we have just followed—that is, if he will first take the trouble to familiarize himself as thoroughly as may be with the actual facts concerning the planes with which ordinary clairvoyance deals. If he will learn what there really is to be seen with astral and etheric sight, and what their respective limitations are, he will then have, as it were, a standard by which to measure the cases which he observes. Since all instances of partial sight must of necessity fit into some niche in this whole, if he has the outline of the entire scheme in his head he will find it comparatively easy with a little practice to classify the instances with which he is called upon to deal.

We have said nothing as yet as to the still more wonderful possibilities of clairvoyance upon the mental plane, nor indeed is it necessary that much should be said, as it is exceedingly improbable that the investigator will ever meet with any examples of it except among pupils properly trained in some of the very highest schools of occultism. For them it opens up yet another new world, vaster far than all those beneath it—a world in which all that we can imagine of utmost glory and splendour is the commonplace of existence. Some account of its marvellous faculty, its eneffable bliss, its magnificent opportunities for learning and for work, is given in the sixth of our Theosophical manuals, and to that the student may be referred.

All that it has to give—all of it at least that he can assimilate—is within the reach of the trained pupil, but for the untrained clairvoyant to touch it is hardly more than a bare possibility. It has been done in mesmeric trance, but the occurrence is of exceeding rarity, for it needs almost superhuman qualifications in the way of lofty spiritual aspiration and absolute purity of thought and intention upon the part both of the subject and the operator.

To a type of clairvoyance such as this, and still more fully to that which belongs to the plane next above it, the name of spiritual sight may reasonably be applied; and since the celestial world to which it opens our eyes lies all round us here and now, it is fit that our passing reference to it should be made under the heading of simple clairvoyance, though it may be necessary to allude to it again when dealing with clairvoyance in space, to which we will now pass on.

CHAPTER IV.

CLAIRVOYANCE IN SPACE: INTERNATIONAL.

WE have defined this as the capacity to see events or scenes removed from the seer in space and too far distant for ordinary observation. The instances of this are so numerous and so various that we shall find it desirable to attempt a somewhat more detailed classification of them. It does not much matter what particular arrangement we adopt, so long as it is comprehensive enough to include all our cases; perhaps a convenient one will be to group them under the broad divisions of intentional and unintentional clairvoyance in space, with an intermediate class that might be described as semi-intentional—a curious title, but I will explain it later.

As before, I will begin by stating what is possible along this line for the fully-trained seer, and endeavouring to explain how his faculty works and under what limitations it acts. After that we shall find ourselves in a better position to try to understand the manifold examples of partial and untrained sight. Let us then in the first place discuss intentional clairvoyance.

It will be obvious from what has previously been said as to the power of astral vision that any one possessing it in its fullness will be able to see by its means practically anything in this world that he wishes to see. The most secret places are open to his gaze, and intervening obstacles have no existence for him, because of the change in his point of view; so that if we grant him the power of moving about in the astral body he can without difficulty go anywhere and see anything within the limits of the planet. Indeed this is to a large extent possible to him even without the necessity of moving the astral body at all, as we shall presently see.

Let us consider a little more closely the methods by which this super-physical sight may be used to observe events taking place at a distance. When, for example, a man here in England sees in minutest detail something which is happening at the same moment in India or America, how is it done?

A very ingenious hypothesis has been offered to account for the phenomenon. It has been suggested that every object is perpetually throwing off radiations in all directions, similar in some respects to, though infinitely finer than, rays of light, and that clairvoyance is nothing but the power to see by means of these finer radiations. Distance would in that case be no bar to the sight, all intervening objects would be penetrable by these rays, and they would be able to cross one another to infinity in all directions without entanglement, precisely as the vibrations of ordinary light do.

Now though this is not exactly the way in which clairvoyance works, the theory is nevertheless quite true in most of its premises. Every object undoubtedly is throwing off radiations in all directions, and it is precisely in this way, though on a higher plane, that the âkâshic records seem to be formed. Of them it will be necessary to say something under our next heading, so we will do no more than mention them for the moment. The phenomena of psychometry are also dependent upon these radiations, as will presently be explained.

There are, however, certain practical difficulties in the way of using these etheric vibrations (for that is, of course, what they are) as the medium by means of which one may see anything taking place at a distance. Intervening objects are not entirely transparent, and as the actors in the scene which the experimenter tried to observe would probably be at least equally transparent, it is obvious that serious confusion would be quite likely to result.

The additional dimension which would come into play if astral radiations were sensed instead of etheric would obviate some of the difficulties, but would on the other hand introduce some fresh complications of its own; so that for practical purposes, in endeavouring to understand clairvoyance, we may dismiss this hypothesis of radiations from our minds, and turn to the methods of seeing at a distance which are actually at the disposal of the student. It will be found that there are five, four of them being really varieties of clairvoyance, while the fifth does not properly come under that head at all, but belongs to the domain of magic. Let us take this last one first, and get it out of our way.

1. *By the assistance of a nature-spirit.*—This method does not necessarily involve the possession of any psychic faculty at all on the part of the experimenter; he need only know how to induce some denizen of the astral world to undertake the investigation for him. This may be done either by invocation or by evocation; that is to say, the operator may either persuade his astral coadjutor by prayers and offerings to give him the help he desires, or he may compel his aid by the determined exercise of a highly-developed will.

This method has been largely practised in the East (where the entity employed is usually a nature-spirit) and in old Atlantis, where "the lords of the dark face" used a highly-specialized and peculiarly venomous variety of artificial elemental for this purpose. Information is sometimes obtained in the same sort of way at the spiritualistic *séance* of modern days, but in that case the messenger employed is more likely to be a recently-deceased human being functioning more or less freely on the astral plane—though even here also it is sometimes an obliging nature-spirit, who is amusing himself by posing as somebody's departed relative. In any case, as I have said, this method is not clairvoyant at all, but magical; and it is mentioned here only in order that the reader may not become confused in the endeavour to classify cases of its use under some of the following headings.

2. *By means of an astral current.*—This is a phrase frequently and rather loosely employed in some of our Theosophical literature to cover a considerable variety of phenomena, and among others that which I wish to explain. What is really done by the student who adopts this method is not so much the setting in motion of a current in astral matter, as the erection of a kind of temporary telephone through it.

It is impossible here to give an exhaustive disquisition on astral physics, even had I the requisite knowledge to write it; all I need say is that it is possible to make in astral matter a definite connecting-line that shall act as a telegraph-wire to convey vibrations by means of which all that is going on at the other end of it may be seen. Such a line is established, be it understood, not by a direct projection through space of astral matter, but by such action upon a line (or rather many lines) of particles of that matter as will render them capable of forming a conductor for vibrations of the character required.

This preliminary action can be set up in two ways—either by the transmission of energy from particle to particle, until the line is formed, or by the use of a force from a higher plane which is capable of acting upon the whole line simultaneously. Of course this latter method implies far greater development, since it involves the knowledge of (and the power to use) forces of a considerably higher level; so that the man who could make his line in this way would not, for his own use, need a line at all, since he could see far more easily and completely by means of an altogether higher faculty.

Even the simpler and purely astral operation is a difficult one to describe, though quite an easy one to perform. It may be said to partake somewhat of the nature of the magnetization of a bar of steel; for it consists in what we might call the polarization, by an effort of the human will, of a number of parallel lines of astral atoms reaching from the operator to the scene which he wishes to observe. All the atoms thus affected are held for the time with their axes rigidly parallel to one another, so that they form a kind of temporary tube along which the clairvoyant may look. This method has the disadvantage that the telegraph line is liable to disarrangement or even destruction by any sufficiently strong astral current which happens to cross its path; but if the original effort of will were fairly definite, this would be a contingency of only infrequent occurrence.

The view of a distant scene obtained by means of this "astral current" is in many ways not unlike that seen through a telescope. Human figures usually appear very small, like those on a distant stage, but in spite of their diminutive size they are as clear as though they were close by. Sometimes it is possible by this means to hear what is said as well as to see what is done; but as in the majority of cases this does not happen, we must consider it rather as the manifestation of an additional power than as a necessary corollary of the faculty of sight.

It will be observed that in this case the seer does not usually leave his physical body at all; there is no sort of projection of his astral vehicle or of any part of himself towards that at which he is looking, but he simply manufactures for himself a temporary astral telescope. Consequently he has, to a certain extent, the use of his physical powers even while he is examining the distant scene; for example, his voice would usually still be under his control, so that he could describe what he saw even while he was in the act of making his observations. The consciousness of the man is, in fact, distinctly still at this end of the line.

This fact, however, has its limitations as well as its advantages, and these again largely resemble the limitations of the man using a telescope on the physical plane. The experimenter, for example, has no power to shift this point of view; his telescope, so to speak, has a particular field of view which cannot be enlarged or altered; he is looking at his scene from a certain direction, and he cannot suddenly turn it all round and see how it looks from the other side. If he has sufficient psychic energy to spare, he may drop altogether the telescope that he is using and manufacture an entirely new one for himself which will approach his objective somewhat differently; but this is not a course at all likely to be adopted in practice.

But, it may be said, the mere fact that he is using astral sight ought to enable him to see it from all sides at once. So it would if he were using that sight in the normal way upon an object which was fairly near him—within his astral reach, as it were; but at a distance of hundreds or thousands of miles the case is very different. Astral sight gives us the advantage of an additional dimension, but there is still such a thing as position in that dimension, and it is naturally a potent factor in limiting the use of the powers of its plane. Our ordinary three-dimensional sight enables us to see at once every point of the interior of a two-dimensional figure, such as a square, but in order to do that the square must be within a reasonable distance from our eyes; the mere additional dimension will avail a man in London but little in his endeavour to examine a square in Calcutta.

Astral sight, when it is cramped by being directed along what is practically a tube, is limited very much as physical sight would be under similar circumstances; though if possessed in perfection it will still continue to show, even at that distance, the auras, and therefore all the emotions and most of the thoughts of the people under observation.

There are many people for whom this type of clairvoyance is very much facilitated if they have at hand some physical object which can be used as a starting-point for their astral tube—a convenient focus for their will-power. A ball of crystal is the commonest and most effectual of such foci, since it has the additional advantage of possessing within itself qualities which stimulate psychic faculty; but other objects are also employed, to which we shall find it necessary to refer more particularly when we come to consider semi-intentional clairvoyance.

In connection with this astral-current form of clairvoyance, as with others, we find that there are some psychics who are unable to use it except when under the influence of mesmerism. The peculiarity in this case is that among such psychics there are two varieties—one in which by being thus set free the man is enabled to make a telescope for himself, and another in which the magnetizer himself makes the telescope and the subject is simply enabled to see through it. In this latter case obviously the subject has not enough will to form a tube for himself, and the operator, though possessed of the necessary will-power, is not clairvoyant, or he could see through his own tube without needing help.

Occasionally, though rarely, the tube which is formed possesses another of the attributes of a telescope—that of magnifying the objects at which it is directed until they seem of life-size. Of course the objects must always be magnified to some extent, or they would be absolutely invisible, but usually the extent is determined by the size of the astral tube, and the whole thing is simply a tiny moving picture. In the few cases where the figures are seen as of life-size by this method, it is probable that an altogether new power is beginning to dawn; but when this happens, careful observation is needed in order to distinguish them from examples of our next class.

3. *By the projection of a thought-form.*—The ability to use this method of clairvoyance implies a development somewhat more advanced than the last, since it necessitates a certain amount of control upon the mental plane. All students of Theosophy are aware that thought takes form, at any rate upon its own plane, and in the vast majority of cases upon the astral plane also; but it may not be quite so generally known that if a man thinks strongly of himself as present at any given place, the form assumed by that particular thought will be a likeness of the thinker himself, which will appear at the place in question.

Essentially this form must be composed of the matter of the mental plane, but in very many cases it would draw round itself matter of the astral plane also, and so would approach much nearer to visibility. There are, in fact, many instances in which it has been seen by the person thought of—most probably by means of the unconscious mesmeric influence emanating from the original thinker. None of the consciousness of the thinker would, however, be included within this thought-form. When once sent out from him, it would normally be a quite separate entity—not indeed absolutely unconnected with its maker, but practically so as far as the possibility of receiving any impression through it is concerned.

This third type of clairvoyance consists, then, in the power to retain so much connection with and so much hold over a newly-erected thought-form as will render it possible to receive impressions by means of it. Such impressions as were made upon the form would in this case be transmitted to the thinker—not along an astral telegraph line, as before, but by sympathetic vibration. In a perfect case of this kind of clairvoyance it is almost as though the seer projected a part of his consciousness into the thought-form, and used it as a kind of outpost, from which observation was possible. He sees almost as well as he would if he himself stood in the place of his thought-form.

The figures at which he is looking will appear to him as of life-size and close at hand, instead of tiny and at a distance, as in the previous case; and he will find it possible to shift his point of view if he wishes to do so. Clairaudience is perhaps less frequently associated with this type of clairvoyance than with the last, but its place is to some extent taken by a kind of mental perception of the thoughts and intentions of those who are seen.

Since the man's consciousness is still in the physical body, he will be able (even while exercising the faculty) to hear and to speak, in so far as he can do this without any distraction of his attention. The moment that the intentness of his thought fails the whole vision is gone, and he will have to construct a fresh thought-form before he can resume it. Instances in which this kind of sight is possessed with any degree of perfection by untrained people are naturally rarer than in the case of the previous type, because of the capacity for mental control required, and the generally finer nature of the forces employed.

4. *By travelling in the astral body.*—We enter here upon an entirely new variety of clairvoyance, in which the consciousness of the seer no longer remains in or closely connected with his physical body, but is definitely transferred to the scene which he is examining. Though it has no doubt greater dangers for the untrained seer than either of the methods previously described, it is yet quite the most satisfactory form of clairvoyance open to him, for the immensely superior variety which we shall consider under our fifth head is not available except for specially trained students.

In this case the man's body is either asleep or in trance, and its organs are consequently not available for use while the vision is going on, so that all description of what is seen, and all questioning as to further particulars, must be postponed until the wanderer returns to this plane. On the other hand the sight is much fuller and more perfect; the man hears as well as sees everything which passes before him, and can move about freely at will within the very wide limits of the astral plane. He can see and study at leisure all the other inhabitants of that plane, so that the great world of the nature-spirits (of which the traditional fairy-land is but a very small part) lies open before him, and even that of some of the lower devas.

He has also the immense advantage of being able to take part, as it were, in the scenes which come before his eyes—of conversing at will with these various astral entities, from whom so much information that is curious and interesting may be obtained. If in addition he can learn how to materialize himself (a matter of no great difficulty for him when once the knack is acquired), he will be able to take part in physical events or conversations at a distance, and to show himself to an absent friend at will.

Again, he has the additional power of being able to hunt about for what he wants. By means of the varieties of clairvoyance previously described, for all practical purposes he could find a person or a place only when he was already acquainted with it, or when he was put *en rapport* with it by touching something physically connected with it, as in psychometry. It is true that by the third method a certain amount of motion is possible, but the process is a tedious one except for quite short distances.

By the use of the astral body, however, a man can move about quite freely and rapidly in any direction, and can (for example) find without difficulty any place pointed out upon a map, without either any previous knowledge of the spot or any object to establish a connection with it. He can also readily rise high into the air so as to gain a bird's-eye view of the country which he is examining, so as to observe its extent, the contour of its coast-line, or its general character. Indeed, in every way his power and freedom are far greater when he uses this method than they have been in any of the previous cases.

A good example of the full possession of this power is given, on the authority of the German writer Jung Stilling, by Mrs. Crowe in *The Night Side of Nature* (p. 127). The story is related of a seer who is stated to have resided in the neighbourhood of Philadelphia, in America. His habits were retired, and he spoke little; he was grave, benevolent and pious, and nothing was known against his character except that he had the reputation of possessing some secrets that were considered not altogether *lawful*. Many extraordinary stories were told of him, and amongst the rest the following:—

"The wife of a ship captain (whose husband was on a voyage to Europe and Africa, and from whom she had been long without tidings), being overwhelmed with anxiety for his safety, was induced to address herself to this person. Having listened to her story he begged her to excuse him for a while, when he would bring her the intelligence she required. He then passed into an inner room and she sat herself down to wait; but his absence continuing longer than she expected, she became impatient, thinking he had forgotten her, and softly approaching the door she peeped through some aperture, and to her surprise beheld him lying on a sofa as motionless as if he were dead. She of course did not think it advisable to disturb him, but waited his return, when he told her that her husband had not been able to write to her for such and such reasons, but that he was then in a coffee-house in London and would very shortly be home again.

"Accordingly he arrived, and as the lady learnt from him that the causes of his unusual silence had been precisely those alleged by the man, she felt extremely desirous of ascertaining the truth of the rest of the information. In this she was gratified, for he no sooner set his eyes on the magician than he said that he had seen him before on a certain day in a coffee-house in London, and that he told him that his wife was extremely uneasy about him, and that he, the captain, had thereon mentioned how he had been prevented writing, adding that he was on the eve of embarking for America. He had then lost sight of the stranger amongst the throng, and knew nothing more about him."

We have of course no means now of knowing what evidence Jung Stilling had of the truth of this story, though he declares himself to have been quite satisfied with the authority on which he relates it; but so many similar things have happened that there is no reason to doubt its accuracy. The seer, however, must either have developed his faculty for himself or learnt it in some school other than that from which most of our Theosophical information is derived; for in our case there is a well-understood regulation expressly forbidding the pupils from giving any manifestation of such power which can be definitely proved at both ends in that way, and so constitute what is called "a phenomenon." That this regulation is emphatically a wise one is proved to all who know anything of the history of our Society by the disastrous results which followed from a very slight temporary relaxation of it.

I have given some quite modern cases almost exactly parallel to the above in my little book on *Invisible Helpers*. An instance of a lady well-known to myself, who frequently thus appears to friends at a distance, is given by Mr. Stead in *Real Ghost Stories* (p. 27); and Mr. Andrew Lang gives, in his *Dreams and Ghosts* (p. 89), an account of how Mr. Cleave, then at Portsmouth, appeared intentionally on two occasions to a young lady in London, and alarmed her considerably. There is any amount of evidence to be had on the subject by any one who cares to study it seriously.

This paying of intentional astral visits seems very often to become possible when the principles are loosened at the approach of death for people who were unable to perform such a feat at any other time. There are even more examples of this class than of the other; I epitomize a good one given by Mr. Andrew Lang on p. 100 of the book last cited—one of which he himself says, "Not many stories have such good evidence in their favour."

"Mary, the wife of John Goffe of Rochester, being afflicted with a long illness, removed to her father's house at West Malling, about nine miles from her own.

"The day before her death she grew very impatiently desirous to see her two children, whom she had left at home to the care of a nurse. She was too ill to be moved, and between one and two o'clock in the morning she fell into a trance. One widow Turner, who watched with her that night, says that her eyes were open and fixed, and her jaw fallen. Mrs. Turner put her hand upon her mouth, but could perceive no breath. She thought her to be in a fit, and doubted whether she were dead or alive.

"The next morning the dying woman told her mother that she had been at home with her children, saying, 'I was with them last night when I was asleep.'

"The nurse at Rochester, widow Alexander by name, affirms that a little before two o'clock that morning she saw the likeness of the said Mary Goffe come out of the next chamber (where the elder child lay in a bed by itself), the door being left open, and stood by her bedside for about a quarter of an hour; the younger child was there lying by her. Her eyes moved and her mouth went, but she said nothing. The nurse, moreover, says that she was perfectly awake; it was then daylight, being one of the longest days in the year. She sat up in bed and looked steadfastly on the apparition. In that time she heard the bridge clock strike two, and a while after said: 'In the name of the Father, Son and Holy Ghost, what art thou?' Thereupon the apparition removed and went away; she slipped on her clothes and followed, but what became on't, she cannot tell."

The nurse apparently was more frightened by its disappearance than its presence, for after this she was afraid to stay in the house, and so spent the rest of the time until six o'clock in walking up and down outside. When the neighbours were awake she told her tale to them, and they of course said she had dreamt it all; she naturally enough warmly repudiated that idea, but could obtain no credence until the news of the other side of the story arrived from West Malling, when people had to admit that there might have been something in it.

A noteworthy circumstance in this story is that the mother found it necessary to pass from ordinary sleep into the profounder trance condition before she could consciously visit her children; it can, however, be paralleled here and there among the large number of similar accounts which may be found in the literature of the subject.

Two other stories of precisely the same type—in which a dying mother, earnestly desiring to see her children, falls into a deep sleep, visits them and returns to say that she has done so—are given by Dr. F. G. Lee. In one of them the mother, when dying in Egypt, appears to her children at Torquay, and is clearly seen in broad daylight by all five of the children and also by the nursemaid. (*Glimpses of the Supernatural*, vol. ii., p. 64.) In the other a Quaker lady dying at Cockermouth is clearly seen and recognized in daylight by her three children at Settle, the remainder of the story being practically identical with the one given above. (*Glimpses in the Twilight*, p. 94.) Though these cases appear to be less widely known than that of Mary Goffe, the evidence of their authenticity seems to be quite as good, as will be seen by the attestations obtained by the reverend author of the works from which they are quoted.

The man who fully possesses this fourth type of clairvoyance has many and great advantages at his disposal, even in addition to those already mentioned. Not only can he visit without trouble or expense all the beautiful and famous places of the earth, but if he happens to be a scholar, think what it must mean to him that he has access to all the libraries of the world! What must it be for the scientifically-minded man to see taking place before his eyes so many of the processes of the secret chemistry of nature, or for the philosopher to have revealed to him so much more than ever before of the working of the great mysteries of life and death? To him those who are gone from this plane are dead no longer, but living and within reach for a long time to come; for him many of the conceptions of religion are no longer matters of faith, but of knowledge. Above all, he can join the army of invisible helpers, and really be of use on a large scale. Undoubtedly clairvoyance, even when confined to the astral plane, is a great boon to the student.

Certainly it has its dangers also, especially for the untrained; danger from evil entities of various kinds, which may terrify or injure those who allow themselves to lose the courage to face them boldly; danger of deception of all sorts, of misconceiving and misinterpreting what is seen; greatest of all, the danger of becoming conceited about the thing and of thinking it impossible to make a mistake. But a little commonsense and a little experience should easily guard a man against these.

5. *By travelling in the mental body.*—This is simply a higher and, as it were, glorified form of the last type. The vehicle employed is no longer the astral body, but the mind-body—a vehicle, therefore, belonging to the mental plane, and having within it all the potentialities of the wonderful sense of that plane, so transcendent in its action yet so impossible to describe. A man functioning in this leaves his astral body behind him along with the physical, and if he wishes to show himself upon the astral plane for any reason, he does not send for his own astral vehicle, but just by a single action of his will materializes one for his temporary need. Such an astral materialization is sometimes called the mâyâvirûpa, and to form it for the first time usually needs the assistance of a qualified Master.

The enormous advantages given by the possession of this power are the capacity of entering upon all the glory and the beauty of the higher land of bliss, and the possession, even when working on the astral plane, of the far more comprehensive mental sense which opens up to the student such marvellous vistas of knowledge, and practically renders error all but impossible. This higher flight, however, is possible for the trained man only, since only under definite training can a man at this stage of evolution learn to employ his mental body as a vehicle.

Before leaving the subject of full and intentional clairvoyance, it may be well to devote a few words to answering one or two questions as to its limitations, which constantly occur to students. Is it possible, we are often asked, for the seer to find any person with whom he wishes to communicate, anywhere in the world, whether he be living or dead?

To this reply must be a conditional affirmative. Yes, it is possible to find any person if the experimenter can, in some way or other, put himself *en rapport* with that person. It would be hopeless to plunge vaguely into space to find a total stranger among all the millions around us without any kind of clue; but, on the other hand, a very slight clue would usually be sufficient.

If the clairvoyant knows anything of the man whom he seeks, he will have no difficulty in finding him, for every man has what may be called a kind of musical chord of his own—a chord which is the expression of him as a whole, produced perhaps by a sort of average of the rates of vibration of all his different vehicles on their respective planes. If the operator knows how to discern that chord and to strike it, it will by sympathetic vibration attract the attention of the man instantly wherever he may be, and will evoke an immediate response from him.

Whether the man were living or recently dead would make no difference at all, and clairvoyance of the fifth class could at once find him even among the countless millions in the heaven-world, though in that case the man himself would be unconscious that he was under observation. Naturally a seer whose consciousness did not range higher than the astral plane—who employed therefore one of the earlier methods of seeing—would not be able to find a person upon the mental plane at all; yet even he would at least be able to tell that the man sought for was upon that plane, from the mere fact that the striking of the chord as far up as the astral level produced no response.

If the man sought be a stranger to the seeker, the latter will need something connected with him to act as a clue—a photograph, a letter written by him, an article which has belonged to him, and is impregnated with his personal magnetism; any of these would do in the hands of a practised seer.

Again I say, it must not therefore be supposed that pupils who have been taught how to use this art are at liberty to set up a kind of intelligence office through which communication can be had with missing or dead relatives. A message given from this side to such an one might or might not be handed on, according to circumstances, but even if it were, no reply might be brought, lest the transaction should partake of the nature of a phenomenon—something which could be proved on the physical plane to have been an act of magic.

Another question often raised is as to whether, in the action of psychic vision, there is any limitation as to distance. The reply would seem to be that there should be no limit but that of the respective planes. It must be remembered that the astral and mental planes of our earth are as definitely its own as its atmosphere, though they extend considerably further from it even in our three-dimensional space than does the physical air. Consequently the passage to, or the detailed sight of, other planets would not be possible for any system of clairvoyance connected with these planes. It *is* quite possible and easy for the man who can raise his consciousness to the buddhic plane to pass to any other globe belonging to our chain of worlds, but that is outside our present subject.

Still a good deal of additional information about other planets can be obtained by the use of such clairvoyant faculties as we have been describing. It is possible to make sight enormously clearer by passing outside of the constant disturbances of the earth's atmosphere, and it is also not difficult to learn how to put on an exceedingly high magnifying power, so that even by ordinary clairvoyance a good deal of very interesting astronomical knowledge may be gained. But as far as this earth and its immediate surroundings are concerned, there is practically no limitation.

CHAPTER V.

CLAIRVOYANCE IN SPACE: SEMI-INTERNATIONAL.

UNDER this rather curious title I am grouping together the cases of all those people who definitely set themselves to see something, but have no idea what the something will be, and no control over the sight after the visions have begun—psychic Micawbers, who put themselves into a receptive condition, and then simply wait for something to turn up. Many trance-mediums would come under this heading; they either in some way hypnotize themselves or are hypnotized by some "spirit-guide," and then they describe the scenes or persons that happen to float before their vision. Sometimes, however, when in this condition they see what is taking place at a distance, and so they come to have a place among our "clairvoyants in space."

But the largest and most widely-spread band of these semi-intentional clairvoyants are the various kinds of crystal-gazers—those who, as Mr. Andrew Lang puts it, "stare into a crystal ball, a cup, a mirror, a blob of ink (Egypt and India), a drop of blood (among the Maories of New Zealand), a bowl of water (Red Indian), a pond (Roman and African), water in a glass bowl (in Fez), or almost any polished surface" (*Dreams and Ghosts*, p. 57).

Two pages later Mr. Lang gives us a very good example of the kind of vision most frequently seen in this way. "I had given a glass ball," he says, "to a young lady, Miss Baillie, who had scarcely any success with it. She lent it to Miss Leslie, who saw a large square, old-fashioned red sofa covered with muslin, which she found in the next country-house she visited. Miss Baillie's brother, a young athlete, laughed at these experiments, took the ball into the study, and came back looking 'gey gash.' He admitted that he had seen a vision—somebody he knew under a lamp. He would discover during the week whether he saw right or not. This was at 5.30 on a Sunday afternoon.

"On Tuesday, Mr. Baillie was at a dance in a town some forty miles from his home, and met a Miss Preston. 'On Sunday,' he said, 'about half-past five you were sitting under a standard lamp in a dress I never saw you wear, a blue blouse with lace over the shoulders, pouring out tea for a man in blue serge, whose back was towards me, so that I only saw the tip of his moustache.'

"'Why, the blinds must have been up,' said Miss Preston.

"'I was at Dulby,' said Mr. Baillie, and he undeniably was."

This is quite a typical case of crystal-gazing—the picture correct in every detail, you see, and yet absolutely unimportant and bearing no apparent signification of any sort to either party, except that it served to prove to Mr. Baillie that there was something in crystal-gazing. Perhaps more frequently the visions tend to be of a romantic character—men in foreign dress, or beautiful though generally unknown landscapes.

Now what is the rationale of this kind of clairvoyance? As I have indicated above, it belongs usually to the "astral-current" type, and the crystal or other object simply acts as a focus for the will-power of the seer, and a convenient starting-point for his astral tube. There are some who can influence what they will see by their will, that is to say they have the power of pointing their telescope as they wish; but the great majority just form a fortuitous tube and see whatever happens to present itself at the end of it.

Sometimes it may be a scene comparatively near at hand, as in the case just quoted; at other times it will be a far-away Oriental landscape; at others yet it may be a reflection of some fragment of an âkâshic record, and then the picture will contain figures in some antique dress, and the phenomenon belongs to our third large division of "clairvoyance in time." It is said that visions of the future are sometimes seen in crystals also—a further development to which we must refer later.

I have seen a clairvoyant use instead of the ordinary shining surface a dead black one, produced by a handful of powdered charcoal in a saucer. Indeed it does not seem to matter much what is used as a focus, except that pure crystal has an undoubted advantage over other substances in that its peculiar arrangement of elemental essence renders it specially stimulating to the psychic faculties.

It seems probable, however, that in cases where a tiny brilliant object is employed—such as a point of light, or the drop of blood used by the Maories—the instance is in reality merely one of self-hypnotization. Among non-European nations the experiment is very frequently preceded or accompanied by magical ceremonies and invocations, so that it is quite likely that such sight as is gained may sometimes be really that of some foreign entity, and so the phenomenon may in fact be merely a case of temporary possession, and not of clairvoyance at all.

CHAPTER VI.

CLAIRVOYANCE IN SPACE: UNINTENTIONAL.

UNDER this heading we may group together all those cases in which visions of some event which is taking place at a distance are seen quite unexpectedly and without any kind of preparation. There are people who are subject to such visions, while there are many others to whom such a thing will happen only once in a life-time. The visions are of all kinds and of all degrees of completeness, and apparently may be produced by various causes. Sometimes the reason of the vision is obvious, and the subject matter of the gravest importance; at other times no reason at all is discoverable, and the events shown seem of the most trivial nature.

Sometimes these glimpses of the super-physical faculty come as waking visions, and sometimes they manifest during sleep as vivid or oft-repeated dreams. In this latter case the sight employed is perhaps usually of the kind assigned to our fourth subdivision of clairvoyance in space, for the sleeping man often travels in his astral body to some spot with which his affections or interests are closely connected, and simply watches what takes place there; in the former it seems probable that the second type of clairvoyance, by means of the astral current, is called into requisition. But in this case the current or tube is formed quite unconsciously, and is often the automatic result of a strong thought or emotion projected from one end or the other—either from the seer or the person who is seen.

The simplest plan will be to give a few instances of the different kinds, and to intersperse among them such further explanations as may seem necessary. Mr. Stead has collected a large and varied assortment of recent and well-authenticated cases in his *Real Ghost Stories*, and I will select some of my examples from them, occasionally condensing slightly to save space.

There are cases in which it is at once obvious to any Theosophical student that the exceptional instance of clairvoyance was specially brought about by one of the band whom we have called "Invisible Helpers" in order that aid might be rendered to some one in sore need. To this class, undoubtedly, belongs the story told by Captain Yonnt, of the Napa Valley in California, to Dr. Bushnell, who repeats it in his *Nature and the Supernatural* (p. 14).

"About six or seven years previous, in a mid-winter's night, he had a dream in which he saw what appeared to be a company of emigrants arrested by the snows of the mountains, and perishing rapidly by cold and hunger. He noted the very cast of the scenery, marked by a huge, perpendicular front of white rock cliff; he saw the men cutting off what appeared to be tree-tops rising out of deep gulfs of snow; he distinguished the very features of the persons and the look of their particular distress.

"He awoke profoundly impressed by the distinctness and apparent reality of the dream. He at length fell asleep, and dreamed exactly the same dream over again. In the morning he could not expel it from his mind. Falling in shortly after with an old hunter comrade, he told his story, and was only the more deeply impressed by his recognizing without hesitation the scenery of the dream. This comrade came over the Sierra by the Carson Valley Pass, and declared that a spot in the Pass exactly answered his description.

"By this the unsophistical patriarch was decided. He immediately collected a company of men, with mules and blankets and all necessary provisions. The neighbours were laughing meantime at his credulity. 'No matter,' he said, 'I am able to do this, and I will, for I verily believe that the fact is according to my dream.' The men were sent into the mountains one hundred and fifty miles distant direct to the Carson Valley Pass. And there they found the company exactly in the condition of the dream, and brought in the remnant alive."

Since it is not stated that Captain Yonnt was in the habit of seeing visions, it seems clear that some helper, observing the forlorn condition of the emigrant party, took the nearest impressionable and otherwise suitable person (who happened to be the Captain) to the spot in the astral body, and aroused him sufficiently to fix the scene firmly in his memory. The helper may possibly have arranged an "astral current" for the Captain instead, but the former suggestion is more probable. At any rate the motive, and broadly the method, of the work are obvious enough in this case.

Sometimes the "astral current" may be set going by a strong emotional thought at the other end of the line, and this may happen even though the thinker has no such intention in his mind. In the rather striking story which I am about to quote, it is evident that the link was formed by the doctor's frequent thought about Mrs. Broughton, yet he had clearly no especial wish that she should see what he was doing at the time. That it was this kind of clairvoyance that was employed is shown by the fixity of her point of view—which, be it observed, is not the doctor's point of view sympathetically transferred (as it might have been) since she sees his back without recognizing him. The story is to be found in the *Proceedings of the Psychical Research Society* (vol. ii., p. 160).

"Mrs. Broughton awoke one night in 1844, and roused her husband, telling him that something dreadful had happened in France. He begged her to go to sleep again, and not trouble him. She assured him that she was not asleep when she saw what she insisted on telling him—what she saw in fact.

"First a carriage accident—which she did not actually see, but what she saw was the result—a broken carriage, a crowd collected, a figure gently raised and carried into the nearest house, then a figure lying on a bed which she then recognized as the Duke of Orleans. Gradually friends collecting round the bed—among them several members of the French royal family—the queen, then the king, all silently, tearfully, watching the evidently dying duke. One man (she could see his back, but did not know who he was) was a doctor. He stood bending over the duke, feeling his pulse, with his watch in the other hand. And then all passed away, and she saw no more.

"As soon as it was daylight she wrote down in her journal all that she had seen. It was before the days of electric telegraph, and two or more days passed before the *Times* announced 'The Death of the Duke of Orleans.' Visiting Paris a short time afterwards she saw and recognized the place of the accident and received the explanation of her impression. The doctor who attended the dying duke was an old friend of hers, and as he watched by the bed his mind had been constantly occupied with her and her family."

A commoner instance is that in which strong affection sets up the necessary current; probably a fairly steady stream of mutual thought is constantly flowing between the two parties in the case, and some sudden need or dire extremity on the part of one of them endues this stream temporarily with the polarizing power which is needful to create the astral telescope. An illustrative example is quoted from the same *Proceedings* (vol. i., p. 30).

"On September 9th, 1848, at the siege of Mooltan, Major-General R——, C.B., then adjutant of his regiment, was most severely and dangerously wounded; and, supposing himself to be dying, asked one of the officers with him to take the ring off his finger and send it to his wife, who at the time was fully one hundred and fifty miles distant at Ferozepore.

"'On the night of September 9th, 1848,' writes his wife, 'I was lying on my bed, between sleeping and waking, when I distinctly saw my husband being carried off the field seriously wounded, and heard his voice saying, "Take this ring off my finger and send it to my wife." All the next day I could not get the sight or the voice out of my mind.

"'In due time I heard of General R—— having been severely wounded in the assault of Mooltan. He survived, however, and is still living. It was not for some time after the siege that I heard from General L——, the officer who helped to carry my husband off the field, that the request as to the ring was actually made by him, just as I heard it at Ferozepore at that very time.'"

Then there is the very large class of casual clairvoyant visions which have no traceable cause—which are apparently quite meaningless, and have no recognizable relation to any events known to the seer. To this class belong many of the landscapes seen by some people just before they fall asleep. I quote a capital and very realistic account of an experience of this sort from Mr. W. T. Stead's *Real Ghost Stories* (p. 65).

"I got into bed but was not able to go to sleep. I shut my eyes and waited for sleep to come; instead of sleep, however, there came to me a succession of curiously vivid clairvoyant pictures. There was no light in the room, and it was perfectly dark; I had my eyes shut also. But notwithstanding the darkness I suddenly was conscious of looking at a scene of singular beauty. It was as if I saw a living miniature about the size of a magic-lantern slide. At this moment I can recall the scene as if I saw it again. It was a seaside piece. The moon was shining upon the water, which rippled slowly on to the beach. Right before me a long mole ran into the water.

"On either side of the mole irregular rocks stood up above the sea-level. On the shore stood several houses, square and rude, which resembled nothing that I had ever seen in house architecture. No one was stirring, but the moon was there and the sea and the gleam of the moonlight on the rippling waters, just as if I had been looking on the actual scene.

"It was so beautiful that I remember thinking that if it continued I should be so interested in looking at it that I should never go to sleep. I was wide awake, and at the same time that I saw the scene I distinctly heard the dripping of the rain outside the window. Then suddenly, without any apparent object or reason, the scene changed.

"The moonlit sea vanished, and in its place I was looking right into the interior of a reading-room. It seemed as if it had been used as a schoolroom in the daytime, and was employed as a reading-room in the evening. I remember seeing one reader who had a curious resemblance to Tim Harrington, although it was not he, hold up a magazine or book in his hand and laugh. It was not a picture—it was there.

"The scene was just as if you were looking through an opera-glass; you saw the play of the muscles, the gleaming of the eye, every movement of the unknown persons in the unnamed place into which you were gazing. I saw all that without opening my eyes, nor did my eyes have anything to do with it. You see such things as these as it were with another sense which is more inside your head than in your eyes.

"This was a very poor and paltry experience, but it enabled me to understand better how it is that clairvoyants see than any amount of disquisition.

"The pictures were *apropos* of nothing; they had been suggested by nothing I had been reading or talking of; they simply came as if I had been able to look through a glass at what was occurring somewhere else in the world. I had my peep, and then it passed, nor have I had a recurrence of a similar experience."

Mr. Stead regards that as a "poor and paltry experience," and it may perhaps be considered so when compared with the greater possibilities, yet I know many students who would be very thankful to have even so much of direct personal experience to tell. Small though it may be in itself, it at once gives the seer a clue to the whole thing, and clairvoyance would be a living actuality to a man who had seen even that much in a way that it could never have been without that little touch with the unseen world.

These pictures were much too clear to have been mere reflections of the thought of others, and besides, the description unmistakably shows that they were views seen through an astral telescope; so either Mr. Stead must quite unconsciously have set a current going for himself, or (which is much more probable) some kindly astral entity set it in motion for him, and gave him, to while away a tedious delay, any pictures that happened to come handy at the end of the tube.

CHAPTER VII.

CLAIRVOYANCE IN TIME: THE PAST.

CLAIRVOYANCE in time—that is to say, the power of reading the past and the future—is, like all the other varieties, possessed by different people in very varying degrees, ranging from the man who has both faculties fully at his command, down to one who only occasionally gets involuntary and very imperfect glimpses or reflections of these scenes of other days. A person of the latter type might have, let us say, a vision of some event in the past; but it would be liable to the most serious distortion, and even if it happened to be fairly accurate it would almost certainly be a mere isolated picture, and he would probably be quite unable to relate it to what had occurred before or after it, or to account for anything unusual which might appear in it. The trained man, on the other hand, could follow the drama connected with his picture backwards or forwards to any extent that might seem desirable, and trace out with equal ease the causes which had led up to it or the results which it in turn would produce.

We shall probably find it easier to grasp this somewhat difficult section of our subject if we consider it in the subdivisions which naturally suggest themselves, and deal first with the vision which looks backwards into the past, leaving for later examination that which pierces the veil of the future. In each case it will be well for us to try to understand what we can of the *modus operandi*, even though our success can at best be only a very modified one, owing first to the imperfect information on some parts of the subject at present possessed by our investigators, and secondly to the ever-recurring failure of physical words to express a hundredth part even of the little we do know about higher planes and faculties.

In the case then of a detailed vision of the remote past, how is it obtained, and to what plane of nature does it really belong? The answer to both these questions is contained in the reply that it is read from the âkâshic records; but that statement in return will require a certain amount of explanation for many readers. The word is in truth somewhat of a misnomer, for though the records are undoubtedly read from the âkâsha, or matter of the mental plane, yet it is not to it that they really belong. Still worse is the alternative title, "records of the astral light," which has sometimes been employed, for these records lie far beyond the astral plane, and all that can be obtained on it are only broken glimpses of a kind of double reflection of them, as will presently be explained.

Like so many others of our Theosophical terms, the word âkâsha has been very loosely used. In some of our earlier books it was considered as synonymous with astral light, and in others it was employed to signify any kind of invisible matter, from mûlaprakṛiti down to the physical ether. In later books its use has been restricted to the matter of the mental plane, and it is in that sense that the records may be spoken of as âkâshic, for although they are not originally made on that plane any more than on the astral, yet it is there that we first come definitely into contact with them and find it possible to do reliable work with them.

This subject of the records is by no means an easy one to deal with, for it is one of that numerous class which requires for its perfect comprehension faculties of a far higher order than any which humanity has yet evolved. The real solution of its problems lies on planes far beyond any that we can possibly know at present, and any view that we take of it must necessarily be of the most imperfect character, since we cannot but look at it from below instead of from above. The idea which we form of it must therefore be only partial, yet it need not mislead us unless we allow ourselves to think of the tiny fragment which is all that we can see as though it were the perfect whole. If we are careful that such conceptions as we may form shall be accurate as far as they go, we shall have nothing to unlearn, though much to add, when in the course of our further progress we gradually acquire the higher wisdom. Be it understood then at the commencement that a thorough grasp of our subject is an impossibility at the present stage of our evolution, and that many points will arise as to which no exact explanation is yet obtainable, though it may often be possible to suggest analogies and to indicate the lines along which an explanation must lie.

Let us then try to carry back our thoughts to the beginning of this solar system to which we belong. We are all familiar with the ordinary astronomical theory of its origin—that which is commonly called the nebular hypothesis—according to which it first came into existence as a gigantic glowing nebula, of a diameter far exceeding that of the orbit of even the outermost of the planets, and then, as in the course of countless ages that enormous sphere gradually cooled and contracted, the system as we know it was formed.

Occult science accepts that theory, in its broad outline, as correctly representing the purely physical side of the evolution of our system, but it would add that if we confine our attention to this physical side only we shall have a very incomplete and incoherent idea of what really happened. It would postulate, to begin with, that the exalted Being who undertakes the formation of a system (whom we sometimes call the Logos of the system) first of all forms in His mind a complete conception of the whole of it with all its successive chains of worlds. By the very act of forming that conception He calls the whole into simultaneous objective existence on the plane of His thought—a plane of course far above all those of which we know anything—from which the various globes descend when required into whatever state of further objectivity may be respectively destined for them. Unless we constantly bear in mind this fact of the real existence of the whole system from the very beginning on a higher plane, we shall be perpetually misunderstanding the physical evolution which we see taking place down here.

But occultism has more than this to teach us on the subject. It tells us not only that all this wonderful system to which we belong is called into existence by the Logos, both on lower and on higher planes, but also that its relation to Him is closer even than that, for it is absolutely a part of Him—a partial expression of Him upon the physical plane—and that the movement and energy of the whole system is *His* energy, and is all carried on within the limits of His aura. Stupendous as this conception is, it will yet not be wholly unthinkable to those of us who have made any study of the subject of the aura.

We are familiar with the idea that as a person progresses on the upward path his causal body, which is the determining limit of his aura, distinctly increases in size as well as in luminosity and purity of colour. Many of us know from experience that the aura of a pupil who has already made considerable advance on the Path is very much larger than that of one who is but just setting his foot upon its first step, while in the case of an Adept the proportional increase is far greater still. We read in quite exoteric Oriental scriptures of the immense extension of the aura of the Buddha; I think that three miles is mentioned on one occasion as its limit, but whatever the exact measurement may be, it is obvious that we have here another record of this fact of the extremely rapid growth of the causal body as man passes on his upward way. There can be little doubt that the rate of this growth would itself increase in geometrical progression, so that it need not surprise us to hear of an Adept on a still higher level whose aura is capable of including the entire world at once; and from this we may gradually lead our minds up to the conception that there is a Being so exalted as to comprehend within Himself the whole of our solar system. And we should remember that, enormous as this seems to us, it is but as the tiniest drop in the vast ocean of space.

So of the Logos (who has in Him all the capacities and qualities with which we can possibly endow the highest God we can imagine) it is literally true, as was said of old, that "of Him and through Him, and to Him are all things," and "in Him we live and move and have our being."

Now if this be so, it is clear that whatever happens within our system happens absolutely within the consciousness of its Logos, and so we at once see that the true record must be His memory; and furthermore, it is obvious that on whatever plane that wondrous memory exists, it cannot but be far above anything that we know, and consequently whatever records we may find ourselves able to read must be only a reflection of that great dominant fact, mirrored in the denser media of the lower planes.

On the astral plane it is at once evident that this is so—that what we are dealing with is only a reflection of a reflection, and an exceedingly imperfect one, for such records as can be reached there are fragmentary in the extreme, and often seriously distorted. We know how universally water is used as a symbol of the astral light, and in this particular case it is a remarkably apt one. From the surface of still water we may get a clear reflection of the surrounding objects, just as from a mirror; but at the best it is only a reflection—a representation in two dimensions of three-dimensional objects, and therefore differing in all its qualities, except colour, from that which it represents; and in addition to this, it is always reversed.

But let the surface of the water be ruffled by the wind and what do we find then? A reflection still, certainly, but so broken up and distorted as to be quite useless or even misleading as a guide to the shape and real appearance of the objects reflected. Here and there for a moment we might happen to get a clear reflection of some minute part of the scene—of a single leaf from a tree, for example; but it would need long labour and considerable knowledge of natural laws to build up anything like a true conception of the object reflected by putting together even a large number of such isolated fragments of an image of it.

Now in the astral plane we can never have anything approaching to what we have imaged as a still surface, but on the contrary we have always to deal with one in rapid and bewildering motion; judge, therefore, how little we can depend upon getting a clear and definite reflection. Thus a clairvoyant who possesses only the faculty of astral sight can never rely upon any picture of the past that comes before him as being accurate and perfect; here and there some part of it *may* be so, but he has no means of knowing which it is. If he is under the care of a competent teacher he may, by long and careful training, be shown how to distinguish between reliable and unreliable impressions, and to construct from the broken reflections some kind of image of the object reflected; but usually long before he has mastered those difficulties he will have developed the mental sight, which renders such labour unnecessary.

On the next plane, which we call the mental, conditions are very different. There the record is full and accurate, and it would be impossible to make any mistake in the reading. That is to say, if three clairvoyants possessing the powers of the mental plane agreed to examine a certain record there, what would be presented to their vision would be absolutely the same reflection in each case, and each would acquire a correct impression from it in reading it. It does not however follow that when they all compared notes later on the physical plane their reports would agree exactly. It is well known that if three people who witness an occurrence down here in the physical world set to work to describe it afterwards, their accounts will differ considerably, for each will have noticed especially those items which most appeal to him, and will insensibly have made them the prominent features of the event, sometimes ignoring other points which were in reality much more important.

Now in the case of an observation on the mental plane this personal equation would not appreciably affect the impressions received, for since each would thoroughly grasp the entire subject it would be impossible for him to see its parts out of due proportion; but, except in the case of carefully trained and experienced persons, this factor does come into play in transferring the impressions to the lower planes. It is in the nature of things impossible that any account given down here of a vision or experience on the mental plane can be complete, since nine-tenths of what is seen and felt there could not be expressed by physical words at all; and, since all expression must therefore be partial, there is obviously some possibility of selection as to the part expressed. It is for this reason that in all our Theosophical investigations of recent years so much stress has been laid upon the constant checking and verifying of clairvoyant testimony, nothing which rests upon the vision of one person only having been allowed to appear in our later books.

But even when the possibility of error from this factor of personal equation has been reduced to a minimum by a careful system of counter-checking, there still remains the very serious difficulty which is inherent in the operation of bringing down impressions from a higher plane to a lower one. This is something analogous to the difficulty experienced by a painter in his endeavour to reproduce a three-dimensional landscape on a flat surface—that is, practically in two dimensions. Just as the artist needs long and careful training of eye and hand before he can produce a satisfactory representation of nature, so does the clairvoyant need long and careful training before he can describe accurately on a lower plane what he sees on a higher one; and the probability of getting an exact description from an untrained person is about equal to that of getting a perfectly-finished landscape from one who has never learnt how to draw.

It must be remembered, too, that the most perfect picture is in reality infinitely far from being a reproduction of the scene which it represents, for hardly a single line or angle in it can ever be the same as those in the object copied. It is simply a very ingenious attempt to make upon one only of our five senses, by means of lines and colours on a flat surface, an impression similar to that which would have been made if we had actually had before us the scene depicted. Except by a suggestion dependent entirely on our own previous experience, it can convey to us nothing of the roar of the sea, of the scent of the flowers, of the taste of the fruit, or of the softness or hardness of the surface drawn.

Of exactly similar nature, though far greater in degree, are the difficulties experienced by a clairvoyant in his attempt to describe upon the physical plane what he has seen upon the astral;

and they are furthermore greatly enhanced by the fact that, instead of having merely to recall to the minds of his hearers conceptions with which they are already familiar, as the artist does when he paints men or animals, fields or trees, he has to endeavour by the very imperfect means at his disposal to suggest to them conceptions which in most cases are absolutely new to them.

Small wonder then that, however vivid and striking his descriptions may seem to his audience, he himself should constantly be impressed with their total inadequacy, and should feel that his best efforts have entirely failed to convey any idea of what he really sees. And we must remember that in the case of the report given down here of a record read on the mental plane, this difficult operation of transference from the higher to the lower has taken place not once but twice, since the memory has been brought through the intervening astral plane. Even in a case where the investigator has the advantage of having developed his mental faculties so that he has the use of them while awake in the physical body, he is still hampered by the absolute incapacity of physical language to express what he sees.

Try for a moment to realize fully what is called the fourth dimension, of which we said something in an earlier chapter. It is easy enough to think of our own three dimensions—to image in our minds the length, breadth and height of any object; and we see that each of these three dimensions is expressed by a line at right angles to both of the others. The idea of the fourth dimension is that it might be possible to draw a fourth line which shall be at right angles to all three of those already existing.

Now the ordinary mind cannot grasp this idea in the least, though some few who have made a special study of the subject have gradually come to be able to realize one or two very simple four-dimensional figures. Still, no words that they can use on this plane can bring any image of these figures before the minds of others, and if any reader who has not specially trained himself along that line will make the effort to visualize such a shape he will find it quite impossible. Now to express such a form clearly in physical words would be, in effect, to describe accurately a single object on the astral plane; but in examining the records on the mental plane we should have to face the additional difficulties of a fifth dimension! So that the impossibility of fully explaining these records will be obvious to even the most superficial observation.

We have spoken of the records as the memory of the Logos, yet they are very much more than a memory in an ordinary sense of the word. Hopeless as it may be to imagine how these images appear from His point of view, we yet know that as we rise higher and higher we must be drawing nearer to the true memory—must be seeing more nearly as He sees; so that great interest attaches to the experience of the clairvoyant with reference to these records when he stands upon the buddhic plane—the highest which his consciousness can reach even when away from the physical body until he attains the level of the Arhats.

Here time and space no longer limit him; he no longer needs, as on the mental plane, to pass a series of events in review, for past, present and future are all alike simultaneously present to him, meaningless as that sounds down here. Indeed, infinitely below the consciousness of the Logos as even that exalted plane is, it is yet abundantly clear from what we see there that to Him the record must be far more than what we call a memory, for all that has happened in the past and all that will happen in the future is *happening now* before His eyes just as are the events of what we call the present time. Utterly incredible, wildly incomprehensible, of course, to our limited understanding; yet absolutely true for all that.

Naturally we could not expect to understand at our present stage of knowledge how so marvellous a result is produced, and to attempt an explanation would only be to involve ourselves in a mist of words from which we should gain no real information. Yet a line of thought recurs to my mind which perhaps suggests the direction in which it is possible that that explanation may lie: and whatever helps us to realize that so astounding a statement may after all not be wholly impossible will be of assistance in broadening our minds.

Some thirty years ago I remember reading a very curious little book, called, I think, *The Stars and the Earth*, the object of which was to endeavour to show how it was scientifically possible that to the mind of God the past and the present might be absolutely simultaneous. Its arguments struck me at the time as decidedly ingenious, and I will proceed to summarize them, as I think they will be found somewhat suggestive in connection with the subject which we have been considering.

When we see anything, whether it be the book which we hold in our hands or a star millions of miles away, we do so by means of a vibration in the ether, commonly called a ray of light, which passes from the object seen to our eyes. Now the speed with which this vibration passes is so great—about 186,000 miles in a second—that when we are considering any object in our own world we may regard it as practically instantaneous. When, however, we come to deal with interplanetary distances we have to take the speed of light into consideration, for an appreciable period is occupied in traversing these vast spaces. For example it takes eight minutes and a quarter for light to travel to us from the sun, so that when we look at the solar orb we see it by means of a ray of light which left it more than eight minutes ago.

From this follows a very curious result. The ray of light by which we see the sun can obviously report to us only the state of affairs which existed in that luminary when it started on its journey, and would not be in the least affected by anything that happened there after it left; so that we really see the sun not as he *is*, but as he was eight minutes ago. That is to say that if anything important took place in the sun—the formation of a new sun-spot, for instance—an astronomer who was watching the orb through his telescope at the time would be quite unaware of the incident while it was happening, since the ray of light bearing the news would not reach him until more than eight minutes later.

The difference is more striking when we consider the fixed stars, because in their case the distances are so enormously greater. The pole star, for example, is so far off that light, travelling at the inconceivable speed above mentioned, takes a little more than fifty years to reach our eyes; and from that follows the strange but inevitable inference that we see the pole star not as and where it is at this moment, but as and where it was fifty years ago. Nay, if to-morrow some cosmic catastrophe were to shatter the pole star into fragments, we should still see it peacefully shining in the sky all the rest of our lives; our children would grow up to middle age and gather their children about them in turn before the news of that tremendous accident reached any terrestrial eye. In the same way there are other stars so far distant that light takes thousands of years to travel from them to us, and with reference to their condition our information is therefore thousands of years behind time.

Now carry the argument a step farther. Suppose that we were able to place a man at the distance of 186,000 miles from the earth, and yet to endow him with the wonderful faculty of being able from that distance to see what was happening here as clearly as though he were still close beside us. It is evident that a man so placed would see everything a second after the time when it really happened, and so at the present moment he would be seeing what happened a second ago. Double the distance, and he would be two seconds behind time, and so on; remove him to the distance of the sun (still allowing him to preserve the same mysterious power of sight) and he would look down and watch you doing not what you *are* doing now, but what you *were* doing eight minutes and a quarter ago. Carry him away to the pole star, and he would see passing before his eyes the events of fifty years ago; he would be watching the childish gambols of those who at the very same moment were really middle-aged men. Marvellous as this may sound, it is literally and scientifically true, and cannot be denied.

The little book went on to argue logically enough that God, being almighty, must possess the wonderful power of sight which we have been postulating for our observer; and further, that being omnipresent, He must be at each of the stations which we mentioned, and also at every intermediate point, not successively but simultaneously. Granting these premises, the inevitable deduction follows that everything which has ever happened from the very beginning of the world *must* be at this very moment taking place before the eye of God—not a mere memory of it, but the actual occurrence itself being now under His observation.

All this is materialistic enough, and on the plane of purely physical science, and we may therefore be assured that it is *not* the way in which the memory of the Logos acts; yet it is neatly worked out and absolutely incontrovertible, and as I have said before, it is not without its use, since it gives us a glimpse of some possibilities which otherwise might not occur to us.

But, it may be asked, how is it possible, amid the bewildering confusion of these records of the past, to find any particular picture when it is wanted? As a matter of fact, the untrained clairvoyant usually cannot do so without some special link to put him *en rapport* with the subject required. Psychometry is an instance in point, and it is quite probable that our ordinary memory is really only another presentment of the same idea. It seems as though there were a sort of magnetic attachment or affinity between any particle of matter and the record which contains its history—an affinity which enables it to act as a kind of conductor between that record and the faculties of anyone who can read it.

For example, I once brought from Stonehenge a tiny fragment of stone, not larger than a pin's head, and on putting this into an envelope and handing it to a psychometer who had no idea what it was, she at once began to describe that wonderful ruin and the desolate country surrounding it, and then went on to picture vividly what were evidently scenes from its early history, showing that that infinitesimal fragment had been sufficient to put her into communication with the records connected with the spot from which it came. The scenes through which we pass in the course of our life seem to act in the same manner upon the cells of our brain as did the history of Stonehenge upon that particle of stone: they establish a connection with those cells by means of which our mind is put *en rapport* with that particular portion of the records, and so we "remember" what we have seen.

Even a trained clairvoyant needs some link to enable him to find the record of an event of which he has no previous knowledge. If, for example, he wished to observe the landing of Julius Cæsar on the shores of England, there are several ways in which he might approach the subject. If he happened to have visited the scene of the occurrence, the simplest way would probably be to call up the image of that spot, and then run back through its records until he reached the period desired. If he had not seen the place, he might run back in time to the date of the event, and then search the Channel for a fleet of Roman galleys; or he might examine the records of Roman life at about that period, where he would have no difficulty in identifying so prominent a figure as Cæsar, or in tracing him when found through all his Gallic wars until he set his foot upon British land.

People often enquire as to the aspect of these records—whether they appear near or far away from the eye, whether the figures in them are large or small, whether the pictures follow one another as in a panorama or melt into one another like dissolving views, and so on. One can only reply that their appearance varies to a certain extent according to the conditions under which they are seen. Upon the astral plane the reflection is most often a simple picture, though occasionally the figures seen would be endowed with motion; in this latter case, instead of a mere snapshot a rather longer and more perfect reflection has taken place.

On the mental plane they have two widely different aspects. When the visitor to that plane is not thinking specially of them in any way, the records simply form a background to whatever is going on, just as the reflections in a pier-glass at the end of a room might form a background to the life of the people in it. It must always be borne in mind that under these conditions they are really merely reflections from the ceaseless activity of a great Consciousness upon a far higher plane, and have very much the appearance of an endless succession of the recently invented *cinematographe*, or living photographs. They do not melt into one another like dissolving views, nor do a series of ordinary pictures follow one another; but the action of the reflected figures constantly goes on, as though one were watching the actors on a distant stage.

But if the trained investigator turns his attention specially to any one scene, or wishes to call it up before him, an extraordinary change at once takes place, for this is the plane of thought, and to think of anything is to bring it instantaneously before you. For example, if a man wills to see the record of that event to which we before referred—the landing of Julius Cæsar—he finds himself in a moment not looking at any picture, but standing on the shore among the legionaries, with the whole scene being enacted around him, precisely in every respect as he would have seen it if he had stood there in the flesh on that autumn morning in the year 55 b.c. Since what he sees is but a reflection, the actors are of course entirely unconscious of him, nor can any effort of his change the course of their action in the smallest degree, except only that he can control the rate at which the drama shall pass before him—can have the events of a whole year rehearsed before his eyes in a single hour, or can at any moment stop the movement altogether, and hold any particular scene in view as a picture as long as he chooses.

In truth he observes not only what he would have seen if he had been there at the time in the flesh, but much more. He hears and understands all that the people say, and he is conscious of all their thoughts and motives; and one of the most interesting of the many possibilities which open up before one who has learnt to read the records is the study of the thought of ages long past—the thought of the cave-men and the lake-dwellers as well as that which ruled the mighty civilisations of Atlantis, of Egypt or Chaldæa. What splendid possibilities open up before the man who is in full possession of this power may easily be imagined. He has before him a field of historical research of most entrancing interest. Not only can he review at his leisure all history with which we are acquainted, correcting as he examines it the many errors and misconceptions which have crept into the accounts handed down to us; he can also range at will over the whole story of the world from its very beginning, watching the slow development of intellect in man, the descent of the Lords of the Flame, and the growth of the mighty civilisations which they founded.

Nor is his study confined to the progress of humanity alone; he has before him, as in a museum, all the strange animal and vegetable forms which occupied the stage in days when the world was young; he can follow all the wonderful geological changes which have taken place, and watch the course of the great cataclysms which have altered the whole face of the earth again and again.

In one especial case an even closer sympathy with the past is possible to the reader of the records. If in the course of his enquiries he has to look upon some scene in which he himself has in a former birth taken part, he may deal with it in two ways; he can either regard it in the usual manner as a spectator (though always, be it remembered, as a spectator whose insight and sympathy are perfect) or he may once more identify himself with that long-dead personality of his—may throw himself back for the time into that life of long ago, and absolutely experience over again the thoughts and the emotions, the pleasures and the pains of a prehistoric past. No wilder and more vivid adventures can be conceived than some of those through which he thus may pass; yet through it all he must never lose hold of the consciousness of his own individuality—must retain the power to return at will to his present personality.

It is often asked how it is possible for an investigator accurately to determine the date of any picture from the far-distant past which he disinters from the records. The fact is that it is sometimes rather tedious work to find an exact date, but the thing can usually be done if it is worth while to spend the time and trouble over it. If we are dealing with Greek or Roman times the simplest method is usually to look into the mind of the most intelligent person present in the picture, and see what date he supposes it to be; or the investigator might watch him writing a letter or other document and observe what date, if any, was included in what was written. When once the Roman or Greek date is thus obtained, to reduce it to our own system of chronology is merely a matter of calculation.

Another way which is frequently adopted is to turn from the scene under examination to a contemporary picture in some great and well-known city such as Rome, and note what monarch is reigning there, or who are the consuls for the year; and when such data are discovered a glance at any good history will give the rest. Sometimes a date can be obtained by examining some public proclamation or some legal document; in fact in the times of which we are speaking the difficulty is easily surmounted.

The matter is by no means so simple, however, when we come to deal with periods much earlier than this—with a scene from early Egypt, Chaldæa, or China, or to go further back still, from Atlantis itself or any of its numerous colonies. A date can still be obtained easily enough from the mind of any educated man, but there is no longer any means of relating it to our own system of dates, since the man will be reckoning by eras of which we know nothing, or by the reigns of kings whose history is lost in the night of time.

Our methods, nevertheless, are not yet exhausted. It must be remembered that it is possible for the investigator to pass the records before him at any speed that he may desire—at the rate of a year in a second if he will, or even very much faster still. Now there are one or two events in ancient history whose dates have already been accurately fixed—as, for example, the sinking of Poseidonis in the year 9564 B.C. It is therefore obvious that if from the general appearance of the surroundings it seems probable that a picture seen is within measurable distance of one of these events, it can be related to that event by the simple process of running through the record rapidly, and counting the years between the two as they pass.

Still, if those years ran into thousands, as they might sometimes do, this plan would be insufferably tedious. In that case we are driven back upon the astronomical method. In consequence of the movement which is commonly called the precession of the equinoxes, though it might more accurately be described as a kind of second rotation of the earth, the angle between the equator and the ecliptic steadily but very slowly varies. Thus, after long intervals of time we find the pole of the earth no longer pointing towards the same spot in the apparent sphere of the heavens, or in other words, our pole-star is not, as at present, α Ursæ Minoris, but some other celestial body; and from this position of the pole of the earth, which can easily be ascertained by careful observation of the night-sky of the picture under consideration, an approximate date can be calculated without difficulty.

In estimating the date of occurrences which took place millions of years ago in earlier races, the period of a secondary rotation (or the precession of the equinoxes) is frequently used as a unit, but of course absolute accuracy is not usually required in such cases, round numbers being sufficient for all practical purposes in dealing with epochs so remote.

The accurate reading of the records, whether of one's own past lives or those of others, must not, however, be thought of as an achievement possible to anyone without careful previous training. As has been already remarked, though occasional reflections may be had upon the astral plane, the power to use the mental sense is necessary before any reliable reading can be done. Indeed, to minimize the possibility of error, that sense ought to be fully at the command of the investigator while awake in the physical body; and to acquire that faculty needs years of ceaseless labour and rigid self-discipline.

Many people seem to expect that as soon as they have signed their application and joined the Theosophical Society they will at once remember at least three or four of their past births; indeed, some of them promptly begin to imagine recollections and declare that in their last incarnation they were Mary Queen of Scots, Cleopatra, or Julius Cæsar! Of course such extravagant claims simply bring discredit upon those who are so foolish as to make them but unfortunately some of that discredit is liable to be reflected, however unjustly, upon the Society to which they belong, so that a man who feels seething within him the conviction that he was Homer or Shakespeare would do well to pause and apply commonsense tests on the physical plane before publishing the news to the world.

It is quite true that some people have had glimpses of scenes from their past lives in dreams, but naturally these are usually fragmentary and unreliable. I had myself in earlier life an experience of this nature. Among my dreams I found that one was constantly recurring—a dream of a house with a portico over-looking a beautiful bay, not far from a hill on the top of which rose a graceful building. I knew that house perfectly, and was as familiar with the position of its rooms and the view from its door as I was with those of my home, in this present life. In those days I knew nothing about reincarnation, so that it seemed to me simply a curious coincidence that this dream should repeat itself so often; and it was not until some time after I had joined the Society that, when one who knew was showing me some pictures of my last incarnation, I discovered that this persistent dream had been in reality a partial recollection, and that the house which I knew so well was the one in which I was born more than two thousand years ago.

But although there are several cases on record in which some well-remembered scene has thus come through from one life to another, a considerable development of occult faculty is necessary before an investigator can definitely trace a line of incarnations, whether they be his own or another man's. This will be obvious if we remember the conditions of the problem which has to be worked out. To follow a person from this life to the one preceding it, it is necessary first of all to trace his present life backwards to his birth and then to follow up in reverse order the stages by which the Ego descended into incarnation.

This will obviously take us back eventually to the condition of the Ego upon the higher levels of the mental plane; so it will be seen that to perform this task effectually the investigator must be able to use the sense corresponding to that exalted level while awake in his physical body—in other words, his consciousness must be centred in the reincarnating Ego itself, and no longer in the lower personality. In that case, the memory of the Ego being aroused, his own past incarnations will be spread out before him like an open book, and he would be able, if he wished, to examine the conditions of another Ego upon that level and trace him backwards through the lower mental and astral lives which led up to it, until he came to the last physical death of that Ego, and through it to his previous life.

There is no way but this in which the chain of lives can be followed through with absolute certainty: and consequently we may at once put aside as conscious or unconscious impostors those people who advertise that they are able to trace out anyone's past incarnations for so many shillings a head. Needless to say, the true occultist does not advertise, and never under any circumstances accepts money for any exhibition of his powers.

Assuredly the student who wishes to acquire the power of following up a line of incarnations can do so only by learning from a qualified teacher how the work is to be done. There have been those who persistently asserted that it was only necessary for a man to feel good and devotional and "brotherly," and all the wisdom of the ages would immediately flow in upon him; but a little commonsense will at once expose the absurdity of such a position. However good a child may be, if he wants to know the multiplication table he must set to work and learn it; and the case is precisely similar with the capacity to use spiritual faculties. The faculties themselves will no doubt manifest as the man evolves, but he can learn how to use them reliably and to the best advantage only by steady hard work and persevering effort.

Take the case of those who wish to help others while on the astral plane during sleep; it is obvious that the more knowledge they possess here, the more valuable will their services be on that higher plane. For example, the knowledge of languages would be useful to them, for though on the mental plane men can communicate directly by thought-transference, whatever their languages may be, on the astral plane this is not so, and a thought must be definitely formulated in words before it is comprehensible. If, therefore, you wish to help a man on that plane, you must have some language in common by means of which you can communicate with him, and consequently the more languages you know the more widely useful you will be. In fact there is perhaps no kind of knowledge for which a use cannot be found in the work of the occultist.

It would be well for all students to bear in mind that occultism is the apotheosis of commonsense, and that every vision which comes to them is not necessarily a picture from the âkâshic records, nor every experience a revelation from on high. It is better far to err on the side of healthy scepticism than of over-credulity; and it is an admirable rule never to hunt about for an occult explanation of anything when a plain and obvious physical one is available. Our duty is to endeavour to keep our balance always, and never to lose our self-control, but to take a reasonable, commonsense view of whatever may happen to us; so shall we be better Theosophists, wiser occultists, and more useful helpers than we have ever been before.

As usual, we find examples of all degrees of the power to see into this memory of nature, from the trained man who can consult the record for himself at will, down to the person who gets nothing but occasional vague glimpses, or has even perhaps had only one such glimpse. But even the man who possesses this faculty only partially and occasionally still finds it of the deepest interest. The psychometer, who needs an object physically connected with the past in order to bring it all into life again around him, and the crystal-gazer who can sometimes direct his less certain astral telescope to some historic scene of long ago, may both derive the greatest enjoyment from the exercise of their respective gifts, even though they may not always understand exactly how their results are produced, and may not have them fully under control under all circumstances.

In many cases of the lower manifestations of these powers we find that they are exercised unconsciously; many a crystal-gazer watches scenes from the past without being able to distinguish them from visions of the present, and many a vaguely-psychic person finds pictures constantly arising before his eyes without ever realizing that he is in effect psychometrizing the various objects around him as he happens to touch them or stand near them.

An interesting variant of this class of psychics is the man who is able to psychometrize persons only, and not inanimate objects as is more usual. In most cases this faculty shows itself erratically, so that such a psychic will, when introduced to a stranger, often see in a flash some prominent event in that stranger's earlier life, but on other similar occasions will receive no special impression. More rarely we meet with someone who gets detailed visions of the past life of everyone whom he encounters. Perhaps one of the best examples of this class was the German writer Zschokke, who describes in his autobiography this extraordinary power of which he found himself possessed. He says:—

"It has happened to me occasionally at the first meeting with a total stranger, when I have been listening in silence to his conversation, that his past life up to the present moment, with many minute circumstances belonging to one or other particular scene in it, has come across me like a dream, but distinctly, entirely involuntarily and unsought, occupying in duration a few minutes.

"For a long time I was disposed to consider these fleeting visions as a trick of the fancy— the more so as my dream-vision displayed to me the dress and movements of the actors, the appearance of the room, the furniture, and other accidents of the scene; till on one occasion, in a gamesome mood, I narrated to my family the secret history of a sempstress who had just before quitted the room. I had never seen the person before. Nevertheless the hearers were astonished, and laughed and would not be persuaded but that I had a previous acquaintance with the former life of the person, inasmuch as what I had stated was perfectly true.

"I was not less astonished to find that my dream-vision agreed with reality. I then gave more attention to the subject, and as often as propriety allowed of it, I related to those whose lives had so passed before me the substance of my dream-vision, to obtain from them its contradiction or confirmation. On every occasion its confirmation followed, not without amazement on the part of those who gave it.

"On a certain fair-day I went into the town of Waldshut accompanied by two young foresters, who are still alive. It was evening, and, tired with our walk, we went into an inn called the 'Vine.' We took our supper with a numerous company at the public table, when it happened that they made themselves merry over the peculiarities and simplicity of the Swiss in connection with the belief in mesmerism, Lavater's physiognomical system and the like. One of my companions, whose national pride was touched by their raillery, begged me to make some reply, particularly in answer to a young man of superior appearance who sat opposite, and had indulged in unrestrained ridicule.

"It happened that the events of this person's life had just previously passed before my mind. I turned to him with the question whether he would reply to me with truth and candour if I narrated to him the most secret passages of his history, he being as little known to me as I to him? That would, I suggested, go something beyond Lavater's physiognomical skill. He promised if I told the truth to admit it openly. Then I narrated the events with which my dream-vision had furnished me, and the table learnt the history of the young tradesman's life, of his school years, his peccadilloes, and, finally, of a little act of roguery committed by him on the strong-box of his employer. I described the uninhabited room with its white walls, where to the right of the brown door there had stood upon the table the small black money-chest, etc. The man, much struck, admitted the correctness of each circumstance—even, which I could not expect, of the last."

And after narrating this incident, the worthy Zschokke calmly goes on to wonder whether perhaps after all this remarkable power, which he had so often displayed, might not really have been always the result of mere chance coincidence!

Comparatively few accounts of persons possessing this faculty of looking back into the past are to be found in the literature of the subject, and it might therefore be supposed to be much less common than prevision. I suspect, however, that the truth is rather that it is much less commonly recognized. As I said before, it may very easily happen that a person may see a picture of the past without recognizing it as such, unless there happens to be in it something which attracts special attention, such as a figure in armour or in antique costume. A prevision also might not always be recognized as such at the time; but the occurrence of the event foreseen recalls it vividly at the same time that it manifests its nature, so that it is unlikely to be overlooked. It is probable, therefore, that occasional glimpses of these astral reflections of the âkâshic records are commoner than the published accounts would lead us to believe.

CHAPTER VIII.

CLAIRVOYANCE IN TIME: THE FUTURE.

EVEN if, in a dim sort of way, we feel ourselves able to grasp the idea that the whole of the past may be simultaneously and actively present in a sufficiently exalted consciousness, we are confronted by a far greater difficulty when we endeavour to realize how all the future may also be comprehended in that consciousness. If we could believe in the Mohammedan doctrine of kismet, or the Calvinistic theory of predestination, the conception would be easy enough, but knowing as we do that both these are grotesque distortions of the truth, we must look round for a more acceptable hypothesis.

There may still be some people who deny the possibility of prevision, but such denial simply shows their ignorance of the evidence on the subject. The large number of authenticated cases leaves no room for doubt as to the fact, but many of them are of such a nature as to render a reasonable explanation by no means easy to find. It is evident that the Ego possesses a certain amount of previsional faculty, and if the events foreseen were always of great importance, one might suppose that an extraordinary stimulus had enabled him for that occasion only to make a clear impression of what he saw upon his lower personality. No doubt that is the explanation of many of the cases in which death or grave disaster is foreseen, but there are a large number of instances on record to which it does not seem to apply, since the events foretold are frequently exceedingly trivial and unimportant.

A well-known story of second-sight in Scotland will illustrate what I mean. A man who had no belief in the occult was forewarned by a Highland seer of the approaching death of a neighbour. The prophecy was given with considerable wealth of detail, including a full description of the funeral, with the names of the four pall-bearers and others who would be present. The auditor seems to have laughed at the whole story and promptly forgotten it, but the death of his neighbour at the time foretold recalled the warning to his mind, and he determined to falsify part of the prediction at any rate by being one of the pall-bearers himself. He succeeded in getting matters arranged as he wished, but just as the funeral was about to start he was called away from his post by some small matter which detained him only a minute or two. As he came hurrying back he saw with surprise that the procession had started without him, and that the prediction had been exactly fulfilled, for the four pall-bearers were those who had been indicated in the vision.

Now here is a very trifling matter, which could have been of no possible importance to anybody, definitely foreseen months beforehand; and although a man makes a determined effort to alter the arrangement indicated he fails entirely to affect it in the least. Certainly this looks very much like predestination, even down to the smallest detail, and it is only when we examine this question from higher planes that we are able to see our way to escape that theory. Of course, as I said before about another branch of the subject, a full explanation eludes us as yet, and obviously must do so until our knowledge is infinitely greater than it is now; the most that we can hope to do for the present is to indicate the line along which an explanation may be found.

There is no doubt whatever that, just as what is happening now is the result of causes set in motion in the past, so what will happen in the future will be the result of causes already in operation. Even down here we can calculate that if certain actions are performed certain results will follow, but our reckoning is constantly liable to be disturbed by the interference of factors which we have not been able to take into account. But if we raise our consciousness to the mental plane we can see very much farther into the results of our actions.

We can trace, for example, the effect of a casual word, not only upon the person to whom it was addressed, but through him on many others as it is passed on in widening circles, until it seems to have affected the whole country; and one glimpse of such a vision is far more efficient than any number of moral precepts in impressing upon us the necessity of extreme circumspection in thought, word, and deed. Not only can we from that plane see thus fully the result of every action, but we can also see where and in what way the results of other actions apparently quite unconnected with it will interfere with and modify it. In fact, it may be said that the results of all causes at present in action are clearly visible—that the future, as it would be if no entirely new causes should arise, lies open before our gaze.

New causes of course do arise, because man's will is free; but in the case of all ordinary people the use which they will make of their freedom can be calculated beforehand with considerable accuracy. The average man has so little real will that he is very much the creature of circumstances; his action in previous lives places him amid certain surroundings, and their influence upon him is so very much the most important factor in his life-story that his future course may be predicted with almost mathematical certainty. With the developed man the case is different; for him also the main events of life are arranged by his past actions, but the way in which he will allow them to affect him, the methods by which he will deal with them and perhaps triumph over them—these are all his own, and they cannot be foreseen even on the mental plane except as probabilities.

Looking down on man's life in this way from above, it seems as though his free will could be exercised only at certain crises in his career. He arrives at a point in his life where there are obviously two or three alternative courses open before him; he is absolutely free to choose which of them he pleases, and although some one who knew his nature thoroughly well might feel almost certain what his choice would be, such knowledge on his friend's part is in no sense a compelling force.

But when he *has* chosen, he has to go through with it and take the consequences; having entered upon a particular path he may, in many cases, be forced to go on for a very long way before he has any opportunity to turn aside. His position is somewhat like that of the driver of a train; when he comes to a junction he may have the points set either this way or that, and so can pass on to whichever line he pleases, but when he *has* passed on to one of them he is compelled to run on along the line which he has selected until he reaches another set of points, where again an opportunity of choice is offered to him.

Now, in looking down from the mental plane, these points of new departure would be clearly visible, and all the results of each choice would lie open before us, certain to be worked out even to the smallest detail. The only point which would remain uncertain would be the all-important one as to which choice the man would make. We should, in fact, have not one but several futures mapped out before our eyes, without necessarily being able to determine which of them would materialize itself into accomplished fact. In most instances we should see so strong a probability that we should not hesitate to come to a decision, but the case which I have described is certainly theoretically possible. Still, even this much knowledge would enable us to do with safety a good deal of prediction; and it is not difficult for us to imagine that a far higher power than ours might always be able to foresee which way every choice would go, and consequently to prophesy with absolute certainty.

On the buddhic plane, however, no such elaborate process of conscious calculation is necessary, for, as I said before, in some manner which down here is totally inexplicable, the past, the present, and the future, are there all existing simultaneously. One can only accept this fact, for its cause lies in the faculty of the plane, and the way in which this higher faculty works is naturally quite incomprehensible to the physical brain. Yet now and then one may meet with a hint that seems to bring us a trifle nearer to a dim possibility of comprehension. One such hint was given by Dr. Oliver Lodge in his address to the British Association at Cardiff. He said:

"A luminous and helpful idea is that time is but a relative mode of regarding things; we progress through phenomena at a certain definite pace, and this subjective advance we interpret in an objective manner, as if events moved necessarily in this order and at this precise rate. But that may be only one mode of regarding them. The events may be in some sense in existence always, both past and future, and it may be we who are arriving at them, not they which are happening. The analogy of a traveller in a railway train is useful; if he could never leave the train nor alter its pace he would probably consider the landscapes as necessarily successive and be unable to conceive their co-existence.... We perceive, therefore, a possible fourth dimensional aspect about time, the inexorableness of whose flow may be a natural part or our present limitations. And if we once grasp the idea that past and future may be actually existing, we can recognize that they may have a controlling influence on all present action, and the two together may constitute the 'higher plane' or totality of things after which, as it seems to me, we are impelled to seek, in connection with the directing of form or determinism, and the action of living beings consciously directed to a definite and preconceived end."

Time is not in reality the fourth dimension at all; yet to look at it for the moment from that point of view is some slight help towards grasping the ungraspable. Suppose that we hold a wooden cone at right angles to a sheet of paper, and slowly push it through it point first. A microbe living on the surface of that sheet of paper, and having no power of conceiving anything outside of that surface, could not only never see the cone as a whole, but he could form no sort of conception of such a body at all. All that he would see would be the sudden appearance of a tiny circle, which would gradually and mysteriously grow larger and larger until it vanished from his world as suddenly and incomprehensibly as it had come into it.

Thus, what were in reality a series of sections of the cone would appear to him to be successive stages in the life of a circle, and it would be impossible for him to grasp the idea that these successive stages could be seen simultaneously. Yet it is, of course, easy enough for us, looking down upon the transaction from another dimension, to see that the microbe is simply under a delusion arising from its own limitations, and that the cone exists as a whole all the while. Our own delusion as to past, present, and future is possibly not dissimilar, and the view that is gained of any sequence of events from the buddhic plane corresponds to the view of the cone as a whole. Naturally, any attempt to work out this suggestion lands us in a series of startling paradoxes; but the fact remains a fact, nevertheless, and the time will come when it will be clear as noonday to our comprehension.

When the pupil's consciousness is fully developed upon the buddhic plane, therefore, perfect prevision is possible to him, though he may not—nay, he certainly will not—be able to bring the whole result of his sight through fully and in order into this light. Still, a great deal of clear foresight is obviously within his power whenever he likes to exercise it; and even when he is not exercising it, frequent flashes of fore-knowledge come through into his ordinary life, so that he often has an instantaneous intuition as to how things will turn out even before their inception.

Short of this perfect prevision we find, as in the previous cases, that all degrees of this type of clairvoyance exist, from the occasional vague premonitions which cannot in any true sense be called sight at all, up to frequent and fairly complete second-sight. The faculty to which this latter somewhat misleading name has been given is an extremely interesting one, and would well repay more careful and systematic study than has ever hitherto been given to it.

It is best known to us as a not infrequent possession of the Scottish Highlanders, though it is by no means confined to them. Occasional instances of it have appeared in almost every nation, but it has always been commonest among mountaineers and men of lonely life. With us in England it is often spoken of as though it were the exclusive appanage of the Celtic race, but in reality it has appeared among similarly situated peoples the world over. It is stated, for example, to be very common among the Westphalian peasantry.

Sometimes the second-sight consists of a picture clearly foreshowing some coming event; more frequently, perhaps, the glimpse of the future is given by some symbolical appearance. It is noteworthy that the events foreseen are invariably unpleasant ones—death being the commonest of all; I do not recollect a single instance in which the second-sight has shown anything which was not of the most gloomy nature. It has a ghastly symbolism which is all its own—a symbolism of shrouds and corpse-candles, and other funereal horrors. In some cases it appears to be to a certain extent dependent on locality, for it is stated that inhabitants of the Isle of Skye who possess the faculty often lose it when they leave the island, even though it be only to cross to the mainland. The gift of such sight is sometimes hereditary in a family for generations, but this is not an invariable rule, for it often appears sporadically in one member of a family otherwise free from its lugubrious influence.

An example in which an accurate vision of a coming event was seen some months beforehand by second-sight has already been given. Here is another and perhaps a more striking one, which I give exactly as it was related to me by one of the actors in the scene.

"We plunged into the jungle, and had walked on for about an hour without much success, when Cameron, who happened to be next to me, stopped suddenly, turned pale as death, and, pointing straight before him, cried in accents of horror:

"'See! see! merciful heaven, look there!'

"'Where? what? what is it?' we all shouted confusedly, as we rushed up to him and looked round in expectation of encountering a tiger—a cobra—we hardly knew what, but assuredly something terrible, since it had been sufficient to cause such evident emotion in our usually self-contained comrade. But neither tiger nor cobra was visible—nothing but Cameron pointing with ghastly, haggard face and starting eyeballs at something we could not see.

"'Cameron! Cameron' cried I, seizing his arm, "'for heaven's sake, speak! What is the matter?'

"Scarcely were the words out of my mouth when a low, but very peculiar sound struck on my ear, and Cameron, dropping his pointing hand, said in a hoarse, strained voice, 'There! you heard it? Thank God it's over' and fell to the ground insensible.

"There was a momentary confusion while we unfastened his collar, and I dashed in his face some water which I fortunately had in my flask, while another tried to pour brandy between his clenched teeth; and under cover of it I whispered to the man next to me (one of our greatest sceptics, by the way), 'Beauchamp, did *you* hear anything?'

"'Why, yes,' he replied, a curious sound, very; a sort of crash or rattle far away in the distance, yet very distinct; if the thing were not utterly impossible, I could have sworn it was the rattle of musketry.'

"'Just my impression,' murmured I; 'but hush! he is recovering.'

"In a minute or two he was able to speak feebly, and began to thank us and apologize for giving trouble; and soon he sat up, leaning against a tree, and in a firm, though still low voice said:

"'My dear friends, I feel I owe you an explanation of my extraordinary behaviour. It is an explanation that I would fain avoid giving; but it must come some time, and so may as well be given now. You may perhaps have noticed that when during our voyage you all joined in scoffing at dreams, portents and visions, I invariably avoided giving any opinion on the subject. I did so because, while I had no desire to court ridicule or provoke discussion, I was unable to agree with you, knowing only too well from my own dread experience that the world which men agree to call that of the supernatural is just as real as—nay, perhaps, even far more real than—this world we see about us. In other words, I, like many of my countrymen, am cursed with the gift of second-sight—that awful faculty which foretells in vision calamities that are shortly to occur.

"'Such a vision I had just now, and its exceptional horror moved me as you have seen. I saw before me a corpse—not that of one who has died a peaceful natural death, but that of the victim of some terrible accident; a ghastly, shapeless mass, with a face swollen, crushed, unrecognizable. I saw this dreadful object placed in a coffin, and the funeral service performed over it. I saw the burial-ground, I saw the clergyman: and though I had never seen either before, I can picture both perfectly in my mind's eye now; I saw you, myself, Beauchamp, all of us and many more, standing round as mourners; I saw the soldiers raise their muskets after the service was over; I heard the volley they fired—and then I knew no more.'

"As he spoke of that volley of musketry I glanced across with a shudder at Beauchamp, and the look of stony horror on that handsome sceptic's face was not to be forgotten."

This is only one incident (and by no means the principal one) in a very remarkable story of psychic experience, but as for the moment we are concerned merely with the example of second-sight which it gives us, I need only say that later in the day the party of young soldiers discovered the body of their commanding officer in the terrible condition so graphically described by Mr. Cameron. The narrative continues:

"When, on the following evening, we arrived at our destination, and our melancholy deposition had been taken down by the proper authorities, Cameron and I went out for a quiet walk, to endeavour with the assistance of the soothing influence of nature to shake off something of the gloom which paralyzed our spirits. Suddenly he clutched my arm, and, pointing through some rude railings, said in a trembling voice, 'Yes, there it is! that is the burial-ground I saw yesterday.' And when later on we were introduced to the chaplain of the post, I noticed, though my friends did not, the irrepressible shudder with which Cameron took his hand, and I knew that he had recognized the clergyman of his vision."

As for the occult rationale of all this, I presume Mr. Cameron's vision was a pure case of second-sight, and if so the fact that the two men who were evidently nearest to him (certainly one—probably both—actually touching him) participated in it to the limited extent of hearing the concluding volley, while the others who were not so close did not, would show that the intensity with which the vision impressed itself upon the seer occasioned vibrations in his mind-body which were communicated to those of the persons in contact with him, as in ordinary thought-transference. Anyone who wishes to read the rest of the story will find it in the pages of *Lucifer*, vol. xx., p. 457.

Scores of examples of similar nature to these might easily be collected. With regard to the symbolical variety of this sight, it is commonly stated among those who possess it that if on meeting a living person they see a phantom shroud wrapped around him, it is a sure prognostication of his death. The date of the approaching decease is indicated either by the extent to which the shroud covers the body, or by the time of day at which the vision is seen; for if it be in the early morning they say that the man will die during the same day, but if it be in the evening, then it will be only some time within a year.

Another variant (and a remarkable one) of the symbolical form of second-sight is that in which the headless apparition of the person whose death is foretold manifests itself to the seer. An example of that class is given in *Signs before Death* as having happened in the family of Dr. Ferrier, though in that case, if I recollect rightly, the vision did not occur until the time of the death, or very near it.

Turning from seers who are regularly in possession of a certain faculty, although its manifestations are only occasionally fully under their control, we are confronted by a large number of isolated instances of prevision in the case of people with whom it is not in any way a regular faculty. Perhaps the majority of these occur in dreams, although examples of the waking vision are by no means wanting. Sometimes the prevision refers to an event of distinct importance to the seer, and so justifies the action of the Ego in taking the trouble to impress it. In other cases, the event is one which is of no apparent importance, or is not in any way connected with the man to whom the vision comes. Sometimes it is clear that the intention of the Ego (or the communicating entity, whatever it may be) is to warn the lower self of the approach of some calamity, either in order that it may be prevented or, if that be not possible, that the shock may be minimized by preparation.

The event most frequently thus foreshadowed is, perhaps not unnaturally, death—sometimes the death of the seer himself, sometimes that of one dear to him. This type of prevision is so common in the literature of the subject, and its object is so obvious, that we need hardly cite examples of it; but one or two instances in which the prophetic sight, though clearly useful, was yet of a less sombre character, will prove not uninteresting to the reader.

The following is culled from that storehouse of the student of the uncanny, Mrs. Crowe's *Night Side of Nature*, p. 72.

"A few years ago Dr. Watson, now residing at Glasgow, dreamt that he received a summons to attend a patient at a place some miles from where he was living; that he started on horseback, and that as he was crossing a moor he saw a bull making furiously at him, whose horns he only escaped by taking refuge on a spot inaccessible to the animal, where he waited a long time till some people, observing his situation, came to his assistance and released him.

"Whilst at breakfast on the following morning the summons came, and smiling at the odd coincidence (as he thought it), he started on horseback. He was quite ignorant of the road he had to go, but by and by he arrived at the moor, which he recognised, and presently the bull appeared, coming full tilt towards him. But his dream had shown him the place of refuge, for which he instantly made, and there he spent three or four hours, besieged by the animal, till the country people set him free. Dr. Watson declares that but for the dream he should not have known in what direction to run for safety."

Another case, in which a much longer interval separated the warning and its fulfilment, is given by Dr. F. G. Lee, in *Glimpses of the Supernatural*, vol. i., p. 240.

"Mrs. Hannah Green, the housekeeper of a country family in Oxfordshire, dreamt one night that she had been left alone in the house upon a Sunday evening, and that hearing a knock at the door of the chief entrance she went to it and there found an ill-looking tramp armed with a bludgeon, who insisted on forcing himself into the house. She thought that she struggled for some time to prevent him so doing, but quite ineffectually, and that, being struck down by him and rendered insensible, he thereupon gained ingress to the mansion. On this she awoke.

"As nothing happened for a considerable period the circumstance of the dream was soon forgotten, and, as she herself asserts, had altogether passed away from her mind. However, seven years afterwards this same housekeeper was left with two other servants to take charge of an isolated mansion at Kensington (subsequently the town residence of the family), when on a certain Sunday evening, her fellow-servants having gone out and left her alone, she was suddenly startled by a loud knock at the front door.

"All of a sudden the remembrance of her former dream returned to her with singular vividness and remarkable force, and she felt her lonely isolation greatly. Accordingly, having at once lighted a lamp on the hall table—during which act the loud knock was repeated with vigour—she took the precaution to go up to a landing on the stair and throw up the window; and there to her intense terror she saw in the flesh the very man whom years previously she had seen in her dream, armed with the bludgeon and demanding an entrance.

"With great presence of mind she went down to the chief entrance, made that and other doors and windows more secure, and then rang the various bells of the house violently, and placed lights in the upper rooms. It was concluded that by these acts the intruder was scared away."

Evidently in this case also the dream was of practical use, as without it the worthy housekeeper would without doubt from sheer force of habit have opened the door in the ordinary way in answer to the knock.

It is not, however, only in dream that the Ego impresses his lower self with what he thinks it well for it to know. Many instances showing this might be taken from the books, but instead of quoting from them I will give a case related only a few weeks ago by a lady of my acquaintance—a case which, although not surrounded with any romantic incident, has at least the merit of being new.

My friend, then, has two quite young children, and a little while ago the elder of them caught (as was supposed) a bad cold, and suffered for some days from a complete stoppage in the upper part of the nose. The mother thought little of this, expecting it to pass off, until one day she suddenly saw before her in the air what she describes as a picture of a room, in the centre of which was a table on which her child was lying insensible or dead, with some people bending over her. The minutest details of the scene were clear to her, and she particularly noticed that the child wore a white night-dress, whereas she knew that all garments of that description possessed by her little daughter happened to be pink.

This vision impressed her considerably, and suggested to her for the first time that the child might be suffering from something more serious than a cold, so she carried her off to a hospital for examination. The surgeon who attended to her discovered the presence of a dangerous growth in the nose, which he pronounced must be removed. A few days later the child was taken to the hospital for the operation, and was put to bed. When the mother arrived at the hospital she found she had forgotten to bring one of the child's night-dresses, and so the nurses had to supply one, which was *white*. In this white dress the operation was performed on the girl the next day, in the room that her mother saw in her vision, every circumstance being exactly reproduced.

In all these cases the prevision achieved its result, but the books are full of stories of warnings neglected or scouted, and of the disaster that consequently followed. In some cases the information is given to someone who has practically no power to interfere in the matter, as in the historic instance when John Williams, a Cornish mine-manager, foresaw in the minutest detail, eight or nine days before it took place, the assassination of Mr. Spencer Perceval, the then Chancellor of the Exchequer, in the lobby of the House of Commons. Even in this case, however, it is just possible that something might have been done, for we read that Mr. Williams was so much impressed that he consulted his friends as to whether he ought not to go up to London to warn Mr. Perceval. Unfortunately they dissuaded him, and the assassination took place. It does not seem very probable that, even if he had gone up to town and related his story, much attention would have been paid to him, still there is just the possibility that some precautions might have been taken which would have prevented the murder.

There is little to show us what particular action on higher planes led to this curious prophetic vision. The parties were entirely unknown to one another, so that it was not caused by any close sympathy between them. If it was an attempt made by some helper to avert the threatened doom, it seems strange that no one who was sufficiently impressible could be found nearer than Cornwall. Perhaps Mr. Williams, when on the astral plane during sleep, somehow came across this reflection of the future, and being naturally horrified thereby, passed it on to his lower mind in the hope that somehow something might be done to prevent it; but it is impossible to diagnose the case with certainty without examining the âkâshic records to see what actually took place.

A typical instance of the absolutely purposeless foresight is that related by Mr. Stead, in his *Real Ghost Stories* (p. 83), of his friend Miss Freer, commonly known as Miss X. When staying at a country house this lady, being wide awake and fully conscious, once saw a dogcart drawn by a white horse standing at the hall door, with two strangers in it, one of whom got out of the cart and stood playing with a terrier. She noticed that he was wearing an ulster, and also particularly observed the fresh wheel-marks made by the cart on the gravel. Nevertheless there was no cart there at the time; but half an hour later two strangers *did* drive up in such an equipage, and every detail of the lady's vision was accurately fulfilled. Mr. Stead goes on to cite another instance of equally purposeless prevision where seven years separated the dream (for in this case it was a dream) and its fulfilment.

All these instances (and they are merely random selections from many hundreds) show that a certain amount of prevision is undoubtedly possible to the Ego, and such cases would evidently be much more frequent if it were not for the exceeding density and lack of response in the lower vehicles of the majority of what we call civilized mankind—qualities chiefly attributable to the gross practical materialism of the present age. I am not thinking of any profession of materialistic belief as common, but of the fact that in all practical affairs of daily life nearly everyone is guided solely by considerations of worldly interest in some shape or other.

In many cases the Ego himself may be an undeveloped one, and his prevision consequently very vague; in others he himself may see clearly, but may find his lower vehicles so unimpressible that all he can succeed in getting through into his physical brain may be an indefinite presage of coming disaster. Again, there are cases in which a premonition is not the work of the Ego at all, but of some outside entity, who for some reason takes a friendly interest in the person to whom the feeling comes. In the work which I quoted above, Mr. Stead tells us of the certainty which he felt many months beforehand that be would be left in charge of the *Pall Mall Gazette* though from an ordinary point of view nothing seemed less probable. Whether this fore-knowledge was the result of an impression made by his own Ego or of a friendly hint from someone else it is impossible to say without definite investigation, but his confidence in it was fully justified.

There is one more variety of clairvoyance in time which ought not to be left without mention. It is a comparatively rare one, but there are enough examples on record to claim our attention, though unfortunately the particulars given do not usually include those which we should require in order to be able to diagnose it with certainty. I refer to the cases in which spectral armies or phantom flocks of animals have been seen. In *The Night Side of Nature* (p. 462 *et seq.*) we have accounts of several such visions. We are there told how at Havarah Park, near Ripley, a body of soldiers in white uniform, amounting to several hundreds, was seen by reputable people to go through various evolutions and then vanish; and how some years earlier a similar visionary army was seen in the neighbourhood of Inverness by a respectable farmer and his son.

In this case also the number of troops was very great, and the spectators had not the slightest doubt at first that they were substantial forms of flesh and blood. They counted at least sixteen pairs of columns, and had abundance of time to observe every particular. The front ranks marched seven abreast, and were accompanied by a good many women and children, who were carrying tin cans and other implements of cookery. The men were clothed in red, and their arms shone brightly in the sun. In the midst of them was an animal, a deer or a horse, they could not distinguish which, that they were driving furiously forward with their bayonets.

The younger of the two men observed to the other that every now and then the rear ranks were obliged to run to overtake the van; and the elder one, who had been a soldier, remarked that that was always the case, and recommended him if he ever served to try to march in the front. There was only one mounted officer; he rode a grey dragoon horse, and wore a gold-laced hat and blue Hussar cloak, with wide open sleeves lined with red. The two spectators observed him so particularly that they said afterwards they should recognize him anywhere. They were, however, afraid of being ill-treated or forced to go along with the troops, whom they concluded to have come from Ireland, and landed at Kyntyre; and whilst they were climbing over a dyke to get out of their way, the whole thing vanished.

A phenomenon of the same sort was observed in the earlier part of this century at Paderborn in Westphalia, and seen by at least thirty people; but as, some years later, a review of twenty thousand men was held on the very same spot, it was concluded that the vision must have been some sort of second-sight—a faculty not uncommon in the district.

Such spectral hosts, however, are sometimes seen where an army of ordinary men could by no possibility have marched, either before or after. One of the most remarkable accounts of such apparitions is given by Miss Harriet Martineau, in her description of *The English Lakes*. She writes as follows:—

"This Souter or Soutra Fell is the mountain on which ghosts appeared in myriads, at intervals during ten years of the last century, presenting the same appearances to twenty-six chosen witnesses, and to all the inhabitants of all the cottages within view of the mountain, and for a space of two hours and a half at one time—the spectral show being closed by darkness! The mountain, be it remembered, is full of precipices, which defy all marching of bodies of men; and the north and west sides present a sheer perpendicular of 900 feet.

"On Midsummer Eve, 1735, a farm servant of Mr. Lancaster, half a mile from the mountain, saw the eastern side of its summit covered with troops, which pursued their onward march for an hour. They came, in distinct bodies, from an eminence on the north end, and disappeared in a niche in the summit. When the poor fellow told his tale, he was insulted on all hands, as original observers usually are when they see anything wonderful. Two years after, also on a Midsummer Eve, Mr. Lancaster saw some men there, apparently following their horses, as if they had returned from hunting. He thought nothing of this; but he happened to look up again ten minutes after, and saw the figures, now mounted, and followed by an interminable array of troops, five abreast, marching from the eminence and over the cleft as before. All the family saw this, and the manœuvres of the force, as each company was kept in order by a mounted officer, who galloped this way and that. As the shades of twilight came on, the discipline appeared to relax, and the troops intermingled, and rode at unequal paces, till all was lost in darkness. Now of course all the Lancasters were insulted, as their servant had been; but their justification was not long delayed.

"On the Midsummer Eve of the fearful 1745, twenty-six persons, expressly summoned by the family, saw all that had been seen before, and more. Carriages were now interspersed with the troops; and everybody knew that no carriages had been, or could be, on the summit of Souter Fell. The multitude was beyond imagination; for the troops filled a space of half a mile, and marched quickly till night hid them—still marching. There was nothing vaporous or indistinct about the appearance of these spectres. So real did they seem, that some of the people went up, the next morning, to look for the hoof-marks of the horses; and awful it was to them to find not one foot-print on heather or grass. The witnesses attested the whole story on oath before a magistrate; and fearful were the expectations held by the whole country-side about the coming events of the Scotch rebellion.

"It now comes out that two other persons had seen something of the sort in the interval—viz., in 1743—but had concealed it, to escape the insults to which their neighbours were subjected. Mr. Wren, of Wilton Hall, and his farm servant, saw, one summer evening, a man and a dog on the mountain, pursuing some horses along a place so steep that a horse could hardly by any possibility keep a footing on it. Their speed was prodigious, and their disappearance at the south end of the fell so rapid, that Mr. Wren and the servant went up, the next morning, to find the body of the man who must have been killed. Of man, horse, or dog, they found not a trace and they came down and held their tongues. When they did speak, they fared not much better for having twenty-six sworn comrades in their disgrace.

"As for the explanation, the editor of the *Lonsdale Magazine* declared (vol. ii., p. 313) that it was discovered that on the Midsummer Eve of 1745 the rebels were 'exercising on the western coast of Scotland, whose movements had been reflected by some transparent vapour, similar to the Fata Morgana.' This is not much in the way of explanation; but it is, as far as we know, all that can be had at present. These facts, however, brought out a good many more; as the spectral march of the same kind seen in Leicestershire in 1707, and the tradition of the tramp of armies over Helvellyn, on the eve of the battle of Marston Moor."

Other cases are cited in which flocks of spectral sheep have been seen on certain roads, and there are of course various German stories of phantom cavalcades of hunters and robbers.

Now in these cases, as so often happens in the investigation of occult phenomena, there are several possible causes, any one of which would be quite adequate to the production of the observed occurrences, but in the absence of fuller information it is hardly feasible to do more than guess as to which of these possible causes were in operation in any particular instance.

The explanation usually suggested (whenever the whole story is not ridiculed as a falsehood) is that what is seen is a reflection by mirage of the movements of a real body of troops, taking place at a considerable distance. I have myself seen the ordinary mirage on several occasions, and know something therefore of its wonderful powers of deception; but it seems to me that we should need some entirely new variety of mirage, quite different from that at present known to science, to account for these tales of phantom armies, some of which pass the spectator within a few yards.

First of all, they may be, as apparently in the Westphalian case above mentioned, simply instances of prevision on a gigantic scale—by whom arranged, and for what purpose, it is not easy to divine. Again, they may often belong to the past instead of the future, and be in fact the reflection of scenes from the âkâshic records—though here again the reason and method of such reflection is not obvious.

There are plenty of tribes of nature-spirits perfectly capable, if for any reason they wished to do so, of producing such appearances by their wonderful power of glamour (see *Theosophical Manual, No. V.*, p. 60), and such action would be quite in keeping with their delight in mystifying and impressing human beings. Or it may even sometimes be kindly intended by them as a warning to their friends of events that they know to be about to take place. It seems as though some explanation along these lines would be the most reasonable method of accounting for the extra-ordinary series of phenomena described by Miss Martineau—that is, if the stories told to her can be relied upon.

Another possibility is that in some cases what have been taken for soldiers were simply the nature-spirits themselves going through some of the ordered evolutions in which they take so much delight, though it must be admitted that these are rarely of a character which could be mistaken for military manœuvres except by the most ignorant.

The flocks of animals are probably in most instances mere records, but there are cases where they, like the "wild huntsmen" of German story, belong to an entirely different class of phenomena, which is altogether outside of our present subject. Students of the occult will be familiar with the fact that the circumstances surrounding any scene of intense terror or passion, such as an exceptionally horrible murder, are liable to be occasionally reproduced in a form which it needs a very slight development of psychic faculty to be able to see and it has sometimes happened that various animals formed part of such surroundings, and consequently they also are periodically reproduced by the action of the guilty conscience of the murderer (see *Manual V.*, p. 83).

Probably whatever foundation of fact underlies the various stories of spectral horsemen and hunting-troops may generally be referred to this category. This is also the explanation, evidently, of some of the visions of ghostly armies, such as that remarkable re-enactment of the battle of Edgehill which seems to have taken place at intervals for some months after the date of the real struggle, as testified by a justice of the peace, a clergyman, and other eye-witnesses, in a curious contemporary pamphlet entitled *Prodigious Noises of War and Battle, at Edgehill, near Keinton, in Northamptonshire*. According to the pamphlet this case was investigated at the time by some officers of the army, who clearly recognized many of the phantom figures that they saw. This looks decidedly like an instance of the terrible power of man's unrestrained passions to reproduce themselves, and to cause in some strange way a kind of materialization of their record.

In some cases it is clear that the flocks of animals seen have been simply hordes of unclean artificial elementals taking that form in order to feed upon the loathsome emanations of peculiarly horrible places, such as would be the site of a gallows. An instance of this kind is furnished by the celebrated "Gyb Ghosts," or ghosts of the gibbet, described in *More Glimpses of the World Unseen*, p. 109, as being repeatedly seen in the form of herds of misshapen swine-like creatures, rushing, rooting and fighting night after night on the site of that foul monument of crime. But these belong to the subject of apparitions rather than to that of clairvoyance.

CHAPTER IX.

METHODS OF DEVELOPMENT.

WHEN a man becomes convinced of the reality of the valuable power of clairvoyance, his first question usually is, "How can I develop in my own case this faculty which is said to be latent in everyone?"

Now the fact is that there are many methods by which it may be developed, but only one which can be at all safely recommended for general use—that of which we shall speak last of all. Among the less advanced nations of the world the clairvoyant state has been produced in various objectionable ways; among some of the non-Aryan tribes of India, by the use of intoxicating drugs or the inhaling of stupefying fumes; among the dervishes, by whirling in a mad dance of religious fervour until vertigo and insensibility supervene; among the followers of the abominable practices of the Voodoo cult, by frightful sacrifices and loathsome rites of black magic. Methods such as these are happily not in vogue in our own race, yet even among us large numbers of dabblers in this ancient art adopt some plan of self-hypnotization, such as the gazing at a bright spot or the repetition of some formula until a condition of semi-stupefaction is produced; while yet another school among them would endeavour to arrive at similar results by the use of some of the Indian systems of regulation of the breath.

All these methods are unequivocally to be condemned as quite unsafe for the practice of the ordinary man who has no idea of what he is doing—who is simply making vague experiments in an unknown world. Even the method of obtaining clairvoyance by allowing oneself to be mesmerized by another person is one from which I should myself shrink with the most decided distaste; and assuredly it should never be attempted except under conditions of absolute trust and affection between the magnetizer and the magnetized, and a perfection of purity in heart and soul, in mind and intention, such as is rarely to be seen among any but the greatest of saints.

Experiments in connection with the mesmeric trance are of the deepest interest, as offering (among other things) a possibility of proof of the fact of clairvoyance to the sceptic, yet except under such conditions as I have just mentioned—conditions, I quite admit, almost impossible to realize—I should never counsel anyone to submit himself as a subject for them.

Curative mesmerism (in which, without putting the patient into the trance state at all, an effort is made to relieve his pain, to remove his disease, or to pour vitality into him by magnetic passes) stands on an entirely different footing; and if the mesmerizer, even though quite untrained, is himself in good health and animated by pure intentions, no harm is likely to be done to the subject. In so extreme a case as that of a surgical operation, a man might reasonably submit himself even to the mesmeric trance, but it is certainly not a condition with which one ought lightly to experiment. Indeed, I should most strongly advise any one who did me the honour to ask for my opinion on the subject, not to attempt any kind of experimental investigation into what are still to him the abnormal forces of nature, until he has first of all read carefully everything that has been written on the subject, or—which is by far the best of all—until he is under the guidance of a qualified teacher.

But where, it will be said, is the qualified teacher to be found? Not, most assuredly, among any who advertise themselves as teachers, who offer to impart for so many guineas or dollars the sacred mysteries of the ages, or hold "developing circles" to which casual applicants are admitted at so much per head.

Much has been said in this treatise of the necessity for careful training—of the immense advantages of the trained over the untrained clairvoyant; but that again brings us back to the same question—where is this definite training to be had?

The answer is, that the training may be had precisely where it has always been to be found since the world's history began—at the hands of the Great White Brotherhood of Adepts, which stands now, as it has always stood, at the back of human evolution, guiding and helping it under the sway of the great cosmic laws which represent to us the Will of the Eternal.

But how, it may be asked, is access to be gained to them? How is the aspirant thirsting for knowledge to signify to them his wish for instruction?

Once more, by the time-honoured methods only. There is no new patent whereby a man can qualify himself without trouble to become a pupil in that School—no royal road to the learning which has to be acquired in it. At the present day, just as in the mists of antiquity, the man who wishes to attract their notice must enter upon the slow and toilsome path of self-development—must learn first of all to take himself in hand and make himself all that he ought to be. The steps of that path are no secret; I have given them in full detail in *Invisible Helpers*, so I need not repeat them here. But it is no easy road to follow, and yet sooner or later all must follow it, for the great law of evolution sweeps mankind slowly but resistlessly towards its goal.

From those who are pressing into this path the great Masters select their pupils, and it is only by qualifying himself to be taught that a man can put himself in the way of getting the teaching. Without that qualification, membership in any Lodge or Society, whether secret or otherwise, will not advance his object in the slightest degree. It is true, as we all know, that it was at the instance of some of these Masters that our Theosophical Society was founded, and that from its ranks some have been chosen to pass into closer relations with them. But that choice depends upon the earnestness of the candidate, not upon his mere membership of the Society or of any body within it.

That, then, is the only absolutely safe way of developing clairvoyance—to enter with all one's energy upon the path of moral and mental evolution, at one stage of which this and other of the higher faculties will spontaneously begin to show themselves. Yet there is one practice which is advised by all the religions alike—which if adopted carefully and reverently can do no harm to any human being, yet from which a very pure type of clairvoyance has sometimes been developed; and that is the practice of meditation.

Let a man choose a certain time every day—a time when he can rely upon being quiet and undisturbed, though preferably in the daytime rather than at night—and set himself at that time to keep his mind for a few minutes entirely free from all earthly thoughts of any kind whatever and, when that is achieved, to direct the whole force of his being towards the highest spiritual ideal that he happens to know. He will find that to gain such perfect control of thought is enormously more difficult than he supposes, but when he attains it it cannot but be in every way most beneficial to him, and as he grows more and more able to elevate and concentrate his thought, he may gradually find that new worlds are opening before his sight.

As a preliminary training towards the satisfactory achievement of such meditation, he will find it desirable to make a practice of concentration in the affairs of daily life—even in the smallest of them. If he writes a letter, let him think of nothing else but that letter until it is finished if he reads a book, let him see to it that his thought is never allowed to wander from his author's meaning. He must learn to hold his mind in check, and to be master of that also, as well as of his lower passions he must patiently labour to acquire absolute control of his thoughts, so that he will always know exactly what he is thinking about, and why—so that he can use his mind, and turn it or hold it still, as a practised swordsman turns his weapon where he will.

Yet after all, if those who so earnestly desire clairvoyance could possess it temporarily for a day or even an hour, it is far from certain that they would choose to retain the gift. True, it opens before them new worlds of study, new powers of usefulness, and for this latter reason most of us feel it worth while; but it should be remembered that for one whose duty still calls him to live in the world it is by no means an unmixed blessing. Upon one in whom that vision is opened the sorrow and the misery, the evil and the greed of the world press as an ever-present burden, until in the earlier days of his knowledge he often feels inclined to echo the passionate adjuration contained in those rolling lines of Schiller's:

> Dien Orakel zu verkünden, warum warfest du mich hin
> In die Stadt der ewig Blinden, mit dem aufgeschloss'nen Sinn?
> Frommt's, den Schleier aufzuheben, wo das nahe   Schreckniss droht?
> Nur der Irrthum ist das Leben; dieses Wissen ist der Tod.
> Nimm, O nimm die traur'ge Klarheit mir vom Aug' den blut'gen Schein!
> Schrecklich ist es deiner Wahrheit sterbliches Gefäss zu seyn!

which may perhaps be translated "Why hast thou cast me thus into the town of the ever-blind, to proclaim thine oracle by the opened sense? What profits it to lift the veil where the near darkness threatens? Only ignorance is life; this knowledge is death. Take back this sad clear-sightedness; take from mine eyes this cruel light! It is horrible to be the mortal channel of thy truth." And again later he cries, "Give me back my blindness, the happy darkness of my senses; take back thy dreadful gift!"

But this of course is a feeling which passes, for the higher sight soon shows the pupil something beyond the sorrow—soon bears in upon his soul the overwhelming certainty that, whatever appearances down here may seem to indicate, all things are without shadow of doubt working together for the eventual good of all. He reflects that the sin and the suffering are there, whether he is able to perceive them or not, and that when he can see them he is after all better able to give efficient help than he would be if he were working in the dark; and so by degrees he learns to bear his share of the heavy karma of the world.

Some misguided mortals there are who, having the good fortune to possess some slight touch of this higher power, are nevertheless so absolutely destitute of all right feeling in connection with it as to use it for the most sordid ends—actually even to advertise themselves as "test and business clairvoyants!" Needless to say, such use of the faculty is a mere prostitution and degradation of it, showing that its unfortunate possessor has somehow got hold of it before the moral side of his nature has been sufficiently developed to stand the strain which it imposes. A perception of the amount of evil karma that may be generated by such action in a very short time changes one's disgust into pity for the unhappy perpetrator of that sacrilegious folly.

It is sometimes objected that the possession of clairvoyance destroys all privacy, and confers a limit-less ability to explore the secrets of others. No doubt it does confer such an *ability*, but nevertheless the suggestion is an amusing one to anyone who knows anything practically about the matter. Such an objection may possibly be well-founded as regards the very limited powers of the "test and business clairvoyant," but the man who brings it forward against those who have had the faculty opened for them in the course of their instruction, and consequently possess it fully, is forgetting three fundamental facts: first, that it is quite inconceivable that anyone, having before him the splendid fields for investigation which true clairvoyance opens up, could ever have the slightest wish to pry into the trumpery little secrets of any individual man; secondly, that even if by some impossible chance our clairvoyant *had* such indecent curiosity about matters of petty gossip, there is, after all, such a thing as the honour of a gentleman, which, on that plane as on this, would of course prevent him from contemplating for an instant the idea of gratifying it; and thirdly, in case, by any unheard-of possibility, one might encounter some variety of low-class pitri with whom the above considerations would have no weight, full instructions are always given to every pupil, as soon as he develops any sign of faculty, as to the limitations which are placed upon its use.

Put briefly, these restrictions are that there shall be no prying, no selfish use of the power, and no displaying of phenomena. That is to say, that the same considerations which would govern the actions of a man of right feeling upon the physical plane are expected to apply upon the astral and mental planes also; that the pupil is never under any circumstances to use the power which his additional knowledge gives to him in order to promote his own worldly advantage, or indeed in connection with gain in any way; and that he is never to give what is called in spiritualistic circles "a test"—that is, to do anything which will incontestably prove to sceptics on the physical plane that he possesses what to them would appear to be an abnormal power.

With regard to this latter proviso people often say, "But why should he not? it would be so easy to confute and convince your sceptic, and it would do him good!" Such critics lose sight of the fact that, in the first place, none of those who know anything *want* to confute or convince sceptics, or trouble themselves in the slightest degree about the sceptic's attitude one way or the other; and in the second, they fail to understand how much better it is for that sceptic that he should gradually grow into an intellectual appreciation of the facts of nature, instead of being suddenly introduced to them by a knock-down blow, as it were. But the subject was fully considered many years ago in Mr. Sinnet's *Occult World*, and it is needless to repeat again the arguments there adduced.

It is very hard for some of our friends to realize that the silly gossip and idle curiosity which so entirely fill the lives of the brainless majority on earth can have no place in the more real life of the disciple; and so they sometimes enquire whether, even without any special wish to see, a clairvoyant might not casually observe some secret which another person was trying to keep, in the same way as one's glance might casually fall upon a sentence in someone else's letter which happened to be lying open upon the table. Of course he might, but what if he did? The man of honour would at once avert his eyes, in one case as in the other, and it would be as though he had not seen. If objectors could but grasp the idea that no pupil *cares* about other people's business, except when it comes within his province to try to help them, and that he has always a world of work of his own to attend to, they would not be so hopelessly far from understanding the facts of the wider life of the trained clairvoyant.

Even from the little that I have said with regard to the restrictions laid upon the pupil, it will be obvious that in very many cases he will know much more than he is at liberty to say. That is of course true in a far wider sense of the great Masters of Wisdom themselves, and that is why those who have the privilege of occasionally entering their presence pay so much respect to their lightest word even on subjects quite apart from the direct teaching. For the opinion of a Master, or even of one of his higher pupils, upon any subject is that of a man whose opportunity of judging accurately is out of all proportion to ours.

His position and his extended faculties are in reality the heritage of all mankind, and, far though we may now be from those grand powers, they will none the less certainly be ours one day. Yet how different a place will this old world be when humanity as a whole possesses the higher clairvoyance! Think what the difference will be to history when all can read the records; to science, when all the processes about which now men theorize can be watched through all their course; to medicine, when doctor and patient alike can see clearly and exactly all that is being done; to philosophy, when there is no longer any possibility of discussion as to its basis, because all alike can see a wider aspect of the truth; to labour, when all work will be joy, because every man will be put only to that which he can do best; to education, when the minds and hearts of the children are open to the teacher who is trying to form their character; to religion, when there is no longer any possibility of dispute as to its broad dogmas, since the truth about the states after death, and the Great Law that governs the world, will be patent to all eyes.

Above all, how far easier it will be then for the evolved men to help one another under those so much freer conditions! The possibilities that open before the mind are as glorious vistas stretching in all directions, so that our seventh round should indeed be a veritable golden age. Well for us that these grand faculties will not be possessed by all humanity until it has evolved to a far higher level in morality as well as in wisdom, else should we but repeat once more under still worse conditions the terrible downfall of the great Atlantean civilization, whose members failed to realize that increased power meant increased responsibility. Yet we ourselves were most of us among those very men let us hope that we have learnt wisdom by that failure, and that when the possibilities of the wider life open before us once more, this time we shall bear the trial better.

THE MONAD

FOREWORD

THE essays included in this book are all upon subjects which it is of the highest importance that our students should try to understand. They have appeared during the last seven years in our various magazines. I have been asked to put them all together in a permanent form convenient for reference. Hence this volume.

C. W. L.

CHAPTER I

THE MONAD

THE information available on the subject of the Monad is necessarily scanty. We are not at present in a position to supplement it to any great extent; but a statement of the case, as far as it is at present comprehended among us, may save students some misapprehensions, such as are often manifested in the questions sent in to us.

That many misconceptions should exist on such a subject is inevitable, because we are trying to understand with the physical brain what can by no possibility be expressed in terms intelligible to that brain. The Monad inhabits the second plane of our set of planes—that which used to be called the paranirvanic or the anupadaka. It is not easy to attach in the mind any definite meaning to the word plane or world at such an altitude as this, because any attempt even to symbolise the relation of planes or worlds to one another demands a stupendous effort of the imagination in a direction with which we are wholly unfamiliar.

Let us try to imagine what the consciousness of the Divine must be—the consciousness of the Solar Deity altogether outside any of the worlds or planes or levels which we ever conceived. We can only vaguely think of some sort of transcendent Consciousness for which space no longer exists, to which everything (at least in the Solar System) is simultaneously present, not only in its actual condition, but at every stage of its evolution from beginning to end. We must think of that Divine Consciousness as creating for Its use these worlds of various types of matter, and then voluntarily veiling Itself within that matter, and thereby greatly limiting Itself. By taking upon Itself a garment of the matter of even the highest of these worlds, It has clearly already imposed upon Itself a certain limitation; and, equally clearly, each additional garment assumed, as It involves Itself more and more deeply in matter, must increase the limitation.

One way of attempting to symbolise this is to try to think of it in connection with what we call dimensions of space. If we may suppose an infinite number of these dimensions, it may be suggested that each descent, from a higher level to a lower, removes the consciousness of one of these dimensions until, when we reach the mental plane or world, the power of observing but five of them is all that is left to us. The descent to the astral level takes away one more, and the further descent to the physical leaves us with the three which are familiar to us. In order even to get an idea of what this loss of additional dimensions means, we have to suppose the existence of a creature whose senses are capable of comprehending only two dimensions. Then we must reason in what respect the consciousness of that creature would differ from ours, and thus try to image to ourselves what it would mean to lose a dimension from our consciousness. Such an exercise of the imagination will speedily convince us that the two-dimensional creature could never obtain any adequate conception of our life at all; he could be conscious of it only in sections, and his idea of even those sections must be entirely misleading. This enables us to see how inadequate must be *our* conception even of the plane or world next above us; and we at once perceive the hopelessness of expecting fully to understand the Monad, which is raised by many of these planes or worlds above the point from which we are trying to regard it.

It may help us if we recall to our minds the method in which the Deity originally built these planes. We speak with all reverence in regard to His method, realising fully that we can at most comprehend only the minutest fragment of His work, and that even that fragment is seen by us from below, while He looks upon it from above. Yet we are justified in saying that He sends forth from Himself a wave of power, of influence of some sort, which moulds the primeval pre-existent matter into certain forms to which we give the name of atoms.

Into that world or plane or level, so made, comes a second life-wave of divine energy; to it those atoms already existing are objective, outside of itself, and it builds them into forms which it inhabits. Meantime the first down-flowing wave comes yet again, sweeping through that newly-formed plane or level, and makes yet another, a lower plane, with atoms a little larger and matter therefore a little denser—even though its density may as yet be far rarer than our finest conception of matter. Then into that second world comes the second outflowing, and again in that finds matter which to it is objective, and builds of that its forms. And so this process is repeated and the matter grows denser and denser with each world, until at last we reach this physical level; but it will help us if we bear in mind that at each of these levels the ensouling life of the second outpouring finds matter already vivified by the first outpouring, which it regards as objective, of which it builds the forms which it inhabits.

This process of ensouling forms built out of already vivified matter is continued all through the mineral, vegetable and animal kingdoms, but when we come to the moment of individualisation which divides the highest animal manifestation from the lowest human, a curious change takes place; that which has hitherto been the ensouling life becomes itself in turn the ensouled, for it builds itself into a form (symbolised as the cup, the Holy Grail) into which the ego enters, of which he takes possession. He absorbs into himself all the experiences which the matter of his causal body has had, so that nothing whatever is lost, and he carries these on with him through the ages of his existence. He continues the process of forming bodies on lower planes out of material ensouled by the first outpouring from the Third Aspect of the Deity; but he finally reaches a level in evolution in which the causal body is the lowest that he needs, and when this is attained we have the spectacle of the ego, which represents the third outpouring from the First Aspect of the Deity, inhabiting a body composed of matter ensouled by the second outpouring.

At a far later stage the earlier happening repeats itself once more, and the ego, who has ensouled so many forms during the whole of a chain-period, becomes himself the vehicle, and is ensouled in his turn by the now fully active and awakened Monad. Yet here, as before, nothing whatever is lost from the economy of nature. All the manifold experiences of the ego, all the splendid qualities developed in him, all these pass into the Monad himself and find there a vastly fuller realisation than even the ego could have given them.

Of the condition of consciousness of the Solar Deity outside the planes of His system, we can, form no true conception. He has been spoken of as the Divine Fire; and if for a moment we adopt that time-honoured symbolism, we may imagine that Sparks from that Fire fall into the matter of our planes—Sparks which are of the essence of that Fire, but are yet in appearance temporarily separated from it. The analogy cannot be pushed too far, because all sparks of which we know anything are thrown out from their parent fire and gradually fade and die; whereas these Sparks develop by slow evolution into Flames, and return to the Parent Fire. This development and this return are apparently the objects for which the Sparks come forth; and the process of the development is that which we are at the present moment concerned to try to understand.

It seems that the Spark, as such, cannot in its entirety veil itself beyond a certain extent; it cannot descend beyond what we call the second plane, and yet retain its unity. One difficulty with which we are confronted in trying to form any ideas upon this matter is that, as yet, none of us who investigate are able to raise our consciousness to this second plane; in the nomenclature recently adopted we give to it the name of monadic because it is the home of the Monad; but none of us have yet been able to realise that Monad in his own habitation, but only to see him when he has descended one stage to the plane or level or world below his own, in which he shows himself as the triple Spirit, which in our earlier books we call the Âtmâ in man. Even already he is incomprehensible, for he has three aspects which are quite distinct and apparently separate, and yet they are all fundamentally one and the same.

The Monad in his first aspect cannot (or at least does not) descend below that spiritual level; but in his second aspect he does descend into the matter of the next lower world (the intuitional), and when that aspect has drawn round itself the matter of that level we call it divine wisdom in man, or the intuition. Meanwhile, the Monad in his third aspect descends also to that intuitional plane and clothes itself in its matter, and adopts a form to which as yet no name has been attached in our literature. It then moves forward or downward one more stage, and clothes itself in the matter of the higher mental world, and then we call it the intellect in man. When that threefold manifestation on the three levels has thus developed itself, and shows itself as Spirit, intuition and intellect, we give to it the name of the ego, and that ego takes upon himself a vehicle built of the matter of the higher mental plane, to which we give the name of the causal body. This ego, so functioning in his causal body, has often been called the higher self, and sometimes also the soul.

We see the ego then to be a manifestation of the Monad on the higher mental plane; but we must understand that he is infinitely far from being a perfect manifestation. Each descent from plane to plane means much more than a mere veiling of the Spirit; it means also an actual diminution in the amount of Spirit expressed. To use terms denoting quantity in speaking of such matters is entirely incorrect and misleading; yet if an attempt is to be made to express these higher matters in human words at all, these incongruities cannot be wholly avoided; and the nearest that we can come, in the physical brain, to a conception of what happens when the Monad involves himself in matter of the spiritual plane, is to say that only part of him can possibly be shown there, and that even that part must be shown in three separate aspects, instead of in the glorious totality which he really is in his own world. So when the second aspect of the triple Spirit comes down a stage and manifests as intuition, it is not the whole of that aspect which so manifests, but only a fraction of it. So again when the third aspect descends two planes and manifests itself as intellect, it is only a fraction of a fraction of what the intellect-aspect of the Monad really is. Therefore the ego is not a veiled manifestation of the Monad, but a veiled representation of a minute portion of the Monad.

As above, so below. As the ego is to the Monad, so is the personality to the ego. So that, by the time we have reached the personality with which we have to deal in the physical world, the fractionisation has been carried so far that the part we are able to see bears no appreciable proportion to the reality of which it is nevertheless the only possible representation for us. Yet it is with and from this ridiculously inadequate fragment that we are endeavouring to comprehend the whole! Our difficulty in trying to understand the Monad is the same in kind, but much greater in degree, as that which we find when we try really to grasp the idea of the ego. In the earlier years of the Theosophical Society there were many discussions about the relations of the lower and the higher self. In those days we did not understand the doctrine even as well as we understand it now; we had not the grasp of it which longer study has given us. I am speaking of a group of students in Europe, who had behind them the Christian traditions, and the vague ideas which Christianity attaches to the word "soul".

The ordinary Christian by no means identifies himself with his "soul", but regards it as something attached to himself in some indefinite way-something for the saving of which he is responsible. Perhaps no ordinary man among the devotees of that religion attaches any very clear idea to the word, but he would probably describe it as the immortal part of him, though in ordinary language he talks of it as a possession, as something separate from him. In the *Magnificat*, the Blessed Virgin is made to say: "My soul doth magnify the Lord, and my spirit hath rejoiced in God my Saviour". She may here be drawing a distinction between the soul and the spirit, as St. Paul does; but she speaks of them both as possessions, not as the I. She does not say: "I as a soul magnify; I as a spirit rejoice". This may be merely a question of language; yet surely this loose language expresses an inaccurate and ill-defined idea. That theory was in the air all about us in Europe, and no doubt we were influenced by it, and at first to some extent we substituted the term "higher self" for "soul".

So we used such expressions as "looking up to the higher self", "listening to the promptings of the higher self", and so on. I remember that Mr. Sinnett used sometimes to speak a little disparagingly of the higher self, remarking that it ought to take more interest than it seemed to do in the unfortunate personality struggling on its behalf down here; and he used jokingly to suggest the formation of a society for the education of our higher selves. It was only gradually that we grew into the feeling that the higher self was *the man,* and that what we see down here is only a very small part of him. Only little by little did we learn that there is only one consciousness, and that the lower, though an imperfect representation of the higher, is in no way separate from it. We used to think of raising "ourselves" till we could unite "ourselves" with that glorified higher being, not realising that it was the higher that was the true self, and that to unite the higher to the lower really meant opening out the lower so that the higher might work in it and through it.

It takes time to become thoroughly permeated by Theosophical ideas. It is not merely reading the books, it is not merely hard study even, that makes us real Theosophists; we must allow time for the teaching to become part of ourselves. We may notice this constantly in the case of new members. People join us, people of keen intelligence, people of the deepest devotion, truly anxious to do the best they can for Theosophy, and to assimilate it as rapidly and perfectly as possible; and yet with all that, and with all their eager study of our books, they cannot at once put themselves into the position of the older members; and they will sometimes show that, by making some crude remark which is not at all in harmony with Theosophical teaching. I do not mean to suggest that the *mere* efflux of time will produce these effects, for obviously a man who does not study may remain a member for twenty years and be but little forwarder at the end of that time than he was at the beginning; but one who patiently studies, one who lives much with those who know, enters presently into the spirit of

Theosophy—or perhaps it might be better said that the spirit of Theosophy enters into *him.*

Evidently, therefore, new members should never intermit their studies, but try to understand the doctrines from every point of view. Year by year we are all growing into the attitude of those who are older than ourselves, and it comes chiefly by association and conversation with those older students. The Masters know almost infinitely more than the highest of Their pupils, and so those highest pupils continue to learn from association with Them; we who are lower pupils know much less than those who stand above, and so we in turn learn by association with them; and in the same way those who are not yet even at our level may learn something from similar association with us. So always the older members can help the younger, and the younger have much to learn from those who have trodden the road before them. It was in this gradual way that we came to understand about the higher and the lower self.

It is a matter of exceeding difficulty to express the relation of the personality to the ego; as I have said above, I think that on the whole, the best way to put it is to say that the former is a fragment of the latter, a tiny part of him expressing itself under serious difficulties. We meet a person on the physical plane; we speak to him; and we think and say that we know him. It would be a little nearer the truth to say that we know a thousandth part of him. Even when clairvoyance is developed—even when a man opens the sight of his causal body, and looks at the causal body of another man—even then, though he sees a manifestation of the ego on his own plane, he is still far from seeing the real man. I have tried, by means of the illustrations in *Mar, Visible and Invisible,* to give some indication of one side of the aspect of these higher vehicles; but the illustrations are in reality absolutely inadequate; they can give only faint adumbrations of the real thing. When anyone of our readers develops the astral sight, he may reasonably say to us, as the Queen of Sheba said to King Solomon: "The half was not told me". He may say: "Here is all this glory and this beauty, which surrounds me in every direction and seems so entirely natural; it should be easy to give a better description of this". But when, having seen and experienced all this, he returns to his physical body and tries to describe it in physical words, I think he will find much the same difficulties as we have done.

For when, using the higher mental sight, a man looks at the causal body of another, it is not actually the ego that he sees, but only matter of the higher mental plane which expresses the qualities of the ego. Those qualities affect the matter, cause it to undulate at different rates, and so produce colours, by examining which the character of the man can be distinguished. This character, at that level, means the good qualities which the man has developed; for no evil can express itself in matter so refined. In observing such a causal body, we know that it has within it in germ all the characteristics of the Deity—all possible good qualities, therefore; but not all of them are unfolded until the man reaches a very high level. When an evil feature shows itself in the personality, it must be taken to indicate that the opposite good quality is as yet undeveloped in the ego; it exists in him, as in every one, but it has not yet been called into activity. So soon as it is called into activity its intense vibrations act upon the lower vehicles, and it is impossible that the opposite evil can ever again find place in them.

Taking the ego for the moment as the real man, and looking at him on his own plane, we see him to be indeed a glorious being; the only way in which down here we can form a conception of what he really is, is to think of him as some splendid angel. But the expression of this beautiful being on the physical plane may fall far short of all this; indeed, it must do so—first, because it is only a tiny fragment; and secondly, because it is so hopelessly cramped by its conditions. Suppose a man put his finger into a hole in the wall, or into a small iron pipe, so that he could not even bend it; how much of himself as a whole could he express through that finger in that condition? Much like this is the fate of that fragment of the ego which is put down into this dense body. It is so small a fragment that it cannot represent the, whole; it is so cramped and shut in that it cannot even express what it is. The image is clumsy, but it may give some sort of idea of the relation of the personality to the ego.

Let us suppose that the finger has a considerable amount of consciousness of its own, and that, being shut off from the body, it temporarily forgets that it is part of that body; then it forgets also the freedom of the wider life, and tries to adapt itself to its hole, and to gild its sides and make it an enjoyable hole by acquiring money, property, fame and so on—not realising that it only really begins to live when it withdraws itself from the hole altogether, and recognises itself as a part of the body. When we draw ourselves out of this particular hole at night and live in our astral bodies, we are much less limited and much nearer to our true selves, though we still have two veils—our astral and mental bodies—which prevent us from being fully ourselves, and so fully expressing ourselves. Still, under those conditions we are much freer, and it is much easier to comprehend realities; for the physical body is the most clogging and confining of all, and imposes upon us the greatest limitations.

It would help us much if we could suppose away our limitations one by one; but it is riot easy. Realise how in the astral body we can move quickly through space—not instantaneously, but still quickly; for in two or three minutes we might move round the world. But even then we cannot get anywhere without passing through the intervening space. We can come into touch at that level with other men in their astral bodies. All their feelings lie open to us, so that they cannot deceive us about them, although they can do so with regard to their thoughts. We see in that world many more of the earth's inhabitants—those whom we call the dead—the higher nature-spirits, the angels of desire, and many others. The sight of that plane enables us to see the inside of every object, and to look down into the interior of the earth; so that in many ways our consciousness is greatly widened.

Let us go a step further. If we learn to use the powers of the mental body, we do not therefore lose those of the lower, for they are included in the higher. We can then pass from place to place with the rapidity of thought; we can then see the thoughts of our fellow men, so that deception is no longer possible; we can see higher orders of the angels, and the vast host of those who, having finished their astral life, are inhabiting the heaven-world. Rising yet another step, and using the senses of the causal body, we find further glories awaiting our examination. If then we look at a fellow man, the body which we see within his ovoid is no longer a likeness of his present or his last physical body, as it is on the astral and mental planes. What we now see is the Augoeides, the glorified man, which is not an image of any one of his past physical vehicles, but contains within itself the essence of all that was best in each of them—a body which indicates more or less perfectly, as through experience it grows, what the Deity means that man shall be. By watching that vehicle we may see the stage of evolution which the man has reached; we may see what his past history has been, and to a considerable extent we can also observe the future that lies before him.

Students sometimes wonder why, if this be so, the evil qualities which a man shows in one life should so often persist in later lives. The reason is not only that because the opposing good quality is undeveloped there is an opportunity for evil influences to act upon the man in that particular direction, but also that the man carries with him from life to life the permanent atoms of his lower vehicles, and these tend to reproduce the qualities shown in his previous incarnations. Then, it may be asked: "Why carry over those permanent atoms?" Because it is necessary for evolution; because the developed man must be master of *all* the planes. If it were conceivable that he could develop without those permanent atoms, he might possibly become a glorious archangel upon higher planes, but he would be absolutely useless in these lower worlds, for he would have cut off from himself the power of feeling and of thinking. So that we must not drop the permanent atoms, but purify them.

The task before most of us at present is that of realising the ego as the true man, so that we may let him work, instead of this false personal self with which we are so ready to identify ourselves. It is so easy for us to feel: "I am angry; I am jealous"; when the truth is that that which is pushing us to anger or to jealousy is merely the desire-elemental, which yearns for strong and coarse undulations, which help him on his downward way into grosser matter. We must realise that the true man can never be so foolish as to wish for such vibrations as these— that he can never desire anything but that which will be good for his own evolution, and helpful for that of others. A man says that he feels impelled by passion. Let him wait and think: "Is it really I?" And he will discover that it is not he at all, but something else that is trying to get hold of him and make him feel thus. He has the right and the duty to assert his independence of that thing, and to proclaim himself as a free man, pursuing the road of evolution which God has marked out for him.

Thus it is at present our business to realise ourselves as the ego; but when that is fully accomplished, when the lower is nothing but a perfect instrument in the hands of the higher, it will become our duty to realise that even the ego is not the true man. For the ego has had a beginning—it came into existence at the moment of individualisation; and whatever has a beginning must have an end. Therefore even the ego, which has lasted since we left the animal kingdom, is also impermanent. Is there then nothing in us that endures, nothing that will have no end? There is the Monad, the Divine Spark, which is verily a fragment of God, an atom of the Deity. Crude and inaccurate expressions, assuredly; yet I know of no other way in which the idea can be conveyed even as well as in words such as these. For each Monad is literally a part of God, apparently temporarily separated from Him, while he is enclosed in the veils of matter, though in truth never for one moment really separated.

He can never be apart from God, for the very matter in which he veils himself is also a manifestation of the Divine. To us sometimes matter seems evil, because it weighs us down, it clogs our faculties, it seems to hold us back upon our road; yet remember that this is only because as yet we have not learned to control it, because we have not realised that it also is divine in its essence, because there is nothing but God. A Sufi sage once told me that this was his interpretation of the cry which rings out daily in the call of the muezzin from the minaret all over the Muhammadan world: "There is no God but God, and Muhammad is the Prophet of God". He told me that in his opinion the true mystical meaning of the first part of this cry was: "There is nothing but God". And that is eternally true; we know that all comes from Him, and that to Him all will one day return, but we find it hard to realise that all is in Him even now, and that in Him it eternally abides. All is God—even the desire-elemental, and the things which we think of as evil; for many waves of life come forth from Him, and not all of them are moving in the same direction.

We, being Monads, belonging to an earlier wave, are somewhat fuller expressions of Him, somewhat nearer to Him in our consciousness than the essence out of which is made the desire-elemental. In the course of our evolution there is always a danger that a man should identify himself with the point at which he is most fully conscious. Most men at present are more conscious in their feelings and passions than anywhere else, and of this the desire-elemental craftily takes advantage, and endeavours to induce the man to identify himself with those desires and emotions.

So when the man rises to a somewhat higher level, and his principal activity becomes mental, there is danger lest he should identify himself with the mind, and it is only by realising himself as the ego, and making *that* the strongest point of his consciousness, that he can fully merge the personality in the individuality. When he has done that, he has achieved the goal of his present efforts; but immediately he must begin his work over again at that higher level, and try gradually to realise the truth of the position we laid down at the beginning, that as the personality is to the ego, so is the ego to the Monad. It is useless at our present stage to endeavour to indicate the steps which he will have to take in order to become a perfect expression of the Monad, or the stages of consciousness through which he will pass. Such conceptions as can be formed of them may be arrived at by applying the ancient rule that what is below is but a reflection of that which exists in higher worlds, so that the steps and the stages must to some extent be a repetition upon a higher level of those which have already been experienced in our lower efforts.

We may reverently presume (though here we are going far beyond actual knowledge) that when we have finally and fully realised that the Monad is the true man, we shall find behind that again a yet further and more glorious extension; we shall find that the Spark has never been separated from the Fire, but that as the ego stands behind the personality, as the Monad stands behind the ego, so a Planetary Angel stands behind the Monad, and the

Solar Deity Himself stands behind the Planetary Angel. Perhaps, even further still, it may be that in some way infinitely higher, and so at present utterly incomprehensible, a greater Deity stands behind the Solar Deity, and behind even that, through many stages, there must rest the Supreme over all. But here even thought fails us, and silence is the only true reverence.

For the time, at least, the Monad is our personal God, the God within us, that which produces us down here as a manifestation of him on these all but infinitely lower levels. What his consciousness is on his own plane we cannot pretend to say, nor can we fully understand it even when he has put upon himself the first veil, and become the triple Spirit. The only way to understand such things is to rise to their level, and to become one with them. When we do that we shall comprehend, but even then we shall be utterly unable to explain to anyone else what we know. It is at that stage, the stage of the triple Spirit, that we who investigate can first see the Monad, and he is then a triple light of blinding glory, yet possessing even at that stage certain qualities by which one Monad is somehow distinct from another.

Often a student asks: "But what have we to do with it while we are down here—this unknown glory so far above us? "It is a natural question, yet in reality it is the reverse of what should be; for the true man is the Monad, and we should rather say: "What can I, the Monad, do with my ego, and through it with my personality?" This would be the correct attitude, for this would express the actual facts; but we cannot truthfully take it, because we cannot realise this. Yet we can say to ourselves: "I know that I am that Monad, though as yet I cannot express it; I know that I am the ego, a mere fraction of that Monad, but still out of all proportion greater than what I know of myself in the personality down here. More and more I will try to realise myself as that higher and greater being; more and more I will try to make this lower presentation of myself worthy of its true destiny; more and more will I see to it that this lower self is ever ready to catch the slightest hint or whisper from above—to follow the suggestions from the ego which we call intuitions—to distinguish the Voice of the Silence and to obey it".

For the Voice of the Silence is not one thing always, but changes as we ourselves evolve; or perhaps it would be better to say that it is in truth one thing always, the voice of God, but it comes to us at different levels as we ourselves rise. To us, now it is the voice of the ego, speaking to the personality; presently it will be the voice of the Monad, speaking to the ego; later still the voice of the Deity, speaking to the Monad. Probably, (as we have already suggested,) between these last two stages there may be an intermediate one, in which the voice of one of the seven great Ministers of the Deity may speak to the Monad, and then in turn the Deity Himself may speak to His Minister; but always the Voice of the Silence is essentially divine.

It is well that we should learn to distinguish this voice—this voice which speaks from above and yet from within; for sometimes other voices speak, and their counsel is not always wise. A medium finds this, for if he has not trained himself to distinguish, he often thinks that every voice coming from the astral plane must necessarily be all but divine, and therefore to be followed unquestioningly. Therefore discrimination is necessary, as well as watchfulness and obedience.

Does the Monad, in the case of the ordinary man, ever do anything which affects or can affect his personality down here? I think we may say that such interference is most unusual. The ego is trying, on behalf of the Monad, to obtain perfect control of the personality and to use it as an instrument; and because that object is not yet fully achieved, the Monad may well feel that the time has not yet come for him to interfere from his own level, and to bring the whole of his force to bear, when that which is already in action is more than strong enough for the required purpose. But when the ego is already beginning to succeed in his effort to manage his lower vehicles, the real man in the background does sometimes intervene.

In the course of various investigations it has come in our way to examine some thousands of human beings; but we found traces of such intervention only in a few. The most prominent instance is that given in the twenty-ninth life of Alcyone, when he pledged himself before the Lord Gautama to devote himself in future lives to the attainment of the Buddhahood in order to help humanity. That seemed to us then a matter of such moment, and also of such interest, that we took some trouble to investigate it. This was a promise for the far-distant future, so that obviously the personality through which it was given could by no means keep it; and when we rose to examine the part borne in it by the ego, we found that he himself, though full of enthusiasm at the idea, was being impelled to it by a mightier force from within, which he could not have resisted, even had he wished to do so. Following this clue still further, we found that the impelling force came forth unmistakably from the Monad. He had decided, and he registered his decision; his will, working through the ego, will clearly have no difficulty in bringing all future personalities into harmony.

We found some other examples of the same phenomenon in the course of the investigations into the beginnings of the Sixth Root Race. Looking forward to the life in that Californian Colony, we recognised instantly certain well-known egos; and then arose the question: "Since men have freewill, is it possible that we can already be absolutely certain that all these people will be there as we foresee? Will none of them fall by the way?" Further examination showed us that the same thing was happening here as with Alcyone. Certain Monads had already responded to the call of the higher Authorities, and had decided that their representative personalities should assist in that glorious work; and because of that, nothing that these personalities might do during the intervening time could possibly interfere with the carrying out of that decision.

Yet let no one think, because this is so, that he is compelled from without to do this or that; the compelling force is the real you; none else than yourself can ever bind you at any stage of your growth. And when the Monad has decided, the thing will be done; it is well for the personality if he yields gracefully and readily, if he recognises the voice from above, and co-operates gladly; for if he does not do this, he will lay up for himself much useless suffering. It is always the man himself who is doing this thing; and he, in the personality, has to realise that the ego is himself, and he has for the moment to take it for granted that the Monad is still more himself—the final and greatest expression of him.

Surely this view should be the greatest possible encouragement to the man working down here, this knowledge that he is a far grander and more glorious being in reality than he appears to be, and that there is a part of him—enormously the greater part—which has already achieved what he, as a personality, is trying to achieve; and that all that he has to do down here is to try to make himself a perfect channel for this higher and more real self; to do his work and to try to help others in order that he may be a factor, however microscopic, in forwarding the evolution of the world. For him who knows, there is no question of the saving of the soul;

the true man behind needs no salvation; he needs only that the lower self should realise him and express him. He is himself already divine; and all that he needs is to be able to realise himself in all the worlds and at all possible levels, so that in them all the Divine Power through him may work equally, and so God shall be all in all.

CHAPTER II

HIGHER CONSCIOUSNESS

STUDENTS who have not yet experienced the buddhic consciousness—consciousness in the intuitional world—frequently ask us to describe it. Efforts have been made in this direction, and many references to this consciousness and its characteristics are to be found scattered through our literature; yet the seeker after knowledge finds these unsatisfactory, and we cannot wonder at it.

The truth is that all description is necessarily and essentially defective; it is impossible in physical words to give more than the merest hint of what this higher consciousness is, for the physical brain is incapable of grasping the reality. Those who have read Mr. Hinton's remarkable books on the fourth dimension will remember how he tries to explain to us our own limitations with regard to higher dimensions, by picturing for us with much careful detail the position of an entity whose senses could work in two dimensions only. He proves that to such a being the simplest actions of our world must be incomprehensible. A creature who has no sense of what we call depth or thickness could never see any terrestrial object as it really is; he could observe only a section of it, and would therefore obtain absolutely wrong impressions about even the commonest objects of everyday life, while our powers of motion and of action would be utterly incomprehensible to him.

The difficulties which we encounter in trying to understand the phenomena even of the astral world are precisely similar to those which Mr. Hinton supposes to be experienced by his two-dimensional entity; but when we try to raise our thoughts to the intuitional world we have to face a state of existence which is lived in no less than six dimensions, if we are to continue at that level to employ the same nomenclature. So I fear we must admit from the outset that any attempt to comprehend this higher consciousness is foredoomed to failure; yet, as is but natural, the desire to try again and again to grasp something of it arises perennially in the mind of the student. I do not venture to think that I can say anything to satisfy this craving; the utmost that one can hope is to suggest a few new considerations, and perhaps to approach the subject from a somewhat different point of view.

The Monad in its own world is practically without limitations, at least as far as our solar system is concerned. But at every stage of its descent into matter it not only veils itself more and more deeply in illusion, but it actually loses its powers. If in the beginning of its evolution it may be supposed to be able to move and to see in an infinite number of these directions in space which we call dimensions, at each downward step it cuts off one of these, until for the consciousness of the physical brain only three of them are left. It will thus be seen that by this involution into matter we are cut off from the knowledge of all but a minute part of the worlds which surround us; and furthermore, even what is left to us is but imperfectly seen. Let us make an effort to realise what the higher consciousness may be by gradually supposing away some of our limitations; and although we are labouring under them even while we are thus supposing, the effort may possibly suggest to us some faint adumbration of the reality.

Let us begin with the physical world. The first thing that strikes us is that our consciousness, even of that world, is curiously imperfect. The student need feel no surprise at this, for he knows that we are at present only just beyond the middle of the fourth round, and that the perfection of consciousness of any plane will not be attained by normal humanity until the seventh round. The truth is that our whole life is imprisoned within limitations which we do not realise only because we have always endured them, and because the ordinary man has no conception of a condition in which they do not exist. Let us take three examples; let us see how we are limited in our senses, our powers and our intellect respectively.

First, as to our senses. Let us take the sense of sight for an example, and see how remarkably imperfect it is. Our physical world consists of seven sub-planes or degrees of density of matter, but our sight enables us to perceive only two of these with anything approaching perfection. We can usually see solid matter, if it is not too finely subdivided; we can see a liquid that is not absolutely clear; but we cannot see gaseous matter at all under ordinary conditions, except in the rare instances in which it has an especially brilliant colour (as in the case of chlorine) or when it happens to be dense, to be much compressed, and to be moving in a particular way—as in the case of the air which may sometimes be seen rising from a heated road. Of the four etheric subdivisions of physical matter we remain absolutely unconscious so far as sight is concerned, although it is by means of the vibration of some of these ethers that what we call light is conveyed to the eye.

Let us then commence the imaginary process of removing our limitations by considering what would be the effect if we really possessed fully the sight of the physical world. I am not taking into consideration the possibility of any increase in the *power* of our sight, though no doubt that also will come in due course, so that we shall be able so to alter the focus of the eye as to make it practically a telescope or a microscope at will. I am thinking for the moment only of the additional objects that would come into our view if our sight were perfected.

Nothing would any longer be opaque to us, so that we could see through a wall almost as though it were not there, and could examine the contents of a closed room or of a locked box with the greatest ease. I do not mean that by etheric sight a man could see through a mountain, or look straight through the earth to the other side of it; but he could see a good way into the rock, and he could see down to a considerable depth in the earth, much as we can now see through many feet of water to the bottom of a clear pool.

One can readily see a score of ways in which the possession of such a faculty would be practically valuable, and it would manifestly add to our knowledge in many directions. All surgical work could be performed with an ease and certainty of which at present we have no conception, and there would be fewer cases of inaccurate diagnosis. We could see the etheric bodies of our friends, and so we should be able to indicate unfailingly the source and cause of any nervous affection. A whole fresh world would come under the observation of the chemist, for he would then be able to deal with ethers as he now deals with gases. Our sight would instantly inform us as to the healthiness or otherwise of our surroundings, just as even now our noses warn us of the presence of certain forms of putrefaction. We could see at once when we were in the presence of undesirable germs or impurities of any kind, and could take our precautions accordingly. We could study the great hosts of the fairies, of the gnomes and the water-spirits, as readily as now we can study natural history or entomology; the world would be far fuller and far more interesting with even this slight augmentation of our sense.

But remember that even this would not take us beyond the physical world; it would simply enable us to see that world more fully. We should still be liable to deception, we should still be capable of error with regard to the thoughts and feelings of others. We should still be blind to all the most beautiful part of the life which surrounds us, even though we should see so much more of it than we do now. But even with the fullest physical sight we could see nothing as it really is, but only, at most, what corresponds to a looking-glass reflection of it. The two-dimensional entity could never see a cube; he would be quite incapable of imagining such a thing as a cube, and the nearest he could come to its comprehension would be to see a section of it as a square. However difficult it may be for us to grasp such an idea, we are at the present moment seeing only a section of everything that surrounds us; and because that is so, we think many things to be alike which are in reality quite different—just as to the two-dimensional creature the thinnest sheet of metal would appear precisely the same as a heavy block of it, the base of which had the same shape and area.

Then as to our powers. Here also we are strangely limited. However strong a man may be, however clever he may be at his speciality, whether that speciality be physical or mental, he can never work at it beyond a certain strictly limited extent without beginning to suffer from fatigue. Most people do not realise that this fatigue is always and entirely a physical disability.

We speak of the mind as tired; but the mind cannot be tired; it is only the physical brain through which that mind has to express itself that is capable of fatigue. And even when the man is fresh and strong, how great are the difficulties in the way of a full expression of his thought! He has to try to put it into words; but words are feeble things at best, and can never really convey what the man feels or thinks; they are often misinterpreted, and the impression that they give is generally not at all what the speaker or writer originally intended.

The physical body is a serious obstacle in the way of rapid locomotion. Wherever we wish to go we have to carry with us this dense vehicle, this heavy lump of clay, that weighs the man down and checks his progress. At great expense and discomfort we must convey it by train or by steamer; and even with all our latest inventions, and with the wonderful progress that has been made with regard to all means of transportation, what a difficulty is this question of physical distance! How it stands in the way of the acquisition of knowledge; how it troubles the heart and lacerates the feelings of separated friends! The moment that we are able to raise our consciousness into a higher world all these difficulties are transcended.

Then as to our intellect. We are in the habit of boasting of it as some great thing. We speak of the march of intellect, of its great development, and generally speaking regard it as something of which we may reasonably be proud. Yet the truth is that it is nothing but a ridiculous fragment of what it presently will be—a fact which is abundantly clear to those of us who have had the privilege of coming into contact with some of the Masters of the Wisdom, and seeing in Them what a fully developed intellect really is. Here again our studies ought to save us from the common error, for we know that it is the fifth round in each chain which is specially devoted to the development of the intellectual faculties; and as we are still in the fourth we naturally cannot expect that they should as yet be at all fully unfolded. In fact, at this stage they would be scarcely unfolded at all, if it were not for the stupendous stimulus that was given to the evolution of humanity by the descent of the Lords of the Flame from Venus in the middle of the Third Root Race.

All this is true; the physical consciousness is sadly limited; but how are we to transcend it? It might seem that in the ordinary process of evolution we ought to perfect the physical senses before we acquire those of the astral world; but our powers do not unfold themselves exactly in that way. In order that the man shall be able to function in his physical body at all, there must be an uninterrupted connection between the ego and that vehicle; and this involves the existence of the mental and astral bodies. At first they are employed chiefly as bridges across which communication passes; and it is only as our development progresses that they come into use as separate vehicles. But inevitably while the consciousness is sending down messages through them, and receiving in return impressions through them, they become to a certain small extent awakened; so that even in a savage, who cannot be said to have any consciousness worth speaking of outside of the physical vehicle, there is yet a faint dawning of intellect and often a considerable amount of emotion. At the stage where the ordinary man of civilised countries stands at the present moment, his consciousness is on the whole more centred in his astral body than in the physical, even though it is true that the powers of the physical are as yet by no means fully unfolded. Their stage of unfoldment corresponds to the round in which we are now engaged; at this period only a partial development can be expected, but that partial development shows itself to some extent in the mental and astral bodies, as well as in the purely physical.

A good deal can be done even with the physical body by careful training, but much more can be done in proportion with the astral and mental bodies, the reason being that they are built of finer matter and so are much more readily amenable to the action of thought. Even the physical body may be greatly affected by that action, as is shown by the remarkable performances of faith-healers and Christian Scientists, and also by the well-authenticated examples of the appearance of the stigmata upon the bodies of some of those who have meditated strongly upon the alleged crucifixion of the Christ. But while only the few by determined exercise of thought-power can succeed in thus moulding the physical vehicle; anyone may learn how to control both the astral and the mental bodies by this power.

This is one of the objects which we seek to gain by the practice of meditation, which is the easiest and safest method of unfolding the higher consciousness. A man works steadily at his meditation year in and year out, and for a long time it seems to him that he is making no headway; yet all the while in his steady upward striving he is wearing the veil between the planes thinner arid thinner, and at last one day there comes the moment when he breaks through and finds himself in another world. So wondrous, so transcendent, is that experience that he exclaims with startled delight:

"Now for the first time I really live; now at last I know what life means! I have thought before that life on the physical plane could sometimes be fairly keen and brilliant—yes, even vivid and full of bliss; but now I realise that all that was the merest child's play—that even in my most exalted moments I had no comprehension, no faintest suspicion of the glorious reality."

And yet all this, which the man feels so intensely when for the first time he touches the astral world, will be repeated with still stronger force of contrast when he transcends that world in turn, and opens himself out to the influences of the mental level. Then again he will feel that this is his first glimpse of actuality, and that even the most wonderful incidents of his astral life were to this but "as moonlight unto sunlight and as water unto wine". Again and again this happens to him as he climbs the ladder of evolution and comes nearer and nearer to reality; for verily it is true, as the old books have said, that "Brahman is bliss", and ever as one approaches the realisation of Him that bliss increases.

But the higher the joy the greater the contrast between the inner life and the life of the physical world; so that to return from that to this seems like sinking into a profound abyss of darkness and despair. The contrast is indeed great; so great that one cannot wonder that many of the saints of old, having once tasted this higher bliss, forsook all in order to follow it, and retired to cave or to jungle that there they might devote themselves to this higher life, in comparison with which all else that men hold valuable seems but as dust before the wind. I remember that, in the early days of this Society, we were told in one of the letters which came through Madame Blavatsky that when an adept had spent a long time in the nirvanic consciousness (leaving his body in a trance for weeks together), when he came back again into physical life he found the contrast so severe that he fell into a black depression which lasted for many days. Our terms were used very loosely in those days, and in this case the word adept must have referred to some one in the early stages of occult development—an adept merely in the sense that he was sufficiently accustomed to occult gymnastics to be able to leave his body and reside for a time upon a somewhat higher level—not what we now mean by nirvana, for only a real Adept (in the sense in which we now use the word) could repose long upon the nirvanic level; and He is far too highly evolved and far too unselfish to allow Himself to indulge in depression, however intensely He may feel the change when He returns to this grey, dull earth from worlds of unimagined splendour. Nevertheless the contrast is severe, and one who has found his true home in those higher worlds cannot but feel something of nostalgia while his duty compels him to dwell at the lower levels of ordinary life.

This has been spoken of as the great renunciation, and no doubt it is so; it would indeed be infinitely great if one who has reached that point did not retain the powers of the higher consciousness even while still functioning in the physical body. One who has reached the Asekha stage habitually carries His consciousness on the nirvanic level, even though He still possesses a physical body. I do not mean that He can be fully conscious on both the planes simultaneously. When He is actually writing a letter or conducting a conversation on the physical plane, His consciousness is centred there, just like that of the ordinary man, though the spiritual splendour is still present in the background; but the moment that His physical work is over, the consciousness naturally springs back again to its accustomed condition, and though He still sits in the same physical chair, though He is fully alive and alert to all that is going on around Him, He is in reality living on that higher level, and earthly objects, though still present to Him, are slightly out of focus. This being His condition, the retaining of the physical body is only a modified sacrifice, although it involves a good deal of annoyance in the way of waste of time in eating, dressing, and so on.

When a man definitely attains the astral consciousness he finds himself much less hampered along all the three lines which we have instanced. In the astral body he has no longer sense-organs, but he does not need them, for what in that world corresponds to our senses works without needing a specialised organ. Strictly speaking, the word sight is hardly applicable to the perception of things in the astral world; but that knowledge of surrounding objects which we gain by seeing them is as readily and much more perfectly acquired in that higher vehicle. Every particle of the astral body is responsive, though only to vibrations of its own sublevel; thus in that higher life we get the effect of seeing all round us simultaneously, instead of only in one direction.

Since, as has frequently been explained, all solid physical objects have counterparts of that lowest type of astral matter which corresponds on that plane to a solid, we see practically the same world around us when utilising the astral senses. But it is a far more populous world, for now we are able to see the millions of the sylphs or air-spirits, and also the hosts of the dead who have not yet risen above the astral level. Higher beings also are now within our purview, for we can see that lowest order of the Angel evolution which we have frequently called the desire-angels. All our friends who still have physical bodies remain just as visible to us as before, although we see only their astral vehicles; but now all their emotions and passions lie open before us, and it is no longer possible for the conventionalist to deceive us as to the real state of his feelings on any point. His thoughts, however, are still veiled, except in so far as they affect his feelings, and so show themselves through them.

The limitation of space has not yet disappeared, but its inconveniences are reduced to a minimum. We no longer need the clumsy methods of transportation with which we are familiar down here; the finer matter of this higher world responds so readily to the action of thought that merely to wish to be at any place is at once to begin to journey towards it. The journey still takes an appreciable time, even though the amount is small and we can reach the other side of the world in a few minutes. But the few minutes are necessary, and we still have the sensation of passing through space, and can check ourselves at any moment of our journey, so as to visit the intermediate countries.

The intellect is far freer here than in the lower world, as it has no longer to exhaust most of its strength in setting in motion the heavy and sluggish particles of the physical brain. We gain greatly also from the fact that fatigue has disappeared, so that we axe able to work steadily and continuously. Another advantage is that we are far less hampered at this level by pain and suffering. I do not mean that there is no suffering in the astral world; on the contrary, it may be in many ways more acute than it can be down here, but on the other hand it can much more readily be controlled. The astral world is the very home of passion and emotion, and therefore those who yield themselves to an emotion can experience it with a vigour and a keenness mercifully unknown on earth. Just as we have said that most of the strength of thought is spent in setting in motion the brain-particles, so most of the efficiency of any emotion is exhausted in transmission to the physical plane, so that all that we ever see down here is the remnant which is left of the real feeling, after all this work has been done by it. The whole of that force is available in its own world, and so it is possible there to feel a far more intense affection or devotion than we can ever gain amid the mists of earth. Naturally, the same thing is true with regard to the less pleasant emotions; accessions of hatred and envy, or waves of misery or fear, are a hundred times. more formidable on that plane than on this. So that the man who has no self-control is liable to experience an intensity of suffering which is unimaginable amidst the benignantly-imposed restrictions of common life.

The advantage is that, little as most people realise it, in the astral world all pain and suffering is in reality voluntary and absolutely under control, and that is why life at that level is so much easier for the man who understands. No doubt the power of mind over matter is wonderful in all the worlds, and even down here it frequently produces marvellous and unexpected results. But it is exceedingly difficult to control by the mind acute physical pain. I know that it can often be done from outside by mesmerism, or even by determined exertion along the lines of Christian Science, and that it is frequently done in India and elsewhere by yogis who have made a speciality of it; but the power so to control severe pain is not yet in the hands of most people, and even where it is possible, such an effort absorbs so much of the energy of the man as to leave him capable of little else for the time but holding the pain at bay.

The reason of this difficulty lies in the density of the matter; it is so far removed in level from the controlling forces that their hold on it is by no means secure, and great practice is required before definite results can be produced. The far finer astral matter responds immediately to an exertion of the will, so that while only the few can perfectly and instantly banish severe physical pain, every one can in a moment drive away the suffering, caused by a strong emotion. The man has only to exert his will, and the passion straightway disappears. This assertion will sound startling to many; but a little thought will show that no man *need* be angry or jealous or envious; no man *need* allow himself to feel depression or fear; all these emotions are invariably the result of ignorance, and any man who chooses to make the effort can forth-with put them to flight.

In the physical world fear may sometimes have a certain amount of excuse, for it is undoubtedly possible for one who is more powerful than we to injure our physical bodies. But on the astral plane no one can do hurt to another, except indeed by employing methods congruous to the plane, which are always gradual in their operation and easy to be avoided. In this world a sudden blow may actually injure the texture of the physical body; but in the astral world all vehicles are fluidic, and a blow, a cut, or a perforation can produce no effect whatever, since the vehicle would close up again immediately, precisely as does water when a sword has passed through it.

It is the world of passions and emotions, and only through his passions and emotions can man be injured. A man may be corrupted, and persuaded to harbour evil passions, unworthy emotions; but these after all can be induced only slowly, and any man who wishes to resist them can do so with perfect ease. Therefore there is no reason whatever for fear upon the astral plane, and where it exists it is only through ignorance—ignorance which can be dispelled by a few moments' instruction and a little practice. Also, most of the reasons which cause suffering amid terrestrial surroundings are quite unrepresented. When we lay aside this body, there is no longer hunger or thirst, cold or heat, fatigue or sickness, poverty or riches; what room is there then for pain and suffering? One sees at a glance that that less material world cannot but be a happier one, for in that, far more than even in this, a man makes his own surroundings and can vary them at his will.

One of the greatest causes of suffering in our present life is what we are in the habit of calling our separation from those whom we love, when they leave their physical bodies behind them. Having only his physical consciousness, the uninstructed man supposes himself to have "lost" his departed friend; but this is really an illusion, for the departed friend stands beside him all the time, and watches the variations of feeling expressed in his astral body. It will at once be seen that it is impossible for the departed friend to be under any delusion that he has "lost" the loved ones who still retain physical vehicles, for since they must also possess astral bodies (or those physical vehicles could not live) the "dead" man has the living fully in sight all the time, though the consciousness of his living friend is available for the interchange of thought and sentiment only during the sleep of that friend's physical body. But at least the "dead" man has no sense of loneliness or separation, but has simply exchanged the day for the night as his time of companionship with those whom he loves who still belong to the lower world.

This most fertile source of sorrow is therefore entirely removed from one who possesses the astral consciousness. The man who has evolved to the point at which he is able to use fully both the astral and physical consciousness while still awake, can naturally never be separated from his departed friend, but has him present and fully available until the end of the latter's astral life, when that body in turn is dropped, and he enters upon his sojourn in the heaven-world. Then indeed an apparent separation does take place, though even then it can never be at all the same thing as what we call loss down here; for a man who has already fully realised the existence of two of the planes has thoroughly convinced himself of the plan of Nature's arrangements, and has a certainty with regard to them and a confidence in them which puts him in an altogether different position from the ignorance of the man who knows only one plane and cannot imagine anything beyond it.

In addition to this, a man who possesses astral consciousness has broken through the first and densest of the veils, and will find it no great effort to penetrate that which divides him from the mental world, so that it frequently happens that before the so-called "dead" person is ready to leave the astral plane, his friend has already opened the door of a yet higher consciousness, and is therefore able to accompany his "dead" associate in the next stage of his progress. Under any and all circumstances, and whether the man who is still in physical life is or is not conscious of what takes place, the apparent separation is never more than an illusion, for in the heaven-world the "dead" man makes for himself a thought-image of his friend, which is instantly observed and utilised by the ego of that friend; and in that way they are closer together than ever before.

Let us see what further advantages are gained by the man who has opened for himself the mental consciousness. Once again he passes through the experience already described, for he finds that this higher plane is thrilling with a glory and a bliss beside which even the wonderful vigour of the astral life pales its ineffectual fires. Once more he feels that now at last he has reached the true life, of which before he had only an inefficient and inaccurate reflection. Again his horizon is widened, for now the vast world of the Form-Angels opens before his astonished eyes. He sees now the whole of humanity—the enormous hosts who are out of incarnation as well as the comparatively few who possess vehicles upon the lower planes. Every man who is in physical or astral life must necessarily possess a mental body, and it is that which now represents him to the sight of the student who has come thus far on his way; but, in addition to this, the great army of those who are resting in the heaven-world is now within his view—though, as each is confined entirely within his own shell of thought, these men can hardly be regarded as in any sense of the word companions.

The visitor to their world can act upon them to the extent of flooding them with thoughts, say of affection. Sometimes these thoughts cannot so far penetrate the shell of the men who are enjoying their heaven-life as to carry with them any feeling of definite affection from the sender which could make them conscious of him, or evoke in them a reply directed personally towards him; but even then, the stream of affection can act upon the inhabitant of the heaven-world in precisely the same way as the warmth of the sun can operate upon the germ within the egg and hasten its fructification, or intensify whatever pleasurable sensations it may be supposed to have. Again, though these men in the heaven-world are not readily accessible to any influence from without, they are themselves pouring forth vibrations expressing the qualities most prominent in them; so the visitor to that world may bathe himself in such emanations as he chooses, and may go round selecting his type of emanation just as a visitor to Harrogate selects the variety of mineral water which he will drink, testing first one spring and then another.

Between those who are fully conscious on the mental plane there is a far closer union than has been possible at any lower level. A man can no longer deceive another with regard to what he thinks, for all mental operations lie open for every one to see. Opinions or impressions can now be exchanged not only with the quickness of thought but with perfect accuracy, for each now receives the exact idea of the other—clean, clear-cut, instantaneous—instead of having to try to puzzle his way to it through a jungle of inexpressive words. At this level a man may circle the world actually with the speed of thought; he is at the other side of it even as he formulates the wish to be there, for in this case the response of matter to thought is immediate, and the will can control it far more readily than on any lower level.

It has often been said in connection with meditation that there is much greater difficulty in governing thoughts than emotions, and that the mental elemental is less susceptible to control than the astral. For us down here this is usually so, but if we wish to understand the matter aright we must try to see why it is so. The physical body is along certain lines obedient to the action of the will, because we have carefully trained it to be so.

If we desire to lift an arm, we can lift it; if we desire to walk to a certain place, if the physical body is in health, we can get up and walk to it with no more resistance on the part of the body than the expression of its ordinary indolence or love of ease. When, however, the physical body has set up bad habits of any kind, it often proves exceedingly refractory and difficult to restrain. It is in such cases that the distance and difference in density between the controlling ego and its lowest vehicle becomes painfully evident. The management of the astral vehicle is in reality much easier, though many people find it difficult because they have never previously attempted it. The moment that one really thinks clearly of the matter this is obvious. It is not easy to banish by thought-power a raging toothache, though even that can be done under certain conditions; it is comparatively easy by thought-power to banish depression or anger or jealousy. The desire-elemental may be persistent in obtruding these feelings upon the man's notice; but at any rate they clearly are under his control; and by repeatedly throwing them off immunity from them can unquestionably be obtained.

Still more definitely is this true, and easier still ought to be our task, when we pass to the mental world. It seems to us more difficult to bridle thought than emotion because most of us have made at least some experiments in the direction of repressing emotion, and we have been taught from childhood that it is unseemly to allow it to display itself unchecked. On the other hand, we have been in the habit of allowing our thoughts to roam fancy-free, and it is probably only in connection with school lessons that we have reluctantly torn them back from their wanderings and tried to concentrate them on some definite task. To induce us to do even this much, exterior compulsion is usually required in the shape of constant exhortation from the teacher or the stimulus of emulation among our fellows in the class. It is because so little effort has been made by the average man in the direction of the regulation of thought that he finds it so difficult, and indeed almost impossible, when he begins the practice of meditation. He finds himself in conflict with the habits of the mental elemental, who has been used to have things all his own way, and to drift from subject to subject at his own sweet will.

Our struggle with him is in some ways different from that which we have already waged against the desire-elemental; and the reason for this will be obvious if we remember his constitution. He represents the downward-pouring life of the Solar Deity at the earliest stage of its immeshing in matter—that which we usually call the First Elemental Kingdom. Consequently, he is less used to material confinement than is the desire-elemental, who belongs to a later kingdom, and is one whole stage lower down in the scale of matter. He is consequently more active than the desire-elemental—more restless, but less powerful and determined; he is in the nature of things easier to manage, but much less used to management; so that it takes far less actual exertion of strength to control a thought than a desire, but it needs a more persistent application of that strength. Remember that we are now at the level of thought, where literally thoughts are things; and this restive mental matter which we find so difficult to govern is the very home and definite vehicle of the mind with which we are to control it. That mind is here on its own ground and is dealing with its own matter, so that it is only a question of practice for it to learn to manage it perfectly; whereas, when we endeavour to rule the desire-elemental, we are bringing down the mind into a world which is foreign to it, and imposing an alien ascendency from without, so that we are badly equipped for the struggle.

To sum up then: control of mind is in itself far easier than control of the emotions, but we have had a certain amount of practice in the-latter, and as a rule almost no practice at all in the former; and it is for that reason only that the mental exercise seems so difficult to us. Both of them together constitute a far easier task than the perfect mastery of the physical body; but this latter we have been to some extent practising during a number of previous lives, though our achievements along that line are even yet notably imperfect. A thorough comprehension of this matter should be distinctly encouraging to the student; and the result of such comprehension is vividly to impress upon him the truth of the remark made in *The Voice of the Silence* that this earth is the only true hell which is known to the Occultist.

Let us now take one step farther, and turn our attention to the upper part of the mental plane, which is inhabited by the ego in his causal body. Now at last the veils have fallen away, and for the first time we meet man to man without possibility of misunderstanding. Even in the astral world the consciousness is already so different from that which we know down here, that it is practically impossible to give any coherent idea of it, and this difficulty increases as we attempt to deal with higher planes. Here thoughts no longer take form and float about as they do at lower levels, but pass like lightning-flashes from one soul to another. Here we have no newly-acquired vehicles, gradually coming under control and learning by degrees more or less feebly to express the soul within; but we are face to face with one body older than the hills, an actual expression of the Divine Glory which ever rests behind it, and shines through it more and more in the gradual unfolding of its powers. Here we deal no longer with outer forms, but we see the things in themselves—the reality which lies behind the imperfect expression. Here cause and effect are one, clearly visible in their unity, like two sides of the same coin. Here we have left the concrete for the abstract; we have no longer the multiplicity of forms, but the idea which lies behind all those forms.

Here the *essence* of everything is available; we no longer study details; we no longer talk round a subject or endeavour to explain it; we take up the essence or the idea of the subject and move it as a whole, as one moves a piece when playing chess. This is a world of realities, where not only is deception impossible but also unthinkable; we deal no longer with any emotions, ideas or conceptions, but with the thing in itself. It is impossible to express in words the ordinary traffic of ideas between men in fully-developed causal bodies. What down here would be a system of philosophy, needing many volumes to explain it, is there a single definite object—a thought which can be thrown down as one throws a card upon a table. An opera or an oratorio, which here would occupy a full orchestra for many hours in the rendering, is there a single mighty chord; the methods of a whole school of painting are condensed into one magnificent idea; and ideas such as these are the intellectual counters which are used by egos in their converse one with another.

There also we meet a higher order of Angels, more splendid but less comprehensible to our dull faculties. There for the first time we have fully unrolled before us all the stories of all the lives which have been lived upon our globe, the actual living records of the past; for this is the lowest plane on which the Divine Memory reflects itself. Here for the first time we see our lives as one vast whole, of which our descents into incarnation have been but the passing days. Here the great scheme of evolution is unfolded before us, so that we can see what is the Divine will for us.

The ordinary man is as yet but little developed as an ego; he needs the grosser matter of far lower planes in order to be able to sense vibrations and respond to them. But an ego who is awakened and is truly alive upon his own plane is indeed a glorious object, and gives us for the first time some idea of what God means man to be. The egos are still separate, yet intellectually they fully realise their inner unity, for they see one another as they are and can no longer blunder or fail to comprehend.

Strange as even that must seem when looked at from below, and far removed as it is from our ordinary conceptions of life, our next step brings us into a region even less possible to be grasped by the lower mind; for when we follow the man into the intuitional world, developing the buddhic consciousness, we are in the presence not only of an indefinite extension of various capacities, but also of an entire change of method. From the causal body we looked out upon everything, understanding, seeing everything exactly as it is and appraising it at its true value, yet still maintaining a distinction between subject and object, still conscious that we *looked upon* that which we so thoroughly comprehended. But now a change has come; the comprehension is more perfect and not less, but it is from within instead of from without. We no longer *look upon* a person or upon an object, no matter with what degree of kindliness or of sympathy; we simply *are* that person or that object, and we know him or it as we know the thought of our own brain or the movement of our own hand.

It is not easy even to suggest the subtle change which this casts over everything—the curiously different value which it gives to all the actions and relations of life. It is not only that we understand another man still more intimately; it is that we feel ourselves to be acting through him, and we appreciate his motives as our own motives, even though we may perfectly understand that another part of ourselves, possessing more knowledge or a different view-point, might act quite differently. All through our previous evolution we have had our own private view-point and our own qualities, which were cherished because they were our own—which seemed to us in some subtle way different from the same qualities when manifested in others; but now we lose entirely that sense of personal property in qualities and in ideas, because we see that these things are truly common to all, because they are part of the great reality which lies equally behind all. So personal pride in individual development becomes an utter impossibility, for we see now that personal development is but as the growth of one leaf among the thousands of leaves upon a tree, and that the important fact is not the size or shape of that particular leaf, but its relation to the tree as a whole; for it is only of the tree as a whole that we can really predicate permanent growth.

Down here we meet people of different dispositions; we study them, and we say to ourselves that under no conceivable circumstances could we ever act or think as they do, and though we sometimes talk of "putting ourselves in the other man's place", it is generally a feeble, half-hearted, insufficient substitution; but in the intuitional world we see clearly and instantly the reason for those actions which here seem so incomprehensible and repugnant, and we readily understand that it is we ourselves in another form who are doing those very things which seem to us so reprehensible, and we recognise that to that facet of ourselves such action is quite right and natural. We find that we have ceased altogether to blame others for their differences from ourselves; we simply note them as other manifestations of our own activity, for now we see reasons which before were hidden from us. Even the evil man is clearly seen to be part of ourselves—a weak part; so our desire is not to blame him, but to help him by pouring strength into that weak part of ourselves, so that the whole body of humanity may be vigorous and healthy.

When in the causal body, we already recognised the Divine Consciousness in all; when we looked upon another ego, that consciousness leaped up in him to recognise the Divine within us. Now it no longer leaps to greet us from without, for it is already enshrined within our hearts. We *are* that consciousness and it is *our* consciousness. There is no longer the "you" and the "I", for we both are one—both facets of something that transcends and yet includes us both.

Yet in all this strange advance there is no loss of the sense of individuality, even though there is an utter loss of the sense of separateness. That seems a paradox, yet it is obviously true. The man remembers all that lies behind him. He is himself, the same man who did this action or that in the far-off past. He is in no way changed, except that now he is much more than he was then, and feels that he includes within himself many other manifestations as well. If here and now a hundred of us could simultaneously raise our consciousness into the intuitional world, we should all be one consciousness, but to each man that would seem to be his own, absolutely unchanged except that now it included all the others as well.

To each it would seem that it was *he* who had absorbed or included all those others; so we are here manifestly in the presence of a kind of illusion, and a little further realisation makes it clear to us that we are all facets of a greater consciousness, and that what we have hitherto thought to be our qualities, our intellect, our energy, have all the time been His qualities, His intellect, His energy. We have arrived at the realisation in actual fact of the time-honoured formula: "Thou art that". It is one thing to talk about this down here and to grasp it, or think that we grasp it, intellectually; but it is quite another to enter into that marvellous world and *know* it with a certainty that can never again be shaken.

Yet it must not be supposed that when a man enters upon the lowest subdivision of that world, he at once becomes fully conscious of his unity with all that lives. That perfection of sense comes only as the result of much toil and trouble, when he has reached the highest subdivision of this realm of unity. To enter that plane at all is to experience an enormous extension of consciousness, to realise himself as one with many others; but before him then there opens a time of effort, a time of self-development, analogous at that level to what we do down here when by meditation we try to open our consciousness to the plane next above us. Step by step, sub-plane by sub-plane, the aspirant wins his way; for even at that level exertion is still necessary if progress is to be made.

A stage below this, while we were still in the higher mental plane, we learned to see things as they are, to get behind our preconceptions of them, and to reach the reality which lay behind what we had been able to see of them. Now we are able to see the reality which lay behind other people's divergent views of that same object; coming simultaneously up their lines as well as our own, we enter into that thing and we realise all its possibilities, because now it is ourselves, and its possibilities are possible also for us. Difficult to put into words; impossible fully to comprehend down here; and yet approaching and hinting at a truth which is more real than what we call reality in this world.

If we could instantly be transported to that level without passing slowly through the intermediate stages, most of what we found ourselves able to see would mean but little to us. To change abruptly even into the astral consciousness gives one so different an outlook that many familiar objects are entirely unrecognisable. Such a thing, for example, as a book or a water-bottle presents to us a certain appearance with which we are familiar; but if we suddenly find ourselves able to see that object from all sides at once, as well as from above and below, we shall perhaps realise that it presents an appearance so different that we should require a considerable amount of mental adjustment before we could name it with certainty. Add to that the further complication that the whole inside of the body is laid out before us as though every particle were separately placed upon a table, and we shall again see that additional difficulties are introduced. Add to them again yet another fact—that while we look upon all these particles as described, we are yet at the same time within each of those particles and are looking out through it, and we shall see that it becomes an absolute impossibility to trace any resemblance to the object which we knew in the physical world.

That is, of course, nothing but an illustration—a coarse and concrete example of what takes place; and in order really to understand, one must spiritualise it and add to it many other considerations—all of which, however, tend to make the recognition more difficult rather than less. Fortunately in nature no sudden leap of this kind is possible. The method of evolution is gradual unfoldment, so that we are led on little by little until we are able to face without flinching glories which would dazzle us if they burst unexpectedly upon our view.

At this level man still has a definite body, and yet his consciousness seems equally present in vast numbers of other bodies. The web of life (which, you know, is constructed of buddhic matter—matter of the intuitional world) is extended so that it includes these other people, so that instead of many small separate webs we get one vast web which enfolds them all in one common life. But remember that many of these others may be entirely unconscious of this change, and to them their own private little part of the web will still seem as much separated as ever—or *would* do so if they knew anything at all about the web of life. So from this standpoint and at this level it seems that all mankind are bound together thus by golden threads, and make one complex unit, no longer a man, but man in the abstract.

What can we say of the next stage of consciousness, that which has often been called nirvana? This noble word has been translated to mean annihilation, but nothing could be further from the truth than this, for it represents the most intense and vivid life of which we know anything. Perhaps it may not unfairly be described as annihilation of all that we on the physical plane know and think of as the man; for all his personality, all his lower qualities, have long ago utterly disappeared. Yet the essence is there; the true man is there; the Divine Spark, descended from the Deity Himself, is still there, though now it has grown into a Flame—a Flame that is becoming consciously part of That from which it came; for here all consciousness merges into Him, even though it still retains all that was best in the feeling of individuality. The man still feels himself, just as he does now, but full of a delight, a vigour, a capacity, for which we have simply no words down here. He has in no way lost his personal memories. He is just as much himself as ever, only it is a wider self. He still knows that "I am I"; but he also realises, and far more prominently, that "I am He".

In the intuitional world his consciousness had widened so as to take in that of many other people. Now it seems to include the entire spiritual world, and the man feels that he is on the way to realising the divine attribute of omnipresence; for he exists not only in all those others, but also at every point of the intervening space, so that he can focus himself wherever he will, thus realising exactly the well-known phrase that he is a circle whose centre is everywhere and its circumference nowhere. He has transcended intellect as we know it, yet he knows and understands far more fully than ever before. On lower planes (lower than this, yet to us high beyond all reaching) he has seen the great Angels and Archangels in all their glorious order. In this spiritual world he comes face to face with the powers that rule, with the great Administrators of Karma, with the great Leaders of the Occult Hierarchy; with Planetary Spirits of stupendous power and wondrous beauty.

It is hopeless to attempt to describe this life which transcends all life that we know, and yet is so utterly different from it as to seem almost a negation of it—a splendour of purposeful life as compared with a mere blind crawling along darkened ways. For this indeed is life and this is reality, as far as we can reach it at present; although we doubt not for a moment that beyond even this indescribable glory there extend yet greater glories which surpass it even as it surpasses this catacomb life of earth. There, all is God, and all these august Beings are obviously great manifestations of Him; and so thoroughly is this conviction borne in upon a man's consciousness, so entirely does it become part of him, that when he descends once more to the physical globe of this sorrowful star he cannot forget it, but ever thereafter he sees the Divine Spark, even in the most unlikely surroundings. Down here it is often hard to recognise; we need to dig so deeply in order to find it. In that spiritual world it is self-evident, and we know, because we see it, that there is nothing but God—no life anywhere in all the worlds but the Divine Life.

For at that level the man himself has become as a god among gods, a lesser light among the greater lights, yet truly an orb of splendour, even though so much less than the Masters, than the Great Devas, than the Mighty Spirits who rule the destinies of men and worlds. There we see face to face all these great Beings of whom down here we hear and read, of whom sometimes we make faint images. There we see with open face the beauty of which down here we can but catch the faintest reflections. There we hear the glorious music of the spheres, of which only occasional echoes can reach us in this lower world.

Truly terrible as is the descent from that great world to this, yet one who has once touched that consciousness can never again be the same as he was before. He cannot wholly forget, even amidst the darkness and the storm, that his eyes have seen the King in His beauty, that he has beheld the land which is very far off, and yet at the same time is near, even at our doors, close about us all the while, if we will but lift up our eyes to see it, if we will but develop the God within us till He can respond to the God without.

"The land which is very far off"; from the days of our childhood the phrase has been familiar to us, and it falls upon our ears with all the magic of holy associations; yet it is a mistranslation of the original Hebrew, and perhaps the real meaning of the text is even more beautiful and more appropriate, for the expression which Isaiah used is "the land of far distances", as though he were contrasting in his mind the splendid spaciousness of the star-strewn fields of heaven with the noisome narrowness of the cramped catacombs of earth. Yet even here and now, imprisoned in densest matter, we may lift our thoughts to the sun, for when once we know the truth, the truth has made us free. When once we have realised our unity with God, no darkness can ever shade us again, for we know that He is Light of Light, and the Father of Lights, with whom is no variableness, neither shadow of turning; and in Him is no darkness at all.

All this knowledge, all this glory, is within our reach, and must inevitably come to every one of us in the course of our evolution, as surely as day follows night. It is beyond all words now, beyond all feelings—beyond our intuition even. But there will come a time when we shall know even as now also we are known. All that will come to us in the course of nature (in the seventh round, as we have said), even though we drift along and make no exertion; but far earlier if we are willing to undertake the labour which earns it—hard work indeed, yet noble work and pleasant in the doing, even though at times it may bring with it much of suffering. Yet the way is the Way of Service, and each step that we take is taken not for ourselves but for others, that through our realisation others may realise, that through our exertion others may find the Path, that through the blessing which comes to us the whole world may also be blessed.

Chapter III

The Buddhic Consciousness

MUCH has been written about the buddhic or intuitional world, and all students are theoretically acquainted with its wonderful characteristic of unity of consciousness; but most of them probably regard the possibility of obtaining any personal experience of that consciousness as belonging to the far-distant future. The full development of the buddhic vehicle is for most of us still remote, for it belongs to the stage of the Fourth or Arhat Initiation; but it is perhaps not entirely impossible for those who are as yet far from that level to gain some touch of that higher type of consciousness in quite another way.

I was myself brought along what I should describe as the ordinary and commonplace line of occult development, and I had to fight my way laboriously upward, conquering one subplane after another, first in the astral world, then in the mental, and then in the buddhic; which means that I had the, full use of my astral, mental and causal vehicles before anything came to me that I could define certainly as a real buddhic experience. This method is slow and toilsome, though I think it has its advantages in developing accuracy in observation, in making sure of each step before the next is taken. I have no doubt whatever that it was the best for a person of my temperament; indeed, it was probably the only way possible for me; but it does rot follow that other people may not have quite other opportunities.

It has happened to me in the course of my work to come into contact with a number of those who are undergoing occult training; and perhaps the fact which emerges most prominently from my experience in that direction is the marvellous variety of method employed by our Masters. So closely adapted is the training to the individual, that in no two cases is it the same; not only has every Master His own plan, but the same Master adopts a different scheme for each pupil, and so each person is brought along exactly that line which is most suitable for him.

A remarkable instance of this variability of method came under my notice not long ago, and I think that an explanation of it may perhaps be useful to some of our students. Let me first remind them of the curious inverted way in which the ego is reflected in the personality; the higher *manas* or intellect images itself in the mental body, the intuition or *buddhi* reflects itself in the astral body, and the spirit or *atma* itself somehow corresponds to the physical. These correspondences show themselves in the three methods of individualisation, and they play their part in certain inner developments; but until lately it had not occurred to me that they could be turned to practical account at a much earlier stage by the aspirant for occult progress.

A certain student of deeply affectionate nature developed an intense love for the teacher who had been appointed by his Master to assist him in the preliminary training. He made it a daily practice to form a strong mental image of that teacher, and then pour out his love upon him with all his force, thereby flooding his own astral body with crimson, and temporarily increasing its size enormously. He used to call the process "enlarging his aura". He showed such remarkable aptitude in this exercise, and it was so obviously beneficial to him, that an additional effort along the same line was suggested to him. He was recommended, while holding the image clearly before him, and sending out the love-force as strongly as ever, to try to raise his consciousness to a higher level and unify it with that of his teacher.

His first attempt to do this was amazingly successful. He described a sensation as of actually rising through space; he found what he supposed to be the sky like a roof barring his way, but the force of his will seemed to form a sort of cone in it, which presently became a tube through which he found himself rushing. He emerged into a region of blinding light which was at the same time a sea of bliss so overwhelming that he could find no words to describe it. It was not in the least like anything that he had ever felt before; it grasped him as definitely and instantaneously as a giant hand might have done, and permeated his whole nature in a moment like a flood of electricity. It was more real than any physical object that he had ever seen, and yet at the same time so utterly spiritual. "It was as though GOD had taken me into Himself, and I felt His Life running through me", he said.

He gradually recovered himself and was able to examine his condition; and as he did so he began to realise that his consciousness was no longer limited as it had hitherto been—that he was somehow simultaneously present at every point of that marvellous sea of light; indeed, that in some inexplicable way he was himself that sea, even though apparently at the same time he was a point floating in it. It seemed to us who heard, that he was groping after words to express the consciousness which, as Madame Blavatsky so well puts it, has "its centre everywhere and its circumference nowhere".

Further realisation revealed to him that he had succeeded in his effort to become one with the consciousness of his teacher. He found himself thoroughly comprehending and sharing that teacher's feelings, and possessing a far wider and higher outlook on life than he had ever had before. One thing that impressed him immensely was the image of himself as seen through the teacher's eyes; it filled him with a sense of unworthiness, and yet of high resolve; as he whimsically put it:

"I found myself loving myself through my teacher's intense love for me, and I knew that I could and would make myself worthy of it."

He sensed also a depth of devotion and reverence which he had never before reached; he knew that in becoming one with his earthly teacher he had also entered the shrine of his true Master, with whom that teacher in turn was one, and he dimly felt himself in touch with a Consciousness of unrealisable splendour. But here his strength failed him; he seemed to slide down his tube again, and opened his eyes upon the physical plane.

Consulted as to this transcendent experience, I enquired minutely into it, and easily satisfied myself that it was unquestionably an entry into the buddhic world, not by toilsome progress through the various stages of the mental, but by a direct course along the ray of reflection from the highest astral sub-plane to the lowest of that intuitional world. I asked as to the physical effects, and found that there were absolutely none; the student was in radiant health. So I recommended that he should repeat the effort, and that he should with utmost reverence try to press higher still, and to raise himself, if it might be, into that other August Consciousness. For I saw that here was a case of that combination of golden love and iron will that is so rare on this our Sorrowful Star; and I knew that a love which is utterly unselfish and a will which recognises no obstacles may carry their possessor to the very Feet of GOD Himself.

The student repeated his experiment, and again he succeeded beyond all hope or expectation. He was able to enter that wider Consciousness, and he pressed onward and upward into it as though he were swimming out into some vast lake. Much of what he brought back with him he could not comprehend; shreds of ineffable glories, fragments of conceptions so vast and so gorgeous that no merely human mind can grasp them in their totality. But he gained a new idea of what love and devotion could be—an ideal after which to strive for the rest of his life.

Day after day he continued his efforts (we found that once a day was as often as it could be wisely attempted); further and further he penetrated into that great lake of love, and yet found no end to it. But gradually he became aware of something far greater still; he somehow knew that this indescribable splendour was permeated by a subtler glory yet more inconceivably splendid, and he tried to raise himself into that. And when he succeeded he knew by its characteristics that this was the Consciousness of the great World-Teacher Himself. In becoming one with his own earthly teacher he had inevitably joined himself to the consciousness of his Master, with whom that teacher was already united; and in this further marvellous experience he was but proving the close union which exists between that Master and the Bodhisattva, Who in turn had taught Him. Into that shoreless sea of Love and Compassion he plunges daily in his meditation, with such upliftment and strengthening for himself as may readily be imagined; but he can never reach its limits, for no mortal man can fathom such an ocean as that.

Striving ever to penetrate more and more deeply into this wondrous new realm which had so suddenly opened before him, he succeeded one day in reaching a yet further development—

a bliss so much more intense, a feeling so much more profound, that it seemed to him at first as much higher than his first buddhic touch as that had been above his earlier astral experiences. He remarked:

"If I did not know that it is impossible for me to attain it yet, I should say that this must be Nirvana."

In reality it was only the next sub-plane of the buddhic—the second from the bottom, and the sixth from the top; but his impression is significant as showing that not only does consciousness widen as we rise, but the rate at which it widens increases rapidly. Not only is progress accelerated, but the rate of such acceleration grows by geometrical progression. Now this student reaches that higher sub-plane daily and as a matter of course, and is working vigorously and perseveringly in the hope of advancing still farther. And the power, the balance and the certainty which this introduces into his daily physical life is amazing and beautiful to see.

Another phenomenon which he observes, as accompanying this, is that the intense bliss of that higher plane now persists beyond the time of meditation and is becoming more and more a part of his whole life. At first this persistence was for some twenty minutes after each meditation; then it reached an hour; then two hours; and he is confidently looking forward to a time when it will be his as a permanent possession—a part of himself. A remarkable feature of the case is that this prodigious daily exaltation is not followed by any sign of the slightest reaction or depression, but instead produces an ever-augmenting radiance and sunniness.

Becoming gradually more accustomed to functioning in this higher and more glorious world, he began to look about him to some extent, and was presently able to identify himself with many other less exalted consciousnesses. He found these existing as points within his extended self, and he discovered that by focusing himself at any one of these points he could at once realise the highest qualities and spiritual aspirations of the person whom it represented. Seeking for a more detailed sympathy with some whom he knew and loved, he discerned that these points of consciousness were also, as he put it, holes through which he could pour himself down into their lower vehicles; and thus he came into touch with those parts of their lives and dispositions which could find no expression on the buddhic plane. This gave him a sympathy with the characters, a comprehension of their weaknesses, which was truly remarkable, and could probably have been attained in no other way—a most valuable quality for the work of a disciple in the future.

The wondrous unity of that intuitional world manifested itself to him in unsuspected examples. Holding in his hand one day what he regarded as a specially beautiful little object, part of which was white, he fell into a sort of ecstasy of admiration of its graceful form and harmonious colouring. Suddenly, through the object, as he gazed at it, he saw unfolded before him a landscape, just as though the object had become a tiny window, or perhaps a crystal. The landscape is one that he knows and loves well, but there was no obvious reason why the little object should bring it thus before him. A curious feature was that the white part of that object was represented in the landscape by huge piles of cumulus clouds, which he saw as floating in the sky of his picture.

Impressed by this wholly unexpected phenomenon, he tried the experiment of raising his consciousness while he revelled in the beauty of the prospect. He had the sensation of passing through some resisting medium into a higher plane, and found that the view before him had changed to one which was strange to him, but even more beautiful than that which he knew so well. The piles of white cloud had become a towering snow-covered mountain, with its long line sweeping down to a sea of colour richer than any that in this incarnation he had seen. The rocky bays, the buildings, the vegetation, were all foreign to him, though well-known to me; and by a little careful questioning I soon ascertained without room for doubt that the scene upon which he was looking was that which I suspected—a real physical view, but one many thousands of miles from the spot where he sat gazing at it. Since that hallowed spot is often in my mind, though I was not thinking of it at that moment, what the student saw may have been a thought-form of mine.

I imagine that up to this point what had happened may be quite simply described. I presume that the student's emotion was excited by his admiration, and that the heightened vibrations which were caused in this way brought into operation his astral senses, and this enabled him to see a view which was not physically visible, but well within astral reach. The endeavour to press on further temporarily opened the mental sense, and by it he was able to see my thought-form-if that second view was a thought-form of mine.

But the student did not rest satisfied with that; he repeated his attempt to push on still higher, or as he put it, still deeper into the real meaning of it all. Once more he had the experience of breaking through into some more exalted and more refined state of matter; and this time it was no earthly scene that rewarded his effort, for the foreground burgeoned forth into an illimitable universe filled with masses of splendid colour, pulsating with glorious life, and the snow-covered mountain became a great White Throne vaster than any mountain, veiled in dazzling golden light.

A strange fact connected with this vision is that the student to whom the experience came is entirely unacquainted with the Christian scripture, and was unaware that any text existing therein had any bearing upon what he saw. I asked him whether he could repeat this experience at will; he did not know, but later on he tried the experiment, and succeeded in passing again through those stages in the same order, giving some additional details of the foreign landscape which proved to me that this was not merely a feat of memory; and this time the awestricken seer whispered that amidst the coruscations of that light he once had a passing glimpse of the outline of a Mighty Figure Who sat upon the Throne. This also, you may say, might be a thought-form, built by some Christian of vivid imagination. Perhaps; but when a few days later an opportunity occurred, and I asked a Wise One what signification we might attach to such a vision, He replied:

"Do you not see that, as there is but One Love, so there is but One Beauty? Whatever is beautiful, on any plane, is so because it is part of that Beauty, and if it is pushed back far enough, its connection will become manifest. All Beauty is of GOD, as all Love is of GOD; and through these His Qualities the pure in heart may always reach Him."

Our students would do well to weigh these words, and follow out the idea contained in them. All beauty, whether it be of form or of colour, whether it be in nature or in the human frame, in high achievements of art or in the humblest household utensil, is but an expression of the One Beauty; and therefore in even the lowliest thing that is beautiful all beauty is implicitly contained, and so through it all beauty may be realised, and He Who Himself is Beauty may be reached. To understand this fully needs the buddhic consciousness by which our student arrived at its realisation; but even at much lower levels the idea may be useful and fruitful.

I fully admit that the student whose experiences I have been relating is exceptional—that he possesses a strength of will, a power of love, a purity of heart and an utter unselfishness which are, unfortunately, far from common. Nevertheless, what he has done with such marked success may surely be copied to some extent by others less gifted. He has unfolded his consciousness upon a plane which is not normally reached by aspirants; he is rapidly building for himself a capable and most valuable vehicle there—for that is the meaning of the ever-increasing persistence of the sense of bliss and power. That his is a definite line of progress, and not a mere isolated example, is shown by the fact that even already the abnormal buddhic development is producing its effect upon the apparently neglected causal and mental bodies, stimulating them into action from above instead of leaving them to be laboriously influenced from below as is usual. All this success is the result of steady effort along the line which I have described.

"Go thou and do likewise." No harm can come to any man from an earnest endeavour to increase his power of love, his power of devotion, and his power to appreciate beauty; and by such endeavour it is at least possible that he may attain a progress of which he has not dreamed. Only be it remembered that, in this path as in every other, growth is achieved only by him who desires it not for his own sake, but for the sake of service. Forgetfulness of self and an eager desire to help others are the most prominent characteristics of the student whose inner story I have here told; these characteristics *must* be equally prominent in any who aspire to follow his example; without them no such consummation is possible.

CHAPTER IV

AN INSTANCE OF PSYCHIC DEVELOPMENT

PSYCHIC development of all kinds is wonderfully quickened just now by the great inrush of spiritual force which is preparing the world for the Coming of its Teacher; and naturally the opportunities for such development offer themselves most readily to those who put themselves directly in the way of that mighty current of force by working in connection with the expected Advent. In the previous chapter I gave an instance of the abnormally rapid unfoldment of the buddhic faculty by means of the power of love; this case which I shall describe belongs to another line, for this time it is the faculty of the causal body which is aroused through the mental vehicle, by putting an undue strain upon the physical brain. But I cannot say to our readers in this case, as in the other: "Go thou and do likewise"; for the mental strain is a serious danger. It happened for once to lead to psychic development; but far more often it results in nervous breakdown of the gravest character, or even in brain lesion and insanity. The account sent to me is as follows:

"When I was at College (about 1910) I took up the study of the calculus, which, as you know, is the mathematics of variable quantities, the study of moving bodies and the like. From a variety of causes I was unable to do justice to the work day by day, and toward the end of the second term, when the day of examination in this was approaching, I was told by the lecturer that my work had been so unsatisfactory that unless I performed some miracle in the forth-coming examination he could not recommend me for a pass in the subject. I fully realised that he was quite right, and set about finding out how I could possibly score a high grade in the examination in order to offset the bad work during the year. I soon found that it would be impossible in the few days left to me really to understand the ground covered, and that the only hope would lie in memorising the formulae and applying them in a mechanical fashion to problems given in the examination. I therefore set to work, first to understand the definitions used in the textbooks, and second to learn by rote all the important formulae. I worked very hard, far into the night, neglected other subjects, in which I felt sure of myself in any case, and resorted to all sorts of devices to gain time and keep awake. Bit by bit I covered all the important ground, but only by memorising, sometimes even visualising the *appearance* of a page or paragraph. The day of the examination I was utterly weary physically, but extraordinarily vivid mentally. I duly appeared, applied my crammed-up facts to the examination, and, as I subsequently found, wrote a paper with only one small mistake in arithmetical computation, or something like that. This was the unexpected performance that the lecturer demanded, and he duly gave me a pass.

"Now the point of this episode comes in the sequel. I found in a few days, as is usual in such cases, that all the material which I had stuffed into my head was a rapidly-vanishing jumble; but as it disappeared, and as I resumed my physical norm (chiefly by long hours of sleep), I discovered that I had actually done something, either damage or benefit, to my mental machinery, and that my ability to picture things in my mind was tremendously enlarged. I now found that if I turned my mind upon something I had seen or experienced even years before, the image returned to me, not in the ordinary vague way, but with the most extraordinary clarity in detail, with accompanying attributes of all sorts. For instance, if I was recalling a scene in a wood, I could actually *smell* the damp earth or the burning fire! This amused me very much, as it was quite possible to get back into the past in momentary flashes of the utmost brilliancy. After a time, however, the power of commanding this strange faculty wore off, and I had to be content with spontaneous outbursts which arose now and then through association. By the sight of a colour or some passing odour this latent power would suddenly put me into another time and place. Fortunately I could always banish the mental image, even though I could not call it up.

"After a time this gradually wore away into a lesser degree of brilliancy, and I was only occasionally edified by this annihilation of time and space.

"But now, just lately, there has been a return, in a new phase, of the old thing. I have had to learn, during the last year or so, the Government regulations of a business which I am carrying on. This bad to be accomplished quickly, and I find that with this effort there is a return of the result which followed the previous effort, and, it is pleasant to note, with two new aspects; first that I am much more able to command and sustain any image that arises, and second that I can *magnify* the scene to a certain extent. Thus, if the picture includes a wall in the distance I can occasionally magnify it until the crannies are visible. And, what astonished me exceedingly, if there is a perfume, say, of flowers present, the same microscopic power can be turned on! Now the result is not intensification of the perfume, as one might hastily conclude, but a *roughening* of it. I mean by this that instead of getting thicker, in the sense that a heavy oil is thicker than water, the smell loses its smoothness and becomes (if one could feel it) like woollen cloth, or a basin of sand. For some reason I cannot perform this same enlarging trick with sound. At present there is no sign of any diminution of this curious phase of memory, but I have no doubt that it will fade away in large part, as I am too busy to undertake its cultivation."

What is happening in this case is obvious to anyone who has had experience in the use of the higher faculties. Instead of using his memory in the ordinary way, the student is coming into touch with the Records; and that means that he is to a certain extent employing the faculties of his causal body. We are far from certain as to the exact method of ordinary memory, for the subject has not yet been investigated; but it is clear that a vibration in the mental body is part of what occurs, and that the causal body is not in any way involved. In the reading of the Records it is precisely this latter sheath through which the work is done, and the mental body vibrates only in response to the activity of the causal. For that reason no satisfactory or reliable reading of the Records can be done without definite development of the vehicle of the ego.

From the description which our student gives, it is clear that he was using his causal body in the glimpses of the past which he relates. It is also evident that that vehicle was aroused by the undue pressure put upon the mind by his reckless overwork. Most men would have ruined their health for life if they had pushed the strain as far as he did; he happens to be the one in a million who managed to do this thing and survive. The result is that his steady persistence in keeping up high mental undulations has stirred his causal body into activity, and thus endued him with a faculty different from any which he has before possessed.

So far it seems to waken only when he turns his thoughts to the past, and only in connection with scenes already familiar to him; but it is probable that he will soon find that he can extend its working in various ways. When a scene is clearly in mind it might be possible to move backwards or forwards from it, and so recover detailed memory of large sections of early life. Perhaps one could in this way push back recollection into childhood—back to birth itself, and even beyond; there have been those who in this manner have attained full knowledge of previous incarnations. Practice makes perfect; and it is encouraging that the power is much more under control now than formerly. The faculty of magnification is another conclusive proof that it is the causal body which is being used; this feature also might by degrees be largely increased, and when fully at the student's disposal might be used (for example) to undertake researches into occult chemistry.

The description of the "roughening" of the smell is most characteristic. The actual process of magnifying consists not in increasing the size of the object examined, but in lessening the psychic lens through which that object is seen. In ancient scriptures it is said that the operator makes himself as small as he will, and so the organ of vision which he is using becomes commensurate with the microscopic size of that at which he looks. Consequently the tiny physical particles which call into action the sense of smell become separately appreciable, like the grains upon sandpaper, and so the sense of roughness is produced. It is a thing difficult to put into words, but anyone who has used the higher faculty will at once recognise our student's attempt to express it.

He is much to be congratulated upon his result, though we certainly cannot recommend his method for imitation by others. Such development will come easily and naturally when, in the course of human evolution, the mind has grown more nearly to the limit of its capabilities; but at our present stage such pressure is distinctly dangerous. That even this partial unfoldment should have been safely achieved is a sign of the times—a sign of the strength of the spiritual outpouring which even now is flooding the world.

CHAPTER V

TIME

THERE are two kinds of time: our time and God's time; two at least, but probably many more; for while we know something of our own capacity, we have no means of gauging the divine capacity. Our consciousness is a point, moving ever from the past to the future, and we give the name of "the present" to the passing moment which divides the two; but this "present" is an illusion; it is evanescent—a mere knife-edge. Even while we think of that moment, it has already become the past, and another moment is to us the present.

Our consciousness moves along a certain line—say, for the sake of illustration, from south to north. Our memory includes more or less accurately that part of the line over which we have already passed, but not that which still lies before us; and we usually regard what we call the past as irrevocable, whereas we recognise that we possess a certain amount of power to mould our future. That is because we think that the point which is our consciousness has already moved along a certain line which cannot now be altered; but that its future movements may to some extent be controlled, since to us it appears that the events of the future have not yet happened. It is true that they have not yet happened to us; perhaps it would be truer to say that we have not yet come to them. It will help us if we can grasp the idea that we are not in reality that point of consciousness—or rather, we are much more than that. We are *the whole line*, and the point of consciousness is passing from one part of ourselves to another part which is equally ourselves. It is within our possibilities to awaken the whole of ourselves, to be conscious of ourselves as a line and not merely as a point; and when we have succeeded in reaching that, we have transcended the delusion of *our* kind of time, for the past and the future lie simultaneously before us.

Take the analogy of a railway train, which we may suppose to be running from south to north. We move along that line and at any given moment we see what is visible from the particular point at which we happen to be. We remember as much as we have observed of the scenery through which we have passed; but we are ignorant of the scenery which lies before us, if it is our first journey along that line. We know, however, that the whole railway exists all the time, and that the objects which we see in succession are really simultaneously in existence; and it is not difficult for us to imagine a condition in which, by being simultaneously present at every point, we could have the whole panorama before us at the same time. By climbing a high mountain or ascending in a balloon we could to some extent realise this idea, except that in that case the point of view would be entirely changed and so the analogy would be imperfect.

But we have still to realise that there is quite another motion going on—one of which we are, normally, entirely unconscious. We may typify this by a lateral motion of the line—say from west to east. So that if we suppose all this motion to be taking place in a square, it would seem to us that our evolution consisted in a northward movement in a line parallel to the side of the square, and to attain the northern side would seem the end and object of that evolution. Yet the real goal is all the while not the northern side but the north-east corner, and there is another time moving at right angles to our time, which carries our past and our future with it just as surely as that fleeting illusion which we call our present. In the analogy of the railway, this time is typified by the rotation of the earth, which is all the while carrying the whole railway (with our train upon it) from west to east, though of this we know nothing by our physical sensations.

That other time is God's time; and in *that* time what we call our past is not irrevocable, but is constantly changing, though always in the direction of improvement, or evolution. It may be said that the events of the past cannot be changed; but that statement is after all an assumption. The important events of the past are our contacts with other egos, our relations with them; and these relations *are* being changed, whether we know it or not; for they are in this direction at right angles to what we call time, which at present we are unable to appreciate.

But just as it is now possible for us to become conscious all along our line instead of only at one point of it, so will it in the far-away future be possible for us to acquire a consciousness which shall contain *the whole square*—a consciousness equivalent to that which now seems to us the Divine Consciousness. Probably then the whole process will be repeated, and we shall find that the whole square is moving at right angles to itself; but it is better to try to grasp one facet of the idea at a time. In the same way our railroad is not only being carried round from west to east as the earth rotates upon its axis, but it is also being carried through space at a far swifter rate as the earth revolves round the sun; and it has yet again an additional and quite different motion as the whole solar system revolves in its incalculable orbit round some far greater central sun.

This transcendental view of time has been very beautifully expressed by the late Mr. C. H. Hinton in his story *Stella*:

If you felt eternity, you would know that you are never separated from anyone with whom you have ever been. You come to a different part of yourself every day, and you think the part that is separated is time is gone, but in eternity it is always there.

If you felt eternity, you would know that what you did to a person and what he did to you is gradually changing. You think it is over and done with, but in eternity what you and he did to each other is always there and always changing and altering. As you grow better, he will act quite differently and you will act quite differently.

If you felt eternity, you would know that you are always living in your *whole life*, that it is always changing, though with your eyes you can see only the part you are in now. The present is just a concentration, like attending to one thing at a time.

The Present is the child of the Past; the Future the begotten of the Present. And yet, O present moment! knowest thou not that thou hast no parent, nor canst thou have a child; that thou art ever begetting but thyself? Before thou hast even begun to say: "I am the progeny of the departed moment, the child of the past," thou hast become that past itself. Before thou utterest the last syllable, behold! thou art no more the Present, but verily that Future. Thus are the Past, the Present, and the Future the Ever-living Trinity in one—the Mahamaya of the Asolute Is.—The *Secret Doctrine*, Vol. II, p. 466.

"Time" is only an illusion produced by the succession of our states of consciousness as we travel through Eternal Duration ... The Present is only a mathematical line which divides that part of Eternal Duration which we call the Future, from that part which we call the Past. Nothing on earth has real duration ... and the sensation we have of the actuality of the division of Time known as the Present, comes from the blurring of the momentary glimpse, or succession of glimpses, of things that our senses give us, as those things pass from the region of ideals, which we call the Future, to the region of memories that we name the Past ... No one would say that a bar of metal dropped into the sea came into existence as it left the air, and ceased to exist as it entered the water, and that the bar itself consisted only of that cross-section thereof which at any given moment coincided with the mathematical plane that separates, and, at the same time, joins, the atmosphere and the ocean. Even so persons and things; which—dropping out of the "to be" into the "has been", out of the Future into the Past—present momentarily to our senses a cross-section, as it were, of their total selves, as they pass through Time and Space (as Matter) on their way from one eternity to another.—The *Secret Doctrine*, Vol. I, p. 69.

CHAPTER VI

INSPIRATION

As our consciousness begins to open to influences from higher worlds, we are likely to come more and more intimately into contact with the phenomenon called inspiration. In all great spiritual movements outpourings of force from higher planes have taken place, and there is no reason to suppose that the latest of such movements will vary in that respect from the older manifestations. Most of our members know that we had a remarkable example of such a downflow at one of the meetings of the Order of the Star, at Benares, on December 28th, 1911, and there must be many who have felt the same thing in a lesser degree at other meetings.

The whole subject of such inspiration, of such pouring out of influence, is one of great interest; one that it is profitable for us to try to comprehend. We talk habitually of inspiration, but it is not generally at all understood, and the word is used to cover phenomena of different types. The manifestation to which I have just referred, though entirely spontaneous and unexpected, partook to some extent of the nature of those periodical effluxes of power from above upon a number of people simultaneously, upon which religions largely rely for the helping and strengthening of their followers. These public and general inspirations, if we may call them so, are in themselves a subject of enthralling interest to which but little scientific attention has been devoted. I have recently made a careful study of it in connection with certain Christian services, and have published the results in a book called *The Science of the Sacraments*. I hope to see the same work undertaken by some qualified exponent for each of the great religions of the world; for it is a side of religious influence that has been much neglected, and it seems to me to be one of great importance.

It is not, however, of these endeavours to affect the collective consciousness of a congregation that I wish to write here, but rather of individual inspirations, and the possibility of our encountering them in the course of our progress. There is, however, another sense in which the word is used, to which it will be well first to make a passing reference.

The less intelligent among the Christians tell us that their scriptures are directly inspired by the Holy Ghost; many Christians hold to a general inspiration, which would prevent any serious error, but there are also many who carry it further, and say that the actual words are so inspired. I am sorry to say that they sometimes make themselves ridiculous by carrying it further still, and saying that every word of the English translation must necessarily also be directly inspired by God. In fact, I fancy that many of the people who hold that view believe that the original messages were given in English! The nearest approach to rationality along this line is the theory that the same Holy Spirit who inspired the original writers also descended upon the translators and made them do their work with verbal accuracy.

I am afraid the verbal accuracy occasionally fails us, but there is this much to be said in favour of their idea, that the English translation of the Christian Scriptures is far finer in many respects than the original. If it ever comes in your way, as it did in mine as a student of divinity, to consult the original and compare it in considerable detail with the translation, I think you cannot but be struck, especially with regard to the Old Testament, with the fact that the original does not seem so poetical, so splendid in many respects, so beautiful and so musically expressed. There is some justification for the theory that King James' translators were the really inspired people, and those who know something of the influence which He whom we now call the Comte de St. Germain exercised over that translation, will be prepared to believe that there is a great deal of truth behind that theory of the rendering into such magnificent English of the scripture which was to have under that particular guise so worldwide an influence. If we compare the French translation of the Bible with the English, I think we shall agree that the former is a poor thing in comparison, and does not give at all the same effect—that our Christian brothers in France lose much by the fact that their scripture is by no means so poetically and so felicitously expressed as our own translation. Luther's translation into German is somewhat better, but even that, I think, falls much below the English version. I mean the old English authorised version; the revised version is more accurate in some respects, but in many cases it has lost the old poetry and the old inspiration.

But the reality of inspiration is not quite as orthodox people imagine it. Some Christians apparently believe that God the Holy Ghost dictated word by word those very scriptures, and are not at all disturbed by the fact that that is obviously untrue, as the books contain numerous mistakes. Yet, apart from such foolish belief, there is a vast amount of inspiration of different sorts going on, not perhaps from so high a source as the ill-instructed Christian supposes, but perfectly real inspiration nevertheless, even though it does not take just that form.

Any student of Theosophy must be aware that our Masters, the true Leaders of the Society, have frequently inspired its speakers and writers; but They have not done so, as a rule, by any sort of verbal dictation. Far more frequently They have done it by projecting into the mind of the speaker or writer certain ideas, leaving the man to clothe them in his own words. That is unquestionably an inspiration, because *spiro* means "I breathe"; so inspiration is something breathed into one from without, and those ideas in that sequence would not have occurred to the speaker or writer without that interference. Of that kind of inspiration I think we have had a great deal.

Those who have heard the lectures of our revered President can hardly fail to have been struck by the wonderful eloquence with which she speaks. That is of course native to her; it is a priceless talent which she holds in this life because she has won it by many lives of assiduous practice in public speaking. But one who hears her as often as I have done, many hundreds of times probably, will soon learn that besides her magnificent flights of eloquence other and different forms of speech sometimes fall from her lips, and that she is unquestionably sometimes guided from without as to what she shall say. I think she would herself say: "Sometimes I feel that my Master is putting ideas info my mind, and I simply express them"; she would even tell you that there have been occasions when He has actually used her organs and spoken through her Himself. I have myself heard that happen on several occasions, and the change is most marked. When left to herself our President speaks always in splendid flowing sentences. I have heard her say, when asked about her eloquence: "While I am speaking one sentence I see the next sentence in the air before me in two or three different forms, and I select from those that which I think will be most effective". I have no personal experience of that sort of thing; that talent has not been given to me; I have not this wonderful gift of eloquence. We use that expression, "a gift", because as far as this life is concerned it is a gift; but remember that it is the result of work done in the past.

Those glowing periods, those balanced and modulated sentences—that is her style when left to herself; but her Master speaks usually in short, sharp sentences. In this incarnation, before He resigned His place in the world and became—not an ascetic exactly, but at least one who devotes the whole of His life entirely to spiritual work—He was a King in India, a commander of troops, accustomed to state exactly what He wanted in strong, brief, military sentences. He does so still, and it is striking indeed to watch the President's style suddenly change into the tone of command, to hear it alter from measured cadences to short, strong sentences—a most interesting study for a student of psychology. That is another form of inspiration.

Sometimes a spiritualist says to us: "In what way does such a condition as that which you thus describe differ from mediumship, to which, I am told, you have a decided objection?"

I answer that the difference is fundamental; the two conditions are wide as the poles asunder. In mediumship a person is passive, and lays himself open to the influence of any astral entity who happens to be in the neighbourhood. When under the influence he is usually unconscious, and knows neither what is being done through his organism nor who is doing it; he remembers nothing when he awakens from his trance. His state is really one of temporary obsession. There is generally supposed to be a dead man in charge of the proceedings, who is called a spirit-guide; but I have seen several cases in which such a guide proved utterly unable to afford efficient protection, for he encountered a force far stronger than his own, with results disastrous to his medium.

If one of our Masters chooses to speak through one of His pupils, the latter is fully conscious of what is being done, and knows perfectly to whom he is for the moment lending his vocal organs. He stands aside from his vehicle, but he remains keenly alert and watchful; he hears every word that is uttered through him, follows with reverent interest all that occurs, and remembers everything clearly. There is nothing in common between the two cases, except that in both of them the body of one man is temporarily used by another.

Our Masters not infrequently make use of Their pupils, not always in speaking or writing only, but in quite other ways. In the great case at Benares on the 28th December nothing was spoken by Alcyone beyond a word or two of benediction at the end of the meeting—nothing more than that; but still the outpouring of the influence was clearly felt by many. It is the custom of the Master to pour influence through His pupil, and often that influence may be not such as we class under the term "inspiration"; that is to say, it will not prompt the pupil to do or to say anything whatever, but it will be simply a tremendous outpouring of spiritual force which may be employed for various purposes; sometimes for the healing of some disease, but more often for the comforting of some one who is in trouble, for the guidance of some one who is in great difficulty.

Perhaps that is one of the ways in which prayers are answered. Most students would say that prayer, in the ordinary sense of the word, is not a thing to which they attach great importance—not a thing which they would recommend. I myself feel, not only as a Theosophist but as a bishop of the Christian Church, that to pray to God for anything personal for oneself implies a lack of faith in Him; it distinctly implies that He needs to be told what is best for His people. I never felt myself so sure of what was best for me as to think that I was in a position to dictate to the Supreme Ruler of heaven and earth. It always seemed to me that He must know so far better than I, and that, being a loving Father (as I am absolutely certain that He is), He is already doing all for me that can be done, and needs no requests from me—more especially as my request might very likely be for something which I wish, though in reality it may not be at all the best thing for me. Therefore I have always felt that anything in the nature of personal prayer is to some extent an exhibition of distrust. I am so absolutely convinced that what is being done is beyond all question the best that can be done under all circumstances and taking everything into account, that it would never occur to me to ask the Great Architect of the Universe to alter His arrangements in order to suit me. I cannot think, therefore, that prayer is a commendable thing. I should consider meditation or aspiration a better form in which to express one's spiritual need.

But vast numbers of people do pray; and the Christians, the Hindus, the Muhammadans all agree in telling us that prayers are often answered. They *are*. It may be that theoretically they ought not to be, but they *are*, and it is useless for scientific investigators to blink facts. If prayers are sometimes answered, how does it happen? for of course we cannot suppose that the Supreme Ruler of the Universe turns aside in His scheme at the request of man. Who then hears these smaller prayers, and to some extent deals with them? Obviously lower entities of some sort. Our Roman Catholic friends tell us that each man has his guardian Angel, that there are great hierarchies of Angels always surrounding us, and that any one of these may be reached by a prayer, and may do in response to it whatever "in the providence of God", as they would say, he is permitted to do.

There is a great deal of truth in that idea. There are hosts of non-human beings peopling the space around us. As a general rule they have nothing to do with us nor we with them; but it is humanity that loses by that state of affairs, and it exists only because people know as a rule nothing about them. It would indeed be well for humanity that it should sometimes be helped by these greater people; and indeed even now it often is so helped without knowing it. I have given some instances of this in *Invisible Helpers,* and they are only examples; one could find hundreds more in which external assistance of one kind or another is given.

Some such cases of help are instances of the vigilance of those disciples of our Masters who are working constantly during sleep in the astral world; they see cases where they think some help can safely be given, and they step in and give it. Others show the interference of some non-physical being, but there is no evidence to show who the being was. It may have been what is commonly called a dead man, or it may have been one of those other non-human spirits; but the facts that such entities do surround us, and that now and then interference of some sort does take place—these are facts which we can verify for ourselves. We may read the published accounts of such interventions; we may look round and inquire whether any such instances can be found in the lives of those whom we know. Remember that we do not as a rule lay ourselves out at all for any such assistance, or for any suggestion from non-physical sources. Remember that the world around us is blankly unintelligent on such matters, and blatantly sceptical about them, and that those are clearly not the conditions which would encourage such intervention.

But if we go to Catholic countries where people do realise the possibility of such interventions, we shall find that they much more often take place there, simply because the people, believing in the possibility, lay themselves open to it in various ways. The ignorant sceptic always says: "These things do not come to me, because of my superior discrimination; I should at once see through the fraud, whatever it may be". That is a foolish attitude to take; and the reason which his vanity gives him for his lack of experience is not the true one. The sceptic erects a barrier round himself by his aggressive unbelief—a barrier which it is not worth the while of the non-physical entity to pierce; and so he goes unhelped, and consequently does not believe that anyone else can be helped. But such help does undoubtedly come, and sometimes it takes the form of inspiration.

It has often been my own experience, and I think it will be that of many public lecturers and preachers, that when speaking on any given subject new ideas are suddenly put into one's mind. Sometimes those come from one's ego, the higher self, who takes an interest in the work which is being done by the lower self, and contrives to flash down a fragment of information; but also sometimes they come quite distinctly from outside and from somebody else. It does not at all follow that the suggestions are necessarily in every respect accurate. They represent the opinion of the person who gives the suggestion, and a person in the astral world is no more infallible than one in the physical world. Here on this plane, if we heard a person talking about some subject, and had the opportunity without seeming intrusive, we should probably suggest to him anything that we knew on the matter. We hear a person explaining something to others, perhaps, and we observe some gaps in his explanation which we happen to be able to fill. If we are on friendly terms with that person, so that we can do it without hurting his feelings, we shall make our contribution in order that the instruction given may be fuller and better. Just as we should do that in a friendly way on the physical plane, so does the dead man, so does the Angel, from the astral plane.

Many students of the occult have passed over into the other world, but naturally they still retain their interest not only in the subjects which they studied, but in their own friends who are studying them. They still come back and attend meetings and lectures, and if an idea occurs to them on the subject under consideration which is not in the mind of the speaker or the lecturer, they will endeavour to insert such an idea. They do not materialise (which would be a great waste of force) in order to get up and speak themselves, but they can without much difficulty put the idea into a mind which is already in sympathy with them, and that is often done. Some entirely new idea, some fresh illustration, is as it were thrust before the mind of the speaker. He may think, especially if he does not know much about the matter, that this is his own cleverness, that he himself has invented this new illustration. It does not matter. The point is to get the idea put before the people; the entity does not care who gets the credit of it, naturally enough. So there is a great deal of inspiration about, even now, and there might be much more if people had an intelligent grasp of the subject, and if they laid themselves out for such inspiration.

It will frequently happen to a man who is writing an article, that these new ideas will come into his mind. He has no means of knowing whether they are his own ideas sent down by the ego, or thoughts sent down by some other agency; but after all it does not matter; there is no question of plagiarism here. Whoever gives them, gives them voluntarily. Any man preparing a subject should prepare it meditatively, with his mind open to new impressions; and he will often get those impressions. What of our poets? A poet is generally a man who is open to impressions. Whence those impressions come matters but little, so long as the ideas themselves are good. They may come from other poets who have passed over; they may come from Angels; they may come from his own higher self. What does it signify, so long as the thoughts are good and beautiful? They are sent down for him to utilise, but it must not be forgotten that it is his responsibility to see that the ideas *are* good and true.

If a man accepts every idea which comes to him, he may truly claim that he is acting under inspiration, but he will often find that the inspiration is not a reliable one, because he cannot as a rule know the source from which it comes. There are cases in which a man does know perfectly well. Those of us who have the privilege—the stupendous privilege—of communication with some of our Masters, soon come to know at once Their touch, Their magnetic influence, and so to recognise immediately when an idea comes to us from Them. Such ideas we should of course accept with the deepest reverence; but be very sure of their source, for there are those who are eager to deceive, and diabolically clever at the work of misrepresentation.

Remember, too, that anybody, with the best possible intentions, may put before us ideas which are not correct. A man is no more infallible because he happens to be dead, than he was when he happened to be alive. He is the same man. He certainly has now the *opportunity* of learning more than he knew before, but not every man takes his opportunities in that world any more than in this. One meets numbers of people who have been for twenty years in the astral world, and yet know no more than when they left this physical life, just as there are many people who have lived through fifty, sixty or seventy years of human life, and have contrived to imbibe remarkably little wisdom in the process. The advice or suggestion of those who have taken advantage of their opportunities is worth a great deal, whether it is given from the astral world or the physical world; but the two admonitions stand absolutely parallel, and we must attach no more importance to communications from the astral world, or from any higher plane, than we should to a suggestion made on the physical plane. We ought to be equally willing to receive them both, and we should attach to them just such importance as we feel they intrinsically deserve—that and no more, whencesoever they may come.

Inspiration is not infrequent: neither is that other form of influence of which I spoke—the spiritual force which is poured through a man who is in connection with a Great One. That also takes place quite often: and it is not only our own Masters who make use of physical people in that way. Other entities of all sorts may have their channels, through whom their force is poured out, and a great deal may be done in the world either by those who are dead or by those who belong to other systems of evolution than our own—those whom the Indians call Devas, whom in the West we know as Angels.

To take the ordinary sceptical or indifferent attitude would in many cases shut one off from the possibility of learning a great deal about these higher matters. When we come back to the more childlike attitude, which is at least receptive, though it may not be critical, we shall certainly find that there are possibilities of which now in our self-sufficiency we hardly dream.

Inspiration is a mighty reality, and so is the possibility of the outpouring of helpful force. Those who come into daily contact with it know well how constantly these things take place; and the blank prejudice against them, the sceptical attitude taken by so many people, is a source of wonder and pain to those who know, because it would seem as though men were intentionally, of malice prepense, shutting themselves away from one of the most interesting aspects of life—from one that may often be useful and helpful beyond all expectation.

Let us keep, then, an open mind with regard to such things. Inspiration may come to *us*; helpful force in some measure may flow through *us*. Let us be ready to be utilised in that way if our karma is so good that we can be so utilised; and when we see evidence that the same thing is happening through others, again let us keep an open mind, and not shut ourselves up in our own prejudice against the possibility of being helped and guided. That, I think, is the best line that we can take with regard to it.

Of course the other side needs emphasis too. We should not too readily believe that which comes. We must take everything on its own merits, no matter though it appears to us to come from a great Master—from a source to which we look for inspiration and for help. Even then, we must weigh it always on its own merits, because these higher planes are full of pitfalls to those who are unaccustomed to them. It is always possible that a higher power may be imitated by a lower one; it is possible that there may be some one who is jealous of the influence over us of a greater soul, some one who may take the shape for the moment of that greater soul, and endeavour to mislead us. It has happened often—terribly often; and we have seen the saddest results from it. Therefore the one and only safe ground is to keep our minds open. It is foolish rashly to reject, but equally foolish blindly to accept, merely because the message comes to us with a high name attached, or with an influence which seems to us to be beautiful. Most things from other planes seem beautiful to us down here, just because they come from a higher level, and bring with them something of its greater luminosity, of its more delicate vibrations, and of all the glamour of the inner world. As St. Paul said long ago, every man should be fully persuaded in his own mind; he should try the spirits and what comes from them, whether they be of God. Let us see for ourselves by all means, but do not let us shut out the possibility of influence by prejudging the whole question, and saying that inspiration is an affair of thousands of years ago, and can never take place now and here in the present day.

Chapter VII

Plagiarism

When our Consciousness develops sufficiently to enable us to understand a little of the working of Nature on the higher planes, we soon find it necessary to revise our judgment in various directions. As we comprehend conditions better, we see the reason for many things which previously seemed unaccountable, and we learn to make allowances for actions which we had before considered inexcusable. In this and the following chapter I am endeavouring to present some thoughts which have occurred to me along these lines.

In the newspapers lately have appeared reports of two legal actions for plagiarism in connection with stories or plays, and in each case the defendant declared that he had not read the work which he was accused of imitating. A man of the world would probably find it difficult to credit such a disclaimer, especially if the points of resemblance between the two stories or plays were many; yet the student of Occultism knows that such a plea may be perfectly true, and that there are more ways than one in which such a coincidence may happen without the slightest intention or consciousness of plagiarism on the part of anybody concerned.

In the second volume of *The Inner Life* I have already explained that in the mental world there are certain definitely localised thought-centres—that thoughts of the same type are drawn together by the similitude of their vibrations, just as men who speak the same language are drawn together. Philosophical thought, for example, has a distinct realm of its own, with subdivisions corresponding to the chief philosophical ideas, and all sorts of curious interrelations subsisting between these various centres, exhibiting the way in which different systems of philosophy have linked themselves together. Anyone who thinks deeply on philosophical subjects thereby brings himself into touch with this group of vortices; if he is asleep or dead—that is, if he is away from the limitations of his physical body—he is drawn spatially to that part of the mental plane; if the lump of earth to which he is attached for the moment prevents that, he rises into a condition of sympathetic vibration with one or other of those vortices, and receives from them whatever he is capable of assimilating, though somewhat less freely than if he actually drifted to it.

This collection of ideas represents all that has been thought upon that subject, and is therefore in itself far more than enough for any ordinary thinker, yet there are further possibilities behind it and in connection with it which are within the reach of the few who are strong enough and persevering enough to penetrate to them.

First, through those centres of thought the living minds of those who generated their force may be reached, and so the modern thinker who is at once strong and eager, yet reverent and teachable, may actually sit at the feet of the great thinkers of the past, and learn how the problems of life envisaged themselves to the mightiest intellects which our world has produced.

Secondly, there is such a thing as the Truth in itself—or we may perhaps put, as the representative to us of such an utterly abstract idea, the conception of that Truth in the mind of our Solar Deity—surely a notion sufficiently lofty for the boldest. The man who has attained conscious union with the Deity is able to contact this thought, but no one below that level can reach it. Reflections of it are to be seen, cast from plane to plane, and growing ever dimmer as they descend; and some at least of these reflections are within the reach of the man whose thought can soar up like a strong eagle to meet them.

It is obvious that many earnest thinkers may simultaneously be drawn to the same mental region, and may there gather exactly the same ideas; and when that happens it is at least possible that their expression of those ideas in the physical world may also coincide; and then there is always the danger that the ignorant multitude may accuse one or the other of them of plagiarism. That this synchronous expression does not happen more frequently is due to the density of men's brains, which rarely allow their owners to bring through clearly anything which has been learned upon higher levels. Not only in the field of literature does synchronal manifestation occur; officials connected with the Patent Office of any country will tell us that applications with regard to practically identical inventions often arrive simultaneously; and when this fact is disclosed each of the applicants is very ready to accuse the other of stealing his ideas, even where physical theft is obviously impossible.

It is not, however, among the promulgators of philosophical ideas that we most frequently hear complaints of plagiarism, but rather among dramatists and writers of fiction. Is there, then, in connection with this form of literature any such thought-centre as we have just described in relation to philosophy? Not precisely—at any rate not for fiction as a whole. But there is a region for what may be called romantic thought—a vast but rather ill-defined group of forms, including on one side a host of vague but brilliant combinations connected with the relation of the sexes, on another the emotions characteristic of mediaeval chivalry and the legends illustrating them, and on yet another masses of fairy stories.

Many writers of certain kinds of fiction and poetry derive much inspiration from excursions into these regions; others come into contact with the shoreless ocean of past history. No untrained person can actually read the records of that history, for that needs the full awakening of the ego, so that he can function in the atomic matter of his causal body. But confused reflections of the more brilliant episodes from those records are thrown down to lower mental levels, and even into the astral world, and those may readily be contacted by wandering voyagers in these realms. So it happens that many a writer finds himself in possession of a splendid idea, a dramatic climax perhaps, and he builds a story to lead up to it, and gains much fame thereby, never knowing all the while that he is but relating a tiny fragment of the world's true history.

Years ago, on board a steamer, I myself read a remarkable novel—one with a plot absolutely out of the ordinary run—and I mentally applauded the ingenuity of the author, though even then it stirred within me a vague remembrance which told me that some reality lay behind it. I did not pursue the subject, and it was only comparatively recently, in following out the history of a series of past incarnations, that I came across the fact of which this story was the expression. Yet neither I, who recorded in those lives the incident as it occurred, nor the novelist who had expanded it into a charming story, was in the least guilty of plagiarism, any more than a traveller who visits and describes the beauties of the River Rhine is guilty of a plagiarism from Baedeker.

In some cases the writer of fiction does not need to search the higher worlds for plots and ideas, for these are provided for him ready-made. One leading novelist of the day has himself told me that his stories come to him he knows not whence—that they are in reality written not by him but through him. in this case the writer understands and recognises the state of affairs; but I believe that there are many other writers in the same case who are blankly unconscious of it. We know so little what is our own (if indeed anything ever is); for not only may we roam the realms of thought and pick up unconsidered trifles on our journey, but others may do for us the roaming and the collection, and we may be nothing but their mouthpiece, even while we marvel at the rapidity and lucidity with which new ideas (new to us, at least) are pouring forth from our brains. Those who during earth-life have written on any subject retain their interest in it after the casting-off of the physical body. In their new and less trammelled life they see sides of it which before were imperceptible to them, they obtain broader views of it, because their whole horizon is widened. As they continue their study under these far better conditions, new light dawns upon it as upon all else, because of their greatly enhanced power of vision; and often they yearn to put their newer and greater conceptions before their fellow men.

But in that new life there are restrictions as well as opportunities; they can learn far more if they will, but they can no longer obtain a physical publisher for their lucubrations. If they wish to reach this lower world they must do so through some one living in it. Here arise difficulties in their way—difficulties which most of them never learn how to overcome. Some few do, and succeed in getting their ideas before the world which they have left, but only under the name of some other man, and often very imperfectly. Naturally enough, the unconscious medium through whom they work mingles their ideas with his own, and colours them with his idiosyncrasies. In some cases the brain upon which alone they find themselves able to work is incapable of transmitting the full value of the thought which they try to pour into it; and in some cases defective education or lack of special knowledge stands in the way of perfect transmission. I very clearly remember, for example, the annoyance and the impatience of old Mr. Cayley when he endeavoured to give to the world through me some new discovery which he declared would revolutionise the whole science of mathematics. As I unfortunately know very little of that science, I was quite unable to understand what he was talking about, and so I was compelled to forego the honour which he destined for me; but I must admit that his language was distinctly uncomplimentary, and I can quite understand that his disappointment may have been keen, as he told me that he had already tried many of his colleagues in vain.

Yet the fact remains that we have but little title to much which we think to be our own. Goethe wrote:

What would remain to me if the art of appropriation were derogatory to genius? Every one of my writings has been furnished to me by a thousand different persons, a thousand things; wise and foolish have brought me, without suspecting it, the offering of their thoughts, faculties and experience. My work is an aggregation of beings taken from the whole of nature; it bears the name of Goethe.

If the great German admits this to be so with regard to the splendid sunlight of his genius, how much more must it be true of the farthing rush-lights of minor writers! It is sometimes not only the ideas that are borrowed, but even the forms of expression; I have seen instances in which two people entirely unconnected put down the same thought in the very same words. This may be due to the zeal and enthusiasm of some dead man; he dictates the same sentence to two or more people, because he is not certain which of them will be able to carry it through successfully to the physical plane. It may, however, also happen without the intervention of a dead man, for an author himself, when assimilating some thought, often finds it less troublesome to take it exactly as it stands than to find for it a new expression in words of his own. In all these matters the natural tendency is to flow along the line of least resistance, and the line of least resistance is that which is already established.

It is very difficult to give, to one who has not seen them, any idea of the appearance of such reservoirs of thought as I have been attempting to describe. One might partially image it by saying that each thought makes for itself a track—burrows out a way for itself through the matter of the plane; and that way, when once established, remains open for the treading—or rather, it may readily be reopened and its particles re-vivified by any fresh effort. If this effort be at all in the general direction of that old line of thought, it is far easier for it to adapt itself sufficiently to pass along that line than it is for it to hew out for itself a slightly different line, however closely parallel that may be to what already exists.

All these considerations show us that it is not wise to hurl reckless accusations of plagiarism at the heads of those who happen to express themselves much as we have done—or even exactly as we have done. I have sometimes seen a certain impatience manifested among Theosophists because writers or speakers who are not members of our Society frequently use what we call Theosophical ideas without any acknowledgment of their source. As there are quarters in which the name of Theosophy is unpopular, I have little doubt that this is sometimes intentionally done, and credit withheld from the. Society in order to avoid the mention of the hated name. Even in that case, however, I cannot see that we as Theosophists need complain, for our one wish is to circulate the teaching of the truth, not to obtain credit for the knowledge of it.

There are, however, a number of other cases in which information about truths well known to us is acquired quite outside our organisation. For example, we have been at some pains to map out the subdivisions of the astral and mental planes, and to describe their inhabitants and the conditions which prevail there; but we must remember that all living people pass on to the astral plane during sleep, and that dead people permanently reside there during the earlier stage of their *post-mortem* life; so it must inevitably happen that among these many millions of people some will be sufficiently sensitive either when alive to bring back into physical existence some clear recollections, or when dead to discover some method of communicating reasonably accurate information to those whom they have left behind. Whenever one of these things happens, we immediately have what we are in the habit of calling a confirmation of Theosophical teaching. But this is in no sense of the word a plagiarism; it is an independent observation of the same phenomenon, and the observer has just as much right to describe his impressions as I should have to give mine of a visit to Italy, even though there are already many hundreds of books upon that country far better than anything that I could write. I have no wish to defend plagiarism, which is indeed nothing but a form of robbery. I wish merely to point out that it is not well to make reckless accusations along that line, since the conditions of the holding of property upon higher planes are very different from those which obtain in the physical world, and in this case, as in so many others, the man who most fully understands is also the man who will take the most charitable view.

Chapter VIII

Exaggeration

We all know people who have a tendency to exaggerate—who never can relate an incident exactly as it happened or pass on a story without improving upon it. After a time we get used to them, and learn to allow a certain discount off everything which they say. Usually we regard them as untruthful, and often also as conceited, especially if their magnifications refer (as they generally do) chiefly to their own part in the stories which they tell.

A considerable amount of experience, however, with those who have this peculiarity has convinced me that in most cases the exaggeration is unconscious. A person finds himself in a certain position, and in that position he (being in all probability quite an ordinary man) acts or speaks much as any average human being would do. In thinking over the situation afterwards, he often realises that he might have met that little emergency much more effectively and dramatically—that he might have covered himself with glory by making some particularly apposite remark, if only it had occurred to him at the time. If he happens to be the type of man who cannot put aside an event when it is past, and forget it in a sane and healthy manner, he continues to brood over the trifling incident and reconstruct it, imagining how the conversation would have proceeded if he had made what he now sees to be the most effective retort, or how the drama would have worked itself out if he had not lost his head (as so many of us do) just at the critical moment. And after he has rehearsed the occurrence a few times along these lines, he begins actually to believe that he really did make that splendidly witty remark, or that he was in fact that hero of romance which he feels that he ought to have been, and indeed would have been if only he had thought of it.

Such a man is no doubt acutely self-conscious, otherwise he would not continue to worry himself about an event which is past and cannot be recalled; and he has also a certain amount of imagination and sensitiveness. The former quality enables him to make strong thought-forms of himself as doing or saying what he feels ought to have been done or said, while the latter quality enables him to sense these thought-forms and to feel their reaction upon him until he fails to distinguish them from the actual memory of the event; and so after a time he relates in all good faith a story which departs widely from the facts as recollected by a more prosaic spectator. Indeed, I have myself on more than one occasion been put in a most awkward position by being appealed to in public to confirm a highly-coloured account of some experience which the narrator and I had shared in the past, but in regard to which my recollection was distinctly less dramatic than that of my poetically-inclined partner. I have even in some cases had the interesting experience of watching a story grow—having in the first place myself witnessed what really happened, and heard the principal actor give at the time a reasonably exact account of it. Coming back a week later, I have found that the tale had considerably expanded; and after a few months it has even become wholly unrecognisable, the embroidery of self-glorification having completely disguised its substratum of fact. Yet I am sure that this inaccuracy is wholly unintentional, and that the narrator who is so entirely misrepresenting the story has no thought of deceiving us, and indeed would shrink with horror from any deliberate falsification.

This is a curious phenomenon; and although, in the extreme form which I have described, it is fortunately confined to comparatively few, we may all of us detect what may be regarded as a sort of germ of it in ourselves. Many of us find it difficult to be absolutely accurate; we are conscious of a certain desire to make a story more dramatically complete than it is in reality—to round it off, or to introduce into it the element of poetic justice which is so often sadly lacking in the very limited views which alone we are able to take of mundane affairs. Quite a number of people who have every intention of being perfectly truthful will yet, if they watch themselves carefully, find that they are not entirely free from this curious instinct of magnification—that in repeating a story they instinctively increase the size or the distance or the value of that of which they speak.

Why does this tendency exist? It is no doubt true that in many cases there is something of conceit, of desire for approbation, of the wish to shine or to appear clever; and even where these terms would be too strong, there is an instinctive self-consciousness which causes the person concerned to look back to past events in which he took part, with the desire that that part had been more distinguished. Yet quite apart from that, and where the story has no connection with ourselves, we still perceive the same curious tendency.

The reason lies deeper than that; and in order to understand it we must think of the nature of the ego, and of the stage which he has reached in his evolution. It has often been mentioned in our literature that one of the characteristics of the ego is his remarkable power of dramatisation. In another chapter I endeavoured to explain that he deals with abstractions as we on the physical plane deal with concrete facts—that to him a whole system of philosophy (with all that it involves) is a single idea which he uses as a counter in his game, which he throws down in the course of a conversation, just as we down here might quote a fact in support of some contention which we were urging. Thus we see that, when dealing with matters on his own plane and those below him, all his ideas are complete ideas, properly rounded off and perfect. Anything incomplete would be unsatisfactory to him—would in fact hardly be counted as an idea at all. For him a cause includes its effect, and therefore, in the longer view which he is able to take, poetic justice is always done, and no story can ever end badly. These characteristics of his reflect themselves to a certain extent in his lower vehicles, and we find them appearing in ourselves in various ways. Children always demand that their fairy-tales shall end well, that virtue shall be rewarded and that vice shall be vanquished; and all unsophisticated and healthy-minded people feel a similar desire. Those who (on the pretext that things do not happen this way in real life) clamour for an evil realism are precisely those whose views of life have become unhealthy and unnatural, because in their short-sighted philosophy they can never see the whole of any incident, but only the fragment of it which shows in one incarnation and usually only the merest outside husk even of that.

Let us notice the influence exercised upon the manifestation of this characteristic by the stage of evolution at which we now are. It has often been explained that each root-race has its special quality to develop, and that in that respect each of the sub-races also manifests the influence of its own special peculiarity upon the root-race quality. The Fourth Root-Race, we are told, was chiefly concerned with the development of the astral body and of its emotions, while our Fifth Root-Race is supposed to be evolving the mental body and the intellect which is intended to work through it. Thus in the fifth or Teutonic sub-race we should be intensifying the development of intellect and discrimination, whereas in the fourth or Keltic sub-race we may see how its combination makes easier both artistic and psychic development, though probably at the cost of scientific accuracy in detail. In fact, this passion for scientific accuracy, for perfect truth in minutest detail, is comparatively a recent development; indeed, it is that characteristic which has made possible the achievements of modern science. We now demand first of all that a thing shall be true, and if it is not, it is of no interest to us; whereas the older sub-races demanded first of all that it should be pleasing, and declined to be limited in their appreciation by any such consideration as whether the thing had ever materialised or could ever materialise on the physical plane.

You may see this clearly in the old Keltic stories. Notice how in the legends which cluster round King Arthur, a knight tilts with some casual stranger, overthrows him and brings him as a prisoner, and how, in narrating his exploit, he describes his unlucky victim as a gigantic ogre, a monster towering to the skies, and so on; and yet nobody present appears to notice any discrepancy between his account and the actual appearance of the unfortunate person then and there before them. We see at once, as we read those stories, that for their reciters and their hearers the limitations of what we call fact simply did not exist. Their one desire was to make up a good and soul-satisfying romance, and in this they succeeded, That the alleged occurrence was manifestly impossible did not trouble them in the slightest degree. It troubles us who read these fables now, because we are developing the discriminative faculty, and therefore, though we like a rousing tale of adventure just as well as our forefathers did, we cannot feel satisfied with it unless an air of probability is cleverly thrown around each incident to satisfy this new yearning for verisimilitude and accuracy of statement.

This desire for accuracy is only the coming through of another of the qualities of the ego—his power to see truly, to see a thing as it is—as a whole and not only in part. But because down here we are so often unable to see the whole as he sees it, we are beginning to demand that the part which we do see shall be to a certain extent complete in itself, and shall harmonise with such other parts as we can dimly glimpse. Our little fragments are usually very far from complete. They do not end properly, they do not show off the characters to the best advantage; and because down here we cannot yet see the real ending which would explain everything, our instinct is to inset an imaginary ending which at least to some extent meets our requirements.

That is the real reason for our desire to improve upon a story. In some of us the newly-developed desire for truth and accuracy overpowers the older craving to please and be pleased; but sometimes the other element is victorious. Then comes in, as we have already said, the influence of vanity and the desire to make a good appearance, and our newly-developed quality of truthfulness falls ignominiously into the background. In most cases all this takes place entirely in the subconscious mind, and so our ordinary waking consciousness is unaware of it. Thus it comes about that some people are still quite mediaeval in their accounts of their personal adventures.

When we understand this, it is clearly our business to assist the ego in his present efforts at development. We must encourage and insist on the quality of accuracy, and we must keep our record of facts apart from our thoughts and wishes with regard to those facts. Yet in thus cultivating truthfulness we need by no means extinguish romance. It is necessary to be accurate; it is not necessary to become a Gradgrind. If we wish to pass an examination in botany we must load our memories with uncouth, pseudo-Latinised terms, and we must learn to distinguish the dicotyledonous from the monocotyledonous; but that need not prevent us from recognising that there is a higher side to botany in which we study the existence of the life of the tree and its power occasionally to manifest in quasi-human form, nor need we ignore the folk-lore of the trees and plants and the action of the nature-spirits who help in the moulding and the colouring of the blossoms—though we shall do well to keep all these rigidly out of our examination papers. The knowledge of the beauty and romance which lies behind need not be lost because we have to acquire arid, superficial details, any more than we need lose sight of the fact that sugar is sweet and pleasant to the taste because we have to learn that its chemical formula is $C_{12}H_{22}O_{11}$.

To mingle our imagination with our facts is a wrong use of a very mighty power; but there is a right use of it which may be of great help to us in our progress. One who desires to meditate is often told to make an image of the Master and fix his attention upon it; and when he does this, the love and devotion which he feels attract the attention of the Master, and He immediately fills that image with His thought, and pours through it His strength and His blessing upon its creator, if the student has been fortunate enough to see the Master, his thought-image is naturally far clearer and better than in cases where it is a mere effort of the imagination. The clearer the image, the more fully can power be sent through it; but in any and every case something at least is gained, and some considerable return is received. This then is a case of the legitimate use of the imagination—a case in which its results are most valuable.

It comes into play also in one of the many lines of psychic development. A pupil who desires to open the etheric sight is sometimes told to take some solid object and endeavour to imagine what the inside of it would be like if he could see it. For example, a closed box might be set before such a pupil, and he might be asked to describe the objects inside it. He would probably be directed to try to imagine what was inside, to "guess", as the children would say, but always with an effort of strained attention, with an endeavour to see that which by ordinary sight he could not see. It is said that after many such attempts the pupil finds himself "guessing" correctly much more frequently than is explicable on any theory of coincidence, and that presently he begins really to see before him the objects which at first he only imagined.

A variant of this practice is that the student calls up before his mind's eye the room of a friend, and endeavours to make a perfect image of it. After a certain number of attempts he will probably be able to do this readily, and with considerable wealth of detail. Then lie should watch closely for anything new or unusual in his mind-picture of that room; or perhaps he may be conscious of the presence of certain people in it. If that happens to him it may be worth his while to write and ask whether such people have been there, or whether there is any foundation for his idea that certain changes have been made; for if he proves to be right on a number of occasions he will realise that he is beginning to develop a certain impressibility which may in process of time evolve into true clairvoyance.

To sum up: Like other powers, imagination may be used rightly or wrongly. Exaggeration is clearly wrong, and is always a bar to progress, even when it is unintentional. Accuracy is essential; but its achievement does not preclude the study of the higher and more romantic side of nature.

Chapter IX

Meditation

The readiest and safest method of developing the higher consciousness is by means of meditation, and it is already the habit of many of our members to begin each morning by spending a few minutes in a meditation which is intended to be devoted to aspiration towards the Masters. I should like to say a few words about this, because it seems to me that some of us are not getting quite as much out of it as we might do.

There are so many various types among us that it is not possible that one method of meditation can produce equally good results with all. Broadly speaking, we may divide into two classes the ways in which such a time as that may be most profitably occupied, and each person must decide for himself or herself to which class he or she belongs, which method will come most naturally and be most profitable.

We have the habit of calling all our exercises of that sort by the general name of meditation, though it is appropriate only to some of them. I have often spoken of three stages through which people have to pass: Concentration, Meditation, and Contemplation; it is this last at which on the whole we ought to be aiming, when that is possible and comparatively easy for us. There may be, however, some of us whose minds are not constructed along that particular line, and they may find meditation more useful and more profitable for them.

The art of acquiring perfect concentration is a slow process, and most of us are only in process of acquiring it. We have not fully succeeded in it yet, because wandering thoughts still come in to trouble us. But supposing we have sufficient concentration to keep out those thoughts which we do not want, it yet remains to be considered how we shall think during these few minutes. We speak of the time as devoted to aspiration towards the Master; but there are different lines of aspiration. The nearest to what is really meant by meditation would be to hold the mind firmly upon our own image of Him, if we are able to construct a good strong thought-image. Some cannot visualise as easily as others. If we can visualise strongly for ourselves, it is well to make our own thought-image and close our eyes. Having made such an image, our thought would then run along some such line as this:

"This," we should say, "is the Master whom have chosen, to whom I am devoting myself. He is the incarnation of love, of power, of wisdom. I must try to make myself like Him in all these respects. Have I succeeded so far in doing this? Not as fully as I should wish in such-and-such ways; I can think, in looking back, that I have not shown these qualities as I should. I shall endeavour in the future to remember Him always, and to be, and to act, and to think as I believe He would be and act and think". And so on with a strong effort to realise those qualities in Him. I take it that that is really what is meant by the word meditation.

If a man finds after some effort that it is impossible for him to make a clear thought-image, it will be well for him to seat himself before a portrait of the Master, and fix his gaze earnestly upon it while thinking as above suggested.

There is something still better, perhaps, for those who find that they can do it readily and easily; and that is contemplation. In that case one forms the image of the Master and, having formed it, throws one's whole strength into an effort to reach Him, an effort which I can best describe by saying that we are straining upwards towards Him, trying to unify our consciousness with His. That effort will not immediately bring a result, in all probability; but if we make it every day in our regular meditation, the time will certainly come when it will meet with full success.

That is the best thing to do for those who can do it. But there are types of mind to which such an effort would be barren; and it is not well for them to waste their time over it if it is a thing which they cannot at all do, while the other form of meditation might be much more fruitful for them.

But for those who can reach upward in that particular way with any sort of success, with any kind of feeling that it is for them a path which will be likely (even though it should take a long time) to lead to a direct union with Him, contemplation is clearly best, for such union when attained is most fruitful, most helpful. With deepest reverence we say to the Master:

"Holy Master, Father, Friend, I lay myself open to Your influence. It shall flow into me to the uttermost degree in which I am capable of receiving it."

We need not ask Him to pour it out on us, because He is doing that all the time. We do not *pray* to the Masters to do this or that. They know very much more about it than we do, and are already doing all that can be done; but it is on our side necessary that we should make ourselves open to it, that we should remove the barriers of self that stand in the way. That is the old story. It must be told over and over again, because the separated self is the one great difficulty in our path—the personality first and then the individuality. That is insisted upon in *At the Feet of the Master*, and in every book that has been written on occult progress. When there is anything hindering our progress it is always the lower self which stands in the way of the Great Self.

Having visualised and realised the Master as intensely as possible, the effort must be to clear away our own barriers, to break through them and reach up to Him, because He is ever ready to be gracious to us, always pouring out His influence just in such measure as we are capable of receiving. We have nothing to ask Him. We have only so to deal with ourselves that His light shall shine through.

That effort will eventually lead us towards an extension of consciousness. When we succeed we shall break through into a different world, a different way of looking at everything.

Along that line is the most rapid and the most satisfactory progress, but as I have said, it is strictly for those who can take it, and for whom that happens to be the way. The man whose nature instinctively runs the other way would probably waste his time by making this effort, whereas he might make distinct progress by following that other line.

One or other of those things we ought to be trying to do, and we must not let it become vague. It has a great tendency to become vague; and it is odd that although we believe that all these advancements are within reach, we are never so much astonished as when anything happens, and we do really get any result. That ought not to be so. It is no doubt a touching example of our humility, but there is a humility that sometimes actually hinders progress. We may feel so sure that we are far away from the possibility of doing anything, that we stand in our own light. It is better, so far as may be, with humble confidence (humble unquestionably, but still confidence) to take the line: "Others have succeeded in this. I intend to succeed, and I am going to persevere until I do".

Then we certainly shall succeed. It may not be immediately, but "immediately" from our point of view matters very little really, so long as we do the thing; and every human being *can* do it; it is only a question of the time it may happen to take, and the time is well spent anyhow.

I think if we remember these ideas it may help us to make more use of the time set apart for meditation. The natural tendency of the age generally is towards vagueness and looseness of thought. Some people just relapse into what is called "feeling good" for a few minutes. Better to feel good than to feel bad, of course; but still it is not quite all that is meant.

Many people meditate daily alone, and obtain great help by so doing; but nevertheless there are even greater possibilities of result when a group of people concentrate their minds on the one thing. That sets up a strain in the physical ether as well as in the astral and mental worlds, and it is a twist in the direction which we desire. For once, just for the time of that group meditation, instead of having to fight against our surroundings (which we always have to do practically, everywhere else) we find them actually helpful. That is to say, they ought to be so, if all present succeed in holding their minds from wandering, and that of course they must try to do, not only for their own sakes but for the sake of their comrades in the effort. A wandering mind in such a group constitutes a break in the current. Instead of having a huge mass of thought moving in one mighty flood, we should in that case have little eddies in it, such as are made by rocks or snags in a river which deflect the water. Anyone who allows his mind to wander is thereby making things not quite so easy for those around him.

A number of people all sending their thought in the same direction offers a fine opportunity for progress if the direction is a good one; but it rarely happens in ordinary life. When it does occur it means great possibilities.

A striking instance, which I have described before, arises in my mind as apposite. I had the privilege of being present at the Diamond Jubilee of Her Majesty Queen Victoria. It was one of the most wonderful manifestations in the way of occult force that I ever saw. Just for a few moments, as the Queen's carriage passed, thousands of people were swept into one line of thought, and it was a very good line, of intense love and loyalty. It was a sight from the inner side which is rarely equalled. Before that came; we had to wait a long time for the procession. Thousands and thousands of people who were within sight had each his own set of thoughts. I happened to be in the heart of the city of London, where those present were mostly commercial or professional men with their wives. The men were chiefly occupied in calculations, and their heads were surrounded by figures, just like a swarm of bees flying round them all the time. The various ladies were thinking about one another's dresses and about domestic affairs of all sorts. There was no unity, as is always the case with any crowd anywhere.

When the procession came along, the people were awakened, and by degrees began to take a stronger and stronger interest in it, and the culmination arrived when the Queen herself passed. For a few minutes all those thousands were thinking and feeling alike. The effect was quite prodigious even on the physical plane, though they did not know why. Here were hard city men, absolutely with tears in their eyes, shaking each other by the hand; while practically all the ladies were weeping unrestrainedly.

The effect was amazing in those few minutes of utter exaltation. Perhaps for the first time in their lives they all of them simultaneously forgot themselves altogether, and were lifted right out of themselves by a high emotion. Now that was an opportunity. In such moments as that, if the excitement is religious, wholesale conversions take place—tremendous temporary upliftments of the soul. I daresay those people afterwards wondered why they had been so shaken. It was exceedingly good for them, but it is rarely that such an opportunity comes.

We make a little current something like that on a small scale by our group meditation. We are perhaps only a score or so instead of many thousands, but in its way such a meeting is a real opportunity; if we could take better advantage of it we should make more rapid progress, we should feel ourselves more greatly helped.

It is a great assistance if in a group there are a few who are capable of rising to high levels. It is a great uplift that we should be for a few moments in the presence of thought on a higher plane. It is one of the advantages that we gain from our association, from "the assembling of ourselves together" for such work as this.

Collective meditation, such as some Lodges have at the public lectures for a mixed crowd, is frankly not of much use. It just keeps the audience quiet for a few moments, but it does little more, because the average man does not know how to think at all.

The unfolding of the higher consciousness is one of the possibilities which lie open to humanity at the stage which it has now reached. Therefore it is to a greater or less extent open to every one of us and it is well worth our while to make some attempt in that direction, for the addition to our usefulness which success would bring is almost incalculable. That the greatest caution must be exercised is true, for the pitfalls are many; nothing should be undertaken without the advice and supervision of a trained psychic. But the world needs helpers possessed of these powers, and it is among Theosophical students that we may reasonably expect to find them. It is hardly necessary to point out how advantageous to our work is the ability to communicate at will with the Angels and with the so-called dead, and the force and precision which definite experience of the higher life will give to our teaching. The knowledge gained is of the greatest comfort to him who acquires it, for it removes for ever from his life all doubt and all sorrow; yet man should strive for that transcendent wisdom not for his own sake, but that he may render himself more extensively serviceable to his fellow creatures, for that is the aim of all true and faithful brethren throughout the world.

www.ingramcontent.com/pod-product-compliance
Lightning Source LLC
Chambersburg PA
CBHW070720160426
43192CB00009B/1258